MAY WE BE SPARED TO MEET ON EARTH

MAY WE BE SPARED TO MEET ON EARTH

Letters of the
Lost Franklin Arctic Expedition

Edited by
RUSSELL A. POTTER, REGINA KOELLNER,
PETER CARNEY, AND MARY WILLIAMSON

*With the assistance of Alison Alexander, William Battersby, Matthew Betts,
Rick Burrows, A.J. Campbell, Jonathan Dore, Alison Freebairn, Andrew Hill,
D.J. Holzhueter, Olga Kimmins, Jonathan Moore, Alexa Price,
Frank Michael Schuster, Michael Smith, and Michael Tracy*

Foreword by
SIR MICHAEL PALIN

McGill-Queen's University Press
Montreal & Kingston • London • Chicago

ISBN 978-0-2280-1139-2 (cloth)
ISBN 978-0-2280-1336-5 (ePDF)
ISBN 978-0-2280-1337-2 (ePUB)

Legal deposit third quarter 2022
Bibliothèque nationale du Québec

Printed in Canada on acid-free paper that is 100% ancient forest free (100% post-consumer recycled), processed chlorine free

Funded by the Government of Canada   Financé par le gouvernement du Canada   Canada Council for the Arts   Conseil des arts du Canada

We acknowledge the support of the Canada Council for the Arts.
Nous remercions le Conseil des arts du Canada de son soutien.

Library and Archives Canada Cataloguing in Publication

Title: May we be spared to meet on earth : letters of the lost Franklin Arctic expedition
/ edited by Russell A. Potter, Regina Koellner, Peter Carney, and Mary Williamson ; with
the assistance of Alison Alexander, William Battersby, Matthew Betts, Rick Burrows, A.J.
Campbell, Jonathan Dore, Alison Freebairn, Andrew Hill, D.J. Holzhueter, Olga
Kimmins, Jonathan Moore, Alexa Price, Frank Michael Schuster, Michael Smith, and
Michael Tracy ; foreword by Sir Michael Palin.
Names: Potter, Russell A., 1960- editor. | Koellner, Regina, editor. | Carney, Peter (Blogger),
editor. | Williamson, Mary (Descendent of Sir John Franklin), editor.
Description: Includes bibliographical references and index.
Identifiers: Canadiana (print) 20220187673 | Canadiana (ebook) 20220187770
| ISBN 9780228011392 (cloth) | ISBN 9780228013365 (ePDF) | ISBN 9780228013372
(ePUB)
Subjects: LCSH: John Franklin Arctic Expedition (1845-1851)—Sources. | LCSH:
Great Britain. Royal Navy—Officers—Correspondence. | LCSH: Sailors—Great Britain
Correspondence. | LCSH:Explorers—Great Britain—Correspondence. | LCSH: Northwest
Passage—Discovery and exploration—British—Sources. | LCSH: Arctic regions
Discovery and exploration—British—Sources. | LCGFT: Personal correspondence.
Classification: LCC G640.M39 2022 | DDC 910.9163/27—dc23

This book was typeset in 10.5/13 Sabon.

Contents

Foreword

I would earnestly recommend to you to keep a correct account of all
your private thoughts and observations; and above all don't sleep
<u>too much</u>.

*John Goodsir to his son Harry, naturalist
and assistant surgeon aboard* HMS *Erebus*

The most eerie and haunting aspect of Sir John Franklin's expedition
to the Northwest Passage is the sudden and complete silence which followed the departure from Greenland. We know pretty well that at least
some members of the expedition were still alive four or even five years
later and yet, apart from the terse Victory Point note, there is not a word
to tell us what became of them.

Which is what makes this collection not only rich and fascinating but
unbearably poignant. The letters paint a picture of warm friendships,
bright hopes, and the unbounded expectations of largely young men,
embarking on a big adventure.

Letters provide rich seams for anyone wanting to delve deeper than
the formal and the official. Officers on a Royal Navy expedition were
required to keep journals, but these all had to be handed in to the
Admiralty at the end of the commission, so they were invariably cautious
and informative – facts and figures rather than opinions and emotions.
Letters, on the other hand, were not censored, and in writing my account
of the journeys of *Erebus* and *Terror*, it was only through letters that
I was able to hear the human as well as the professional voices and to
understand a little better all the things that fascinated me – the characters, the personalities, the pressures of close contact, the fear and apprehension when things went wrong, the restlessness and dissatisfaction as
more demands were made, the sense of achievement and wonder as the
crews witnessed things that no-one in human history had seen before.

The letters in this collection vividly bring to life the hopes and expectations of the Northwest Passage expedition that were to be so cruelly

dashed in the ice-locked Arctic waters. So overwhelming is the sense of optimism that some are almost painful to read. But others sound a different tone.

Captains Franklin and Crozier, the objects of almost universal approval in the officers' letters home, express, in their own letters, serious doubts as to their suitability to be leading the expedition at all.

Of particular interest are the relatively few letters from non-officers, many of whom had limited educations and were less able to express themselves in writing. This makes what they did write even more valuable. In marked contrast to the almost uniformly gung-ho note of the officers, the crew directly faced the risks and the dangers ahead and the possibility of never seeing their loved ones again. For them, crossing the Northwest Passage was not a path to glory, but a test which only God could see them through.

Along the way, there is much rich detail to enjoy. We learn that one of the officers thinks that taking four dozen shirts with him "will be amply sufficient," that one of the doctors on board had never been to sea before, and that of the fourteen bullocks on board as they crossed the North Atlantic, only three survived as far as Greenland.

The editors have done a remarkable job in tracking down so many letters from so many sources. They, and we the readers, have been rewarded not just by the volume but also by the quality of so much of the writing.

The Franklin expedition may have been written off as a tragic failure, but it is impossible to ignore. It is only in the last decade that both ships have been discovered, and who knows what a thorough exploration of them will reveal? These letters offer a tantalizing hint of the eloquence of the men who sailed with Franklin, and the tantalizing hope that some evidence will one day come to light of what they must have recorded in those grim years after they sailed away from Greenland and disappeared over the horizon.

Michael Palin
Actor, Author, and Traveller
London

Figure 1 | James Fitzjames's cabin. Collection of Russell A. Potter. See Letter 90, where Goodsir says: "If you purchase the next Saturdays Nos. of the Illustrated London News & the Pictorial Times you will have views of both ships & various parts of them." Not all were pleased; in Letter 105 Fairholme wrote: "We were disappointed about the Illustrated London News. The sketches are very bad & do not give any idea of the cabins."

Figure 2 | Graham Gore, "HMS Erebus, 22 May 1845, 3AM, off Aldborough." Courtesy Scott Polar Research Institute, University of Cambridge. No letters of Gore's are known, but this sketch was sent by him to Jane Franklin.

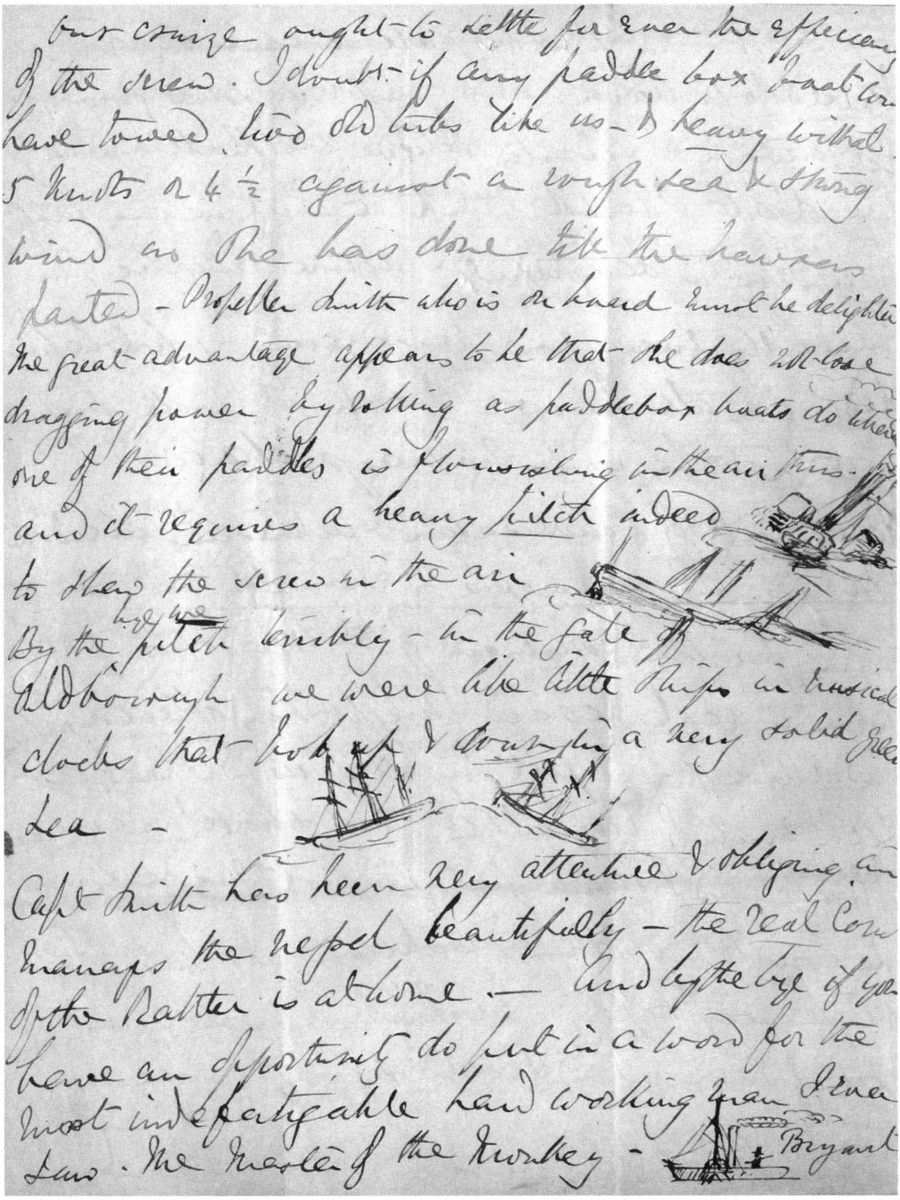

our cruize ought to settle for ever the efficien[cy]
of the screw. I doubt if any paddle box boat co[uld]
have towed two old tubs like us — & heavy withal.
5 knots or 4½ against a rough sea & strong
wind as she has done till the hawsers
parted — Propeller Smith who is on board must be delighted
the great advantage appears to be that she does not lose
dragging power by lolling as paddlebox boats do when
one of their paddles is flourishing in the air thus —
and it requires a heavy pitch indeed

to stay the screw in the air
by the pitch visibly — in the gale off
Aldborough we were like little ships in musical
clocks that bob up & down in a very solid green
sea —

Capt Smith has been very attentive & obliging in
managing the hopeful beautifully — the real Com[mander]
of the Rattler is at home — And by the bye if yo[u]
have an opportunity do put in a word for the
most indefatigable hard working man I ever
saw. the master of the Monkey — Bryant

Figure 3 | James Fitzjames, page from Letter 112, showing ships pitching. © Royal
Geographical Society (with IBG).

Our friend and Pitcher   May. 30 1845

Figure 4 | Owen Stanley, "Our friend and pitcher." Fitzjames in Letter 115 wrote: "Stanley calls the Terror his friend and <u>pitcher</u>." National Library of Australia.

 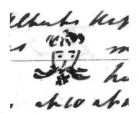

Figure 5 | James Fitzjames opened his letter of 1 June
to John Barrow Jr (Letter 115) with a bad joke:
"Why is Prince Albert's kiss like this ship? – 'Cause its
a hairy bus," adding a small cartoon of the prince. Jane
Franklin, who copied out sections of these letters for her
own reference, included her own version of the sketch in
her transcript. Fitzjames's cartoon © Royal Geographical
Society (with IBG); Jane's sketch is preserved at the Scott
Polar Institute, University of Cambridge (MS 248/380)
and is used with their permission.

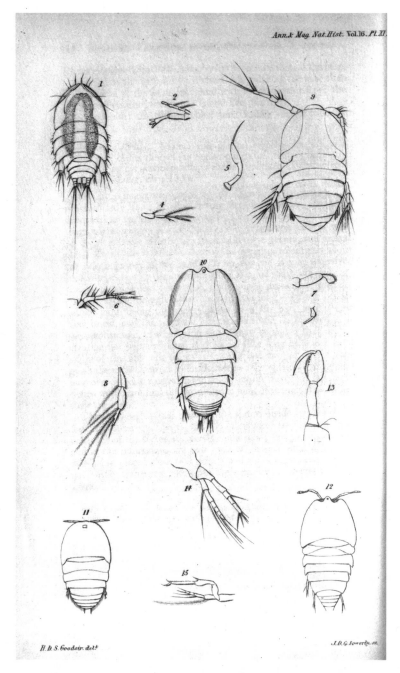

B.D.S.Goodsir.delt.

J.D.G.Sowerby.sc.

Figure 6 | Engraved plate showing crustaceans, based on sketches by Harry Goodsir for the *Annals and Magazine of Natural History*, mentioned by him in Letter 119. Collection of Russell A. Potter.

Figure 7 | James Fitzjames, "The Arctic Expedition Leaving Stromness 3 June 1845 9 am." Courtesy Scott Polar Research Institute, University of Cambridge.

Figure 8 | Owen Stanley, "Signal to Terror, Opportunity for sending Letters to England, 4 June 1845." National Library of Australia.

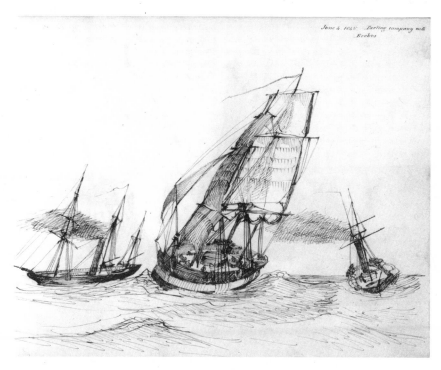

Figure 9 | Owen Stanley, "Parting Company with the North Pole Squadron." National Library of Australia.

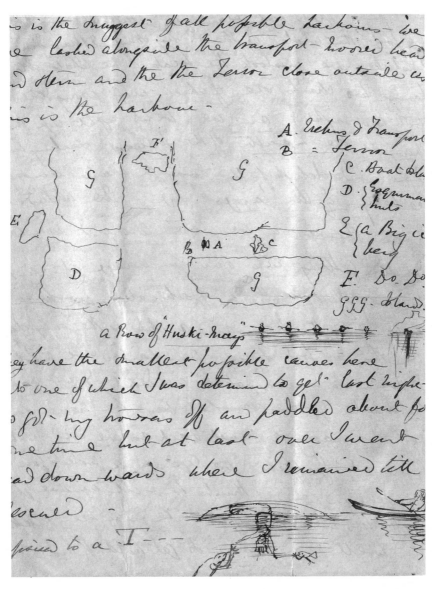

is the snuggest of all possible harbours — we
lashed alongside the transport — moored head
and stern and the the Terror close outside us
is the harbour —

A. Erebus & Transport
B = Terror
C. Boat Isla
D. { Esquimaux
     { huts
E { a Big i
   { bay
F. Do. Do
GGG. Island.

a Row of "Huski-mays"

they have the smallest possible canoes here
to one of which I was determined to get last night
got my trousers off and paddled about fo
some time but at last over I went
and down wards where I remained till
rescued —
posed to a T---

Figure 10 | James Fitzjames, sketch map of the Whalefish Islands, letter of 1–11
July. The key to this map is in Letter 141. © Royal Geographical Society (with
IBG).

Figure 11 | Henry Thomas Dundas Le Vesconte, sketch of *Erebus* and *Terror* at anchor off Disko Island. Courtesy Jersey Heritage.

Figure 12 | John Irving, sketch of *Erebus* and *Terror* at anchor in the Whalefish Islands. Collection of Douglas W. Wamsley.

MAY WE BE SPARED TO MEET ON EARTH

Introduction

Russell A. Potter

UNDERSTANDING THE FRANKLIN EXPEDITION

Our modern sense of the fate of the Franklin expedition has been shaped by more than 170 years of searching for its traces. At first, of course, when there remained some possibility of rescue, there was a great urgency to this search; in time, the gradual realization that all were lost seeped in, and the question arose: what could possibly have happened? How could an expedition often referred to as the most technologically advanced of its day, hoping only to close the last modest blank space between two well-surveyed shores, led by Arctic veterans, not only have failed in its mission but have seemingly disappeared, ships, men, and all? Despite dozens of searches, the whole sum of what was found amounted to little more than a small scattering of bones, an empty boat, some scientific instruments and utensils, and a few "lonely cairns of stones." The paucity of evidence has given unusual value to the few traces that could be found, and has also made the "mystery" of the expedition's fate a recurrent spur to both imaginative works and historical speculations.

The initial phase of intensive searches persisted over more than a decade, from 1848 to 1859, involving a mixture of government- and privately funded endeavours. The recurring theme of these expeditions was their lack of success in obtaining much information – if any – about Franklin's fate; but their repeated coverage in the illustrated press, and the many books and leaflets that came with them, established the Arctic searching expedition as a cultural touchstone, one so familiar that Mark Twain could mockingly compare it to the quest for the Holy Grail:

The boys all took a flier at the Holy Grail now and then. It was a several years' cruise. They always put in the long absence snooping around, in the most conscientious way, though none of them had any idea where the Holy Grail really was, and I don't think any of them actually expected to find it, or would have known what to do with it if he had run across it. You see, it was just the Northwest Passage of that day, as you may say; that was all. Every year expeditions went out holy grailing, and next year relief expeditions went out to hunt for them.[1]

All this "grailing" came to an initial close with Leopold McClintock's discovery of the Victory Point note, the expedition's only official record, which, though unclear about other vital matters, stated: "Sir John Franklin died on the 11th June, 1847; and the total loss by deaths in the expedition has been to this date 9 officers and 15 men." Facsimiles of the note about the discovery were included in every copy of McClintock's book *The Voyage of the 'Fox' in the Arctic Seas*[2] and reproduced in newspapers around the world. *The Times* of London could now opine: "Alas! there can be no longer those sad wailings from an imaginary Tintagel to persuade the credulous that an Arthur still lives."

This period of active searching was followed by a longer period, punctuated by two significant private searches, the first led by the American journalist Charles Francis Hall in 1864–69, and the second by Lieutenant Frederick Schwatka, a US Cavalry officer, in 1878–80. While the material discoveries of these two expeditions were relatively slight – utensils, bits of telescopes and other equipment, buttons, sledge-harnesses, and two more or less complete skeletons – they both gathered the testimony of local Inuit, including – in Schwatka's case – that of an eyewitness who had been aboard one of the ships. This evidence was not taken seriously enough, however, and much of it remained in Hall's notebooks, as the official account published after his death only quoted from them selectively. For many years the published narratives of Hall and Schwatka – as well as those of Schwatka's companions William Gilder and Heinrich Klutschak – remained chiefly as obelisks marking a realm of uncertainty.[3]

It was not until the 1920s that new searchers came to the places where Franklin and his ships were last seen – Knud Rasmussen, on his fifth Thule expedition (1921–24), interviewed the descendants of some of Hall and Schwatka's informants; their accounts were remarkably unchanged. Not long afterward, Lachlan Taylor Burwash, whose position with the government of the Northwest Territories gave him an ideal opportunity for travel in the region, began anew to collect both physical artifacts and Inuit oral traditions.[4] Nothing of what he found significantly altered the understanding of the expedition's fate, but it reinforced the sense that, with time and opportunity, a good many unturned stones yet might be turned. Burwash was followed by others in the employ of either the territorial government or the Hudson's Bay Company: Richard Finnie, L.A. Learmonth, and Henry Larson in the 1930s and '40s, followed by Stu Hodgson, Bob Pilot, and J.J. Ootes in the 1970s.[5] The fact that these men could readily travel – indeed, it was part of their jobs – and search without restriction, gave them an unparalleled opportunity, but the results of their investigations did little to resolve the uncertainty and ambiguity of the evidence as to the expedition's demise. Furthermore, few of these figures published full accounts of their searches; anyone seeking to compile their finds in the pre-digital era would have faced significant obstacles.

The year 1939 was a watershed for Franklin studies, as it marked the appearance of *Sir John Franklin's Last Arctic Expedition* by Richard J. Cyriax (1885–1967).[6] Cyriax, by day a physician and public health official in Leamington Spa in central England, indulged his interest in naval history, particularly that of the Franklin expedition, in his spare hours. His extraordinary diligence and careful work with primary sources made his book a standard reference, even after some aspects of it were supplanted by later discoveries. Cyriax continued to publish articles on the expedition throughout his life, many in collaboration with the noted Polar historian A.G.E. Jones (1914–2002). These included papers on specific Franklin relics, among them the medicine chest recovered from King William Island by McClintock, as well as the notorious "Peglar" papers, a bundle of cryptic documents written almost entirely backward, found with the skeleton of one of Franklin's men.[7] While it might have been hoped that they would help solve the Franklin mystery, these papers – insofar as they have been deciphered – contain almost no certain references to the expedition itself, but consist largely of doggerel verse and accounts of visits to warmer climes.

The 1960s saw a renewal of interest in the area identified in the Inuit accounts given to Hall and Schwatka. If, indeed, a ship (or ships) was in the area west of the Adelaide Peninsula, it seemed possible that its large iron ex-railway engines might show up via a magnetometer survey. The first such attempt was made in 1965 by a team from Canada's Department of Mines and Technical Surveys led by Ben Ackerman, James Shearer, Nick Stuifbergen, and Fred Roots. They searched the area north of O'Reilly Island with a snowmobile-towed magnetometer, but found that a seemingly promising magnetic anomaly was in fact a natural feature. In 1967, in connection with the observance of the centennial of Canadian Confederation, a renewed search in this area – originally proposed by W.G. Mackenzie of Toronto, Ontario – was undertaken by the Ministry of National Defence. Land searches were conducted near the former site of the North Magnetic Pole (where Mackenzie believed Franklin to have been buried), and scuba divers searched the waters near O'Reilly Island. Nothing was found in the underwater search, although a piece of wood found on the island by diver Bob Shaw may have been part of one of the ships; it was later carved with the names of the divers and saw service as an ashtray in his home!

The next major breakthrough in our understanding of Franklin's fate began in the 1980s. Owen Beattie, an anthropologist who had caught "Franklin Fever" from his colleague Jim Savelle, instigated the boldest plan to date: the exhumation of the three Franklin sailors buried in the first winter of the expedition at Beechey Island. Securing permits for this, as well as funding for the planned forensic examinations of the bodies, took time; the first body, that of John Torrington, was exhumed in 1984; his grave-mates John Hartnell and William Braine were exhumed in 1985. Beattie performed autopsies on these bodies, even setting up an x-ray tent on the island; photographs, tissue samples, and small squares of the men's clothing were brought back for further examination in the laboratory. It was this work, and the realization that the men all had elevated levels of lead, that produced the first grand theory of what had gone wrong. In this hypothesis, first set forth in Owen Beattie and John Geiger's *Frozen in Time* (1987), it was proposed that the tins of preserved meat, supplied to the expedition by Stephen Goldner, were the source of the lead; and moreover that the effects of these high lead levels would have produced increasingly serious cognitive issues, along with other symptoms (fatigue, anorexia) that could have doomed the expedition entirely.

Although this hypothesis was striking in its scope and influence, it should be noted that renewed laboratory studies in the past decade have significantly altered our understanding of the issue. There had always been concern about whether the levels of lead in the men's bodies were really higher than average for sailors of that era. As early as 2006, Franklin searcher Stephen Trafton published an essay in which he asked this question.[8] Clearer evidence emerged in 2017, when a study by K.L. Griffin of the bodies of Royal Navy sailors buried in Antigua at nearly the same time as Franklin's men showed very similar lead levels, without the benefit of Goldner's tins.[9] Simultaneously, a number of studies which included bone samples from later in the expedition's progress demonstrated via a more advanced use of x-ray fluorescence that new bone growth between these timeframes did not indicate increased lead absorption.[10] Given this new evidence, lead poisoning can no longer be seen as the sole or primary cause of the expedition's downfall, though it certainly may have been one factor. And, as demonstrated by co-editor Peter Carney, the vilification of Goldner's tins was entirely unjustified.[11] Goldner was, however, late with his shipment; this volume of letters includes several that allude to a delay in sailing, explained by Lieutenant Irving in his letter of 16 May (Letter 78): "We have been detained by some preserved meat not being ready" – the ships did not in fact sail until the morning of 19 May.

Following Beattie's work on the bodies at Beechey Island, the next significant period of new historical and archaeological work began in the 1990s with the work of the gifted amateur historian David C. Woodman. Woodman began with a very thorough analysis of all the historical Inuit oral tradition, including field notebooks and other papers of Hall in the collections of the Smithsonian Institution, which had never been published. The result of this work, *Unravelling the Franklin Mystery: Inuit Testimony* (1991), proved to be a turning point in our understanding of exactly what, where, and when things went wrong.[12] Woodman demonstrated that, carefully examined, the Inuit evidence – which was still being dismissed by historians at this stage – was, when painstakingly cross-referenced, remarkably consistent. Through a series of field searches he conducted himself, he was able to corroborate a great many of these oral histories, and he came surprisingly close to where Franklin's ship HMS *Erebus* was later found; only lack of resources and time prevented him from making that discovery. At around this same period, inspired by Woodman's book, another amateur historian – Barry Ranford, a high-school teacher in Ontario – made his own way to King William Island, where in 1994 he identified a site at Erebus Bay, known by its Borden coordinates as NgLj-2, whose full significance had been missed by previous searchers.[13] The following year an archaeological team led by Margaret Bertulli and Anne Keenleyside excavated the site. Their study, published in 1997, established clear evidence for cannibalism among at least one group of Franklin's men, corroborating Inuit accounts given to Hall and Schwatka, as well as to Dr John Rae some years earlier, in 1854.[14]

Woodman's searches continued through to 2004, and some members of his team, particularly Tom Gross, have continued searching in the years since.[15] During this period, their attention turned toward uncovering a "vault" spoken of in Inuit oral tradition, which may have contained the remains of Franklin himself, as well as written records, but it has proven elusive. The next significant epoch of field research came with the move by the Canadian government to support a team of Parks Canada underwater archaeologists in their initial efforts to locate one of Franklin's vessels. Their first field season took place under the supervision of Robert Grenier, and included the assistance of Louie Kamookak, an Inuk from Gjoa Haven who brought his own family's oral histories to bear on the search; having served as a guide for a number of earlier searches, he himself had taken a passionate interest in the story. The Parks Canada team made use of Woodman's earlier surveys, hoping to continue to narrow the area – somewhere to the west of the Adelaide Peninsula south of King William Island – to which the Inuit evidence pointed.

It was a lengthy process, given each year's short season; at this point the search was made mainly using side-scan sonar towfish pulled by boats, with support from the icebreaker *Sir Wilfrid Laurier*, which required open water in the area of the search. Further investigations, in 2010, 2012, and 2013, narrowed the search area, reaching a point where it was determined to shift the search from the coast of the Adelaide Peninsula northward to the Victoria Strait, where – it was surmised – one or both of Franklin's vessels might have sunk in the pack ice. The 2014 search, the most ambitious to that date, was accordingly dubbed the "Victoria Strait Expedition." The ice itself, though, had one final say; since the ice in the strait was too thick to deploy some of the specialized search equipment, an area closer to the original search zone became the focus. Thanks in part to the fortuitous find of a heavy iron davit pintle on an adjacent island – the assumption being that such a piece could not have drifted far – the search was directed there, where, on 2 September, a vessel later determined to be HMS *Erebus* was located, roughly halfway between the areas pointed to by the Inuit testimony given to Hall, and that recounted to Schwatka.[16]

The discovery of *Erebus* was followed, quite beyond expectations, scarcely two years later, by that of HMS *Terror* in Terror Bay. Sir Francis Leopold McClintock had named the bay in 1859, quite unaware that its eponymous ship lay secretly berthed in its depths. The chain of events leading to this discovery began with Gjoa Haven resident and Canadian Ranger Sammy Kogvik.[17] Aboard a support vessel operated by the Arctic Research Foundation which was headed up the western coast of King William Island to rendezvous with Parks Canada, Sammy told a story about how he had seen a large wooden pole – a mast, by his reckoning – sticking out of the ice on the east side of Terror Bay. The support vessel, the *Martin Bergmann*, decided to investigate despite the fact that the permit they were operating under – granted to Parks Canada – forbade any searches at Terror Bay. In that one regard, they acted rightly, although their failure to communicate with the Parks Canada team for the following eight days has stained what would have otherwise been the credit due to them. The Parks Canada team returned and in 2017, 2018, and 2019 began the long process of investigating the wreck of the *Terror*. In the last of these three seasons, via the deployment of a small remotely operated underwater vehicle (ROV), they obtained interior video footage showing the excellent preservation of HMS *Terror*, following the offi-cers' companionway through to Captain Crozier's "great cabin," where imagery of his desk was obtained. The contents of its drawers, alas, will have to wait until the ship, more confined than *Erebus* below decks and therefore better preserved, can be safely reached by the dive team.

So stands the archaeological and scientific investigation into the Franklin story – and certainly, it is quite possible that written records discovered aboard either vessel could entirely alter our present under-standing. For now, the wreck of HMS *Erebus* has been the main focus of artifact recovery, given that its shallow depth and vulnerability to strong waves have already – even since its discovery – compromised the integrity of the wreck. In the 2019 field season on *Erebus* – the best yet – more than 350 artifacts were brought up, but it remains to be seen what more can be discovered. Among those finds, though, one – a small stamp, the property of the captain's steward Edmund Hoar – stands out. Apparently intended to mark clothing, the stamp bears his name, "Ed. Hoar," and the device of an anchor. His life is one of those that intersect with the letters transcribed here; in Letter 159 – Franklin's very last epistle to his wife, Jane – he enclosed a note from Hoar to Mary Foster, Lady Franklin's maid. Of its contents we know nothing, but its existence demonstrates that the effects of this tragedy were felt not only by the Franklins but also by their respective personal servants, of whom this lately excavated artifact is a poignant reminder.

In addition to the extraordinary ongoing archaeological work of the Parks Canada team, land-based archaeology has carried on in its own bailiwick. Anne Keenleyside has continued to be associated with many of these studies, which include contributions by Robert Park and Douglas Stenton. In recent years Dr Stenton has set the ambitious goal of determining which reported Franklin sites and remains are in fact associated with the expedition, and making fresh visits to all sites whose authenticity is clear.[18] He has excavated bones reburied by the Schwatka expedition and also completed a recent excavation of Two Grave Bay.[19] In March of 2021 it was announced that his team had made the very first identification of the remains of one of Franklin's men by means of DNA evidence – that of Warrant Officer and 1st Engineer John Gregory of HMS *Erebus*, which was matched to a living descendant in South Africa.[20] The identified remains were from NgLj-3, a site on Erebus Bay where the Schwatka expedition had reburied Franklin expedition bones; over the years, this skull had come loose from the deposit and lay on open ground, where it was first spotted by Barry Ranford in 1993. The bones remained on the site until 2013, when they were removed for study by the team led by Dr Stenton. It is entirely possible that there will be additional identifications of this kind in the future; for now, we count it fortunate that Gregory is represented here in his own words, in Letter 155.

It should be mentioned at this point that two nearly complete skeletons were brought back in the nineteenth century, one by Hall in 1869 and one by Schwatka in 1880. Hall's skeleton was shipped back to Britain, and examined by no less a light than Thomas Henry Huxley; it was his conclusion that the bones were likely those of Lieutenant Henry Le Vesconte.[21] Notwithstanding this, they were interred – initially under the floor of the Painted Hall at Greenwich, and later within a marble memorial in the nearby Chapel – only as the remains of "one of Sir John Franklin's companions." When this memorial was moved in 2009, the bones were given a fresh examination; the isotope ratio of the teeth clearly indicated an origin among the granites of the eastern coast of Scotland (rather than chalky Devon, where Le Vesconte grew up); in addition, a facial reconstruction showed a strong resemblance to the daguerreotype of Harry Goodsir.[22] The existence of a gold filling also suggested a connection to the pioneering dentist Robert Nasmyth, who originated the use of gold for fillings in Scotland, and for whom Harry's brother John had worked as an assistant. It is not a 100 per cent certainty, but it is highly likely that these bones were Harry's; his strong connections with his family are richly evidenced in these letters, which even make reference to Nasmyth (see Letter 3 and note). The second skeleton, identified as that of John Irving by a maths medal found near the gravesite, was reinterred in Edinburgh and the remains have not yet been re-examined.

The archaeological finds – so far – from the ships have included only a relatively small number of items that can be identified with a single individual. In addition to Hoar's stamp already mentioned, a pair of epaulettes retrieved from an interior space in Lieutenant Fairholme's cabin are likely his, although since we know from Letter 105 that he posed for his daguerreotype wearing Fitzjames's borrowed jacket, they are *not* the same ones as in his photograph. Quite beyond personal contexts, of course, the materials brought up by Parks Canada are giving us a *collective* sense of life on board ship – plates, patent-medicine bottles, epaulettes, and scientific instruments all had their place, and the letters transcribed in his volume, similarly, give a broader picture of life on board. These two threads – the material histories and the historical documentation – may yet bring us a clearer picture of the expedition's overall work and progress; aboard HMS *Terror*, Captain Crozier's desk yet sits, equipped with the world's most intriguing drawers. The Parks Canada team has indicated that conditions there – darkness, low oxygen content of the water, and cold – are nearly ideal for the preservation of written documents.

The history – and historiography – of the expedition is another dimension of its meaning; here, the goal is not to "solve a mystery" but rather to trace its reception and articulation throughout the cultural and literary histories that have ensued from the first hints of the ships' disappearance in 1849 to the present day. Here, the change over time is due not to additional information alone, but to the differing cultural and ideological structures through which the expedition's story has been disseminated. The earliest period – that of the original search up through McClintock's remarkable finds in 1859 – is almost a separate phenomenon; it was, in a sense, the first mass-media disaster the world had ever seen. Every means of representing it and understanding it available in the mid-Victorian era was employed: panoramas, dioramas, coloured lantern slides, and public lectures fed on both the fame and the mystery of Franklin, while some searchers – particularly Dr Elisha Kent Kane in the United States – became for a time the stars of their own subsidiary shows.[23] Quite early on, the story attracted the theatre, with Wilkie Collins's 1857 play *The Frozen Deep* produced in close cooperation with his mentor Charles Dickens appearing as the first dramatization.[24] Dickens had already stepped into the controversy between the Inuit testimony of cannibalism reported by Dr John Rae in 1854 and the collective denial of Lady Franklin and much of the British public – and yet the play, as produced, slyly made cannibalism one of its central subjects, with a cook named "John Want" who prepares a soup of pounded bones (something that had indeed been tried – albeit with animal bones only – on Franklin's first land expedition, when he lost several men to starvation).

The literary aftershocks continued throughout the rest of the century. Joseph Conrad, reflecting in one of his last essays, "Geography and Some Explorers" (1925), recalled that it was reading McClintock's account at the age of ten that first stirred his interest in geography, and ultimately his career as a novelist as well:

My copy was probably in French. But I have read the book many times since. I have now on my shelves a copy of a popular edition got up exactly as I remember my first one. It contains a touching facsimile of the printed form filled in with a summary record of the two ships' work, the name of "Sir John Franklin, commanding the expedition," written in ink, and the pathetic underlined entry "All Well." It was found by Sir Leopold M'Clintock under a cairn, and is dated just a year before the two ships had to be abandoned in their deadly ice-trap and their crews' long and desperate struggle for life began. There could hardly have been imagined a better book for letting in the breath of the stern romance of polar exploration into the existence of a boy whose knowledge of the poles of the earth had been till then of an abstract, formal kind, as the imaginary ends of the imaginary axis upon which the earth turns.[25]

Conrad's reference to the facsimile of the Victory Point note shows the expedition's continuing influence and the intrinsic contrast between its initial hubris and its year-later documentation of disaster. It seems no coincidence that at the beginning of Conrad's own masterwork, *Heart of Darkness*, his narrator Marlow speaks of Franklin among the "knights-errant" of the sea who sailed down the Thames; nor that, as Marlow ascends the dark river into the interior of the African continent, one of the things he comes upon is a book about the use of magnetic compasses abandoned by a sailor.

Much of the other early literature inspired by the Franklin story is far less well-known. There were quite a few poems, including an elegy by Algernon Charles Swinburne that was entered in a Franklin-themed poetry contest at Oxford in 1860 (it did not win). R.D. Blackmore, among the most successful novelists of the later nineteenth century, penned a lengthy but now-forgotten poem, "The Fate of Franklin," that same year. Later poetic framings of the expedition include Canadian poet Gwendolyn MacEwen's "Terror and Erebus" (1965) as well as David Solway's book-length poetic cycle *Franklin's Passage* (2003). In modern times, a number of noted novelists have returned to the subject, among them Sten Nadolny (*The Discovery of Slowness*, 1983), Steven Heighton (*Afterlands*, 2006), and Richard Flanagan (*Wanting*, 2009).

In the era following news of his death, Franklin also received the usual hagiographies, most prominently Sir Albert Hastings Markham's *Life of Sir John Franklin and the North-west Passage* (1891) and *The Life of Sir John Franklin* by Henry Duff Traill (1896). Modern biographies include those of Roderic Owen (*The Fate of Franklin*, 1978), Andrew Lambert (*Franklin: Tragic Hero of Polar Navigation*, 2009), and Martyn Beardsley (*Deadly Winter: The Life of Sir John Franklin*, 2002). Owen, who was a descendant of Franklin, produced a very finely grained portrait, drawing from many of the letters reproduced here which are now in the hands of his niece (and this book's co-editor) Mary Williamson; for his part, Lambert chose to focus much of his book on the role of the expedition in the Magnetic Crusade,[26] and Beardsley's, although it paints a lively portrait, is marred by its deprecation of the Inuit testimony.

The nineteenth-century view of Franklin tended to obscure any of the disturbing or uncertain sides of his story and elevate him to the highest firmament of Polar heroism; even Conrad, who clearly steered his own narratives into darkness, spoke of Franklin's "professional prestige and high personal character," qualities of a man who "served geography, even in death." And, to be sure, there is ample evidence of his character in the letters collected here; every single officer and sailor who mentions him seems to speak highly of him, with Charles Hamilton Osmer, purser of HMS *Erebus*, perhaps the most effusive, even florid in his praise: "The more I see of our worthy chief, the more I like and admire him, in that he is deservedly <u>beloved</u> by us <u>all</u>, Seamen as well as Officers, and I cannot but prognosticate that success will certainly follow one whose moral character is so every way deserving of encomiums" (Letter 136). Franklin's merits seem indeed to have been singular, while his flaws – a degree of ethnocentrism, the naval habit of sticking close to orders, or not having planned for every exigency – were common ones among his peers. His death and those of his men, though often referred to today as a "failure," were memorialized to an almost sanctifying degree, with the small bits of rediscovered domestic clutter – forks, dessert spoons, and eyeglasses – revered and referred to as "relics."

The degree of this early memorialization is nowhere clearer than in Wilkie Collins's title and introduction to the letters of James Fitzjames (an uncensored version of which is among those in this volume), which appeared in Dickens's journal *All the Year Round* in 1859. Under the title "Last Leaves of a Sorrowful Book," Collins opined:

In the history of our lives there is one touching domestic experience, associated with the solemn mystery of Death, which is familiar to us all. When the grave has claimed its own; when the darkened rooms are open again to the light of heaven; when grief rests more gently on the weary heart, and the tears, restrained through the day, fall quietly in the lonely night hours, there comes a time at which we track the farewell journey of the dead over the familiar ways of home by the simple household relics that the lost and loved companion has left to guide us. At every point of the dread pilgrimage from this world to the next, some domestic trace remains that appeals tenderly to the memory, and that leads us on, from the day when the last illness began, to the day that left us parted on a sudden from our brother or sister-spirit by the immeasurable gulf between Life and Eternity. The sofa on which we laid the loved figure so tenderly when the first warning weakness declared itself; the bed, never slept in since, which was the next inevitable stage in the sad journey; all the little sick-room contrivances for comfort that passed from our living hands to the one beloved hand which shall press ours in gratitude no more; the last book read to beguile the wakeful night, with the last place marked where the weary eyes closed for ever over the page; the little favourite trinkets laid aside never to be picked up again ... these mute relics find a language of their own, when the first interval of grief allows us to see them again; a language that fills the mind and softens the heart, and makes the sacred memory of the dead doubly precious; a language that speaks to every nation and every rank, and tells, while the world lasts, the one solemn story that exalts, purifies, and touches us all alike.[27]

This same backward glance, rich with nostalgia and tragic atmosphere, remained the dominant mode through which Franklin and his men were seen throughout the rest of the nineteenth and most of the twentieth centuries. It remained for Canadian historian Pierre Berton to begin to desanctify such beatific reveries, and point out what perhaps had been obvious all along: that by eschewing Inuit ways of knowledge – how to travel, hunt, and live off the land using dog-drawn sleds and living in igloos or tents – Franklin and those who sent him had doomed the expedition. This mistake was now, by Berton, couched as cultural blindness and ethnocentrism; Franklin's loss was no longer a tragedy but a telling tale of the cost of cultural myopia. This view, which Berton expressed in his magisterial volume *The Arctic Grail* (1988), set the tone for a sea-change in the public view of the Franklin expedition. Among its natural consequences was the elevation of figures such as Dr John Rae – who used the Inuit's hunting and survival techniques and was on good terms with them – at the expense of Franklin. The most widely read proponent of this new view is Ken McGoogan, whose 2002 book *Fatal Passage: The Untold Story of John Rae, the Arctic Hero Time Forgot* initiated a reappraisal of Rae that has had wide influence; Rae has now been celebrated in films (John Walker's 2008 *Passage*), festivals (an annual

John Rae festival now takes place in Orkney, sponsored by the John Rae Society), and in the purchase and restoration of Rae's home, the Hall of Clestrain, by that same society.

It is a welcome correction, of course, but by no means the last neces-sary one. The most recent development in Franklin studies has been with critical reappraisals, not so much of the histories themselves, but of the underlying bias of the historiographical methods and tone continued in even the most recent work on Franklin. The leading voice of this critique has been Adriana Craciun, whose 2016 study *Writing Arctic Disaster: Authorship and Exploration* offers dual criticisms both of the original explorers' narratives, and of the narratives contemporary scholars and writers have made of them. One of her key areas of critique is the treat-ment accorded the Franklin "relics":

> Beginning with the earliest collections of Franklin disaster debris, not only the message but the relics themselves were indistinct and unsta-ble artifacts verging on ecofacts, further losing ontological cohesion and categorical integrity as searches proliferated more objects and they in turn more questions.[28]

It's an apt apothegm of the way the relics have been seen and writ-ten about, one to which Craciun joins the question of the disposition of cultural artifacts generally. Craciun argues that, for far too long, we have experienced the Franklin story, along with others of explorers *in extremis*, in a manner rather too similar to that of our Victorian fore-bears. Like them, we read and reread the explorers' original narratives, letting the woodcuts and engravings with which they were illustrated carry us north on imaginary wings; like them, we dote over relics, seek-ing amid spoons and eyeglasses the vital clues that might solve it all.

And yet, despite this, nostalgia and memorial tones remain persistent elements. This was vividly demonstrated by the travelling exhibition "Death in the Ice: The Mystery of the Franklin Expedition." This exhibit, which began in Greenwich in 2017–18 and also appeared in Ottawa, Mystic Connecticut, and Anchorage Alaska, was warmly received by the museum-going public.[29] There they could see two sorts of objects – some of the original "relics" brought back at the time (including the Victory Point record, in its first exposure outside the UK) alongside items recovered from HMS *Erebus* by the Parks Canada team. Also included, very pointedly, were items in which Inuit had repurposed some of the materials found on land or in the ships, along with recordings of the words of Inuit elders – Louie Kamookak's among them – describing the oral tradition of the encounter with these strangers. Such an exhibition of course must give the public what it wants – but here the objects of reverence were purposefully juxtaposed with those of utility, and the Inuit story told, not as ancillary, but as one equally as vital as the European perspective, providing as it did the long-sought solution to the mystery of Franklin's ships. It might be noted at this point that a number of the letters in this volume describe crew-members' encounters with Inuit – although in West Greenland rather than the Canadian Arctic – and it must be admitted that nearly all the writers regarded the Inuit as implicitly inferior (Fairholme calls them "the <u>dirtiest</u> race I ever came across" in Letter 140), while praising the efforts of the Moravian missionaries to bring them closer to the twin goods of Christianity and Civilization. Perhaps significantly, it's a non-naval man, ship's engineer James Thompson, who offers the most empathetic view: "they appear to be A harmless set of People and very honest I had two of the Men to supper on Munday Night" (Letter 156).

Doubtless the most widely seen version of the Franklin story is that of the AMC television series *The Terror* (2018). Based on Dan Simmons's 2007 novel of the same name, it is set firmly within the horror genre, with a monstrous bear-like spirit creature conjured by an Inuit shaman as its antagonist – and a far more hubristic Franklin than will be encountered in these pages. And yet, at the same time, it made use of extraordinarily careful historical research and gave each of the persons represented his own character arc based on his personal histories and traits. This is especially evident with Harry Goodsir, who – as portrayed by Paul Ready – is a sympathetic character, taking a keen interest in the Inuit and even at one point working to compile a comparative grammar of Inuktitut. And indeed, the real historical Goodsir actually did so, as evidenced here in one of Lieutenant James Fairholme's letters: "I assisted Goodsir yesterday in collecting words for a vocabulary, & we were very much struck with the resemblance between their language & what we know of the Tartar & Kamschatadate. Every word almost begins & ends with a <u>K</u> which makes the language harsh" (Letter 140). Inuktitut indeed is related to languages in the Mongolian family; that a non-linguist would have had this kind of insight is remarkable in and of itself. Ready's Goodsir is also sympathetic to, and makes the most concerted effort to communicate with, "Lady Silence," played by the Greenlandic Inuk Nive Nielsen. Along with her, Johnny Issaluk and several other Canadian Inuit actors appear in all the Inuit roles – a welcome departure from the usual Hollywood and television-drama practices.

All of which brings us to the present moment when, after a period of relative obscurity, the story of the Franklin expedition is becoming increasingly well known outside of historical and archaeological circles. Since the ships' original disappearance, the public's interest has never been so pronounced, and it is for those readers that this book is primarily intended. We, the editors, have been at pains to make this text as readily accessible as possible, while at the same time making it as accurate as can be. Many of the sources for our letters – original manuscripts retained by the explorers' families, faded old photostats and typed copies, and – when no other copy can be located – even newspaper clippings, have posed many and various challenges in making sure we have followed consistent rules and procedures in rendering their text. The great majority of these letters have never before appeared in print, and it is to the families of these men, present and past, that we owe the greatest debt. It is our hope that the letters here will now go forth into the world and someday perhaps be joined by preserved writings from the same individuals, brought up from the cold Arctic waters by the skilled hands of Parks Canada divers. And so, as both underwater and land-based archaeologists continue their slow and careful work, and as scholars and historians evaluate and sift through new evidence as it emerges – they and we will continue to weigh it, seeking always to better understand the ultimate meaning of this singular chapter in the history of exploration.

THE LETTERS THEMSELVES

What you are about to read is a remarkable, never-before-assembled collection of personal letters from the era of the planning, departure, and first few months of sailing of HMS *Erebus* and HMS *Terror*. All the long history of the expedition's aftermath, of searches and theories and evidence, was as yet far in the future, neither knowable nor determined. From the viewpoint of Franklin and his men, many possible futures still lay ahead, and while some writers, such as Harry Goodsir's father, John, initially looked upon the voyage as a "fearful hazard," the general feeling seems to have been one of optimism and high expectation.

It should be cautioned, though, that while this is the largest collection yet assembled, it is almost certainly only a small portion of the total number of letters likely sent from the ships. Included here are letters from seventeen of the officers and crew; eleven of the writers are from the *Erebus,* and just six from the *Terror*. This represents only about 12 per cent of the 134 on board both ships at the onset of the voyage (five were sent home from Greenland for various reasons, leaving 129). Not only is there a significant bias toward the men of the *Erebus* but the list is officer-heavy, with thirteen officers, two warrant officers, one marine, and one petty officer. Not one of the ordinary sailors, rated able seamen – of whom there were thirty-nine – is represented. A lower level of literacy among this group may have been a factor, but the majority of men at this time would have been literate to some degree.[30] Lastly, the more senior officers tended to write far longer letters, and more frequently, than their juniors; Franklin's last letter to his wife, Jane, alone runs to over 5,700 words.

We also felt, right from the start, that we would want to include all the letters we could find that were sent *to* the men by their friends and families. With these letters we faced one additional disadvantage; those mailed early on had a reasonably good chance of reaching their recipients, in which case they were lost when the ships were lost. Most of the surviving letters, therefore, date from a later time, at which point concerns about the fate of the expedition were growing. The Admiralty periodically offered to take letters from family members aboard search ships such as the *Plover* and the *North Star*, which are mentioned by a number of the writers. Jane Franklin, who as the sponsor of many of the searchers wrote more letters than anyone else, sent one with nearly every vessel and, when they were returned undelivered, sent them out again.

Those whose letters were eventually returned – and not all may have been – would then have had to preserve them over a long period of time. Cherished at first, the letters would have been passed down through many generations to reach the present moment. Some were kept by the families, some donated to public archives, and some laid aside only to be rediscovered years later in attics and old suitcases. Even those thought to be safely preserved in libraries have sometimes gone astray, due to gaps in catalogues, particularly when these were transferred to digital systems. One example of such missing letters is those of James Reid, ice master aboard HMS *Erebus*; his family emigrated to Australia, and at one point in the 1930s shared excerpts of them with a local newspaper. Nevertheless, and although his descendants there searched diligently, they were not relocated in the archives of the State Library of New South Wales until 2020, when the original card catalogue was fully digitized. More may yet be discovered – only time will tell how many.

Not all of the letters that appear here are being published for the first time; some were published in full or in part in the *Arctic Blue Books* printed for the Admiralty; others appeared in newspapers or magazines, or were privately published (Fitzjames's letters to his sister-in-law Elizabeth Coningham appeared in both forms). In a very few cases, such as Esther Blanky's quotation from a letter of her husband's, a newspaper version is all we have; in three cases, such letters were published with no attribution (these are given in Appendix B). Our aim here has been to present them in chronological order, while providing some context and notes to explain any references that time has rendered obscure. In the case of Harry Goodsir, we also felt it appropriate to include a selection of correspondence from his family and friends, written well prior to the expedition, as they offer unique documentation of his lengthy and ultimately successful campaign to be selected as the expedition's naturalist.

Unlike the letters *from* the men, the undelivered letters *to* them were written by family members and friends who knew all too well that something – though they did not yet know what – had gone wrong. The earliest are full of news and the expectation of soon hearing word of the expedition's success; over time, the tone shifts to one of hopes diminished, with words of religious faith and comfort. Even Jane Franklin, not usually given to strong religious sentiments, reached that point at last: "If the prayers of all who love you can have availed with that Merciful God whose ear is ever open to the cry of all who trust to Him, you will yet be spared to us" (Letter 181). From Lady Franklin down to the families of the humblest members of the crew, the sentiments expressed were much the same. Sarah Hartnell, who as the mother of two of Franklin's sailors – John and Thomas – must have felt a double burden of anxious anticipation, was among them. Fittingly, it is the closing words of her letter to them – written, although she was not to know it, after John had already died and been laid to rest on Beechey Island – that give this book its title: "if it is the Lords will may we be spared to meet on earth if not God grant we may all meet around his throne to praise him to all eternity" (Letter 175).

I have stood before John Hartnell's grave on Beechey Island and read this letter aloud to groups of expedition travellers who have made a special pilgrimage to the place. Her words are as poignant and resonant today – indeed, more so – as they were before their ink was dry. Her deep religious faith, her heartfelt hope that her letter would reach her sons, yet with an acceptance of the fact that, despite all hope, it might not – all ring loudly and clearly in her simple yet eloquent words. It is the kind of letter we seem to have forgotten how to write – but not how to appreciate. Here before you are the testimonies of many others that such faith was not misplaced; nor was the men's resolve any less firm for knowing the risk they undertook. If we see, amid the fateful clamour of their impending doom, some light, some ray of possibility, it is here, in their own words, with all the particulars of their yet-undimmed expectations.

A NOTE ON THE TEXTS

In the transcriptions of these letters, we have aimed for the highest possible degree of accuracy. All the letters that survive in manuscript have been gone over by numerous editors to make certain that the texts accurately reflect the originals. We have retained *all* original spelling, no matter how archaic or idiosyncratic; usage that might be unfamiliar is glossed in the notes. We have also – to the extent possible – preserved their format, along with different forms of dates, headers, and postscripts.

That said, in the interests of readability, we have made some slight emendations:

- Abbreviations have for the most part been silently expanded, with the exception of common breviagraphs such as *&c.* (spelled in various ways; we follow the usage of the original) or @, along with *inst.* (meaning the same month) and *ult.* (the previous month); HMS (or H.M.S. in some instances) is given as in the originals. Individual writers' habits of using periods (or not) after "Mr," "Mrs," and "Dr" have been respected; initials or abbreviations in signatures have been retained exactly as written. "V.D.L." and "VDL," which both Sir John and Lady Franklin used as shorthand for Van Diemen's Land (modern Tasmania), have been retained as such.
- To the extent possible, the formatting of the letters reflects that of the originals, including varying degrees of indentation along with different forms of dates, headers, and postscripts.
- Where needed for clarity, we have at times added some very light punctuation (many of the writers, of sundry backgrounds, seem to have ended quite a few sentences without a period).
- Where, despite all efforts, a word could not be definitively deciphered, our best guess is marked with a (?) and conjectural readings of missing letters are in square brackets. Physical gaps in the text, due to paper loss or being obscured behind wax seals or inkblots and so forth, are designated thus: [...] and, if extensive, are commented on in the notes.
- Superscript words have not been noted as such, and when a writer has crossed out one word and replaced it with another, we have treated that as an editorial change and followed the text as edited; any such changes that could be seen as altering the substance of the letter are described in the notes.

- Various writers employ many forms of ampersands and "+" symbols; in the interests of readability these are all represented by "&"; however, if a writer spells out "and" this is *always* followed.
- Any specific issues related to sources are mentioned in the notes, such as when the only source may be a faded photostat, typed copy, or printed version.

Rather than sprinkle the letters with numerous footnotes, we have chosen to use endnotes keyed to each letter. Every proper name, every object, every place, and every reference that would be unfamiliar to today's reader is explained there. Generally, the names or references that occur more than once are glossed on their first appearance, although in a few cases we have chosen to do so in a letter where they are specifically mentioned in greater detail (all others are cross-referenced). In addition, we have sought, in the introductions to the several sections, to give the most important backgrounds and highlights of what follows. For each correspondent, we have supplied a capsule biography, with an emphasis on the writer's circumstances current at the time of sailing.

It should also be noted that some writers penned "serial" letters, continuing the text with a new header and date. Some of these are presented here as written, while others – such as James Fitzjames's self-described "journal" or Osmer's short daily jottings – have been separated out into parts, in order for the text not to get too far ahead of the overall chronology, and to keep (for instance) references to the approach to Greenland near one another. In such cases, we have made these divisions only where and when the writer has put in a fresh indication of the date.

Some of the letters included or were accompanied by sketches or drawings; wherever possible these are reproduced here with them. We have also provided maps to show the progress of the expedition during the time the letters were sent and also to show the anticipated routes through the Arctic, which were – quite understandably – the subject of much conversation among the men as they drew closer and closer to uncharted waters. Our hope is that, to the fullest extent possible, readers will feel as if they are just over the shoulders of these writers and can have an uninterrupted experience of their collective testimony.

NOTES

1   Mark Twain, *A Connecticut Yankee in King Arthur's Court* (Toronto: Rose Publishing Co., 1890), 119.

2   Francis Leopold McClintock, *The Voyage of the 'Fox' in the Arctic Seas* (London: John Murray, 1859).

3   See Charles Francis Hall (ed. J.E. Nourse), *Narrative of the second Arctic expedition made by Charles F. Hall: his voyage to Repulse bay, sledge journeys to the straits of Fury and Hecla and to King William's land, and residence among the Eskimos, during the years 1864–'69* (Washington, DC: Government Printing Office, 1879); Schwatka, Frederick, *The Long Arctic Search: The Narrative of Lieutenant Frederick Schwatka* (Mystic, Connecticut: Marine Historical Association, 1965); Gilder, William H., *Schwatka's Search: Sledging in the Arctic in quest of the Franklin records* (London: S. Low, Marston, Searle and Rivington, 1881); and Heinrich Klutschak, *Overland to Starvation Cove: With the Inuit in Search of Franklin, 1878–1880*, tr. and ed. by William Barr (Toronto: University of Toronto Press, 1993) (a translation of *Als Eskimo unter den Eskimos: eine Schilderung der Erlebnisse Schwatka'schen Franklin-Aufsuchungs-Expedition in den Jahren 1878–80* (Vienna: A. Hartlemben, 1881).

4   L.T. Burwash, *Canada's Western Arctic: Report on Investigations in 1925–26, 1928–29, and 1930* (Ottawa: F.A. Acland, 1931).

5   Hodgson, Pilot, and Ootes were the leading members of an informal group, the "Franklin Probe," whose periodic reports were self-published in very limited numbers; a collection of these is in the archives of the Royal Geographical Society, SJF/10.

6   Richard J. Cyriax, *Sir John Franklin's Last Arctic Expedition: A Chapter in the History of the Royal Navy* (London: Methuen, 1939).

7   Richard J. Cyriax, "A Historic Medicine Chest," *Canadian Medical Association Journal* 57, no. 3 (1947): 295–300; with A.G.E. Jones, "The Papers in the Possession of Harry Peglar, Captain of the Foretop, H.M.S. Terror, 1845," *The Mariner's Mirror* 40, no. 3 (1954): 186–95. These papers have been the subject of further research by one of the present editors; see Russell A. Potter, "The 'Peglar' Papers Revisited," *Trafalgar Chronicle: The Yearbook of the 1805 Club*, 2014.

8   Stephen Trafton, "Did Lead Poisoning Contribute to the Death of Franklin Expedition Members?" in Alan Day, *Dictionary of the Discovery and Exploration of the Northwest Passage* (Landham, Maryland: Scarecrow Press, 2006).

9   K.L. Giffin, T. Swanston, I. Coulthard, A.R. Murphy, D.M.L. Cooper, and T.L. Varney, "Skeletal Lead Burden of the British Royal Navy in Colonial Antigua," *International Journal of Osteoarchaeology* 27 (2017): 672–82.

10 See Ronald Richard Martin, Steven Naftel, Sheila Macfie, Keith Jones, and Andrew Nelson, "Pb Distribution in Bones from the Franklin Expedition: Synchrotron X-ray Fluorescence and Laser Ablation/Mass Spectroscopy," *Applied Physics A* 111 (2013): 23–9; and K. Millar, A. Bowman, and W. Battersby, "A Re-analysis of the Supposed Role of Lead Poisoning in Sir John Franklin's Last Expedition, 1845–1848," *Polar Record* 51, no. 3 (2015): 224–38.

11 See Peter Carney's blog "Erebus and Terror Files," particularly the posts for 11 June, 16 and 24 November, and 6 December 2020: http://erebus-andterrorfiles.blogspot.com.

12 A second edition, unchanged save for a new introduction, was published by McGill-Queen's University Press in 2015; Woodman also wrote a second book, *Strangers Among Us* (Montreal and Kingston: McGill-Queen's University Press, 1995), which offers further reconstructions of the Inuit testimony specific to the Melville Peninsula area.

13 Barry Ranford, "Bones of Contention," *Equinox* magazine, spring 1994, 69–87.

14 Anne Keenleyside et al., "The Final Days of the Franklin Expedition: New Skeletal Evidence," *Arctic* 50, no. 1 (1997): 36–46.

15 See the webpage index "David C. Woodman Franklin Search Expeditions," hosted by Russell Potter at Rhode Island College's website: https://w3.ric.edu/faculty/rpotter/woodman/mainpage.html.

16 This is based on the map prepared by Rupert Thomas Gould for L.T. Burwash, officially known as Admiralty Chart 5101. It indicates the locations of all Franklin remains as reported by both European and Inuit sources; the site reported to Schwatka is marked "S" and that reported to Hall is marked "H." LAC, R11630–3307-8-E, Box number: 2000358357.

17 Steve Ducharme, "Ship Director and Inuk Ranger Tell the Tale of Terror," *Nunatsiaq News*, 23 September 2016, https://nunatsiaq.com/stories/article/65674ship_director_and_inuk_ranger_tell_the_tale_of_terror/.

18 Douglas R. Stenton, "Finding the Dead: Bodies, Bones and Burials from the 1845 Franklin Northwest Passage Expedition," *Polar Record*, 2018.

19 Douglas R. Stenton, Anne Keenleyside, and Robert W. Park, "The 'Boat Place' Burial: New Skeletal Evidence from the 1845 Franklin Expedition," *Arctic* 68, no. 1 (March 2015): 32–44; Douglas R. Stenton, Anne Keenleyside, Philippe Froesch, and Robert W. Park, "A Franklin Expedition Officer's Burial at Two Grave Bay, King William Island, Nunavut," *Journal of Archaeological Science:* Reports 35 (2021).

20 Douglas R. Stenton, Stephen Fratpietro, Anne Keenleyside, and Robert W. Park, "DNA Identification of a Sailor from the 1845 Franklin Northwest Passage Expedition," *Polar Record* 57 (e14), 1–5.

21   Thomas Henry Huxley (1825–1895) was an eminent biologist specializing in comparative anatomy; his outspoken advocacy of the theory of natural selection earned him the moniker "Darwin's Bulldog."

22   S. Mays, A. Ogden, J. Montgomery, S. Vincent, W. Battersby, and G.M. Taylor, "New Light on the Personal Identification of a Skeleton of a Member of Sir John Franklin's Last Expedition to the Arctic, 1845," *Journal of Archaeological Science*, July 2011, 1571–82.

23   See Russell A. Potter, *Arctic Spectacles: The Frozen North in Visual Culture, 1818–1875* (Seattle and London: University of Washington Press, 2007).

24   See Robert Louis Brannan, *Under the Management of Mr. Charles Dickens: His production of "The Frozen Deep"* (Ithaca: Cornell University Press, 1966).

25   Joseph Conrad, "Geography and Some Explorers," *National Geographic Magazine* 45 (March 1924): 241–356. http://www.conradfirst.net/view/serialisation-id=53.html.

26   While Lambert is correct that mapping of the earth's magnetic field was a key scientific goal of the expedition, I believe he is wrong to say that it was its *primary* overall goal. The "Magnetic Crusade" was that of Edward Sabine (1788–1883) to map the earth's magnetic field, particularly on common "term dates." He is represented in this volume by Letters 126 (Franklin), 130 (Fitzjames), 153 (Franklin), and 164 (Fitzjames), which discuss the magnetic measurements being undertaken.

27   [Wilkie Collins], "Last Leaves of a Sorrowful Book," *All the Year Round* 1, no. 14 (30 July 1859): 318–23, https://www.djo.org.uk/indexes/articles/the-last-leaves-of-a-sorrowful-book.html.

28   Adriana Craciun, *Writing Arctic Disaster: Authorship and Exploration* (Cambridge: Cambridge University Press, 2016), 44.

29   The lead curator for this exhibition was Karen Ryan of the Canadian Museum of History, Gatineau, Quebec.

30   Inferred literacy (based on the percentage of those able to sign their names in marriage registries) suggests a literacy rate of 69 per cent among men in 1840, but this was unevenly distributed; those living in larger cities, for instance, were considerably more likely to be literate than those in small towns or rural areas. See W.B. Stephens, "Literacy in England, Scotland, and Wales, 1500–1900," *History of Education Quarterly* 30, no. 4 (1990): 555.

I

Anticipation

When I look upon the fearful hazard ...

John Goodsir

These, the earliest letters related to the Franklin expedition, date back to the time before it was fully planned and assembled; indeed, in some cases (as with Harry Goodsir) they predate any definite plans for such an undertaking. The context for these first letters was the period following the return of James Clark Ross's highly successful Antarctic expedition (1839–43), which took place using the same two ships – HMSS *Erebus* and *Terror* – that would later be Franklin's. There was some expectation at that moment that Ross would soon be despatched on a fresh expedition, to either the Antarctic or the Arctic, and those whose interest in serving in such an endeavour was keenest clutched at every rumour. Harry Goodsir, though just recently appointed as the conservator of the Surgeons' Hall Museum in Edinburgh, was the keenest of all; he peppered his family with anxious queries, and they in turn peppered every contact they had within the Admiralty (it is for this reason that, in this section only, we have included letters from these other correspondents). It is possible that another expedition under Ross might have been proposed, save for the apparently surprising news contained in a note from Lord Haddington (then first lord of the Admiralty) that "Sir James Ross has married a wife – & is publishing a book !!!" Ross having, in addition to that, apparently withdrawn from any consideration for command, key figures such as Sir John Barrow, who still sought to launch a fresh mission for the Discovery Service, turned their attention to other possible candidates, and – with Ross's support – Sir John Franklin was eventually selected to command a fresh search for a navigable Northwest Passage. Goodsir, in the meantime, having already ingratiated himself sufficiently, turned his attention to securing the title of *naturalist* – a point of professional pride for him, given that he would have to step aside from his other duties; the role of naturalist meant an appointment as a mere assistant surgeon, and would make him one of the few members of the expedition with no naval or maritime background. James Fitzjames, another early candidate for a senior position, had the singular advantage of a close friendship with John Barrow Jr, Sir John Barrow's son, although in the end he was given command of neither ship but was assigned at the rank of commander to serve as Franklin's second aboard *Erebus*. Unbeknownst to him, Franklin (with the support of Ross) had another candidate in mind for second-in-command: Francis Crozier. Crozier, then in the midst of a holiday in Italy, heard from his old friend of the possibility of his serving as Franklin's second and replied that he was very much ready to do so. Others, as their appointments were made, wrote to let their families know, as – one by one – they headed for London and Woolwich. Newcomers such as Goodsir found that they had to purchase their own uniforms, while veterans like Crozier, his appointment confirmed, wrote to his sister Charlotte – affectionately known to him as "Small" – to be sure that she got his uniform and epaulettes out of his dresser drawer and shipped along to him. There was an air of expectation in every letter, as all those who were summoned to the undertaking wrote in optimistic terms to their comrades and confidantes. Truly, it seemed that this expedition, more than any other before it, was sure to meet with success.

CHRONOLOGY

24 December 1844: First mention of the possibility of Franklin's appointment to the expedition (Letter 10)

30 December 1844: First mention of Crozier's possible appointment as second-in-command (Letter 11)

27 January 1845: Sir John Barrow retires from the Admiralty (Letter 20)

7 February 1845: Franklin receives word from Lord Haddington that he has been given command of the expedition (Letter 24)

3 March 1845: HMS Erebus and HMS Terror are officially commissioned; first trial of the "Halkett" inflatable boat (Letter 40)

11 March 1845: Date of Harry Goodsir's letter of appointment as assistant surgeon on hms Erebus (Letter 41)

24 March 1845: Alexander McDonald writes that he has been appointed as assistant surgeon on hms Terror (Letter 43)

1. JOHN GOODSIR TO HARRY GOODSIR [SON], 11 JUNE 1844

Manse Largo
11 June 1844

My dearest son Harry

I am quite happy my letter of Thursday with its contents, of all sorts, reached in safety. I have no doubt Mr. O. would get your letter & the B.

What you mention to me regarding Captain Ross' expedition, on first sight, appears fair & desireable, but I have a great misgiving when I look upon the fearful hazard, altho I would allow, that on reading accounts of such voyages, my enthusiasm has always been raised, and at your time of life, I would myself have undertaken such a voyage. It is necessary at some time to take a cool and dispashionate view of the whole matter & to reflect upon the circumstances connected with your present situation as Curator of the College of Surgeons for granting you were allowed to undertake the appointment of Surgeon & Naturalist to Captain Ross' expedition, is it not likely the College might grant an interim appointment only, to your substitute, for a limited period, and were the expedition to be delayed beyond the expected period, you might be shoved out of the Curatorship. Well without saying more about the certainties & uncertainties, I wish you to write to me by return of post who appoints to this situation, whether the Admiralty or Captain Ross &c. &c., and as I know of no one save Admiral Durham to whom I can write, I will only delay doing so till I hear from you; so do answer this tomorrow afternoon.

I was at Carnbee yesterday with Jane. She went to Grangemuir & I made calls at Drumrack, Kingsmuir, &c. Mrs. Farmer has not gained that full state of health, a nurse ought to enjoy nor has her infant been quite the thing. For the mother whose appetite is miserably bad, & who sweats profusely – he (Trotter) has ordered regular exercise in open air, – without medicine of any kind, denying all such – for the child who suffers greatly from flatulence in the stomach & bowels, he ordered hot whisky toddy – here is practice for you. & here likewise is a total loss of sight of his own gain – not a penny for medicine.

Lady William Douglas told Jane, that she had sent for him (Trotter) a good while ago to see two of the young ladies with cough. He said there was little the matter – ordered no medicine whatever – & has never once called again. – Here is the man of Edinburgh – London – & Dublin. His <u>skull is filled with peat moss.</u>

Love to John & Archie and yourself – the post at hand – Let have a letter on Thursday.

Your very affectionate Father

John Goodsir

2. ROBERT GOODSIR TO HARRY GOODSIR [BROTHER], 11 JUNE 1844

London, 27 Surry Street
11th June 1844

My dear Harry

Upon calling on Forbes today he shewed me a letter from you regarding the Arctic expedition. Forbes says he is completely at a loss as to some of the particulars. In the first place, are you certain that such an expedition is actually on foot, for no one here has heard anything about it. In the next place, Forbes would like to know, if you are certain that you would be appointed naturalist, if the expedition really went on. Write to him & let him know fully what are the sources of your information concerning the expedition & your hopes of being appointed Naturalist.

I would have sent Johns shirts & your socks &c before this, but that I could not find a box that would hold them suitably. I have however fallen in with one today, & will send them off without delay. I am afraid John has been put to inconvenience from the want of his linen.

Mr. Cleghorn called on me here today. He sets off for the continent end of the week.

Yours

Robert A Goodsir

I delivered your parcel safely to Professor Bell.

3. HARRY GOODSIR TO JOHN GOODSIR [FATHER], 11 JUNE 1844

Royal College of Surgeons
Edinburgh 11th June 1844

My Dear Father

It was very stupid of me to forget in my letter of last night to ask you to write to Admiral Durham about Captain Ross expedition. It was only when I was talking to Mr. Nasmyth that it came into my head. Mr. N. recommended me to write to the Admiral without delay which I did. I was at one time uncertain whether it would be altogether right in me writing him but after consulting John it was aggreed upon to send the letter off. I wish however you would write to the Admiral by tomorrows Post & ask him to use his interest in my favour. I offered to send testimonials if they were thought necessary. Mr. Nasmyth told me this morning that after consulting with Sir George Ballingall Sir George freely aggreed with him that it would be of advantage to the College to in the way of procuring specimens and that if Dr. Gairdners influence could be gained I could go out as Conservator for apparently Gairdner's opinion has great weight with the College. Now fortunately I have had a great deal to do with Gairdner of late with regard to these Hydatids & have prepared a number of drawings for him of them so that I will be able to secure him & all that is necessary then is the obtaining the appointment under Ross which with Lord Williams & Admiral Durhams influence will be almost certain. If there is any other person however which you think may be of service write to them without delay but it would be needless to write to anyone unless they were to be decidedly useful for we do not want the thing spread abroad. Do you think Captain Nairne would be of any service?

I spoke to Dr. Henderson to day about John Reekie but he said he could say nothing decided unless he were coming up to Edinburgh. Do you suspect any thing like Pthisis in this case?

The whole of one of my last papers has been translated into one of the French Journals. I intended to have written Bob tonight but I do not know his address let me know it when you write and write by return of Post,

With Love to Jane Joseph &

Believe me
Ever Your Affectionate Son
Harry D. S. Goodsir

P.S. Tell Jane to send the Plants for I must get up my Botany now.

4. JOHN GOODSIR TO HARRY GOODSIR [SON], 12 JUNE 1844

Manse Largo
12 June 1844 – 5 P.M.

My dearest Harry

I have not been forgetful or negligent in regard to the application in your letter of this day. – I have written a long letter to Sir Philip & it is now ready for the P.O. and I trust it may be of use to you. – I hope you will obtain Dr. Gairdners friendly interest, as a prominent member, of the College of Surgeons and should you be fortunate enough to obtain the appointment of Surgeon & naturalist in Captain Ross' expedition, and at same time retain the Conservatorship in the Museum, it will certainly be fortunate. I cannot at same time divest myself of much anxiety as regards the extreme danger attendant upon such an expedition; and should you gain the situation it will surely be of great service in many ways; and we must place our reliance upon a Supreme Superintending Power, being with you in the midst of the many dangers we must all lay our account with. –

In such a situation as this you will naturally mix with men of science & extensive information; and you ought without delay, to take every means to improve yourself, in general information; – in a correct manner of recording your observations & acquirements, and in adding industriously to your stock of knowledge. – Try & obtain a neat style in your correspondence, & do attend to your orthography; – in your last letter, e.g. you spell the word agree with two gs, & in several other words you are constantly inattentive. – I presume you will be constrained to keep a regular journal; & I would earnestly recommend to you to keep a correct account of all your private thoughts and observations; and above all don't sleep too much. I have no patience for unnecessary indulgence in this sleeping propensity – I say the truth of my heart – Joseph, has but two faults – too much, of the abomination of snuff – & more sleep than nature requires – at least I think so.

Love to John, – dear Archie & yourself – I am – My dearest Son Harry
Your very affectionate Father
John Goodsir

5. JOSEPH GOODSIR TO HARRY GOODSIR [BROTHER], 12 JUNE 1844

Carnbee 12th. June 1844

My dear Henry

I have just seen Lord William Douglas – He told me to write you immediately and say that it [is] his opinion you should get some such person
as Professor Jamieson or Dr. Abercrombie to write Lord Haddington
recommending you not on the grounds of professional fitness alone but
also as a Naturalist – He took my promise to write you thus by this
nights Post –

It is more than likely I think that you have got something of this sent
down already – I forgot to mention to him that Forbes was working for
you in London – Indeed I know so little of your movements that I could
give him no more information than he had – As he seems interested in
the thing you had better write him again and tell what you have done.

Things are going on very well with us at Largo – Come down some
Saturday evening soon when my Father will perhaps go up with you
for a day or two as a change does him good – All are well however –
Remember us to all at Lothian Street and Believe me

Your affectionate Brother
J. T. Goodsir

6. JOHN GOODSIR TO HARRY GOODSIR [SON], 14 JUNE 1844

Largo Manse
14 June 1844

My dearest Harry

I received yours of the 12th. but had not time to answer it yesterday. I am very happy to hear of excellent Lord William Douglas' speedy attention to your application to him. Any letter from Lord William to the first Lord of the Admiralty, must have its own great weight and importance. You would learn by my letter yesterday that I had written to Sir P. Durham, by Wednesday's Post.

I did explain to him the chief nature of your object should you obtain the appointment, & I spoke of you as <u>Surgeon</u> and <u>Naturalist</u>; because you so stated the case to me yourself; but I had my own misgivings, from the conviction, that as the expedition will be a Government one – it necessarily follows, that a Naval Surgeon will be appointed qua Surgeon. I also asked Sir P. to apply to Captain Ross; and I doubt if I could, with propriety, trouble Sir Philip again, at least till I may hear from him. Will the simple circumstance of putting Surgeon before Naturalist have any bad effect? I should think not; for certainly a naval Surgeon must go out as such, & should your wished-for appointment take place you will be rated qua Naturalist. I have not heard again from Robert; but I have heard of him, & I enclose Mr. Scotts letter, & his son's note which will give you all I know at present – Robs address is 27 Surry Street – Strand. –

What you tell me of C. Trotter does not at all surprize me – there is surely some hidden cause for such repeated instances of gross stupidity – [...] that we were but clean with him. – I have really a great deal to do at present, & however anxious I may be to get done with T. I will not be able to go to Anstruther till Wednesday next, & I must be there for two, if not three days & I intend to be at Carnbee during the night, & to breakfast & dine there all the time. I approve of both John & you getting your money out of Trotter.

Jane will attend to what you say about the Algæ &c.

Should Mr. Roughead send any false shirt collars for me to 21 – tell Archie to send them on by the Balcarras & to write to me. – To return to Mr. Scott, – I know him so well, & am so confident he will do much for Robert I would wish John & you to call for him at Mr. Formans – together or separately.

I do thank him for his kind intentions toward Robert.

Joseph & Jane dine this afternoon at 6 o c – a ceremonious party – at Mr. Lumsdaines [in] Lathallan; – & Joseph & I with Mr Urquhart [in] Newburn, dine at Mr. Nairnes at Elie, on Tuesday.

When you hear anything regarding the Expedition let me know without delay; and when I get any word from Sir P. I will write to you.

We join in love to you all.

I am – My dearest Harry

Your affectionate Father

John Goodsir

P.S. I am sorry Dr. H. can say nothing about Mr. Reekie.

7. WILLIAM DOUGLAS TO HARRY GOODSIR, 15 JUNE 1844

Private
Grangemuir 15 June 1844

Dear Sir

You will see by the enclosed letter from Lord Haddington that no expedition is intended for the Antarctic Regions. Yours truly

Wm R K Douglas

8A. WILLIAM DOUGLAS TO THOMAS HAMILTON, 11 JUNE 1844 [ENCLOSED WITH 7]

11 June 1844

My dear Lord Haddington

I take the liberty of sending you enclosed two letters which I have received this morning from the Messrs Goodsir. They are both natives of Anstruther & have by their [...] talents & endeavours forced their way into Edinburgh where the one is assistant in the Anatomical Class of the University, the other Henry Curator of the Museum of the College of Surgeons. Their father & Grandfather were very eminent medical practitioners in their neighbourhood.

If the appointment Mr H Goodsir desires be still open, I believe you will find it will be very difficult for you to find any man more qualified for the situation than he is. He is very well known to all the leading Medical Men in Edinburgh. & if you think it is desirable to make particular enquiries about him, I feel satisfied that you will obtain every assurance of his capacity from any of them you may apply to & I can from my own knowledge say that his zeal & industry is rarely equalled.

On an occasion of this sort I am persuaded you will forgive me for troubling you with my testimony in favour of Mr Goodsir.

Believe me to be with much regard
Yours truly
W R K D

8B. THOMAS HAMILTON, TO WILLIAM DOUGLAS, 13 JUNE 1844 [ENCLOSED WITH 7]

Admiralty
June 13th /44
My dear Lord William

No such Captain & no such Ship are intended for the Arctic Regions.
It is an invention – I presume – to mislead & disappoint Zoologists &
Botanists !!
I am yours truly
Haddington

Sir James Ross has married a wife – & is publishing a book !!!

9. JAMES FITZJAMES TO JOHN BARROW JR, 3 NOVEMBER 1844

November 3 – Brighton Sunday evening

Dear Barrow
I wrote a note on Saturday to Captain Beaufort which I sent by hand
and expected an answer to day – it was to ask him whether he thought it
likely the Admiralty would send me if I volunteered to attempt the journey
to the North Pole on the original plan which I sent you from Bombay –
My plan being to go in the summer as far North as possible of
Spitzbergen winter there in the ice – (not at Spitzbergen) and then walk
to the Pole in the winter or long night when the ice is hard – with sledge
boats &c &c or at all events attempt it in the spring before the melting
of the ice – there are few better walkers in the service then I have proved
myself and I have some perserverence.
Captain Beaufort is I hear unwell – But if you could find out from him
whether he would support such an undertaking and what chance there
might be of success this would do better than going third in the N. W.
expedition
I mention Captain Beaufort because he once urged me to volunteer and
because in his position of Hydrographer his opinion would have some
weight. Sabine could in the mean while measure a degree at Spitzbergen

your sincere friend
James Fitzjames

10. JOHN FRANKLIN TO JAMES CLARK ROSS, 24 DECEMBER 1844

Castle Hedingham
Essex
24th December 1844

My dear Ross,

I am sincerely obliged by your confidential communication which I have shewn to no one but my dear wife in whom I know you would yourself at all times fully confide – I purpose going up to London on Thursday next and will then make a point of seeing Sir John Barrow, Beaufort & Parry though you may rely on my not giving to them the slightest intimation as to my having received any such communication as yours – I shall go in fact to them for the purpose of enquiring of them how the question stands as to the Expedition and to let them know that providing you do not go in the command of it I hope to do so. This is the language which I have constantly held to each of these friends and if I find that the Expedition, as your note seems to imply, has been approved by the Admiralty and is in course of preparation I shall certainly offer myself for the Command of it. This will bring the matter to a point and develop the under-current if such exists. I wish very much to see you while I am in Town and will gladly come down to Black-Heath for that purpose unless it should be more convenient for you to meet me in London Will you have the goodness to send a letter for me to the Athenaeum Club – by the Thursdays post so that I may get it on the Friday Morning. My wife wishes to write a few lines. I leave the remainder for her – With my kind regards to Lady Ross & best wishes for the Baby – Believe me
    most faithfully yours
    John Franklin

11. FRANCIS CROZIER TO JAMES CLARK ROSS, 30 DECEMBER 1844

December 30th 1844

My dear James

I have this instant received yours of 19th and call at Reading Room to answer it as I find it has been laying in the office some days – I hesitate not a moment to go second to Sir John Franklin – pray tell him so – if

too late I cannot help it – of Course I am too late to volunteer to command but in truth I sincerely feel I am not equal to the leadership – I
would not on any terms go second to any else, Captain Parry or yourself
excepted – Act for me my dear friend in this as you see fit and I will carry
it out in every particular – I will write you by tomorrows post more fully
but to the same purpose – Kindest love to dear "Thot"

Ever yours
FRM Crozier

12. FRANCIS CROZIER TO JAMES CLARK ROSS, 31 DECEMBER 1844

Casa del Bello
Via della Fornace
Florence
December 31ˢᵗ 1844

My dear James

Many thanks for yours of 19ᵗʰ which I in a very hurried manner
answered on a scrap of paper I begged at the News Room – As it may
not have reached you, I will repeat the substance of my reply which I
trust is at all events as decided as you could wish – I was so run for time
that I had to take a coach to save the post, which must plead my excuse
for the extraordinary production – If not too late I am quite ready to
go second to our kind friend Sir John – with none else save and except
yourself and Captain Parry would I go – I am in truth still of opinion
as to my own unfitness to lead, you on that subject as well as all others
know my whole mind – whatever you arrange for me, I will hasten on
hearing from you, to carry out to the fullest of my ability –

Now my dear James I leave all with you, and have only to say that
whatever you settle I will be quite content with – I am delighted to hear of
dear kind Thot such good accounts as well as of Master James. If I hear
from you that Sir John would accept of my Services I would start from
here immediately for London if not I purpose accompanying my friends
from here to Rome and Naples. – till I hear from you I will not leave my
present abode – Your letter was ten days coming I therefore cannot expect
an answer from you before 19 or 20ᵗʰ of January so that I could not be

in London before February, but as ships would not sail before May there would be plenty of time – I had not the least idea there would have been another knowing you had declined – Several people here having been asking me about Back and I am sorry to say from what an old Gentleman said of him last evening he has not left a very favourable impression behind him – Talking I apprehend very absurdly of ladies here who shewed him much attention, the old fellow said it was he was a very pleasant fellow, but if he was in love with himself he had no right to suppose every lady he met was the same. There is a great deal of Society here (English) both gay and otherwise, but as my friends with whom I am staying are very quiet people we do not belong to the gay world, which certainly pleases me much – There is much to be seen of painting and sculpture which we take very quietly, going each day for some hours to one or other of the galleries which are open to the public – Many things have indeed much delighted me more than I imagined such things would, but then being with dear friends to whom I am much attached adds to the pleasure – I am sorry to hear the Book is such a trouble to you – What of Wilkes, is he out yet? The weather in the South of France after I wrote you was very cold indeed I positively was nearly frozen to death in the Diligence not having with me any warm clothing and generally being alone and going so slow – France is a horrid country but full of fight – They were going to eat me at Toulouse for walking over the battle ground – The Guide although paid could not or would not tell the name of a single place. We had however with us Allisons account of the Battle, I met then a Welsh acquaintance of Colonel Sabine a Mr. Thomas a neighbour of Lord Adare – I know not whether to be glad or sorry I am from England at this time, but I am induced to think I am as well here knowing that you my dear friend will act for me – I shall be anxious to hear how things are arranged – There is one thing I would recommend whoever goes that is to have if possible a captain of a whaler as acting Master and two 2nd Masters as before, it would get rid of our annoyance on returning and then is a precedent for it – Poor Humphreys would I dare say be glad – what think you of that? – Give my love to dear "Thot" and tell her I am not so unreasonable as to expect to hear from herself, but let me return to England when I may, I will not be long then before I see her & the dear little stranger James Coulman. To you and dear Thot I wish you many very many returns of this joyous Season and believe me my dear James your ever attached and obliged friend

FRM Crozier

13. JOHN FRANKLIN TO JANE FRANKLIN [WIFE], 31 DECEMBER 1844

Athenaeum
31st December 1844

My dearest Love,

I have just left Parry and come here to write to you – He had not heard anything more about the Expedition – We discussed several points together and I told him the opinions I had formed from the reading of his Melville Island Voyage & that of Wrangel on which he concurred – He also thought that I had better not go to either Beaufort or Barrow until the paper of the latter has been sent to me, but continue my reading of the voyages which I had told him I was doing – We have agreed to talk over the points together as they suggest themselves to me.
I could not get down today to Ross –

My first business today was to call upon Mr Copeland to talk to him about Montagu's treatment of his friend Nairne. He was on the point of starting into the country, but remained a sufficient time for me to let him know the history of Montagu's treatment of Nairne & as to the appointment of Seymour – of which he had heard only some of the particulars.

Mr Copeland told me Spode was quite in anger at the way he had been treated which I also pointed out to him had its origin with the maneuvering of Montagu – Lord Stanley it seems declines giving the pension to Spode and has written out to ask his age and whether he could not be provided for in any other Department. Nairne has been confirmed by Lord Stanley – neither Nairne or Spode had written to Copeland for a long time at which he was surprised – He told me also that he had heard Lord Stanley had found that matters were very different in the Colony from what Montagu had given him to understand especially as regards the Convict Discipline and that he was very angry with him, for he had ascertained that his system did not work as he had been led to expect – Copeland of course did not disclose his authority – but said when he returned to Town [in] February he should be happy to see me again – and he would then endeavor to find out more about Master Montagu as he termed it – and to do anything he could to assist me. He told me that both Nairne & Spode had written to him to say that Montagu had promised to call upon him as their friends among the first things he should do after his arrival – but he never came near him!!

Having received a note from the Reverend Mr Bawdler wanting some information respecting the proposed College in V D Land previous to the meeting of the Society for Promoting the Gospel on Monday next – I called on him and had an hours conversation with him on the subject – so that he is prepared to advocate its cause with the Society for a grant of money – He hopes the Archdeacon will come up to tell his own views & had written to him to that effect yesterday – He also promised to write again tonight. I also will tell the Archdeacon that I shall be in Town and quite ready to give him every assistance & advice in my power on the Convict question.

I return your paper which I copied and sent it with the others to Richardson.

Two observations Copeland made deserve mention viz that Lord Stanley had allowed Montagu to Ear-Wig him and that Lord S had got his information on many points from paragraphs in newspapers which he had found were not correct – Finding he was in a hurry I said nothing upon these remarks but will bear them in mind when we next meet for I fancied they had reference to my case.

On my way hither I met Lord Haddington to whom I rose my hat immediately he recognized me & turning round gave me a very kind nod.

The Times has a short paragraph alluding to the Expedition & says it is to be offered to Ross, if he declines the command falls to me – Tomorrow will be the New Year, may it prove to you & my dear Eleanor and to all your family circle through the blessing of God – all that we could desire.

Ever yours most affectionately
John Franklin

14. JAMES FITZJAMES TO JOHN BARROW JR, 2 JANUARY 1845

Brighton 2nd January 1845

My dear Barrow

I have just received a letter from Mr Abraham Rose Bradford Surgeon of the Actaeon wanting to go with me – He is just the man for an expedition – being active & energetic – a capital shot & a pleasant fellow – but he is no 'ologist – he c'ant stuff birds – give long names to shiny things – or put moss in blotting paper. However if I have a choice – he is the man – so pray put him down in the list – a youngster who was with me in the Clio (from Conway) & now in St Vincent is very anxious to go with me. I suppose I could get him appointed without interfering with my "first entry" – if it be advisable to take a boy of 14 to the ice –

Will you let me know this that I may write to his mother – who will then know he is out. – I wrote to Mrs. Basil Hall telling her to write to you when her son is old enough to go to sea – if he be not old enough now – If you want a wife she has two cute daughters – especially the youngest. do make their acquaintance

Thank you for your letter.

Charlewood is getting dolefully enthusiastic on the subject –

I have been reading a french account of N. P. voyages from Zeno to Ross & Back – which makes me quite au fait in the matter.

It appears the Fury is broken up – so the supernumerary Commander c'ant get her if he would. It does not appear clear to me what led Parry down Prince Regents Inlet after having got as far as Melville Island before – the N. W. passage is certainly to be gone through by Barrows Straits but whether <u>South</u> or <u>North</u> of Parrys group remains to be proved. I am for <u>North</u> edging N.W till in Longitude 140° if <u>possible</u> – however <u>Bakalim</u>.

I have written to Beecher to find out where a Master named Forster is who was with Captain Bethune in Conway & since in Cornwallis – he is a first rate surveyor & observer & a capital fellow & I intend asking him if he would like to go –

The Campbells are with Charlewood at New X. <u>Colonel & all !</u>

Yours ever sincerely

James Fitzjames

15. JAMES FITZJAMES TO JOHN BARROW JR, 4 JANUARY 1845

Brighton 4th January 1845

My dear Barrow

Another volunteer for the Arctic regions has appeared – Robert Jenner who wishes to go with me as First Lieutenant or with any <u>one else</u>.

Do pray speak to Sir John Franklin or get Captain Beaufort to do so – in case he may not have any one. Jenner is a first rate officer, and very nice fellow – he was Gunnery Lieutenant of Edinburgh & got promoted for inventing fuzes or something.

Young D'Arcy Wynyard a Naval Cadet in St. Vincent is also a volunteer put both their names down.

Mrs Hall's boy is only 11 years old so cannot go with me. I shall therefore give you the nomination, to change with Wynyard if I cannot get him appointed.

I see by the papers the Firebrand is ordered to South America.

Cannot Le Vesconte be appointed to the College again? to wait for me he never wanted to go in the Firebrand to which they appointed him from the Superb whose complement they chose to reduce.

I do hope they will decide soon on sending us, they ought to be thinking of it or the ships will not be ready to sail this year – they will want much repairing after the Southern Cruize –

I hope we shall have a steamer also à la screw –

[rest of letter missing]

16. JOHN FRANKLIN TO JAMES CLARK ROSS, 9 JANUARY 1845

21 Bedford Place
9th January 1845

My dear Ross

You may be sure that if I get the appointment I should be glad to have so fine a fellow as Crozier for my second, and I am really flattered, & so you may tell him, at his cordial answer to your suggestion.

I remain however, as to the plan & equipment of the Expedition in the same position as to information as I was when I had the pleasure of dining with you at Black-heath. because I have considered it right still to adhere to my determination not to go to the Admiralty until I know that some decision has been arrived at whether or not I am to have the command.

Rumour however says that point has been spoken of as nearly if not quite settled, and farther, that the Board contemplate having a Commander only in the 2nd ship. I understand moreover there are two persons of that rank whom they have in their eye, and are said to possess considerable scientific qualifications, besides having the advantage of youth.

On this point it must not be shirked that they will be disposed perhaps to put my age and Croziers together and fancy that it makes a somewhat heavy amount – However as soon as I get my appointment I shall be ready to take steps with you as to Crozier, till then I think it would be unwise for me to recall him.

I am suddenly called away to night to attend the sick bed of a sister in Lincolnshire, or I should have been at the Royal Society, where I understand you will be in the chair. I trust to be back in the course of Tuesday next.

Pray say everything kind to Lady Ross for me & mine
      Ever yours most faithfully
        John Franklin

PS. But though I don't think I can ask for Crozier till I get my own appointment, you might be working for him, & certainly make known his willingness to go as my second
      J F

17. JOHN FRANKLIN TO JAMES CLARK ROSS, 17 JANUARY 1845

                 Spring Gardens Parry's Office
                 17th January 1845
My dear Ross

Parry being up to his eyes in business has asked me to say to you that in a private letter from young Barrow he says to Parry "His father would be glad if he would show you & myself his original notes relative to the proposed expedition – before either of us see Lord Haddington which Parry was desired to communicate to you & to me that his Lordship intended to require to see us on the subject of the Expedition

These notes are now with Parry here – Will you say when you will call to read them
      Very faithfully Yours
        John Franklin

18. JAMES FITZJAMES TO JOHN BARROW JR,
19 JANUARY 1845

13 Royal Crescent Brighton
19th. January /45

My dear Barrow

You will get this on the 20th January – on which day the vessels destined for the Arctic regions should have been at least a week commissioned & half manned.

The last week has passed contrary to my expectations without anything having been settled. Should the next week have ended in a similar manner, I shall have given up all idea of going this year. – And although as far as the good to the country and benefit to science are concerned – the Expedition would be as useful next year as this, I for one should regret its not having been sent during the continuance in office of your father – it appears to me that if the Admiralty really intend immortalizing their administration, by a last attempt to perform what has so nearly been brought to a conclusion after so many attempts since the time of Elizabeth, that it is but due to the man who for so many years has been the untiring advocate of these discoveries, to mark his retirement from the public service – by the commissioning of the vessels destined for a final attempt to explore the North West passage – or rather to sail through it? – –

The orders conveying the intentions of the Admiralty – should bear the signature of "John Barrow" – and that signature [s]o attached would be a fitting termination of a service of 40 years –

That signature would be a connecting link to the chain of icy enterprize from the Reign of Queen Elizabeth to the reign of Queen Victoria may her shadow never be less.

[rest of letter missing]

19. FRANCIS CROZIER TO JAMES CLARK ROSS, 23 JANUARY 1845

Casa del Bello
Via della Fornace   Florence
January 23rd 1845

My dear James yours of 10th only reached me yesterday (too late for Post) Several Mails were due from inundation, I believe in Northern Italy – Thank you much and dear "Thot" for your kind wishes to have me with you, I have however resolved to remain <u>here</u> the result of NW Expedition we had planned a party to visit Rome Naples & Venice which is for the present abandoned, but should I not be required however it will go on so soon as I hear from you what the arrangements are – I can easily fancy that Barrow will not be so strenuous an advocate since he learned your determination to decline the command, indeed it would not surprize me if it was even yet given up. they must however soon resolve as time is drawing on – I feel quite satisfied in my own mind that I was right in volunteering to go second to Sir John and also in <u>not</u> volunteering as a leader, come of it what may I am resolved to be content, indeed if I had not been staying with such kind and dear friends I would in probability have been now on my homeward passage, now however I think I will make up my year and return by Switzerland & the Rhine.

There is much to be seen in this city and indeed I like much what I have seen – Several naval people here I do not see much of them, my friends being rather of the quiet order – Smith of China I meet frequently, he is a kind <u>fellow</u> and so is his <u>wife</u> – There is a great deal of society here amongst the English, it is of two kinds the serious and the gay – The Grand Duke is attentive to those who attend his Levees & Balls, for my part I do not belong to that gang although Mrs. Smith wishes to matronize me – Oh but James dear were you not distressed to see the death of our poor friend Richards, I cannot tell you how <u>much</u> it <u>shocked</u> me, he was one amongst ourselves as it were, true it is that many of our old shipmates & messmates have been called away, but then who amongst the number looked more like a long liver than poor Richards his poor widow I grieve for her had I known he had been ill I certainly would not have left England without seeing him, but from some cause or other I fancied he was abroad and frequently enquired about him amongst the English families I fell in with – 'Tis James dear a road we must all travel sooner or later and to be ready is or ought to be the chief buisiness of our pilgrimage here below – I wrote old Bird some time ago but have not heard of him, I was glad to hear that your sister and George were to be with you pray remember me kindly to them. I hope you have seen Sir William Parker since his return they are keeping him going. I am glad of it as he is sure to have the vessels under his command in good working order Lord George Paulet I see is coming home with a freight just what he will like – I see by Athenaeum that some Volumes of Wilkes have made their appearance – I would be glad to see it but I fear it will be beyond my price – The librarian to the Grand Duke of Tuskany has given me the reports of the Geographical Society of Italy during our absence wherein he has made handsome mention of our discoveries in contradistinction to Wilkes, he seems a fine old fellow a Swede by birth – Speaks English well.

Thanks many my dear "Thot" for sending the things for the Belfast Bazaar, had I been near I would have had them myself, however I have no doubt they sold readily, my old sisters could not make out about them, they however fortunately sent them to the right place. I have been getting an alabaster head done of myself, here it is considered like 'tis however I would say much too young looking, although he has not given me one hair more on my head than I have in reality. 'tis very small but being so pure a white it makes a nice little toy, therefore will do just as well as if it was a good likeness – Well my dear friends if I have not tired you I have at least come to an end of my yarn. I shall be anxiously looking for your next as on that my future proceedings will depend – If to go home I will loose no time in reaching London via France. – From the ship I will loose no time in going to Blackheath – I have not written a word to the auld sisters about this business as I thought there was no use in bothering them about a thing that may never take place – Well God love you both or as I might now say in the language of my own country "all three both together" little Sir James making the third – and believe me ever yours

sincerely

FRM Crozier

[on the envelope]

P.S.

your last was 12 days coming & we have here usually the London papers in 9 days – that is from Saturday evening to Monday week in morning

FRMC

20. EDWARD FORBES TO HARRY GOODSIR, 24 JANUARY 1845

3 Southwick Street
Hyde Park Square
January 24. 1845

Dear Harry

I have put off writing from day to day in the hopes of getting definite information about the northern expedition – which, after all will not I fear come off for some time. It seems Sir John Barrow is retiring from the Admiralty – that the plan of the Expedition is entirely his – & that unless he is in the way there is but little hope of it's being put into execution.

I have however laid all in train for you. Stokes & Broderip have promised to stir for you in case of arrangements being made & as Stokes is Ross's confidential friend I have no doubt the matter rests in the best quarter. So much for that.

Did you not tell me that the bivalve shell of Cypris & shield of Daphne were formed out of the transformed joints of the Legs? Please explain this to me as I am anxious about it, having a notion concerning trilobites bearing on it.

Best love to John & David. Is the book out yet? I find in carrying away my copy of Deshayes Conchology that the plates are not with it. Would you look for them. When will you be here? Please let me know in time beforehand.

Ever Dear Harry

Your friend

Edward Forbes

21. JOHN FRANKLIN TO THOMAS HAMILTON, 24 JANUARY 1845

21 Bedford Place Russell Square
24th January 1845

My Lord

In obedience to your Lordships commands I lose not a moment in giving my written opinion on the questions your Lordship did me the honor of putting to me this morning.

1st As to whether I considered the question of a NW passage as one which ought again to be entertained; to which I have no hesitation in answering in the affirmative, for the following reasons. The discoveries of Parry & Ross have narrowed the parts in which the passage should be sought, to two of farthest, viz. that space between Cape Walker & Banks's land of Parry: where I should recommend the trial first to be made and in case of the Passage not being forced in that direction, then, to the northward by the Wellington Channel.

The ships commanded by these officers had not the advantage of steam, and I need hardly say that the benefits to be derived from the aid of such a power are incalculable. Having pointed out to your Lordship today some of these advantages I will not dwell farther on the matter than to say the addition of steam to the ships is in my opinion indispensable. It is gratifying also, to know that it may be efficiently applied to the ships without destroying their capacity for stowing the requisite stores of provisions.

If the proposed Expedition should unfortunately not be entirely successful in effecting a passage, it must contribute to our Geographical knowledge; and it cannot fail to make important additions to the series of Magnetical observations which are now carrying on in every part of the world. I concede that the greatest impediments from Ice will probably be met between the 95° & 125° degrees of Longitude, the latter meridian being passed, I should expect to find the ice less heavy and such as may be penetrated with comparative facility. We know of no Islands to the North, westward of 120°.

Should there be any who say of these Arctic Expeditions, to what purpose have they been? I should desire them to compare our present map of that region and of the Northern Coast of America, with that of 1818 when these Expeditions commenced. They will find in the latter only three points marked on the Coast of America and nothing to the northward of it. Surely it cannot be denied that so large an addition to the Geography of the Northern parts of America and of the Arctic Regions is in itself an object worthy of all the Efforts that have been made in the course of former Expeditions.

> I have the Honor
> > to be
> > My Lord
> > Your Lordships
> > Most obedient Servant
> > John Franklin
> > Captain RN

22. JOHN FRANKLIN TO JAMES CLARK ROSS, 31 JANUARY 1845

> 21. Bedford Place
> 31st January 1845

My dear Ross

Parry being again very busy has turned over to me John Barrow's Junior – letter – and he wishes me to ask your opinion as to the suggestion of an engraving on the pedestal of the ships wintering should there be room for it –

Parry had not time to consider the question but it was evident to him as to me that if this device of the ships be adopted, it must be instead of Sir John Barrows Coat of Arms. Will you send your opinions & return these papers direct to Parry. Not a word more about the Expedition! – but very little more loss of time in arriving at the decision – will put to risk its going this season –

My kind regards to Lady Ross, and pray say to her that if she makes up her mind to lend me the Baby to go as your Representative to the North – there shall be the nicest bed prepared for it that the best upholsterers can furnish –

> Ever yours most faithfully
> John Franklin

23. JAMES FITZJAMES TO JOHN BARROW JR,
ON OR BEFORE 7 FEBRUARY 1845

My dear Barrow –

I have been very anxious to hear about the Northern business which I had hoped would have been settled last Wednesday -

I tried to see you on my way down here from Hertfordshire but could not spare time – having an engagement here

I have heard that the command of the expedition has been offered to Sir James Ross who has refused it and that Captain Stokes was to be appointed if Sir John Franklin refused which looks like Captain Stokes going 2ⁿᵈ if Sir John <u>does</u> go

Now Captain Stokes is a Commander very little senior to me and being in an expedition of the sort I should either like to go un[der] such men as Franklin & Ross of known experience in icy affairs or in command myself – for I think I could do as well as Captain Stokes. in fact I should feel much disappointed at having to go 2ᵈ to Stokes. of course if <u>appointed</u> by their lordships I would go second to anybody or third

Besides all this if the ships be not commissioned immediately and fitted out as quickly as possible they will be too late to start this year with advantage. Parry's 1ˢᵗ expedition sailed on the 1ˢᵗ May and arrived off Lancaster sound on the 1ˢᵗ August – <u>too late</u>. Parry's Second expedition sailed on April 29ᵗʰ and arrived at Resolution Island at the entrance of Davis Strait on 5ᵗʰ July – <u>Too late</u>: Parry's 3ᵈ expedition sailed on the 10ᵗʰ May and prepared for winter in Prince Regents inlet at the end of October – <u>too late</u>

Franklin's <u>last</u> expedition should sail on the 20ᵗʰ of April and being towed to the ice by a large steamer should arrive off Lancaster sound where the <u>work is to begin</u> on the 1ˢᵗ July – not a bit <u>too early</u> –

From the late mild winter it is probable this will be a peculiarly fine season with less ice than usual and I have the vanity to suppose that if the thing is to be done it will be done by Charlewood and myself – either together – or under such a man as Sir John Franklin

I write this in heaviness of heart for I have now nearly given up all idea of Going this is a great disappointment to me and will be a sad one to those officers who have been hoping to go with me.

Write me a line and tell me what you think about it now – Shall we go ?

    Yours ever sincerely

    James Fitzjames

24. JOHN FRANKLIN TO JAMES CLARK ROSS, 8 FEBRUARY 1845

21 Bedford Place
8th February 1845

My dear Ross,

I have just received your note & give you many thanks for it. I am glad you have determined on writing to Crozier at once – I was in the act of writing to you when your note came to tell you that I had received a note last evening written in the absence of Beaufort by desire of Lord Haddington to tell me I was to have the command of the Expedition –

I have seen this morning the assistant Surgeon of whom you spoke I think very well of him – he is known to Richardson, I shall therefore Endeavour to do what I can to promote his wishes – Lady F was very sorry to hear of Lady Ross' indisposition and thanks her for her love She will certainly come to see her in a few days –

Ever Yours most faithfully
John Franklin

25. SIR JOHN FRANKLIN TO ISABELLA CRACROFT [SISTER], 8 FEBRUARY 1845

21 Bedford Place
8th February 1845

My dear Sister

I have only a few minutes to spare, but I have the pleasure of telling you that the information was last evening communicated to me by desire of Lord Haddington that his Lordship intended to appoint me to the command of the Expedition – and this morning Ross has informed me that Lord H told him last evening that he approved of Crozier going as my second – This is what I desired Ross to ask of his Lordship – I shall probably get my appointment in a few days –

I am sorry to hear you have not be[en] well – but I hope you are now better – Pray send me the amount of the Cabinet Makers Bill as soon as you can –

Jane & Eleanor are well and Mr Griffin is gradually getting better
    Love to all –
        Your affectionate Brother
            John Franklin

Eleanor has just informed me that your letter tells her Jarman's Bill is £24 . 10 . 6 ½ – I therefore send you a draft for the money payable to his order – and will thank you to get the receipt from him – I have not drawn for the ½ – Will you enquire after the carriage & ascertain when it will be finished.

Eleanor begs me to say with her love that she will be unable to write to day. I think she is writing to VDL as a ship is to sail on Monday

JF

26. JOHN FRANKLIN TO JAMES CLARK ROSS,
10 FEBRUARY 1845

Athenaeum
10th February 1845

My dear Ross

I was much concerned at the cause which has taken you & Lady Ross so suddenly into Yorkshire – but I trust you found your father in law in a less dangerous state than you expected – and that you have hope of his getting better

I have been this morning to Lord Haddington and learnt from himself that he had decided on Crozier being my second – He has promised to write to him himself – but Hamilton said that was no reason why I should not give Crozier the information at once – which I have done – On arriving here I found your letter addressed to this place and am happy to find that you had also written to him before you left Blackheath so we may hope Crozier will soon be on his way home I mentioned to Lord Haddington that I thought I should have a Commander. He said that point should be taken into consideration – We had not then time to talk over other matters, though I did ask his Lordship to promote Kendall.

If the state of your father in law should permit it I feel confident you will not let slip the occasion of your being so near Hull to obtain all the information you can for me as to the ice in Davis Straits and whether any ship has been into the Wellington Channel, & if so to obtain from her Commander or the ships Log Book all the information you can respecting it –

Will you also be good enough to enquire after the Ice Masters and leading men for both ships.

I suppose that I shall get my Commission in a few days – will you therefore tell me where I can find the Clerk you spoke of – or any of the Warrant officers. Mr Innes of the Admiralty speaks well of the Purser who was with Beechey & recommends him. His name is Osmer – I shall perhaps see Beechey – for I am sorry to learn he has come to town on account of the dangerous illness of his Father in law – Mr Griffin I am happy to say is daily gaining strength.

Lady Franklin desired me when I wrote to express her deep sympathy with Lady Ross – & yourself under your present affliction –

Pray write to me when you can for you know your advice will be most valuable to me

      Believe me
      Ever Your attached friend
        John Franklin

1st. the experience of the Masters of the Whalers for some years past as to the favourable Latitude for getting through the Ice on Davis Straits to Lancaster Sound – It would also be desirable to ascertain the best season for accompl[ish]ing this object with expedition & safety

2nd. Have the Whalers of late years been accustomed to seek for fish in Lancaster Sound & Westward of it –

3rd. Have any of these ships been to the Westward of Prince Regent Inlet – or along the Northern Coast of Parrys North Somerset.

4th. Have any been as far to the West along that Coast as Cape Walker of Parry ?

5th. Have any been to the South & West of that Cape Walker.

6th. What was the state of the Ice to the sw of it – ?

7th. did they see any land or appearance of it to the sw or West of Cape Walker

8th. Is the Coast of North Somerset continuous from Cape Clarence to Cape Walker – ?

9th. Have they gone up Wellington or any oth[er] bays opening to the north of Lancaster Sound

10 General Remarks

27. JAMES FITZJAMES TO JOHN BARROW JR, 11 FEBRUARY 1845

Brighton 11th February 1845

Dear Barrow

In case of Crozier's appointment I send you a letter to Beaufort asking him to try for Le Vesconte which pray send <u>at once</u> as soon as you know I am not to go – <u>if I am appointed tear it up</u> – as also his two letters to Captains Curry & Sir Thomas Herbert.

I forgot to tell you that I saw Mrs Gee at Abbots Langley – (Marianne Jackson as was) and a nice little lady she is.

They are very anxious about their brother John Milbourne Jackson who is in Daphne in South America & very uncomfortable – Could not anything be done for him? I was thinking of asking Captain Kellett to take him – he is a good mathematician & I should think would take to surveying. He is nearly 5 years passed – and lost the commission at the college by a severe illness got on the coast of Africa – tell me if you think if his mother was to memorialize it would do any good. For he is a good fellow & ought to be promoted, his father & grandfather were old Commanders in the Navy.

We have a delightful clear day here at Brighton while you are doubtless full of joy I shall be laid up for a day or two – vaccination having come out strong in my right arm.

Mind I am in confident expectations of the Second Ship in Franklin's Expedition nothing else is worth having
                    Yours ever
                    James Fitzjames

28. JAMES FITZJAMES TO JOHN BARROW JR, 12 FEBRUARY 1845

Dear Barrow

Hodgson has just written to me saying that if I do not go Northward that he still wishes to go – therefore do not forget him as he is worth having.

I wrote to Forster (Master) & Bradford (surgeon) of Actaeon telling them I should probably not go & if they in that case did not wish to go – that they had better write to you & have their names erased as they have not done so I conclude they wish to go – Forster is a triumph I look upon Fairholme as due of going with Franklin therefore remember [my picks] which are

√ Le Vesconte   Lieutenant
           }
√ Hodgson.

Forster   Master

Bradford   –   Surgeon

√ Des Veaux   Mate

---

and above all

        Yours ever
√ James Fitzjames

Brighton 12th February

I had thought he was Senior therefore recollect if I go – my two
Lieutenants are Le Vesconte & Hodgson. Hodgson volunteered to me
on the express condition he was to be 2nd Lieutenant in one of the ships –
    Another Lieutenant also volunteers – just made – a splendid chap who
was in Columbine when we landed in the Euphrates Expedition Francis
Marten put him down and d'ont forget Mr Charles Des Veaus (Mate) √
        Ever yours sincerely
        James Fitzjames
13 Royal Crescent
Brighton
Friday

29. JAMES FITZJAMES TO JOHN BARROW JR, PROBABLY 13 FEBRUARY 1845

Dear Barrow
    Do you think I ought to write to Sir John Franklin offering to go as
his Commander now that I am sure of not being able to have the second
ship ? –
    You said nothing in answer to a note I wrote you about young Jackson
– Can anything be done for him ? Will Kellett take him do you think ? he
is in the Dido & very uncomfortable – Excuse another note
        Yours ever
        James Fitzjames
Brighton
Thursday Evening

30. FRANCIS CROZIER TO JAMES CLARK ROSS, 15 FEBRUARY 1845

February 15th 1845

Florence

My dear James

Many thanks for yours of 6th which has just reached me, I had in truth began to think your letter had gone astray – I am <u>all ready</u> should <u>I be required</u> – I will write a line to my agent to pay £ 5 to the Barrow plate. Would you be kind enough to mention to Sir John F- the name of a Lieutenant Reginald Levinge (son of Sir Richard Levinge who lives in my brothers Parish in Ireland) – a volunteer for the New Expedition. My brother tells me he is a very fine young man – I know not his standing – he is however a Gentleman his family being amongst the oldest in the County Meath – The weather here is most desparately cold nothing but snow – I will write you fully when I again hear from you which I hope may be soon and decided. I must come to a finish to save <u>this days post</u> Kindest regards to dear "Thot"

& believe me ever yours <u>FRMCrozier</u>

31. FRANCIS CROZIER TO JAMES CLARK ROSS, 18 FEBRUARY 1845

Florence, February 18th 1845

My dear James

Yours of 18th reached me this morning for which a thousand thanks for all the trouble you have had on my account – I find I cannot leave Leghorn by Steamer for Marseilles for some days therefore have determined to await your next at this place, which I hope will give me Lord Haddington's final decision. I was indeed to start on the moment till I found 3 days must elapse waiting for Steamer – In the meantime I will have my passport and all things in readiness and so loose not a moment should I be required – It has kept me in a sad state of anxiety here, my kind friends will be glad to get rid of me as I have upset all their plans, and I could not even write the auld sisters as I did not wish to mention the thing till was settled one way or the other. The truth is I am of opinion

Sir George C. will not approve of two captains being employed on that service <u>Expense etc.</u>

Blame me not my dear James for not going immediately but the truth is when there is a <u>doubt</u> in the case, I would not like to leave Italy without seeing Rome & Naples, in company with my kind friends – I hope you excused my last mentioning Mr. Levinge (Lieutenant) he is a <u>gentleman</u> therefore would be an acquisition to Sir John – God bless you and dear "Thot" not forgetting the little stranger and believe
> me ever yours
> FRMCrozier

32. HARRY GOODSIR TO JOHN GOODSIR [FATHER], 18 FEBRUARY 1845

> 21 Lothian Street
> Edinburgh 18th 1845

My Dear Father

I have been very busy getting some certificates regarding my qualifications as a Naturalist & likewise as regards my knowledge of Medicine & Surgery for this Arctic Expedition. I send off some to Forbes tonight and others tomorrow. I hope Joseph or you have written to Sir William Burnett & that it was done on Saturday for no time can be lost in such a case and a word from Admiral Durham to Sir William Burnett would without doubt settle the thing at once. However I hope it hase been determined on ere this that I should go. Professor Simpson is going to London in the course of a week and is going to speak for me to some people of influence. He says he could have been sure of it had the Earl of Haddington been in but I suppose the Earl has not resigned yet & if so a word from Simpson will do a great deal. Has Lord William been written to?

What has been done about Trotter. I saw Mr. T. Trotter today but did not speak to him. It is to be hoped the whole matter will be brought to a favourable termination. Let me hear by return of post in haste

> Your affectionate Son

> Harry D. S. Goodsir

33. FRANCIS CROZIER TO CHARLOTTE CROZIER [SISTER], 19 FEBRUARY 1845

Florence 19 February 1845

My dear Small

I have been many times going to write you but the truth is I knew not for the last <u>two months</u> what my movements were likely to be, as if a North-West expedition went out it was not my place to be one of the party to be left at home. The thing <u>has been now decided</u> and I this day heard from my old & kind friend Sir John Franklin that Lord Haddington had told him that I am to be his second and command "Terror".

Now, Small of course, you and my dear sister will congratulate me on my appointment, well knowing that idleness on shore would not suit me. I did not wish to write to you on the subject so long as there was a doubt of my going, well knowing what your kindly feelings are. But I assure you, I often felt I ought to give you a line but then I could not sit down and write when I would not, and indeed could not, write fully and freely. Of course you are aware 'tis a service more congenial to my feelings <u>than any other</u> and we all know that the same God rules in all places whether on sea or shore, he is ever with us. – I leave my dear friends here tomorrow, Henry accompanys me to Leghorn which will be a great pleasure reducing a long trip just so much.

Now Small you must send me to London directed to Hills Hotel Charing Cross my tin case with my uniform (it is in a handkerchive in one of my drawers) my Epaulet case and belts (sword) as well as any Uniform coats and waistcoats in short any <u>blue</u> clothing that <u>you can put</u> into the case – cap etc. You will also my dear Small muster all my traps – such as shirts Stockings Flannels etc. not forgetting gloves or any little warm clothing I may have. I will write you from London as soon as I arrive and I hope [to] be able to say at what time I will be with you. Do however have all my traps repaired that you may think will be of service to me.

Will you write the Parson that I received his communication about Mr. Levinge and write Captain Ross on the subject, but I fear too late to be of service if he Mr. L. had not written himself to the admiralty. I wrote also to Sir John Franklin but <u>do tell</u> him that his letter reached me not for one fortnight after its date – therefore my application must have been nearly the same time going home which makes me fear that the vacancy may be filled up – I would be only to happy to have had him with me in Terror – the day I arrive in London I will send you a paper and will not probably write till I see my way clear – this business has disarranged all our plans here each day have I been kept in a state of anxiety, so long have they at admiralty been in coming to a decision and till the very last it was not decided whether a Captain was to go as Second – of course you and my dear sister will agree with me that employment I must have and when is there any more honourable as under such a man as Sir John Franklin and on such an Expedition – You will have the tin case with my traps booked by mail steam boat for Liverpool and on to London by Railroad and at the same time write a line by post to Mr. Hill to keep it till my arrival. You can give me a line at same time. – You cannot conceive how much I abhor the idea of starting off to travel post haste so many miles land travelling – however Small we that belong to the public must be at all calls – had I only to go by sea all the way I would enjoy it amazingly – God love you both, and believe me my dear Sisters yours ever,

<u>F. R. M. Crozier</u>

34. JAMES FITZJAMES TO JOHN BARROW JR, 20 FEBRUARY 1845

Brighton 20th February

My dear Barrow

If it be finally settled that I am to go with Sir John Franklin I can only say that I am very glad but I hope it is with the full wish of Sir John Franklin.

In case it should turn out after all that Crozier does not go – I hope no one <u>else</u> will step in between me and the command of the second ship –

In all that I have written to you I hope there is nothing to make you imagine that I underestimated Sir John Barrow's exceeding kindness on my account. I know that he has done more for me than he would for any one else and more than any one else would have done for me

And if I have expressed the disappointment it is natural I should feel at not obtaining the command of the 2nd ship I was far from imputing any fault to him. As to <u>your own</u> unvaried kindness my dear fellow I shall say nought about it to <u>you</u> –

Will you get the Enclosed forwarded to Mr Dawson some time member for Derry from John Boyd – Captain Beaufort has applied to Sir John

Franklin to take LeVesconte whose father was with Captain Beaufort in Ville de Paris

What can I now do for Hodgson – I shall write to him to apply to Sir John – Des Veaux the mate I should think there will be no difficulty about and young Wynyard –

Ever yours
James Fitzjames

35. JOHN FRANKLIN TO JAMES CLARK ROSS, 21 FEBRUARY 1845

21. Bedford Place
Friday 21st

My dear Ross,

I received your letter respecting Beverley and will take it this forenoon to Parry – and afterwards sign in myself –

I contrived the day before yesterday to pick up a bad cold – it is better today and I think will not prevent my having the pleasure of being with you by the ½ past 4 omnibus.

If I do not then turn up – you will know the cause –

I was with Sir William Gage yesterday about the Lieutenants. I also saw Beaufort Parry & Sabine – I have therefore much to say to you –

Most Sincerely yours
John Franklin

36. JOHN FRANKLIN TO JOHN RICHARDSON, 22 FEBRUARY 1845

21 Bedford Place
22 February 1845

My dear Richardson,

I write a few words of heartfelt congratulation on my own part and that of my wife & Eleanor – on dear Mary's safe accouchement – May God continue to preserve her & the baby –

I do not think we shall have room for any Naturalist –

I like all you are doing for poor Mary Anne – Mr Paine too is indefatigable – I have just received a note from him which I have not time to answer – nor to say more to you

John Franklin

37. JOHN FRANKLIN TO JAMES CLARK ROSS, 24 FEBRUARY 1845

21 Bedford Place
24th February 1845

My dear Ross

Many thanks for your note for I had this morning met Crozier's Agent at the Admiralty who shewed me a letter just received from him dated 15th February in which Crozier says not having heard any thing further about the Expedition he supposes it has blown over and that when the bad weather has passed he purposes setting off Rome & Naples – but your letter I trust will reach him and bring him back as you think in a few days –

You will be happy to learn that I have been this morning with Sir George Cockburn and Sir William Gage – and made all the arrangements respecting the officers – with the exception of the 1st Lieutenant of the Terror which of course I left open for Crozier to select – If he reaches Mr Levinge he can of course have him – Lieutenant Little is however quite ready to go if Crozier wishes to have him and I learn from Mr Little he has some knowledge of Crozier though it is slight – Fitzjames is to be the Commander and I believe the ships will be commissioned in a day or two. I told Sir George they ought positively to be so by the 1st March –

I forwarded the letter to Beverly with Parrys Certificate & one from me attached – Parry is doing well and I walked with him from the Admiralty to his Bankers & then home on Saturday – He has not ventured out to day –

I regretted not seeing you at Lord Northamptons – was the Treakle Posset the cause? I hope not – for it would have been a proof that your cold unlike mine had not disappeared. How did the young Hero bear the inoculation ? Mama's fears as to his crying were no doubt abundantly realized & yet no great cause for it was given – Preserve me from the 10 o'clock omnibus – we did not reach Charing Cross before ¼ to twelve I was reminded of the old Greenwich Coaches stopping as it did at numerous public houses –

Ever Yours Sincerely
John Franklin

Written in haste to save post under half darkness

38. EDWARD FORBES TO HARRY GOODSIR, 24 FEBRUARY 1845

Monday

Dear Harry

I have had Sir John Franklin spoken to. I am advised to be easy. If you go – it must be as Assistant Surgeon – so be prepared. I have not given in your testimonials for you have sent <u>no application</u> with them. Perhaps you have done so to Sir William Burnett.

in haste

E Forbes.

39. JOHN IRVING TO CATHERINE IRVING [SISTER-IN-LAW], 28 FEBRUARY 1845

H.M.S. "Excellent,"
Portsmouth, February 28, 1845

My dear Katie, –

Many thanks for your very kind letter. You see I am determined to give you no chance of indulging in a scold. I am still in suspense whether or no I am to go on the Arctic Expedition. I shall be glad to be put off it, as it affects my prospects for the summer very materially, there being some difference between the regions of thick-ribbed ice and perpetual snow, and the green fields I might visit if I did not get appointed, for I had some idea of coming down to see you then ; but I imagine going would probably assist me in getting advancement in the service ; and in the usual routine there is but a poor prospect. I do not believe I have much chance of going, so your wicked wishes are likely to be gratified. It is not a service of much danger, and they take provisions for only two years ; so they must come back in that time, if at all. The " Excellent " is very comfortable ; but it is a tiresome kind of life, and Portsmouth is a nasty place. I want something more exciting, and not to be lying in a harbour. It is now nineteen months since I last saw you. It seems a long time. Give my kindest love to Lewie ; I suppose he is too busy to write to me ; your letters of course tell me everything he could tell me. – I am ever, my dear Katie, your very affectionate brother,

John Irving.

40. JOHN FRANKLIN TO JOHN RICHARDSON, 1 MARCH 1845

21. Bedford Place
1st March 1845

My dear Richardson

I saw Mr Grant yesterday and made arrangements with him about the Pemmican, also as to the supply of condensed fuel and of square Biscuits to be packed in tin – I did not see Sir William Burnet yesterday and therefore had not heard of Mr Stanleys appointment. He seems however to be a proper man. I will take care that Mr Goodsir has every proper support, and convenience in my cabin for drawing – and as for any jealousy in his Chief I will do all I can to prevent that appearing –

We rejoice to have received your account of Mary this morning – and of the thriving condition of the Baby – The ships are to be commissioned on Monday we are going to Richmond to see Lieutenant Halketts experiments on the Thames in his Cloaks

Yours affectionately,
John Franklin

I heard from Crozier yesterday, he may be daily expected in England

41. HARRY GOODSIR, RECIPIENT UNSPECIFIED, 13 MARCH 1845

Surgeons Hall Edinburgh
13th. March 1845

Sir

I have the honor to acknowledge the receipt of your letter of the 11th. Inst: directing me to repair immediately to the Captain Superintendant of

Woolwich Dockyard for my appointment as Acting Assistant Surgeon of
Her Majesty's Ship Erebus during the period of the North Pole Expedition

> I am
>> Sir
>>> Your very humble Servant
>
>>> Harry D. S. Goodsir.

42. JAMES REID TO ANN REID [WIFE], 22 MARCH 1845

8 Smiths Place High Street Wapping March 22/45

Loving wife

I hope you have received my yesterdays letter with the one pound chake
from William –
There is a Letter come from Quebec from the Owner stating that if
Captain Reid can be found to get him if not engaged to take charge of
the Neptune and sail for Quebec 1st April – now you see how mean some
Scotsmen is to pay a Master of[f] for a few weeks. I called on them to
day and told them that i wase engagen with Sir John Franklin <u>R.N.</u> to go
with him to the North as ice Captain, but I would give them an answer
on Tuesday. During th[at] time i will call on Sir John, at Woolwich, [and]
if he puts me <u>on pay just now</u> @ £18 pe[r Month], I fix and I take my
chance of the Voyage. I go [as] Master & Pilot, it is sure pay and good
c[ompany]. I dined with all the officers, we are fo[und] no servant, we
must find one amongst [us]. You will have half pay, if I should never
return, then there will be something for you and the family. Mr. Enderby
will see after that what I have mentioned all Depends on putting me on
pay just now, if not I take command of the old ship –

William is Quite well he wants to go to sea, it hurts me very much to
think how bad of[f] we are but I hope god will Spare me, on any of the
ships we will get over this. If I wase clear of all in Aberdeen. & you & the
family in London or any other Place I would bee happy – Aberdeen will
never see me again and I Rather think William is the same. I Received
my parcel from the Mate of the Steamer, If I Engage with Sir John I
will Draw Money some way or other & [s]end for you, you will bring
all my warm things up, my things here is in [b]ad order [n]ever tuched
since we Landed [O]ld James would be handy here with me. I am Quite

happy with Mr Ronald's sister and hir Husband, I am due him three weeks Lodgins, say 36/ that is nothing, I am informed from sum of the officers that we Receive three months pay, before we sail, then your pay commence[s]. I will write you on Tuesday again when All will be settled. Hoping this finds you and my three Darulins well.

in Hast[e],

Remains your Loving
Husband
Jas. Reid

43. ALEXANDER MCDONALD TO WILLIAM PENNY, 24 MARCH 1845

6 Buckingham Street
Strand, London
March 24th 1845

My dear Penny

Here I am again. How are you all in the north? I was paid off from the Belvidere about a fortnight ago and have been in town ever since preparing for the final examinations which will render me eligible for promotion. I flattered myself that I should have the pleasure of seeing you in Scotland on this occasion, but that is not now likely, as I am already appointed to a ship. I go out in the expedition under Sir John Franklin.

The object is to discover the northwest passage. So if you happen to be in Davis Straits this year we may meet. I belong to the "Terror" Captain Crosier. The appointment is a good one. I have twice written to Mr Hogarth but have never heard from him. On the last occasion I wrote him concerning some pecuniary affairs but I find that he has not attended to that either. Is it possible that my letters have not reached him? Has he changed his residence or what?

I heard some story of change of fortune, but I treated it as an idle tale. Were it not to trouble you too much I would ask you to send me particulars of his address as soon as you conveniently can, as I am anxious to correspond with him. Remember me most kindly to him if you have an opportunity & also to Mr George Davidson

My kind compliments to Mrs Penny

Is Miss Kennedy still living. I will write you more fully when I have got my examinations over.

Mean time Believe me

My Dear Penny

Yours most sincerely
Alex McDonald

44. JAMES REID TO ANN REID [WIFE], 26 MARCH 1845

8 Smiths Place High St. Wapping
London March 26/45

Loving wife

I Received Anns most welcome Letter this moment sorry to see by it that your Leg is so sore but I hope it will not come to any height this leaves me Quite well. Williams work got done with Mr Ronald and left on Saturday but shipped on board of a fine Barque belongen to Greenwick lying in St. Catreenes Dock Bound for Montreal, it is above Quebec it will be some time before he sails, he went on board this after noon Quite will and happy The Ships name I dount know as yet, but he will write you himself he stopes in the same house with me and sleeps in the same bed – I called yesterday on the Neptunes Brokers and told him that owen to the mean way i wase used I would not go in Neptune, he wase very sorry to here that – to lose a good man for the sake of a few pounds, –

so now I Shipped yesterday with Sir John Franklin R.N. to go with him to Daviss Straits, and up Langester sound in search of a passage through, it may be two years and it may be three & four but I am quite willing to go. It is no use lying at home being allwise in measurie the thoughts of your leg and leaving the family is worse than the Voyage. Sir John told me that if I went the voyage with him, and landed safe in England again, i would bee looked after all my life. The ship I go in is the Erebus, and the other is the Terror. just such ships as the Hecla but not Quite so Large. Sir John is a man about 60 years old. Quite a Hero he is very fond of me as is the officers, as i answer all the quistences they put to me about the Land and ice about the Quarter we are going to.

My wages is £18,, ,, per Month. 13 Months to the year. I receive three months pay before we sail and then half pay at home pabil at the first Month but that will bee all settled before wee sail. my things is in very bad order just as the[y] came from Quebec if you are not able to come to London it will bee a bad job for me it will be <u>May</u> before we will sail. Mr. Enderby hase bean a good friend to me at this time, he will Look after you if I should never return, but that never comes in my head, there is a number thinking it strange of me going, but they would go if they knew about ice is i know – I got all my <u>Instructions</u> yesterd[ay], so you m[a]y consider me on Mond[ay] one of hir Majesties Servants for this Voyage. I have Received orders to ship, another ice Captain & 6 Leadin men. I wrote to Charles about a week ago to see if he could Recommend any in Dundee but not yet Rec'd an answer. Sir John told me yesterday that he would send me down to Hull or any other place, and Look after them myself and all my expencess paid. I will know that on Monday when I get my Commission. I will Try Mr. Enderby for a little mony untill we get our advancess, if you bee able to come up we will stope at Woolwich.

Remains your Loving
Husband
James Reid

[cross-written on first leaf]

P.S. no doubt there will bee a greate talking about me going this voyage, it will show that I am not frightened for my life, like some men, it is for you and the family, why should a man stope at home and Bring them <u>bagen</u>.

[on envelope]

Daeent mention that I want another master for the other Ship. Clark might write me about that berth: I daeent think he would go Shame may he think to Spend the best of his days and not try something. Keep your hart up there is no fere of me, do the best you can for a short time, you will bee will of soon sorry am i that things hase been so backward this long time, God knows perhapes is for my good, keep the Letter by yourself I will as soon as I Receive my Commission. Hopping you are going about keep your hart up. I am Happier now then I have bean these three months, Hopping this this finds my three Darlings Quite well not forgetting yourself.

45. JAMES FITZJAMES TO JOHN BARROW JR, 27 MARCH 1845

14 Francis Street Woolwich
27th March 1845

My dear Barrow

    I have been speaking to Colonel Sabine and Sir John Franklin about coming home through Siberia after we get through Behrings Straits.

    <u>In whatever year</u> we do get through, the month will be August or September so that there will be time to go at once to Okhotsk – and start off for Petersburg. But in case of its being too late in the season to attempt the journey (for travelling in Siberia in the winter is I believe impossible) a winter passed at either Okhotsk – Yakoutsk Irkoutsk Tomsk or Tobolsk would be profitably employed in taking magnetic observations which would form a chain of them <u>round the world</u> Besides the éclat it would give to the Expedition –

    Sir John tells me that he had thought of such a journey for some officer – and Colonel Sabine says it would be highly desirable & interesting -tell me therefore whether I ought to volunteer by letter <u>and how</u> ? or whether you or Sir John Barrow if he approve of the plan would speak to Sir John Franklin in order that application might be made to the Emperor of Russia before starting – for leave to traverse the country

    Having landed me the ships could then go on to Panama & send an officer to England before going round Cape Horn – or go on [to] China & send one overland via Bombay & Suez –

    Yours ever

    James Fitzjames

14 Francis Street Woolwich

27th March

2

Preparation

I have now got every thing in fair trim...

Harry Goodsir

This next batch of letters brings us more proximate to the final preparations for Franklin's voyage. The speed with which they proceeded was indeed remarkable – from rumour to plan to actual expedition, all in the course of scarcely six months. We travel now with the men who were to serve as they converge on London and then Woolwich, where the ships were being re-outfitted. Some, it seems, were eager to be aboard and arrange their berths; others took rooms nearby, from which they could read of the public excitement attending their plans in the daily papers. Old friendships were renewed, and new ones begun; these letters often included requests to family and friends to send particular items – books, clothing, and equipment – wanted for the voyage. Harry Goodsir, after laying out the required sum for his undress uniform, found himself short of the resources he needed for the required set of silver spoons and forks; his needs were supplied by his family (this is borne out by the fact that the utensils of his that have been recovered since bear different hallmarks and years of manufacture). Everyone seemed in need of warm socks and coats, or their families felt them to be so – rather like kindly parents sending a child out into the snow, the emotional comfort of these items was as significant as their physical warmth. So many of the men were young, a fact borne out in the records of the "allotment" of pay each was entitled to assign to a relative; in most cases, it was to parents rather than wives.

We also get some further details here as to the daily lives of the men during their last weeks of relative freedom of movement. Goodsir found time to see the opera – a performance of Rossini's *William Tell* by the noted singer Gilbert Duprez – while Le Vesconte (who, unlike many of his brethren, preferred to lodge aboard ship) still managed to "run to town on a Saturday evening and perhaps remain Sunday," though of his activities there he gives no details. On 9 May an official entertainment for Franklin and his senior officers was hosted by the lords of the

Admiralty; a rumour went around that the ships were to be visited by Her Majesty the Queen (a visit that seems not to have occurred); and public fascination with the expedition's departure was so great that, as Franklin remarked, "the visitors to inspect the ships became so numerous as to impede the men in their work."

There was one sad note – as preparations were underway, Franklin had word that his niece Mary, the wife of his old comrade Sir John Richardson, had died. Franklin was in Brighton, having been advised, it seems, that the sea air might help him recover from a recent bout of influenza; he replied that he hoped to call on his friend on his return to London in a few days. Richardson had been Franklin's stalwart on his first land expedition in 1819–22, and their bond was to prove an even more enduring one – for, in 1848 Richardson, though by then over sixty years of age, joined with Dr John Rae in the first of the many searches for his friend.

CHRONOLOGY

31 March 1845: Franklin takes temporary lodgings
at 40 Lower Brook Street in London (Letter 47)

2 April 1845: Henry Le Vesconte writes to his father that he has
been appointed to the expedition (Letter 49)

Before 4 April 1845: The steam engine meant for HMS *Erebus*
arrives at her berth (Letter 52)

After 5 April 1845: Franklin removes to Brighton for his health
(Letter 54)

10 April 1845: Franklin's old companion John Richardson's
wife, Mary, dies (Letter 58)

14 April 1845: Franklin returns to London from Brighton (Letter 58)

9 May 1845: The Admiralty hosts a reception for Franklin and Crozier

12 May 1845: *Erebus* and *Terror* depart Woolwich and arrive at
Greenhithe (Letters 66, 67, 70)

13 May 1845: Several men are struck from the muster rolls
for physical problems (Letter 71)

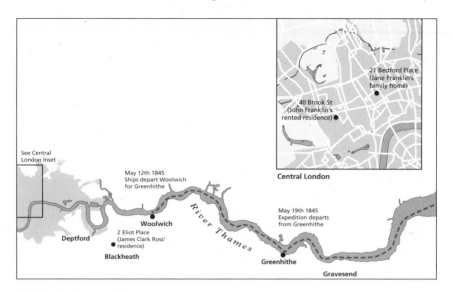

London and environs

46. FRANCIS CROZIER TO JOHN FRANKLIN, MARCH OR APRIL 1845

1 George Street Woolwich
Tuesday Morn

My dear Sir John

The post only allows me time to write you a line to say you are not required here this day (Tuesday) all is going on <u>well</u> indeed more swimmingly than I could have <u>dared</u> to hope

I will send you some letters by the next post also the weight of articles for Transport that you can look over at your leizure. It would be well to be early on the morrow as I think it will be requisite for you to see Sir John Hill on your return to Town.

Post about starting yours in
　　　much haste <u>FRM Crozier</u>

47. JOHN FRANKLIN TO JANE FRANKLIN [WIFE], 1 APRIL 1845

> 40 Lower Brook Street
> Grosvenor Square
> 1st April 1845

My dearest Love,

We took possession of the lodgings last evening. I think them good & moderate considering their situation.

I am fully sensible of the natural anxiety you feel respecting the completion of the pamphlet and very grateful for your self devotion to it, most happy indeed should I be if I could render you the personal assistance in its preparation which it is no less my duty than my earnest desire to do.

I have had however very complete occupation since my appointment to the Expedition in preparing the lists of provision & stores, the Astronomical Instruments – the materials for the collection of Natural History and in the general arrangements of the details of the ships – which as they involve a constant reference to the authorities at the Admiralty & Somerset House as well as at Woolwich have required my undivided & closest attention especially during Croziers absence. He returned on Friday last and on Saturday we spent the whole day at the Admiralty & Somerset House in giving more detailed information respecting the stores & instruments we required than the general demands for them had afforded – We have now therefore got every-thing in a fair way. I have taken advantage therefore to keep quiet for a day or two that I may get rid of my cold – which I now suspect to have been a slight attack of Influenza from the weakness it has produced as well as loss of appetite. Mr Phillot has given me Quinine with some other mixture to be taken twice a day – which has been beneficial. He has also desired me to take wine again – I begin now to be quite myself again & shall tomorrow go to Woolwich – I have preferred remaining in Town today the first of our being in our lodgings, or I might have gone today.

Parry told me that Lady Parry would not go to the Drawing Room and I fancied from what he said that she never did go – I am sure also from what I heard Lady Ross say of her only appearance there on her marriage that she has no desire to repeat the visit & encounter such another squeeze – she is very delicate I perceive – and her habits and inclinations are to be retired and domestic. I have not seen either Ross or her since I dined with them for Blackheath lies completely out of my track to Woolwich – and to go there would completely cut up a day – The same observation applies

to the Sabines – I will make a point however of seeing both very soon &
then making the enquiry you wish about lodgings there – which I am of
opinion with you, would be better than you remaining at Brighton.

I regret your not having been informed of the substitution in the news
papers of my return from foreign service, for the Government of VDL – it
was an unlucky charge – but I presume they are published from the lists
furnished by the Clerks in the Chamberlains office –

It might perhaps have been amended as you propose but I think the
doing so would have been injudicious, in as much as it would have
betrayed a degree of self consequence & importance little in accordance
with my habits. I am afraid that I cannot persuade you to feel more
indifference to what may be thought of the omission in VD Land. The
parties there who would take advantage of it are really not worth so
much concern. They themselves have learnt by experience not to look
upon Lord Stanley's favour or that of the Colonial Office as the greatest
blessing – Love to Sophy –
– yours most affectionately,
John Franklin

48. JOHN FRANKLIN TO JANE FRANKLIN [WIFE], 2 APRIL 1845

> 40 Lower Brook Street
> 2 April
> 1845.

My dearest Love

I have just returned from Woolwich & Deptford victualling offices, the
latter being the place whence all our provision is shipped – Crozier &
the Purser accompanied me and the final arrangements were made as
to sending some of the earlier required articles to the ships for stowage.

The ships had made much progress in the rigging which is the only part
they can do as long as the shipwrights are at work – The engineers are
kept to their promise by daily reminders from Parry.

This Influenza for such Mr Phillot admitted it to be yesterday still keeps
me weak though I am much better & gaining strength & my cough is

decidedly better. I thought best however to engage a Fly from Town that I might not be exposed to either the Drafts in the Steam Carriages or in the Boats. I knew too that I should have to take Crozier & the Purser to Deptford. I have been kept free from rest and quiet by this proceeding.

Lady Ross accompanied Crozier yesterday to see the ships – Ross himself being away house hunting in Warwickshire. I would have called on her today to see her if I had not to go out of the way to Deptford.

I saw Mr Grant who is superintending the making of our pemmican at the Clarence Yard – He distressed me much by saying that when he left Gosport yesterday the medical men were much alarmed at the state of poor dear Mary Richardson. She had recovered from her confinement but ague & low fever succeeded which has brought her to the brink of the grave. I fear Richardson is quite worn out with watching & overwhelmed with grief – I am afraid to write to him – Mr Grant thought I had better not.

Pray come up on which day suits you – I shall be happy to see you on either, but I beg of you if you set out Friday not to fatigue or weary yourself – or arrive too late to get your requisite rest before you go to Lady Haddington.

Your going there I consider of immense importance to you & me. I feel certain you will there meet many of the Ministers & perhaps Lord Stanley and Mr Hope who may see you – though I hope & trust neither of these will have the assurance to notice either of us.

The post man's bell has rung some time. Eleanor has gone to the Bath in Great Coram Street in a fly & of course William has gone with her.

I will make an effort to get in tonight but if I do not succeed do not fancy me negligent if it does not get to Brighton before the morning train.

Ever yours affectionately

John Franklin

49. HENRY T.D. LE VESCONTE TO HENRY LE VESCONTE [FATHER], 2 APRIL 1845

HMS Erebus Woolwich
April 2 1845

My dear Father

You may perhaps see by some stray paper before this reaches you that I have succeeding in joining the Polar expedition. My friend Fitzjames worked hard to get me appointed first on one of the ships but it was of no use – we got our appointments March 4th Just too late to tell you know and I have had no letter from you since I last wrote from London in the beginning of March I sent you some newspapers at the same time. There were three wrapped in the same paper. I joined and soon as I got my appointment and have been here ever since. There are a great many officers a commander on the Erebus – my ship – and three lieutenants three mates and an Ice Master. that is a Greenland skipper with the temporary rank of Master – men came forward very readily and the ships are making good progress under the first Lieutenants Gore of the Erebus and Little of the Terror Several of us are already employed in studying the use of instruments and making the calculations for magnetic observations. this is a very tedious affair the more so as being quite new. it is very little understood even by those who have devoted their whole attention to it, and there is at present no practical use to be made of these observations. all you know is that magnets on such a day with a certain state of the atmosphere &c did vary at different places in different ratios besides this I have been selected by Sir John Franklin at the instance of Captain Beaufort to manage the surveying part of the affair – there is not much to be done in this way as far as the explorers have hitherto been. but we do hope to get further perhaps through I consider this was a good thing for me and I shall certainly be able to make some returns and it may help me to employment in the same department at another time it is at present the most lucrative practicality to commandeer and I must say that I do hope this voyage will lead to promotion.

The ships are at present in dock where we are rigging each stowing them while the shipwrights are altering their sterns by bracing on abaft the stern posts an large mass of timber of the same thickness in which to work the screw propellers the engines will be put in next week we take a large supply of welsh coal and patent fuel – being bricks of coal dust and bitumen – we take a transport to the edge of the ice and shall from there start with three years stores and provisions we have seventy men in Erebus and 68 in Terror – Sir Edward Parry has been directed to make out our orders on the part of the Admiralty. what they will be is rather an interesting question to us the more so that there is a report that we shall be ordered if possible not to winter in the ice. this is I know Sir John Barrow's and Captain Beaufort's opinion – but not Sir John Franklins. He having been on the north coast before wants to push down to that coast again and says if he could once reach the mouth of the Mackenzie river he would be able to get through.

We shall be ready early in May what is as soon as will be of use if we are at all late in the present state of affairs there will be no difficulty in getting steam to tow us out – I do not myself think we shall reach the American coast at least until we get to Icy Cape but if we do there will be explorers sent along it I should think and it is possible I may at some future time find my way down to you in the shape of a messenger. but I shall stick to the expedition as long as my health lasts and there's any thing good to be done. We get double pay from the dates of our commissions – and are allowed six months advance. I dont think this will cover the expense but it is a long way towards it and there will be more afterwards – I very seldom leave this. never except to run to town on a Saturday evening and perhaps remain Sunday but I have promised myself a trip to Southampton in a few days. William Le Feuvre was in town two days hence but as usual

[rest of letter missing]

50. HARRY GOODSIR TO JOHN GOODSIR [FATHER], 3 APRIL 1845

H.M.S. Erebus
Woolwich Dockyards
April 3d 1845

My Dear Father

I have now got every thing in fair trim & feel myself much more comfortable. As none of the Officers live in the hulk but in Lodgings on shore I have thought it necessary to do the same as it would not do to be singular in that respect.

I met Captain Fitzjames & gave him the letter from Dr. Kerr. The first Lieutenant – Gore – I also know & find both of them very pleasant.

The Surgeon – Stanley is a very excellent fellow. We have been at work all morning preparing lists of things which shall be required during the voyage. All the books which were laid aside & which you put into the boxes be so good as send by the very first opportunity with the exception of those marked thus X Direct them to H.M.S. Erebus Woolwich Dockyards. You will recollect of course to send up all the Portfolios just as they are.

I hope you got my last letter which was written from London & also one to John from Newcastle. I have been expecting an answer both yesterday & today but have been disapointed. My money is now almost gone & it will place me in a very awkward predicament if any thing is required. The Vessels will be ready by the 1st week of May so that we shall get our money then & when I will be able to repay all that I have got from John & Joseph also my outstanding accounts in Edinburgh.

I hope every thing is going on well, that the College of Surgeons is attended to and that Archie is working there so that he may have an opportunity of getting in. Tell Bob Robertson that I spoke to John about the money that was still due him & also that I hope he will remain with John until I come home again.

As long as I reccollect be so good as send me the Edinburgh & Fife Papers regularly I will send them on to Roberts Lodgings as he will be up soon now surely. I hope also John will be here as he intended when we start. Love to Jane & Joseph when you write them I will do so soon – Joseph has not answered my letter from Newcastle. Hoping you will write without delay.

Believe me
Your affectionate Son
Harry D. S. Goodsir

51. HARRY GOODSIR TO JOHN GOODSIR [BROTHER], 3 APRIL 1845

H.M.S. Erebus
Woolwich Dockyards
April 3ᵈ, 1845

My Dear John

I have now got every thing settled & in working order there is not much to do only requiring to visit the Ship once a day to see if there are any sick You will see the arrangements I have made as regards my living during the time I am here – in the letter to my Father. I went to the Linnean Club dinner & afterward to the Society on Tuesday last & met Bell, Yarrell, Falconer, Spence, Dr. Good, Forster, & a number of others. I go with Forbes on Sunday morning to Cumming the Conchologist who is to give me all the information he can. I was also at the Geological Society last night.

Milne Edwards has been in London but only for a few days. Kolliker is at present – I will see him on Tuesday next. Forbes says he is a very good fellow.

With regard to the Planairy[?] unless you have done anything about it already, I think it will be needless to lay them before the Royal Society You can let me know – however regarding

[rest of letter missing]

52. JAMES FITZJAMES TO JOHN BARROW JR, BEFORE 4 APRIL 1845

My dear Barrow

Will you kindly forward this letter to the Cape – it is to get old Kelly of Conway to sign my young friend Wynyard's certificate – I have told his mother to send it you in a letter when she gets it – and I am sure you will forward it to him in the Pandora.

Will you to oblige Charlewood go to the Royal Society – and vote for Peter Barlow – son of the Professor and get as many votes for him as you can.

Thank you very much for the little Franklins – we dine on Friday next with Becher – do mind you get a cab and call for me at Albemarle St., 5 minutes before ½ past 6

The ships are getting on famously – our engine is down alongside. It came drawn by 10 coal black horses & weighs 15 tons.

[rest of letter missing]

53. HARRY GOODSIR TO JANE ROSS GOODSIR [SISTER], 5 APRIL 1845

H.M.S. Erebus
Woolwich Dockyard
April 5ᵗʰ. 1845

My Dear Jane

I was in such a hurry during my short stay at Largo that I entirely forgot to speak to you about the work you imposed upon me some time before. I had no proper opportunity of arranging it before leaving Edinburgh & so placed it in Johns hands who promised to manage it all speedily. I have no doubt it will succeed but at any rate One should always go on with such things for if we do not make strenuous efforts we cannot expect to advance in any thing of the kind.

I have got every thing comfortably settled here now but occasionally some few rather irksome things occur – always the case on entering upon a new mode of life. These however will soon pass away. All the Officers are very pleasant gentlemenly men with whom one can be always at ease. Government had a man down yesterday taking all our measures for large outer clothing. I missed him along with my others but all the clothes will require to be made so large that the tailor cannot go wrong.

The Queen it is said is going to pay us a visit on Tuesday, but unfortunately I have not got my uniform yet!!

I got my certificate from Sir John Franklin today which entitles me to draw £130 as soon as I please being six months pay in advance from the 11th of March With this however I have to get my ou[tfit &] my share of the mess & have to pay my various accounts in Edinburgh if any can be spared when I start for I cant carry any with me you shall know.

> Believe me
> Ever your Affectionate Brother
> Harry D. S. Goodsir

P.S. I got Josephs letter with order for £8 today tell him I will write him soon & will also attend to his other directions. [Further postscript, written on the back] This letter has been delayed till this day the 8th: in consequence of my being in London where also it is now Posted I have many things to do so cannot at present at least write much to any one. There is a letter lying for me at the Ship I believe but do not know from whom. I go today to get my outfit &c: bedding &c: Went to Drury Lane last night to hear Duprez as Arnold in William Tell. I will write soon.

54. JOHN FRANKLIN TO JAMES FITZJAMES, 5 APRIL 1845

> 40 Lower Brook Street
> 5th April 1845

My dear Sir,

Thank you for your note of yesterday and for its information.

The Sketch Books in the Demand are for the purpose of entering Bearings & angles – and sights etc – this I will explain to day to Mr Miles.

I am glad that you have entered an Armourer & Carpenters Mate and to hear your opinion of our men. The one exception we must part with.

Sir George Cockburn immediately acquiesced in my opinion that a new Gunner should not be appointed – & gave instruction to reduce our Complement accordingly. We have therefore no further inconvenience about the Cabins to fear.

I am happy to say that my cold which has proved an attack of Influenza, is much better, but my medical man & many of my Brother Officers, Sir James Ross included, have so strongly urged my going down to Brighton as the only chance of my getting rid of it, that I have determined on running down there for two or three days for change of air – Brighton has on former occasions instantly relieved me & I trust it will do so now. I will write to Captain Crozier and inform him of my determination which has only been arrived at this morning – Have the goodness to take any official letters that may come to Captain Crozier whom I will request to open & act upon them. I hope to get back to Woolwich on Wednesday –

Mr Stanley has been with me this morning with additional demands for articles required for the preservation of specimens of Natural History which I have approved & given to him to put into the proper channel. Hoar has also been here & has informed me that his discharge from the St Vincent has not yet been sent. I will enquire about it at the Admiralty.

I was at Lord Haddingtons last Evening & was happy from your note on being able to tell him that the Topmasts were up – & that the ships were getting on well. I feel obliged to Gore for his exertions which however I was fully prepared to expect.

I hope the officers are keeping steadily at their instruction in Surveying & Magnetism.

Believe me
my dear Sir
yours very sincerely
John Franklin

55. HENRY T.D. LE VESCONTE TO SARAH LE VESCONTE [MOTHER], 8 APRIL 1845

Erebus Woolwich Apr. 8 1845

My dear Mother

I have already related the little news I have to tell so do not expect a very interesting letter from me for I fear I am not quite in a writing vein being much puzzled with new and sharp calculations and observations we have to make – I am most anxious to hear what you think of the expedition or rather of my having embarked on it. it has been an object of much solicitude to me for a year and a half but it was at first so uncertain in itself besides being classed among dangerous enterprises that I thought it better to say nothing about it until it was likely to be decided. I am and have been since the 4th March 2nd Lieutenant of the Erebus under Captain Sir John Franklin & Commander Fitzjames. The other ship the Terror is commanded by Captain Crozier who commanded her in the South before We hope to sail in middle of May and to return – as soon as we can get through Behring Straits.

They are very strong good ships and very well provided with every thing that can add to our comfort or convenience connecting with the service we are on. We shall be in every way provided for three years and may perhaps get into the Ice and be cut off from all communication with the rest of the world for a couple of years but beyond this and the recollection of those we leave behind us there is nothing to be troubled about. Wherever we are we are assuredly in Gods hands – I do not think the danger or inconvenience are at all equal to China or the coast of africa and we are all hoping for promotion – dont you hope we may get it – dont say I said so at present – but I am wanting promotion and a quick return to England for the reason that I am more than half in love with with – who – you could not easily guess for she was a very young lady when you left England – indeed she is scarcely nineteen now – The only piece of advice on this subject I remember receiving was from my Father "never marry an older woman" so far well – at any rate

Miss Sarah Le Feuvre will insist on being my aunt and I have received lately some very nice letters from <u>her</u> niece you may suppose I have not had much time for courtship but they are all very good people and I have never missed an opportunity of passing a day or two there but enough of this when I know more I will tell you if it is good – if not I shall say no more about it. I am very sorry I cannot give you any news of Philip but I still think he is all right but too proud to write because he is not doing exactly what he could wish – I do not hear much from Devonshire. They are poor hands at writing. I tried to get Mrs John into correspondence but it is no use and I regretted more that she really can write a very good sensible and witty letter – Mary Kendell is getting my worsted things knitted for me – I preferred asking her because I thought she could do it with more ease than aunt Betsy but I took the precaution to ask her to say nothing about it. William writes from Ipplepen a hurried scrawl to know if I can find any one to take his house and practice at Totnes. I certainly should not recommend any <u>friend</u> of mine to go there for I know his practice was worth very little and there is a crowd of doctors in the Town but I shall mention it when I think it <u>may</u> be serviceable – I think he will do much better in the country and Mrs W will be much pleased with it she is such a good little woman that I cant help having a greater regard for her than for any of them – I got a very odd letter from Mr Nantes on the Polar voyage which he talk[s] of leading to great honor and rich rewards or something of that sort. I don't know if he is yet gone to Windsor nor can I guess whether he would let me know when he does go – you must promise any letters that I will write before I sail give them all my love and believe me ever your very affectionate son

HTD LeVesconte

56. HARRY GOODSIR TO JOHN GOODSIR [FATHER], 9 APRIL 1845

H.M.S. Erebus
Woolwich Dockyards
April 9th 1845

My Dear Father

I have only got your letter of 5th today (Wednesday) in consequence of having been in London since Sunday but hope it will not put you to any inconvenience its not having been answered sooner. In regard to money I had a letter from Joseph, containing two Orders, the end of last week (Saturday) & was therefore supplied in time but no more for I had to meet Forbes in town on Sunday & could not have gone but for Joseph's timely letter. I am sorry about the trouble you have had with my books but at the same time hope you will be able to get them or rather have sent them off ere this. I thought I had acknowledged receipt of Commission &c. – It came safely to hand.

After paying Rickards that last Bill I was only due him £7 & other things of course which have been got since will mount it up a little. You must just see about as well as you can he cannot expect money for some time and in fact since he has got so much favours of late he must be patient, you need not pay it. I wrote to Jane a few days ago but only posted the letter last night from London.

I have been up looking after my outfit & find it will be rather expensive The Queen visits us on Tuesday next & if we all require to attend it will be a cause of great expense as we must appear in full dress uniform & a cocked Hat alone costs £4 As it is I have been obliged to get a suit of undress uniform which I hope will be all that I need at present in that way. My suit of Furs alone will cost from 8 to £10 & what with shirts outer clothing bedding &c. it will come to something considerable.

Government only gives us a certain amount of clothing annually, the rest we provide ourselves. Regarding these matters however I will let you hear more again, but at present & as long as there is time want to ask a few questions which you can let Jane know of as I am uncertain of the people we deal with here.

1st. About shirts. Of these I would require a considerable number as there will be little or no washing during winter months. but perhaps 3 dozen & ½ or 4 dozen will be sufficient of common coarse cotton similar to night shirts, some blue striped. 4 dozen I think will be amply sufficient.

2d. Stockings worsted to come a little above the knee, & a little large to come over a pair of socks, & if knitted very much better than the bought kind. 3 or 4 dozen ☞ I have been looking with some of the other officers at the worsted work in a Shetland house in London but am quite sure that the knitted things I have got from Aunt Ann were much better. & if Aunt could only get some pairs of large stockings & some mits made I would like it very much I will of course be at all the expence. My best plan however will be to write her myself which I will do tonight.

3d. Ask Jane what blankets, sheets & other bedding will be necessary. I will get a matrass or feather bed here for the purpose as it requires a particular form.

I took with me from Edinburgh a considerable number of towels so that I wont require them to be got on purpose.

Will you be so good as tell me what you pay for your suit of Chamois leather.

I got Johns letter containing Traills letter &c. but have determined not to deliver them as I know Sir John Franklin already & it would be only troubling him. I will however think of Walkers when I go to town again. Tell John also I had a letter written to him last week but did not send it off in consequence of Joseph's letter coming in time. In it I asked him to send up the small phial containing the Beetle with the intestinal Filaria it is lying in the parlour press Expecting to hear from you soon.

> Believe me
> Ever your Affectionate Son
> > Harry D.S. Goodsir

57. HARRY GOODSIR TO JOHN GOODSIR [BROTHER], 11 APRIL 1845

H.M.S. Erebus
Woolwich Dockyards
April 11th. 1845

My Dear John

Your letter of Monday I have just received & am glad to hear that every thing is going on so well. I posted a letter on Tuesday in London for Jane in which there was an acknowledgement of receipt of Josephs money. Every thing goes on smoothly and comfortably here. I am very little in Town & therefore do not see Forbes often but will probably be up tomorrow. So long as I recollect of it I had better mention that the Officers are anxious to have a good dog on board, So we may take Cæsar. One of the Lieutenants is very anxious to get a small Scotch Terrier. Tell Bob to look out for that Dandy Dinmont John Christie offered him it must be good one of that or the Skye breed. Bob could also easily bring them up with him when he comes which will be soon now I suppose. Do you come up as you intended? There is a spare bed in my lodgings which you can easily get. It is my intention however as soon as I get all the microscope observations made on shore & as soon as I get my bedding to live on board which will be very soon now I hope.

I was to have sent my paper to Taylor today but have been on board the ship all the day in consequence of the absence of all the other Surgeons. I have got very little of my outfit yet as it will be better to wait to see what kind and quality of things the others get I have decided what should be got but will learn what is best after I see the others. A Sealskin greatcoat & set of undress uniform are all I have got yet – All the Officers are in great hopes of making the passage & expect to be in the Pacific end of next summer However from all that I hear and see I have no doubt that every facility will be allowed for the observation of animals.

You can let Forbes know that the probable route is up the west coast of Greenland & then directly into Lancasters Sound.

The books for which we have just made enquiries have not come yet. The dredge will be with them I hope. As I am in haste you must excuse this letter which is written with a ships pen. I will write more fully soon. Look after the dogs but of them you shall hear more explicitly.

Believe me
Your Affectionate Brother
Harry D. S. Goodsir

58. JOHN FRANKLIN TO JOHN RICHARDSON, 12 APRIL 1845

Brighton 12th April

My dear Richardson

I have been for some days apprehensive of learning the awful announcement which your letter of the 10th, received here to day, has made to me. God's ways are inscrutable, but we know them to be all ordered in infinite wisdom. His will be done in Earth, as it is in Heaven!

I cannot my dearest friend venture at this time to write more – than to assure you that I praise the Lord most heartily for his merciful support of you through the present trial, and that I feel a humble trust in God that he will continue to give your dear family his all-sufficient help.

I have been for several weeks suffering from a severe attack of Influenza, and I was strongly advised to change the air & come to Brighton for a few days. The change has been most beneficial to me, and on Monday I should have returned to my duties on board the ships.

I am glad to learn that Eleanor has told you of my being here – had it been otherwise I should have been with you by the first train after your letter reached me – I shall be in London on Monday afternoon and if you would let me have one line at No. 40 Lower Brook Grosvenor Square to state your wishes as to seeing me before the funeral I will immediately comply with them. Say also when the funeral is to be. My wife & Sophy C. who alone are with me, join me in the deepest grief & Condolence.

Ever yours affectionately
John Franklin

59. HARRY GOODSIR TO JOHN GOODSIR [BROTHER], 13 APRIL 1845

H.M.S. Erebus
Woolwich Dockyards
April 13th. 1845

My Dear John

I suppose you have received the letter posted in London on Sunday Evening. I am busy now with the Collections here & have got full liberty from Gray to examine all the specimens in the British Museum.

There are apparently, at the utmost only 10 or 12 Seals known so that I hope to be able to do something with them. Gray has promised me his book – which forms one of the Antarctic Series – if Government wont supply it; He tells me also he thinks it is a false step going out but I told him I had made up my mind to all the disadvantages but even taking all of them into account had no doubt that a great deal could be done he said Hookers Surgeon was mad and did every thing in his power to prevent any thing being done. I have no doubt however that Stanley is a very different person & at all events under Sir John Franklin there can be no doubt that every thing will go on well. I gave in my paper today to the Annals but am afraid it will be too late for this next month. I called upon Mr. Nasmyth and Wardrop yesterday, sat with the latter for a long time while he was reading to me part of his new work on the heart. by the way he is going to notice the book soon in some periodical.

Mr. Nasmyth asked me to dine with him on Saturday where I meet Forbes, Waterhouse, Dalrymple, King (the letter man) &c. I meet Kolliker tomorrow night at the Linnean go to the Geological on Wednesday, dine at the Red Lions on Thursday & Richard Taylor on Friday. At present I live in Town in Roberts Lodgings. I hope that he as Young tells me is coming up this week for I will be able to help him. If my letter of yesterday reaches you in time I hope you will tell him, before leaving, to look after the dogs I must speak more definitely to Captain Franklin or Lieutenant Gore before any thing can be done about Cæsar & I will do that tomorrow.

As long as I remember I had a long conversation at the British Museum today with Falconer he is busy with his new work. He is particularly anxious to see you about the Teeth as he says he has [...] out all the principal characters about the [...] of the Eliphants. Expecting to hear f[rom] you soon.

Believe me

Your Affectionate Brother

Harry D. S. Goodsir

Tell Joseph when you are writing him that he will hear from me in a few days.

60. HARRY GOODSIR TO ANNE MONRO TAYLOR [AUNT], 17 APRIL 1845

H.M.S. Erebus
Woolwich Dockyards
April 17th. 1845

My Dear Aunt

I received your kind letter, of the 12th, yesterday & now hasten to answer it that you may know actually what I have got already of my outfit, & I now begin to think that with what we get from Government it will be quite enough.

1st Suit of Undress Uniform
Pilot Jackets & trowsers

One pair Deer Skin Trowsers	– – – £	2 .. – – –
– – – – – Racoon Skin Ditto	– – – –	2 .. – – –
One Lambskin Waistcoat	– – – –	1 .. 10 –
One large Sealskin Greatcoat	– – – – –	5 .. – – –
One Sealskin Cap	– – – – – – – – – – – 15 –
3 pairs – – – – Gloves	– – – – – – – – – – – 15 –
3 pairs Strong boots – – – – – –	

each average 5/– 4 of each, of 4 various kinds, of woollen clothing

Chamois skin shirts	2 – – each –	.. 10 .. 6
– – – – – trowsers	1 – – – – –	.. 12 .. 6
½ dozen Grampian stockings	– – –	1 .. 4 .. –
1 dozen Black Shetland Ditto	– – –	1 .. 4 .. –
1 dozen strong silk Handkerchiefs	– – –	2 .. 2 .. –

The above is a list of all the things I have yet ordered & believe myself they are sufficient except as regards the stockings of which I think 2 dozen or 2½ will be little enough we require however to cautious in not ordering too many things as our berths are so very small that they wont hold very much. I have not yet ordered shirts but believe that with what I have one dozen or one dozen & ½ will be sufficient as of most of these things Government gives us so much annually. I got my six months pay yesterday in advance amounting to £114 but am sorry to say that it will very soon go as what with my outfit & mess money the bills soon mount up. Each of the officers are obliged to give £60 for mess & the outfit itself will be £40 or 50 so you see everything is taken up. Regarding our mess I must have my own spoons &c. about which I will write Jane myself but as I am uncertain when & as there is little time to loose now I take the present opportunity of letting her know as I suppose you will let Jane know about it. Each officer is required to have at least 2 pairs of each I mean 2 of each not 2 pairs, he may have three if he chooses Silver forks, dessert ditto – Table spoons, dessert, & Tea spoons. I was bargaining yesterday for a set but found they would cost me £11 at least which is too much money for me.

Sir John Barrow is out of the Admiralty now and from all I can gather is in bad understanding with some of the parties so that it would not do to come in contact in that way. Nevertheless I am much obliged to Lord William but do not think it would do to write to him until I get further information at least regarding Sir John Barrow.

I call upon Captain Nairne today at 2 at the Marine Insurance Office & I expect to get a great deal of information from him. I will not write to La[rgo o]r Edinburgh till tomorrow so that I c[an] send further information but be so good as let J[ane] see this letter so soon as you get it so that I may receive an answer without delay – We start, it is supposed, almost certainly on the 8th of next month & therefore have little time to spare. Let me know what you think of the prices affixed to the articles of clothing I have got.

> Believe me
> Your Affectionate nephew
> Harry D. S. Goodsir

Jane has never written yet.

Do you say the Dogs name is Fernie who is coming from Scotland. Love to Uncle.

The woman, who comes originally from Edinburgh, that supplies the Woollen, Shirts &c. asks 30/ a dozen for the coarse stripe shirt. Is that much? You must excuse my letters how far these things cant be well done under present circumstances.

61. JAMES FITZJAMES TO JOHN BARROW JR, 17 APRIL 1845

April 17, Thursday

My dear Barrow

Mind you call for me in Albemarle Street at ½ past 6 or sooner if you like – on Friday.

I think if you want to see the Erebus before she leaves the Dock that you ought to bring Sir John here next week – say <u>Wednesday</u> to be here at 3 o'clock – that is leave Hungerford Market Waterman's pier, the second street below Hungerford Market at ¼ before 2 –

D'ont go down the street with "Steam Boats" in tin across the bottom of it – but go on 2 streets. If you miss this boat then go back to the "Steam Boat" street & leave ¼ <u>past</u> 2 –

Captain Beaufort was here today & daughters – also wife

Believe me always

    Yours sincerely
    James Fitzjames

I hope the Queen will come & see us – it will give them a spur in the Dockyard – She ought to give Sir John Franklin his "broad pendant" – he should look very respectable I think – amongst the ice

62. JOHN IRVING TO CATHERINE IRVING [SISTER-IN-LAW], 18 APRIL 1845

H.M.S. "Terror,"
Woolwich, 18th April 1845.

My dear Katie,

Many thanks for your very kind letter of the 11th, which would have been replied to before now ; but I did not get it owing to one of our fellows taking care of it for two days instead of telling me of its arrival. As you say, my visit was one of the shortest, but better that than none at all. I can assure you there was no one it grieved me more to part with than yourself; for somehow or other, from the very first time we met, you and I seemed to understand each other wonderfully well. I got back here on the Monday morning to breakfast, and went about my occupations as usual. We make some show now, having got the masts up and rigging complete, ready for sea, and are now busy stowing away everything, provender, etc. etc., for two years' consumption. They talk of sailing on the 1st of May ; but I suspect it will be some days later. As you observe, there must now be a long blank in our correspondence. However that may be, I hope when we meet next we shall not be obliged to part so quickly. . . . Whatever happens, it is the will of God.

I hope you do not think me so weak as to labour under any presentiment of evil ; but remember this is no common voyage, and two years is a long period to look forward to in the life of the healthiest and the least exposed to risks. Only one half of Sir John Franklin's former party returned with him, and our " Terror " in her last voyage with Captain Back was so crushed by the ice that she could not have been kept afloat another day, when they got into Loch Swilly. Two years is a long time without any tidings, and perhaps we may be three years at least. Do not give us up, if you hear nothing.

But now I will throw over a new leaf with the rest of my letter, and tell you that I am very sanguine of succeeding in the object of our expedition. Everything has been done that the latest improvements in the various branches of arts relating to nautical matters could suggest ; and every preservation against the climate provided for the health and comfort of the crews ; and we must for the rest put ourselves, and, what is dearer, our hopes, into the hands of our Maker. Should it please Him to permit us to return to reap the fruits of our labours, I trust the greater the dangers we may have passed the more gratitude we may be enabled to show in our future lives for the protecting Hand without which, after all, our skill and devices and contrivances are in vain.

I intended to write something to amuse you, but I find I cannot help being serious. Everything around me, and every duty I am engaged in, tend at present to make me so, – I mean all keep so much alive the feeling of a long separation from those near and dear to me. Even in writing I am reminded that a terrible long pause of anxious suspense is before me, when I can only hope, without a prospect of tidings of good or ill. So, my dear Katie, do not blame me that you should have been, whilst reading this mass of scribbling, obliged to banish your usual smiles. I will write you yet again, so I shall not take a very formal farewell of you this time. My most brotherly love to my dear Lewis. – Yours very affectionately,

John Irving.

63. HARRY GOODSIR TO JOHN GOODSIR [BROTHER], 21 APRIL 1845

26 Surry Street Strand, London
April 21st. 1845

My Dear John

Your letter came safely to hand and 1st. with regard to David Forbes I have not yet had a proper opportunity of speaking to his brother but will do so without delay. I have been so much engaged in London this last week that I thought it better to take lodgings here for the time but generally go down to Woolwich every second day to see about letters &c. I dined with Nasmyth last night & had a night of microscopic examinations, Dalrymple, Gulliver, King, Carpenter, Dr. Grant, & Waterhouse were present. Did you send a copy of the book to Carpenter or to the Review? He has not got it apparently. I do not think Richard Taylor has got a copy for the Annals of Natural History. Breakfasted yesterday morning with Robert Brown & spent the whole forenoon with him looking over the collections of Arctic plants brought home by Parry & others; He gave me a great deal of information & promised me a copy of his appendix to the voyage with a small collection of the plants, he also told me that he spoke particularly to Franklin so that the work will not likely be meddled with by any of the officers. He (Mr. Brown) is exceedingly anxious to examine that small shrubby plant from Ichaboe could you get a small but characteristic specimen from Dr. Wilson or Dr. Maclagan. he is very anxious to examine it & I am anxious to be able to do any thing for such a man in return for his kindness. Some of his observations of the development of cells in fossil plants are very similar to those brought forward in the book on which account it would be useful to give him a copy. Nasmyth says his views regarding the development of cells are exactly similar & he can now bring forward his views more confidently, Dalrymple is not sure about the placenta. Forbes thinks he is the author of the review in the last Lancet, which I suppose you have seen Kolliker is still here yet I am going to call upon him in the course of a day or two to give him a copy both of the book & also of my other papers which he wants. It would be a good opportunity of sending over presentation copies to the continent to Oken, Siebold, &c. He is anxious to do it, a few, Dined with Richard Taylor on Friday & met Owen & Robert Brown. Owen is very kind & is to give every assistance I will visit the Collection tomorrow & the British Museum again on Tuesday when I also dine with Grey, I go to the Ethnological Society on Wednesday where Nasmyth is to read [...] on the peculiar form of the Skull in some [...] The Society are also to give me a series of queries & observations to make. King is a very pleasant little fellow – I had a great deal of Conversation with him.

I received Janes letter on Friday but I have got all the outfitting already, my only fix now being Silver forks, spoons, &c which are required for mess three of each kind viz table spoons 3. Forks 3 dessert spoons 3 & Forks 3. teaspoons 3. I mentioned in a letter to Aunt Ann all the Outfit I have got & the expense, which together with mess will take up almost all my pay so that if I can get the spoons &c. without buying them here – they would cost £10 2d hand – it would be much better [if] Bob could bring them with him As there are no dessert silver forks at home I would buy them here second hand. By the bye send up a Highland plaid, Mackenzie tartan, directed to Frederick Hornbey Esquire. H.M.S. Terror Woolwich with the Account enclosed.

I called last Thursday upon Captain Nairne he is an old messmate of Sir John Franklins & knows him intimately so he intends going down to Woolwich some day soon to meet him. I am not sure from your letter whether you are to be up or not but expect to hear from you soon. Tell

Jane, or Archie to write to her, not to do any thing as I have got all my outfit ready Boxes have come but are not yet opened. Love to all at home.

Believe me &c &c
Harry D. S. Goodsir

64. HENRY T.D. LE VESCONTE TO HENRY LE VESCONTE [FATHER], 2 MAY 1845

HMS Erebus Woolwich May 2, 1845

My dear Father

Since I wrote to you last I have received your letter of March I acknowledge the justice of your complaints about badly managed correspondence, but I have been much harassed and often so uncertain about my daily movements that I have deferred writing with the hope of telling you something more satisfactory. I think Lord Haddington's answer very good and I shall leave a copy of it and of the memorial with William Le Feuvre to be used by him if there is an opportunity and I will tell Henrietta how it may be done with much advantage that she may prompt him if a proper time occurs for he is very much occupied the idea of Madame Adelaide is a good one she is the same lady but I do not think anything should be done there until after I am gone. It is very likely that the senior lieutenants will be promoted while absent or at least our first Mr Gore who has strong claims and bears a very high character. If this happens you might bring forward my claims successfully. perhaps. but I feel so much interest in this voyage now and I feel so satisfied that it will place one in so much better a position for future employment that I have not any very great need to get the step before the ships sail, poor little Henrietta says she does not like these dangerous enterprises but she is fully aware of the necessity of doing something – and I tell her we may be back in a year this is quite true but the most probable time is two years and a half – we shall be ready about the 12th and sail very soon after.

Proceeding to Disco and then as soon as possible into Lancaster sound and try to get down to the coast about the M'Kenzie River and to the Behring straits. I have heard from Miss Kendell who says there is not a young man to be found willing to go out with the prospect of becoming a landed proprietor in Canada. I have answered abusing them all for being faint hearted and saying what fine things they are losing. One objection is so many are married I do not know if this would not be a commendation for I suppose female servants are as difficult to procure as male. but Miss K will I think write to you about it – She has sent me some capital socks and Guernsey frocks knitted as I like I have told her most particularly not to let Aunt Betsy know she has done so so I hope none of you will mention it for the latter good lady would be vexed that I did not ask her and you know Mary Kendell was the best hand. I am sorry I should have so libelled the Erebus and Terror. I mean the Red Rover and water witch but you may in return abuse the old discovery ships as much as you please – Sarah will not share the blame with me but she certainty was concerned in the joke. I think when I spoke of Aunt Judith it must have been meerly from frequently hearing her so called but I do sometimes call her Auntie now she is staying with Maria Kilroy at Plymouth while he is gone to Bermuda with convicts – I hope to get down to Southampton for a few days but our time is very much taken up just now and every body wants to say good bye. we were discussing the ships last night and I urged my claim to a few days leave very strongly – and said I would run if I could not otherwise get away so I think it will be so arranged that I go down on Tuesday morning. We have every prospect of being most comfortable. Sir John Franklin is a very good man. I need not again say what I think of Fitzjames – in writing to me just before he got appointed he says "I shall get promoted" and then I will never rest until you are. He came to me yesterday to request particularly if I wanted money to fit out. I would not think of asking any other person – he has had something left him lately but he is not much richer than I am. Our two lieutenants are very fine fellows. Fairholme was on the Niger expedition he is talented and very persevering – he was civil enough to take me to his uncle's on saturday last, "Lord Forbes". I remained with them until Sunday evening – The surgeon was in the Cornwallis with Fitzjames and myself. We have a queer fellow for an acting master – or Ice Master most of us think we should be better without him but it appears the Admiralty are anxious to supply every thing that can be of use. The provisions will be very good. we take flour in preference to bread as we have to keep up fires to make ourselves warm it may as well be employed in baking bread a very great quantity of pickles mustard and cranberries are sent for the use of the ships company and the spirits are thirty five degrees above proof. There will be enough for three years if we get down on the coast you will perhaps hear from us. I hope there will be some means of communicating

I have spoken about being sent home through North America if we get through it may be managed Fitzjames wants to go through Siberia – and I think he will be allowed The ships are to come round Cape Horn but most people shrug there shoulders when we speak of these things. Captain Austin whom I was speaking to about it a few days since says they were always just as sanguine as we are & considered themselves the expedition to be successful. This is said to be the 79th sent to make discoveries in the Polar seas. Of one thing I feel assured we should not readily give it up whatever may be our luck. I hope you will write to William Le Feuvre I do not think it necessary to ask if you approve of my engagement with his daughter. Knowing how much you esteem him and that all their family approve. I have not named it to the General but Mrs Le F says he has expressed his approbation. altho he did write to Henrietta something about poverty driving love out at the window. I have not the least idea of letting them suppose I expect anything from him. but I am well pleased that he likes it for he has been always very civil to me and she is a great favorite of his at least so his sisters tell me – there is one consideration here which I always reflect on with pleasure although there is a large family of William Le Feuvres there is no one of them either silly ugly or ill tempered. Edmund is a very steady and intelligent fellow and will certainly rise rapidly. Frederick is eleven and very spirited. the other boys are too young to say much of. poor Mary is a very sweet tempered girl, what a pity she is so lame it is of no use my praising Henrietta but I do not doubt you will hear many good accounts of her from our aunt with fondest love to my dear father & mother believe me your very affectionate son,

HTD LeVesconte

[In margin of first leaf] I shall write to Charles this evening if I have time

65. HARRY GOODSIR TO JOHN GOODSIR [BROTHER], 2 MAY 1845

H.M.S. Erebus
Woolwich Dockyards
May 2[d] 1845

My Dear John

I have just received yours of the 30th. & have in the first place to thank you for the Plaid & Silver spoons. The parcel has not yet come but I will

look for it now every day. I am sorry you have been at the expence &
trouble of sending me silver spoons for I find I will be able – at least I
hope to get it arranged tomorrow – to procure money enough to settle
every thing. If so I will arrange about the silver things, for I know you
cant well want them & besides it is only two that is required. Since
however you have already put my initials upon them all it had better
just remain as it is & I will send you down the money you have paid out
together with as much as I can spare, for the Edinburgh accounts.

Speaking of writing I hope you received a letter from me a few days
ago. I also sent one to my Father. I hope you will be able to send the dogs
& if so it must be done without delay as we will sail very shortly now. It
is impossible for any one to say exactly when but every one agrees that it
will not be later than the 10th. or 15. We are all however kept in such darkness regarding the motions that it is impossible for me to let you know any
thing farther at present. I hope you will also send my boottrees. I am very
glad that Bob has made up his mind to begin Medicine & of course if any
thing is to be done the sooner it is begun the better. I do not know however
how my things are to be got up if he or you does not come.

I suppose you have got a letter from Falconer a few days ago He was
down with a brother of Miss Edgeworths at the Vessels. Great numbers of visitors are down daily, & it is expected that immense numbers
will visit the ships before the day of sailing. I wish you would come up
if Robert does not come for there are many things we require to talk
about of which we cannot write. The Admiralty have now determined to
appoint a Naturalist to every Expedition in consequence of something
Prince Albert said to the Earl of Haddington a few days ago. Accordingly
Forbes was applied to for the Californian Expedition who mentioned
me, but I will remain here as I am, with this Exception, that the title of
Naturalist must be added to that of Assistant Surgeon and this I expect
to get done tomorrow or next day when I will call upon Robert Brown
about it. By the way I hope you have got specimens of the Ichaboe plant
from George Wilson for R. Brown. I will call upon him tomorrow &
give him a copy of the book – I wish we had one or two more here as
they are all g[one] now & Kolliker leaves tomorrow.

I dine with […] tomorrow – Cumming on Sunday 4th. & Captain
Nairne on Monday. I do not know whether I have told you or not that
I am living on board the hulk now where we all mess together & a
better set of men you could not meet with any where. McDonald the
Assistant Surgeon of the Terror is a very good hearted fellow. & is very

much better than either of the others Peddie of the Terror is a Montrose man who will do nothing unless to bring in money but at the same time does not bother other people much with attempts at working & much speaking he is one however who neither exerts himself & will not do so in any way for other people. Stanley is a would be great man who as I at first supposed would not make any effort at work after a time. He is at present however altho he knows nothing whatever about subject & is ignorant enough of all other subjects showing it more than any other person I ever met with in consequence of his speaking so much. I will therefore for securities sake procure the above title which will enable me to be much more independent. Love to all at home.

Your affectionate Brother
Harry D. S. Goodsir

I am busy with all my papers & will get them all finished in time

66. HARRY GOODSIR TO JOHN GOODSIR [FATHER], 6 MAY 1845

H.M.S. Erebus
Woolwich Dockyards
May 6th. 1845

My Dear Father

I have just returned from London. I was dining last night with Captain Nairne and hasten now to write the information I have gained regarding Robert. Before going to Captain Nairne's I was told by Young that he was likely to leave the situation which he now holds in the house of Harris & Co in the course of a month or 6 weeks & thought it very likely that Robert would be able to get it. Mr. William Scott whom I met at Captain Nairne's says that he will speak to Harris & Co about Robert if he still wishes to obtain the situation but would far rather advise him to go on with the study of medicine – if he is at all inclined to the profession. – seeing that as a banker or wine merchant he never can expect to rise above a Clerkship which neither produces a good return as regards money nor any thing like a respectable standing. Explain this to Robert as I have not time to write him direct. We sail on Monday first for Greenhithe & start from that place for good on the 15th. The

1st. Lieutenant of the Erebus has got a dog if therefore you have not sent off Cæsar yet it is just as well to keep him at home poor brute as he is rather old for the voyage altho not so advanced in years as the one we are taking. I have received the Plaid for Hornby together with the Silver spoons. I have a very great deal to do yet before starting for the papers I have promised to John & the Annals of Natural History one is printed already for the latter & all the others I have got so far finished & hope to get them finished altogether very shortly there is so much bustle now however in consequence of the two vessels being alongside the hulk that is by no means easy. This will be the last letter, I am afraid I will be able to write you from Woolwich but will if possible send you one from Greenhithe, at all events you will all hear by means of the Steamers which are to tow us beyond the Orkney's. After Monday therefore unless you have further information, you need not send or direct any more letters to this place – Before leaving this I have to write to John with a small parcel but farther than that, seeing I have so much to do, it will be impossible for me to manage. Captain Nairne & Mr. Scott are to be down to the Vessels on Friday. You must excuse this short letter as I am very hurried

Believe me
Your affectionate Son
Harry D. S. Goodsir

67. JAMES FITZJAMES TO ELIZABETH CONINGHAM [SISTER-IN-LAW], 10 MAY 1845

Woolwich Saturday 10th May

My dearest Elizabeth

When I left you for many years – on a former occasion I knew you merely (which to me was much) as the wife of him I love best – I now leave you knowing you as <u>yourself</u> – and you will believe me when I say that now that you are gone I have felt parting from you to the full as much as from William –

I look back with pleasure to the quiet time at Brighton and trust when I come back that I shall find you in a nice permanent residence near Town which I know will suit you both as well as me.

William's letter came this morning & Shell who is with me grinned when he gave it. I really do not know what I should do without Shell he is packing my books & clothes – & has been up to Town – & back twice to day. – He brought his wife & Parry down in a Cart & they went on board (barring the wife who was afear'd) and came back and eat beef steaks & drank beer & tea & laughed & were quite happy –

On Thursday I dined with Lord Haddington – the pleasantest party I recollect – he had Franklin Parry Ross – Back, Crozier Sir John Pelly (Chairman of the Hudson's Bay Company) Barrow – Beaufort, Sabine and the Lords of the Admiralty & their secretaries. I sat between Sir William Gage and Sir Edward Parry –

Sir William Gage made me tell him all about Icheboe the account of which he passed across the table to Lord H – he chatted all dinner time, & Lord H spoke of "Caesar passing the Rubicon" Sir Edward Parry – told me he was sure it would be perfectly possible & _easy_ to reach the Pole and that every body said _I was_ to do it – when we come back.

After dinner a little black long-haired, short-sighted little goose hopped in whom they announced as Lord Northampton – But the best thing remains to be told – and which you shall have the pleasure of telling William – Sir John Barrow attacked Sir George Cockburn & Lord Haddington – and then came to me in the dining room & told me that Sir George Cockburn had promised him that my commission as Captain should be sent out with us, if the board agreed – and that he would propose it immediately Lord Haddington said he would be delighted if the Board recommended it – & Sir William Gage said he should support the proposition Now as they are the majority of the board. I think I am safe – expecially as Sir John Barrow never promised me anything of the sort before.

I was up till 3 o'clock this morning at the Observatory the stars having appeared to make up for my _disappointment_ on Wednesday. I was up again at ½ past 5 and am now nearly ready – We have crowds of people looking at the ships, who quite fill the vessels –

On Monday at 3 o'clock the ships go to Green Hythe 12 miles down – and I remain here & go down early on Tuesday morning – the instruments not having yet all arrived

Tomorrow Sunday I shall take Shell on board the Great Britain Captain Hoskins having asked me and then shall see the children. Shell desires me to say he saw them yesterday (Friday) looking well & happy.

And now God bless you, I shall write from Green Hythe and again when the steamers leave us & again when the Transport leaves us in the ice and again from the Sandwich Islands. Remember me with all kindness to Anthony & Charlotte & tell them Clark is really too ill to go with us.

I have had a long letter from Mrs Campbell begging me to try & persuade you to go to Portsmouth, in which Missie joins both of whom I wish you knew – The Colonel was here yesterday – write pray to the care of John Barrow for I do not think we shall finally leave the river till

next Saturday the 16th being Friday & I d'ont think we can be ready on Thursday – Believe me
>Ever yours with sincere affection
>James Fitzjames

68. JAMES FITZJAMES TO ELIZABETH CONINGHAM [SISTER-IN-LAW], 10 MAY 1845

>Woolwich 10th May

My dear Elizabeth

I leave you these two letters from my little friends – as I am sure anything that gave me pleasure will gratify you.

I think little Fanny's hand is improving, and I believe both letters to be written of themselves – without any supervision.

I also enclose you a letter written in a very extraordinary hand which I should like you to consult before you look at the signature.

Perhaps you will think I am foolish to care for the little children's letters – but so it is – I am as much pleased with their expressions of regard – exaggerated though they be – as I should be with the more studied, but probably not so genuine, effusions of many grown up people.

I think the love of a child is a thing not to be thrown away lightly.

There are some grown up people too, whose love I would not exchange for any worldly good. And of these I need not say you & William stand far highest in the heart
>of your affectionate
>James Fitzjames

68A FANNY CAMPBELL TO JAMES FITZJAMES [ENCLOSED WITH 68]

My very dearest Fitzjames

I am very sorry indeed to hear you are going to leave England so soon we shall think of you when you are far away in the snow and some times when your poor toes are freezing with cold you must think of us as we shall be longing for your return when I hope you will pay us a very long visit as I can tell you Mama very often says you have not taken any trouble to stay with us this time pray do write to me before you leave
>and believe me your very fond and affectionate
>Fanny Campbell

68B MARIA-JANE CAMPBELL TO JAMES FITZJAMES
[ENCLOSED WITH 68]

Northend House

My very dearest Fitzjames

Captain Fisher came to see us today and told us that you will leave England next week As Fanny gave you the little marker so I send you this little picture of Missie's dog I hope you will write me a very long letter before you go. I am very sorry you are going so soon as I was in hopes you would have paid us another visit as on the 24 of this month is my birthday and it would have been so delightful to have you with us I hope you will spare us a few minutes so as to write us a very nice long letter I hope you will not forget us when you are in among the snow and when you come home you will pay us a nice long visit

Give my very best love to Mrs Gambier if you see her I must now say good bye with many many loves and kisses I hope you will have a pleasant voyage and come back again quite well and safe again And believe me to remain ever

Your ever affectionately and attached friend
Maria Jane Campbell

Missie says just as _if_ you care a <u>fig</u> for our attachment to you

69. JAMES FITZJAMES TO WILLIAM CONINGHAM [BROTHER],
11 MAY 1845

Woolwich Sunday 10th

Dearest William

Today I went up with Shell and I saw the children; looking well & very happy. I had some dinner with them & they appeared quite delighted to see me.

I also took Shell to the Great Britain which is well worth seeing, so I charge you to go & see her before she leaves England, which will be in the middle of June. Get a note from Captain Hoskins to some of the officers who will make you see everything.

The ship goes to Green Hythe tomorrow & we shall sail on Thursday if we possibly can. I d'ont think it will be before Saturday.

I called on the Barrows to day to take leave – and saw Fitzgerald Gambier & his wife to both of whom I really feel much attached for I cannot but be certain of their real regard for me.

Sir John will see the Admiralty people tomorrow and John B says that I shall know before I go whether the commission is to go with me or not.

I wrote to Elizabeth yesterday to Antwerp so good night I am quite tired & have to go to the Observatory at 6 tomorrow morning

Ever yours affectionately,

James F————

70. JAMES FITZJAMES TO ELIZABETH CONINGHAM [SISTER-IN-LAW], 12 MAY 1845

My dear Elizabeth

The ships Erebus & Terror are this day gone to Green Hythe – and I remained behind to finish observations – but got away in time to get Sarah & the children into the Dockyard from which we saw the ships moving off – Minney was quite delighted & it was a great pleasure to me to have them in your absence – I told Sarah to bring them over in a fly – & that I was sure William would be pleased they should see us sail –

The day was clear and beautiful – & I did not keep them long enough in the yard to get cold. Poor Minney was quite put out of Countenance by Hodgsons mother kindly telling her she looked like a little boy.

It is finally settled as I suspected that we sail on Saturday – Friday not being a propitious day – I go down tomorrow morning early – I got your letter from Bruges this afternoon for which I thank you. I write this late at night & have to get up early tomorrow so God bless you both – Ever your affectionate J.F.

Woolwich Monday 12th.

Of course Sarah sends her love & duty and desires me particularly to say that the children are well

Old Shell has a new lease of his life I am sure – Excuse small paper my desk is gone to the ship

71. JAMES REID TO ANN REID [WIFE],
13 MAY 1845

Green Hine London River,
May 13/45

Loving wife

I Received your last of the 9 Inst. happay to see you and the young ones is well, as this Leaves me the same we left Woolwich – yesterdy and will Remain hear a few days. I hope you have Received my last of the 9 inst. with a ten pound note inclosed, and yesterday I gave Mr. Laws king of Denmark Wapping £18 to put in the Bank in London and you to Receive the same through the British Linnin Company /,, Bankers – Aberdeen, which I inclose a Line of the same Houses. When you Receive this you will call on the above Bankers If they have got no notice of the same you will write to Mr. Laws King of Denmark Wapping he Received the money from me In Regard to the officers mese I wase under the necessity of paying £63,, ,, sore against my will. I wrote Sir John Franklin about it he told me it wase high but if Possiable to Pay it is not the wine nor the Spirits that is the Expense it is other things, there is a Store of Every thing for three years – – on that account I insured my Life for £100 @ 5 per Cent out of that I Received £50 from a Navy Agent @ 2 ½ percent which I gave him my will to secure his £50 – if I never Return he Receives his £50 – and you the Remand – I inclose to you his name & his adress, na doubt he will write you him self. The other Ice Master is from Whitby, the name of Brinkly, he hase don the same. the Monthly Line will bee sent to you from the Trinity House will be drawn at the Custom House, this hase bean a very expencif Jobe, Silver forks & Spoons each officer must find them – if it bee in your paur call on Mr. Finlason the Tailor and pay him a little and a little when you Receive your months pay but that will bee some time before that comes due. I wase Quite happy when I saw John. I gave him several things to the amount of £2, 12. Cash 5/ I am Rather surprised he did not take my chest along with him it would [have] saved 5/ –

Mr. Valentin[e] wase casten for the Scurvey in his Leges and the others for several things an the Black Ladi wase casten for his Leg having once Broken. – – I Received a Letter from aunty at Dundee mentioning she had Received the four Pound, I would like to here if you have Received the Money. in all sent £4[...] I will write before I Leave the River.

Remains,
your Loving Husband
James Reid

72. HARRY GOODSIR TO JOHN GOODSIR [FATHER], 13 MAY 1845

Greenhithe
May 13th. 1845

My Dear Father

I have just received yours of the 8th enclosing Johns letter to you about the old House at Anstruther. It appears to me that you are quite right in not parting with it at the sum you mention especially since property is rising in value besides there can be no doubt that it will sell well in consequence of the Herring fishery succeeding. We sailed from Woolwich yesterday. This place is about 5 or 6 miles farther down the River & we remain here till Saturday or Sunday when we will sail for good. So long as we remain here the Officers are busy with what they call swinging the vessels for the purpose of testing the compasses. We have all been very busy for the last week up every morning sometimes as early as 4 o clock so as to get our things arranged & packed away – a matter by no means easy seeing our room is so limited. I have however got my cabin very comfortably arranged & a great number of my books put away in it. The rest are in the Mess room & first Lieutenant's cabin. When we get every thing arranged I suppose all my natural History books will be put into Sir John Franklins Cabin where we are to work. This is a most beautiful place the banks on each side of the river being very green & covered with trees surrounding fine Houses. All the way up & down the river on both sides is very rich.

I am not sure what you intend doing with the dogs because in a letter received from John a week or ten days ago he said that Joseph would not part with Cæsar, and in answer to this letter I told him not to send Cæsar as we had already got a dog for the Erebus. But altho this answer must have reached you long ere this you tell me in your letter of the 8th. & Robert also writes in the same way, that the dogs are both coming up by the Granton Steamer & were to be shipped on Saturday last. To prevent anything like mistakes I have written to Young to look after them & if Cæsar does come to take care of him till I make arrangements. I hope however you have not sent him after my letter already mentioned. With regard to Mr. Scott I have not seen him again but Captain Nairne called on me at the vessel as we were hauling off from the hulk into the river & saw Sir John Franklin. We will not be longer of starting for good, than Sunday so that if you think a letter will reach in time be so good as let me hear from you before I start. I will write, altho not today, to all in Carnbee, Largo, & Edinburgh before leaving this & I will also take the opportunity of letting you have a letter from Stromness, if we should call there, but at all events by means of the Steamers that go out with us beyond the Orkneys. I called upon Sir William Burnett yesterday before leaving town when he told me to look after the Museum at Haslar as an appointment likely to come in my way on my return home. In consequence however of the Admiralty making this new appointment of Naturalist at the rate of £300 a year I will remain in this service provided another expedition fits out on my return, a thing which is very likely to take place. I wont get I believe the actual title of Naturalist attached to my commission in consequence of what Mr. Brown has said, also since the Admiralty have made this new appointment.

I will attend to all you say in your letter and hope that in course of a two years or so we will all meet again in good health. & believe me if we take care of ourselves there is little doubt with the naturally good constitutions we have there is little doubt of such a meeting. I will write John tomorrow & each in succession afterwards.

Believe me
Your most Affectionate Son
Harry D. S. Goodsir

73. JAMES FITZJAMES TO JOHN BARROW JR,
14 MAY 1845

Dear Barrow

In looking over our books I find we have not got your father's
"Chronology of North Polar Voyages" which I should much like to have
if you can get it for us. And Beechy's last book on Polar Voyages –

I fear we are too late to make a 2^d application to the Admiralty – but
still perhaps it may be done before we go on Saturday. –

I do hope you will see us before we sail –

Yours ever sincerely

James Fitzjames

Greenhithe

14th May 1845

74. JAMES FITZJAMES TO WILLIAM CONINGHAM [BROTHER],
14 MAY 1845

Dearest William

I have been hard at work all day observing with the compass, (what
is technically called "swinging the ship") ie bringing the ships head to
each point of the compass & observing the correct bearing of a mark
on shore – from which an observer simultaneously observes the bearing
of the compass on board – these two bearings should be opposite but in
consequence of local attraction of iron on board they are not so excepting at two points nearly North & South, where there is no deviation and
two points where the deviation is greatest – in some vessels 26 degrees
have been found shewing that if a ship imagined herself steering East
she would be steering 2 ¼ points from it – thereby losing Her Majestys
ship &c –

We hope to get this done tomorrow – & then Terror begins but the
weather has been squally, which is against keeping a ship at one point &
I much fear we shall not get away before Saturday or Sunday.

People crowd down to see us & the Pictorial times has been on board
– The Pictorial Times expressed itself much pleased and said it would
like to go with us. – Captain Robert Gambier came from Southampton
to day on purpose to see me, and Fitzgerald & a party come tomorrow.

I go no more out of the ship – I have written to you & Elizabeth 3
times, the last time telling of the children's visit to the Dockyard – Old
Shell stood on the wharf staring at us on the day I left like I could not see

him – I write this at night & commence work at 3 in the morning – so good night God bless you both

J Fitzjames

Greenhithe 14th. May

75. HENRY T.D. LE VESCONTE TO SARAH LE VESCONTE [MOTHER], 15 MAY 1845

May 15, Greenhithe

My dear Mother –

Your anxious considerations and endeavours to convey to me your last good wishes before I set out for the North have been successful – I have got your very delightful letter with dear Rose's addition. I do not think you should trouble yourself much about this Northern voyage – there is no more work than in other countries – not half so much as in China and India – and there is a sure advantage in the pay with a very fair chance of promotion – indeed I cannot help feeling myself sure of it when we return – the affair is so very popular in what the newspapers call high quarters and there are some things I know on the subject besides but which I am not at liberty to mention that will transpire soon after we leave or I am much decieved besides these things the service brings me in contact with people of rank and superior attainments, people of influence – I do hope to get something out of it bye and bye – I cannot conjecture how long we shall be absent – but I hope not more than two years or a certain young very dear friend of mine may be much disappointed – I do not fear that I shall lose her affection but surrounded by so many Aunts – I have great respect for them and they have been extremely civil to me – but while I cannot help thinking if any sleek son of the Church should offer himself the poor girl might be subjected to much annoyance – at any rate after two or three years have passed away – but Henrietta is a very dutiful child yet she has plenty of firmness and direction she will not be readily led to do what her conscience tells her is wrong – she is very religious almost to excess but this is in the beginning of course but the force of example yet it has led her to think deeply on sacred subjects and she is a quiet unaffected good christian. I do not know if I am talking this much on this subject but it is all interesting to me and I hope will be pleasing to you – I hope we may introduce her to you – I suppose you will write to Mrs Kendell now and then I think I told you before she had kindly procured me some very good worsted things they are I think the best in the ship but they cannot get a labourer for you. what strange animals to prefer poverty and rags at home rather than make a trifling exertion – we do not sail so soon as was anticipated or quite so soon as some people think desirable but we shall have steam vessells to help us to the northwards and then good strong ships and everything needful to help us along. I have provided myself liberally and nearly exhausted my means altho' they were greater than I had a right to calculate on there being another hundred coming from the Emperer of China – I shall leave about 150 behind but part of it is advanced pay – I am going to leave this in the hands of Edward Le Feuvre who will do something with it to increase it if he can – if not it can't be helped. I do not think I want Messrs. Shewells services any more and they make a great hole in the pay charging on full pay 2 ½ percent – I cannot stand this and now I have new relations at home I can manage better – I sent you by the Vesuvius a box the contents were nearly all chosen by Henrietta. altho I deputed Sarah as being the most experiensed but she very kindly by way of pleasing me left her fair niece to do the active part of the business merely assisting if required They tell me the things are very good and that by getting those of patterns out of fashion just now – but which would not make the least difference in Canada they got them for less than half their value there are some muffles and gloves – of which Sarah said it would be prudent to put in and I sent you some numbers of a Pictorial Paper – which I think will be interesting – only fancy There is a man onboard sent down by Lady Franklin to take <u>all</u> our portraits. I suppose we shall all be in print before we come home for Lady Franklin can write if she pleases – she is a very amiable woman but very enterprising would willingly go with us – when she was in Van Dieman's Land she set out with Sir John and a party to explore a large tract of country they were on foot in the woods and for ten days had nothing to eat but 2 ounces of salt pork except that once or twice they caught some fish – I do not know who will write to you from Southampton

I should be very curious to know what <u>Aunt</u> Judith would say – she is very civil but is more reserved than the others. I have such a lot of lady correspondents that they really take up a fearful deal of time but I suppose it is my fault for provoking it. Aunt Lily & Cousin Nymphe and Mr John Wills sometimes with – you may suppose – lots of letters from Southampton but some of them are too much prized not to be preferred before every other consideration – I have promised my good old friend Mr Rainier a letter about the expedition but I don't know when I shall write it perhaps not till we get among the ice May you enjoy many happy days my dear mother and again see and bless your affectionate son   HTD LeVesconte

76. HENRY T.D. LE VESCONTE TO ROSE LE VESCONTE [SISTER] [ENCLOSED WITH ABOVE LETTER]

My dear Sister Rose.

What can I say to you except that as I cannot see you it gives me pleasure to hear from you and to write but I hope I may be able to cross the atlantic one day. It has pained me much to hear of your indifferent health. Is it too cold in Canada Mr Kay says the climate is much finer than ours this I know that I have been very cold the last two or three days What shall we do in latitude 74. We shal[l] soon be nearly North of you so that you will be able to point out the very star we are under as they pass across the heavens & the fine evenings Papa has spoken much of my sisters. I hope you will all think that I am and always will be your brother indeed. Other ties I may form but these will not weaken my regard for you I hope you will love those I love & always believe me your very
    affectionate brother

                                        Henry

77. JAMES REID TO ANN REID [WIFE], 16 MAY 1845

                          Green Hithe London River May [16]

Loving wife

I Received yours of the 11 inst. [happy] to here you Received the ten pounds. by the [time] you Receive this I hope you have Received [the] sume of Eighteen pounds through the Ba[nk] & A. Newes paper, you will call on C[aptain] Hay of the Brig Flora, Aberdeen [I hope] you will receive a Parcel, containing [a quantity] of Pr[int] for Alexanderina to make her [summer] frok and whate is over will answer [for Mary] & Ann but Alexanderina first.

The Hands is to bee paid To morrow [& we] sail in the Evening on Mondy and to [be] Towed with Steam to the Orkneys [first] I have now every thing on board, and lef[t] London & Woolwich, cleare of every one, not Due one farthing, and my stoke is 7 Shillings even, – I sined the Books yesterdy, about the Half Pay, to be paid at the Custom House Aberdeen, it will bee sent by Steam to you Payable about the 10th Sept. you may [depen]nd all will be Right in Regard of the [ha]lf Pay after you Receive the first every [28] days after – – I shall Spare no opportunity in writing you, I had a Letter yesterday from Aunty Edger Liverpool Mentioning that David hase Fall on a pice of Timber [and] broke one of his Ribes, poor David – [after] one thing comes another, wrote a [few] lines to Liverpool, she mentions she [is] still with Mrs. Reid. You will Receive [my] chest with the city Steamer I though[t it] very straing John did not take it [wi]th him. I wase not so uncind to him [he] might [have] saved 4/6 or 5/ Mr. Arguant – [pu]shed him to take it, but he sade a very bad word & told her he would not take it.

Loving wife, mind yourself. Dount you trust to one of them for as soon as they can do for themselves they will never mind you nor me, you dount see so much of the world as I see. Let them from Home, then the Chief Part of <u>young men</u> Forgets there <u>Parents</u> and friends. Take all but give nothing, <u>mind this Take care</u> of yourself & the three young Lasess they are not able to mind themselves. –

Mr. Bannerman & Mr. Adam of the [news] Paper called on me Sunday Last, he [wase] Looking well wase Quite Happy to see me Looking so well we hade a glass of B[eer] together in my Lodgin House at Wolwic[h] I Called on the Messrs. Enderbys. I [saw] Mr. George but not Charles nor H[enry] I Forgot to mention the office th[at] My Life is insured in it is [called] Economic Life Insurens office, Bridge [Street] Black fraier, but the Navy Ag[ents] will put you all to Rights write h[im if] you wint any newes about any th[ing] They are very fine Gentlemen I write you again before we start Good Vouge keep your hart up about me we have a good ship & strong and Sir John Franklin is a fine man and I Rely think all the officers is all fine young men. – I am still sorry I did not bring you up to London, you would saved your Passage money to me, at the same time you would have the Pleasure of seeing the Ships. there is no help for it now,

Remains,
Your Loving Husband
James Reid

P.S. this Leaves me Quite well. Hope [this] will find you the same, and the young [ones] I have lost all nothing of Murray th[e] Watch Maker, he is a proper De[vil] with Drink and his young family [none] of them is at a School I Realy th[ink] he will go all to wreck again – David Leyes is due him a few pounds he is – Coming down to Morrow when the Ships is Paying I tauld David to mind his wife & not Pay him a farthin he wase a Bankrupt when it wase due – tell his wife this if you see her.

J.R.

3

Sailing

No ships could go to sea better appointed than we are.

John Franklin

On 12 May, the ships departed Woolwich for Greenhithe, where the visitors became rather less numerous; among them, though, was one especially important party – Lady Jane Franklin, Franklin's niece Sophia Cracroft, and his daughter Eleanor. They were invited aboard, given a hearty round of cheers, and joined the men for a service of thanksgiving personally conducted by Sir John. At her ladyship's request, a camera "operator" from the firm of Richard Beard came on board, and the officers of the *Erebus* – along with Francis Crozier of the *Terror* – sat for their portraits (copies of which, Harry Goodsir noted, were available to the public at Beard's shop on King-William Street). Fitzjames, who had stayed behind to receive some overdue scientific instruments, rejoined the ship in time to be photographed; all the other officers who had taken local lodgings had already moved into their cabins.

The letters now began to take on tones of farewell, for while it was still possible that mail might make it to the ships at Stromness, their final port of call, everyone realized that further letters would be too late for any reply to reach them. And yet this circumstance rather led most men to write *more* rather than less; all seemed eager to put something in every mail-bag, anxious to give their loved ones the most up-to-date account of their progress possible.

We also get glimpses of life aboard ship, for although they had not yet sailed, everyone was already becoming better acquainted, both with each other and with the vessels and their equipment. We hear from James Fairholme of the monkey, "Jacko," given by Lady Franklin; "Neptune" is mentioned, as well as an unnamed dog and a cat. Fairholme also describes an evening where a fiddle was "going on as hard as it can," accompanying songs from the forecastle (by implication, somewhat more rough and bawdy ones). Franklin's habit of presiding over Divine Service is first mentioned by him (as it will be shortly by many others); in a last letter to a friend in Tasmania, he describes his fellow officers as "a fine set of young men, active, zealous, and devoted to the Service." Only Crozier seems immune to the festive spirit; he alludes to having visited his old friend James Clark Ross an "hours walk" away, but describes himself aboard *Terror* – now on the eve of her expected sailing – as "alone."

Although the ships had been expected to sail on 16 May, there was an unexpected delay; the tinned provisions provided by Stephen Goldner – and which would later be the subject of considerable interest in terms of whether the haste of their preparation played a role in the expedition's demise – had not yet arrived. On 17 May, Crozier wrote that he was "hoping to sail on the morrow" but it wasn't until 19 May, at 10:00 a.m., according to Goodsir, that the ships were finally "under way."

CHRONOLOGY

15–17 May 1845: A photographer from the firm of Richard Beard takes daguerreotype portraits of the officers of *Erebus*, as well as Francis Crozier (Letters 75, 80, 90, 93)

16 May 1845: Crews test *Erebus* and *Terror* steam engines (Letter 78)

17–18 May 1845: Lady Franklin, Sophia Cracroft, and Franklin's daughter Eleanor visit the ships; they attend Divine Service on Sunday, 18 May (Letters 81, 84, 90)

19 May 1845: *Erebus*, *Terror*, and transport *Barretto Junior* depart Greenhithe at 10:00 Greenwich Time en route to the Thames Estuary (Letter 90)

78. JOHN IRVING TO CATHERINE IRVING [SISTER-IN-LAW], 16 MAY 1845

H.M.S. "Terror"
Greenhithe, May 16, 1845.

My dear Katie, – I have sat down to bid you farewell, for we sail to-morrow on our voyage. We came down from Woolwich to this place, which is near Gravesend, two days ago. We have been detained by some preserved meat not being ready. We take two years' provisions, and a transport accompanies us with a third year for each ship ; so if you do not hear of us for three years, you need not think we are starved. We tried our screws, and went four miles an hour. Our engine once ran somewhat faster on the Birmingham line. It is placed athwart ships in our afterhold, and merely has its axle extended aft, so as to become the shaft of the screw. It has a funnel the same size and height as it had on the railway, and makes the same dreadful puffings and screamings, and will astonish the Esquimaux not a little. We can carry twelve days' coal for it ; but it will never be used when we can make any progress at all by other means. We have the same spars and sails as before ; but Parry found that during the few days the sea was a little clear of ice he had no wind ; and we hope then to feel the power of our screws.

It is thought probable that we shall pass the winter near Melville Island, and next summer try to get westward to Behring's Straits. See the Map. I think we shall be all bons compagnons de voyage. I like my skipper very well, and nothing seems to be left undone in the way of providing for our wants and comforts. We have a large hand-organ in each ship. One plays fifty tunes, ten of which are psalms and hymns. We bought it by subscription. "Music has charms," you see. We are laden as deep as we can swim ; and I hope we may have good weather crossing the Atlantic in this state. We must, like mice in a haystack, eat away and make a little room for ourselves.

Our decks are crowded with casks, and even the cabins are nearly filled up. However, as our Captain says, we have not shipped for comfort. We are all most sanguine of success. I am afraid, however the voyage may terminate, that I shall have little chance of promotion, as I am the junior lieutenant, and there are three in each ship, and it is hardly to be expected that they will promote them all. I daresay that long before I return you will be quite snug in your new house. Excuse this, but I have much to occupy me for the rest of our stay, which is only a few hours. We shall pass the Orkneys, and perhaps, should it be foul winds, may anchor at Stromness. Now, my dear Katie, I shall bid you farewell. I shall let you know our position and prospects in August when the transport leaves us. – My kindest love to Lewie, and believe me ever, my dear Katie, your most affectionately,

John Irving.

79. JAMES FITZJAMES TO HORATIO AUSTIN, 16 MAY 1845

My dear Austin

Thank you very much for your kind parting note and your paper of "hints" which I have not had time to read but intend to study during our passage to Lancaster sound.
    You will I am sure think of us often – and be glad to hear of our arrival in the Pacific – which I doubt not will happen eventually if not sooner
    I have no time to write more than that I am always yours most sincerely

James Fitzjames
Erebus
    Greenhithe
16th May 1845

80. JAMES FITZJAMES TO WILLIAM CONINGHAM [BROTHER], 16 MAY 1845

Erebus Greenhithe Friday
16th. May

My dearest William
    John Barrow rode down to day and brought me your welcome letter of the 14th. from Antwerp – we have done our "swinging" – all our grub is in the last instalment of 6000 cases of soup having been taken in to day the ships Company are to be paid tomorrow – and why we should not sail tomorrow evening I d'ont know – except that perhaps it is as well not sailing at night. But I fear Sir John w'ont sail on Sunday so Monday will

be our day not time however for you to answer this – which will <u>not</u> be my last from England. We are now <u>comfortable</u>. Lady Franklin lives here – & came on board this evening – I like her very much and she appears most fond & proud of Sir John which I was not prepared to find.

She has taken it into her head to have a portrait of <u>all</u> our officers, & sent a man down who takes us all with the Daguerrotype – I have got a second for Elizabeth to whom I shall send it when set. I believe it is very like me though I fear Lady Franklin will have the best – He comes on board tomorrow & I shall try & get 2 more one for Fitzgerald & one for Mrs Campbell & you shall have the best of the three –

<u>All</u> the Gambiers came down yesterday to see me William, Fitzgerald & both their wives and Gloucester also came from Dover on purpose Captain Robert came up from Southampton on purpose – and they were really all so cordial and kind that I can have no doubt of their real feeling of regard for me – Fitzgerald & his wife, I really love Mrs. Norris has also written me a very affectionate note which I think you would like to see so I shall leave it, and when read tear it up. By the bye the Board w'ont promote me that is they w'ont send the Commission out <u>with</u> us But have decided on taking the first opportunity &c See good John Barrow & ask him to shew you Hamilton's note.

Yours ever
J.F.

81. JAMES FAIRHOLME TO GEORGE FAIRHOLME [FATHER], 17 MAY 1845

Greenhithe
Saturday night May 17th. 1845

My dear Father

..... All well with the Expedition & very comfortable. Lady Franklin has given us, among other presents, a capital monkey, which with old Neptune & a Newfoundland dog which is coming & one cat will be all the pets allowed. At present, Saturday night seems to be kept up in due nautical form, around my cabin, a fiddle going on as hard as it can & 2 or 3 different songs from the forecastle; in short, all seem quite happy...... I do not think there is a thing which is likely to be really wanted that I have not got.

Our people have just sent to ask us to give a <u>spare</u> fiddle. Lady Franklin is down here, & Sir John has begged that all his officers attend Divine

Service on board the ship tomorrow forenoon, when they will <u>all</u> be off here. It will be an unusually interesting occasion, & I trust that true prayers will be offered up by all, both for those going & those we leave behind us.

J. W. Fairholme

82. FRANCIS CROZIER TO CHARLES MAGEE
[BROTHER-IN-LAW], 17 MAY 1845

Terror <u>May 17th 1845</u>

My dear charles

I have been intending to write you but the truth is I have been in such a bustle I scarcely have known which way to turn. – In the first place I wished to thank you for the trouble you have had on my account with my little affairs – I forget all about them now but as I talked all over with Small she will tell you how I stand etc. – I would be glad if you give poor Mrs. Crozier so long as god spares her some thing say 5 Shillings a Quarter or more if you see right – Mary Little I would like you to do something for as you may see right – Remember me most kindly to Mae & Mrs and tell her with my best regards that I really think I will be able to send her the paper on my <u>immediate</u> return as the trip has rather brought things to a crisis – I have often regretted I had not had a few days to run down amongst you, but these things always come upon one after the opportunity has passed – Bird has been with me pretty much and I have been within an hours walk to Ross's during my Stay at Woolwich – I am now however all alone on board Terror hoping to Sail on the Morrow –

With Kind Rems to
the boys and Jenny believe
me sincerely yours
FRMCrozier

83. JAMES FITZJAMES TO JOHN BARROW, 17 MAY 1845

Hms Erebus Greenhithe 17th May 1845

My dear Sir John Barrow

I cannot leave England on the most interesting Expedition that has ever left her shores – without attempting to express to you how deeply grateful I am to you for all your acts of kindness and exertions to procure my advancement in the Service.

Whether I obtain the Rank of Captain within a short time, or on our return is a matter of small worth as I look upon it as a matter of certainty when we <u>do</u> return and on looking back I perceive that – I shall have risen to the highest attainable rank solely by your exertions in my behalf –

I never can forget that it is to you, I owe my first footing – when you procured me the rating of midshipman in the St Vincent – and the time which I never otherwise could have hoped to have secured. To your recommendation I was appointed to Sir William Parker's Flag ship which procured me the Commander's step; to your great exertions I was put in command of the Clio – and here I now am in a position which besides securing my final step, places me before the serv[ice] in a most honorable point of view –

I beg you will express to Lady Barrow my grateful sense of her kindness, to your glorious son John I shall say nothing – because I can say nothing that would express my real affection for him – and with kind regards to Miss Barrow – Believe me my dear Sir
    yours most sincerely & gratefully
    James Fitzjames

84. JOHN FRANKLIN TO ISABELLA CRACROFT [SISTER], 18 MAY 1845

HMS Erebus
Greenhithe
18th May 1845

My dearest Isabella,

I must not leave the Thames – without saying to you Goodbye – though I know you hear constantly of our proceedings –

We sail tomorrow – my wife Sophy & Eleanor are now on board arranging my books – they will soon be going to Hedingham and will therefore tell you all that we have been doing and that we have an excellent set of officers & men –

I have not time to say more than God bless you & yours will be my earnest prayer

Yours affectionately

John Franklin

85. JAMES FITZJAMES TO JOHN BARROW JR, 18 MAY 1845

Erebus Greenhithe 18th. May /45

My dear Barrow

Good bye – we are off tomorrow morning early – The men are quite satisfied at the prompt payment of their <u>river</u> pay – although they never expressed any <u>dissatisfaction</u> but much <u>dis-appointment</u>.

D'ont put yourself in a cast iron fever about my promotion which must come eventually if not sooner.

If you were to send me my Captains commission on condition I left the Expedition, I would not take it – and I would rather have the good <u>opinion</u> of the present Board of Admiralty and the good wishes of a man like Lord Haddington or Captain Hamilton than <u>promotion</u> in an ungracious way from "qui que ce soit" –

To you my dear fellow I feel much as you must know – but can say little –

I delight in Sir John Franklin who is delightful. <u>Mind I say</u>, we shall get through the North West passage <u>this year</u> & I shall land at Petro Paulovski, and shake you by the hand on the 22nd February 1846.

Give my kind regards to your father (to whom I have written) and Lady Barrow and believe me always

your very sincere friend
James Fitzjames

86. HARRY GOODSIR TO JOHN GOODSIR [BROTHER],
18 MAY 1845

The cabin is leaking most tremendously thro the Bulls eye
Greenhithe Erebus
May 18th. 1845

I will let you know all about money matters of both Forbes & my own from Orkney. But I think you will find Forbes in my account Book which my Father has got.

My Dear John

In a letter to my Father posted some days ago I mentioned that I would write regularly every day until we left this place but my time has been so much taken up that it has made it quite impossible for me to fulfil my intention. We start however tomorrow morning so that I now take this last opportunity, at present, of writing to all of you. I went up to London on Thursday last to procure some few things which I required & returned to the Ship again yesterday morning but was obliged to go back to London in the afternoon again, so that you see the whole of my time has been fully occupied. I went up to the Dockyards at Woolwich on Friday to procure a couple of dredges, in consequence of those which had been ordered in the demand sent into Government, being almost useless – the most absurd things you ever saw, which I have no doubt has been the cause of so little haveing been got in former expeditions, & also a good proof that the Surgeon or whoever ordered them knows very little about the subject.

I have met Newport twice lately when we have had a long conversation about the book he is very much pleased with it and is going to review it in Forbes Journal. In his paper on the blood globules of the Articulata he has corroborated the metamorphosis of cells as well as the 4 different generations besides many other things.

I saw Thompson of Belfast on Friday at the meeting of the Royal Society I hope you will take out all the publications as well as those of the Sydenham. You have heard of course, I think I wrote you, about the appointment of Naturalists to all Expeditions after this also that Edmonston has got the one for the Californian Coast. I have met him several times & the first night he came [...] Forbes Van Hoorst & Davy came down with him & dined on board the Hulk with us. He is a desperately outspoken obstreperous fellow, but goodhearted.

With regard to the Dogs, I hope Robert did not send Cæsar after my letter about him but I am anxious as I received a letter from Robert evidently written after mine had reached you stating that Cæsar & the terrier were to be sent by the Steamer that very night. Perhaps how[ever] my lette[r] never reached you as I gave it t[o] Stanley t[o] be put into the Post Office It will be a great pity if it has not as I have not had a moments opportunity to look after their arrival & Young to whom I wrote was only able to learn in one of the Leith Boats that there was no dog in the vessel. Robert should write Young without delay & make arrangements about the Lodgings which are due from February last for he very stupidly had kept them on ever since he went to the Country until I gave information about his change. Tell him to look after this & to write Young without delay for Y. is a most honorable fellow & should not be lost sight of. I will have to send the papers for you per Steamers from the Orkneys as I have not got them finished yet. You will have also, I am afraid, to go over them yourself carefully as in consequence of the hurry & bustle here it is quite impossible to do any thing well. You have not told me any thing about Archies prize &c. I heard of it thro Davy. Tell D. Forbes that I have not had a moments time to write to him but have always expected to hear from him about the order he gave me. I hope you will attend to him on his brothers account who has been v[er]y kind

Believe me Your Affectionate Brother Harry D. S. Goodsir

87. JOHN FRANKLIN TO JOHN GRIFFIN [FATHER-IN-LAW], 18 MAY 1845

H M S Erebus
Greenhithe
18th May 1845

My dear Sir

It was a great disappointment for me not to have found you at home when I called to take leave – I will not however forego the pleasure of conveying to you by this means – my earnest hope and prayer that the blessing of God may attend you. Your recent recovery seems to have been so complete that if you are careful of yourself we may endulge the hope of meeting you again after my return –

In the mean time I am confident that I need not commit my dearest Jane to your affectionate kindness & protection – She doubtless has many friends, but none of them can be so dear to her as yourself & her sisters – My daughter also I would beg to recommend to your kind offices.

I wish you could see the ship now – she is almost as clear as she will be at sea and quite ready for sailing. The Officers & the Crew all fine young men & in excellent spirits. This day we had the happiness of joining together on board in Divine Worship, to praise God for his past mercies and to implore his guiding and Protecting Providence – In this spirit we all hope to begin, continue & end our voyage –

May the Almighty preserve and comfort you – may you be rooted & grounded in his faith & joyful in the hope of his Redeeming Love will ever be the fervent prayer of your affectionate Son in Law

    John Franklin

We sail tomorrow – love to all your family circle.

88. JAMES FITZJAMES TO WILLIAM CONINGHAM [BROTHER], 18 MAY 1845

Dearest William

The men were paid their money yesterday but in consequence of a slight mistake – which caused another payment to day we did not sail as intended – tomorrow morning we are off – and the wind has just shifted from NE to Westerly. The Rattler is here to tow us – and a small steamer for the Transport (called "Baretto Junior.") I got your letter from Bruges which Barrow brought down. I hear there is to be a brevet on the 18th. June & I suppose I shall be included but d'ont care <u>much</u>.

We are now off and I am more pleased than ever at my position Franklin is quite delightful – and the ship is comfortable – all are nice people – and to crown all my old steward Richard joined us, as he "did not like to see me go without him".

You will see all about us in the Pictorial Times – (or Illustrated London) In which you will probably find some truth and much humbug –

I continue daily to get most affectionate letters from all the Gambiers which I believe answer the purpose intended –

To Elizabeth I have written occasionally – and now may God protect you both my best beloved friends It is now midnight – & I have to be up at 4 – though we shall not sail till 8 or 9 – But I feel as if I was talking to you –

    Always your affectionate

    James Fitzjames

Sunday 18th. May

89. JAMES FITZJAMES TO JOHN BARROW JR, N.D.
(BEFORE 19 MAY)

Dear Barrow

I have returned the Admiralty Bibles &c with a public letter –
   Will you explain to Captain Hamilton the real reasons – viz that we
have now <u>more</u> than one for each man
                    yours in haste
                      J Fitzjames

90. HARRY GOODSIR TO JANE ROSS GOODSIR [SISTER],
19 MAY 1845

Greenhithe 19th May
H.M S Erebus

My Dear Jane

It is a long time since I have written to you but my time has been too
much occupied with matters of considerable importance to me for my
voyage to allow me time for other things. The vessels start however this
day at 10 O.C a.m. so that I am anxious to write to you all before starting, if I can make it out seeing it is now 7. Lady Franklin was on board
& took leave of the Officers yesterday (Sunday) she appeared to be very
much overcome for Sir John is an old man now for such an expedition as
the present & most people are afraid about his return. I have no doubt
however that every thing will go well with us all at least if it was to
depend on the good wishes of the people here. We are all very sanguine
regarding the success of the passage. Great numbers of people have been
to visit us I had a long conversation with the Bishop of Norwich about
the Natural History of Greenland and found that our Surgeon who is a
humbug had been stuffing the Right Reverend with all sorts of nonsense.

My cabin which is about the size of one of the leaves of your dining table
is completely stuffed with clothing &c. and there is just room for me to
move about & nothing more. If you purchase the next Saturdays Nos. of
the Illustrated London News & the Pictorial Times you will have views
of both ships & various parts of them. The Artist for the News took a
sketch of the Gun room during the time I was sitting in it but not being
aware that he was including me I left & only found when I returned that

he was blotting me out so I cannot tell whether I remain or not We will not have an opportunity of seeing either publications. I hope Joseph got the Gazzete which I sent him. Lady Franklin has sent down a Talbotypist to take the portraits of all the Officers of the Erebus. As I have other letters to write home it will be impossible for me to write more at present I will write if possible either from Orkney or Greenland per Transport.

Believe me
Ever your Affectionate Brother
Harry D. S. Goodsir

I write in my own Cabin & have just room for my arms to move. You may get all or any of the likenesses to purchase at the following address in London Mr. Beard 85, King William Street, City.

91. HARRY GOODSIR TO JOSEPH GOODSIR [BROTHER], 19 MAY 1845

Greenhithe May 19th
1845
H.M.S. Erebus

My Dear Joseph

It has always been my intention to write and thank you for your assistance as regards money during the time I was at Woolwich, but have had so much to do that it has always been out of my power. We are now however on the point of Starting & will not have another opportunity for some time to come if I do not take the present.

I am glad to hear your catechism &c. so much talked of. it will just have come out at the proper time during the sitting of the General Assembly. I wish I could hear more of these things & others of Johns & my own before leaving There are observations making now which would be of great importance to me could I know the result before leaving.

I hope that every thing is going on well about Largo – one has a curious feeling at leaving for such a length of time in such an Expedition as this for no one can be certain when we are to return, But this is only at starting so soon as we get fairly off all will be lost in anxiety to get on.

Every one of the Ships Company is in excellent spirits & all of them very aggreeable, – the most pleasant set of people you could possibly meet with. I have not time for more,

Believe me
Ever your most Affectionate Brother
Harry D. S. Goodsir

[Possibly enclosed in the preceding to Jane]

92. JOHN FRANKLIN TO ADAM TURNBULL,
19 MAY 1845

H.M.S. Erebus
Off Greenhithe
19th May 1845

My dear Turnbull,

I must devote to you some of the very little time which remains to me for letter writing, and thank you for the very interesting letters I have from time to time received from you.

I need not say to you how shocked I was by the display of falsehood and treachery afforded by Montagu in his correspondence with yourself. It arrived most opportunely for the pamphlet which I have printed and in which I have exposed much, though not all of the dastardly policy which has been suffered to triumph against me.

Montagu's own testimony is invaluable and I have placed the whole correspondence in the form of a postscript to my pamphlet before my friends. This postscript has already been sent by me in Print to Lord Stanley by way of assurance that the Pamphlet will soon follow. Finding a week ago that with all my exertion that it was improbable that the whole of the M.S.S. could be got correctly through the printer's hands before my departure I thought it right to apprise Lord Stanley of the painful step to which I was reduced, that of publication and to forward to him the Postscript as affording a strong reason for the necessity. I expressed in the same letter to his Lordship my regret in being unable to get the whole of my pamphlet through the Printer's hands before my departure and requested his attention to the sheets I enclosed. I said also that without his

Lordship's permission I could not venture to forward [it] when the other portions of the sheets [were] in their unfinished state. I have received no reply to this letter and cannot regret there has been none.

Lord Stanley can now only be <u>forced</u> into renouncing his determined advocacy of Montagu but I have no doubt that he heartily repents his rejection of my statements respecting him – and Lord Stanley cannot be ignorant that many men of sound judgment and high station, conceive and have said, that I have been most unjustly and harshly treated – I know too that Mr. Hope the partizan and I suspect the mouthpiece and ear wigger of Lord Stanley, has heard some plain truths on this point from different quarters – It is evident that the boldness of Montagu's policy has ensured its success for a time – and the want of principle in Lord Stanley prevents his own avowal of his having been deceived by it. I think you have been rather over-indulgent to Montagu in reply to his letters and statements : and one very important point is unnoticed by you altogether, viz the statement that you were directly a party to the letter written to Mr. Aislabie on Lady F's supposed interference in the Coverdale case. Since you last heard from me I have found a memo to the effect that on a day <u>after</u> Mr. Montagu's departure from V.D. Land, I mentioned to you the correspondence between Mr. Aislabie and Montagu, of which you had up to that moment heard nothing ; it is therefor plain that the whole of the minute details given by Montagu of your active participation in the framing and sending his reply to Mr. Aislabie are false from beginning to end. I cannot but regret that you did not in any way meet this point as if uncontradicted it affords to Montagu a decided advantage, but I am sure that the light I am enabled to throw upon it will afford you sincere pleasure. You will of course have heard of my Expedition and will be glad to learn from myself that the appointment has been given to me unsolicited and in a manner most gratifying. It is considered by my friends so directly indicating that Montagu's slanders have failed to injure me and that Lord Stanley's conduct towards me has been altogether without the participation of his colleagues except perhaps that of Sir James Graham (who as a statesman is equally unpopular as Lord Stanley). Indeed I cannot speak too highly of the unvarying kindness and consideration I have received from the Admiralty, from the First Lord down to the Junior of the Department. The Expedition excites the strongest interest in England among all parties and likewise on the Continent, the most flattering testimonies of these facts have reached me from numerous quarters whence such compliments are highly gratifying.

The visitors to inspect the ships became so numerous as to impede the men in their work, and we were glad to hasten from Woolwich to this place, that we might get the ships to rights before proceeding to sea.

My friend Crozier is my Second and the Admiralty have appointed a Commander unsolicited on my part to my ship – all the officers have been of my own selection in both ships and they are a fine set of young men, active, zealous, and devoted to the Service. Equally good are the crew – and many say that no ships could go to sea better appointed than we are. I trust also my dear friend that we shall all proceed on our voyage, not trusting in our own strength or judgement but in the merciful guidance of the Almighty, with whom alone must rest the issue of it – it was gratifying to me that yesterday (Sunday) the Officers and Crew assembled on board their respective ships to offer their thanksgiving to God for his infinite mercies already vouchsafed to them and their prayers for the merciful continuance of His Gracious protection and blessing to them.

I had the happiness of seeing my dearest wife my child and niece assembled with the crew of this ship on that occasion, whose prayers no doubt were as fervent on our behalf as ours were on theirs.

This circumstance tended with many others to soothe their sorrow at the prospect of my long separation from them – and they were also much supported in becoming personally known to the officers and seeing that there was every prospect of our living and acting most happily together – no one ever embarked on an expedition with more causes of rejoicing than ourselves – it is not therefore to be wondered at that we commenced our hazard in the highest spirits and full of hope that it may please God to prosper our effort to successful termination. You must not discontinue writing to my dear wife, nor to me, for I assure you on my return to England I shall have pleasure in reading your letters. My interest in your welfare will not abate – nor my personal desire, to be of all the assistance I can to V.D. Land. And on the latter point I will not despair, but trust that the seed we have endeavoured to sow for its improvement since our return to this country, tho not at headquarters exactly, may be of some service. May God bless you, Mrs. Turnbull, and your family in safety amidst all the evils we now hear of as prevailing in that land – will ever be my fervent prayer. Again God bless you.

Ever your friend,
John Franklin

P.S. the present state of V.D.L. is well known in England and the causes of it – but I must not say more on that painful subject.

93. JAMES REID TO ANN REID [WIFE], 19 MAY 1845

Green Hithe London River
May 19th/45

Loving wife

we are now all clear for a Start. will sail to day we are to bee towed with steam Down to the orkness – Lady Franklin hase ordered all the officers Likeness to bee taken and mine amongst the Rest, with my uniform on – She keeps them all by herself – Sir John Franklin Gave us prayers yesterday his Lady wase in Company, your order will bee sent to you when due. I got 6 Month's Pay – I joined the Erebus 27 March, bee sure and Call on Mr. Finlason the Tailor and make arrangement with him, you know more about his account than I do, once you are underway with your half pay, you will bee abale to pay him part Every month, once you get the account below twenty pounds he canat Hurt you – the other Ice Master wase taken out of the ship for £37, but I Rather think he hase got it settled, we paid the Ships Comp[an]y on Saturday last. David Leys is not Quartermaster. I have nothing more in the meen time will write by the steamer if we dount go into the orkness. Good Biy keep your hart up we will both meate again, this voyage perhapes will [be] the last that ever I make. I have nothing to doo my work is Coming. I am sorry to say I am badly of[f] for Quarter Masters, and we are the leading ship, it will keep me much on my legs – I think I have Every thing Right but short of White Shirts, and whate I have are Quite gone. This Leave me Quite well. Hopes it will find you and the family the same, by this time you have Received my Chest. –

Remains
your Loving Husband
James Reid

94. HARRY GOODSIR TO ANNE MONRO TAYLOR [AUNT], 19 MAY 1845

Greenhithe May 19th. 1845
Erebus

My Dear Aunt

As you may well believe it is no easy matter to get every thing settled and put to rights under the present circumstances. There is such a bustle & confusion so much noise & hurry occuring that one cant even hear oneself speak. As we start this day however at 10 A.M. I am anxious to write you before leaving I thought to have had more time to do so here than at Woolwich but it has been quite otherwise. But we are now getting into something like order the regular routine is commencing and no doubt tomorrow or next day when we have got fairly to sea every thing will be in Order. Yesterday we had divine service performed on board for the first time by Sir John who is very strict with regard to all religious duties. He is a most excellent man & one of the pleasantest persons I ever met with. Captain Nairne came down just as were starting from Woolwich & had a long conversation with Sir John. Be so good as write to Captain or Mrs. Nairne & Mr. Scott and thank them for me, they have been very kind & I cannot write them myself. I hope Uncle will not be offended with me for not writing to him when he knows how my time has been occupied. I will write him either from Orkney or Greenland.

Give my respects to the Grangemuir Family & thank Lord William as I do not think – this only strikes me now – I have ever written to thank him explain how my time has been taken up I must also write Robert Macadam as in a letter he particularly requested it D[o] not forget the Wakifeild[?]

Believe me
Ever Your Affectionate nep[hew]

[rest of letter missing]

95. HARRY GOODSIR TO JOHN GOODSIR [FATHER], 19 MAY 1845

Greenhithe 19th. May
Erebus

My Dear Father

We are just starting and I take this last opportunity of writting you from England for the present. I have been engaged since early this morning & last night in writing to the rest at home. I received a letter from you a few days ago containing one to the Surgeon of a Greenland Ship. I wish I had had more time to write you more fully but that was impossible & at all events cant be helped now I got all my bills paid here but one to the Shoemaker Dowie to whom I gave a note to send to you for the amount £2.18 or so There is also another of £3 to Dr. Lankester Golden Square from whom I got a loan of some money when up in London the first time about a month ago. This is all I owe here & hope you will be able to clear it for me. I will be able to repay you all on my return as I will be then more or less independent that is if we stop out long enough.

I wish you would write Mr. Scott & Captain Nairne & thank them for their kindness as I have not time to do it myself. I am only sorry that Mr. Scott could not accompany Captain Nairn when the latter visited the Ships at Woolwich but at any rate be so good as write & thank them for me. I have written to all at home but Robert & Archie for whom I will not now have time as the Ship is just starting.

I hope you will take care of yourself & that we will all meet again in health on my return.

Believe me
Ever Your Affectionate Son
Harry D. S. Goodsir

P.S. of all the money which I got & a considerable sum which I received afterwards & which I shall write about when I have more time – from Ork[n]ey I have only a few shillings left. Fortunately I do not require much or any where we are going.

96. JAMES FITZJAMES TO ELIZABETH CONINGHAM
[SISTER-IN-LAW], 19 MAY 1845

1 Am.   19ᵗʰ. May 1845

Dearest Elizabeth

Read these two notes and tear them up – they pleased me much – more than I can express –

You will be glad to see them <u>because</u> they gave me pleasure, but you will make out more by their handwriting than I can probably do by what is written. Mrs. Norris is Sir James' eldest daughter a widow – whose daughter is an agreeable girl of about eighteen – Yet with all their affection I cannot feel towards them as I do to you – How is this? – I feel <u>grateful</u> to them for their kindness which I believe to be genuine and of <u>course</u> I feel partial to them – that is I <u>like</u> them. To Mrs. F. Gambier I feel really most warmly – but I cannot discover that I care any more for any of them than I should for utter strangers who had taken the same pains to be liked –

To you it is not so – I love you for <u>yourself</u> and above all for the sake of him who is to me more than all in this world – and you <u>know it</u> – and this is the <u>real</u> reason of our mutual regard, esteem and affection

God for ever bless you

James Fitzjames

4

London to Stromness (May–June 1845)

I do most fervently hope and pray that nothing may occur to loosen
the ties which at present so very happily bind us to each other.

Charles Osmer

As their ships sailed along familiar shores – down the Thames into the
North Sea, then north along the east coast of England and Scotland to
Stromness in the Orkney Islands – the men aboard *Erebus* and *Terror*
marked time more than anything else. The "contrary winds" reported
early on by many writers slowed the voyage, though with the help of
the steamers *Rattler* and *Monkey* – the latter damaged and replaced by
Blazer – the ships ended up making relatively good progress. Whenever
a port, or a friendly ship, offered the chance of getting out a message, the
men – particularly the ordinary seamen – took the opportunity to send a
line. There was still a chance that they might even get a reply – in Letter
105 Fairholme mentions having received several letters – while others,
such as Alexander Wilson, the carpenter's mate on HMS *Terror*, express
disappointment that no letter was waiting for them at Stromness.

Stromness was a storied town – and the home, though none of the men
remarked on it, of a key recruiting station for the Hudson's Bay Company,
which was operated for some years by the father of Dr John Rae, who
would later distinguish himself as the first man to find concrete traces of
Franklin's eventual fate. The relations between the HBC – a private concern, founded in 1670 – and the Royal Navy could be a bit chilly at times,
but when it came to the Arctic, their fates were to be intertwined. Some of
the men took advantage of the port call to visit local sights; others, such
as Osmer, had work to do – the more so as Franklin himself never worked
upon the Sabbath day – securing oxen and other livestock that were to
be transported to Greenland and there slaughtered, to start the ships off
with some fresh meat. The ships also took on fresh water at Login's Well,
located near the waterfront in Stromness, which to this day bears a plaque
commemorating the event (the well was sealed in the 1930s, and is now
shielded by a wall of plexiglass, installed, I was told when I visited, to prevent local pub patrons from making improper use of it).

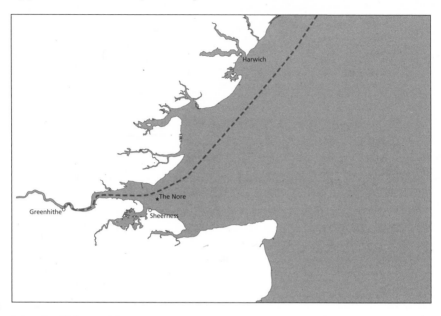

Mouth of Thames Estuary

CHRONOLOGY

20 May 1845: The ships are in tow of the steamers *Monkey* and
Rattler, "somewhere or other below the Nore," a sandbank near
where the Thames meets the North Sea
(Letter 97)

22 May 1845: *Monkey,* having been damaged in a gale, is forced
back to Harwich for repairs, and does not rejoin *Rattler*
(Letters 110, 118, and note)

22–23 May 1845: The ships are off Aldeburgh, Suffolk (known as
"Aldborough" at the time), having had to anchor due to heavy winds
(Letters 98, 99)

24–25 May 1845: *Rattler* tows both ships
(Letter 110)

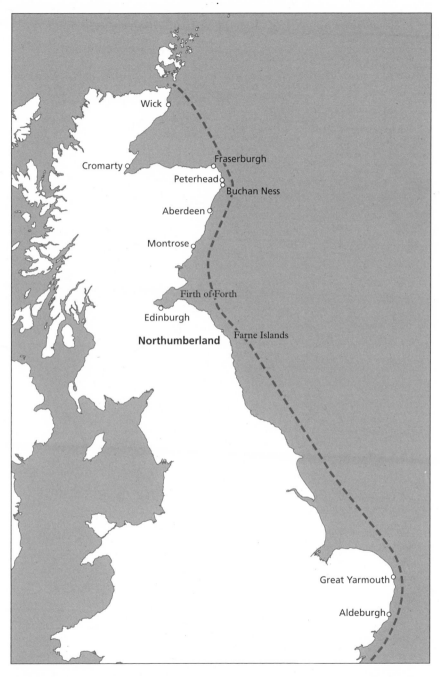

Route up the Eastern Coast of Britain

c. 26 May 1845: The ships are in sight of the Farne Islands
(Letter 100)

c. 26 May 1845: *Rattler* parts company in a storm off Northumberland
(Letter 105)

29 May 1845: *Erebus* and *Terror* are four miles off Aberdeen; *Blazer*
finds and joins them (Letters 107, 109); *Rattler* takes on coal at
Cromarty (Letter 104)

30 May 1845: The ships pass Fraserburgh, John O'Groats, Caithness,
and Duncansby Head (Letters 105, 110, 112)

31 May 1845: *Rattler* returns to join *Blazer* (Letter 110)

31 May 1845: The ships arrive at Stromness (Letters 110, 114)

97. JAMES FITZJAMES TO JOHN BARROW JR, 20 MAY 1845

Dear Barrow
   Last night – we anchored somewhere or other below the Nore because
the North wind and flood tide d'ont do –
   Today d[itt]o – off Harwich
   Anchor for the evening & Stanley has come off in a cutter & takes
this ashore
   We are all very happy Nobody wishes anyb[ody] out of the way –
Every body shakes hands with himself & wishes [for] a sight of Cape
Farew[ell]
   Rattler tows <u>both</u> of u[s] 3/6 and 4 knots –
Sir John is delightful an[d] [a]s energetic as possible
   God bless you
   J Fitzjames

off Harwich 20th May

98. CHARLES OSMER TO ELIZA OSMER [WIFE], PROBABLY 23 MAY 1845

HMS Erebus
Off Aldborough
Coast of Norfolk
May 1845

A boat has just come off from this place and will wait just five minutes – I therefore must scribble a line or two to say that my health has much improved – by the sea air. We have had nothing but strong winds against us since we left Greenhithe, and God only knows when it will change to cause us to advance to the Northward – I understand that we shall be one day at Stromness in the Orkneys. Jane will be gratified to hear that we are all very comfortable & in high spirits at the idea of our soon completing our voyage –

99. JOHN FRANKLIN TO THE REVEREND PHILIP GELL, 23 MAY 1845

HMS Erebus at Sea off Aldborough
23rd May 1845

My dear Mr Gell,
I am sincerely obliged to you for all your kind wishes as conveyed in your letter of March last, and I am sure you will excuse my not having written to thank you for them sooner.

You know how short a period has been given us for our equipments, and this was curtailed to me by my own indisposition from Influenza, and by the death of my much esteemed niece Mrs Richardson, so that I have had little time to think of or do any thing that was not absolutely necessary. I have a very fine set of Officers & Men and they are all very sanguine & full of eager interest in the success of our objects. I sincerely trust with you, that this Expedition may Eventually, though in ways perhaps undiscernible by us, promote the cause of true religion; at all events it will be no less my duty than my delight to lay before my own officers & crew the blessing it imparts, to all who humbly seek to embrace & follow its holy precepts through faith in the Crucified Redeemer.

I have just received a letter from your Son, he seems much pleased by the efforts that have been made about the College – but when he wrote he did not know of the Subscriptions that are now going on. We must see the result of these, and if they amount to a sufficient sum to make it desirable to commence, we should all be sorry I think, that your Son had not the honor of being the 1ˢᵗ Warden. It will be time enough perhaps to think of this subject in connection with my daughter when I return, if it please God that I should do so, from my Expedition.

I can assure you I am thoroughly satisfied with my future Son in Law, and I believe Eleanor to be firmly attached to him, as to my wife, she loves him and has long done so, as a Son.

I believe I can give but little hope of Eleanor's being disposed to leave her mother in my absence or of Mama's liking to part from her. I am not the less obliged by your kindness to Eleanor, and I hope they may both have the pleasure of meeting you abroad. I trust your health has benefitted by the change. Pray give my kind regards to Mrs Gell & to the other members of your family who are with you & believe me

  Most sincerely yours
  John Franklin

P.S. should the Expedition prove successful this Season we may hope to reach England again in 18 months, but if we have to winter we must be about three years.

100. JOHN FRANKLIN TO JOHN PHILIP GELL, 23 MAY 1845

       HMS Erebus 23ᵈ May 1845
       at ⚓ off Aldborough

My dear Gell,

Eleanor's recent letters have I doubt not informed you of my present appointment – or the above address would surprise you. I parted with my dearest Jane, Eleanor & Sophy on Monday Morning 19ᵗʰ inst, – They had been remaining at Greenhithe for a few days that they might take the latest farewell of me. There was much benefit in their so doing – since their being on the spot enabled them to become personally acquainted with my officers, and to ascertain from them that it was their desire to be very careful of me at the same time that they knew from the tenor of their conversations that their hearts were in the right place as respects the objects of the Expedition. These convictions soothed their minds and broke the sorrow my dearest ties would have felt at my separation from them – they bore it I assure you with a very proper spirit, as persons who would not close their eyes against the fact that the service upon which I was going will be attended with difficulties & dangers – but who in fervent prayer committed me & my companions & our cause to the infinite Mercy of God who alone can order the issues of the voyage, and trusted that the Lord would graciously receive their petitions.

We all had the happiness of assembling together on the preceding day at the first performance of divine worship on board, and you can imagine that our prayers for each other were fervent and sincere. I am sure that more than myself thought of you on that interesting occasion; it was our desire then, as it will ever be to be kindly remembered in your prayers. Only one day before I left London, I was gratified by receiving your note of 5 October brought by Dayman, in which you thank me for having written to Lord Stanley about the College – Badly as I think of him & of the manner in which his Department is managed, I could not forget what I owed to you, to the Colony & to myself – and permit the College labours to slip through unnoticed, nor let the efforts of the party inimical to them prevail without a remonstrance from me. I am glad you approve of the manner in which this was done. Lord Stanley's answer was the only civil thing he has done towards me. Before this note can reach you, the intelligence will have reached you – that we are still making efforts among the people of the Church of England to raise subscriptions for a College to be placed entirely under the Bishop – some good subscriptions have been promised and I hear Marriott has been put into high spirits again on the subject by the success of his recent visit to Cambridge. It is happily to be independent of the Government, home & local – Marriott is most anxious that you should have the power of being its 1st Warden and I can fancy you would be equally desirous on that point and providing you saw any immediate prospect of the College succeeding, that you would remain out for a time longer. On this point I should advise you to act precisely as you think best. I know if you thought you could do good to the cause by staying longer you would cheerfully do so – but unless there were a prospect of such an appointment being made soon I cannot feel it right that you should sacrifice your time & happiness & health, perhaps, by remaining longer in that demoralized place.

I believe these are the sentiments of Eleanor also & of my wife – and certainly I believe them to be those of your parents & your family – indeed except for the Establishment of the College I should consider your longer stay there as wasting the most precious years of your life – if you should determine on coming to England at no distant period, you will probably arrive there much about the time I shall return from my Expedition – and truly rejoiced shall I then be to welcome you – I have already spoken to my friend Parry on who you must call early to introduce you to the Bishop of Norwich – you must yourself get at the Arch Bishop of Dublin through Mr Arnold and we must make our united efforts available to get you some certain employment – either a perpetual Curacy or small living if no other better thing offered. I have no doubt however of your own talents & energy being quite sufficient for your having a competency wherever there is a field for you to work in free from the base & ceaseless intrigues which have everywhere crossed your path in VD Land.

You will regret to learn that Dayman only reached England just in time to say good bye to me and that was after our departure from Woolwich. I had at the first left a vacancy open for him to accompany me – but was obliged to get it filled – He is equally sorry with me at this disappointment for he would have gladly gone. He told me that he had many papers and drawings for me which I was unable to stop for – indeed we had only time for one hour's chat together on account of his having to return to London by the Steamer – Scott came also with him. From their accounts as well as from my own letters I hear very wretched accounts of the Colony. Indeed they are now well known to every body – and the causes spoken of freely – the conduct of the Chief also is well known in England – and many most influential persons have Exclaimed against the appointment of such a man. The last Exclamation of the kind was openly made to me in the Antechamber of the Queens Drawing Room. It has been told me too that Lord Stanley did not really know the Extent of his demerits and that Sir Robert Peel has spoken to the same effect. They knew of his poverty and of the inconveniences arising there from but not the other points of his character which are very generally spoken of – The <u>Times</u> had an article a few days since on VDL – and promises to continue the subject at intervals of its present condition till there be amendment or the subject be brought before Parliament.

I suspect also that Sir Eardley has had some <u>raps</u> from the Colonial Office on several points of his policy which of course he keeps secret. As respects the Bishop Sir E has been advised I hear to be more considerate and recommended to act more cordially with him. I hear however that on some points the Bishop was too precipitate & may have given the Government the advantage. I think on the whole Marriott has managed his business well – he has been constantly with us – but he has never ventured on mentioning my name either to Lord Stanley or Mr Hope at any of his interviews – this he has been advised not to do I dare say, & perhaps he is right.

My pamphlet will soon be from the Printer's hands – I regret with all my exertion that it could not be got out before I sailed – I have told Lord S. of its coming out & that the Printer had received my direction to send him the 1st copy – I have already sent him in Print the Postscript containing Montagu['s] last letter to Turnbull and the reply of the latter – which if any thing will convince Lord Stanley of Montagu's real character, these letters will do it. I should have failed in getting anything so fully established against Montagu as is contained in his own letters – which I also think compromises Lord Stanley – You will very soon receive your copy of the Pamphlet – which you know is printed by me for the information of my friends. I trust you will find that though I have been firm in my statements – yet I have been temperate and I have refrained from implicating any one beyond what was necessary for the Establishment of my facts – and in the defense of my wife or my self –

It will probably make some stir in VDL and of course it will give rise to all kinds of invention, scurrility, and falsehood – it is not improbable that some person or friend of Montagu may attempt to answer it – if so I have left some very able and judicious friends well supplied with matter & willing to take up the Cudgel on my behalf. Here I am on a fair field – known to a very extensive Society – especially the Scientific branches of it who will not be bamboozled by the unblushing lies of such men as Lathrope Murray and such like, who are the supporters of the Party in VDL. I have not at all refrained from talking of the injustice of Lord Stanley and of the Subtlety of Montagu – with men of influence whom I have found take an interest in my welfare – Which I can assure you is felt by many persons. My present appointment is considered by all such persons as having given the lie to all the statements of the Colonial Office – and so in fact it may be considered with propriety.

The Expedition has excited very general interest from all parties in the Country – and the feeling in its favour is scarcely less strong on the Continent – which has been Evinced by presents of magnificent books to me from thence – The Admiralty have been most kind to me from the 1st

Lord to the Junior Clerk of the Department. The officers have all been of my own selection and a fine set of fellows they are, so are the men. The ship has been in every respect well-fitted and provisioned – and if these advantages could ensure success – ours might be considered certain – but I trust we all feel that "We are not sufficient of ourselves to do anything as of ourselves – but our sufficiency is of God" – and that in all our ways we acknowledge him and seek his Grace & Strength, his guidance & protection. Under these feelings and putting forth our Earnest Endeavours to perform our duties we leave the issue to his Almighty will –

Now my dear Gell I must stop – may the Lord bless and protect you and restore you to us in his good time – blest with health and happiness – I close my note off the Farn Islands – the scene of Grace Darling's memorable Exploit – but the weather is too thick for our seeing the land.

     Ever yours most faithfully,

     John Franklin

I have written to your Father

101. HARRY GOODSIR TO JOHN GOODSIR [FATHER], 23 MAY 1845

> H.M.S. Erebus
> Off Aldborough
> Friday 23ᵈ May 1845

My Dear Father

We have been lying here for the last two days in consequence of a storm from the north east which has prevented us proceeding. We will however be able to go on tomorrow & expect to reach Stromness in the course of a few days where we will wait for a day or two. Be so good if this reaches in time to write a few lines to that place (Stromness) You can easily direct it to be returned if too late for the Ships. Let me know what you have done about Cæsar. In haste love to all believe me

     Your Affectionate Son
     Harry D. S. Goodsir
P.S. The boat which has come off from the shore is just leaving.

102. DANIEL BRYANT TO MARY ANN BRYANT [WIFE], 25 MAY 1845

Erebus Sunday 25th May 1845

Dearest Wife

With feelings of Pleasure I now take the opportunity of writing to you hoping they will find you and Luisa in good health as it leaves me at present. Dearest Anne I wrote to you two letters while we was lying of Herridge which I hope you received my Love we are now on ower passage to Stromness Orkney with a Buetiful fair wind. Besides the Ratler Steam Boat has got us in tow and the Monkey Steam Boat has got the other vesell in tow and we expect to get to Stromness about Wednesday next. Please god my Dearest Anne we had Church this morning and Sir John Franklin read to us a very Beautifull Sermon. Sir John took his Text from the 17th Chapter of the first Book of Kings and 16th verse – and the Barrell of meal wasted not neither did the cruse of oil fail According to the word of the Lord. Sir John Called the Ship's Companys Attention to that Part of the Sermon and the whole of the Ship's Company was very much Pleased with Sir Johns Appropriate text and unite in the Point of view as Sir John and that is to accomplish ower object wich we have in view and that with the hialp of the Allmighty I verely Believe and my dearest Wife I will never go away – Oh what would I give if I could But see you and Embrace you one Before we Begin our work my dearest Anne I give you All my Best wishes and All the Blessings upon earth and I hope you and me shall meet again as we have often done before and that with the blessing of god, we shall be happy yet. My dearest Anne rest assured that you are my only Treasure on Earth and such you shall find me, my Love. I hope by the time this arives you will be Quite Comfortable and Setled. Dearest Ann I am quite Comfortable myself. I have had no complaints from no one everything goes on very quite and regular and my Duty is Done at 10 o Clock untill 6 o'clock in the morning. I must conclude by wishing good night my Love And I remain your Affectionate Husband, Daniel Bryant So untill death [do] us part I will send another please to excuse [my haste] [as] soon as [pos]able
[Cross written on final leaf]
our ship is [making up lost] time please to excuse

103. CHARLES OSMER TO ELIZA OSMER [WIFE], 29 MAY 1845

H.M.S. Erebus Stromness Orkney.
May 29th 1845

My hurried and short note from off Aldborough will have informed you of our progress to that date. The following morning the wind having somewhat abated as well as slackened its power we got under weigh in tow of the Rattler and made another good progress during the next twenty four hours, but the wind once more changed and brought with it a chopping head-sea, which rendered the motion of the vessel anything but pleasant, but notwithstanding all this the jokes and the anecdotes went round with us at the mess table, and to judge from the merry looking fases, they heeded not the storm's rageing over their heads – and we all please God willing hope to be in England in August 1846. Then love you will be pleased to hear that I have found a set of Messmates that are in every way deserving. Tis a rare thing to find met together twelve men of different ranks, and age, who combine the scholar with the Gentleman such are those it has been my fortunate lot to mix with, and I do most fervently hope and pray that nothing may occur to loosen the ties which at present so very happily bind us to each other – Sir John is particularly attentive and even pointed in his attention to me. I have dined with Sir John twice a week since we left. With such a Leader to command us tis next to impossible that we shall be other than most happy and comfortable. August or September 1846 sees me God willing in England that is the first step in the ladder, the next will be a permanent appointment where neither north or south pole will cause me to leave my home.

104. JAMES FITZJAMES TO JOHN BARROW JR, 29 MAY 1845

Dear Barrow
Stanley just found in Blazer – been looking for us to Northward.
Rattler parted company – to unwind a few <u>fathoms</u> of hawser got round her <u>screw</u>.

She has been in to Cromarty to coal. Blazer has been looking for us for 3 days – we were determined not to go "West about" and didn't, and here we are off <u>Peterhead</u>
Will be at Stromness tomorrow or next day & then off – Boat co[ming]
    so adieu
        J Fitzjames
off Buchan Ness 29th May

105. JAMES FAIRHOLME TO GEORGE FAIRHOLME [FATHER],
29 MAY–1 JUNE 1845

off Aberdeen May 29th 1845

My dear Father

Being off Aberdeen, with a prospect of being in Stromness tomorrow night, I begin a letter which, however, I shall keep open till the last moment. We have had rather a rough passage thus far, & I could not help rejoicing that William was not on board as he proposed as he would have been very unwell in all probability. We saw a good deal of the coast as we came up, particularly about the Fern Islands as the wind has been generally foul so we were obliged to stand close inside to take advantage of the tides. We made Montrose on Monday night, & have been ever since getting as far as Aberdeen, where we now are (that is about 4 miles off it) The Rattler parted company from us in a hard blow which we had off Northumberland, but we really manage better than I expected in such heavy looking ships. All goes on most comfortably on board. I like Sir John more & more every day. The officers are in 4 watches, with one to spare in case of sickness etc. This is just as it ought to be & does not make the duty too heavy. For I had from midnight till 4 a.m. this morning, then I am off till 6 p.m. this evening when I have duty till 8 & nothing more till 8 next morning & so on, so that we have an undisturbed night every fourth.

Now that we have daylight at ½ past 1 in the morning & twilight till 11 at night one thinks nothing of night watches. They are very different to the long drowsy nights of 12 hours in the tropics. The principal employment in the watch is taking hourly observations with about half a dozen different kinds of <u>ometers</u> for the metereological journal, & each officer writes these in the log <u>himself</u> instead of the log being written by one person as is usually done We have done nothing yet in magnetism but are to commence observing the dip as soon as we leave land. Our dinner hour is 3 & Sir John's 4. As yet he has always invited 3 of the officers to dine with him, but I do not know whether that will be kept up. He dines with us on Sunday & a most pleasant dinner party we had last Sunday when he remarked that we seemed as well settled & to know each other as well as if we had been 3 years together. We were very fortunate in getting a good steward only 2 days before we sailed. Without him we should not have been nearly as comfortable in our mess. I have made my cabin very snug & found it best to be my own carpenter, which has kept me well employed. Now I am settled & shall take to more profitable employment. I hope Elizabeth got my photograph. Lady Franklin said she thought it made me look too old, but as I had Fitzjames coat on at the time, to save myself the trouble of getting my own, you will perceive that I am a Commander, & have anchors on the epaulettes so it will do capitally when that is really the case.

Stromness June 1st We got in here last night & I believe we shall start today if we can possibly get the supplies we want. We yesterday met with the Rattler again off Fraserburgh, & as it was a perfectly calm day, we had a most delightful cruise along the N. E. coast of Scotland, passing John O'Groat's house about 6 in the evening. I never saw anything more lovely than the scene last night, as we ran through the narrow passages among these little islands. In themselves there is nothing of the beautiful, as they are perfectly bare, but there was such a sky, & such a sunset & such a glass like sea that it was quite worthy of the Gulf of Smyrna. The sun did not set till half past 9 – at midnight I had the pleasure of receiving all your letters & papers, which I read in the open air, in almost broad daylight. I fear we shall see little of this place, but if we do stay today, I shall try to get over to see Kirkwall. We were disappointed about the Illustrated London News. The sketches are very bad & do not give any idea of the cabins. Mine is certainly the most comfortable one in the ship & the fittings etc. but <u>the</u> drawback is the draft from the hatchway which makes it rather cold. N'importé with the buffalo cloak for a curtain. I hear we stay till tomorrow. June 2nd

I have just returned from a most agreeable trip to Kirkwall, & find that after a walk of 30 miles with but little rest I have to dine out as a matter of duty. We are under orders for 9o'c tonight but the wind is still foul & we shall not do much. I shall send you a long letter by the next opportunity & shall now say once more a kind goodbye.

J.W.F

106. FRANCIS CROZIER TO CHARLOTTE CROZIER [SISTER], 29 MAY 1845

Terror May 29th 1845

My dear Small

I find a boat coming along side (off Aberdeen) we are only this far from a long continuance of adverse winds – all getting on otherwise as I could wish – We have still time enough before us, but it was the chain of contrary winds that made me so anxious to be off – I was sadly vexed to sail without hearing again from you or our dear friends at Fortfield but I must hope all things – Poor Lady Franklin was in a sad state before we left – I was obliged to row her – She tells me if anything should take her to Dublin before we return she will certainly make you out – You would like her much she is so full of Kindness – I will write from Stromness (Orkney) when we shall land our Pilot

God love you all and

Believe me ever yours

FRM Crozier

P.s. our progress has been – so
slow I could not bear to sit
down to write

FRM

107. JAMES FITZJAMES TO WILLIAM CONINGHAM [BROTHER], 29 MAY 1845

Dearest William

This goes in to Aberdeen or some such place by the Blazer which has just joined and goes in for coal & comes out tomorrow and will help to tow us to Stromness – where we shall be tomorrow or next day – Rattler we lost in a fog – but expect to find her soon as she has been in to Cromarty to get coal & to unwind a few fathoms of hawser which had got wrapped round her screw.

We have had a continual NE wind but being determined to go this way – did go this way – and the Admiralty – finding we were at Harwich sent the Blazer to tell Sir John to go down the channel and go "West about" as it is called –

We have pitched & pounded thus far however & of course d'ont care for orders and being only 100 miles or so from Stromness intend going there for water –

I like Sir John amazingly and we all get on most capitally – Stanley commands the Blazer and takes this ashore –

I shall write from Stromness which will be the last letter you will have till the Transport leaves us – I see by Lyon's journal that they were only 9 days getting to Cape Farewell (Greenland) from the Orkneys.

I wish I had told you to write to Stromness – By the bye will you get something (<u>not</u> a <u>fork</u> or a <u>spoon</u>) and send to my new Goddaughter which the Charlewood's have got. I forgot it – or rather I was too busy when I sailed to do what I intended & <u>wish</u> – so I leave it to you –

What a delightful cruize you must have had in Holland – I often think of you.

We have this day the most delightful clear weather possible & cold. the sun sets at 8. and it is daylight till 11 – and again at 3 – & twilight the rest of the night.

I think I cleared Shell but if I left any thing unpaid I told him to ask you for it. will you ask him if there is anything

Now that we are off you have no idea how happy we all feel – how determined we all are to be frozen, and how anxious to be amongst the ice –

I never left England with less regret – and I account for this by the ardent hope I have of doing what we are going to try and of being back again <u>soon</u>.

Please God when I <u>do</u> come back I will have a little quiet with you Barring one more attempt to reach the Pole – God bless you and dear Elizabeth and believe me ever

Your affectionate
James Fitzjames

Erebus 29th May <u>8 Pm</u>
Off Peterhead or
Buchan Ness.

108. JAMES FITZJAMES TO WILLIAM CONINGHAM [BROTHER], 29 MAY-2 JUNE 1845

HMS Erebus 29th. May 1845.
Off Peterhead

Dearest William

I have occasionally sent you or Elizabeth I forget which, a flying note which if you have received will have accquainted you that we have been struggling ever since we left the Thames against one of the most obstinate NE breezes that ever blew which NE wind if we had been clear of the Orkneys would have been fair for Cape Farewell. It did occasionally blow a gale – once we had to anchor off the coast between Aldborough & Southwold – and though we had 100 fathoms of cable out, drifted about 2 miles but we were determined not to go into any harbour – and therefore didn't –

We got a gale off the Farn islands, which we have since heard sent the Blazer into an anchorage – but we remained outside pile driving like the little ships one sees in a very blue sea in musical clocks But everything must have an End – and we are now beating up with a fine breeze going within a mile of the land at each tack near Peterhead. the said land being barren enough in appearance barring the corn fields – with very desolate looking Castles some of which have pointed tops on their towers like extinguishers – The Rattler which towed us and the Terror most beautifully – got a few fathoms of hawser wrapped round her screw – we lost her in a fog – and have since heard that after looking for us she went in to Cromarty for coal – and to unwind her screw which she did – as the Blazer which had been ordered by the Admiralty to find us out – followed the Rattler there – We are now anxiously looking for the Rattler who with the Blazer will take us into Stromness immediately if not sooner, and when there we shall get water – and be off –

The Blazer brought orders to go round by the Lizard – but happily we are not now going that way. – The little Monkey – a small steamer that towed the Transport –lugged her hawseholes out in the gale off Aldborough – & then got short of coals – so we sent her back. The Rattler on this cruize has proved beyond a doubt the great power of the screw for I doubt much if any paddle boat would have towed two old tubs like us 4 ½ knots against a head sea & wind – "Propeller Smith" is on board her – Be sure you do not let the Great Britain go without seeing her – She is well worth a trip I assure you.

Read Beechey's voyage towards the North Pole published in /43 it is I think well done – it is curious that no account of Buchan's voyage should have appeared – Franklin commanded the Trent with him –

Franklin is really a most delightful person and full of anecdotes of his adventures and journeyings – it appears he was with Captain Flinders on the first survey of New Holland – and was in Dance's squad of merchant ships what licked Linois – He was at Copenhagen & Trafalgar & in all the minor affairs of the war – then with Buchan & crowned all with his own Expeditions – The other day he mentioned a curious fact that I do not remember to have seen – After an American forest has been burnt to the ground – another forest springs up consisting of a different species of tree – <u>not one</u> of the original species appearing –

We have just tacked (2 Pm) within ¼ mile of the pier of Peterhead & all I could see with a glass, was (or were) 3 Custom house officers looking at us through a glass – an old scotch woman scratching her head, and a few cocks & hens on a dung hill. Except the town clock which was going (I mean the hands were) there was no other sign of life in the good town of Peterhead –

<u>11</u> Pm Before going to bed I finish the sheet. the weather is heavenly – but the little wind there is NE – Blazer having lugged us clear of the NE corner of Scotland – called Kinnairds Point – has gone for Terror – where Rattler is we c'ant guess – Stanley came on board this evening & brought us from Aberdeen – bread – fish – milk & newspapers to 27th. by which I see we have been in a gale of wind, very dreadful, glad we know it before leaving – Greenwich time only 12 minutes from this so you are now sending Elizabeth to bed – I conclude you are back from Holland. Good night.

3rst. May at Noon – Crossing the Murray Firth with a smooth sea. Clear blue sky – cool air & fresh. Rattler came on us at 4 this morning and took us in tow. The Blazer is out of sight with Terror – but Rattler saw her this morning – – the sun rose at ½ past 2 – Mountains are in sight ahead – somewhere about John O'Groats – and we shall probably be in to Stromness tonight or tomorrow morning – as the Rattler is towing us 6.2 knots an hour – .

I said Kinnairds' Point was the NE extreme of Scotland but it is'nt – there is a <u>Northerer</u> and Easterer, which rejoices in the name of Duncansby Head and which is now in sight – blue and rugged.

I hope O'Callaghan's friend (whose name I forget) is getting on well in the library – I feel a strange interest in young East, who I have taken it into my head is to be a great man in the service I was so anxious to get him into the Vesuvius knowing how pleased Elizabeth would be that I looked upon him as a very old accquaintance I hope when I come back he will have turned out well.

<u>6.30 Pm</u>. John O'Groats House is a low hut which is seen from the sea on passing Duncansby Head – and the pilot has a long story about 7 sons who quarrelled about sitting at the bottom of the table – so the father had it made broad enough to hold them <u>all</u> at the bottom, & from what I can make out found he had only got a table athwartships in his hall the sons all sitting on <u>one</u> side –

Some say John O'Groats <u>house</u> is a remarkable cliff or rock jutting into the sea at or near Duncansby Head – from which we passed only about 100 yds in the smoothest possible water – with the clearest sky going 6 ½ knots towed by Rattler 10 minutes ago – and are now threading our way among the barren looking islands called Skereys

<u>Midnight</u> we are anchored in Stromness. Terror and Blazer here – and I get an immense heap of notes and newspapers dated to 24th. from Fitzgerald and Barrow – and a letter from Elizabeth dated the Hague 10th. which is worth 'em all – Tell her how delighted I am to get it – though she does indulge in a tirade against crazy North Polar Expeditions –

Now that we <u>have</u> got here the winds begin to veer round to the N.W. and perhaps we may have a gale against us again – but this time will be clear off into the big ocean – the Rattler is gone out again to bring the Transport in – good night –

1st. <u>June</u> We have been here all day and the good people of Stromness w'ont move or shew themselves seeing that it is the Sabbath – so we can get nothing done – Transport came in at 4 this morning – so here we are 5 vessels – I have been the whole day on a small dissolute island scratching at the dipping needle – and tomorrow go again. We shall get water &c and probably sail at 8 in the evening with the ebb tide of tomorrow

<u>Monday 2nd. June</u> so I shall finish my letter this night – and send a line if I have time again. Sir John wisely intends waiting the post which only comes twice a week & is expected tomorrow evening – I <u>may</u> get a letter from you if you have sent one to John Barrow – I forget whether I ever asked you to get something & send to Charlewood for his daughter just born to whom I am supposed to be Godfather.

Whether we go tomorrow or next day – we shall be clear off by the time you get this – and you will hear once again by the return of the Transport – I have written all this in snatches and really d'ont know what I may have said – God bless you my beloved William and equally beloved Elizabeth – kiss the children for me give my regards to Sarah who I have no doubt took good care of them while you were away – Believe me always

Your affectionate
James Fitzjames

109. CHARLES OSMER TO ELIZA OSMER [WIFE], 30 MAY 1845

Off Peterhead 30th May the Blazer joined us about 10 o'clock and the Terror was a long way astern. The Erebus beats the Terror very much, we are both now in tow of the steamers but she has too little power to enable us to advance much should however this fine weather continue I have no doubt that we shall get to Stromness on Sunday. I had almost omitted to mention that we have had Divine Service every Sunday since we left Greenhithe and you would be perfectly delighted at the beautiful and impressive manner in which Sir John reads both the Service and the Sermon, he has quite astonished us all in this respect. Every officer, Seaman, and Marine, and boy have each a Bible, Prayer Book. I assure you tis with unalloyed feeling of delight that I witnessed their fervent and audible responses.

110. HARRY GOODSIR TO JOHN GOODSIR [FATHER], 31 MAY 1845

H.M.S. Erebus
Stromness
May 31st 1845

I have written a latter letter to John both go by same Post

My Dear Father

We arrived here last night when I received your most welcome letter. We have had a long time of since we left Greenhithe & for the first week very stormy weather & contrary winds during which time we lost sight of both steamers. One was damaged considerably & obliged to return the third day after we left so that the one (Rattler) had to tow both ships for two days after which she was driven away altogether so that we had to beat up as far as Aberdeen before any assistance reached us. At that place the Blazer Steamship met us, she had been on to Orkney to look after us.

The Steamer which we had lost came upon us yesterday morning off Buchan Ness after which we got well & quickly on & reached this anchorage about ten last night. We are all uncertain of the time of starting but think it will be either tonight or early tomorrow morning. Perhaps later so that there was abundance of time for receiving letters; none however had much expectation of remaining here so that we have been rather diss-apointed as regards letters. I wish I had written to John from Aldborough for I was anxious to hear from him about several things; I also forgot to ask you to send a paper about the General Assembly &c. and any other news for we are all anxious to hear any news before leaving, seeing it will be in all probability so long before we have an opportunity of hearing again.

I was very much pleased with the intelligence regarding Jane & hope that every b[l]essing will attend her. Let her know that my time is so much occupied with the papers for John that it is out of my power to write her at present but was gratified at receipt of her letter I am afraid also that it will not be in my power, from the same cause, to write as I intended to Uncle Anstruther but you will perhaps send this letter to them at Carnbee. We passed so rapidly the Coast of Caithness, in consequence of the power of the Steamer (a Screw propeller) & I was so busy down below at the time writing that I missed seeing Wick a thing I regretted very much we were not however very near the coast seeing we crossed the Firth from Kinairds to Duncansby head. We passed within a stones throw of John O'Groats & the sail through amongst the Orkney Islands to Stromness in the still of the beautiful evening was very pleasant after the late stormy weather. I will write by any opportunity which offers in the shape of Whalers but at all events you shall hear from me per Transport from the edge of the ice. I am sorry you have had any trouble regarding my money matters but will be able to repay it all on coming home as I will then be more or less independent at which time I hope to be able to repay John for all the outlay on my account. The accounts regarding the success of all at home pleases me much & my only wish is that all may be going on in like manner when I reach home again with love to all.

Believe me
Your Affectionate Son
Harry D. S. Goodsir

I have no time to read my letters over

III. CHARLES OSMER TO ELIZA OSMER [WIFE],
31 MAY 1845

Off Caithness 40 miles from Stromness 31st May – this morning the Rattler again made her appearance and took us in tow whilst the Terror was towed by the Blazer. It is a delightful and lovely morning barely a

breath out of the heavens and we are consequently propelled at an amazing rate, of six knots an hour. Sir John being too strict in his observance of
the Sabbath for any duty to be done on that day, my time in Stromness will
be fully occupied in purchasing Oxen for the two vessels as well as getting
ready despatches for the Admiralty. The Officers of the Rattler have given
us a return Dinner to day, in that from the Captain to the lowest boy in
every Vessel, but one feeling appears predominant and that is anxiety for
the result of our Labours, added to a sincere and ardent wish for our success – if such a feeling prevales the hearts and minds of the almost uninter-
ested, what must be the feelings of our <u>dear</u> <u>relations</u> at <u>home</u>.

112. JAMES FITZJAMES TO JOHN BARROW JR, 31 MAY 1845

> Erebus 31st May off Duncansby
> Head
> near John O'Groat's

My dear Barrow

You will have received divers notes from me written in a hurry as the
opportunity offered for sending – and they will have served to acquaint
you that though bothered with a NE wind we were none of us very
unhappy about it. On the contrary "d'ont care" is the order of the day –
I mean d'ont care for difficulties – or stoppages – go ahead; is the wish
– we look to the <u>result</u> not to the means of attaining it. So then you
Admiralty people wanted to make us go round by the Lizard – It is a
question whether in the first instance it might not have been better but
once having started to go this way – I would have gone through a hur-
ricane rather than "put back" at the beginning of the voyage – no one
could possibly have foreseen such a continuance of N.E. winds – Here we
are however going 6.2 Rattler towing us – Duncansby Head in sight and
Blazer got Terror <u>out</u> of sight – ahead – as we sent her on last night before
Rattler got hold of us – Transport is also somewhere about the Pentland.

So Inshallah! tonight or tomorrow morning early, we shall all be in
Stromness, where we shall only remain long enough to see the Transport
filled with water and a few more bullocks. – D'ont think we are <u>late</u>

we are in plenty of time. if the thing is to be done <u>at all</u> it is to be done only between 1ˢᵗ August & September I do hope and trust that if we get through we shall land at Petro Paulovski – and that I may be allowed to come home through Siberia – I shall do all in my power to urge Sir John Franklin to let me go. – and I do wish the Russian Government had been asked to send to their Governors etc so that they may expect me and not oppose my going on. This was done in former Expeditions as I have just read in Beechey's account of the Dorothea and Trent's voyage – the best written book I have seen for some time & the most interesting.

It is not now too late to send to Petersburg. It <u>could</u> do no harm, and might do some good – get through I firmly believe we shall – and if we d'ont I do not think it will be our fault. Sir John is delightful – active, energetic, and evidently even now persevering – what he <u>has</u> <u>been</u> we all know – I think it will turn out that he is in no ways altered. He is full of conversation & interesting anecdotes of his former voyages – I would not lose him for the command of the Expedition for I have a real regard, I might say <u>affection</u> for him and believe this is felt by all of us – I have not seen much of Crozier yet – but what I have seen I like – and I think he is just made for a second to Sir John Franklin. – In our mess we are very happy – we have a most agreeable set of men – and I could suggest no change except that I wish you were with us. –

Our cruize ought to settle for ever the efficiency of the screw. I doubt if any paddle box boat would have towed two old tubs like us – & <u>heavy</u> withal 5 knots or 4 ¼ against a rough sea & strong wind as she has done till the hawsers parted – Propeller Smith who is on board must be delighted the great advantage appears to be that she does not lose dragging power by rolling as paddlebox boats do when one of their paddles is flourishing in the air thus and it requires a heavy <u>pitch</u> indeed to shew the screw in the air. By the bye <u>we</u> pitch terribly – in the gale off Aldborough we were like little ships in musical clocks that bob up & down in a very solid green sea – Captain Smith has been very attentive & obliging and manages the vessel beautifully – the <u>real</u> Commander of the Rattler is at home – And by the bye if you have an opportunity do put in a word for the most indefatigable hard working man I ever saw – the master of the Monkey – Bryant.

[rest of letter missing]

113. JAMES FITZJAMES TO ELIZABETH CONINGHAM
[SISTER-IN-LAW], 31 MAY 1845

HMS Erebus 31 May near Stromness

I have been writing a sort of rambling letter to William, my dearest Elizabeth – and that you may not fancy I have forgotten you yet. I send you these few lines, written with the old porcupine quill which you are quite right in thinking I should be glad to have – I really was quite delighted to see it and had it not been for your letter from Bruges announcing its advent it would have remained wrapped up with the needles.

You will imagine us in the clearest of days – going head to wind past the rough Coast of Northern Scotland – we shall remain a few hours at Stromness – where I shall add a few lines to you and William if I have time, but if not, I sh'ant – you will imagine us wending our way (without steam) across the Antlantic and you will picture to yourself a smooth passage if you please. for we have had rolling & pitching enough to last us all the voyage – the old Terror pitches so much we call her our friend & pitcher no doubt we appear to do so likewise from her decks.

We are very happy – I never was more so in my life but you must not imagine that it is really the happiness of getting away – On the contrary I think it is the determination to get back – which makes us so contented with ourselves – perhaps a few weeks may alter our ideas on the subject

I have recommended William to read Beechys North Polar Voyage – which is well done I think – and you will like it I venture to assert.

I d'ont know why I am writing all this nothing but shall go to another she[et]

[rest of letter missing]

114. JAMES THOMPSON TO CHARLES THOMPSON [BROTHER],
1 JUNE 1845

H. M. Ship Terror June 1st 1845
Storm Ness Oarkneys

Brother

I take this opportunity of writing to you hopeing to find you and all friends well as I am my self at present, we left Green High on Monday 18th at 11 O clock Towed by the Ratler astern of the Erebus but the wind not been very favourable we cast ancor at 4 in the afternoon below the Nore Light on Tuesday we set sail at 9 O Clock in the Moarning but the wind being still against us we cast ancor in the afternoon of[f] Harwick on the Essex coast on Wednesday we set sail again at 11 O Clock and cast ancor at 3 O Clock off Alborough on the Suffock Coast and there we remaind at ancor till Saturday Morning at 6 O Clock when we set sail once more we had been from Monday till Saturday and had not got to the Yarmouth Roads but we have [been] sailing ever since as we have not had to drop the ancor till our arrival at the Oarkneys.

the weather has been cold for the time of the year since we left the Thames the Thermometer never standing above 55° but upon the whole it [h]as been A pleasant voyage comeing very oft in sight of Land on the Yorkshire Coast Derham and Northumberland and the coast of Aberdeen and the North of Scotland. Saturday the 31 has been the finest day since we set sail and we have been in sight of Land all the day for after we leave the Land North of Scotland we then come to the Oarkney Islands which is a large track of Hilley Land at each side of the Rivver and appears to be in no manner of Cultivation you may see A few sheep grazin in Different parts but there is no such A thing as tree to be seen.

We arrived hereabout 8 O Clock in the Evening of the 31st but how long we shall remain no one appears to know as it depends on Sir John Frankling and he is in the other Ship but no one has been allowed to go on Shore this day Sunday has been very fine and we have A pleasant view from the Ship we are laid about A Quarter of A Mile from Stoarm Ness which is the principle town at the Oarkneys it is A small place situated on A Hill side the Ho[u]ses appears to be chiefly built on stone after we leave hear we shall soon been in the western Ocean and the next place we make be the accounts of the Sa[ilor]s that has been A whale Fishing will be Davis Straits.

I shall never have an opportunity of hearing from you but there may some times be A chance of me sending you A few lines as I expect the Transpoart will go with us to the Ice or perhaps we may meet with A whaler, the Erebus is laid A short distance from us but I have not yet had an opportunity of Seeing Gregory you must give my kind Respects to Mother January and all Enquiring Friends especily Bob & Beard likewise Bienham. So I Remain yours

James Thompson

There is laid heare at Pesent the Erebus & Terror the Transpoart and the Ratler and the Blazer I expect the two Steamers will stop to take us out of the Harbour and then they will Return to London and leave us to do the best we can for ourselves ——

115. JAMES FITZJAMES TO JOHN BARROW JR, 1 JUNE 1845

Erebus Stromness 1ˢᵗ June 1845 Sunday

Why is Prince Albert's kiss like this ship? – 'Cause its a hairy bus my last. –

Here we are at Stromness – got here last night in a lovely calm <u>day</u> (at 10 at night). smooth sea Rattler towing us 6 ½ good by Massey's log as proved to the satisfaction of <u>both</u> Smiths who were on board & who only gave themselves credit for 5.6 –

Blazer brought Terror in just before us, and Rattler went out immediately and brought in the Transport this morning at 5 o'clock. –

I got a heap of notes & letters from you and some papers for which I thank you as they are the only ones we have – we could do nothing in the way of getting water or bullocks to day, as the good people of Stromness make it <u>Sabbath</u> strictly – Our voyage here has been so much longer than we contemplated that we want to fill up water especially the Transport and 4 bullocks having died we want to fill up their stalls. – A Post is expected tomorrow afternoon and I think it probable we shall sail with the first of the Ebb tomorrow evening at 8 – the day is calm rather cloudy – and I fear we are now going to have a Westerly wind – as the barometer is falling. but we are in plenty of time I believe for all purposes – and so we d'ont care for much –

I was on shore on a dissolute island all to day observing with Fox – after all our trouble they have given us a rotten old Fox. one of the first that was made – badly marked & of little use – giving the new one intended for us to Kellett to whom it might have been sent. We are much disgusted at this, now that we find the increase of trouble & loss of <u>time</u>. Crozier has one of his own, or he would have fared as bad. and he is much annoyed because he asked the Hydrog[raph]er people in the Admiralty to pay his bill for repairing it & putting it to rights and they refused. I cant conceive what the deuce they have gone to such an expense to provide us with first rate magnetic instruments and then give us a disabled Fox –

I intended filling this sheet but am so sleepy I must go to bed as it is 2 o'clock 2nd June and I have to get up at 5 – so goodbye for the present if I have more to say – or hear from you by tomorrow's post I will let you know – and you mus'nt mind postage – I have no stamps – I have written to Coningham also – so he will know the last of me – I will write [via] the Transport – have a letter waiting at Panama on Speck – next January – do – [it] would be curious to have a letter wa[iting] there – whenever we do get through we shall be passing Behring's straits in [the] end of September or <u>early</u> in October. Kindest regards to Sir John & Lady Bar[row] if you please – also to your brother sc[ribes] in the room of musty books and the old p[...] with the reheumatis. – –

Will you also give my remembrances to Beaufort and Becher – and also to Captain Hamilton I beg – I won't go [...] the Admiralty but having finished sheet <u>nearly</u> – I'll say good night

     Ever your sincere friend
      James Fitzjames
Stanley calls the Terror his friend and <u>pitcher</u>.

116. JOHN FRANKLIN TO JANE FRANKLIN [WIFE], 1–3 JUNE 1845

                   HMS Erebus Stromness
My dearest Love,   1st June 1845

  I was delighted last evening on my arrival at this anchorage to receive your very interesting letters with those from Eleanor & Sophy and the papers accompanying them. It was especially gratifying to me to find that you were not alarmed by the reports which the newspapers had given of our position off Aldborough though they appear to have caused the Admiralty to send me an order if the NE winds continued, that I should immediately proceed down Channel. This order was dated on 23rd May & sent to Harwich for Captain Stanley to bring to me – He however did not overtake the ships before the afternoon of the 29th then to the north of Aberdeen. The return to the Channel course was in that position out of the question – indeed the taking the course we have done has never been a matter of question after leaving Aldborough. We have had only one other strong breeze and that off the Farr Islands in which during thick weather we separated from the Rattler & the Transport. The old Erebus & Terror however managed very well together and were making tolerable progress when we were joined by the Blazer and afterwards rejoined by the Rattler. It is satisfactory to perceive that the Erebus & Terror sail so nearly together that they will be good company keepers. The Transport sails better than either but we must keep her close in hand going across the Atlantic.

Our squadron is now anchored around us and by tomorrow afternoon will I hope have finished the little fittings we required and be ready to sail – I propose retaining the two Steamers to tow us about 30 or 40 miles off the land where we must part with them but we shall be thankful for the assistance they have given us. You will be glad to learn that the most experienced Davis Strait seamen here and at Peterhead declare that we are quite in time. This intelligence ought to please Beaufort & Sir James Ross. What a kind note the latter has written me – which I will answer by the Rattler. His conduct towards me has been kind throughout as regards the Expedition and he has acted as a man ought to do who is convinced that I should have spurned taking the least advantage of him by proposing my own services had he the least desire to have gone. I was aware, for he told me that the suggestion was made to him that if he would go the next year the Expedition might be post-poned for that time, and also that a Baronetcy and a good Service Pension were spoken of as inducements for him, but I suspected then and believe now, that each of these propositions were suggested to him by Beaufort & Sabine as considerations and rewards which would follow his acceptance of the Command and that they had received no express authority to make them as promises to be immediately fulfilled, however he richly deserved these honors for his past services. I agree with him in the opinion that the navigation of the Arctic Sea is not near so full of danger as that of the Antarctic, nor as far as I can learn of the Spitzbergen Sea. It is very consolatory to me that you, my dear girl & Sophy have such correct views of the nature of our service – it is one unquestionably attended with difficulty & dangers – but not greater than those of former voyages – and we may trust in Gods merciful support & protection if we humbly seek them, putting forth at the same time our earnest endeavours to over- come them.

I am flattered by Sabines reasons for his supposing me so well fitted for the command of the Expedition. Even so in some respects you tell me he thinks, better than Ross. I think perhaps that I have the tact of keeping the officers & men happily together in a greater degree than Ross – and for this reason – he is evidently ambitious and wishes to do everything by himself – I possess not that feeling, but consider that the Commander of any Service having established his character before – maintains it most by directing the exertions of his officers and studiously encouraging them to work under the assurance that their merits will be duly brought forward <u>and</u> appreciated – Sabine's remark is a just one, that my officers are from a different class of society and better informed than those on any former Expedition – so says Parry – and certainly if we call to mind those officers who were with Ross – there was scarcely one with the exception of Hooker above the ordinary run of the Service. However I feel my responsibility the greater from having these men to govern – and I pray God to aid me in this work – I have the satisfaction of perceiving that they all defer to my opinion – even on points not immediately connected with our present pursuits – Fitz-james even looks surprised when it comes out that I have been in this or that kind of service – of which he had not been previously informed. The more I see of Gore the more convinced am I that in him I have a treasure & a faithful friend – I am particularly pleased with the manner in which he commenced and continues making the sketches for you – I expect to derive very great assistance from him if we have to winter from his previous knowledge of the Terror situated when encumbered with Ice. Stanley who is often with us tells me he is a very valuable fellow to have near you – I like the Ice Master Reid and so do the other officers – he begins to feel himself approaching the field of his labours – he opens out & becomes communicative on the subject of Ice and its Motions.

Crozier has not had the opportunity of being much on board on account of the weather – but when he does come he is cheerful & happy – and seems to think we are making good progress – he could not bear the thought of going down channel – Captain Smith of the Rattler has been uniformly attentive, both he and his friend Mr Smith the great improver if not the Inventor of the Screw – a passenger on board are quite delighted with the manner & speed in which against wind & swell the Rattler has towed the Erebus & Terror together. Yesterday she towed the Erebus alone in calm weather near 6½ miles an hour – this has proved on repeated trials –

I greatly rejoice at the progress you are making towards the conclusion of the Pamphlet – the written portions of that part seem to be good and sufficiently explanatory – I have not time to study them or do more than read them which I have done attentively. I have however the most perfect reliance on your own judgment and on that of each of my dear friends to whom you refer each sheet – your present portion is of course directed against Lord Stanley & the practices of the Colonial Office being that approaching the writing up of my statements. I fervently pray that he may have wisdom bestowed on him from above to receive the just rebukes he has received in a proper spirit. I perceive by the papers that Dayman has had an interview with him, and Sophy tells me that Marriott was to have dined with him on the 28th ult. The Arch Bishop of Canterbury has likewise been with him recently – all these circumstances have given me pleasure because I receive them as an index of better feeling by Lord Stanley towards VDL and especially towards the Bishop and his cause – if His Lordship & Mr Hope do not willfully shut their ears to the truth, they must by this time be informed of Sir E Wilmots real character and of his conduct in the Colony – and I hope they will feel the duty incumbent on them to rebuke him. The poor Bishop I must again exclaim after reading Gells letters and the extract you have sent me from Mr Nixon's letter – think of old Bedford doing the mischief to the Church which he does – as for Edward Bedford he only shews the character which I have attributed to him, and as for Fry I think now that even Gell will agree with me in designating him a Jesuit. Gells letter to you is an excellent one and proves him to be of sterling worth. I like much also the extracts from his letters to Eleanor which she has copied for me – you will consider what I had written to him before your letters came. I think you will not disagree with me on the sentiments I have expressed except perhaps that as to his returning to England in case the College does not immediately make progress – I send you as you wished to see them, all the other letters I have written to VDL and I hope you will think that I have not been idle in the way of writing since my departure. The letter you have sent me from Gregson shall be answered to day if possible. I take precisely the view you do – that it was natural for us not seeing it contradicted – to believe the report in the Advertiser to be correct. I trust you will approve of my letter to Gunn – the subject of purchasing more land even in VDL I will leave to yourself.

Tuesday 3rd June 1845 Eleanors (21st) Birth Day – God Bless her may she be a comfort to you in my absence – we this morning have left Stromness and I retain the Rattler and Blazer that they may tow us & the Transport sufficiently far off the land that we can make sail to the westward – there I hope will probably part company this evening. I am using my utmost efforts to get this letter finished that I may at once have my despatches sent to the care of Captain Smith – whom I have asked if you are still at Shooters Hill to call on you, also to call on your sister – Stanley will likewise see you if he can – he will tell you that he has supplied me with a sopha bed for my lockers from the cabin furniture of Captain Washington which you must write Washington or his wife at Harwich & pay for – Pray do not omit to settle this at once – you will hear of Washington always from Beaufort –

I yesterday signed the Deeds (which I return by this conveyance) in the presence of a notary named Mr Ross of Stromness, to whom you must write if you find from Simpkinson that there ought to have been witnesses to attest my having signed them. There were witnesses present & if requisite Mr Ross & the other party say they will attest to this fact by their signatures providing the Deeds be sent to Mr Ross. Write Stromness for that purpose – this you must enquire after of Mr Simpkinson & send the Deeds back if requisite taking care to pay the Postage for them.

I received your note of the 29th last evening, and I have done all the preceding – it is quite out of my power to answer your points with regularity – I can only assure you that I entirely rely on your judgement in doing every thing for the best – you have too many able & kind friends to advise with – who will be delighted to advise you – I have written to Sabine Brown Parry Richardson Ross and in fact to every one whom I thought it was most desirable for your sake & mine to do so to Eleanor & Sophy I have also written – more I fear I cannot do – indeed as the day is advancing I begin to be anxious about getting all my letters safely on board the Rattler – for this opportunity lost I have none other.

Let me now assure you my dearest Jane that I am now amply provided with every requisite for my voyage and that I am entering on my voyage comforted with every hope of Gods merciful guidance & protection and especially that he will bless and comfort & protect you my dearest love my very dear Eleanor and dear Sophy – and all my other relatives – Oh how I wish I could write to each of them to assure them of the happiness I feel in my officers my crew & in my ship.

I shall not fail to write by any ship we may meet & very fully by the Transport when she returns. Again I remind you that I return you the Deeds signed by me but whether fully or not you must consult Simpkinson again before you transmit that one which has to go to Elliot at Peterborough. By the way I think Colonel Sabine could find whether the Minister Mr Bloomfield has as yet left his Father Lord Bloomfield at

Woolwich, if not he would put you into the way of sending the deed or letter out. Give my affectionate regard to your father & sisters & your Aunt and to your nieces in Bedford Place to whom it is quite impossible to write & thank them for their presents – now my dearest wife I pray that God may bless & preserve you through His infinite mercy & love. To his almighty protection I again commit you & I pray you may ever keep him in sincerity & truth

Your affectionate husband
John Franklin

117. ALEXANDER WILSON TO SARAH WILSON [WIFE],
1–2 JUNE 1845

Sunday June 1st

Dear Wife

I take up my pen to write to you in this place knowing I cant send you another letter fore a good while so now I embrace this opportunity

I hoop you got the last letter I sent you from Aldbrough we have had nothing but contrary winds since we left and the wind has set in from the west we might be here untill the wind changes but it is quite uncertain Dear Wife I Fulley expected a letter here for me when I arrived but I hoop I will get one tomorrow from you Dear Wife I hoop the children is quite well and I hoop Sarahs face has got better and I hoop you send them to [s]chool regular Dear Sarah I hoop you will make yourself as comfortable as possible fore I think we will be verrey comfortable on board here and if it is Gods wills that we should meet again I shall stoop on shore and never go to Sea and lieve you again but Dear Wife you know that I have three Dear Childeren to provide fore and it might be the means of me getting something on shore but I can do at sea as well as aney one but I dont like to be parted from my dear childeren but Dear Wife earnest industerey in your side while I am away and you may depend upon me we will be comfortable when I come home again and I hoop Dear Wife you will go to a place of worship as often as you can and put your trust in the Lord fore their is no comfort niether in this world nor in the world to come fore life is but a span compared with eternity so I comend you and my Dear childeren to the trust of the Almighty with my vervent prayers fore you hooping that we will be able to meet for to lead a good religious life together and if it is Gods wills that we should not meet again I hoop we will meet in heaven their to enjoy life ever lasting so Dear Sarah dont fret about me when I am away nor mind what people tells you for the Lord will be as mercifull to me where I am going as If I had stooped at home Dear Wife every night i lay down in my hammock I offer up a silent prayer for you and my dear childeren and I hoop Dear Wife you Do the same fore their is nothing Done but under his Almighty influence Dear Wife I know this voiage will be a severe trial fore us all but there is every thing here to make us comfortable Dear Wife you may tell Heaton that Handfords jacket lining has got riped and the leather has not been sowed at all onley stuck in and not stiched at all in which it is a great shame fore he got the best price for every thing John Handford got a letter last night from home his mother arrived safe home and they was going to write to you

Walker and all of the mess is quite well their is a good maney sick since we came away but it is with their own bringing on tell Ann that I was verrey sorrey that I could not ask he[r] on board that day we was going away but I hoop I will have the pleasure to ask her when I come back give my kind respects to Mrs Meirifield and Mr Tolpin and Edward and also to Elisabeth and Ann and all enquiring friends and when you write to aney of our friends tell them I left my best wishes with them all give my respects to Spraggon when he comes home and like wise to elisabeth and Isabella and both of my cousans if they correspond with you Dear Wife I hoop you will tend to what I told you in my last letter and take things as comfortable as you can fore earnest industry will surpass all difficulties so I have given you a good long letter for the last in lieving therefore I conclude wishing that we may live to meet again to sit down together and never to be parted untill death give my Dear Childeren a thousand kisses fore me and hoopin that I will return and help them all so no mor from your dear and loving Husband Alexander Wilson so good bye good bye god bless you all

[postscript]

Monday Night my Dear Wife I have not riccieved a letter from you yet and we are going to sail in the morning

So good bye good bye but if you have sent a one perhaps it will follow us and if it does not return to you you may be sure I have got it good bye and god bless you

118. JOHN IRVING TO CATHERINE IRVING
[SISTER-IN-LAW], 2 JUNE 1845

H.M.S. "Terror," Stromness, Orkney,
Monday, 2ᵈ June 1845.

My dear K., – I suppose you know we left the Thames this day fort-night. On our way to the north we have had a bad passage, getting here only on Saturday night. We had steamers to tow us, but off the coast of Suffolk it blew so hard that we had to anchor. We then got separated, and got here as we best could, it being our appointed rendezvous. The steamers came here, two days before us, looking for us, and then went back to Aberdeen and picked us up off there.

We start again to-morrow, having watered and repaired some damages, also replenished our live- stock on board the transport, four of the oxen having died from the weather and pitching of the vessel.

The Orkney people are very kind, and think they cannot be too civil to us. We made a great show in the harbour of Stromness, – two men-of-war steamers, our two ships, and the transport. The third steamer was obliged to return, having suffered considerable damage at the beginning. We are all well and in good spirits; and, I believe, notwithstanding our delay, we shall be in Baffin's Bay quite soon enough for the clearing away of the ice, which does not break up before July. I shall write you by the transport when she leaves us, as that will be the last opportunity of writing for a long time.

We have had very fine weather for the last six days, and it looks likely to last, and afford us a good passage to Greenland. This is of some impor-tance on account of the cattle and sheep on board the transport, as we can get no further supplies after leaving this place. We are commanded by a fine old fellow, of whom you have read, I daresay, eating his own boots – Sir John Franklin; and I have no doubt he will persevere this time also. By the time you get this we shall be far off on the wide Atlantic. By the end of September you may expect to hear from me by the transport. Till then fare-well, my dear Katie. My kindest love to Lewie.– Your affectionate brother,

John Irving.

Tuesday morning. – We are off Stromness now, and I send this on shore by the Orkney pilot, who is about to leave us. The steamers accompany us a hundred miles further. Farewell for a couple of months more.

119. HARRY GOODSIR TO JOHN GOODSIR [BROTHER], 2 JUNE 1845

H.M.S. Erebus
Stromness
June 2ᵈ. 1845

My Dear John

I am sorry I did not write you from Aldborough during the time we were detained there so that I might have had an opportunity of hearing from you as we touched here. We have been 10 days in reaching this from Aldborough so that we only start tonight so that there was abundance of time to get a letter. The letter from my Father had been lying for me here for some days apparently.

I have been very busy for the last few days with the paper for you but am afraid in spite of all my exertions that it will not reach you in anything like a perfect state You will get with this however the drawings arranged & a full description of plates along with what is perfect of the manuscript & the rest I can send by the Transport. You can have no idea of the time which is taken up getting things ready & in a fit state for working, in consequence of which the greater part of my time is taken up.

We have been dining on board the Rattler today a thing which I was very much annoyed at seeing we have so little time to spare, but as it was a particular request that the Gun Room Officers should do so it could not be avoided, since going on board I have heard that we are to sail tomorrow morning early & the Rattler & Blazer Steamers tow us out 100 miles or so on our way. I will therefore send the paper drawings &c all home to you by that opportunity. The former vessel sails for Leith to take in coal so they will be taken to you direct & delivered by the Surgeon whom I hope you will attend to. His name is Chambers & he is apparently a very nice fellow – I told him that you would be very happy to show him the Museum or any other thing in that way. His assistant whose name is Crowner will call with him also. I went to the town last night & met Baillie Robertson who knows you on speaking to him about the Voyages which have been attempted he was anxious to procure a paper which I spoke to him about which I said you might be able to get for him it is a short chronological account of the North West Passages published in the last no. of the Nautical Magazine & sold separately (6d) I wrote to my Father by this opportunity. It gives me great pleasure to hear of the success of all your proceedings & hope that every thing will continue to go on in a like manner with you all. With regard to the prospects of my own success I am very sanguine. All the Officers are very ready & willing to assist & Fairholme our 3^d Lieutenant is very much interested. He is a nephew of Lord Forbes. My only fear is the want of proper accommodation but as soon as we commence proceedings we will be well off. I have no doubt Sir John Franklin will do every thing to assist. Love to all at home hoping we shall all meet again in good health With regard to money matters I must let you know all my proceedings in London by next letter from Rattler.

Believe me in haste Your affectionate Brother
                    Harry D. S. Goodsir

5

Stromness to Greenland

Now we <u>are</u> off at last ...

James Fitzjames

Stromness, on the "mainland" of the Orkney Islands, stood as the very last stage of the ships' progress before the steamers were to part ways and the expedition set forth on what was, to many aboard, the first real leg of their voyage to the Arctic. The departure of the steamers, after a farewell dinner, made an enormous mark on the crews' minds. For Charles Hamilton Osmer, purser of the *Erebus*, it was a moment never to be forgotten: "The exciting and hearty cheers which we received on that day when the Rattler and the Blazer parted company are still ringing in my ears – never no never shall I forget the emotion called forth by the deafening cheering when the above steamers left us, the suffocating jab of delight mingled with the fearful anticipation of the dreary void that would accompany us for <u>months</u>, nay perhaps years, until we again claimed such a <u>welcome</u> instead of a <u>farewell</u>."

Stromness also marked the last definite opportunity for the men to receive mail. Given the development of faster carriage routes on tar-and-gravel roadways, the expansion of railways, and coastal steam packets, it was certainly likely that – by 1845 – a letter mailed from London to a town such as Stromness could have reached its destination in four or five days, far faster than the two weeks it had taken the *Erebus* and *Terror* to reach that point. James Reid, in Letter 121 dated 3 June, mentions receiving two letters from his wife posted on 29 and 30 [May], and since the first of June was a Sunday, they were likely delivered on the second, the latter having been posted from Aberdeen just three days earlier.

This period saw an increasing number of "serial" letters, in which the men added new days' entries to letters they had already begun; such was the nature of "at sea" correspondence. James Fitzjames, of course, was the champion of these, and his is the most detailed accounting of this part of the voyage, extending from 6 to 24 June (Letters 134 and 135).

With some serial letters, we have broken them up so that the parts adjoin single-day letters from others, but here we give his account in two long sections, with the last of his many verbal sketches of his shipmates and the scenery. His accounts of the shortcomings of some of his fellow officers – such as Goodsir's underbite and protruding lip – were seen as unkind, and excised by the Coninghams in their published version of his journal; today, a hundred and seventy-seven years later, that little detail about his chin has proven helpful in identifying the skeleton now believed to be his.

Goodsir, among others, was still concerned with matters back home, principally financial ones, though he also took care that his drawings of specimens, as well as a draft of a scientific article, were sent back. He and James Reid, the ice master of the *Erebus*, found themselves in neighbouring cabins and soon became fast friends, as both their letters attest. And, inevitably, the minds of many turned to the perils ahead and the question of what route should be taken. Everyone seems to have had his own idea, and Franklin's gift as a commander appears to be that he gave each of his officers the sense that he was confiding his innermost thoughts to them; Osmer in particular seems to have been convinced that only he was privy to the truth. And yet even for those with no notion of its details, with the commencement of their most essential endeavour so very nearly at hand, their thoughts seemed most earnestly tuned to the possibilities yet to come.

CHRONOLOGY

3 June 1845: The ships depart Stromness (Letter 117, 120); *Rattler* tows *Erebus* and *Terror*; *Blazer* tows the *Barretto Junior* (Letter 130)

3 June 1845: The ships pass the Stack Rock (Letter 129)

4 June 1845: The ships are 80 miles to the west of Stromness, near Barra and Rona (modern Sula Sgeir and North Rona); *Rattler* and *Blazer* part company (Letter 132)

12 June 1845: The ships are within 60 miles of Iceland "almost in sight of Iceland" (Letters 134, 141, 159)

19 June 1845: The ships are 140–150 miles due east of Cape Farewell (Letter 134)

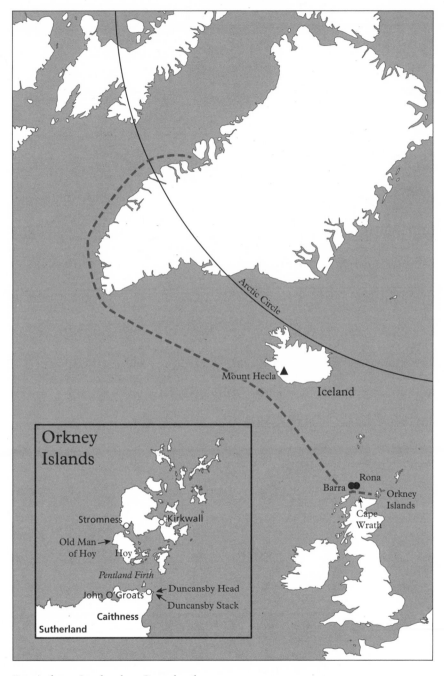

Route from Scotland to Greenland

22 June 1845: The ships reach Cape Farewell (Letter 137)

25 June 1845: The ships "made the coast of Greenland" near
Lichtenfels (Letter 158)

120. JAMES FITZJAMES TO JOHN BARROW JR, 3 JUNE 1845

Dear Barrow

More postage to pay for I have no <u>heads</u> but I think you will like the latest intelligence from me.

We left Stromness this morning early and the two steamers a giving us a good offing before they finally leave us.

All are well as ever and as sanguine.

I hope you have got my notes and letters & that you have been able to make them out – for I have been in a great hurry <u>always</u> this is of <u>course</u> the last letter you will have till the Transport leaves us –

Write on speck to Panama & the Sandwich Islands every six month –
      God bless you
            Ever yours
            James Fitzjames
Erebus 3ᵈ. June
Off the North Coast of Scotland

121. JAMES REID TO ANN REID [WIFE], 3 JUNE 1845

Stromness 3 June 1845

Loving wife

I received yours of the 29 & 30 – Happy to here that you and my Dear young ones is well as this leaves me the same, we are now under way. The Steam Boats is to tow both Ships clear of the Land.

You mention that your old Gray Hare wase not worth the sending to me, I cane only tell you that your old gray Hare is as good to me as ever, and I would [have] been very Happy if you hade inclosed one Lock of it.

I am quite surprised you have never Received my Likeness, the man's Address is as follows, and you will write him – Mr. Beard's Process of Photography 85 King William Street, City <u>London</u>. he told me he would send by Post free of expence. I hope you have Received is before this comes to Hand. I am surprised you never mention if you Received the money I sent through the Bank, but surlay you have Received it be so good and write Aunty Edger tell her I would write her from this but I dount know her adress. I have nothing more to say worth mentioning. I am Quite Happy with Sir John & all the officers Good biy Take care of your self keep your Hart up may the Lord bee with you and all the family. We have Divine Service every sunday Performed by Sir John Franklin. he is a fine old man, his age is 65 years I am Glade John is shipped again, if he is spaired he will make a good Seaman. William will bee in about the 10 July – I would Liket to seen him [if] he is an[d] I hope and trust will Look after you, I hope Alexandrina hase Received her Summers froke.

> Remains,
> Your Loving warm Harted
> Husband
> James Reid

P.S. I hope James will Turn his wages and doo good. If I thought he wood I would be Happy tell him this when you write him.

J.R.

I will write you by the Transport from S.E. Bay and by the Whalers, so goodby again.

JR

122. JOHN FRANKLIN TO JAMES CLARK ROSS, 3 JUNE 1845

> HMS Erebus 3 June 1845
> At sea West of Stromness
> 25 miles

My dear Ross

One more line before the Rattler leaves us to say God Bless you, Lady Ross & the Heir, – and reward you abundantly for your many kindnesses to me in the equipment of this Expedition I wish especially also to thank you for your last heartfelt note written at my wifes lodgings –

I can say no more than again to commit you and yours to the divine blessing – I feel confident of your seeing my dear wife & child as often as you can and that they will always have a sincere friend in you and in Lady Ross

Crozier is well following us as yet in tow of the Rattler,
Ever most faithfully yours
    John Franklin

123. JOHN FRANKLIN TO ELEANOR FRANKLIN [DAUGHTER], 3 JUNE 1845

HMS. Erebus at Sea
20 miles west of Stromness
3rd June 1845

My dearest Eleanor

I rejoice that our western voyage commences on your Birth-Day – another favourable omen I trust!

I am happy at having the opportunity of writing to you on this day and in assuring you that my fervent prayers have been offered to the Almighty on your behalf, and my thanksgiving for the manifold mercies you have received at his hands – nor have I omitted to approach the throne of Grace on behalf of him who is so dear to you & to me. I have written a long letter to him which I now send with others for VDL to your Mama, as she is so desirous to see what I write. My ardent desire is in this as in every other respect to meet her wishes. I am sure my dearest Eleanor that you feel the same desire of meeting and anticipating her wishes –

It is this assurance of your affection for her & of my dearest wishes for you that gives me such comfort. I am persuaded that you will continue to seek & pray for each others welfare –

May the Almighty bless you both in these holy purposes and Graciously preserve you in safety & me also so that we may [have] the happiness of meeting together in Peace & Comfort.

I have many letters to complete & despatches to be closed up which I wish to do now & send off to the Rattler while the wind is light – for if a breeze springs up we may lose the Conveyance –

We are all happy and in good spirits – this perhaps either Captain Smith or Captain Stanley may have the opportunity of telling you personally – for I shall request both if they can to call upon your Mama –

I have received all the letters to the 29th May – and thank you for them but cannot enter into details –

Believe me, my dearest child,
       Your affectionate Father

             John Franklin

124. JOHN FRANKLIN TO SOPHIA CRACROFT [NIECE], 3 JUNE 1845

HMS Erebus at Sea
20 miles west of Stromness
3rd June 1845

My dearest Sophy,

I heartily thank you for all your affectionate notes which I have had the happiness of receiving with regularity up to the 29th May –

I have far too much to engage my attention at the present time to answer them with anything like equal regularity – but I shall read them over again with pleasure as we advance to the westward and reply to them by the Transport – We are drawing off the land being towed by the Rattler – which ship as well as the Blazer I shall retain till we are in a position from which we can make sail alone & get to the West – But as the wind is now light I feel it of the utmost importance to get my letters & despatches delivered into the charge of Captain Smith of the Rattler – I requested of him if you are still at Blackheath to call & see your Aunt & you – or if you be at Bedford Place –

He also takes charge of your Aunts letters –

I rejoice at Mr Lacys safe arrival with his children – pray express my regret that I am leaving England without becoming acquainted with him –

I have written to Tom and to many other friends in VDL – the letters I now send – and I have really not time now to do more – indeed I write in fear that I must cut short my letter to your Aunt – I would have written to Gregson – but I cannot, nor can I write more to Gunn – Lieutenant Dayman do me the kindness of writing to Gregson for me & thank him for his explanatory letter which is very satisfactory.

What a state VDL is in, God in mercy protect it from further ruin.

Now my dearest Sophy be assured that you will often occupy my affectionate thoughts and be the subject of my prayers – I know too that my dear Aunt Jane will continue her kindness & affection for you & towards the members of your family during my absence –

I commit you & them to the gracious protection of the Almighty in full assurance of hope that he will protect you and trust that we may in due time meet again and enjoy the domestic circle –

> Ever my dearest Sophy
> Your affectionate Uncle
> John Franklin

I have written to Richardson, Brown Sabine Parry & Ross – I will write to Sellwood if possible.

[note on envelope]

I like the sheets you have sent written very much & feel that I now know all – except the introductory chapter
JF

125. CHARLES OSMER TO ELIZA OSMER [WIFE], 3 JUNE 1845

3rd June 1845 – off the coast of Sutherlandshire 4 o'clock Afternoon, willing that you should hear of our movements to the very last, I now acquaint you that we left our anchorage at Stromness very early this morning and are slowly but still we are progressing on our voyage with no other depressing of spirits than the occasioned by our leaving our friends behind us otherwise our hearts are as light in in anticipation of success. I dine with Sir John Franklin to day with the Captains of the Blazer & Rattler, tis a farewell dinner preparatory to the hearty cheers which will be given from these Vessels & repeated by us immediately preceding our separation from each other.

126. JOHN FRANKLIN TO EDWARD SABINE, 3 JUNE 1845

Captain G W Smith takes charge of my letters for Lady F – whom I have asked to enquire of you where she is – JF

HMS Erebus   3ᵈ June 1845

My dear Sabine

We are now outside of Stromness & making the best of our way in tow of the Rattler till we get beyond the swell which you are aware sets in on this coast with westerly winds.

I have but a moment to thank you & Mrs Sabine for all your great kindnesses to my dear wife & myself – may God reward you for them – I cannot – but I will offer my prayers to God on your behalf – I feel confident you will – both continue your kindnesses to my dear wife & daughter – which is a comfortable thought to me

Most faithfully yours
John Franklin

127. JOHN FRANKLIN TO ROBERT BROWN, 3 JUNE 1845

H.M.S. Erebus 3ʳᵈ June 1845
20 miles west of Stromness

My dear Brown

I cannot lose sight of the British shores without giving you the assurance of my gratitude for your continued friendship to me & your kindness to my dearest wife and daughter and niece. They are the objects of my greatest solicitude but I leave them with confidence in the care of the Almighty, knowing that they possess in yourself, and others most sound friends & advisers.

We left Stromness this morning in tow of the Rattler Steamer the services of which I shall continue as well as those of the Blazer Captain Stanley until we get far enough to the westward to clear the land under sail on either tack. Pray remember me kindly to those friends who may enquire after me, and particularly to Fitton. I recognized his son as I passed the Blazer yesterday, but had not then time to stop, or I should have gone on board expressly to see him. Had I remained at the ẗage today my intention was to have sent for him

I rejoice to find the Pamphlet drawing to its close, the latter manuscript sheets have been sent me, and all the printed ones, so that I feel quite satisfied that I know every part of it except the introductory chapter which I am sure you will manage very well. My accounts from V.D.L. more recent than when I last saw you, are worse and worse. I heartily wish Bicheno had a better prospect of peace & comfort there. May the Lord protect and bless you shall ever be the prayer of your much attached friend

John Franklin

128. FRANCIS CROZIER TO CHARLOTTE CROZIER [SISTER], 3 JUNE 1845

June 3^d 1845

My dear Small

Once more are we on the broad Atlantic with a favourable breeze for Davis Straits – I wrote you a few hurried lines from Scotch coast to say how slowly we had been getting on – Now all is prosperous therefore all in high spirits – Well my dear Sisters, I am happy to say I am most comfortably fixed with my old Servant – the one I had found was too smart for me and I am delighted I got rid of him as I am induced to think he would have been a troublesome fellow if not a great rogue – The one I have knows me and that is a great matter on a voyage of this kind – we had been two days at the Orkneys when I increased my pets by one pig and 12 Fowls – Eggs out of number at 4 d per dozen – You will be glad to know that I like the officers very much – The first Lieutenant is really a very superior fellow – and the Doctor our only married man again a very nice proper man although perhaps we shall never be the same intimate friends as I was with Robertson still I would not wish a better – Small would you believe it I could have got plenty of Whiskey at Stromness very cheap but would not as I find myself so much more comfortable with a little wine that I mean to go on as I have Commenced – I have been eating a Fortfield ham and it is most delicious do tell dear Jane so, how I would have liked to have heard from them once more – however it was arranged otherwise therefore I must be content – Kind Lady Franklin gave me such

a splendid Scotch Muffling shawl or Plaid, she is a dear good woman – Sir John amused some of us the other day in reading from her note her love to Captain Crozier and kind remembrances to the rest of the officers – I regret to find from Sabines note that dear Lady Ross has been poorly and that he is rather uneasy about her – When I last saw him he was not uneasy but I was as I did not like her appearance I had a kind affectionate note from her before I left Small I must say adieu – I will write by Transport – she will be home some time early in August – With kind love to all not forgetting Sally & Sarah believe me Ever
  my dear Sisters yours
   FRMCrozier

129. HARRY GOODSIR TO JOHN GOODSIR [BROTHER],
3 JUNE 1845

Just reported to be off
the Stack Rock

     Erebus
     About 60 miles to the
     North West of Stromness
     2 oclock Tuesday June 3ᵈ. 1845

My Dear John
 The letter which I sent on shore last night by Baillie Robertson was dated a day too late the 3ᵈ. instead of the 2ᵈ. Owing to the roughness of the weather however this will more than likely reach you, before the letters of last night, It will be delivered by Mr. Chambers Surgeon of the Rattler Steam Frigate which is now towing us fairly out from the land & will continue to do so until evening when she leaves us to return to England. As I explained in my letter last night she goes into Leith to take in coal which is very fortunate. I am only able to send you, at present the drawings of the animals & the Description of the Plates but will more than likely have an opportunity, in the course of a few days, by some of the returning whalers, of sending the Descriptive part of the manuscript. As I have mentioned in the margin of the plates, you will get the figs of the animals from Taylor who is going to give them very much reduced in size so you had better ask for the drawings themselves. I said you would look after the Natural History reports untill another could be got if you did not choose to carry them on. I think you should carry them on. Taylor is a good man & was very kind. You will observe some of the observations are good especially with regard to the reproduction of lost parts, if therefore

you think it will do publish what is now sent & the remainder afterwards.

I have got another additional series of observations to make at the request of Captain FitzJames viz a register of the dew point which is to be kept 6 times daily. So you see with my own work my time will be fully occupied. I do not intend to begin work fairly until we part from the Transport for I have to write at Jerdens request – Captain Crozier also has spoken to me about it – a short account of the proceedings of the Expedition till we reach the ice & as I would like it to be well done it will take up a little time. All my letters &c. will be sent home from the [ice] in one parcell so you will have an opportunity of looking over it before Jerden gets it. You are aware that Jerden is the Proprietor & Editor of the Literary Gazette. As we will however be six weeks at the least in getting across to Davis' Straits there will be abundance of time to do any thing which was intended.

In some of my former letters I think I informed you that owing to the expence of outfitting it would be necessary for me to get more money than the pay I had received. My Great fault at first was not getting an agent to draw my pay &c. & upon whom I could draw Bills &c., if we get through. I did apply to one (Messrs. Stilwell & Co. Arundel Street, Strand London) who gave me all I wanted £50 for which I was obliged to Insure my life at the usual rates. But to secure for themselves in case any thing should take place during the voyage I was under the necessity of having a testament made out in which you were made heir & them executors to any pay that would be due. This is a mere form but it was of course necessary to do it. The firm consists of two brothers – both of them apparently very excellent men – if you think it necessary you can write to them. They are well known all over the world as Navy agents. I got introduced to them through a brother of Sir J. Macgregor, with whom Mr. Nasmyth is very intimate. Captain FitzJames has directed letters to be sent him every six months or so, to Panama in South America. Be so good therefore as write & tell the rest of them to do so to that place in a short while i.e. a few months say 2 or 3 or 4 months after this. Every thing is flying helter skelter just now on account of the tremendous swell Our hawsers which are keeping us all in tow are breaking every now & then & our foretopmast has just snapped right through the middle. As I have to write to Forbes yet I will now have to close this for there is little time now to spare.

Believe me
Ever your most Affectionate Brother
Harry D. S. Goodsir

130. JAMES FITZJAMES TO EDWARD SABINE, 3 JUNE 1845

> HMS Erebus off the North
> Coast of Scotland
> 3^d June 1845

My dear Col Sabine

Your note of the 28th, came to Stromness last night and I thank you for it. We left Stromness this morning and are now being towed (with the Terror) by the Rattler – Blazer has got the Transport – and this will go by the steamers when they leave us – which will be this evening when they shall have towed us some 30 miles from the "Old man of Hoy" – I fear however that we are to have a Westerly wind. While at Stromness I took a complete set of observations with Fox, using both deflectors singly & together and the 3 weights you used –

I also with Hodgson took a set of deflections and vibrations with the Terror's Unifilar. The deflections were tolerably satisfactory – the vibrations not quite so. I think I observed that a small bank of sandstone under which the instrument was placed affected the needle.

I am terribly disappointed with my Fox which is <u>rotten</u> – To crown all it is sunk so low in the gimball stand that the sun exactly comes on with the point of the needle at 70° and at 80° I shall not be able to see it so we <u>raise</u> the table and we intend to try the unifilar on it <u>at sea</u>. Crozier has been trying vibrations with Hansteen at sea very well.

I intended writing you a long letter but find I really have not time – this will assure you however that we are all well & happy. All your friends here desire to be remembered to you – will you kindly remember me to Mrs Sabine – and believe me to be

> yours very sincerely
> James Fitzjames

131. JAMES FITZJAMES TO WILLIAM CONINGHAM [BROTHER], 3 JUNE 1845

Dearest William

Here we are at last launched into the wide world of sea & ice – we left Stromness early this morning – and the Steamers are giving us a good offing before finally leaving us – I hope you have received all my notes & letters

All goes on as well as I could wish

The wind is at present variable and I much fear we shall have it from the Westward however all say that if we are in Baffin's Bay by the 1st. week in July we shall be in plenty of time – and as the distance to Cape Farewell is only some 1100 miles – there is every chance of our doing it by that time, three weeks would be a long passage –

Stromness is a curious quiet primitive place but I saw nought of it as I was busy the whole time –

I have nothing more to say, but to give you the latest tidings With best love to Elizabeth –

believe me ever

Your Affectionate

James Fitzjames

Erebus

3d June –

off the North Coast of Scotland –

Write on speck to Panama & the Sandwich Islands every now and then. I maynt get them but I <u>may</u>

132. JAMES REID TO ANN REID [WIFE], 4 JUNE 1845

Barra & Ronna, about 80 miles to
the west of Stromness, June <u>4/45</u>

Loving wife

This day the Steam Boats, H.M. Rattler & Brazier is to take there Departure from us, and I have taken the opportunity of Droping you a few Lines, acquainting you that I am still Enjoying Good helth thanks bee to God for it. Hopes it will find you & my Dear Little young ones the Same. I have nothing strang[e] to say as I wrote you yesterdy by the Pilot, but I know you will bee Glade when you Receive it, it will bee some Time before you can expect another – So I bid you Good biy. Take care of your self For Gods sake, you will Receive the Half pay Quite Regular when it comes due but it will bee some time yet, paible at the Custom House. I sent you the mans adress that took my Likeness & I send it in this, in case my last bee Miscarried, Mr. Beards Process of Photography At No. 85 King William Str. City London. – we have two Doctors, the 2d one is from Fife Shire a fine young man, him & I is Quite chief his berth is next my one he never wase at sea before and he is very fond of my old yarns. – our 3^d lieutenant is from About Berwick, hase a num[ber] of Friends about Aberdeen a very fine young man His name is Mr. Fairom. On the whole I think I will bee Happy. The 1st lieutenant cales me his Joly Old Hero he is a Good Seaman, & so is Captain Fitz James, he is a fine man he is next to Sir John Franklin. May God bee with you, <u>all</u>

Remains
Your Loving Husband
James Reid

P.S. beesure and write Aunty at Liverpool I would have wrote her but I have no address to her, I have inclosed a few lines to William.

J.R.

[on the envelope] you can forward it to him

133. JAMES FITZJAMES TO ELIZABETH CONINGHAM [SISTER-IN-LAW], 4 JUNE 1845

My dearest Elizabeth

Although I wrote to William only yesterday and sent the letter on board the Rattler fearing a gale should come on before we parted and so prevent my writing – you will I am sure be glad to have a few lines though only a day later, and full of similar nothings

I write this off the island of Rona, 70 miles from Stromness – we have a good breeze not quite in our teeth – but rather foul – it seems inclined however to veer to S.W. we have rather much of a swell – but fine clear weather – the Steamers leave us to day at noon – and you will not hear again till the return of the Transport in about three months.

I do think that I am not fitted for what is called Society – I mean tea & bread & butter Society of a humbugging world – and that I am much better in a portion of the sort I now occupy – than going into the said humbugging world.

I was however very happy with you & William & shall look for a similar period of happiness on my return though I hope I shall have a little less exciting worry at the Admiralty – To shew you how really happy I am I send you what I d'ont want my self and d'ont think you do – but I may want when I come back, so beg you will keep it for me.

I have written occasionally both to yourself and William and I believe got all your notes, as far as it was possible – the last I had was from him dated at Ghent 14th. in which he says "Tomorrow I shall write from the Hague – this I did not get but if he sent it to John Barrow, it will doubtless go to Stromness, where he knows we are going –

You are by this time I doubt not with the children and Minney will have told you how she saw the Erebus and Terror sail – I hope you and William did not disapprove of my getting them down to Woolwich – it was a great pleasure to me –

I love those two children as much as I think it possible I could ever love any of my own – in fact I <u>now</u> think more so – but suppose this cannot be in reality true, and I really do think I have no other wish in this world but to see you and dear William happy – (barring getting through the N W passage)

I leave England with the most intense consciousness of affection for both of you – each for your own sake, and for the sake of the other, and I hope and <u>believe</u> you are both aware of this.

So then I will finish for the present at least, hoping God may bless and preserve you for the happiness of him who I know appreciates you and loves you as you deserve to be loved –

I need not I know tell you to think sometimes, when you are enjoying yourselves of your affectionately attached friend
James Fitzjames

11 Am. the wind since I began writing <u>has</u> veered to SW. So we are going on our course –
With love to the dear children – William and yourself – I am as ever
Your attentive friend
James Fitzjames

HMS Erebus
4th. June
off Rona Island

134. JAMES FITZJAMES TO ELIZABETH CONINGHAM
[SISTER-IN-LAW], 5–25 JUNE 1845

HMS Erebus, at sea, 5th June 1845

My dearest Elizabeth
You appeared very anxious that I should keep a journal for your especial perusal – Now, I do keep a journal such as it is which will be

given to the Admiralty; But, to please you, however I shall note down from time to time such things as may strike me – and in so doing I shall feel a real pleasure – Either in the form of a letter, or in any other that may at the time suit my fancy – I shall probably never read over what I may have written, so you will excuse inaccuracies. I commence tonight, because I am in a good humour – every one is shaking hands with himself. We have a fair wind, actually going 7 knots, sea tolerably smooth, though we <u>do</u> roll a <u>little</u> – but this ship has the happy facility of being very steady below while on deck she appears to be plunging & rolling greatly. Our Latitude is now about 60° 0' Longitude 9° 30' – so you will find out our "whereabouts". The steamers Rattler & Blazer, left us at noon yesterday near the island of Rona, 70 or 80 miles from Stromness. Their Captains came on board & took our letters – one from me will have told you of our doings up to that time – there was a heavy swell – and wind from NW; but it began veering to West & SW – which is fair. The steamers then ranged up alongside us, one on each side, as close as possible without touching, and with the whole force of lungs of officers & men, gave us (not three) but a prolongation of cheers to which of course we responded – having done the same to the Terror – away they went, and in an hour or two were out of sight, leaving us with an old gull or two and the rocky Rona to look at – and then was the time to see if any one flinched from the undertaking – Every one's cry was, Now we <u>are</u> off at last no lingering look was cast behind – we drank Lady Franklin's health at the old gentleman's table. & it being his daughter's birthday – hers too – but the wind, which had become fair as the steamers left, as if to give the latest best news of us – in the evening became foul from N.W. and we were going Northward instead of Westward. The sky was clear. the air bracing & exhilarating. I had had a slight attack of agueish headache the evening before – but am now clear headed, and I went to bed thinking of you and dear William, whose portrait is now looking at me. for I am writing at the little table you will see in the Illustrated London [News], only you must imagine that the said table is 3 feet long, or from the bed to the door. and the picture just looks down at me – as I said I went to bed and read all your last letters & William's –

This morning we began to have a fair wind, before the day was half over it was right aft. Terror is coming after us. the Transport sailing close to us with as little sail as possible – for she could run us out of sight if she chose – only they fear the ice doubtless, not being built to shake it away. In our mess we have the following whom I shall probably from time to time give you descriptions of –

First Lieutenant	Gore – and his black labrador dog.	
Second —	Le Vesconte	Mate — Sargent,
Third —	Fairholme	„ Des Vœux
Purser —	Osmar	„ Couch
Surgeon —	Stanley	Second Master – Collins .
Assistant Surgeon	– Goodsir	Commander, you know
Ice Master so called	– Reid	better than he does himself

The most original character of all. rough, intelligent, unpolished, with a broad North Country accent, but not vulgar – good humored, & honest hearted – is <u>Reid</u> – a Greenland whaler – native of Aberdeen – who has commanded whaling vessels. & amuses us with his quaint remarks & descriptions of the ice – catching whales &c. – For instance – he just said to me, on my saying we should soon be off Cape Farewell at this rate, & asking if one might not generally expect a gale off it (Cape Farewell being the south Point of Greenland). "Ah! Now, <u>Mister Gems.</u> we'll be having the weather fine Sir! Fine! – No ice at <u>arl</u> about it Sir, unless it be the <u>bergs</u> – arl the ice'll be gone Sir only the bergs which I like to see. Let it come on to <u>blow</u> look out for a big'un. Get under his lee. and hold on to him fast Sir fast if he drifts too near the land – why he grounds afore you do!" I think the idea of <u>all</u> the ice being gone except the icebergs, is rich beyond description. I have just had a game of chess (with <u>the</u> big men) with the Purser, Osmar, who is delightful. he was with Beechey in the Blossom when they went to Behrings Straits to look for Franklin at the time he surveyed the North coast of America, and got within 150 miles of them – he was at Petro Paulovski, in Kamschatka, where I hope to go – and served since on the lakes of Canada. I was at first inclined to think he was a stupid old man because he had a chin and took snuff – but he is as merry hearted as any young man, full of quaint dry say-ings – always good humored, always laughing – never a bore, takes his "pinch after dinner" – plays "a rubber," and beats me at chess – and, he is a <u>gentleman</u>.

The second master Collins is the very essence of good nature, and I may say good humour – but he is <u>mad</u>, I am sure – for he squints to him-self with a painful expression of countenance when he is thinking – (or thinking of nothing) and I can get no work out of him, though ever so willing he may be – yet he is not a bore nor a nuisance – but a nonentity. we might be as well without him – We intend however to make some-thing of him – and now, good night, it is past 11 o'clock – I have written without stopping – all with the porcupine quill – God bless you!

<u>Friday 6th</u>. Today Sir John Franklin shewed me such part of his instructions as related to the main purposes of our voyage, and the necessity of observing everything from a flea to a whale in the unknown regions we are to visit – He also told me I was specially charged with the magnetic observations – He then told all the officers that he was desired to claim all their remarks, journals, sketches &c., on our return to England. and read us some part of his instructions to the officers of the Trent – the 1st vessel he commanded in 1818 with Captain Buchan on an attempt to reach the North Pole – pointing out how desirable it is to note every thing – and give ones individual opinion on it – He spoke delightfully of the zealous co-operation he expected from all and his desire to do full justice to the exertions of each.

Today has been a gloomy day, as far as sunshine is concerned, and the wind has drawn round to the Northward, though so little of it, that the old Erebus cannot keep her head the right way – or, as we term it, she "falls off" with the roll of the sea. 7 or 8 large grampusses came shooting past us to the s.w., which Mr. Goodsir declared were delightful animals – last evening a shoal of porpoises were bounding about the bows of the vessel as she plunged into the sea – and a bird called a mollimauk, a sort of peterel which all the arctic people look for as a sign of going towards the icy regions -

At dinner to day Sir John gave us a pleasant account of his expectations of being able to get through the ice on to the coast of America – and his disbelief in the idea that there is open sea to the Northward. he also said he believed it to be possible to reach the Pole over the ice – by wintering at Spitzbergen and going in the spring before the ice broke up and drifted to the south – as it did with <u>Parry on it</u> – I employed myself nearly all day working the observations I made at Stromness, – finished them, bullied the second master about the ship's log which is badly written and which he is to <u>re</u>write by Sunday. Played a game at chess with Couch & beat him, but ought to have lost – Went on deck, found a dead calm. Shall have fair wind tomorrow. remembered we had no congreve rockets to shoot whales with – wrote this page or rather sheet – and commence reading & to bed.

6th towards midnight

I can't make out why Scotch men just caught always speak in a low hesitating monotonous tone of voice which is not at all times to be understood – this is, I believe, called "canny"ness. Mr. Goodsir is "canny". his upper lip projects beyond his lower & his lower beyond his chin producing a gradation thus ⌇ but a whisker comes down beyond the chin so you imagine there is more of it. he is long & straight (like a yard of pumpwater) and walks upright on his toes, with his hands tucked up in each jacket pocket. He is perfectly good humoured – very well informed on general points – in Natural History learned – was Curator of the Edinburgh Museum – appears to be of about 28 years of age – laughs delightfully, cannot be in a passion – is enthusiastic about all 'ologies – draws the insides of microscopic animals with an imaginary pointed pencil – catches phenomenas in a bucket. looks at the thermometer & every other o'meter – is a pleasant companion & an accquisition to the mess. So much for Mr. Goodsir.

Saturday 7th. 11 p.m. – Pitching heavily – breeze increasing from w.n.w. It came on us as the Sun was thinking of setting at about 9 – in the form of a bank, behind which he vanished; & then rose in the form of an arch & I expected wind but having overspread the sky it settled into a steadily increasing breeze – Barometer rising as rapidly as it fell – and I have been prognosticating a sort of gale in consequence – It was calm all last night, cloudy all to day (except in the evening for two hours). Passed the day in working & making observations when the sun did peep out – with Le Vesconte. There is nothing in this day's journal that will interest or amuse you, at all events, and I am not in a humour for describing any more messmates.

Sunday 8th. I like a man who is in earnest – Sir John Franklin read the Church Service to day and a sermon so very beautifully that I defy any man not to feel the force of what he would convey – The first Sunday he read was a day or two before we sailed, when Lady Franklin his daughter, & niece attended. Every one was struck with his extreme earnestness of manner – evidently proceeding from real conviction. He dined with us to day – and at 7 had the evening Service in his cabin for the benefit of those whose watch on deck prevented them being present in the morning. I say the benefit because I am sure every one derives benefit from the earnest supplications of a good man. Those officers who felt inclined attended. – I read the lessons on these occasions –

We had a heavy sea & stiff breeze to day; but it moderated at 4 o'clock, and the sun came out clear and beautiful – In Latitude 62°, at 9 o'clock this evening we tacked (if you know what that is) and stood to the South West. – We saw a ship from Peterhead to day – The meeting at prayers in Sir John's Cabin this evening brought to my mind the day when we went to Hampstead (I think it was) and William read the day's service in a gravel pit – Believe me now when I say that I <u>do pray</u> for you both – God bless you & him.

Monday 9th –

Tuesday 10th I was beginning to write last night – but the ship was tumbling about to such an extent I went to bed and had to turn out again immediately & get the Topsails reefed, as it blew very hard in squalls – The ship pitched about as much as I ever saw any vessel – but still very <u>easily</u> – Read says he does not like to see the wind "seeking a corner to blow into" a cute idea I think for viariable gusts. I worked observations all yesterday – and to day took a number on deck – the weather moderated this morning & all day we have had little wind & tolerably smooth sea – a clear, fine sunset at a ¼ to 10, and Goodsir examining "molusca" in a m<u>ee</u>croscope – He is in extacies about a bag full of blubber like looking stuff, which he has just hauled up in a net, & which turns out to be whales' food & other animals. I have been reading Sir John Franklin's vindication of his Government of Van Diemen's Land, which was to come out a week or two after we sailed. He has ready all the sheets – he cuts up Lord Stanley <u>a few</u>, & says he is a haughty imperious snob.

Here ends I find my third sheet – so if you d'ont like your <u>letter</u> thus far, pray d'ont read the following which I <u>intend</u> to write – There is nothing to interest you now. and we are not far on our journey. So I wind up this and call it a letter, just for the sake of adding that I am as ever your most affectionate friend James Fitzjames

More of the 10th Couch is a little bullet-headed – blackhaired – smooth-faced lump of inanity – good humored however in his own way – writes, reads, works, draws – all <u>quietly</u>. is never in the way of anybody – and always ready when wanted – but I can find no remarkable point in his character – except perhaps that he is I should think obstinate. Stanley, the surgeon I knew in China. he was in Cornwallis a short time, where worked very hard in his vocation – Is rather inclined to be good looking – but is fat or flabby as if from drinking beer. jet black hair – very white hands – which are always abominably <u>clean</u>, with the shirt sleeves tucked up – giving one unpleasant ideas that he would not mind cutting one's leg off immediately –"if not sooner." He is what is called a "good fellow" – inclined to be coarse if it was the <u>fashion</u> – is vulgar to a certain extent – but thoroughly good natured and obliging – and very attentive to our mess. – Le Vesconte you know. He improves if anything on closer accquaintance. Fairholme you know – or may have seen – is a most agreeable companion & a well-informed man. Sargent – a nice pleasant-looking lad, <u>very</u> good natured. But no energy of character, and I fear not <u>too</u> much sense, but fortunately does not (as is usual in such cases) fancy himself very clever. Des Vœux I knew in Cornwallis – he went out in her to join Endymion, & was then a mere boy. he is now a most unexceptionable – clever agreeable – light-hearted – obliging young fellow, and a great favorite of Hodgson's which is much in his favour besides.

Graham Gore the 1ˢᵗ lieutenant – a man of great stability of character, a <u>very</u> good officer and the sweetest of tempers – is not so much a man of the world as Fairholme or Des Vœux, is more of Le Vesconte's style without his shyness. He plays the flute dreadfully well, draws sometimes very well, sometimes very badly – but is altogether a capital fellow.

Here ends my catalogue. I d'ont know whether I have managed to convey an impression of our mess. and I hope you know me sufficiently to be sure that I mention their little faults, failings, and peculiarities in all charity – I wish I could, however, convey to you a just idea of the immense stock of good feeling – good humour, & real kindliness of heart in our small mess. we are <u>very</u> happy, and very fond of Sir John Franklin, who improves very much as we come to know more of him – He is anything but nervous or fidgety – in fact I should say remarkable for energetic decision in sudden emergencies – but I should think he is easily persuaded where he has not already formed a strong opinion -

Our men are all fine hearty fellows mostly North country men – with a few "man of war's men". We feared at Stromness some of them "repenting", and it is usual to allow <u>no leave</u> – the Terror didn't. But two men (one of whom I had got from the Belvidera at Portsmouth) wanted to see – one his wife whom he had not seen for 4 years, & the other his mother, whom he had not seen for 17 – and I let them go to Kirkwall, 14 miles off – I also let a man from each mess go on shore to buy provisions for the rest. they <u>all</u> came on board to their leave – but finding we were not going to sea till the following morning, four men (who probably had taken a <u>leetle</u> too much whiskey, amongst whom was the little old man who had not seen his wife for four years) took a small boat that lay alongside & went on shore without leave – their absence was soon discovered and

Fairholme assisted by Baillie somebody or other, soon brought all on board or rather by 3 o'clock in the morning. I firmly believe each <u>intended</u> coming on board (if he had been sober enough). especially the poor man with the wife; who had a man outside the house looking out on the ship in case she got under weigh – but, according to all rules of the service these men should have been severely punished (one method being to stop part of their pay & give it to the constables or others who apprehended them. It struck me however that punishment is intended to prevent misconduct in others, and not to <u>revenge their</u> individual misconduct – men know very well when they <u>are</u> in the wrong. and there is clearly no chance of any repition of the offence till we get to Valparaiso or the Sandwich Islands. So I got up at 4 o'clock, had every body on deck, sent Gore & the Sergeant of marines below – and searched the whole deck for spirits which were thrown overboard – this took two good hours – soon after which we up anchor and made sail out. I said nothing to any of them, they evidently expected a rowing, and the old man with the wife looked very sheepish, & would not look me in the face – but nothing more was said, and the men have behaved not a bit <u>the worse</u> ever since – I d'ont know why I tell you all this – perhaps you w'ont understand half of it – I meant to go to bed when I finished the other sheet; but went to look at some beautiful specimens of crustaceous animals in the microscope, one of which about ¼ of an inch long is an entirely <u>new</u> animal. & has a peacock's tail. Goodsir is drawing it. And now I must really say good night; it is past one o'clock – ask William what reefing Topsails means –

<u>Wednesday 11th – Thursday 12th.</u>

All yesterday it blew very hard, with so much sea that we shipped one or two over the Quarterdeck by which I got a good drenching once. The sea of the most perfect transparency – a beautiful delicate cold looking green, or ultramarine – long rollers, as if carved out of the essence of glass bottles, came rolling towards us; now & then topped with a beautiful pot-of-porter-looking head. At Sun Set the wind moderated & was calm at night. This morning a fair wind till 4 o'clock <u>Pm</u>, when thick fogs blew over at last, and settled this evening into a strong Northerly breeze (fair for us,) by which we are going on at a good rate, with another sea getting up in the opposite direction to the last, & between the two we are rolling somewhat. We are now only 60 miles from Iceland – South of it.

<u>Saturday 14th.</u> – Yesterday I remained in bed till Noon as I did not feel well. I was all right again in the evening. The sea went down much, and

the wind became very light. This morning the wind was quite fair, having been so more or less all night – but instead of having clear weather, as with the NE wind, it came to SE, and brought hard rain & thick fogs all day. We are now however (11 Pm) going 7 ¼ knots in a thick fog with the Terror on one side & Transport on the other, keeping close for fear of losing sight of us. To day we arranged all our books in the mess and find that we have a very capital library – I find the Carpenter's Mate was with me in the Madagascar in 1832. Read still amuses us – he has just told me how to boil salt fish when it is <u>very salt</u>. he saw the steward towing it overboard – & roared out – "What are you <u>mekking</u> faces at there? That's not the way to get the <u>sarlt oout</u>." – It appears, that when it boils it is to be taken off the fire and kept just <u>not</u> boiling. This is Saturday night – Read & Osmar drinking "Sweet hearts & wives" & wanted me to join – I said I had not the one and did not want the other. Good night.

I left off journalizing on Saturday night & find I said something about "sweethearts & wives" – which if you like you may imagine not said – I remember my <u>friend</u> Griffin Commander of the Ganges telling me & Dobbie that we should be taken for great big Mates because we would'nt wear little bits of lace on our shoulders when wearing jackets – the said bits of lace being <u>customary</u> only & not the real uniform. My answer was, that from the specimen I had lately seen, I would rather be taken for a <u>Mate</u> than for a <u>Commander</u> – Mind I <u>d'ont</u> mean to say <u>this</u> to <u>you</u> – From the specimen I have lately seen I d'ont want a wife – now! down paper and grin – because <u>I am</u> laughing, for Read has just said (scratching his head) "Why, mister Gems, you never seem to me to sleep at arl – you're always a <u>writin</u>" I tell him that when I <u>do</u> sleep, I do twice as much as other people in the same time. Now for the journal.

<u>Sunday 15th</u>. Wind fair & strong, with a high sea but we carried on much sail – heeling over much; & we actually fancy we went 9 knots. Early in the morning – In the evening it moderated, and the weather was clear & cool.

Monday 16th Calm day – sea glassy smooth – cloudy weather, no sun – after breakfast I went on board Terror, to see Captain Crozier about my Fox observations. "Fox" being a dipping needle invented by him. Fairholme & Le Vesconte followed in the India rubber boat, which was being tried when you came to Woolwich to bully me. I found them all with the dolefuls on board the Terror – Hodgson had been ill – and they d'ont look happy, but they say they are. – In the night we were going 7 or 8 knots again with a fair wind. Crozier & Little, (1st Lieutenant) dined on

board with Sir John & Griffiths a little sharp hooked nosed Lieutenant
agent for Transport – who is in a great fright about getting near the ice –

Tuesday 17th. The sun shone out a bit & we had a smooth day & not
much swell – air cold. Since the 11th, the thermometer on deck in the
shade has never been above 50° or below 45 night or day; generally
46 or 48 – At night cloudy, with a bright light on the horizon to the NE
which Gore says is Aurora Borealis. Read calls it Ice blink – I say it is
the reflection of sunset, though it is NE. It looks like a large town on fire
20 miles off.

To day 18th We set to work, and got a catalogue made of all our books &
find we have amongst us a most splendid collection – The "Crows Nest"
is up – which is usually a cask lined with canvas at the Fore Topmast head
for a man to stand in to look out for channels in the ice – with us, it is a
sort of canvas cylinder, hooped, and is at the main Topgallant mast head
(if you know where that is.) Read who will have the peculiar privilege of
being perched up there, says it is a very expensive one. I think I have now
written enough nonsense to last a week so shall conclude this sheet with
the sincerest & warmest love of your affectionate James Fitzjames

At Sea Wednesday 18th June 1845 11 pm about 200 miles East of "Cape
Farewell" (Greenland)
My dear Elizabeth,
Nothing has been written for you these last few days – not because I had
nothing to say – or did not think of you and William -, but because, I
have had plenty to do in the writing & calculating way – and because,
somehow or other just as I was beginning to get paper & ink ready (&
the porcupine) I found I was in bed & fell asleep. To day is "Waterloo
day" & we drank the Duke's health at Sir John's table & our own (where
by the bye I have as yet only dined on Sundays) There was a talk before
we left England of a Brevet on this day – if this be true – I think it more
than probable that I shall come in for a share & get what I now seldom
think about, the rank of Captain. With this idea, I took a glass of Brandy
& water at 10 o'clock, which allowing for difference of Longitude,
answers to 7 ½ in London, and drank your healths, in petto – fancying
that you might be drinking mine – In fact, we took an imaginary glass
of wine together – and I d'ont care how soon we may take a real one.

Thursday 19th 12 o'clock at night – I suppose we are 140 or 50 miles
from Cape Farewell – Blowing hard – but not a rough sea, though there
is a swell – when I say blowing hard however I mean fresh – we can carry

much sail & <u>do</u>. I can scarcely manage to get Sir John to shorten sail at all – Still cloudy. at 10 ½ a Bright light appeared in the N.W., which was set down as Aurora But turned out really to be the reflection of sun set. The clouds & mist moved off as if a blanket were being withdrawn, leaving an orange colored clearness underneath in the form of an arch with a well defined dark horizon – which clearness turned out to be a real clear sky – cold looking & fine; – and now this moment the officer of the watch comes to tell me the wind is lighter, and we certainly <u>are</u> <u>quieter</u>. "Shake a reef out, set the Fore Top Gallant sail" (the main being set.) "Call me at six – and if anything happens" "Good night Will" (to his picture), Good night Elizabeth (to yourself)

Tuesday 24th In Davis's Straits. Cape Desolation at noon today bearing East 90 miles, but we ca'nt see it. We have just done with a glorious gale of wind which has been sending us on in grand style – I wrote to [you] last. on Thursday night – and shall sum up from thence – On Friday 20th (and Thursday night also, though I did go bed so quietly) we kicked and plunged and danced in a tremendous manner, the sea running all manner of ways – the day was nearly calm, with a very heavy swell – the ship rolling deeply, something in this way. a number of "bottle noses" a species of whale, about 25 feet long, came dancing about us – their head is very peculiar, & unless they are close so as to see their <u>beak</u> under water one fancies their foreheads are snouts poked up above the water.

This is the shape of its head which it pokes above the water something in this manner. All this night we jumped and danced again with a strong breeze again dead foul for us, which at midnight had turned into a complete gale; the air cold, though thermometer stood fixed at 42°. <u>On Saturday</u> Calm again, and smooth water Shearwaters, Mollimauks & trees with the bark rubbed off by ice, floating about – Sir John at dinner; most amusing with anecdotes of an Indian Chief, whom he met in the journey in which he suffered so much named, I think, Akatcho, who appears to have been a fine character. this evening we got a fair wind going 8 knots with a smooth sea all night.

On Sunday, 22nd. It began to blow hard suddenly at 7 in the morning from East (you must recollect that all this time our course is <u>Westerly</u>.) We struggled through the church service on the lower deck, the ship rolling & tumbling much, the sea curling astern beautifully. – at 9 <u>Pm</u>

we imagined ourselves to be due South of Cape Farewell 60 miles from it

Yesterday the 23^d . – We had the highest sea I think I ever saw; it was
very fine I know nothing finer than a gale of wind particularly when you
are running before it – we had a few seas on our decks – one of which
found its way down on to our table just as we had done dinner – I dined
at our mess to day Sir John finding his guests could not hold on and eat
too – we are packed close, & c'ant move very _far_ – But the good humour
of every one is perfect; and we do dance before it so finely I mean before
the wind. – It rained hard all yesterday & all night – and this morning
a glorious sun & a clear blue air, sent us all up to dry ourselves & our
clothes – we have gradually altered our course, & are now steering due
North. at noon to day Cape Desolation was due _East_ 90 miles, so we
are _in_ Davis' Straits. The sea is now moderately smooth & the wind still
fair – I am writing this at ½ past 10, in broad daylight. Sir John says
that in his voyage to Hudson's Bay he passed the very spot we were on
yesterday, and was sailing through ice – We have as yet seen no ice or
land. the sea is beginning to get colder. the air still at 41° – but to day it
felt delightfully cold.

I fear all this account of sea & air – wind and weather will not amuse
you but I c'ant help it: I must write whatever comes uppermost or not at
all – and at least you will give me credit for the wish to amuse & interest
you and William –

The monkey has however, just put on a blanket frock & trowsers, which
the sailors have made him (or rather her) so I suppose it _is_ getting cold
– adieu for the present –

Wednesday, 25th. – At 1 this morning, I was on deck looking at the West
Coast of Greenland – and an Ice berg – though the land was 40 miles
off, & the berg 6 or 8 – we sailed along it before the wind till Noon, and
the thermometer, when I went on deck had gone down to 39° though it
still keeps at 42° in the day – The Coast of Greenland looks rugged &
sparkling with snow, the shadows & ravines forming deep black marks
– we regret not being a little nearer to see it better – at 8 this morning
one snowy ice berg was to be seen a long way off – I am now writing
at 11 Pm (as usual) Latitude 63° – near about a place marked on the
chart as Lichtenfels – the sea, as the sun set half an hour ago was of the
most delicate blue in the shadows – perfectly calm – so calm that the

Terror's mast heads are reflected close alongside though she is half a mile off – The air is delightfully cool & bracing, and every body is in a good humour either with himself or his neighbours I have been on deck all day taking observations – so has Le Vesconte. Goodsir is catching the most extraordinary animals in a net, & is in ecstacies. Gore & Des Vœux are over the side poking with nets & long poles, with cigars in their mouths, & Osmer laughing – he is really an original & a delightfully dry fellow. Couch turns out a very nice little obstinate chap with short little feet & high boots like John Coninghams. I am really very sleepy & tired but did not like to go to bed without writing on this day, the first in which we have seen Arctic Land. And I remember William saying one day to me "My dear fellow mark my words, none of you will go" Read says, "we shall soon see the Huski-mays", which he says are "<u>vulgarly</u>" called Yaks by the whalers, – & 'Huski's' for shortness.

Thursday 26 – A delightful day we have had quite calm – <u>hot sun</u>. Thermometer 42° – all sorts of beasts being caught in nets – We take turns to fish with a net at the end of a long pole – & bring up most strange animals – Crozier dined on board, & Hodgson came looking very ill – We saw several ice bergs a long way off, which we hoped would come near us; the scenery and rugged peaks of Greenland 20 miles off –

6

Last Partings

... if I am not happy here, I d'ont know where else I could be.

Charles Osmer

As the ships reached their final anchorage within reach of European contact near the settlement of Lievely – today known as Qeqertarsuaq – the volume of letter-writing picked up. For men who knew that it might well be years before they could be in contact again, the moment was a spur to write as much as they could. And, for the first time for many, visits to Danish settlements and encounters with the Inuit there made a powerful impression. There are, in the writings of some of the men, reflections of a regrettable attitude that is offensive today, and ought to have been then – that the Inuit were dirty, poor, and pitiable. Yet others write of the intelligence and resourcefulness of these same people and of their positive impressions on visiting a mission schoolroom. No one, except perhaps Franklin himself, seems to have reflected on the fact that these were the very people on whose goodwill and honesty any hope of rescue – and, when that proved impossible, any hope of the men's fates finally being discovered – rested.

There was also a frenzy at the last opportunity to practise – before it really began to matter – the many routines of scientific observation that the expedition would be expected to perform from then onward. A magnetic observatory was established; Goodsir supervised the collection of specimens, and those with a gift for the pen took it up to sketch the situation of the ships. Fitzjames, in a letter to John Barrow, included a drawing of their current anchorage, along with a key; Le Vesconte made a capable drawing – preserved today at the museum of the Société Jersiaise next to one of his forks. All these, along with the letters, were stuffed into the final mailbag for each vessel, which was then placed into the hands of each ship's pursers to be taken aboard the *Barretto Junior*. Osmer, ever the resourceful man, took advantage of this circumstance to stuff in one last note of his own – the copy at the Scott Polar Research Institute adds a note, in another hand: "This was the very last letter from the Ships."

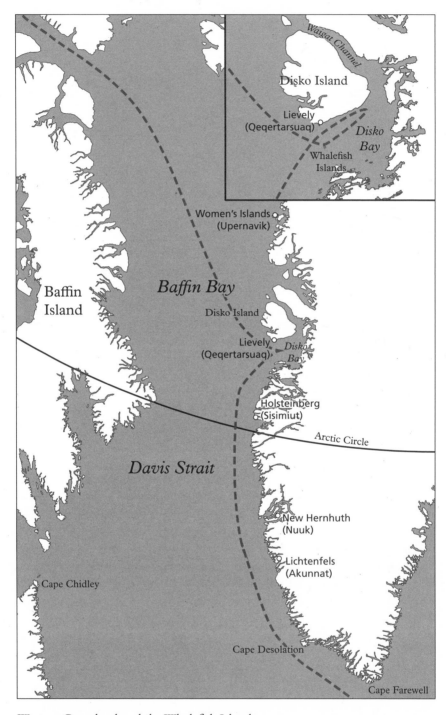

Western Greenland and the Whalefish Islands

CHRONOLOGY

30 June 1845: The ships cross the Arctic Circle, 25 miles from coast of Greenland, at 6 p.m. (Letter 135)

2 July 1845: Ships pass by Lievely, on Disko Island (Letter 135)

3 July 1845: The ships reach the mouth of the Waigat Channel (today's Sullorsuaq Strait) northeast of Disko Bay (Letter 139), mistakenly missing the Whalefish Islands and ascending the strait, thereby having to double back (Letter 135)

4 July 1845: Ships arrive at the Whalefish Islands, piloted to a safe anchorage by Greenlanders (Letter 140)

Evening of 12 July or morning of 13 July 1845: *Erebus* and *Terror* part company with *Baretto Junior* – the last mailbag (Letters 169, 173)

135. JAMES FITZJAMES TO ELIZABETH CONINGHAM [SISTER-IN-LAW], 27 JUNE–6 JULY 1845

<u>Friday</u> 27th. I would not mind betting sixpence that you did not recollect that this is William's birth-day, but I didn't and mentally drank his health at dinner and may God bless him – He is only <u>30</u> I wish I was <u>only</u> 30 – I begin to fancy I am getting old and stupid – I certainly do fancy (now and then <u>only</u>) that a year or two on shore would do me a world of good –

To day has been hot and calm and delightful – got bottom in 40 fathoms & pulled up star fish & shells & all sorts of strange beasts, and what is better pulled up plenty of large Cod-fish, enough for a good feed or two for all hands. This afternoon a thick fog suddenly came over us with a North wind, in which the thermometer fell to 35°, where it now stands – & we are sailing in smooth water, & small whales bounding about in all directions – Latitude 64° – the fog has cleared away, & we have lost the Transport – This morning a brig came close to us and her skipper came on board a rough old fellow, from Shetland. He has come to fish for Cod on the banks & salmon in the "Fiords" – a new scheme quite in these parts – He came to see the little old man who had the wife at <u>Stromness</u> who had been a mate with him.

Dearest William

The day shall not close without my giving you a few lines to wish you all manner of happiness on this the day of your birth, a day which brings to my recollection happy times.

Do you recollect sending up the rockets at Abbots' Langley on your birth day when you were about 8 years old? I do. –

If you have had patience to read all the nonsense I have written for Elizabeth you will understand better than I can express, how dear you both are to one who never lays his head on his pillow without praying for you – I am always your affectionate
James Fitzjames
Erebus Davis' Strait 11Pm 27th. June 1845 –

[Saturday 28] 29th Here goes again for you dear Elizabeth, you will excuse the digression before I went to bed last night – To day we have had sea smooth as glass – very cloudy, & a cold air. Thermometer 35° and to my delight passed several Ice-bergs – within a mile of a large one – The effect was very fine for the horizon happened to be a dark distinct line and these bergs catching an occasional gleam of sun-shine, shone like a twelfth cake I had fancied icebergs, were large transparent lumps or rocks of ice – They look like huge masses of pure snow, furrowed with caverns and dark ravines – I went on board the Terror in the evening for it was quite calm, & found Hodgson better for he had been ill & Crozier looking like a sick owl – I had tea with him and when we came on board we pulled up for Goodsir beasts, star-fish, mud, & shells, from a depth of 250 fathoms or 750 yards & caught more Cod.

Sunday 29th Last night I remained up till a late hour trying to read a watch by the light of certain blubbers, remarkable jelly like fish about this size which emit a bright phosphorescent light when shaken in a basin – To day Cloudy dead calm Land in sight, under dense masses of clouds. We have found the Transport, & a Danish brig is close to us.

This evening a number of large whales came sporting toward us so close as nearly to touch us – we have now all sail set and going smoothly before the wind. The weather feels delightfully cool, though the thermometer is at 37° to 39°. –
11 O'clock I have just been on deck the sea is like glass –

Monday 30th All last night and all to day we have had a delightful breeze
– all sail set & the smoothest possible sea but cloudy weather. The Coast
of Greenland is now very fine – we are nearer than ever about 25 to 30
miles perhaps but it looks close – & dense clouds overhang the whole
rugged and snowy coast. I saw several glaciers to day – but the clouds
were too dense to sketch anything though the effect is very fine of the
masses of cloud & snow, relieved by dark blue craigs –

To day, at 6 o'clock in the evening we crossed the Arctic Circle Latitude
66° 30' – and the Sun's declination happening to be more than 23° 10'
he will not set to us tonight <u>at all</u>. I regret it is too cloudy to see him at
midnight. This evening, sea as smooth as ever – no icebergs wind going
down – Here Ends another sheet so God bless you – I fear you will be
tired of all this trash about sun – sea & snow, but I c'ant help it –
                    Good night J.F –

Hms Erebus 1st July 1845. 10 Pm

                    Latitude 68° N.

My dear Elizabeth
    Tomorrow we expect to get to Disco – or rather to the Whale Fish
Islands close to it – where we shall unload the Transport of provisions &
coals and start as soon as we can – what with this and the observations I
shall have to take, & the reports I shall have to send home, my time will
be so fully occupied that it is just probable I may only be able to find
time for a hurried note to you or William – I shall, therefore, continue
my journal up to the present time – and if you hear nothing more from
me you must be satisfied that we have arrived at Disco and are gone on
in the prosecution of our journey.

This morning was damp & foggy, but it cleared away, and we are
now sailing with a delightful breeze with all sail set, the slightest rip-
ple on the smoothest possible sea the dark blue land on our right 20
miles off, relieved by snowy peaks on which somehow or other the
sun manages to fix a beam or two now & then – and a line of craggy
icebergs, as far as the eye can reach ahead – & on both sides some of
them looking as if they were scratched out of the land – In a few hours
we shall be amongst them. There is no danger in ice bergs – <u>on the
contrary</u> they ground on the shoals, and warn ships to keep clear. We
have now 25 fathoms water. Icebergs have been known to ground in
150 fathoms – I have just been up in the crows nest, & the appearance

of these icy craigs & pinnacles, is beautiful & singular – far in close
to the land is a perfect glacier equal to any Swiss one. – Still on we
go – on – on – the <u>three</u> of us – though the Transport wishes herself
back again no doubt.

This evening we sailed in amongst a shoal of some hundred walrusses
tumbling over one another, – diving – splashing with their fins & tails
& looking at us with their grim solemn looking countenances & small
heads bewhiskered and betusked. – Altogether every thing is delightful
and the weather is cool but not cold – the Thermometer being up to 36°.
– I have just been on deck and there are 65 icebergs in sight –

In talking to Sir John Franklin, whose memory is as good as his judgment appears to be correct, it appears that one great difficulty is to get
from where we are to Lancaster Sound – Parry was fortunate enough,
in his first voyage to sail right across in 9 or 10 days a thing unheard of
before or since – In his next voyage he was 54 days toiling through fields
of ice & did not get in till September, yet Lancaster Sound is the point
we look to as the beginning of our work – If we are fortunate we shall be
there by the 1ˢᵗ August, which will be time enough; <u>sooner</u> would probably put us among the clearing ice – No expedition has ever been able to
leave Disco before the 4ᵗʰ or 5ᵗʰ July , though some have sailed a month
before we did except old Ross; in his first voyage, and he got away by
16ᵗʰ June & was, I believe, a month going 60 miles further. So you see
all is conjecture; we <u>may</u> do well this year, and again, we may not. And
now God bless you and dear William kiss Minney and my little Godson.
I shall often think of their merry faces when they came to Woolwich –
Give my kind regards to Sarah and old Shell and I need not tell you to
think now & then of your affectionate friend
                    James Fitzjames.

Midnight, 1ˢᵗ.
   I have just been on deck to look again at the splendid Ice bergs we are
passing through & saw one about 200 feet high topple over & come
down with a crash, which raised a cloud of foam spray & mist like an
avalanche. – It is a fine clear, sunshiny night – the Danish brig is closer in
shore, occasionally quite hid from our view by a berg.

Wednesday 2ⁿᵈ. Soon after I left the deck last night it came on to rain hard
& we sailed through & past ice bergs in all directions. I was on deck at
4 in the morning looking at one about ½ a mile long – which we nearly

brushed – 180 were in sight at one time when it cleared a little. The weather was so thick, that we could not see when we had gone far enough – but found ourselves in the forenoon right under a dense black looking coast topped with snow – with long furrows & ravines of snow and canopied with a mass of Clouds & mist. In bold relief, at the foot of this black mass, the most fantastically formed & perfectly white Bergs shone out – This was Disko – and we shewed our colors to the Danish flag, hoisted on the house (or hut) of the Governor of the Danish settlement, called Lievely, near its Southern end – We are now beating up to Whale Fish Islands which are in the bay formed by the South end of Disko & the Main land, where we clear the transport, &c. – and shall probably be in tomorrow morning early as we are now (10 p.m.) 15 miles from them – & well past Lievely.

Ice bergs – Grand and fantastic are shining in all directions – But it has rained so hard all day we are quite soaked – thermometer 42°. The wind appears however as if coming from the NW which will be clear, & break up the ice which this Southerly wind must have packed up on the West side of Baffin's Bay – so we shall be just as well here till it clears. –

The scenery is most grand, but desolate beyond expression – I could not help thinking of the Frenchman who after a long account of the misery of the rain & fogs of England, wound up with

'Pour quitter ce triste Sol
Je m'embarque à Liverpol.'
and now I am taking a glass of brandy & water to your health –

Osmar has just come from on deck (midnight) and is dancing with an imaginary skipping rope. I said to him "What a happy chap you are Osmar you are always in a good humour." His answer is, "Well, sir, if I am not happy here, I d'ont know where else I could be." This will show you that we are really like a man shaving; So-appy! – The rain has done and the wind is moderate and the sea is smooth. and the ice is glistening and Read says we shall see the Huski-mays tomorrow morning – so I shall get a few hours sleep

3ᵈ This morning, instead of going into Whale Fish Island, by some mistake, Read fancied we were wrong – & away we went up to the end of the bay 30 miles, and to the mouth of the Waigaut Channel looking for them – the Bay full of most glorious icebergs, packed close along the shore. At noon we found our mistake – & had our sail for nothing which would be good fun but for the delay. I went on board the Terror in the evening – & found Captain Crozier knew the mistake but fancied we had given up the idea of going there. Fortunately the wind favoured us right round the Bay, and had a delightful sail. We are now running in to these Whale Islands – where we ought to have been yesterday evening -

Friday 4th. In the Evening – you will say I have not had much sleep last night for I went to bed (or rather lay down with my clothes on at 11 – and was up again at twelve oclock – You will bear in mind that all this time the <u>sun is up</u>. Finding ourselves at last off these rocky Whale-Fish Islands, we sent LeVescomte in the gig to reconnoitre, as Captain Crozier [who] was here some years ago, did not recognize the place – a certain flagstaff on hill having been carried away. Very soon out paddled 5 "Huskimays" in the smallest possible canoes all in a row and two going ahead kept just near the ship, & piloted her in to a safe place among the rocks – where we are now moored in a channel just four times the ship's length in breadth – and perfectly what we call land locked – this is a ground plan of the place:

All to day I was on shore on Boat Island, observing, with "Fox" – and standing in a damp sodden place whereby I got very wet & very cold – but plunging into cold water, when I got on board made me quite warm – & I dined at 6 ½ with Captain Crozier, who gave a spread & had Sir John on board. It is now 11 o'clock & I want some sleep.

<u>Sunday, 6th</u> A fine sunshiny night, and we have had a delightful Sunshiny Day – quite warm the air clear, ice glistening in all directions. The fine bold land of Disko, black, & topped with snow – Clear – the sea covered with bits of ice which are rushing through the channel as the[y] break from the ice bergs, which fall with a noise like thunder. Every man nearly on shore running about for a sort of holiday being Sunday – getting Eider ducks' eggs, &c. &c. – curious mosses & plants being collected as also <u>shells</u>. &c. Le Vesconte & I on the island since 6 this morning he surveying – and me squinting with him at the compasses and at the sun. It is very satisfactory to me that he takes to surveying, as I <u>said</u> he would Sir John is much pleased with him – – All yesterday I was on the island from <u>6</u> to <u>6</u> with Fairholme with the dipping needle. and it rained hard & was cold. We have a little square wooden house to cover ourselves. Very large musquitoes bite us – I shall send you one.
But to day it is calm & beautiful & I got a good sleep last night and though it is now 12 intend sleeping till 6 in the morning when I shall have more work at the island, which will last while we are here. – The

Transport will probably be cleared tomorrow evening or Tuesday – then we "swing the ship" as we did at Greenhithe for magnetic correction and shall get off on Wednesday night or Thursday that is on the 9th or 10th – and hard work too. A man just come over from Lively a Dane, who has married an Esquimaux – says that they believe it to be one of the mildest seasons & earliest summers <u>ever known</u>. and that the ice is clear away from this to Lancaster Sound. <u>Keep this</u> to yourself, for Sir John is naturally very anxious that people in England should not be <u>too</u> sanguine about the season – in case of disappointment and has begged me not to give too favorable a report to John Barrow. besides, the papers would have all sorts of stories, not true – so pray mind about this point – I do <u>believe</u> we have a <u>good chance</u> of getting through <u>this</u> year, if it is to be done at all – but I hope we shall not as I want to have a winter for the magnetic observations. And now dearest Elizabeth here goes a new pen into the Porcupine to say that your journal is at an end – at least for the present. I do hope it has amused you, but I fear not for what can there be in an old tub like this, with a parcel of sea bears, to amuse a "lady fair". This, however, is a façon de parler, for I think, in reality, that you will have been amused in some parts & interested in others, but I shall not read back, for fear of not liking it, and tearing it up –

This will go by the Transport. If I can keep some more notes of the sort for you I will – but cannot promise for I find I have as much to do as I can well get through. I shall write a note up to the last moment to you or William – but shall have no more time while we are here at all events. You will have seen however by what I have written from time to time that I am well and happy which I do believe and feel will give you and William as much pleasure to know as anything can. And this feeling is to me a great comfort more so than you may imagine – I never have felt it so fully since we lost our beloved and best friend –

Somehow or other William and I did not <u>know</u> each other of late years, as we did in the days of our boyhood – I always felt convinced that he loved me sincerely; and was aware that he knew how much I was attached to him, but we had been so long, and so much apart that I doubt if either of us had the same intensity of affection for the other, which both are now conscious of feeling – he will perhaps say that this was not the case on <u>his</u> part – and will set it down to my carelessness – but I think you will both <u>understand</u> what I mean though I may express myself badly – What I feel convinced however never <u>did</u> exist was a coolness or want of affection between us –

And may God bless <u>you</u> for having been – and being the chief means of the happiness he now enjoys – you must feel how much I love him because you <u>know</u> that I am really sincerely attached to you not only for your own sake – but for his also.

I will not close my nonsense without a word to our dear little children whose merry faces often come up before me in my thoughts.

If you see any more of Fitzgerald Gambier and his wife – you will find that I have in both of them sincere and affectionate friends to whom I feel much attached. and you will like her I am certain. I shall write to him before the Transport goes – and also to John Barrow, who naturally expects from me an account of our movements – this will probably be the whole amount of my correspondence, if I have even time for this much, unless I can find a few moments for Mrs. Campbell – and now I say Adieu in good earnest – on this Monday morning the 7th. July in the Whale Fish Islands near Disko – and always your affectionate friend James Fitzjames

136. CHARLES OSMER TO ELIZA OSMER [WIFE], 27 JUNE–10 JULY 1845

H.M.S. Erebus 300 miles <u>West</u> of Disco Island Davis Strait 27th June 1845

As in all probability three or four days from this date will see us safely Anchored at Disco Island, from where we dispatch the transport on her return home and I well knowing that I shall be fully employed in super-intending the clearing her of the Provisions I must begin and write at once and trust letters will be awaiting us, as this may be in all proba-bility be the last you will receive during our absence, at all events until I write you from the Pacific allowing that we are fortunate enough to succeed in getting through – I will commence this from the day on which I concluded my last, and not withstanding that the exciting and hearty cheers which we received on that day when the Rattler and the Blazer parted company are still ringing in my ears – never no never shall I for-get the emotion called forth by the deafening cheering we received when the above steamers left us, the suffocating jab of delight mingled with the fearful anticipation of the dreary void that would accompany us for <u>months</u>, nay perhaps years, until we again claimed such a <u>welcome</u> instead of a <u>farewell</u>, could not but impress upon every mind the impor-tance and the magnitude of the voyage we have just entered on. There is something so thrilling in the true, hearty British <u>cheer</u>! that whilst its echo delights and thrills the heart of a <u>friend</u>, it has always produced a contrary effect on our enemy, witness the many instances recorded during the Late Wars, either afloat or on shore, nothing can probably withstand a true British cheer!

After a run of twenty days, in any thing but fine or calm weather, we saw the snow capped mountains of Greenland, and altho most inhospitable their looks appeared, yet as being the <u>first</u> stepping stones towards the successful prosecution of our labours, we hailed the sight with pleasure and gratification –up to this time we had seen no Ice, notwithstanding former navigators had been occasionally stopped by it before arriving at our position, but on the following day (25th) three or four large Ice bergs were seen, two of them rather close to us. They could not have been less that 3 to 400 feet high. you should have seen and witness every eye being directed towards them, being the first beheld by them, but as I had seen them before they appeared like things of course – Each day since making the coast of Greenland the weather has been beautiful and comparatively warmer the thermometer standing at 45 degrees with a bright sun and an unclouded sky – I will endeavour to explain what will be our movements provided that formidable enemy the <u>Ice</u> will permit us – You will see Greenland Davis Straits, Baffins Bay, in the latter of which you will perceive, on the left hand side an opening called called <u>Lancaster's</u> <u>Sound</u>, through which the Expedition will pass, after coasting up the <u>East</u> Coast as far as Cape York, you will then perceive a continuation of that sound called Barrow's Strait, & Prince Leopold's Island, we then intend to pass Cornwallis Island, Bathurst Island and so on to <u>Melville</u> Island, this latter you will perceive to be the farthest limit <u>West</u> reached by Captain Sir Edward Parry. It is not our intention, however, unless the <u>Ice</u> is <u>stubborn,</u> to remain at Melville Island, but leaving it on our <u>right</u> push on for what you will see called <u>Bank's</u> Land, and should our passage in this direction not be obstructed by Ice. Should however we be compelled to abandon our attempt to the Southward & Westward, we retrace our steps and pass thro' the <u>Wellington</u> Channel, between <u>Cornwallis</u> <u>Island</u> & Cape <u>Bowden</u> in Barrow's Strait, if this latter route is taken we shall not certainly succeed this year, but shall lay the Vessels up in some snug and secure anchorage for the Winter, in order to be ready to recommence operations in the ensuing Spring or Summer which from our advanced position will give us an advantage not hitherto enjoyed by our predecessors inasmuch as they never tried the passage in question, and never having been furnished with sufficient provisions to risk a long stay in these regions –Another, and a most important thing in our favor is being fitted with the <u>Screw</u> <u>propeller,</u> which was not even dreamt of in former voyages. All these things combined cannot but enliven our hearts & spirits & make us turn a deaf ear to those who imagine we are pursuing a <u>chimerical</u> <u>phantom,</u> but we

put our Trust in <u>Providence</u> to guide us as <u>He</u> <u>will</u> should our course by
the land to the South West (Banks Land) not be impeded, we direct our
course towards the <u>Mackenzie River</u> and still coasting it proceed on to
<u>Point Barrow Icy Cape</u>, and through Bhering's Strait into the Pacific. I
have attempted to give you a little insight as to our intentions, the prosecution of which will and <u>must rest</u> with a <u>much higher power than frail
man</u> – The more I see of our worthy chief, the more I like and admire him,
in that he is deservedly <u>beloved</u> by us <u>all</u>, Seamen as well as Officers, and
I cannot but prognosticate that success will certainly follow one whose
moral character is so every way deserving of encomiums. I shall have a
great deal to say on this head before I finish this letter, & therefore will
reserve it, merely presuming that dear old good Sir John's example &
precepts would do honor and confer everlasting fame and credit on many
men who by their Situations and stations in life, have the care of large
congregations, but whose neglect is <u>proverbial</u>. As this is Sunday, (the 29
June) I cannot have a better or more fit opportunity of again referring to
the excellent moral example set us by our worthy chief. And as this diary
will serve as a sample of what has already taken place on the Lord's day;
And which will, no doubt, be strictly adhered to for the future, I may
enlighten you by describing our observance of it. We assemble at prayers
at 10 o'clock, the beautiful service of the Church of England read by Sir
John in the most impressive manner, after which a sermon, adapted to
our pursuits is also most impressively delivered. Sir John always dines
with us on that day, which we look forward to with much pleasure and
satisfaction. At 7 in the Evening all those who are so desirous assemble
in Sir John's Cabin, when the Evening service is read and another Sermon
delivered. I have mentioned this in order to show you what a contrast it
bears to the performance of Divine Service generally on board a Man of
War in the latter case, I say it with regret many, very many instances found
where both Officers and men use every possible pretext not to attend,
whereas in our <u>instance</u> we look forward to the coming of the Sabbath
with much gratification, and tis rarely you will miss the attendance of
even <u>one</u>, except when duty occurs, then these absentees are sure to be
of the Evening's congregation. We expect to arrive at Disco tomorrow
afternoon, where we shall instead of anchoring make fast to an 'Ice Berg,'
and commence clearing the transport, but where each Vessel is to stow
the Provisions, & Stores she has got in for us remains to be proved, for
they are full as an egg at this moment, however I have no doubt it will be
managed – I think it probable that the transport will leave us on her return
voyage, about the 7th of July and as I do not see what is to hinder her making the passage in three weeks or a month you will I hope receive this very

much earlier than I thought, by the time you are most likely reading this letter, We shall have just entered 'Lancaster's Sound' that is should the Ice not prevent the movements of the Ships – We have been proceeding for the last three or four days at a very slow speed, owing to light winds but we have been repaid for such delay by the appearance of the lofty snow clad mountains of Greenland. Together with the many large Ice Bergs drifting past us to a more Southern clime, there majestic appearance, so unusual to the eye of Land men in general serve to wile away our time on Ship board as well as serving for a topic of conversation when we meet at the mess table, where every thing reigns in the <u>greatest</u> <u>harmony</u>, the <u>joyous laugh</u> and the <u>witty</u> <u>jest</u> and passing round with our glass, and no illnatured remark obtending to mar our happiness if happiness it can be called to be separated from all our relations.

137. HARRY GOODSIR TO JOHN GOODSIR [BROTHER], 28–30 JUNE 1845

Davis Straits off Latitude 63
June 28th. 1845

My Dear John

I begin to write you now, altho the letters do not leave until we reach Disco, in consequence of the weather being at present unfavourable for working. I have been so completely occupied with drawing, preserving, & noting the animals procured within the last few days that I have not had the least time for any thing else. Even in this Latitude the light is constant & for the last 3 days with constant working I have not been able to get to bed for I must take advantage of the calm weather when we have it. I expect also to be constantly engaged during the time we are at anchor in Disco so that this is the only time for me to write Any thing of interest occuring will be of course noted before the letter is sent off. so you will have the latest news. The weather after leaving Stromness was very stormy and we were driven far to the north of our course, beyond 62° & almost in sight of Iceland hourly expecting to see Hecla. As I could not procure animals in such weather the greater part of my time has been occupied with the paper which I have now got finished & which you will receive with this & a box containing the specimens I hope you got the drawings safely through Chambers of the Rattler. The paper has cost me a great deal of trouble the points requiring observation being very difficult

of determination. There are several points in which the descriptions &
the drawings differ of which I will send you a list of corrections enclosed
in this. by means of which I hope you will be able to rectify them.

I will now give you an account of proceedings since we left Stromness
& our mode of doing duty. Our anchorage in Stromness bay was very
good & quiet but so soon as we got beyond Hoy Head the sea became
very heavy. The two steamers accompanied us for two days & then left
on their return Home. The wind had been contrary ever since we left the
Orkneys & has never changed except for a short while occasionally until
we were off Cape Farewell on the 22^d. when it blew tremendously but it
was favourable, we ran before it with only a little rag of sail at the rate
of 9 knots which is remarkably fast sailing for such heavy vessels the Sea
was very high and on Monday during dinner just as the cloth had been
removed when we were taking a little wine – reaching Cape Farewell
– an enormous sea was shipped & in one moment the Gun room was
floating & all drenched. In such a state of things every thing that is not
firmly lashed is knocking about & it is all one can do to keep yourself
up. The whole of this time I got nothing excepting during two days when
it was <u>rather calm</u> but what was got there was exceedingly interesting.
Briareus, Clio, Beroe, the type of a new genus of Crustacean Portia allied
to my Irenæus. A most beautifully characteristic form & very large. In
a letter I have written to Jerden of the Literary Gazette you will see the
characters given, for I have no time to enter into much detail.

Briareus I find is a Ciliograde. Eschricht is correct regarding Clio but has
missed several points I have already got great numbers of specimens &
will send you some but do nothing with them until I get home. The most
interesting animal I have yet got perhaps is a Ciliograde Acalepha of
much more complicated structure than any hitherto known of the same
Class. The ribs, in pairs, are transverse & the body being barrel shaped
the animal is exactly like a small barrel. Of them also I will send you
one or two. These are only the most interesting of the animals got in the
ocean and the two days work was all I got in consequence of the state
of the weather. On Wednesday the 25th. however after we had got fairly
into Davis Straits the weather became exceedingly beautiful, & warm
with a dead calm almost so that I got things under way at once.

The Officers who were taking great interest in the collecting of specimens now became very active & during the whole day a range of them
might be seen sitting in the main chains each with a net in hand dabbing

away for Acalephæ. In this way my time has been fully occupied drawing and taking notes, night & day. It was this morning we saw the first
iceberg, near the shore & the appearance of the land is very curious.

The whole of the 26th. occupied in the same way drawing & writing hard
as the Officers catch they are all quite excited about it, being perfectly new
to them, & the only idle hand is the Surgeon who appears to spend the
greater part of his time reading novels in bed. All the duty he does is to
see one or at most 3 cases in the morning & prescribe. He acts too, which
is the most important part of his duty apparently, as caterer for the mess.
I am thankful however he does not intermeddle much, altho he attempts
sometimes to be lofty. He sees however I don't care much for him, so does
not anoy himself. He as I said to Forbes attempted a little at first, a miserable failure, but has not given up yet altogether, Upon the first appearance
of a flock of the large bottlenoses, Captain FitzJames & Les Vicomte the
2nd. Lieutenant asked me whether or not they were whales laughing at the
same time because Stanley tried to perswade them, they were not. This
morning the 27th. the dredge was put over for the first time attached to
the deep sea lead line & brought up great numbers of animals accounts of
which you will see in the letter to Jerden. The soundings were 40 fathom
with gravelly bottom. A brig from Aberdeen was out on a Speculation
fishing for Cod & Our ships Company caught great numbers in the shortest time with remarkable rapidity They were most beautifull fish mottled
and speckled in the way you see the deep sea Cod at Cellardyke but much
more strongly. Gills as red as scarlet I never saw these organs to such per-
fection before or of such a beautiful colour. Few or no Caligi or Gerneæ[?]
on them. Their stomachs full of Hyas[?] & Ammodytes, two forms new to
me of Cyclopterus which along with an exceedingly beautiful little silvery
fish are all we have got of the same forms Pisces.

Sir John Franklin asked me when dining with him yesterday for the drawings I have made to send to Richardson whom I met by the way before
leaving England. I work constantly in the Captain's Cabin where we
have good light for the Microscope but the ship is not always too steady
for such means of observation but notwithstanding have done a good
deal in that way. Mr. Gore our 1st Lieutenant has drawn some of my best
animals on a black ground & you have no idea how beautiful they are I
had some idea of sending them home to be published but think it safer
to keep them at present. In fact all the Officers are very much interested
in the procuring of animals & as messmates are the most pleasant set of
fellows I ever met with & I now find that if success is to depend on them

I will be successful in all respects. I have got already a great number of drawings of specimens & notes. & expect to do a great deal at Disco.

June 30th. The large dredge was put over on Saturday evening last about 10 o clock in 300 fathoms when we brought up some splendid things. Asteridæ some splendid Isopods, thundering big fellows Oprindidæ[?] Annelides Shells, Corals & curious enough Forbes Brissus Lyrifer and my own Alauna in great abundance. So far as I am aware this is the greatest depth which animals in such variety and nos. have been dredged. The bottoms are curious & all preserved for Sir H. De la Beche. I was kept: up all night almost drawing & noting as nothing can be done here well on Sunday. I have got considerably ease now in sketching & colouring & have got some beautiful coloured figures. Sunday a couple of enormous Whales came alongside & accompanied us for some time. I now see the species are not at all known for it had none of the characters of any of the known forms. I have already got some very good coloured sketches of the Cetacea but our harvest for them will be in Lancaster Sound the Monodons tooth in the young the Sea Horse & in fact every thing I will look at. I have spoken to the Captain & give so soon as it is properly drawn out a list of things to be observed. I have also got a good friend in the Ice Master who will look out for all the Whales, Seals &c. for me. July 3d. Since last I have got some beautiful Shrimps, Cynthia Sagitta, & a small form of Medusa a most valuable specimen this last as it illustrates the mode of generation & development of cells most beautifully.

On Monday evening passed a large flock of Sea Horses enormous animals as big as an Elephant they are not at all known I see the figures given are not good. We have also now got fairly amongst icebergs, but are aware that it is not nearly what we are yet likely to meet with it is however a fine sight & what few can conceive without seeing. You must explain to them all at home how busy I am or I would have written to all. My only letters home are to my Father and Uncle Anstruther. By the way I will enclose a short note of the money got by David Forbes. I hope he is getting on well with you for his brothers sake.

I have written to Edward Forbes & asked him to arrange about the specimens when we get home that I may have the superintendence of them during the time they are in the Admiralty offices also about their distribution, & what with regard to the Assistance from Sir Henry De la Beche & others it will be managed I hope.

In my last to you I asked you send a letter for me to Panama. Be so good as do so addressed to the care of the British Consul. Captain Fitzjames & the others have all done so, so sanguine are they of getting through. It will be time enough the beginning or middle of the coming Winter. Give my respects to, Syme, Duncan and all my other Edinburgh friends.

Be so good as deliver the enclosed packet of Disco Flowers to Mrs. Duncan as the only thing which I can find here worth sending & which is likely to be at all prized from such an out of the way place.

Believe me
Ever Your Affectionate Brother
Harry D. S. Goodsir

P.S. There are several Danes on board of us as seamen so having no difficulty with language.

138. HARRY GOODSIR TO JOHN GOODSIR [FATHER],
30 JUNE–2 JULY 1845

Davis Straits June 30th.
1845
Crossing the Arctic Circle

My Dear Father

My time is so completely taken up with the observations on the animals I am procuring, drawing them and writing descriptions, that you must not expect a finely written letter. We are obtaining so many animals (all of which on account of their rarity, I am so anxious to preserve) both in drawings and otherwise that I am engaged night and day. I am enabled to do so because there is no darkness here the sun being constantly above the horizon so long therefore as I have animals I work on. Since the 25th. when this 1st began I have had little or no sleep and this is likely to continue so long as the sea remains calm for I must not loose the opportunities. It is therefore only when I have finished my observations or when the sea is rough that I can spare time to write letters. Having however finished my work for this day near 1 A.M. I take the opportunity of commencing a letter to you. After leaving Stromness we had desperate weather contrary

winds the whole way to Cape Farewell. We were obliged to run so far
north that we expected to see (on the 11th.) Mount Hecla every hour. The
Ship however was put about in consequence of the wind changing & so
we were all dissappointed. When we reached Cape Farewell on the 22d.
the wind, which had been blowing very strong during the 21st. came on to
blow a perfect storm the Ships running before the wind with almost bare
poles at a great rate. All however was bringing us near the Straits where
we were sure of smooth water. The Captain of the Transport has since told
Captain FitzJames that he was quite astonished at the rate we went at &
also that we did not lie to. Which says a great deal for it is the boast of
merchantmen I understand to out run if possible men of war. The sea was
very high – long heavy waves with the water as green, I cant find a colour
to liken it to. Notwithstanding all this Sir John held Divine Service twice
altho it was quite impossible to stand, without being knocked from one
side of the Ship to the other. Sir John generally dines with us on Sunday
but you can have no idea of a dinner on board of Ship in such a day as this
with a little care however we generally are able to manage it prety well.
You require however to be always on the outlook in case your opposite
neighbours soup or beer or wine does not come pouring into your lap. I
am getting on with my fellow Officers very well & as messmates never
met with better men You will see by Johns letter more fully as I have
written more particularly to him about the animals & my other duties. I
can easily conceive now the knowledge a navy Surgeon must gain of his
Profession. We have not had more than 3 or 4 cases since we came out
& these of no more importance than a cold or so. Our Surgeon is a little
better than Trotter. What is poor Dog doing now?

The appearance of the Coast here is very curious and also very interesting. It is very abrupt & precipitous; the surface also is most irregular as
if an immense no. of highly peaked conical hills had been set down upon
it as thick as they could stand. The hollows at this season having a thick
coating of snow which in many places has melted away & showing the
black rock underneath All of these are bare rock but notwithstanding
there are many villages & settlemen[t]s all along the Coast. A few days
ago we were off New Hernhuth. Where the Moravians formed their 1st.
settlement. Some enormous icebergs are occasionally seen here but close
in shore.

July 2d. My Dear Father since the former part of this was written we
have got to Disco but have not yet anchored. Last night we passed an
immense flock of Sea Horses all tumbling about in the water each as
big as an Elephant, and shortly after got amongst a great many icebergs

many of them as big as Largo Law almost all of them were aground in this deep water, which would make them from their inferior part to the top many 100 feet. Above water they were even as I have already mentioned a couple of 100 feet & when it is considered that there is 9 times as much below the surface of the water you will be able to judge of their size. Altogether it is most beautiful & interesting a sight and voyage I would not have missed for any consideration. It is not however what we have to see yet or any thing like it. & it will only be when I come back or by the Whalers of next year that you will be able to hear of it.

Our Ice Master whose name is Reid is from Aberdeen a good hearted rough old sailor is very friendly & through him whose acquaintance I have always cultivated I expect to get all the Seals, Sea, Horses & Whales, Sea Unicorns &c. which have to be examined & prepared. You will see by Johns letter all that I am doing in that way, where also you will see that I have got many of the same kind of animals got by myself at the mouth of the Firth of Forth. All the Officers assist very much in fishing & procuring specimens for me & are otherwise very kind especially the Commander Captain FitzJames & 1st. Lieutenant Mr. Gore I work in Sir Johns Cabin & Show him every night my days work in which he takes great interest. In case I forget, & because John is apt to do so also I now write to tell you that his Leather Portmanteau was left by accident at Woolwich Dockyards If you think it worth while direct a letter to Mr. Goodall, Samuel St. Woolwich to look after it. I lodged in his house & as he is a Scotchman & was very kind he will do every thing about it I forgot to write about it from Stromness.

139. CHARLES OSMER TO ELIZA OSMER [WIFE], 1 JULY 1845

This afternoon we find ourselves about 90 miles from our destination (Disco) And from the unusual appearance of the sea horses or Walrusses of which we counted no less than 180, we are assured that Ice is in the neighbourhood, as these animals seldom or never are seen at any great distance from the 'Ice' this supposition was soon verified, for as we advanced slowly but in the proper direction towards our Port, sixty five 'Ice Bergs' were reported in sight, many of them large ones. Our proximity to these bergs caused a sensible atten[ua]tion in the temperature of both Air and Sea Water, the former falling from 42° to 34° and the latter from 46° to 36° consequently greatcoats were in requisition, and the quick walking of the promenaders on deck gave those below to

understand that their blood required circulation – I am notwithstanding writing in my Cabin with the thermometer standing at 52° exactly
20 degrees <u>above</u> the freezing point – In the course of conversation to
day 1st July I was so very delighted to find that we shall have one or
more opportunities of sending letters home to England by the Greenland
Whale Ships which we shall be sure to fall in with either in Lancaster
Sound or Barrow Straits.

Toward this evening 2nd of July we saw the high Land of <u>Disco</u>, its
summits covered with snow, our progress was here disputed by immense
bergs of Ice, so that we had literally to thread our way amongst them –
some of these formations were upwards of 500 feet high, and presented
the most fantastic shapes, so much so that it was not at all uncommon
to hear orders given to the Steersman to steer for the Church with the
high Steeple," for the high Obelisk," the Long Barn" and ultimately for
<u>St. Paul's</u>," a berg of unusual size and height having appeared in our
track, which to our imagination mind bore a great resemblance to the
Cathedral of that name. We continued with light winds and heavy rains
to make our way to the small Island that had been selected by Sir John
for a good place to clear the transport but owing to very light airs and
calms, the morning found us but little advanced from our position of the
previous evening –

We have been all this way (3rd July) endeavouring to reach our anchorage, which altho' constantly in sight the light winds and strong current
against us has prevented us from reaching. We are now (8 o'clock evening) 3rd July, slowly approaching our anchorage, comparatively mild
weather, with <u>192 Ice bergs</u>, large and small in sight. Some of them
close to us & as I said before disputing our advance. I do not think we
shall anchor, or commence clearing the transport until tomorrow when
we shall go to it in right earnest. We have Chess, Backgammon, and
draughts, and 1700 Books on board to amuse us.

140. JAMES FAIRHOLME TO GEORGE FAIRHOLME [FATHER],
1–5 JULY 1845

H.M.S. Erebus, Just inside the Arctic **O**
July 1. 1845

My dear Father

Here are we, fairly on our ground, & with the prospect of being at
Disco by tomorrow night, so I will begin my despatches, leaving them

open till the Transport leaves. I promised to give you some account of the Orkneys, but now there seems but little to say about them, except that several of us had a most agreeable walk to Kirkwall where we saw the Cathedral & visited some of the scenes of the "Pirate". The country is quite barren & rather uninteresting & the merry party we had did more to amuse us than anything else. Two of them were quite knocked up with the long walk there, & we had to hire a cart to bring them back to the great amusement of all who saw the party on their return.

On leaving Stromness, the two steamers accompanied us as far as Cape Wrath, where they gave us 3 hearty cheers, & left us, with a fair wind & a fine day. From this day to the 22nd we had every change of weather, some days very lovely & some equally wet & disagreeable. & the southerly wind kept us, much to our annoyance, a good deal to the northward of Cape Farewell. On that day however (the 22nd) a heavy N. E. gale came on which continued for 3 days, with a very high sea running & which carried us (quicker than the old ships had ever been known to go before) right round the Cape, on leaving us on the 24th in a calm sea, & in sight of the high land of Greenland, & a great number of icebergs. During the gale we had rather an anxious time for there was a dense & continued haze, which scarcely ever allowed of our seeing more than a mile ahead, & as we had expected to come on the ice long before, we never knew how soon a berg or a floe might be seen close to us. This obliged us to keep such a lookout as I have never kept before -, or than is generally necessary when running for land of which the position is well known. The gale seems to have set the ice far to the northward, & (we hope) also over the west coast, as all we have seen since our arrival in the straits have been bergs, most of which appear to be aground.

You can imagine nothing finer than this coast. I have seen nothing like it since I was in Switzerland. It is one long unbroken chain of rugged mountains, rising immediately from the sea to a very great height & when we first saw it it was almost entirely covered with snow. A few days of sunshine, however, have made some difference in its appearance & we can now see the black summit & ridges showing out from among the snow. I should think some of these mountains are extinct volcanoes & I observed & took a sketch of one which must, from its form, be an extinct crater.

Fitzjames is, as ever, a fine fellow. His time is principally devoted to magnetic observations. Gore does all the duties of 1st Lieutenant. Sir John still continues to receive 3 of us at dinner every day, & to dine with us on Sundays, & instead of the formal parties these are in most ships, one really looks forward with the greatest pleasure to meeting him. On the voyage across, everything has shaken down into its place. We have got into regular habits. The orders (which will remain) are given for the internal arrangements, subject only, it seems to me to alterations for the <u>comfort</u> of those concerned. Sir John is himself of all scientific observations & encourages it much amongst us all. Indeed he makes all take an equal share in the navigation of the ship in determining positions etc. By this means I have learnt much on these subjects, which, in the common run of the service, would perhaps never have come in my way.

Soon after leaving the Orkneys, Sir John sent for us all into his cabin & read to us such portions of his orders as were not private, particularly as to observing everything & collecting specimens, also his authority from the Admiralty for claiming <u>for them</u> all our logs, journals & everything connected with the expedition. Since we got into the Bay, we have been much employed in assisting our naturalist (Goodsir) in collecting specimens of <u>medusae</u> etc. with which the water abounds & of which he has already got some hundred different kinds.

We have also dredged several times in great depths (1500 ft) & got up some very curious crustacea, & a few shells. We find Goodsir a most superior man (he is scotch) & such an indefatigable naturalist & good companion that he is a great favourite with all. Another grand amusement has been the fishery for cod, which we have had during the calm weather, the last few days. These fish seem to be almost as numerous here as on the banks of Newfoundland, a fact scarcely known though we met an Aberdeen brig out on a speculation for them & the salmon fisheries inshore. What a cruize for William! I thought as the old skipper told me his intention of running into all the rivers & inlets from Cape Farewell to Disco, & perhaps further! It is however very doubtful if this will answer.

You will wonder what sort of climate we have here, under these snowy mountains & among icebergs. Well! at present I must admit that my feet are rather cold, but till today, we have had most lovely weather, the sun shining for 20 hours & upwards, & the mean thermometer at about 38° Tonight the sun will be in sight all the 24 hours, but I fear it looks too cloudy to hope for a meridian altitude at <u>midnight</u> an observation we are all most anxious to make. Lately we have had the most lovely <u>sunsets</u>, & could watch the progress of the brilliant lights along the horizon till they became those of the <u>sunrise</u>, bright daylight continuing all the time. Our appetites are enormous in this sharp weather, & we find a <u>middle watch</u> supper most necessary (an unheard of piece of extravagance in Southern regions) Fortnum & Mason have done their part well, & we find all their stores of the best description. Our mess is very comfortable & after the very rough weather & passage across, & the numerous breakages we enjoy the quiet sea inside the strait.

The coast is deeply indented by numerous fjords or inlets in most of which are rivers & in all, I believe, plenty of Salmon. We have now got slowly along this coast nearly as far as Cape Chidley, which we hope to see in a few hours, & we shall then haul in for Disco, & probably go to Lievely Bay where we may be, I suppose, at least 3 days getting our stores, provisions etc. on board from the Transport. She will then leave us & return home & we shall start for Lancaster Sound.

I will now tell you something about the ship & expedition having given an outline of our voyage up to this time. When I last wrote I told you how comfortable we all were in this ship, & since then everything has tended to make us still more so. We all now know each other probably as well as we ever shall & I really think there could hardly have been selected a set more likely to get on together. Sir John is a <u>new man</u> since we left. He has quite recovered from his severe cold, looks 10 years younger & takes part in everything that goes on with as much interest as if he had not grown older since his first Expedition. We are all delighted to find how <u>decided</u> he is in all that he resolves on, & he has such experience & judgement that we all look on his decisions with the greatest respect. I never felt that the Captain was so much my <u>Companion</u>, with anyone I have sailed with before. He has certainly made a <u>friend</u> of every person on board, & I believe not a thing he has said or done has given rise to the slightest complaint.

I have seen but little of the Terror since we left (internally I mean) having only been on board twice. I fancy they are very happy also but <u>I would not change</u>. One of my visits was paid on a calm day, about half way across, in Peter Halketts boat when the Terror was ½ a mile from us Le Visconte went with me & it carried us capitally. It just holds three, & we got on board the Terror, paid our visit & got back again without the least wet or discomfort, altho we were of course sitting much below the level of the sea. The exertion of paddling is rather severe or rather it was so then from neither of us having had much practice lately. We proved, however, completely the safety & efficiency of the boat, with two heavy persons in it. Sir John looks upon it as a most important invention for land expeditions & says that if they had had one on the Banks of the Coppermine, many lives would probably have been saved.

We have had immense numbers of sea birds about lately, most of them peculiar to these northern seas. They seem hardly to notice us, & a light breeze springing up after a calm (when they all settle on the water) generally carries the ship almost over them before they will get up. I saw one caught with a hook & line the other day, after some hundreds had been fighting with the unlucky fellow for the prize.

There are two important members of the Expedition that I must not forget to mention. Viz Neptune & Jacko. Old Nep has lost much of his unwieldiness since we left & now runs up & down our step ladders with ease. He is the most <u>lovable </u>dog I ever knew & is a general favourite. I often give him an extra kiss on Williams account, & he seems to know that it comes from a friend. The monkey continues to be the annoyance & <u>Pest</u> of the whole ship, & yet not a person in her would hurt him for the whole world. He is a dreadful thief but such a very <u>amusing</u> one that his robberies bring very little sympathy for the unfortunate <u>losers</u>! The Doctor declares that Jacko is in a rapid consumption, & he certainly has a very bad cough, but the only other symptom I see of it, is the rapid consumption of everything eatable he can lay his paws on.

I am happy to say my watch has proved as yet to be one of the best in the ship, its rate with the chronometers varying a few seconds only each day, & I find it of the greatest use. Indeed I do not know what I should have done without this watch, & the Warres kind present of a sextant which also proves an excellent instrument. As yet I have had nothing to do with magnetic observations, nor indeed has anyone but Fitzjames, until the observatory is erected, as there is only one instrument to observe with afloat. Indeed I find my time constantly occupied, so much so, that it is only lately that I have got into the habit of reading. I have been much delighted with "Whewell's Indications" & I was fortunate in getting some further answer to the "Vestiges" from Captain Stanley before he left us. I find Goodsir a most valuable assistant as though the natural history of the lower orders of animals is his favourite subject, he has an immense deal of information on most others & most excellent views on them.

I am now reading a book which I strongly advise you to look at. It was published just as we sailed & is written by Count Strelecki, a particular friend of Sir Johns, & to whom I think I introduced William the last Sunday he was on board. The title of it is "A physical account of N. S. Wales & Van Diemens Land" & it has given me an idea of those countries which I never had before. He was at Moreton Bay & speaks of Darling Downs, & I have no doubt George met him out there, though he could not recollect the name. We have got a Catalogue made of all the books, public & private, that are on board. (& the Terror is doing the same) & we find there is scarcely a book that we can think of as being required that is not in the list. We shall supply each other with these lists, & thus, when a book is wanted, the Librarian (Goodsir) will at once know which ship & what cabin it is in. I fear there has been a great loss amongst our live stock, as by the last accounts, only 5 or 6 of the 18 bullocks were alive. Our provisions however, are of such excellent quality, & Government have been so liberal in the ships supplies that this does not so much matter. Besides the supply of fish which we have had for some days, has been a good substitute for fresh meat.

10 p.m. (Same Day) Disco is in sight & we shall probably be fast by noon tomorrow. I have just been in half an hour in the Crows nest, from which place we counted 65 icebergs of all shapes & sizes, some being very large. Everything around denotes the Arctic circle. The sky is most remarkable <u>iceblink</u> appearing in all directions The land is here rather low & presents a continuous line of dreary bleak cliffs, while the whole coast is lined with sharp & glittering icebergs, many of which are much higher than the hills near them. About 8°ᶜ a man aloft reported "hundreds of <u>sea horses </u>in the lee bow" & by altering course a little we passed right amongst them. They allowed the ship to pass close by them, as they rolled about on the surface. You cannot imagine anything so strange as the appearance of these monsters, as they raised their queer looking faces & long white tusks towards the ship. They are without exception the most hideous & unwieldy creatures I ever saw. Their faces are covered with long & stiff bristles & their skin is of a dirty whitish colour, which makes them look like gigantic sheep wallowing about. They stick close together in groups of 20 or 30 huddled up so close that I cannot imagine how they could move. I hope we may soon see some of them either on shore or amongst the ice, & have an opportunity of examining them closely. We are now going to pass between an iceberg & the land, so I will go up & see it, & leave my letter for tomorrow.

July 3ʳᵈ. We are now at the Whale Fish Islands, where I hope we may be safely at anchor in a couple of hours. Yesterday we were all day threading our way through hundreds of icebergs, some of immense size. While passing near one of these, which I had just remarked was about the size of the North Foreland, it suddenly fell to pieces with an awful crash, sending the spray up to a great height, and leaving one field of sharp & broken ice. We saw many of them turn over, & indeed, in this weather, when the rain & sun are melting them fast it is not safe to go near them. We saw the Island of Disco & the Danish settlement last night & as the anchorage is better there we stood across the bay during the night. Disco is very high land & half covered with snow, & has a most magnificent but desolate appearance. The settlement at Lively Bay consists of two or three small houses on a low point immediately under the high land. It certainly does not look inviting for winter quarters. Bye the bye Williams little sketch gives a capital idea of an iceberg, but you must imagine them of every form & size, some of them of a most fantastic appearance.

Saturday night July 5th. We only arrived here yesterday morning, having missed these islands, & got so far to the northward that we had a good long beat back. Here we are, Terror, Transport & ourselves, close to each other, hard at work, getting stores on board & preparing for a start. I hope we may get away by Tuesday. These islands are only barren rocks, from 1 – 6 miles in circumference, & consisting of gneiss & mica slate, & separated from each other by narrow but very deep channels, in one of which we are lying. We have been constantly employed since we anchored, each having his own duty. Mine has been at the observatory, on a small island near where Fitzjames & I take the magnetic observations, & this will keep us well employed till the ships are ready to go.

Here we have seen the first Esquimeaux, who came off to us in their little canoes, & led the way in from leeward. They are so exactly what everybody has described them that I will not say more about them than that they are the <u>dirtiest</u> race I ever came across. Their canoes are so small that had I seen one on shore, I should have thought it was a model, but having succeeded so well with Halkett's boat, I was determined to try this also. It is quite impossible for a large person to bend his legs so as to get into any of them, however so I was contented to occupy <u>two</u> by putting a board across them, & sitting with one leg in each of the holes, when I managed capitally.

There is much employment here for the naturalist, & the lichens & mosses alone would give him plenty to do. While I have so much on my hands, I shall confine myself to collecting what shells & fossils may come in my way, which I believe will not be many. After the work is over, viz about 6 o'clock we dine, & the parties go out walking or shooting. I took my gun out this evening & got 3 eider ducks & several <u>dovekies</u> a small kind of diver. I hear that some ptarmigan have been seen, but did not myself come across any.

In walking over the hills on which there is still some snow, I found a good deal of Ross' <u>red snow</u> of which I have promised to get some specimens tomorrow. We see numbers of seals about here, & several kinds of sea birds & hawks, besides the pretty little <u>snow bunting</u> which is very common. Tomorrow we are to have a day of rest, after which I hope to be able soon to close this letter & see the anchors up again. We passed Sunday quietly, & after the hard work of the last two days, it was a reasonable rest. In this climate the want of darkness prevents me getting to sleep or even going to bed at the proper time, so that all suffered from want of sleep. Some of us go to bed before 1 or 2^{am}, indeed the walking & shooting parties do not think of starting till about 8 or 9 at night. Sir John performs Divine Service in the fornoon, & also at 7 o'clock in the evening, this last being in his own cabin for those who were on duty before, & also for any others who may wish to attend. He has the most beautiful & impressive manner I ever heard, even in clergymen, & the service here is very different to what it is in most ships.

Thursday 10th. We have been most busily occupied for the last 3 days, & have now nearly got all our stores on board. The business has been much longer than any of us expected, but that is always the case, & what one talks of doing in a day or two in England actually takes much more time to accomplish. I ought to have remembered our delay at the mouth of the Niger, when we were also constantly employed. My station has been at the observatory, where I have been from 6 a.m. till 4 or 5 o'clock p.m. daily. We have now completely all the observations which can be taken without a much longer delay, & after the ships have been again swung for local attraction, which must be done tomorrow, I hope we shall have nothing further to detain us.

I went last night to the Esquimaux village, where I spent 2 or 3 hours among their tents. They are now living in tents of skin (deer & seal) a good deal like the Moorish tents, but much <u>dirtier</u>. In sept they go into winter houses which are built of turf & stones about 4 feet above the ground, the floor being excavated to a depth of 3 or 4 ft below it. A narrow crooked, half underground passage leads into it, looking very much like a large drain. These people are in better condition than most of the Esquimeaux however, as the Danes do much to civilize them, & have actually established a school during the winter months at which a half Esquimaux is the school master! I was surprised to find that nearly all here, especially the young ones, can write & make figures. One of them drew a sketch of some of our party (on a wall) which was really not bad. They are very different in appearance to any Indians that I have seen, having such remarkably <u>broad</u> flat features, projecting cheekbones, & low depressed noses. The outside corners of their eyes are drawn up in a manner like those of the Chinese or Tartars which gives them a most remarkable expression of countenance.

I assisted Goodsir yesterday in collecting words for a vocabulary, & we were very much struck with the resemblance between their language & what we know of the Tartar & Kamschatadate. Every word almost begins & ends with a <u>K</u> which makes the language harsh. I have sent, by the agent of the Transport, a small box which contains the eggs of the Eider duck, tern, snow bunting & one of the ptarmigan, in case you should not have them already. Of the snow bunting eggs & ducks there are 2 pairs & I have promised Sir John to beg you to send a pair of each to a young friend of his who wants them for her collection (Miss Cust) I will give her address when he comes off. Should you have the other eggs already perhaps you will give her all that you do not want.

It is curious how few <u>wants</u> we find. There is scarcely anything that could be of use that has been neglected & I really do not think if I could be in London for an hour or two I should want to get anything! I am delighted with my watch & pray tell Elizabeth that the chains she made me are <u>invaluable</u>. I will not say any more today as I want to write several letters. I write to Mr. Warre & Dr. Richardson. I intended writing to Uncle Walter, but I will not write a short letter & have not time for a long one, so I shall beg you to send him this one to read, when you have read it as he begged me to tell him of our proceedings. Where this letter may find you I have not the least idea but I hope & think the Italian plan was adopted & that you may read it in Rome or Florence. I suppose Charley is now in the Superb & trust he likes her & those in her. If he comes round the Horn, perhaps we may meet! I shall look out anxiously for him in the first boat that comes off at Petropaulowsky. however I fear it is no use looking. I often suggest to myself the different plans you may be pursuing.

Sir John told me to close my letters tomorrow so I will end this with a P.S should I have anything to tell you before sealing it. I have only now to

send my kindest love Libbity, & William & to George & Charley when you write
& believe me to be ever
    my dearest father
      your affectionate son
        James W. Fairholme

P.S. As I remember William has got a Polar Chart I may as well give you some idea of our course after leaving this place which you will see a little to the right of Disco Island. We go if the wind is fair, through the Waygat Passage, & stand north, as far as about Baffin's Island. It then depends on the state of the ice whether we stand straight over to Lancaster Sound or follow the land right round Baffin's Bay. In one case we run the risk of getting beset by floating ice, & drifted to the southward. In the other case the voyage is longer, but there is more chance of open water & always something to secure the ship to, either by land or icebergs aground.

Our Icemaster is in favour of the latter plan which I hope we may adopt, as it will give us a good opportunity of seeing the "Highlands & Highlanders" of Sir John Ross. Our first attempt in the sound will be, I believe by one of the passages to the South of Melville Island, but then all depends on how we find the ice. You may be assured I shall not miss an opportunity of writing by the whalers, some of whom we are sure to see in the Sound.

The Bag is now being closed (sewed up) so I will only add that we have almost completed swinging for local attraction, & shall sail tonight or tomorrow morning, with a fair wind. So goodbye again with my prayers for the safety & health of all my dear friends at home.
    Saturday 12ᵗʰ   J.W.F.

141. JAMES FITZJAMES TO JOHN BARROW JR, 1–11 JULY 1845

HMS Erebus Latitude 68° N.
11 pm 1ˢᵗ July 1845

My dear Barrow

You d'ont often get a letter from <u>this</u> side of the Arctic Circle – you have never got one from any body who has a more sincere regard for you –

We expect to get in to Disco tomorrow and I shall have so much work on my hands that I may not have time to write – so I shall have this letter written ready beforehand.

The fair wind which blew us from our friends the steamers did not last long – and we had one continued succession of Westerly and North Westerly wind (relieved now and then by a fair wind for a day) till the 21st June when we found ourselves 134 miles due East of Cape Farewell – There we had a calm with a most tremendous heavy swell in which we <u>did roll</u>.

During our journey thus far we went within 60 or 70 miles of your old friend Iceland but it was too cloudy to see Mount Hecla – We did not go within 70 miles of Cape Farewell but rounded it with a gale right aft which followed us round – with a heavy sea we kept close reefed Topsails & reefed Foresail and made the old craft go 8 knots through it. We lost no time I can assure you – the only difficulty I had was to get Sir John to shorten sail when it was wanted – he is full of life and energy – with good judgement and a capital memory – one of the best I know his conversation is delightful & most instructive and of all men he is the most fitted for the command of an enterprize requiring sound sense and great perseverance – I have learned much from him & consider myself most fortunate in being with such a man – and he is full of benevolence & kindness withal –

We had the usual allowance of rain, & squalls, (heavy ones too) Shipped a few seas – one or two down in our mess – but satisfied ourselves that the Erebus is very easy – though now & then we did kick & plunge most terribly – We were all in a good humour, in fact there is one incessant laugh from morning to night – We are most comfortable & happy – plenty to do observing all sorts of things all day and eating good dinners into the bargain – On Sunday the 22d we were due South of Farewell on the 24th we flattered ourselves we were in Davis' Straits being in Lat 69°36' for a bright gleam of sunshine enabled us to get this & dry our clothes &selves – We worked for Cape Desolation which sounds Polar enough and we bowled along merrily shaking hands with ourselves and making interesting short cuts through America to the Pacific –

The thermometer had scarcely ever varied 3° for three weeks – being at about – 43° – <u>On the 25th</u> we saw our <u>first ice-berg inshore</u> the beautiful sharp craggy snowy coast of Greenland in sight – an immense distance off and a thing like a rock sticking up this being 10 miles off which might have been an iceberg for aught I could tell – this was at 2 in the morning the sun just rising – the sea smooth – air clear – Read our Ice Master always told us we should see <u>no ice</u> down here "barring the bergs" – which are nothing – Since then we have had delightful smooth Seas – sometimes calm – sometimes a foul wind light & <u>much</u> fair wind – for the last few day[s] we have been nearer the land and yesterday were catching cod near the most glorious assemblage of ice rock snow & clouds – being about 30 miles from the Coast about Lichtenfels – Today we have had a splendid breeze right aft with a strong current in our favour A most splendid semicircle of Icebergs appear ahead & under the land we count 65 from the "crows' nest" – but we d'ont care for we know they are all aground – I always fancied an ice berg was a great transparent looking lump of ice – instead of a white beautiful twelfth cake looking thing as it is – odd shapes enough however some of them.

I have just been on deck looking at one about 200 feet high which came down with a crash & raised a mist like an avalanche. – It is now 12 o'clock, though the sun is up so I shall go to bed and finish this tomorrow – though it is a pity to sleep on such a fine clear sun shiny night –

2nd July Soon after going to bed last night it came on to rain hard and the breeze freshened we got in amongst the icebergs and saw about 180 before morning when we stood in and found ourselves in the forenoon close under the rugged high land of Disko covered with masses of cloud & its ravines filled with white snow We were in fact close to the Settlement called Lievely & shewed our colors to a Danish flag hoisted on a low point – The day has been tolerably miserable – raining hard. Thermometer up to 42° smooth water & we have had to beat up towards the Whale Fish Islands which are in the bay to the SE of Disko. The scenery of Disko is grand in the extreme & well worth the trouble of coming & the beautiful icebergs in bold relief against the dark almost black looking coast look curious – we shall not get into our berth in the Whale Islands before tomorrow.

Whale Fish Islands 10th July 1845 We lost the whole of the 3rd by some extraordinary mistake we mistook the locale of the Whale Islands having two charts one of which was wrong & the other not too right, and we went right up the bay to the mouth of the Waigaut – sailing in the most delightfully smooth water among ice bergs of the largest size – The altitude at Noon shewed us we were wrong & we went back getting into our anchorage at 3 in the morning of the 4th. fortunately we had a breeze right around the bay; and as this is the only day we have lost since we sailed – we must set it down to unavoidable accidents & <u>not care</u>. The master of the Transport says he never saw vessels carry so much sail as we did. I shall give Mr. Griffiths (the agent) a note to you as you desired and I think he will amuse you with his account of us – he is a very intelligent and well read man – so get hold of him –

This is the snuggest of all possible harbours – we are lashed alongside the Transport – moored head and stern and the the Terror close outside us This is the harbour:

A. Erebus & Transport
B = Terror
C. Boat Island
D Esquimaux huts
E a Big iceberg
F. D° D°
GGG – Islands
a Row of "<u>Huski-Mays</u>"

They have the smallest possible canoes here into one of which I was determined to get last night so got my trowsers off and paddled about for some time but at last over I went head down-wards where I remained till rescued. Capsised to a T –

Our observatories where I have passed most of my time are on Boat Island and we have had the most heavenly weather here I ever saw clear calm – with a hot sun & Ice bergs glistening in all directions. Fairholme Hodgson & I counted 280 from the top of a hill the other night – and big mosquitoes biting us all the time. The work of clearing the Transport has been a heavy one – we counted on doing it in two or 3 days at most – but though we have worked from 4 am to 6 pm hard we shall only finish this evening, and I hope swing the ship tomorrow & sail next morning the 12th rather <u>late</u> but we c'ant help it & if we have a good breeze & open sea to Lancaster Sound shall be there before the 1st August which will be plenty of time – but we must remember that Parry was 54 days doing it on one occasion.

We are very deep & full as an egg – the Terror is fearfully deep – and her deck is piled up with coals to the exclusion of all light below from her bull's eyes which is a serious annoyance – however we shall start with three years provisions & the Engine! – You have no conception how happy we all are – Sir John is delightful – I believe however I told you of him & in a former part of this letter.

We hear that this is supposed to be a remarkably clear season – but have had as yet no good authentic intelligence However clear or not clear we must go ahead as the yankees have it – and if we do'nt get through it w'ont be our fault – I can see however that even if there be a good passage that is a perfect lottery what sort of season we have – and whether we happen to be at the particular spots at the most favorable moments.

I like Crozier, he is a most indefatigable man and a good observer. Just suited for his position I should say.

And now you have us as far as Disko and by the time you get this we shall I trust be well into our work – where we may be God knows Give my kindest regards to Sir John and Lady Barrow – we intend to drink Sir John's health on the day we go through Behrings Straits – If we get through this year, we shall have to land somewhere or other to discharge some cargo – for it will not be safe to go into the Pacific laden as we are and now good bye for the present – if there be an opportunity of writing by any of the Whalers I shall give you a line in the meantime believe me always
    Your sincere friend
    James Fitzjames

all your friends here (& you have many) desire to be remembered to you

11th July – The Transport is only this day cleared at Noon – the work has been very heavy – and we are fearfully deep – drawing 17 ft. 4 in forward & no false keel. But we have 3 years provisions in d'ont you Admiralty-people be saying "What have those fellows been wasting their time at Disko for?" – We have done all it was possible to do in the time – besides the wind is NE and we are better here – The weather heavenly – sun quite hot – Adieu.

142. HENRY T.D. LE VESCONTE TO SARAH LE VESCONTE [MOTHER], 2 JULY 1845

HMS Erebus – off Disco in
Baffin's Bay. July 2nd 1845

My dear Mother

I fear that were it not for the affectionate interest you take in every thing relating to your children you would find but little to please you in this letter. There is so little in the monotony of a sea voyage and in the scenes of this wild inhospitable land which will pay for describing – but you will be glad to know that I am in very good health and delighted with the proceedings of the expedition. That I am under the orders and guidance of a most skillful amiable and pious commander – all our proceedings are influenced by the greatest harmony and good will. every one is anxious to render a cheerful obedience to the wise regulations – which emanate from our gallant Captain hitherto the only things of interest we have seen are first the vast number of highly curious – small blubbers and other marine animals and animaliculae which in fine weather we dredge up from the bottom of the sea or catch on its surface this sea abounds with these strange creatures of whose habits and structure very little is known. our skilful naturalist Mr Goodsir provided with powerful microscopes is making collections of them accompanied by drawings and descriptions. I must say I prefer them in their native beauty swimming in the clear water – I do not like – snakes and blubbers in bottles – nor do I admire butterflies with pins stuck through them. altho I can appreciate their beauty when freely flying from flower to flower. but I can admire the zeal of those who labour to d[isclose] the wonderful secrets of nature. our charts of this place are so defective as to be almost useless if the weather permits we shall make a survey of it which will give me much to do I am therefore writing my letters while I have time that a press of work may not give me the sorrow of leaving them unwritten When we shall meet again is known only to the all wise disposer of events – but I hope you & my dear sisters will always believe that I feel the loveliest love for you – and I must ask in return your love for one whom I feel becomes hourly more dear to me I assure you she is a <u>very good</u> girl. believe me my dear mother ever most affectionately your son

HTD LeVesconte

143. HARRY GOODSIR TO ANSTRUTHER TAYLOR [UNCLE], 2 JULY 1845

July 2ᵈ. 1845
Island of Disco
Baffins Bay

My Dear Uncle

I am a very bad letter writer even when I have abundance of time it is not likely therefore that my attempts will improve when hurried as I am very much at present but I hope you will overlook any faults or imperfections in the present instance I promised Aunt when writing from Stromness or perhaps it was Greenhithe to write you by the Steamers which accompanied us so far out of the Orkneys but my time has been so much taken up with observations on the animals procured, drawings and descriptions that it was completely out of my power & even now it is hard work to write this for I have been at work without intermission for the last fortnight day and night writing, drawing and using the microscope – I can do so constantly here because there is constant light ever since we entered Davis Straits & since the 30ᵗʰ. Ult. when we passed the Arctic circle the sun never descends below the horizon. He is always in sight & at times very powerful. During the 25ᵗʰ. 26ᵗʰ. & 27ᵗʰ. water spilt on the Deck steams out with much greater rapidity than it would during the warmest days in Summer with you.

I have already obtained a great number of very valuable specimens and have before this leaves me far above 100 drawings – many more than was expected so early in the voyage My Mess mates are all very active in assisting me & during the warm days a whole range of them from the Commander downwards may be seen over both sides of the vessel dabbing for animals. They are all excellent men. The very purser takes an immense interest & is dabbing constantly. The Officers mess consists of 12 & during meals there is always a great deal of amusement. During our passage out we had very bad weather & when rounding Cape Farewell it blew a tremendous gale, in such weather several handless fellows amongst them were constantly tumbling over their dishes or teacups causing great anoyance to others so I introduced porridge or as they call it Burgoo, to breakfast which has now become a standard dish in both vessels. I took it myself more for a change than anything else from the constant hard biscuit which is the only bread we have. Several on board who had not been at sea for some time before and were suffering from the change improved very much in their health & all on board the Terror were complaining before this change. It was amusing to me to see the way in which it was eat[en] some mixing salt beef & mustard with pepper, others eggs & the rest fish, All however praised the Burgoo!! I never loose my appetite any where & in all likely hood it will increase in these cold climates!!! We have got 10,000 cases of preserved ready cooked meats on board the Erebus alone so you see there is no chance of Starving. Notwithstanding the awful gale which blew as we were rounding Cape Farewell Sir John had Divine Service twice, All the men assemble, with the exception of those who keep the watch on deck, below the main hatchway on the main deck sitting on their chests in rows the officers being arranged on each side of the Captain who reads the Service very beautifully. It is one of the most solemn scenes I ever witnessed hearing the responses under such circumstances; in this case the vessels were running before the wind, with only a little bit of topsail to keep her steady, at the rate of 9 knots an hour, & an enormous sea running, the noise being so great as to prevent you hearing what any person says.

Do you know if Sir Howard Douglas is any relation of Lord Williams? I ask because one of my messmates called Des Veaux (pronounced De Veau) appears to be a relation of Sir Hs. He says he know Lord William & his Family altho not personally; he is 2^d. mate. Captain Fitz James is Commander Mr. Gore 1st. Lieutenant Le Vescomte 2^d. D. Fairholme 3^d. Des Veaux, Sargent, & Couch Mates Fairholme is a nephew of Lord Forbes's

We are now passing great numbers of icebergs many very large floating about; but many more of enormous size – as big almost as Kelly Law – stranded and appearing like islands. We have passed numbers of whales altho no true whales yet, we are not far enough north for them, Sea Horses, Seals &c. Specimens of all which I expect to get and examine.

I hope you are all well and that Aunt will not

[rest of letter missing]

144. HENRY T.D. LE VESCONTE TO HENRY LE VESCONTE [FATHER], 2 JULY 1845

> HMS Erebus off the S End of Disco
> In Baffins Bay heading up in the
> Whale Islands
> 2 July 1845

My dear Father

This is most probably the last letter I shall have an opportunity of writing to you for a time so indefinite that I am afraid to fancy what its length may be. I wrote you before leaving England all that I thought could be of interest to you and to my dear mother – I told you I felt glad that you approved of my proceeding on this voyage it is <u>one</u> of those opportunities which occur but once in a man's life and should by all means be taken advantage of. There is no instance I believe of a person going on a Polar voyage who has not gained one step by it, not always indeed at once. but then where it has not been so as as was the case with the officers of the Isabella and Alexander and Dorothea and Trent in 18 the Government were displeased with the commanders for returning home without making greater exertions Sir John Franklin was Lieutenant commanding the Trent in company with the Dorothea Captain Buchan. They were to attempt to go by Spitsbergen over the North Pole and so down to Behring's Straits. The ships got into the ice the Dorothea Captain Buchans ship was very much damaged and he decided on returning home and taking the Trent with him. Sir John Franklin wished to go on but Captain B said his ships company were discontented at the idea of going in an unsound ship – so there was an end of the expedition it has not been attempted since, and all sensible men agree that it is impracticable – what this at N may turn out I cant say but this I know that we are most ably commanded and if skill and perseverance can do it it will be done now.

You would be much astonished to see our daily operations for finding the variation of the compass. not only its general variation but the difference on each particular point. this is done by a needle hung freely so as to point to the magnetic pole – by a number of observations which require to be taken with much care; to find the dip of the needle; at Greenhithe on the river it hangs 69 degrees from the horizontal when pointed at the magnetic meridian on the same line as the variation here on latitude 68.30 North it dips 83 ½ degrees. The consequence of the needle assuming a nearly vertical position is that the iron of the ship has a great effect on it so much so that here with the ships head SE we allow 57 degrees westerly variation whilst on a West course we have to allow 80 the consequence of making these observations and correcting our courses according to well-tried rules is that we scarcely ever find a current in the open sea when the logs in ancient time or indeed in years but just gone by remarked on the ships being set here and there without any apparent reason. The effect of the ships iron on the compasses is however of much less importance as we proceed on to lower latitudes and the fact of the greater number of ships being employed where the compass is less liable to error may account for its being long unnoticed.

You will be pleased to learn that we are very happy and all goes as well as the most sanguine could wish on board the Erebus. Sir John is a most able and most worthy man he proceeds on the voyage solely from his love of science with I should think a spice of ambition to get a name then I have my old and very good friend Captain Fitzjames and a set of messmates worthy of my highest esteem – we are on a very liberal allowance of provisions &c on board the ship – preserved meats and pickles in abundance but then the climate requires something extra – even now the second of July we have the thermometer from 34 to 36 with much rain and thick weather whilst the land is covered with snow. we are now beating in to anchor at the Whale Islands. to clear our transport and make some observations – there are some Danish settlements about here containing very few of that people and the dependant Esquimaux who hunt for them and recieve knives and snuff in exchange for their skins and oil – this job will take us three or four days and then we go up the East side of the bay and round its head to Lancaster sound it may take us some time to get in here. there are two new kinds of sailing to learn weaving and boring. the former means threading your way in the narrow channels and the latter dashing at the Ice where it is not too heavy and breaking it or moving it on one side by the power of the ship – our efforts after getting as far as Melville Island will be directed to the Southward so as to get if possible on the coast of North America at the mouth of the Mackenzie River or there abouts – there is a variety of opinions about the best road to follow but that appears to be the one thought best of by the ablest judges among whom I reckon Sir John. Sir J Barrow the original promoter of these voyages is in favour of pushing north I think – but the man who has been several years in the north should be preferred before one who has but argued the thing by the fire side.

I have been thinking it possible but I must say it is hugely improbable that in the event of our reaching the coast some one might be sent into Canada with despatches and that that someone might be myself – I fear it is too good a scheme to be realised and yet when first I heard of the Polar expedition at Bromley it was just as remote from probable that I should be now in the Erebus in Baffin's Bay. even up to a few days before I knew it was decided on I was assured by people whose direct informants were cabinet ministers that the story was only spoken of to amuse old Barrow until he retired and then it would be stopped at once but it is the most liberally provided expedition that has yet been fitted out – I am going to send my letters to my good friend Edmund Le F to distribute he will look out for intelligence of Philip – I wish very much you could hear from him. I think he must be gone to some South American place to settle. He has talent and ambition and plenty of pride which if it keeps him from speaking of himself unless he has something good to say will also prevent his doing any thing improper – you may suppose I have written a long story to my dear little

Henrietta I wish you could know her – I hope they will make me a commander in good time even for her sake – I hardly think the scheme on the King of the French would be advisable while there are reasonable objections such as seniors on the same service to be advanced but I have lately heard Sir John Franklin and others here speak of both Louis Phillipe and Madame Adelaide as being very fond of seeing and of serving all those they knew in their days of adversity I have some hopes from William Le Feuvre of course he will do anything he can for me and he can urge a claim better now than he could have done for a distant relative – I wish rather however to consider these things as chances and to trust entirely to my exertions. At present I have no thoughts of being on half pay while I can get full and if they will put me on the shelf as a commander I must try some other road. perhaps in the woods. but I dont know that – would like it. there is nothing I have more to say except that I hope I may be enabled soon to meet you again by your own fireside. to pray you to think I shall always study to do what will be most pleasing to you. and to request you ever to consider me your most affectionate son   HTD LeVesconte

145. CHARLES OSMER TO ELIZA OSMER [WIFE], 4–9 JULY 1845

At 3 o'clock this morning (4th July) we reached our Anchorage, having had to thread our way through innumerable 'Ice Bergs' and masses of <u>Ice</u>.

I must here stop to tell you that now we have passed the 'Arctic Circle' at
66°30' (the sun does not set consequently when the weather is clear we
see that luminary all the day and night, if light can be called night. We
are here snugly anchored, with small islands all round us, that a casual
observer would be puzzled how we got in, and how we are to get out,
but get in we did and get out we certainly shall – We landed the transport alongside the ship this afternoon and the work of clearing her has
commenced, but I much fear that it will occupy more time than I have
already anticipated in a former part of this letter. The Esquimaux, in their
small boats called 'Kyacks,' were early visitors, bringing with them various
rudely constructed articles for barter, but what pleased us most was the
quantities of wild ducks eggs which they had, and which we purchased for
a few Pounds of our ships biscuit. These eggs are very fine, and considered
a great delicacy and we found them every way delicious. Are we not in the
land of the living. At 5 o'Clock this morning (5th July) we commenced our
work of clearing the Transport, we expect to finish with her on Tuesday,
and to sail on the following day – We were visited in the course of the day
by several Esquimaux from the aged grandfather down to the child at the
back, they carry them so here. They had evidently turned out in their best,
had they been cleaner would not have been amiss.

I shall take a strole tomorrow to The Esquimaux Village, when I shall
be able to give you an idea how these poor creatures live. They are so
dirty – I dined again with Sir John to day with a party of our own and
the Terror's Officers I cannot tell you more than I have done how truly,
deservedly beloved Sir John is by us all –

Sunday morning 6th July – this morning has been ushered in by bright
sunshine, so as to enliven the spirits of us all on board. The brightness of
the day forms a striking contrast to the dreary aspect of the rocks around
us but we must make up our minds to prefer them to the beautiful green
fields, otherwise we shall always remain dispirited. We are now preparing
for Divine service – I mentioned yesterday that it was my intention to pay
a visit this day to the Esquimaux village, if it can be so called. After dinner
& divine service, Sir John asked me to accompany him I am constrained to
say that nothing will tell to the Advantage of an Esquimaux they are one
mass of dirt alas that ever human beings should reside in places very much
inferior to our common pig sties in England. We were accompanied by one
of our Sailors (a Dane) who speaks their language, and as there was rather
an intelligent individual on the Island in the person of a 'Danish agent,' we
managed to pick up some little information only fancy not a large strip
of land, very high at one end composed almost entirely of red and white

granite rocks, rising above each other to the height of 100 feet, with not even a blade of grass to divert the eye from the montononey of this huge pile of stones. no trees no shrubs, no anything but <u>rock rock</u> – so you can fancy what Sir John felt on attaining its summit which we did after much toil & trouble, swarms of 'mosquitoes' as large, I was going to say, <u>Eagles</u>, as a blue <u>bottle fly</u> they stung us through our <u>trowsers</u>.

We obtained a good view of Greenland covered with snow, and of the almost innumerable small Islands with which the Coast abounds, this view was certainly worth all the fatigue we had and the annoyance we experienced from our friends the 'mosquitoes' in our descent we came to a small patch of sand and stones, the burying place of the natives. The graves were very rudely constructed and not long like you see in England, from the circumstance of their interring their dead in a sitting posture with their hands drawn up under their chins, I suppose there must be some superstition attached to this. We descended towards the Village and peeped into a crude turf hut, <u>four feet high</u> and about 20 feet square, in which benches were placed traversing each other at right angles, and on enquiring we learnt that this was a <u>genteel</u> <u>establishment</u> for the <u>education</u> of <u>young Esquimaux Ladies and Gentlemen</u>. It appears that the Danish government provides them a teacher, I can vouch that they are apt scholars, as youngsters of both sexes, I heard read portions of the Testament translated in their own tongue. On enquiring I find that at stated intervals they are visited by a Moravian priest who christened, married, & buried them. 7th July this day we got on well with clearing the transport it would astonish you to see the amazing quantities of Provisions and Stores, including 80 tons of Coals which each Ship will receive on board, our decks are full Coals being ranged right round the inside, 8th July, I and Lieutenant Gore went out Shooting with one or two other officers we were not very fortunate.

9th July We are still occupied clearing the Transport a most disagreeable and tedious undertaking the decks being literally impassable from Casks, Cases, Coals, & Wood. I am not even now enabled to say for certain when we leave this, July 10th We cleared the Transport this Afternoon and we have very little left us to do but stow every thing and clear our decks – I think we shall leave this on Saturday (12th) but nothing yet is known, We still continue to have so much beautiful weather so much so that it is warm enough for white jackets, and straw hats. You will hardly conceive this to be the case but I can assure you tis the fact, and all this in 70° North. I dined on board the Terror to day and was much entertained by the surmises of the different Officers as to our intended <u>route</u> – nobody but Sir John and myself being acquainted with it – however it will soon be known. We start in about two <u>hours</u> on our <u>eventful</u> <u>Voyage</u>, with the most beautiful weather, almost insufferably hot. We expect to fall in with the main body of Ice in about ten days, then perhaps we shall not have to complain of the <u>heat</u>.

Charles H. Osmer

146. FRANCIS CROZIER TO JOHN HENDERSON,
4 JULY 1845

Whale Fish Island,
July 4th 1845

My dear Jack

I do sincerely hope this will find [you] recovered from the effects of your most unfortunate accident often indeed have I thought of it since knowing that it was your kindness in executing my commissions led you into such a trap – there is no excuse for them at the ship, in short I have no patience with such carelessness Well old boy we were a long time getting clear of the coast of England & Orkneys our passage across was very boisterous however we are safely moored here & busy clearing the Transport – How full we shall be but I am still in hopes we shall be able to stuff into her three years provisions from the present time – Our steering is decidedly improved by the alterations in the counter we now sail much more evenly with Erebus which is advantageous to us in many ways – Bergs are numerous this year but we did not stand far enough to the west to make the packed ice on our passage up Davis Straits – We were two days at Stromness Steamers towed us about 50 miles to Westward of Land – Rattler towed the two Vessels at about 5 miles an hour – not bad I think – I would rather be on a Sailing Vessel I mean as a Command – Well Jack I wonder when we shall again meet – Some years no doubt – this Season will have a good deal to do with our future operations if we can only make a good hit at the first, it will be most glorious

All going on as well as I could wish, every one has fallen very speedily into their places and things are progressing quietly – My time I find is fully occupied with observations of various kind which I have not as yet instructed our Youths in although they are full of zeal and anxiety to do well Living alone is the great drawback to me but I know well it cannot be otherwise. I belong to the Gregarious tribe of animals I believe but I do not pine much when alone – My Tea and Sugar has not yet turned up the latter is to me a great loss – however that will be a triffle if we only make a good seasons work of it – I am sending three men home in Transport reducing our compliment to 62 from 68 which we know is quite enough too many I would say still – In Fury if you recollect we had only 58 or 60 – but now we have more officers which would make us about the same number of working men – If you see anything in Newspapers about us send one old boy to my sisters 2 Sandford Place Dublin – I mean if it is so that it would give them a favourable impression as to our movements – I intend writing a line to old Bird before we leave – God bless you old Boy and that you may not have any bad effects from your unfortunate accident is the

prayer of your sincere friend

F.R.M.Crozier

147. FRANCIS CROZIER TO AN UNKNOWN CORRESPONDENT, C. 4 JULY 1845 [EXCERPT]

All is getting on as well as I could wish. Officers full of youth and zeal, and indeed everything is going on most smoothly. The Admiralty were exceedingly kind to us, all our demands were readily granted; if we can only do something worthy of the country which has so munificently fitted us out, I will only be too happy; it will be an ample reward for all my anxieties, and believe me, Henry, there will be no lack of them.

148. EDWARD COUCH TO JAMES COUCH AND MARY COUCH [PARENTS], EXCERPTS ONLY [COPY], 4–11 JULY 1845

Erebus.
Whale Islands – close along side of Isle – Disco – Davies Str.
July 4th to 11th 1845 –

Arrival took place this morning at 3 o'clock & one of the rummest snug little places I ever saw. x x x x x I have been on shore with Le Visconte one of the Lieutenants – all over on[e] of the islands taking the bearings of the different points of land & making a sketch or two – Old Sir John came up with us – very rough barren place, so I was obliged to help him up & down every minute – all the climbing places – I was surprised to see him attempt anything so risky but he managed very well considering. x x x x x

We were a long time finding out this place, no one having been here before – there are so many little groups of islands – we went right up S.E. Bay 20 miles – thinking to find there but no, oh no, we were obliged to come back again, so lost a day by it. x x x x Captain Parry came here once to unload the transport – well adapted for the purpose. x x x

I have been very busy all the way across, making Sir John a signal book – painting in etc – a copy of one Sir Edward Parry used – a long job & have only just finished it – So He is pleased – as I took a good deal of pains about it & that, with a little drawing, has been my chief occupation. x x x x x x

Old Franklin is an exceedingly good old chap – all are quite delighted with him and very clever – he is quite a Bishop. – We have church – morning & evening on Sundays – the evening service in the cabin to allow the watch that could not attend in the forenoon to do so in the evening – We all go to the (Terror ?) – gives sermons out of his sermon books & I can assure you – adds a great deal himself – They say they would sooner hear him than half the parsons in England – He has 3 every day to dinner with him and when the weather permits the Captain & officers of "Terror" – He ordered stock & wine to be laid in, enough for 4 every day & a cabin full twice a week for 3 years, so you see what a liberal old man he is –

In our mess – we live uncommon well – too well almost – we commenced preserved meats & soups etc, a day or two ago & find them very good – in fact every thing is most comfortable – couldn't be more so. x x x x We shall have plenty of shooting by & bye – when we arrive at our station – jammed in the ice – a regular set of game laws will come out – that whatever is shot goes as ships provisions, to save the others, so it almost becomes a duty, as well as a pleasure – We saw an English barque yesterday pass by Disco on her way to the Whale fisheries – just from England. x x x x x

They were talking in England about our being too late for the season but we are full early now even & they say it is a very comparatively warm season – x x x x It is not decided where we shall winter but very likely at Melville Island – It is almost an impossibility to think of getting thro' this season – Odd as it appears nobody likes the thoughts of being done out of going through one of the winters to see & pick up every thing worth knowing – So about Sept 1846 we hope to be in Behring's Straits on our way home – which is not over long to look forward to – Coming back this way again is a thing decided against, as a matter of course & no mistake –

Blankey, ice master – in Terror – is a clever, capital chap & much liked – x x x x x

Talking of meridian altitudes, old Sir John has lent me one of his sextants to use instead of my old quadrant, so I have plenty of that work, 2 or 3 times every day – our work is kept in books & bye & bye will be sent to the admiralty, as well as our journals & all drawings, charts – which the Captain distinctly made known to us – they give them up generally in 2 years or so, if they don't want to keep them & all specimens as well, that we shoot or pick up – they are odd fellows

We have about 50 tons of coal on the upper deck besides 2 rows of salt provisions right round the upper deck – the large chocks outside make a make a capital stowing place – all the Booms etc go outside – the lower deck is as full & every hole & corner in her crammed – we stow a great deal more than the "Terror" – as she has left a great deal behind – We have taken more coals than was expected, as the transport had some hundred bags of it which she brought for the Rattler – So we have it now & a "store is no sore" as the saying is. x x x Sargent & I went on shore this afternoon – for the sole purpose of taking a sketch of this place but were obliged to retire with the loss of one pound of flesh each – almost eaten by mosquitos –

149. JOHN FRANKLIN TO ELEANOR FRANKLIN [DAUGHTER], 6 JULY 1845

My dearest Eleanor,   Whale Fish Island near Disco
                                         Sunday 6th July 1845

I commence my letter to you on this day, and I feel certain that you & your Mama have had your thoughts frequently on this day turned towards me and my companions. This has been with us a day of rest and comfort as I trust it has been with you. In addition to our own party at the morning service we were joined by the officers & some of the crew of the Transport – Which is now alongside of the Erebus that the stores may be more easily delivered over. The subject of the sermon was the importunity of Bartemeus as related by Saint Mark which is almost identical with the account of our Saviours compassionate relief of him given by Saint Luke in the 2nd lesson for the day – The evening service is read in my Cabin, that of the morning being on the Main Deck – and all who choose to attend the second service may come, and I am truly grateful by observing that all the officers & seamen not on watch avail themselves of this privilege – May God grant that these opportunities of uniting together in divine worship may prove effectual in bringing each of us nearer to Christ. The evening sermon was taken from the 2nd lesson on the subject David wishing to purchase Araunah's threshing Floor – from whence it was proved that God would not be pleased with sacrifices which cost us nothing to make – and that we must surrender our dearest pleasure if it be contrary to the commandments of God – You have seen on the Fairlie & on the Rajah how very attentive seamen are during service – but I think our men are still more earnest in their desire to hear the word of Truth than these were – I have as yet selected my sermons from those volumes which you know I used to read with so much pleasure on coming home – and as many of them are upon historical subjects and practical points I shall continue to read from these Family sermons – until I have gone through them- I thought that I had Arnolds sermons on board – but I find that I have only his life – & the history of Rome.

I went in the afternoon to visit the station at which the Esquimaux reside – on an island not far from our anchorage. These people are engaged by the Danish Governmentt to kill seals for their oil & skins which are sent for sale to Denmark These about 130 Esquimaux in all belonging to this station but the greater part of these are now absent catching seals and about 30 only remaining here – They appear to me to be well taken care of by the Danish Governmentt – many of them we are told read their Bibles – and when the whole party is here the Children are taught daily. One of the Huts was pointed out to me as the School Room which I noticed was furnished with seats & stools – The women when they came to visit the ships were neatly dressed – in Sealskin, prepared of course by themselves, though one or two had cotton dresses – all of them wore a handkerchief on their heads – within which the hair was neatly tied in an exact queue – Their faces as well as those of their children were clean – I invited them down to my cabin where they sat about

¼ of an hour – talking among themselves but did not touch any thing – I saw them at their Tents cleaning & dressing the Seal skins – I send you a specimen of their work in the shape of a watch holder. – The Danish minister frequently attends to preach to and instruct these poor people – He is now making a Tour round his other stations – The person who seems now to have the charge of the station is a Carpenter apparently an intelligent man who has been in this Country 13 years. He lives in a wooden Hut during summer and in a Turf raised Hut in winter – The store also is of wood.

The other residences are either skin tents or Huts built of Turf – with a step under ground for warmths sake. The Governor being in Denmark on sick leave of absence and the next in command, absent from Disco on a Tour of inspection, I have seen no person of higher rank than the Carpenter of this Exquimaux station under whose charge these people at present seem to be. He however appears an intelligent man -, his information is that the winter has been severe but the spring not a late one – and that he has understood the ice has broken away some degrees farther north, as far as Lat 73, from the shore and he judges from all these circumstances that our passage to Lancaster Sound may be favourable – at any rate he seems to have no doubt of our getting there quite in time for the ice being broken away farther to the west than that Sound – However as to what part or even as to Lancaster Sound he knows nothing – We hope in a few days to have our stores on board from the Transport and to go and examine for ourselves – We all continue full of hope and eager to get forward – May God bless our humble efforts and grant us his protection & favour – and enable us to put forth our own utmost strength & judgment – and then to leave the issue of the voyage to his Almighty will.

I have requested of your Mama not to become over anxious if we do not return to you by the time you may prescribe for our absence – because as the ships on quitting this place will be stored for three years of every needful supply – we can with safety perhaps pass a second winter if the prospect of still farther progress be encouraging – or we should not have tried all the parts which may promise a passage – This can be done without any apprehension being entertained as to our safety – though we could not reach home within the 3ᵈ year –

I am very desirous of impressing the same caution on yourself – do not be over anxious on this point, and pray endeavour to cheer each other with the hope that the Lord will protect us – if we seek by prayer his continual help & guidance – I hope & trust through Gods blessing that for your sake & that of Mr Gell – I may reach England soon after he has established himself at home in some position which would justify his marrying – and which I am sure he would make a point of doing as soon as he can – You may assure him when you write that my esteem & affection for him are great and that nothing shall be left undone on my part to promote his welfare & your united happiness – I do not imagine that he will remain very long in VDLand – nor at all after the Archdeacon returns, longer than may be necessary to set the College going if there is to be one – To remain that time and assist in that good office I conceive to be his duty even if he should not be tempted to accept the office of the First Warden – However, I pray heartily that God may guide his judgment in this, and in every part of his future life – and that he may not take any step unadvisedly – – I have nothing more to say to him than what I last wrote – and I shall not therefore write now – you must say what you think best for me – I shall entirely confide in your Mama's judgment and your own as respects your happiness – and I pray that God will bless you with a right judgments in all things – and keep you under the influence of His Holy spirit –

Believe me ever your most affectionate Father
John Franklin

I refer you to your Mama's letter for details of what we have been doing & of other matters.

150. JOHN FRANKLIN TO JOHN RICHARDSON, 7 JULY 1845

Whale Fish Islands
Disco Bay
7th July 1845

My dear Richardson,

You will be glad to know that we made our passage to this place in good time. We anchored early on the morning of the 4th, and having got the Transport along side, began very soon to unload her. We have however some doubt whether the ships, the Terror in particular will be able to take all she has brought for us without being too deep in the water.

Time & care are also requisite to make the best stowage we can in our very limited room. Crozier and I are resolved to carry all the provision & fuel we can. We have been favoured with the most beautiful weather for the observations on shore and various sets of officers are busy at the Magnetic Instruments. The observations for Lat & Long and in getting Angles for the Survey of the Islands, if our stay permits. Specimens of the rocks & of the few Plants & Birds have been taken. Mr Goodsir has been very assiduous throughout in his dredging and has caught great numbers on our passage of Crustacae – acalepha with some Annelides & Molluscae, many of which are rare – He has kindly supplied me with the enclosed drawings of two fish which he thinks you would be desirous of having – He is now fully installed at a table in my Cabin, where he draws & describes his animals as soon as they are taken. Every one, officer & man is happy to collect for him; in fact he is a very general favourite on the ship. His immediate Senior behaves kindly to him, and I have seen no symptoms as yet of his being jealous of his Assistant. I perceive that Stanley is willing to take his part in collecting & skinning Birds, with which branch of Natural History he is perhaps the most acquainted.

The place where we are anchored is a mere fishing station for the Esquimaux who are employed in Catching Seals for the Danish Government. There are about 130 of them when all assembled, but not more than 30 at this time. They are like those in Hudsons Strait, but stouter, and their clothing manner & appearance bespeak that care is taken of them by their Masters. Several of them read the Bible, men & women. Some can do questions of simple Arithmetic, and I am informed that the children are kept at school when the whole are assembled, the teacher being a half Cast Dane who acts under the Minister. One of their Turf Huts was shown me in which seats & stools were placed, and the School is held.

The Danish Governor of Disco as well as the next officer in rank are absent and I hear that a Super cargo is left in charge, from whom I received a note in reply to one I had written to the Governor acquainting me that he could not read English & therefore could not understand my letter. His answer being in Danish I had to get it translated by one of my men. I found that it offered me any assistance, but referred me to the Cockswain of their Government boat now at this place for information. This I had already obtained from this man as well as from another person who appeared more intelligent than him. Both however, told me that the winter had been Severe, the strongest winds being from the

Eastward. The ice broke away in the Bay at the close of April, and their latest accounts from the Northward state that it is also broken up as far as 74° or the Women's Island, where our Whalers have been catching fish. These men argue from all these circumstances that the prospect is favourable for us as far as the getting in good time into Lancaster Sound is concerned, beyond that they know nothing about the matter. The main point for us at present is to get as quickly as we can across the Barrier of Ice in Baffins Bay and it is satisfactory for all of us to know that these men consider we are in proper time for doing that. We must pray for the guidance of the Almighty in this as in every part of our course, and having the hope of his protection and blessing, put forth our best exertions. The weather is now remarkably fine and even warm on shore, so that the Mosquitoes are troublesome to the thin skinned members of our party. They are of the large kind.

Mr Stanley begged me to remember him to you and I am sure Mr Goodsir wishes me to do so on his part, though he is too diffident to make the request of me.

When we have completed our provision from the Transport we shall have full three years supplies of every thing needful on board, so that if we should be foiled even after this winter we can without apprehension remain a second winter. I have been thinking much of the probability of there being a Chain of Islands, if not a continued shore which connects Wollaston Land with that of Banks as I remember you always imagined would prove to be the case. I cannot else see how the Musk Oxen got to Melville Island, which cannot swim far I suppose. These would hardly cross over the Ice, though the Reindeer would; besides the latter animals can swim, and would perhaps cross over wide channels. Should there exist a chain of islands in the direction we are speaking of, I shall consider the circumstance as favourable and that we shall have the best prospect of getting to the westward through the channels between them. I cannot agree with Sir John Barrow in supposing that the open water is to be found apart from Land. I shall of course despatch parties on boats & by land to examine into and find out passages, in places where it may be difficult & only productive of delay in taking the ships. I have had much pleasure in reading over a letter I received from Krusenstern soon after my return from Russia and Sir John Ross had sailed, to find that he feels certain of an Expedition succeeding in the NW passage if the ships can be got to any point we were at on the Coast of America. I admit with you that Regents Inlet seems to be the most certain way of attaining that point, but the more I reflect upon the voyages hitherto made into that Inlet the more convinced I am that James Ross & Parry are right in supposing that ships of our size if they were once got down among the islets and strong tides at the bottom of that Inlet, they would never be got out again. The Coast in that part must be surveyed in boats. But once to the west of Point Turnagain our ships might with safety go. Should we be entirely obstructed in forcing our passage between the parallels of Banks & Wollaston Lands, we must try the Wellington Channels or some other of the Channels to the North, but I cannot find any good reason for [...] we are to find open water th[...] ill have it.

I trust to your kindness in keeping my dear Jane & Eleanor as much at ease as possible on the subject of the difficulties that may attend our progress, and especially if it should turn out that we find it necessary to prolong our stay, beyond the time they may have fixed for our return. Your own experience will suggest to them many causes of detention quite consistent with our being in perfect safety & health.

I have an excellent set of officers & men who have embarked with the best spirit in the cause. It will [be] my study to keep them united & happy, and to encourage them while they put forth their own strenuous endeavours, to commit the issue of their success to God.
I hope my dear Richardson your dear children are proving themselves a great comfort to you. It is one of the trying circumstances of my present absence, that I am so far separated from you & them

and unable to assure you by my personal presence & help how deeply I sympathize with you all. May God bless & preserve you shall be my frequent prayer as well as that I may in Gods good time be permitted to return and enjoy your society.

Give my affectionate love to the Children and believe me ever most [...]

[John Franklin]
I think Lieutenant Fairholme intends [...]

151. HARRY GOODSIR TO JOHN GOODSIR [FATHER],
7 JULY 1845

July 7th.

My Dear Father

We have at length got to our anchorage in the Whale Fish Islands It was rather a heavy sea when we were beating off & on about 2 o clock in the morning but notwithstanding we very soon saw several specks just like Ducks upon the surface of the water which we very shortly found to be the Esquimaux in their canoes coming off to the Ships It was the strangest sight possible to see them rising up and down upon the tops of the waves in shells exactly the same size as that in the Gallery of the College of Surgeons and going through the water at a tremendous rate most of them without any covering for the head & dripping wet all over. One of them went in to the anchorage, between three or 4 Islands rather, before the ship. I have been working very hard since we got in & have done a great deal in all ways. Going on shore we saw one of the Esquimaux sick consumptive – He was lying in the most wretched hut amongst sea[l] skins on the ground the very grass growing at his feet. One of the men was making a mess of some Eider duck eggs outside and the women all dressed in seal skin jacket & trousers sitting round the inside of the tent, the dogs running about tearing at and eating every thing that came in their way I enclose a drawing of one of the tents. Two of the men gave us a couple of eggs each in return for Tobacco biscuit rum &c. I enclose the eider down taken from the two nests which I found myself on shore Jane should clean it and make a cushion it is valuable I will write another letter but in case of accidents seal up this.

Your Affectionate Son
Harry D. S. Goodsir

152. JOHN FRANKLIN TO ROBERT BROWN,
9 JULY 1845

Whale Fish Island
Disco Bay
9th July 1845

My dear Brown,

Here we are, having been one month from Stromness. Busy as Bees, and like those careful animals laying in plenty of stores. We hope to get our portion from the Transport this Evening, and then we shall have on board three complete years of provision and fuel. The ships however are very deep, which is of little consequence as the sea is for the most part smooth where there is much ice, and by the time we get to Behring's Strait, or through the winter, we shall be in good sailing trim, and have room to stretch out our limbs which we have hardly room now to do, so perfectly full is every hole & corner.

The Danish authorities are all absent from Disco making their Tours of Inspection, so that I have not been able to make enquiries as to the ice at the Fountain Head, but I have conversed with an intelligent man, a Carpenter, who is in charge at a Station near this anchorage, and learnt from him that though the last winter was unusually severe, the spring was not later than usual, and that the Ice broke away from the Land here about at the close of April.

He had also understood that the ice had separated from the land as far North as 73° latitude Early in June, from which circumstance he considers that we have a favourable passage to Lancaster Sound, which is the limit of his knowledge

You will be glad to hear that Goodsir has collected very assiduously on the waters and from Depths, and that he has procured many things which are rare & some of them unknown. I must not however attempt to give you their unwriteable names, but trust to your learning what they are from Professor Forbes or some other of his Correspondents.

He is a most assiduous person, and no sooner bags his game than he sketches & describes what he has got. I have given him one of the tables in my Cabin, at which he works daily. You will be glad to know that there is no feeling of jealousy shewn on the part of his immediate Senior. Their pursuits are not likely to clash, for Stanley likes ornithology, and his stuffed birds are also spread to dry in my Cabin, by permission

Goodsir is a general favourite with officers & men, and every one is ready to assist him.

Let me again thank you my dear friend for all your kindnesses to my wife & my family. The recollection of this has caused me now to beg of them to confer with you whenever they may feel particularly anxious on any point. I know also that they feel a happiness in having the permission to do so.

My last letter from my wife, received at the Orkneys, lead me to feel assured that she will not be much depressed by any attempts the Montague and Forster parties may make to bully and frighten her.

Some of my officers have read the Pamphlet which I brought with me to within a sheet or two of its close in manuscript, beyond what had been printed. They are astonished at the conduct of Lord Stanley which they designate as being disgraceful and to that of Montague they apply the term vilainous.

What I most fear respecting my wife is that if we do not return at the time she has fixed in her mind, she may become very anxious, and I shall in such a case be greatly obliged to my friends to remind her that we may be so circumstanced at the end of the first winter & even of the second so as to wish to try some other part in case we have not previously succeeded, and having abundance of provisions and fuel, we may do that with safety. In order to prevent too great anxiety either on her part & that of my daughter, they should be encouraged not to look for our arrival earnestly, till our provision gets short.

I wish that I could learn your opinion of Streleski's Book, which appears to me to contain very interesting matter and to be well put together. I shall Ever feel indebted to him for its Dedication to me. Such a mark of friendship ought to counterbalance a thousand disappointments which such men as Lord Stanley may throw in your way.

I wrote to Streleski from Stromness, and will do so again from this place if I can, but in case I am not able will you have the goodness to say every thing that is kind from me – and I shall also be obliged if you will tell Dr Fitton that I had the pleasure of seeing his Son on board the Erebus, he having only just recovered from the Sea Sickness. He told me that he liked the profession, & I am happy to think that he is in a good school under Washington and Stanley.

I have enquired of Mr Goodsir whether he had any thing which I could communicate to you. He has begged me to say that "Several Species of Alga were collected at Sea, and all of those growing on the shores of these Islands. All the land plants have also been collected, amounting to about 30 Species."

Your neighbour, Arrowsmith, assured me that before I sailed he would publish a new sheet of the map of V.D.L., for the purpose of introducing the divisions of the land into Counties, and other information with which I furnished him, but I fear no farther steps were taken respecting it. Will it be inconvenient to you to jog his memory as to this matter when you meet him?

Our next chance of writing may be by a Whaler if we chance to meet any – if not, this note must convey to you the sentiments of affection & esteem which I cherish for you. May God bless you.

John Franklin

153. JOHN FRANKLIN TO EDWARD SABINE, 9 JULY 1845

Whale Fish Island
9th July 1845

Dear Sabine

I know that Crozier and Fitz-james mean to write to you so that I need not enter upon the subject of their observations – I must however do them the justice to tell you that they have been assiduous in making them throughout the passage – and at this place – Here the weather has been particularly good for them.

We were just a month from Stromness to this place and we appear in the estimation of every one to have arrived early enough for our future operations. The authorities at Disco are all absent – the Governor in Denmark, the next in rank, as well as the Minister are making their tour of annual inspection so that I have not been able to get information from any of the leading people as to the prevailing winds or the state of the temperature during the winter. I have however consul[ted] with an intelligent Dane (who has been here 13 years) on these points. He is the Carpenter in charge of the Esquimaux station on these Islands. His account states that the winter was unusually severe & windy, the east winds prevailing. The spring he represents to have been much as usual. The Ice hereabout broke at the close of April, and he has heard that early in June it was loose as high up as the Women's Islands, from which circumstance he infers that our prospect is favourable for getting early into Lancaster Sound.

We have had the transport alongside from the morning of our arrival and I hope to have all our things out of her tomorrow, but we shall be as full as an Egg, and as deep as any ships need be. We shall have on board provision fuel clothing & stores for three years. Before this is expended we trust that by Gods blessing we shall have been enabled to give a satisfactory account as to the NW passage –

I hope my dear wife & daughter will not be over anxious if we should not return by the time they may have fixed upon; and I must beg of you to give them the benefit of your advice and experience when that arrives, – for you know well that, even after the second winter, without success in our object, we should wish to try some other channel, if the state of our provisions & the health of the Crew justify it.

I am sanguine in my hope that Mrs Sabine & yourself have been travelling this summer in Company with my wife & Eleanor – I know that they looked forward to the probability of having that pleasure. You would then make them be au fait at Arctic matters and proceedings.

I should also feel your being their Companions a great benefit in case the Montagu party should make any rejoinder to the Pamphlet for the sake of frightening my wife – that you might, as I am sure you would be of assistance in advising with and comforting them. I know however that my wife is not so easily frightened as they may imagine.

I can not thank Mrs Sabine & yourself enough for the aid you have given in the preparation of the Pamphlet and I have the satisfaction in reading it over again since I have been at sea to think that while it has been written in firm language – there has been a tone of moderation preserved throughout. Some of my officers have read it so also has Crozier who speak in the strongest terms of indignation at the conduct of Lord Stanley – and at what they term the villainy of Montagu. I cannot but think if the Pamphlet be read at all that it will produce an unfavourable impression against the lack of principle of Lord Stanley –

[As] for Montagu I really do not think that even his friends will attempt to justify his unmanly attack on Lady Franklin – may God forgive him – and me also for having my mind dwelling so frequently on his baseness – You must excuse me also for writing again on this subject.

This ship will carry away I trust my last thoughts about this painful affair – I at least shall endeavour to shake them from my mind.

I need not tell you that I have an excellent set of officers for you know them, but I will have the satisfaction of saying that we have a most willing and [able] crew likewise, – who have entered into the service with spirit and do their work well –

Our collectors of Natural History specimens are all on the gun line – Mr Goodsir the assistant surgeon whom we consider <u>the Naturalist</u> has been very successful with his Dredges and nets – and has procured many rare and some unknown specimens of Crustacea, Mollusca and of other unpronounceable names – which he no sooner catches than he sketches & describes them – I hope you saw him on board for he is all intelligence & enthusiasm in his pursuits. The Surgeons part is that of ornithology –

There are several fair draftsmen among the officers so that I hope we shall be able to shew our friends what we have seen. We have not as yet been favoured with the sight of a Bear leaping from a floating Iceberg – but as travellers see strange things our Portfolios may be enriched [by a ye]t more remarkable sight than that.

This will in all probability be the last opportunity I may have of writing to you, unless we meet with the Whalers – allow me therefore to assure you & Mrs Sabine of my very sincere attachment & esteem, and that you may rely on my taking every occasion to cause the observations to be made which you desire to have made.

I see well however that Fitz-james will need no spur for he goes at his observations with alacrity & cheerfulness – so I must add, do each of the officers to the observations which they have had more immediately placed under their charge –

May God bless & preserve you & Mrs Sabine & grant to us a happy meeting together.

                                        John Franklin

154. JOHN FRANKLIN TO JAMES CLARK ROSS,
9 JULY 1845

Whale Fish Island
9th July 1845

My dear Ross

Crozier I know is writing to you, but this must not deprive me of a similar pleasure – We are now in the fair way having received almost every thing on board which the Transport brought for us – and as you will imagine deep enough We are having full three years supplies of every thing on board – however the daily consumption will soon cause room to be made and the Yachts will jump up again to their proper trim for sailing – I hope we shall be again moving northwards in a day or two – the Transport I trust will be cleared tomorrow and on the following day we shall get the ships swung – then off we Go – The principal persons are all away from Disco the Governor in Denmark, sick – the next in command as well as the Minister on their tour of annual inspection so that I have not been able to obtain any information from Head Quarters – The person in charge of the station here a Carpenter by trade is the only person of whom I have been able to make enquiries respecting the weather during the Winter & Spring He says the Winter was severe and the winds were strong from the Eastward but that the spring did not appear to be later than usual – the ice broke away here about at the close of April – and he had recently heard that it broke up about the Womens Islands by the close of May – and that our Whalers had been getting fish – from which circumstances he considers we shall meet with but little difficulty from ice to Lancaster Sound Your experience will allow you to judge of the value of such an opinion- we of course sincerely hope that he may prove to have judged correctly and we be able to get early on our working ground.

It is very satisfactory for us to have found that our observations agree very well with the results given by Parry – as to Lat & Long. Crozier & Fitz-James have also been fortunate in having had fine weather for their magnetical observations – and their variations

I have occupied myself on the passage in carefully reading over again the points in the different voyages which bear upon our present pursuits, as well as over several notes of my own which I had drawn up – before Back's expedition – as well of some of Richardson of the same period – I think from these that it is very probable we shall find the space between Bank's Land and Wollastons occupied either by continuous land or a Chain of Islands – more probably by the latter, in which case I consider our prospect of forcing through between those parallels very good and if the channels between the Islands are tolerably wide so much the better. The Musk Oxen on Melville Island have always been considered by me as a proof of there being a track from the continent not greatly broken by wide channels of water – for I never supposed the Musk Oxen swam far – and I do not imagine they would cross over extensive tracts of ice in the Winter or Spring – where of course they could not feed – The Reindeer however can swim well – or travel rapidly across the ice in the spring to the Northern Islands – If the western shore of Boothia should stretch from your Southern point to Cape Walker as I believe you supposed it to do – there would be a direct way for the Reindeer and perhaps for the Musk Oxen to get to Melville Island The traces which you found of the Esquimaux on the Islands North of Barrow Strait – and at Melville Island – afford another interesting topic for thought – are they those of the men you saw in Victory Harbour or where they left by tribes living westward of the Prince Regents Inlet – It appears to me from reading old Ross' book that the people you saw so much of were the same that you had known when with Parry on Winter Island & about the Hecla & Fury Straits – I was looking over Parrys original charts of Barrow Straits with Crozier to day – and we found that Wellington Channel is not laid down more than 30 miles across – and it was seen into about 15 miles – and to my view of the chart it does not appear to be a more promising channel than others you saw However if baffled to the South of Bank's Land it is the next place I shall try – I cannot however yet see the reason upon which those ground their arguments who contend for the water being more open to the North of Melville Island than to the South – nor can I subscribe to the opinion of those who maintain that there must always be open water however far North if there be not land – this is not the case between Spitzbergen & Greenland nor between Nova Zembla & Spitzbergen – and I firmly believe the vicinity of land to be almost necessary, if not entirely so to cause the breaking up of the ice – the experience of Baron Wrangle does not appear to me to be applicable to this question because he was not more distant than 180 miles from the Coast when he came upon the broken ice & water and moreover he was then in shoal water & never in deep which had extended from the coast – and is another circumstance favourable to the wasting and breaking up of ice – I will not say more on these points at present –

I trust Lady Ross & yourself have become quite at home in your new residence – and that you have found it such as you expected it to be – The Country is certainly pretty and I believe healthy – I often think of you both with much interest for your happiness – this indeed I ought to

do as a return for the very kind interest you took in my own welfare and
that of my dear wife. Moreover I feel persuaded that you will continue
to shew the same steady friendship for my wife & child as you have
done – Pray give them every good hope & comfort during my absence
and especially as the time draws nigh which they may have fixed upon
in their minds for our return and yet we do not appear – It is then your
experience will be invaluable to them for you can assure them that there
may be many good reasons for our delay – quite apart from all apprehension for our safety Let me now beg an interest in your prayers and
in those of Lady Ross for the divine protection & blessing to attend us
all – and I will pray for you both & your dear child – that God may
support & comfort you
   Ever your attached friend
    John Franklin

155. JOHN GREGORY TO HANNAH GREGORY [WIFE], 9 JULY 1845

       July 9th 1845
       Desko Whale Fish Islands

My dear Wife
 I long very much to know how you are getting on but that is a gratification I must be content to forego for some time to come. I am however
happy to be able to inform you that my health continues very good and
I hope and trust this will find you and our Dear Children all well.

This is probably the only opportunity I shall have of writing for a long
time without we make the passage through, which if we are fortunate
enough to succeed in we shall send dispatches home via Russia

I shall now give you a short account of our passage from Stromness, we
left there on the 3rd of June in tow of the Rattler and Blazer steamers, on
the 5th they left us in the Western Ocean, when they gave us three cheers
which were heartily returned by our two Ships companys, on the 6th I
saw a great quantity of porpoises sporting around us, until the 23rd we
had variable weather at times rather rough which gave us a good rock-
ing, on this day we saw a large tree close by the ship supposed to have
come from North America, on the 25th we got sight of the east Land
of Davis Straits, saw the first Iceberg and several Whales, on the 27th

the weather was quite warm with nearly a dead calm we found bottom at 350 fathoms and next day at 40, when lines were served out to the Messes and we caught 60 head of fine Cod which made us two or three fresh meals which we enjoyed very much after the salt provisions.

We saw but two ships on our passage from the Orkneys though we have learnt from the Natives here that several Whalers put into this bay as early as the month of april some of which we shall most likely fall in with when we get farther North. July 1st the icebergs greatly increased both in size and quantity, since which we have passed some from one to three miles in circumference and varying from fifty to an Hundred feet in height, they are as white as snow intersected with blue lines. The blue appearance is caused by the shade of the Sun, which when it shines full upon them causes them to glitter like glass and being of all conceiveable shapes and figures they have a most grand and beautiful appearance.

The coast of Greenland several of the men jocosely remarked, should have been named Whiteland for it has that appearance, being still covered with snow it has a most dreary and desolate appearance the Mountains inland rising an immense height the summits of some piercing the clouds, on the 2nd a suit of Clothes was given to each man consisting of a Jacket and Trowsers of blue cloth, 1 pr. snow boots, 1 pr of Sea do. 1 Red worsted shirt, 1 pr stockings, 1 welsh wig, 1 Comforter, and 1 Red worsted shirt, previously to delivering out the clothes Sir John had all the men on deck and gave them to understand that the government intended them as presents, provided the men behaved well, which he hoped he should be able to report of all of them, otherwise they would be charged to them out of their wages, their value is at least Five Pounds, on the 4th at 1 oClock in the Morning we entered a small harbour since which we have been very busy getting in our stores from the Transport which returns to England, the place we are in is called south east bay, it is about 200 yards in width and about half a mile Long The islands on each side are barren rocks, one of them is upwards of 3 hundred feet high, in a few places there is a little coarse grass and some moss, also a kind of stone crop which is in bloom and the only flower I found on the place. There are a few inhabitants of the Esquimaux Tribe most of whom have been on board the ships bartering with the crew for tobacco pouches, shoes, jackets, and various things which they make in a very curious manner from seal skins -they use but one paddle to their canoe, which they use by striking the water alternately right and left which propels them at a rapid rate, they appear an innoff[ensiv]e race o[f] people, subsisting entirely on fish and birds, they kill these by throwing a long dart, to give you an instance of their dexterity with this weapon, one of our men suspended a biscuit to the jib boom when one of them sitting in his canoe threw and cut the string in half, they are under the Danes who have a small settlement about 4 miles from here.

I hope my dear the children will all pay respect to my wishes with regard to their behaviour as written in my last – if Edward has come home which I hope he has in good health I have only to repeat what I before said, I hope you are comfortably situated with regard to a house. I wish you to see Mr Fitzpatrick with respect of the Money you may place in Mr Maudslays hands and arrange it with him. Give my best respects to Mr & Mrs Haviland, also Mr Harts & tell them he is quite well, you can tell them he would have sent them a letter but for being so very busy, give also my respects to Mr Rose, also give my best respects to Mr Pile and ask him if he has spoke to Mr Maudslays about my money I wish you to go to his house and see him upon it as soon as you can. be sure you keep the children to school both on Sunday as well as the week and be careful what acquaintances you make – I hope Fanny is improving in her business and if you think it necessary that she will get some lessons from some one competent to improve her, I hope also James is giving every satisfaction both with regard to his work and behaviour.

Give my best respects to Mr and Mrs Empey and tell them on reconsideration I have thought it better instead of placing my Money in the bank to put it into Messrs Maudslay's hands Give my Kind Love to Edward, Fanny, James, William, and Kiss baby for me – and accept the same yourself

And I remain your ever Affectionate Husband
John Gregory

P.S. tell Mr Pile I should have written him a letter had I not have been so busy taking in my stores, which we are doing as quick as possible as they are hurrying to get away north before the winter sets in as far as they can –

156. JAMES THOMPSON TO CHARLES THOMPSON [BROTHER], 10 JULY 1845

South East Bay Whale Fish Islands
Davis Straits
10th July 1845

Brother

I take this opportunity of writing to you as I do not know when I shall be able to write again the last time I wrote to you was from the Oarkneys and as I stated before we arrived the on Saturday the 31 of May on Monday I [went] on Shore and Bought A quantity of Provisions for private use such as Potaties Bacon Eggs Butter &c. the Ships allowance is 1 Pint of Cocoa for Breakfast and 1£b of Biscuit per Day the Dinners consist Monday Preserved Meat on Teusday Salt Poark and Pea Soup on Wednesday Preserved Meat Thursday Salt Beef Friday Preserved Meat Saturday Salt Poark and Sunday Salt Beef when we Preserved Meat it amounts to ¾ £b Per Man on account of having no bone and A pound of the other Meat to make up for the Bone when we have Salt Beef we have ¾ £b of flour and 1 Oz of Pickels we have 1½ Oz of Sugar and ¼ Oz of Tea per Day and ¼ Pint of Rum Per Day when we have Salt Meat we have half Pint of Lime juice as A preventative against the Scurvey. water is A scarce article we have 2 quarts Per Day for each Man for washing cooking and every thing. I found as great A loss for Water as any thing at first as I can very seldom get more than A Pint to wash in at one time but now I have got quiet used to it.

We left the Oarkneys on Teusday Moarning the Rattler Towed the two Boats one Astern of the other into the Western Ocean when we was left to do the best with the wind we had some very rough Weather in the Western Ocean on Sunday and Monday 22 & 23 it was very Stormy and the Ship rowled about so that we was obliged to tie the pots and any thing that would break togeather to prevent them rowling about and with all their care there was A great quantity of Earthen ware destroyed on Tuesday we entered Davis Straits and had A Ice Burg in sight but A great distance off as this was the first that presented its self it was very anxiously looked for especily by those that had not seen one by fore on Wednesday it was very fine and we had A number of large fish in sight known by the name of Finbacks and Bottle Noses the Thermometer stud at 40° and we have it light all Night so as to be able to reade or do anything on deck the sun went down at ½ Past 10 on thursday Moarning we

met in with an Aberdeen Fishing Boat that was fishing for Codfish and as
soon as it was known that there was plenty of Fish there was Lines and
hooks given out to the Men to fish with and there has been A great quantity catched all the Men that could be spared from the Ships Duty was
busily engaged in fishing hanging the lines from the ship side sometimes
drawing in two fine fish at once the fishing lines are about 3/16 Diameter
and about 60 Yards long with A lump of Lead 5 or 6 Pounds weight tied
about 4 feet from the Bottom to sink them and there was A great quantity
of Cod Fish catch so have had plenty of Fish for Breakfast.

Friday 27 it was very Cold the Thermometer was at 36 some part of the
Day there was four Ice Burges in Sight all the Day the one that came the
nearest to the Ship was considered to be about 100 feet long and 30 feet
high, on Saturday and Sunday it was very Calm the ship scarsely moving
at all we have had some very fine weather in comeing up Davis Straits but
some times very Cold land quiet visible at the East side of the Straits it is
very Mountaneous and Covered with snow and has a very fine appearance when the Sun shines on Friday the 4th July all hands called up at 3
O Clock to get the ship into one of the Whale Fish Harbours so as to
take all the stores out of the Transpoart all Hands quiet busy employed
in removing the store the Erebus is laid along side of the Transpoart,
but we are laid about 200 Yds off so all the stores has to be conveyed
in Small Boats which makes A great deal more trouble as soon as we
got into the Harbour the was A quantity off Esquemaus came alongside
in their Cannoos and there is some comes on Board every Day allways
bringing some skins with them to trade with they will exchange the skins
and Dresses on Sunday it was very fine and went on Shore to look at the
Esquimaus Huts their are rather A superior soart what are heare the are
under the Danish settlement there is A store house here belonging to the
Danes but we are about 6 Miles from where the Danish governer lives the
Hutts at present are the summer Hutts they are made in the same forme
as the gipseys tents in England they are covered over with skins instead
of A Blanket the Men has a large flat Broad face and long Black hair with
large Heads the heads Measures 23 and 24 Inches the Women Dresses
same almost as the men Boot with the Fir inside Britches and A kind of
A smock with Hudd to go on the Head with Firr outside I counted 13 in
one hut Men Women & Children one of the Women was giving suck to
A Child about 6 Years old they appear to be A harmless set of People and
very honest I had two of the Men to supper on Munday Night. Red her-
rins Poark Biscuit and some Rum they said all very good and they liked
the Rum but I thought it would not do to give them much as they had to

go home in their Canoes and not been in the Habit of taking anything of the kind I thought it might make their heads feel painfull.

When I was on shore on Sunday it was so very fine and warm I took my Stocking off and gave my feet A good wash and there was plenty of Misketoes and they bite very bad my arms are very much bitten with them they are more venemous than the English Bugg some of the Men is blisterd all over the Face and Arms On Teusday it was very Hot I do not think you had A finer Day in England each Man in the Ship had his Winters Clothing given to him it was given out sooner than it would have been but the Roome was wanted to stow away the Ship stores as we are very much [full] in every part of the Ship we have not had the Engine at work yet and the Engine House is filled with Cole Wood and other articles, the Clothes that was given out consisted of 1 Jacket 1 Pair of Trousers 1 Pair of Large Boots that comes up to the thighs 1 Red Serge shirt 2 Pair of thick Stockings 2 Comforters and 1 Welch Wig in the Evening I went ashore and had a Comfortable Bathe It looked rather strange to see men bathing with snow on the ground but the Water was very Comfortable the time that I am writing this not the least doubt but Charles and others are enjoying themselves at Leeds Faire you must give my kinds Respects to all enquiring Friends you must have a little patience till you get through this long letter when I first commenced I scarsely knew what to say as you are aware that I do not like Letter Writing there is three of the Men belonging to the Terror going to be sent home 1 A Marien the Armerer and the sale maker by the Transpoart I do not know when you will Receive another letter perhaps I shall be like the Hibernian bring it myself excuse any more at Present as I think I shall weary your Patience
     So I remain your's
     James Thompson

157. JOHN FRANKLIN TO EDWARD PARRY, 10 JULY 1845

Whale Fish Island
10th July 1845

My dear Parry,

Having had the pleasure of seeing the last cask of provisions hoisted from the Transport into the Erebus I have come down to write to you. We are now in every way full & complete for three years – but of course very deep – and shall draw seventeen feet when the anchors & boats are up. Our passage hither to from the Orkneys occupied one month. On the morning of the 4th we took up your former berth – and soon afterwards we brought the Transport alongside as the quickest way of clearing her. The magnetic men were landed with their instruments as were also the other observers, on the Boat Island at the spot you occupied – and you can fancy them all in full play – I am happy also to tell you that their results give the lat & long of their positions within a few seconds of those you assigned to it.

I find that the principal people are absent from Disco – so that I have had to obtain whatever information about the Ice to the North that is to be picked up here, from a Danish Carpenter who is in charge of the Esquimaux at this Station. He tells me the winter was severe and that they had strong winds from the Eastward – but the spring was not later than usual and that the Ice broke up here about at the close of April. He also seems to have had some intelligence from the Northern Coasts about the Women's Islands, from which he considers the ice to have broken up there also by the close of May – or early in June. The whalers, he has heard, have caught fish there about – He fancies from these circumstances that we may not meet with much obstruction from ice in getting to Lancaster Sound, and we hope his conjectures will prove true. At any rate we hope to be able to put them to the test in a few days. Nothing can be finer than the weather we have had here for all our operations. I think it must be favourable for the opening of the ice – and we all feel happy in the idea that we shall be quite in time to avail ourselves of any openings westward of Barrows Straits.

During my passage from England I have carefully read over parts of your voyages – as well as some notes of Richardson & my own which were made on the occasion of Back's Expedition – deduced from our previous observations at & about Point Turnagain. And I am inclined to think from these and from the observations of Dease & Simpson – that there exists much land between the Wollaston and Banks Lands which I hope may be found to be separated into Islands; and also I trust we may be able to penetrate through a channel between them.

One of the arguments that has weighed with me in supposing that there must be land between the above mentioned parallels & not widely disconnected – is the circumstance of your having killed a Musk Ox and seen others on Melville Island. These animals cannot I believe swim far, nor do I consider that they would cross large channels covered with ice where they could not obtain food. The Reindeer can do both they swim well – and over ice their speed is so much swifter than the Musk Ox that they readily pass from Island to Island. I have also been cogitating on the traces of Esquimaux which you found on Melville Island and on other of the shores north of Barrows Strait. Have these men come from Regent Inlet, where Ross in the Victory found the Esquimaux? who were I believe recognized by him as being allied to – or at least in some way intimately connected with those you saw at Winter Island – and near the Hecla & Fury Straits – or have the traces been left by Esquimaux who reside westward of Boothia?

If by the latter they in all probability have come thither along the Coasts or by the Chain of Islands which I have imagined to exist – I think the west side of Boothia will be found to extend from James Ross's Point Felix to Cape Walker.

I have thus communicated my ideas unreservedly to you – because I know that you will kindly receive them if they be different from yours as the opinions of a person as yet comparatively inexperienced as to what may be inferred from circumstances met with in these higher latitudes so far apart from the Main Continent of America.

It would do your heart good to witness how zealously the officers & men in both ships are working and how amicably we all pull together. Knowing what an excellent instructor and fellow worker Crozier was & will prove to Fitz-James, I have left the magnetic observations of the Erebus to the latter – who is most assiduous respecting them. I have also endeavored to encourage each of the officers to take some one branch or other under his more immediate care – from which I trust he will ultimately reap substantial benefit – so that my share of the work at present seems to be more the training and overlooking of these gentlemen than doing the work itself. I have now for instance at the tables in my cabin a Lieutenant constructing the plan of the Survey he has made of the Islands of which this group is composed – and Mr Goodsir the Assistant Surgeon & Naturalist with his microscope sketching & minutely examining the Crustacae Moluscae & which he describes at once while the colours are fresh.

He is very expert at dredging and has found many rare & some unknown creatures – with too long names for me to write. Beyond his table lie lots of skinned birds the handy work of the Surgeon who is skilled in such subjects. Around the deck of the Cabin are arranged the ships store of

Preserved Potatoes – packed in neat tin cases. With the above description you will be able to bring me before your mind at this moment – and in turning my head I recognize you like as life. Was there not in your time a large Station here for the Esquimaux under a commandant? This office is broken up & the establishment of Esquimaux reduced to 130 – only 30 of whom are at present here, the rest are absent hunting seal. Judging from their manner, their dress and more cleanly appearance than other Esquimaux whom I have seen I should say they are well taken care of by the Danish Government –

I must now thank you for your Signal Books – which are so complete that I had only to add some few Nos. to suit the steam purposes – before I sent them to Crozier to copy – we shall use them after leaving this place.

I meant to have had the steam up here to see that all was right – but we really could not at present spare either the space or time. We are satisfied however that all is right and kept in order by the Engineer and it is my intention to take the first opportunity of our being beset to get the steam up, and certainly have every thing ready for its immediate use by the time we reach Lancaster Sound. We find our Engineer Mr Gregory a good & valuable man – and willing to do anything required of him.

Again my dear Parry I will recommend my dearest wife & daughter to your kind regards. I am persuaded that she feels how entirely she may trust to your friendship for advice & comfort whenever she may need them. It will always prove a happiness to know your opinion as to where we may be & what we may be supposed to be employed in doing. I have every confidence in the firmness of her mind and that she will endeavour to repress any undue anxiety as long as the time has not arrived in which she may have fixed upon in her own mind for our return. But I fear if we should not happen to make our appearance by that time she may be become over-anxious. Then it will be, that I more especially entreat of my friends to comfort her, by pointing out that without there being the least occasion for uneasiness as to our safety – there may be reasons for the delay, such as the desire to look into every hopeful place as long as the health of the Crew & the state of the provision justify our doing so.

I know my dear Parry that both my wife & daughter will heartily join with many dear friends in fervent prayer that the Almighty Power may guide and support us – and that the blessing of His Holy Spirit may rest upon us.

Our prayers I trust will be offered up with equal fervour for these ines-
timable blessings to be also vouchsafed to them, and to all who love the
Lord Jesus in sincerity and truth.

I humbly pray that Gods richest blessings may attend yourself, Lady
Parry and your family.

> Believe me
> Ever your affectionate friend
> John Franklin

Will you have the goodness to say every thing most kind to Beaufort,
and perhaps you will have the goodness to let him see any parts of this
note which may interest him. I would most willingly write to him if I
could say anything more about the ship & our prospects than I have to
you – or that I could give to him any farther proof than you will have
the kindness to convey to him, of my most sincere & affectionate regard
for him and of my esteem for Mrs Beaufort and his family. May the Lord
bless & preserve them all –!

I have requested the Agent of Transports, Lieutenant Griffiths, to call
upon you. He is an intelligent person and I have been much pleased with
him. He wishes to obtain either his promotion or some command as a
Lieutenant – though I fear his service on the present occasion would not
add to his claims – I should yet be glad to say a good word for him. Can
you venture on saying this at the Admiralty?

You will be glad to know that I have not had the least return of a cough
since I have been at sea and that I never was in better health.

158. JOHN IRVING TO CATHERINE IRVING [SISTER-IN-LAW], C. 10 JULY 1845

> H.M.S. "Terror,"
> Whalefish Island, Greenland

My dear Kate,

– I sit down at last to take a long farewell of you, for it will be probably a
couple of years, if not more, before I have another opportunity to write.

I wrote you from Orkney, where we stopped three days. We left there on the 2d of June, and had a voyage of a month, with the usual variety of fair and foul weather. We made the coast of Greenland on the 25th, and arrived at the Whalefish Islands on the 4th instant. We have been very busy shifting our stores and provisions from the transport, which has convoyed us so far. We have now cleared her of everything, and we all sail tomorrow, – she on her voyage back to England, and we, in the first place, for Barrow's Strait, and after, as we best can. Only three of the cattle on board the transport have survived the voyage; however, we leave this with three complete years' provisions, so, even should we not cast up for so long, you need not think we have been eating our shoes. About the last week of September we shall fix our ships somewhere for the winter. We shall be frozen up for ten months, several of which in total darkness. At present we have constant daylight, and for the last fortnight we have had sunshine all night. There is plenty of ice floating about and scraping our sides, and we have sometimes a little snow. All very well for July.

I have every cause to be pleased with my shipmates, and barring the want of all communication, I ought to enjoy myself very much, as everything is new, and, after all, there is nothing like variety – at least it is so at sea.

The Whalefish Islands, where we now are, consist of four or five barren rocky islands like Inchkeith, and the openings betwixt some of the islands are choked up with ice. We have passed many icebergs, which are huge piles of ice and snow floating about. Some are 200 feet high. These are formed by avalanches from the Greenland mountains, which are very high and precipitous, and one sheet of snow to the water's edge. There are some families of Esquimaux living here – most wretched people, half- starved, living on seals (when they can catch them); but they seem happy, and they can read their own language, and have Bibles sent from Denmark, printed in Esquimaux, and they have been taught to read by a Danish missionary who was here some years ago. They are dressed in sealskin jackets, etc., women and all alike, and their children, of which there are great numbers, are very curious-looking creatures, more like seals than anything else. They have rosy cheeks, and round, good-humoured faces though rather greasy. Their canoes are just long enough to sit in, and the sealskin frock is tied round the edge of the hole they sit in, to keep the water out; so they can go right under water without taking any in. They are made of sealskins covering a frame made of bones, and are so light that a man can carry them. You will see all these things far better described in the Polar voyages of Parry, Ross, and Back, which perhaps you may now have a little interest in looking at, as they describe exactly what will be our difficulties; and you will, I daresay, like to know a little what I may be about for so long; at least, I am sure you have no friend that takes a greater interest in you than I do. I send you a little Polar chart, and I have put the track of the Expedition in red, and proposed route dotted red. We hope to reach Melville Island before the end of September, and pass the winter there, and try to reach Behring's Straits the following summer.

Should the ice not clear away enough, or should we meet land instead of water, we shall have to pass another winter and try again, and either to go on or come back in the third summer.

The former Expeditions were stopped by a barrier of ice so thick and solid that the summer, which is only ten weeks long, passed away without dissolving it. However, I trust we may have a warmer summer, either this or the next, or find some channel which they overlooked. We have the advantage of all their experience, and will save much valuable time in not looking uselessly for a passage where land has been laid down in their charts, which we have with us. We have a library of the best books of all kinds, consisting of 1200 volumes, and shall be able to pass the time very well, as there shall be some exploring parties sent out on foot while the ships are frozen in; and we will eke out our provisions with all the game our guns can procure. We shall be very busy sawing the ice and working the ships on, whenever a single mile can be gained. I have written my father a letter which is very much to the same effect as this. You might send him the little chart, as our proposed route is shown in it, and he is much interested in geography generally; I daresay you may see my letter to him. And now you are in possession of all I can tell you.

The sudden change from summer back to winter has caused us all to suffer from chilblains. Some are so bad that they cannot put on their shoes. I have had my hands much swollen; but they say that in two or three weeks all this will go away. There are many tons of ice within five or six yards of me now; but it is not cold, and the sun shining all night, we don't think of going to bed, but go shooting after working hours are over, and it is supposed to be night. We shall have it dark for a long time by and by. I must now finish, my dear Katie. May every good attend you and yours. My kindest love to my dear father and Lewis. – Yours ever affectionately,

John Irving.

P.S. – I have been making sketches; but you will see all of them when I next come to Falkirk. I have eight hours' watch out of the twenty-four to keep on deck, and I have charge of our chronometers, which are little clocks. I have to wind them up and compare them, and write an account of their goings on – there are ten of them in each ship, – and also various astronomical observations to make, and calculations. All this is much more interesting than the dull routine in a regular man-of-war, which is like a barrack or a workhouse. Now, good-bye. God bless you.

We are going to have a school for the men. Our Captain reads prayers on Sundays. We are exempt from many of the temptations of the world, and I hope we shall have grace to find that it has been good for us to have been separated from the world, and that God has been with us in all our wanderings. May we submit ourselves to His pleasure in all things.

I send you a small piece of the Tripe de Roche, a sort of lichen growing on the rocks, which was the food of Sir John Franklin in his Expedition. I send you a sketch of our ships at this place; The "Erebus " is alongside of the transport getting her provisions, and the " Terror " is a little to the left. The Danish house is in front, and two Esquimaux sealskin tents, which they live in during summer.

159. JOHN FRANKLIN TO JANE FRANKLIN [WIFE], 1–12 JULY 1845 [HIS LAST LETTER TO HER]

HMS Erebus about 30 miles
distant from the Coast of Greenland
near Holsteinsberg   1st July 1845

I enclose a letter for Mrs Foster from Hoar. He spoke of her yesterday to me in a kind way & expressed his hope that she would remain with you till our return. He is a reliable & careful servant. JF

My dearest Love,

I begin the month in your service. Our voyage hitherto has been favourable – the passage across the Atlantic was, as usual, attended with strong breezes, and these generally from the west & sw so that in mak-ing our way across we were led to the North and even carried to within 60 miles of Iceland before we could get past Cape Farewell – but we did

not see Iceland It would have been contrary to the long experience of the
Greenland Seamen if we had gone round Cape Farewell unattended by a
gale. We had a very strong one from SW with much sea which drove us
rapidly past the Cape on the 22nd June, and continued to favour us till
the 25th June. When the gale gave place to calm, the weather which had
been thick snow became clear, and we obtained our first views of the
shores of Greenland distant about 40 miles, the Astronomical observations told us it was the land in the neighbourhood of Lichterfels. Here to
our surprise we found a Bank of 40 fathoms water on which we caught
many Cod fish. Here also we communicated with an English Brig which
had sailed from Shetland the same day we left the Orkneys and had
come out to procure salmon in some of the Fiords. He had also been
catching fish nearer in shore this morning on a bank of 20 fathoms.

From the last date to this time we have been generally in sight of the
Coast, advancing gradually to the north, aided by light winds as also we
are now doing. This calm weather & smooth water have been particularly favourable to Mr Goodsir's objects as it has enabled us to keep
the dredges worked and to have frequent specimens brought up from the
bottom while other machines capture the molluscs & animacula all that
swim on the surface. He has obtained many specimens that are rare and
some which he considers entirely unknown. It would delight your heart
to watch his eagerness to catch every thing that passes which he instantly
draws & describes while the colours are fresh. He is fairly installed at a
table in my Cabin and is now busily at work having his microscope before
him. I am happy to say that he finds a willing coadjutor in each officer and
Seaman and I think there is no fear of any jealousy as regards the Natural
History on the part of his immediate Senior which Richardson was rather
apprehensive might be the case. The magnetic observations are likewise
carried on with zeal & energy by Fitz-james who never omits an opportunity of obtaining them. Each officer in fact directs his attention to some
point or other of enquiry or observation and it is this mode of fixing their
energies specifically that I have encouraged in them and shall continue
to do so as the best means of the expedition obtaining results on various
points. I impress at the same time upon them the assurance that their individual exertions will prove their best chance to the favourable notice of
the Admiralty. Of this they are all aware so likewise are they that I shall
have pleasure in bringing their services duly before the proper authorities.

I shall be excused <u>by you</u> if I add, that it is gratifying to me to know that
they have the confidence in me that I shall do them justice. It is amusing

to me also occasionally to hear even Fitz-james express his surprise at learning for the first time, or reading of, some points of my professional life. He has more than once said before others at the table – Why Sir it would be difficult to name a place where you have not been, it was last said on learning that I had been at Moscow. He seems to have been aware of your having travelled much, this he probably learnt from the Barrows – with whom I find he has been for many years, if not throughout his life, very intimate, in proof of the intimacy I can tell you that he has been invited to dine several times with Sir John Barrow – and that he has even gone to Sir George Staunton's to meet them – he may perhaps be related to the Barrows – he knows of the unworthiness of their unfortunate son Peter. Fitz-james has read the Pamphlet, so have Gore & Fairholme, the latter having learnt from Fitz-james its contents, requested me to lend it him. They have all expressed their indignation at the treatment of Lord Stanley – and one & all of them exclaimed what a villain that Montagu must be. Crozier has also read it, and on his returning it – he said the conduct pursued towards you is perfectly diabolical – there being others present at the time he could not enter more into detail. From the re-perusal of it, I feel the conduct both of Lord Stanley & Mr Hope to be more indefensible as men & Christians than I perhaps thought at first – as for Montagu I cannot think worse of him than I did from the first development of his wicked scheme – I pray to God to change his heart and that Lord Stanley may do justly, and that I may be forgiven if I have done wrong or injury to either. Such I trust will be the spirit of my fervent prayer to the end of my life – may such be your prayer also!

You have not sent the Appendix with the sheets – which I should like the officers also to have seen – Mr Youngs letter for instance would have placed Montagu's character scarcely inferior to that in which he has exhibited himself in the Postscript. This display of his own course of action shocks & astonishes every one. Lord Stanleys heart must indeed be callous to all righteous feeling if he can read that and continue to defend Montagu!!! I have been daily thinking of you in connection with the Pamphlet since I suppose it to have been published on the 8 or 10 June – and have fervently implored the Almighty to support & comfort you under any trial of patience or feelings which our enemies may endeavour to visit upon you in consequence of its circulation. I know however, that I have left you in the hands of sound judging men to advise you. In this conviction I take comfort. Crozier has only been able to dine twice with me on account of the rough weather – and on these occasions we had objects of immediate interest to talk over and did not enter into other subjects. We hope to be more together while we are at Whale Island unloading the Transport, from which place we shall not be today farther than 90 miles. We have as yet seen but very few icebergs & none of large size. The land we have seen is generally hard & picturesque with openings that indicate the entrances into the numerous fiords which indent the whole Coast – there appears less snow on the lower part of the hills than I had expected to see. We hope to hear from the Danish Commandant at Disco Island what have been the prevailing winds during the winter & spring and in what state he supposes the ice to be now to the North & West and where the Whalers are.

After I had issued such written orders as I thought necessary for the internal discipline & arrangement of the ship, as well as the instructions to the officers respecting the various observations which they would be required to make and for their general guidance, I devoted myself to the preparation of a Code of Signals to be used between the Erebus & Terror when among the ice after parting from the Transport; and in this duty I was mainly assisted by Parry's signals in a similar situation which he had most kindly lent me, indeed I had little more to do than to introduce onto his code some signals that related to the Steam Machinery with which we are furnished. These first duties over, I have employed my time in carefully reading again the voyages of the earlier Navigators as given in Barrows Collection of them & still better in the Edinburgh Cabinet Library Article Polar Seas & Regions – you will conclude of course that Parry's voyages have not been overlooked (nor Ross's (Sir John I mean) in this examination, and yesterday I spent the morning most agreeably in reading the letter which you had kindly collected & put into my writing desk, some of which I find to contain opinions and descriptions of Richardson & myself on the very object of my present Expedition which will be useful to me. The Despatch of Dease & Simpson to the Hudsons Bay Company and the letters of Richardson & myself to the Geographical Society & Beaufort, on which Backs last Expedition was based, are also among them – these likewise will be serviceable as references. These readings I consider matters of duty, but I occasionally take up some of the interesting little volumes with which you furnished my library – I have begun since leaving England reading a Chapter of the Old Testament morning & Evening with the Commentaries of Henry upon it which I hope to continue. The Sunday is by all observed properly, we have divine Service on the Main Deck every forenoon and in the evening of that day all those who choose & are not on watch, may attend the service in my Cabin – which in fact all do – and a most interesting "assembling of ourselves together" it has proved and will I trust prove in future to be. It is a source of sincere gratification to me when I think upon your prayers ascending with Eleanors & mine for our mutual protection and for Gods blessing on each other. The heart is refreshed & comforted by such thoughts and strengthened for the faithful discharge of our relative duties. I rejoice at being able to assure you that my cough has entirely left me – and that I really am in such robust health as to cause the Officers to exclaim what a surprising change the coming to sea has produced in your health & appearance, you look now quite a different man from what you did at Woolwich – I hope Captain Smith of the Rattler gave you the same account of me – Our temperature now varies between 35° & 39°.

July 4th We arrived at the anchorage in Whale Fish Island at 4 this Morning, which but for thick & blowing weather we should have reached on the Evening of the 2nd inst thus making one months passage from Stromness. We made our appearance off Lively the residence of the Governor of Disco on the evening of the 2nd, though we could not communicate with him. The next day proved beautifully fine which afforded us an opportunity of examining the state of the Ice in the Way-gat passage before we came in here – it was satisfactory to find from this view that the ice there about had broken up, though numerous masses were floating about. As Parry has described our ‡age so have we found it to be, a most snug place for clearing the Transport (which is now alongside for that purpose) as well as for the Magnetical & Astronomical purposes, which observations were very soon commenced under Crozier & Fitzjames on the same spot which Parry occupied in 1824. I accompanied Le Vesconte to the top of the highest land that we might procure a view of the groups of islands & rocks in this neighbourhood and take bearings for placing them on the Chart. Nothing can be more sterile than these islands are, a mere collection of rocks with a few mosses and swamp loving plants in the water courses. Mosquitoes however are most abundant and of large size. I have not as yet heard many complaints made as to their biting.

July 5th This is a Danish station at which live several Esquimaux – the officer in charge of them is now absent at Lively where the Governor in Chief resides so that I can give you no account of the establishment at present. The Esquimaux came off before we entered the harbour and two of them piloted the Erebus to the ‡age by keeping their Canoes just ahead of the ship. This morning we had a visit from their wives & children, all of whom had clean washed faces and hair neatly combed & put up, their dresses were likewise clean & good, some of them of the sealskin & others of cotton, all the grown women had handkerchiefs on their head procured I presume from the Danes. The Danish Government or perhaps merchants of that country have several colonies on this side of Greenland at which they procure furs, seal skins & oil from the natives. At each of these Establishments I believe there are Missionaries for the religious instruction of the Esquimaux – several of whom are Moravians. Mr La Trobe could perhaps give you more information than I can as to the latter Establishments. The Esquimaux who have been on board appear to me cleaner in their dress & person than those I have before met which shews I think that attention is paid to them in this respect. I have today employed two of them to convey a letter which I have written to the Governor at Disco. One man would not undertake to go across the Bay (20 miles) alone – Each went in his own Canoe – it in fact holds but one.

Sunday 6th July The Messengers returned this afternoon with a letter from the officer in charge of Lievely who communicated to me that not understanding English he had been unable to read my letter. He however referred me to the Cockswain of a boat which had crossed over from Disco, whom he begged me to acquaint – whether he could render me any assistance from Disco. This man I saw, as well as a still more intelligent person a Carpenter and from the latter received the information that from the last winter having been severe & the winds high and from the ice having broken up hereabouts early in May, our prospects he thought were favourable as to getting to Lancaster Sound. He had heard that our whalers were off the Woman's Islands in 74 North. We of course shall rejoice to find his opinion correct the getting into Lancaster Sound early and across the barrier of ice in Baffins Bay will be great points attained. It seems the Governor of Lievely is absent on leave, the Inspector is likewise away at some other station, and there is a supercargo only, in charge, so that in all probability we shall gain no further information than we have gained from these parties.

I went after Church to day – onshore to visit the Esquimaux Huts & Tents which with one dwelling house & a store built of wood have received the designation of a Station. It belongs to the Danish Government and there are belonging to it 130 Esquimaux all of whom except 30 are away catching seals. I have already mentioned their being comfortably dressed & apparently well taken care of by the Danes and I was delighted that many of them read their Bibles, and that the Children are taught at a school to read & perhaps to write. One of the turf-built huts which I observed to be fitted up with seats & forms was pointed out to me as the School Room. There was nothing to invite your staying long in the midst of a seal catching station therefore I staid but little time longer among these huts than to ask the questions I wished to have answered The parties themselves I prefer seeing alongside of the ships – apart from the odours that surround their residences.

Monday 7th July Still busily employed clearing the Transport which we shall not be able to empty to day – we are cramming the ships as full as possible both care & time are requisite to make the best stowage. This necessary delay is favourable for the magnetic & other observations which are carrying forward on shore – and it will be satisfactory to Col Sabine to know that the results by the observers from both ships accord very well. I have no doubt Crozier & Fitz-james will write to him on the Magnetic matters. I shall also write to him. I shall also write to Richardson and send him tracings of two rare fish which Mr Goodsir thinks he will be glad to have. Mr Fairholme has been so fortunate as to find a nest containing four Eggs of the kind Lady Cust wished me to procure for her daughter, two of which he has given me for that purpose; they will be sent packed up with two others for her father who will forward them to Lady Cust. I yesterday saw Fitz-james making a sketch of the harbour of which he intends sending you a copy. Mr Gore has made a very faithful drawing for you of our parting with the Blazer & Rattler and of their cheering the Erebus – which he has kindly framed also. He is now very much occupied or I am sure he would have further enriched your Collection by a sketch of the ships at this place – My own contribution to your Arctic Stores is a pair of seal skin boots made by one of the Esquimaux and I send to Eleanor & Sophy pockets for holding a watch, also made of seal skin as specimens of the female work. Lieutenant Griffiths the agent of Transport will kindly take charge of them for you – I shall ask him to call on Bedford Place for the purpose of seeing you or some member of the family – He is an intelligent person and will give you full particulars of our progress hitherto.

I had written thus far when Mr Gore brought me in the sketch of our present ‡age for you – taken from the opposite side to that by Captain Fitz-james – The two ships together are the Erebus & Transport & the single one the Terror, it is a correct representation of the land and of our position. Almost immediately afterwards Captain Fitz-james brought me his sketch also to look at, which he will himself send you. This is taken from Boat Island on which Parry took his observations as our officers are now doing. It will therefore be an interesting memento of the scene to shew him.

I feel much gratified by the kind feeling of the officers towards you – and I am sure there is nothing they would not do to please you. Hitherto I have invited them with regularity to dinner, Fitz-james daily and I shall continue to do so, until we get to the ice or in a situation when neither I nor they may be able to spare the time for sitting down to dinner. I have got the Master of the Transport to spare what wine he could, sugar & coffee, which amounts to £7.2 and for this sum I have given him a bill on Messrs Stilwell in whose hands there is perhaps about that money remaining if not, it is of no consequence – he will advance the amount. Let me here remind you if you see the Agent of Transport Lieutenant Griffith RN not to mistake him for the Master whose name is Huggins & from whom I got the above supplies.

Tuesday 8th July – Still unloading the Transport – if we do not quite complete this job to day we shall be able to do so early tomorrow, and at least to ascertain whether or not both ships can carry all she has on board for them – of this we are certain that the two ships will have on board three years supply of provision fuel & clothing. I mention this the more particularly that you may not have the slightest apprehension respecting our welfare though we should have to winter twice, and with respect to this point, let me entreat you & Eleanor not to be too anxious, for it is very possible that our prospects of success and the health of the officers & crew might justify our passing a second winter in these regions. If we do not succeed in one attempt to try in other places, and through Gods blessing we hope to set the question at rest. Parry, Ross & Richardson will be the best persons to consult on every occasion that you may feel anxious each of whom will give you the result of their own judgment & experience and advise you in every way. I have not mentioned the Sabines whom I know you will henceforth consider as dear friends and whom you are sure to look to for comfort. I am much gratified by your account of Mrs Sabines attachment to you and interest on your behalf. I have been just reading over all your letters sent to the Orkneys and there seems to me no point in them to which I have not in some way or other replied. I entirely coincide with your wishes as to having some little land in England on which we could reside. Our means would necessarily cause the purchase to be small, and I feel with you that we should in no case keep any part beyond the garden & the lawn if there be one, in our own possession. I likewise concur with you in the desirableness of instructing Mr Gunn to sell the land at Port Phillip and Mr Gell that in South Australia whenever they can be sold with advantage. I should do the same with that at New Zealand. My only objection to increasing the

purchases of land in VDL rests on the present uncertainty of its prospects
– If Lord Stanley adheres to his unrighteous views as to the treatment
and employment of the Convicts – the settlers of respectability who have
families will not remain if they can get away and property will decrease
in value & become likewise insecure. The returns also from such a distant
Colony must be precarious and if you have mainly to depend on them
must cause you anxiety. I have every confidence in Mr Gunn & believe
he will manage our affairs for the best, but he cannot force the parties
to pay who have not the means. I trust he may now be able to make use
of the Deeds which I have signed at the Orkneys – and make over the
land at the Huon to the parties who have the means of paying for it – I
should however insist on his making such people as Mr Ballantyne pay
their debts first or discharge them from the land. I hope he may be able to
do something with Betsey Island – though I much fear its vicinity to the
Convicts on Tasmans Peninsula will militate against its being occupied
by any respectable tenant. It may ultimately have to be purchased by the
Government which I think would be the best thing that could happen
for us and I hope you will not object to instruct Gunn to sell it to them
if they wish for it. You are quite right in changing your money from
Dunn's Bank to that of McLachlan, the one is a certain friend the other a
doubtful person and a skin-flint. I look upon the placing young Dunn in
the Council as a proof that self interest prevails at Head Quarters. I quite
approve also of your recommending Mr Gell to commence now with the
formation of the College Library at Ancanthe rather than that the shelves
should be kept open for the contributions of Natural History which I
am persuaded will not be given except by Gunn Dr Hobson and two
or three others of that stamp. It is delightful to think of the Tasmanian
Journal going on and that you by this time have received the new number. I hope you have seen the references which Streleski has made to that
"useful journal" in three parts of his book; this notice ought to shame
Lord Stanley for letting such an institution be sacrificed to please the
whim of one selfish & unprincipled man. Streleski also speaks of you
most kindly in connection with the Huon as in other places. I have been
astonished at the mass of important matter which he has collected & of
the pleasing manner in which it is put forth – I really feel the Dedication
of that Book to me as an honor of which I may be justly proud. I am certain it is a Book that will attract the attention of Agriculturists & men of
Science especially if it be reviewed by Buckland to whom I wrote & made
the request. Mr Fairholme had heard of it and wished to read it which
he is now doing and he told me the other day that he should write to his
father, who is a Geologist, to get it.

Tuesday 8ᵗʰ July – I often think of you & the Pamphlet and always with increased thankfulness to God that you managed the points & the arrangements of them so well that every one who has read it here, is struck with the moderation and yet firmness of the language. Montagu's friends may bully and attempt to frighten you, but they cannot succeed and will do the most harm to themselves by such a course for it is evident to every one that he is a bad fellow. I am inclined to think that Forsters friends in this Country will be the most sore at his name having been so deservedly brought in – They are aware of the part he played but did not suppose that his underhand working with Montagu would be exposed. I sometimes imagine that the Archdeacon will be pleased at the Pamphlet and may even take courage to speak out if he should be spoken to on its subjects by either Lord Stanley or Mr Hope – The Bishop I am sure will be pleased at it. I approve of your not sending the Pamphlet to anyone in your own name. I forget whether Sir Robert Inglis is on the List – if not he should be. I think of writing a line to express my regret at having left England without bidding him good bye, because he & Lady Inglis were so kind to us all. Crozier has been dining with me and we had a little conversation about the Pamphlet when alone together. He repeated that the conduct of Lord Stanley & Mr Montagu was disgraceful. I think he intends writing a few lines to you, but of course he will say nothing about the Pamphlet. "<u>Entre nous</u>" – I do not think that he has had his former flow of spirits since we sailed, nor that he has been quite well. He seemed more cheerful & better to day, and has always been very kind & attentive & I endeavor to encourage in him a close intimacy with me, which I think will soon come on. He has never mentioned Sophy – nor made the slightest allusion to her and I sometimes question myself whether or not it would be agreeable or proper for me to speak of her to him. This was the first day in which I have remarked his having spoken of Tom Cracroft and that only observing that he was to have gone with him in the Gig to Launceston had he not been taken ill when Ross and I went there. He is indefatigable in his duties and very kind in instructing & helping Fitz-james as to any doubt he may have respecting the Magnetical Instruments. Fitz-james & he appear to like each other. In speaking to the Sabines or Ross be careful not to mention what I have said about his spirits or to Parry. The officers of the two ships live very amicably together and I trust will continue to do so.

Wednesday 9ᵗʰ July – I trust by the close of this day we shall have all our stores cleared from the Transport and most of them put into some place or other – the weather fortunately continues good for our operations both on board and on shore. I have taken into my Cabin all the Preserved Potatoes which are packed in tin cases and stow conveniently without interfering with either Mr Goodsirs table or my own or another at which I think Mr Le Vesconte will take up his position and make the Charts. The Gun room officers have also taken what can be best stowed under their table so that every hole in the ship will be full and many heavy spars are lashed outside. I have written to Mr Brown & Sir Robert Inglis to day.

Thursday 10th July – I went on shore this morning with Crozier that he might gather some specimens of the plants. He told me that he had last evening been writing to you but had torn his letter up for fear you should judge from it that he was not in good spirits. I begged of him to write another which he half promised me to do. He dined with me and was more cheerful – I have no doubt if there be any cause for lowness of spirits on his part as connected with Sophy, that he will give me by & bye an opportunity of conversing with him on this subject – at present his thoughts are occupied with the stowage of his ship, which requires the utmost care in order that she may carry her supplies. I am confident that he will continue to cultivate his friendship for me and that we shall act together most cordially. He is a fine hearted fellow. He was regretting with me last evening that Ross had not stuck closer at his publication which he feared is even now far behind. I had this evening the pleasure of knowing that all our stores had been received on board from the Transport but the difficulty now is where they are to be stowed, a very large quantity of them will have to be secured on deck but as we have very little sea in these high northern parts that will not matter.

Friday 11th July – Another most lovely day- on which we are fully occupied in filling up every hole & corner of the ship with stores. The Transport will soon remove from alongside to make her own preparations for sailing, and in order to leave us room to swing the ships & find the deviations of the needle on each point of the Compass, after our ships are stowed, as was done at Greenhithe. I have written to Sabine & Parry, to each of my sisters, to Sophy your sister Mary & your Aunt, and I think every other letter which appears to me of importance to write. I have not been able to do any thing with my VDL friends, you must say to them all you wish me to say to those we respect among them. The Transport is removed from us and will sail tomorrow.

Saturday 12th July – This is another lovely & clear day which makes me desirous of getting away – which I think we shall do tonight – for both ships are now busy in swinging the ships to obtain the Dip & Deviation of the Compass – which is our last operation in Harbour. I have just written the sketch of my official letter to the Admiralty for Mr Osmer to copy – Fitz-james has seen the draft and approves of it – it is short and only gives those events the Admiralty wish to receive. Lieutenant Griffiths the Agent of the Transport is waiting for my letters. He kindly takes charge of two small boxes & a tin case containing Fitz-james sketch of this anchorage for you – I hope you will see Mr Griffiths who seems glad of the prospect of making your acquaintance he is an intelligent gentlemanly man and can give you a full account of us all up to the latest moment – Mr Osmer has begged of me to present the kind remembrance of all the officers to you – Be assured that you have their best wishes – and I feel confident of having their cordial cooperation – this observation may also be applied to Crozier & the Officers of the Terror – I hope Crozier has written to you and I have no doubt that he was desirous of doing it. I trust that I have not omitted any point that you wished to be informed upon, if so exercise your own excellent judgment if it relates to any of our personal matters this also I particularly wish you to do with respect to my dear Eleanor & Gell if the latter should come home and get settled before I return – they will both prove blessings and comfort to you & to me. I have written to each of my dearest friends to comfort & assist you with their best counsel. To the Almightys care I commit you & dear Eleanor. I trust He will shield you under his wings and grant the continual aid of His Holy Spirit – again that God bless and support you both is and will be the constant prayer of your most affectionate Husband

John Franklin

160. JOHN FRANKLIN TO HENRIETTA WRIGHT [SISTER],
11 JULY 1845

Whale Fish Island
Bay of Disko
11th July 1845

My dearest Henrietta

You will be glad to learn that we arrived at the first stage of our voyage in the time we expected, and that we have had favourable weather here for all operations. Those on board were unloading the Transport

and leaving all the stores of Field Provision which she had brought
out for both ships. Those on shore were obtaining of Magnetical and
Astronomical Observations, and making the collections of the subjects
of Natural History. We are now supplied with every requisite store for
three years and should we not be fortunate enough in finding a passage
in the first direction in which we seek for it, we have the means of staying
to try in other places which I shall do if God wills, and the health of my
crews continues good so I that I wish to warn you and my other Sisters
as I have done Jane and Eleanor not to become over anxious if we do
not return at the time they may have fixed in their minds that we should.

You may also be gratified by the assurance which I can give you of my
officers and crew being zealous and excellent people, all full of life and
spirit, who have entered upon their duties con amore and are blessed
with health and strength to go through their duties. I rejoice likewise to
say that the coming to sea has entirely removed my cough, and that my
health is so good that the officers often exclaim that I am quite a different looking person since we sailed. When they first became known to
me I was suffering from the severe Influenza which sent me to Brighton.

We have no means of hearing much as to the state of the ice in our future
course and nothing beyond a few hundred miles to the North. What we
have heard of its state so far is good, and we hope in a few days to be in a
situation to judge for ourselves. The Transport sails for England tomorrow and we shall get away I hope in a few hours afterwards.

I am convinced that we bear with us your earnest prayers and those of
Mr. Wright and of the other members of your family, and be assured
you will all be remembered in mine. There are few things which give me
more sincere pleasure to contemplate than the mutual intercession at the
Throne of Grace offered up by the members of a family for the divine
blessing on each other. Whatever be our pursuits God alone can cause
them to issue in success and to his glory, be it our duty then to seek His
guidance, His merciful protection and favour. May we learn to feel the
delight of casting our care upon Him because He careth for us.

Mr. Wright is probably aware that there are several Missionary stations in
Greenland for the instruction of the Esquimaux, many of them under the
Moravians whom I consider the teachers best adapted to teach uncivilized
men whose means of subsistence is so precarious that they cannot live a
stationary life or be assembled together at but few seasons of the year.

The Moravians while they instruct them in the all important duties of religion, teach them improved and practical habits of fishing or culture or whatever be their mode of living, and in fact they identify themselves with the people they have to teach but never intermarry with them I believe.

There is a station near to our present anchorage at which there are 130 Esquimaux when all assembled but the greater part are absent catching seals, the oil and skins of which they sell to the Danish Government. The appearance dress manner and cleanliness of these Esquimaux bespeak that care is taken of them by the Government. Several of them can read the Bible with ease, and I was told that where the families are all collected the children are obliged to attend school daily. I looked into one of the huts arranged with seats for this purpose. When the Minister comes over from Disco he superintends the school at other times the children are taught by a Half Caste Esquimaux.

How delightful it is thus to know that the Gospel is spreading far and wide, and will do so till its blessed truths are disseminated throughout the Globe. Every ship in these days should go forth to strange lands bearing among its officers and crew a Missionary Spirit, and may God grant such a spirit on board this ship! It is my desire to cultivate this feeling, and I am encouraged to hope that we have some among us some who will aid me in this duty. We have Divine Service twice on each Sunday, and I never witnessed a more attentive congregation than we have. May the seed sown among us all fall on good ground and bring forth fruit abundantly to God's honour and Glory.

I trust my dearest Jane and Eleanor and Sophy have been able to pay their long wished for visit into Lincolnshire, and that their minds being free from the ceaseless anxiety which the Pamphlet occasioned, as well as their bodies from the labour it caused them, they may now be really able to enjoy themselves. Each of them has been over worked and wanted relaxation. This visit over I trust they will lose no time in getting abroad where they will be far removed from the scene of their cares and their thoughts turned away from the subject of Mr. Montague and Lord Stanley by change of objects which may be interesting to them.

I have been writing all this day I have written to each of my sisters. I shall not be able to write to _____ may I beg of you therefore to give my affectionate regards to them all. You must do the same to every member of your own family whom I should have liked to have seen more of, than my hasty trip into Lincolnshire permitted. I trust through God's blessing to pass more time among you after my return. May the Almighty keep Mr. Wright your family and yourself under His gracious protection and love.

Ever your affectionate Brother
John Franklin

161. JAMES REID TO ANN REID [WIFE], 11 JULY 1845

Davis' Straits, South East Bay, Whale Fish Island
July 11th, 1845

Loving wife,

This leaves me Quite well hopes it will find you and the family the same we Landed here on the 4 Inst. all well excepting of one who is to bee sent home by the Transport we have got Every thing out of the Transport or will have to day, we will start from this for the North in a day or two. I have seen none of the whalers as yet and I Dount think I will see any of them. By the state of the season, they will be all through Melville Bay & bee over to the west Land before we can see them by what I here from the natives here, Last winter wase very mild and the ice all gon[e] from this Quarter early in May. They Likewise Acquaint me of several of the Whalers having got fish, My Brother 2 if not 3, St. Andrew 1 if not 2, Parker from Hull 2. Several others, but I dount remember there names, bee so good as write To Dundee about this, and a few lines to the Mannager of the Alexander, he is a very fine man, and tell him that I have Great hopes of the Shipes beeing all well fished this season, it hase not been known these many years for the is[e] to brake up so soon.

I trust we will have very little Trouble in Reaching Lancaster Sound and then to Barrows straits. Since I left London I have been thinking how you might Receive 20. Or 30 Pounds from the same man, my life is Insured with, it will pay intre[st] the same as £ 50 I got, no doubt you will bee short before your pay comes on, and If so you write to that gentleman you have his adress, David Leys is Quite well.

I am Glade to acquaint you that Sir John Franklin o[u]r Captain R.N.
is Quite well and enjoying his helth much Better then when in London,
he is a fine Gentleman, we have Divine Service twice Every sunday very
good, indeed he minds me very much of Dr. Kid[d] on the whaler, we
are all happy one with the other he allowes no Swearing on board nor
no high words. whate they have to say they must Repeat it to the 1st
Lieutenant. I hope William is home before this comes to hand. James
must bee in about the same time when you have the Occasion to write
them, Remember there Father to them it will be a long time before I have
it in my paure to write you again. wee have Provisions for three years of
Every Thing. Both Ships is very Deep & no Doubt you will think Long
but you must not trouble your mind about me, it is orderd to me to
bee here wheather it bee for Good or bad no one knows, but God he is
the only one I put my trust in. If I allwise know you wase well, I would
bee mu[ch] happ[i]er whate is to come of my three Dear young ones if
anything is the mater with you, but I trust the Lord will Spaire you and
them so that I may Engage you and them for a number of years yet we
are not to call old. I will Inclose a line to my Broker in London so that
you cane forward to him wh[en] you are short of money and I think he
will forward you a moderate thing untill you Receive your pay and when
it is in your paur pay every one but dount hurt yourself – bear in mind
whate I mentioned to you before Take care of yourself the Growing up
Family would Take all from you some of them

I am sorry to say I Lost my Spy Glass on the Pass[age] out when we
wase Drawing nige the Ice Bergs, that is the only thing I want. but the 1st
Lieutenant is very good and Pusser the[y] both makes me very welcome
to there & S. John Franklin, every officer in the Navy fin[d]es his own
Glass I wase ever in the Hopes of seeing My Brother Charles but Dount
think I will now, after hearing the state of the country, If I hade, I would
no doubt get one from him.

I think I will Drope Mr. Enderby a few lines in London, I have been a
Number of years in this contry but I never saw it so warm as it hase
been this last three days. the Miscatties is Very Thick. I have been sadly
annoyed with them my face and hands is all swolled by them and the
Chief part of the crew the same way. but we will find it cold anough
in a few months – we have hands in all 68 – out of that, one Sargen
& Corpral & six Mareens – I have nothing more to say Give my best

Respects to Robert Forbes, and all Friends, may the Lord bee with you and my Dear Family, for three years if not through before that time, keep yourself easy about me. Trust wee will meet Again. Remember me to William Gaudy wife & family Bidding you all Good By.

Remains your loving
Husband
James Reid

Latitude 68°, 59' N Longitude 53°, 13' W The Transport starts this Evening for London July 12th but I daunt think we will before Monday 14. I Dount think Sir John will Start on Sunday, there wase Blankets served out to day to the people I took two and marked.

JR

P.S. I spoke the Brig Banchory of Aberdeen Mowat master all well 27th June in Latit[ude] 64°03' N Longitude 63° 09' W he wase fishing for Cod it ware calm at the time and the Cod ware thousand all Round the Ship we Caught a number of them, the owners name is A&N. Nichol. If he is not arrived, be so good and call on these gentlemen and mention this to them, they will bee anxious to here about her.

JR

162. ALEXANDER MCDONALD TO JAMES CLARK ROSS, 11 JULY 1845

H.M.S. Terror: Whalefish Islands
July 11th 1845 –

My Dear James

The transport leaves us tomorrow and I cannot let slip the opportunity of writing you for it is probably the last I will have for some time. Our proceedings up to the time of our arrival here were dull enough, but since then we have been all life & activity. In point of professional duty there is little to be done, but things are so arranged that we have no want of employment.

Much is expected from us in the way of collecting specimens of the subject of natural history and assisting generally in the scientific department. It is impossible in the present stage of the proceedings to give an opinion as to the state of the ice, but I am inclined to think that this is what is called an open season. Should this prove correct we will make great & rapid progress: indeed some among us are so sanguine as to believe that we will reach the Pacific without wintering. The possession of steam power certainly gives great advantage over any former expedition but such signal success is, if possible, highly improbable. Altho confident of our ultimate success yet I think it can only be gained by long & unceasing efforts.

I will write you from the first port we reach after we get through, and you would oblige me much by writing me occasionally and forwarding your letters to certain ports at which we will call. There is a port on the coast of Kamtschatka named I Think, Petropolski (anglici St Peter & St Paul) which we will likely visit. Letters to [a]wait the arrival of the arctic expedition would be forwarded to that port if sent to the office of the Russian ambassador in London, with a request that he would forward them via Siberia. We call at the Sandwich Islands and you may write by whatever way you think best, as there is no regular mail. We will also call at or send an officer to Panama and letters addressed to the care of the British Consul there will certainly be looked after. I will confidently expect to hear from you at each of these places and in return will not fail to write when opportunity offers. I may also observe that writing to Kamschatka about the 1st January to Panama about the 1st June you will put me in possession of the latest intelligence. You may continue to do this for several years should you not hear from or of me for that time.

Farewell my dear James may God bless you

Ever affect &c
Yours Alex McDonald

163. JAMES FITZJAMES TO WILLIAM CONINGHAM [BROTHER], 11 JULY 1845

HMS Erebus Whale-fish
Islands, 11th July 1845

Dear Will

Elizabeths bundle of yarns will shew you that I am well and happy – and that I have not forgotten you yet – I have not much time, as the Transport sails tomorrow evening, and we shall be all day at work "swinging" the ship as we did at Greenhithe for deviations of the Compass. It was a heavy job, clearing the Transport, and took us longer than we imagined it would have done, though we worked from 4 till 6. We are now full – very – having three years provisions and coals, besides the engine – The deck is covered with coals and casks, leaving a small passage fore and aft, and we are very deep in the water –

I was on shore with the observations nearly all the time and my work has been increased by losing the book in which I had noted all my observations, when walking on the hills – so I had to begin again – With the exception of one rainy day & a thick fog one afternoon we have had the most heavenly weather you can imagine – clear and calm – and the sun to day is really too hot thermometer in the shade 57° – The mosquitoes are terrible, but they d'ont bite me as much as a great many people – –

We sail if possible tomorrow night, and hope to get to Lancaster Sound by the 1st August, which, however, is a lottery. We have good reason to expect a very favourable season – but do not intend being too sanguine about it – I hope you will be amused with my Journalizing – I really d'ont know half what I have written for at times I wrote when very sleepy just before going to bed.

It is now eleven o'clock, & the sun shining brightly above the snowy peaks of Disko. From the top of one of these islands, the other day, I counted with Hodgson & Fairholme 280 ice bergs – and beautiful objects they are. If you go to John Barrow & ask him he will introduce you to a little old dry Agent of the Transport Lieutenant Griffiths to whom I have given a note for Barrow he will tell you all about us but with countless additions no doubt.

Should you hear nothing till next June, send a letter via Petersburg to Petro Paulowski in Kamschatka, where Osmar was in the Blossom, and had letters from England in three months. And now God bless you and Elizabeth and the children and everything belonging to you. –

Always your affectionate
James Fitzjames.

164. JAMES FITZJAMES TO EDWARD SABINE, 11 JULY 1845

HMS Erebus Whale Fish Islands 11th July 1845

My dear Colonel Sabine.

Captain Crozier has I know written to you fully on what you are most interested about in our expedition – the observations we have made in the magnetic department, or rather those we have not made – for he will have told you that the weather during our voyage to this has been anything but favorable to observations either with Fox or anything else – not that my observations with Fox can ever be of much use. for the instrument being cut only to degrees cannot give a reading of any intrinsic value – I imagine I appreciate to every 5' – and even if I could estimate to minutes I would put no value on the results – besides the vernier is about ¼ of a mile from the limb – and in fact the instrument is rotten and it grieves me much because it prevents my taking the great interest I otherwise should in the observations and experiments I perceive might be made with a good instrument. – why the Admiralty should have palmed off a rotten affair like this on us I am at a loss to determine. I can only suppose that it was supposed my observations would not be of use as compared to Captain Crozier's – if so I cannot see the use of keeping any.

As it is I am determined it shall never be said there was any fault of mine in the matter & consequently I take all the needful observations but with no feeling of pleasure – in fact I look on it as a loss of time & Lord knows my time is of some value to me now. I had begun to prepare a set of results as obtained hitherto but imagining it would be of no use deferred the work. I will say however that the Fox observations I have taken present a tolerably good series of means.

On arrival here I was anxious to get the index error of the needle and for this purpose set up on "Boat island" the "Robinson" which is a most beautiful instrument and has cost me some trouble for I lost the first series of observations – having dropped my book on the hills, and in taking second series I observed that the needle A1 gave a much smaller result than the other. I consequently repeated the observations three times with all the needles and came to the conclusion that the magnets supplied with the instrument were not strong enough to magnetise the needles properly – This morning I repeated the observations magnetising the needle with the strong magnets supplied with Lloyds intensity instrument. This gave a more <u>equal</u> result – but still A2 was less than the others

The two static needles did not give the same results on the separate observations but at times the changes were very great and the instrument is beautifully delicate. The mean of the whole however will I should imagine give a good result of the absolute dip. With Captain Crozier's assistance I took a set of observations with the Lloyd intensity instrument which however good the theory of it may be and however good the result – might be with a good instrument – is I should imagine of not much more for delicate observations – the instrument is evidently put out of hand in a hurry by a contract maker – No reading is to be obtained beyond 85° dip – the Ys are very rough yet in the instructions a "correction for "gravity" is hinted at in using the constant weight – as well might one talk with <u>gravity</u> of a lunar observation to tenths of seconds with an old quadrant. However nothing shall be left untried to get as many and as good observations as possible with the instrument such as it is – at all events it is better than my Fox.

We got the two unifilars on shore and had good sets of vibrations & deflections by Hodgson & Fairholme – Had I the least idea that we should have been here so long and have had such fine weather I would have got the Bifilar up and the Declinometer. We are this day <u>very full</u> having worked from 4 am till 6 pm everyday since the 3^d – Hard work it has been and we & the Terror are <u>fearfully</u> full.

Tomorrow we swing – I shall take the Dip direct[ion] & intensity with Deflection of at each two points – and of course the Compass deviation at every point – Of course I do not intend getting up the Robinson till we are in winter quarters as I am aware it is for the observatory for <u>changes</u>.

So much for magnetics It remains to say that we hope to sail tomorrow evening and have every reason to expect a favourable season for getting to Lancaster Sound from where I trust we shall be by the 1st August at the latest. Sir John is very well and full of life and energy – and we are all as happy as possible looking forward to the commencement of our <u>real</u> work – No one I am sure will rejoice more than yourself at our success which we all anticipate eventually if <u>not sooner</u>.

Pray remember me with all kindness to Mrs Sabine in which Fairholme Hodgson & Levesconte join me. and believe me

yours very sincerely

James Fitzjames

I intend writing to Riddell but should I not have time for I am much harried pray tell him of my kind remembrances.

I observe that neither the static needles belonging to the Robinson – or those found in the case of Lloyds instrument are guarded Captain Crozier agrees with me that this could not have been unintentional – so we leave them.

The static needle of Lloyd instrument A1 – has its North End at B – A2 at A2 –

165. JOHN FRANKLIN TO ISABELLA CRACROFT [SISTER], 11 JULY 1845

Whale Fish Islands
Disco Bay
11th July 1845

My dearest Isabella,

I was delighted to learn by my letters at Stromness that Mr Lacy and his dear children had arrived in England. And I hope they were shortly afterwards under your roof. It would give me sincere pleasure had I been able to see them, and believe me from no member of your family would Mr Lacy & his children have received a more heartfelt welcome than from me. The meeting them is now among the pleasing anticipations which I indulge in. Pray assure him of my affectionate regards for him & them.

This is the first stage of our voyage – and a snug anchorage it is, so that we had great facility in unloading the transport and we are now stored with full supplies for three years consumption. The accounts we have received of the state of the ice to the north is favourable as far as it extends viz to Lancaster Sound – beyond which the information of my informant does not reach – It is gratifying however to hear such an opinion entertained even up to this point – and we hope in a few days to be sufficiently advanced to test it ourselves.

The Transport sails for England tomorrow and I have been writing to all my sisters – with many letters to my friends. All will be gratified to find that I have every reason to be pleased with my officers & crew. They are zealous and ardent in the cause, full of hope & spirit – ready to work well & having the power of working in them. The most perfect unanimity of feeling & harmony exists between the officers & crews of the two ships – Crozier & I continue our friendship, he is an excellent hearted man and the very best second I could have had – He has not once mentioned Sophy's name to me and I have not considered it proper to introduce any mention of her in my conversation. I shall not however avoid doing so if he gives me the opportunity – We often dine together, but for the present both of us have too much to do with our present objects to talk on subjects not connected with them.

We have had a very fair passage hitherto – though in crossing the Atlantic the wind took us within 70 miles of Iceland and we were to have had the hope of seeing Mount Hecla but were disappointed.

Since we have passed round Cape Farewell we have been much in sight of the Greenland coast – keeping generally from 30 to 40 miles off. The snow in the lower parts has disappeared but remains in the upper – The outline of the land is picturesque. The Danes have several mission-ary stations among the Esquimaux on this coast, which I should like to have visited. They are principally I believe under the charge of Moravian Ministers – the very best in my opinion for such purposes among unciv-ilized aborigines. They have succeeded admirably with the Esquimaux on the Labrador Coast. There are a few Esquimaux hereabout under the Danish Government – and Ministers. They are employed catching seal for their oil & skins which are sold to the Government –

Judging from the appearance of these men & women I should say they are well mannered, they are certainly more cleanly & better dressed than any Esquimaux I have before seen – and I am told many of them are able to read their Bibles. The children are taught daily in school and I saw the hut arranged with seats which is used for this purpose.

Do not get over anxious about us if we do no return by the time you have fixed upon. Be earnest in prayers for us as I shall be for you & yours. Give my affectionate regards to all around you and believe me ever yours Most affectionately,

John Franklin

166. HARRY GOODSIR TO JOHN GOODSIR [FATHER], 12 JULY 1845

Whale fish Islands
July 12th. 1845
H.M.S. Erebus

I send a long letter to you in the box addressed to John

My Dear Father

As it is several days since I closed my letter to you dated from Disco I wish to write you from the last moment & as the Transport sails this evening intend giving you all the news since we have come here The weather has been exceedingly beautiful & very warm much more so than I ever experienced it in England upon the face of the Cliffs it is actually burning & the Mosquittoes are very troublesome to all. The bite of these flies is much more troublesome than the sting of a bee leaving the mark for many days. I have been busy for the last week with the animals to be found here and all the other things which come under my department so that my whole time has been taken up. I have got a complete vocabulary of the Esquimaux language here and am only anxious to get casts of their head and face which I hope to get all round the coast of America for the purpose of showing the differences. A few days ago I went out with Sir John and the Captain of the Transport & landed on an Iceberg & went to the very top. I suppose I am the only one in the two ships that has been to the top of an iceberg yet but I am anxious to get a good knowledge of the structure of these immense bodies. The water from the ice is excellent and is quite hard, & when the sun is shining upon the surface of the berg it is the most beautiful thing possible to see the water pouring off the ledges. We have shot great numbers of eider duck and birds of other descriptions but the other Surgeons are great bores regarding all these things. I send home some eider down in a box which is directed to John and will reach you shortly after this. I hope every thing is going on well with you, all. It is almost useless talking about such a thing now but I hope that after this voyage I will be able to spend a time with you all at Largo. After we arrive however my tim[e] will be occupied for some time arranging and describing the animals got during the voyage. This will be however after visiting you & I hope you will be able to return with me to London where of course I must be during the time the descriptions &c. of the animals are being published. To this I look forward with a great deal of pleasure & hope that every thing will go on successfully to forward it. Tell Joseph and Jane that it is only want of time which prevents me writing them & I hope that every thing will go well with them till we meet again. Remember me to all friends and Believe me

Your most Affectionate Son
Harry D. S. Goodsir

167. HARRY GOODSIR TO JOHN GOODSIR [BROTHER], 12 JULY 1845

July 12th 1845
Whale Fish Islands

I send a small box by this same opportunity so be good enough to look out for it. I direct Captain Griffiths agent of the Transport to forward it without delay Baretto Junior Transport Deptford

My Dear John

The Transport leaves us today, so that I hasten to give you information of all that has taken place since I closed my last. We have been lying here now 8 days, & during that time I have got every thing examined – A vocabulary with all the characteristics & peculiarities of the Natives – The Geological features of the Islands which are very simple – and the action of the Ice upon them, a very interesting subject and very prominently marked. I have also obtained specimens of the vertebrate, as well as the invertebrate animals, together with all the plants, mosses and sea weeds. I am anxious to obtain good casts of the head and face of all the various tribes of Esquimaux we meet with, & will do so, if I possibly can.

You can tell Professor Forbes, that I have examined the structure of the ice, & find that it contains, numerous cells, as he describes, but that they do not appear to be air cells (See letter to Jardine & your former one). Its semiopacity depends upon these numerous cells, many portions of it such as veins where the cells do not exist being of a very beautiful ultramarine blue. Regarding the rate of motion of icebergs we are not yet in the country for that. I have also made many interesting observations upon the action of ice on rocks, an action plainly visible over the whole surface of these islands, & have got several sketches illustrative of it.

Upon the superior surface of one of the Islands, which I examined particularly, I was enabled to make out the action of the ice formed in the large
pools of water which collect there every year, all of which observations,
I hope will be important to Geologists.

The invertebrata, here, altho very numerous as regards individuals, are
not so, as Species at least at present, but I have no doubt, that various
forms make their appearance during the year. I have however procured
a great number & cannot complain.

I have already got (what I did not expect at such an early period of the
voyage) more than 150 figures of animals alone, besides all those of their
anatomy &c. and immense numbers of specimens. As we get up the bay,
this will no doubt increase in proportion, and I also expect to make out
there the Cetacea & Seals, which will make beautiful figures. They have
all left this for more northern latitudes, being too warm here for them You
have no idea how warm it is here, much more so than any place I have
ever been in, & the mosquittoes are very troublesome. I do not feel them,
but they tell so much upon some of our officers, that they are obliged to
keep bed, on account of the swelling caused in the face being so great.

After I had got all the Medusæ examined I got a number of naked
Mollusca, such as Tritonia Doris and Eolida by pulling up the sea weed
from the bottom in which way I obtained many valuable animals – One
of which is figured in a german thesis you have got. It is an Annelide quite
transparent, & of a beautiful green colour in the centre. I have also got
a very large & beautiful specimen of Boltenia, which is rather valuable.

From all that I have done already I should think that a more favourable
field is open yet. All that I hope for is that we may meet with as good
success in the latter as the early part of the voyage. I send this by itself
with Captain Griffiths that you may have an opportunity of hearing
sooner as well as to look out for the box containing the paper bottles &c

> Believe me
> Your affectionate brother
> Harry D. S. Goodsir

P.S. I am so much engaged at present, and fatigued at the same time, that
I am not able to write you an Account of the action of the ice over the
Rocks. I hope however Prof. Forbes will get it put into Jardines Gazette
along with the other information, if not he will send it to you.

168. HENRY T.D. LE VESCONTE TO HENRY LE VESCONTE [FATHER], 12 JULY 1845

HMS Erebus Whale Fish Is.
July 12. 1845

My dear Father

I wound up my letters before coming in here knowing we should have a press of work it has been so but we have been much longer than I thought the ships are now loaded we sent the Transport away and sail ourselves to night. The ships are miserably loaded the decks so crowded that there is scarcely room to move but we hope for nothing but very fine weather this is a very commodious place a creek between small rocky islands. we made fast to the rocks and employed ourselves in magnetical astronomical and surveying operations also shooting for the islands are covered with a great variety of chicks – I am expecting to be hurried off every moment so cannot write much more I have to report that the ship is most comfortable and that Sir John Franklin continues to command that respect & esteem he so richly merits. I have sent Henrietta a sketch of an ice berg and some arctic flowers they are not very pretty but there is a variety particularly of mosses. the tripe de roche prevailing – believe me my dear Father your ever affectionate son

HTD LeVesconte

169. JOHN FRANKLIN TO MARY ANNE KENDALL [NIECE], 12 JULY 1845

Whale Fish Islands
Bay of Disco
12. July 1845

My dear Mary Anne,

I will not lose this last opportunity of writing to you in order to assure you of my continued sympathy with you and your dear children – and that it is among my most cherished anticipations, if God spares my life to do what I can in your and their behalf – It is a happiness to reflect how much you have been supported in your affliction and especially to know that you have a most judicious friend to advice you in Mr Paine – I do not remember having met any person who seizes upon and acts with more promptness on the best points of a case – His heart too is truly good – May God bless his endeavours to assist you – You have a sincere friend in Parry – and I recommend you to write to him when you have reason to think he may be of assistance to you –

You will be glad to know that the coming to sea has had its usual good effect on me – all my cough at once disappeared – and every remnant of my attack of Influenza – I never in fact was in better health – I have every reason also to be happy – blessed as I am by having zealous & good young officers – and an active well disposed Crew – Each of whom appears to be ardent in the service we are upon – I trust also that each of us have been taught and see the necessity of placing our trust in God – "We are not sufficient of our selves to do any thing as of our selves but our sufficiency is of God" – His aid protection and guidance we must earnestly seek in the full assurance of faith & hope that he will order all things as seemeth the best to his infinite wisdom – and enable each of us to do our duty to the praise & glory of his Holy Name –

I am sure my dear Mary Anne we shall have the benefit of your prayers also – and I assure you that neither yourself nor your children will be forgotten by me in my humble petitions before the Throne of Grace –

The transport sails for England to day and I think we shall also proceed northwards in the night – or early to morrow morning so that we may be able to get well clear out to sea in time to have prayers – Which we have each Sunday morning & evening –

I must beg of you to say every thing kind & affectionate on my part to your parents & sisters – and do not forget to assure your sister Eliza that my sincere good wishes attend her. I shall not be able either to write to your brothers in VDL – Pray give my love to them.

I have written to Richardson It has just occurred to me on looking up – that the drawing which faces me is that of Fort Enterprize by yourself – so that I have with me a memento – I have another of Fort Franklin by my lamented friend Kendall.

God bless & preserve you is the fervent prayer of
    yours affectionately
      John Franklin

Will you kindly remember me to Miss Garrett – and to Admiral MacKinley & his family –

170. STEPHEN STANLEY TO JOHN RICHARDSON, 12 JULY 1845

H.M.S. Erebus
Whale Fish Islands
July 12th 1845

My dear Sir

I cannot allow the Letter Bag to be closed without dropping you a line to let you know how we all are – Sir John Franklin is in the very best health, certainly much better than when you saw him at Greenhithe – He seldom takes Snuff now more than once a day, and that consists of one pinch only. Whether this broken habit has anything to do with his improved state of health or not I cannot say. Lady Franklin I know had an idea, if the quantity taken was decreased, something of the kind would be the consequence – at all events his health and energy is everything his most anxious friends could wish or desire, and if you are likely to see or write to Lady Franklin you will no doubt mention what I now tell you, and at the same time give our united thanks for her kind consideration of our comfort on board.

We arrived here on the 4th and start I believe this Evening – I have been busy getting all the birds the Islands afford, but I find they are not many. I have I think nearly all. I was very lucky in killing two beautiful specimens of the large black backed gull. The Male Bird measures from the tip of the wings, five feet seven inches, and the plumage of both in excellent condition – they took me the whole of yesterday forenoon to skin. Goodsir is making a large collection of medusa and draws them very nicely – none of us I assure you, are idle – and all hope to have more to do before our return. I have not a man on the list and it is impossible we could be in better health – I send one man home as unfit for the Service and the Terror send one also. –

Trusting our efforts may be successful and our arrival soon and in health which our most anxious friends could wish. I remain, my dear sir,

Yours very faithfully

Stephen S. Stanley

171. THOMAS BLANKY TO ESTHER BLANKY [WIFE], 12 JULY 1845

"The season is a very open one, much such as one when we came out with Captain Ross. We are all in good health and spirits, one and all appearing to be of the same determination, that is, to persevere in making a passage to the north-west. Should we not be at home in the fall of 1848, or early in the spring of 1849, you may anticipate that we have made the passage, or likely to do so; and if so, it may be from five to six years, – it might be into a seventh – ere we return; and should it be so, do not allow any person to dishearten you on the length of our absence, but look forward with hope that Providence will at length of time restore us safely to you."

172. FRANCIS CROZIER TO JAMES CLARK ROSS, 12 JULY 1845

Whalefish Islands July 12
<u>1845</u>

My dear James

I cannot allow Transport to leave without writing you a line, altho' I have little to say and our many detentions keep me in anything but a fit mood for letter writing – We got here on morning of the 4ᵗʰ and have been busily employed ever since clearing and stowing away from Transport 'Tis very tedious work from the small space we have to stow things – We have now a mean draught of 16 feet and all our provisions not yet on board – I send home our largest Cutter (and fill launch with patent fuel –) 2 anchors & cables – Iron Waist Davits and various other things of weight as I think it better to have the provision come what may afterwards. How I do miss you – I cannot bear going on board Erebus – Sir John is very kind & would have me there dinning every day if I would go – He has Fitzjames and 2 officers every day.

All things are going on well and quietly but we are I fear sadly late – From what we can learn the winter here has been very severe with much Easterly wind, there was however an early break up of the Ice and the last accounts of whalers is that Fish were plenty and ships as high as the Women Isles (73°) What I fear is that from our being so late we shall have no time to look round and judge for our selves, but blunder into the

Ice and make a second 1824 of it – James I wish you were here, I would then have no doubt as to our pursuing the proper course – I must have done with this croaking I am not growling mind – indeed I never was less disposed to do so – I am I assure you beginning to be a bit of a philosopher and hope before the season is over to having so tutored myself that I will fret for nothing. I have started the Sergeant for specimens, he has however made a bad beginning having fallen and broken the Stock of my Gun. Sea weed very scarce and plants I have not after yet as my time has been a good deal occupied with dips etc. – I have sent Col. Sabine an abstract for so far – Our passage accross was very unfavourable for observing such constant heavy Sea and a great deal of wet – Very many days I could not manage azimuths, the cards are very heavy and once set in motion no getting them to rest and the unsteady motion of ship made arc of Vibration very irregular. I often wished for my own old one as I am sure I could have managed better. The new compasses are in smooth water perfect I believe but in a heavy irregular Sea I cannot say much for them. I did not try the head for checking the Vibrations, as I found them so irregular I did not want to bother with them as we were so soon to be in smooth water when I knew they would be more valuable –

Why I should have gone so far and not said one word about dear "Thot" who from my heart I do hope has benefited by change of air and getting away from comfortless Blackheath. I would like to have seen your place that I might often picture to myself your little employments – With Gods blessing my Lady I will not fail on my return to soon find my way down to see you to be condoled with peradventure, if on the other hand to rejoice with you at all events one thing is certain, meet when we may it will be to me a source of heartfelt pleasure. I hope the little son is going on well, the mild weather of the interior must be to him beneficial That Bleakheath was a scorching place. Goodsir in Erebus is a most diligent fellow a perfect enthusiast in Mollusca, he seems much in his habits like Hooker never idle making perfect scetches of all he collects very quickly and in the most extraordinary rough way – he has the happy knack of engaging every one around him in the same pursuit – he certainly is a great acquisition – I find Irving (3rd Lieutenant) will do all the chart work that I want quite well enough – he is a diligent hard working fellow – All goes on smoothly but James dear I am sadly alone, not a soul have I in either ship that I can go and talk to. "No congenial Spirit as it were" I am generally busy but it is after all a very hermitlike life – Except to kick up a row with the helmsman or abuse Jobson at times I would scarcely ever hear the sound of my own voice. .

The Transport is nearly clear and my Sugar and Tea have not made their appearance The Sugar is a great loss to me but the Tea I care not for – I cannot at all events say much for Fortnum & Masons punctuality. they directed my things to Captain Fitzjames Terror but by some strange accident they discovered my name sufficiently accurately to send me the Bill & I was fool enough to pay it from their declaring that the things were absolutely delivered on board.

growling again no –

FRMC

"Thot" I will not forget about the sketch from what I have seen we appear to have a number who draw prettily particularly in Erebus – I will take care it shall not be a steam view – how I do wish the Engine was again on the Dover line, & the Engineer sitting on the top of it, he is dead and alive wretch full of difficulties and is now quite dissatisfied because he has not the leading stoker to assist him in doing nothing as on board Erebus – I have been obliged to send home our armourer & Sailmaker being perfectly useless either at their trade or anything else also 2 men invalided which reduces our complement 62 from 68 of course making that saving in provisions and leaving us still a larger complement than Hecla & Fury – I am attending to Barometer observations carefully and get the dew point of Cabin once a day regularly and purpose during the winter months to have it more frequently – Barometer in Erebus a poor thing by Pastorelli only reads off to 100[ths] – 'Tis just as well so as they appear to be strongly tinctured with all the Sabineite notions –

Well my dear friends I know not what else I can say to you – I feel that I am not in spirits for writing but in truth I am sadly lonely & when I look back to the last voyage I can see the cause and therefore no pro[s]pect of having a more joyous feeling The bustle of the season will however be life to me and come what may I will endeavour to sit down at the end of it content – I find by the instructions that Fitzjames is appointed to superintend the Magnetic observations I will therefore take just so much bother then as may amuse without considering myself as one of the staff. God bless you both not forgetting the son and believe me ever

most sincerely

FRMCrozier

173. CHARLES OSMER TO ELIZA OSMER [WIFE], 12 JULY 1845

At the last moment, I have just that time to say God bless you. the Transport is now four miles out of the Harbour whilst I write these few lines. I shall get on board the Erebus by 12 o'Clock to night.

Lat 69° 59° N.
Long 53, 14 W.
12 July 1845

296 Ice bergs in sight from the mast head.

[In another hand] This was the very last letter from the Ships

7

Letters to the Lost

I try to prepare myself for every trial which may be in store for me, but dearest, if you ever open this, it will be because I have been spared the greatest trial of all.

Jane Franklin

It is in the nature of letters – at least, back in their pen-and-ink-and-stamp days – that they are always sent into uncertainty. When will they be delivered? When read? When replied to? And when might that long-desired reply actually arrive in one's mailbox? Even at a space of years, such is the nature of epistolary expectation that one can write a letter, not knowing whether or not it will ever arrive, and still feel in some sense the presence of its intended recipient.

And such are most of these letters. In the earliest of them, there is a strong presence of the present – the loved one has but lately departed, and passing along daily news as to family doings seems entirely sensible. As time goes on, there is a sense that such things fall away, at least to an extent – though families still are anxious to convey the "big" news as to deaths, marriages, and births. In the final phase, with hope of the letter reaching any living being steeply diminishing, there is a plaintive, almost memorial tone, as though the sender well knew that their words were not really for their imagined recipient, but for themselves.

As mentioned in the general introduction, the Royal Navy made it known to the men's families that they would take and attempt to deliver letters; the earliest in this section were sent aboard the *Plover* in January of 1848; another batch went out aboard the *North Star* in April of 1849. Of course, Lady Jane Franklin was the most enduring letter-writer of them all. Having had a role, direct or indirect, in almost every search for her lost husband and his men, she was able to place hers directly in the hands of both Naval and private searchers. When the letters were returned, she often chose simply to send them back again with the next available searcher, making a note on the envelope (for an example of this, see Letter 191).

At the same time, the families of the far more humble ordinary seamen also sent letters forth in the spirit of "Hope on, Hope ever!" – and received them back, stamped (as was the one to John Diggle from his parents), "RETURNED TO THE SENDER THERE HAVING BEEN NO MEANS OF FORWARDING IT." Which was true – and yet today, these letters feel almost as though they had been forwarded to *us* personally, speaking as eloquently as they do of the sorrows of those for whom no return, no comfort, and no consolation remained.

CHRONOLOGY

1847–49: Sir John Richardson and Dr John Rae, overland search for Franklin (Letters 178, 180, 187)

1847–51: Commander Thomas Edward Laws Moore, search from the west aboard HMS *Plover* (Letters 176, 177, 178, 179, 180, 181, 182)

1848–49: Sir James Clark Ross, commanding *Enterprise* and *Investigator* on first maritime search (Letters 177, 180, 182, 187)

1849: William Penny sails aboard the *Advice*, but is turned back by ice (Letter 183)

1850: Charles Forsyth, ineffectual search in command of the *Prince Albert* (Letters 187, 191)

1850–51: Sir John Ross, private search with the *Felix* and *Mary* (Letter 187)

1850–51: Horatio Austin's squadron – HMS *Resolute*, *Assistance*, *Intrepid*, and *Pioneer*; discovery of expedition's first wintering at Beechey Island (Letters 188, 193)

1850–51: Under William Penny, the *Lady Franklin* and *Sophia* search for Franklin; Robert Goodsir, Harry's brother, is aboard in the capacity of surgeon (Letters 188, 189, 193)

1850–51: The American ships *Advance* and *Rescue*, under Edwin De Haven, join the search, with Dr Elisha Kent Kane; this was the "First Grinnell Expedition" (Letters 190, 191)

1850–54: The *Investigator*, under Robert McClure, and the *Enterprise*, under Richard Collinson, embark on a search via Bering Strait (Letter 193)

1851–52: The *Prince Albert* returns, commanded by William Kennedy (Letters 186, 193, 195)

1852–54: Edward Belcher's squadron: *Assistance, Resolute, Pioneer, Intrepid,* and *North Star* (Letter 188)

1853: William Kennedy returns to the search with *Isabel* via the Pacific, but her crew mutinies near Valparaiso and she never reaches the Arctic (Letter 195 – our last – was carried by her)

1853–55: Dr Elisha Kent Kane returns in command of the *Advance* (see note to Letter 190)

1854: In January, the Admiralty announces that, from 31 March, Franklin and his men would be deemed to have died in Her Majesty's service, and struck from the *Navy List*

174. CHARLES HARTNELL TO JOHN AND THOMAS HARTNELL [BROTHERS], 23 DECEMBER 1847

Dear Brothers

This comes with my kind love to you hoping it find you both in good health as thank god it leaves me at preasent it is nearley three year since we parted but I hope it will not be that time before we meat again their as been great changes took place since then.

Uncle Ford is ded and Aunt is now living at borden. I saw Uncle and Aunt Hoar last June and the[y] whear quite well and wished me to let them know as soon as we heard from you. Poor Mrs Goldie poisoned herself yesterday.

But if I tell you all the news now I shall have none to tell you when you come home, which I hope will not be long as three long years has nearley pas[s]ed away but this I have to say that I have three years less to serve.

Betsey is quite well and as Mother is going to Finish I wish you a prosperous passage to return safe home so no more at present from

Your Effectionate Brother
Charles Hartnell

175. SARAH HARTNELL TO JOHN AND THOMAS HARTNELL [SONS], ON OR AFTER 23 DECEMBER 1847

My Dear Children

It is a great pleasure to me to have a chanse to write to you I hope you are booth well I assure you I have many anx[i]ous hours about you but I endeavour to cast my care on him who is to wise to err and to good to be unkind. I know his promises are sure either to be here fulfild there and why should [we] of his goodness doubt.

I still suffer much from rhumatiss[m]s it afflicts my heart and Chest so much I sometimes fear I shall not be spared to see you again I am in the hands of the Lord O may I be resign[e]d to his will in all things.

Mary has been at her place 9 mont[h]s an[d] gives great sattisfaction Betsy is at home at presant but she earns many shillings you will be supprised to hear we have a Soldier in our family nearly all the Dockyard are Soldiers you would not know Charles if you where to meet in his clothes they have sixpence an hour for exercise. J[ohn], your r[i]val is married to C. Barlow and your Goose to Mrs Sextons Brother Miss Green to James Harding and Mary Hammond to a sergeant royal Irish after 5 weeks from first sight and young Hary Bane he has taken a Irish Wife on 9 shillings a week Jane Wort and Martha Dray and Old Dray are all Married and John Gardener and old Beal and Margaret Gardener and Hester Berry and John Robinson young Daniel Harden is a Jo[ur]ne[y]man in Portsm[o]ut[h] if you should ever come then he would be glad to see you.

My Dear children if it is the Lords will may we be spared to meet on earth if not God grant we may all meet around his throne to praise him to all eternity is the Prayers of your Affectionate Mother

Sarah Hartnell

176. JOHN THOMPSON TO JAMES THOMPSON [BROTHER], 3 JANUARY 1848

Dear Brother

It gives me great pleasure in having the opportunity of writing to you at after so long A absense, and I hope that they will arrive safe and find you and your companions all well – for I will assure you that great fears are entertaind as to your safety, there is a great deal of conjetering about you, and A great deal of anxiety amongst amany concerning the safety of the Expedition, for fears are entertaind, at after so long A absense and nothing being heard of you, there has been different articles in the papers concerning you, I have got all the papers that as had any thing for to say upon the subject, and I have preserved them all for you against your return so that you will be able for to read them for yourself and then you will find what has been said in your absense, one party that has had letters in the papers says that those partys that are going out in sirch of Franklin and his brave associats will not be able for to meet with them but I hope that the plover will find you all well at after being so long shut off from the rest of your old friends and associats, I fully expected you home in October 1847 and when you did not come, and Dr Rae returned without either hearing off or seeing you I was greatly disapointed and A great many was that takes a interest in the Expedition, but I hope before another year rolls round that you'll all be safe at home for I will assure you, that there is a great many enquiries, and I wish many A time that I was able for to give them a answer It gives me pleasure for to say that we are all well at home farther and mother is very desirous of hearing from you and says that you have been very foolish for transporting yourself to such a dangerous place perhaps never to return they say, but I hope before this year passes away that all they fears will be dispeld, I don't think that when you do return that you will find much alteration for I am just as you left me, except A little older, you will find books papers and other articles just where you left them there you'll find them, I have not disturbd them nor would I allow them for to be removed, so when you are fast for a subject for to think upon you must practice artificial memory and place your self in your old room and there you will find all the Magazin[es] just has you left them, there as nothing very paticular happend since you have been away, except that their has been a famine in Ireland, and a money panic here, and there has been A kind of Influenza which has took A good many off, you will find A little alteration in Lambeth when you return you will find the Southampton Railway making its way to London Bridge it is for to cross over Marsh gate by Watchorns and proceed almost in a direct line to London Bridge for to join the Dover if that I was sure that these would find you I would have sent you A folio sheet giving you all paticulars both public and private, for I think that there has been A little alteration in all the worlds since you left here, the theatrical world the scientific, and the political world and the Mon[ey] world, in the litriture world there is a great increase of publication, and some has given up you must excuse me at present [h]oping for to see you soon I remain yours truly – John Thompson

Lambeth January 3ᵈ 1848
                    28 Thomas Street
                    gibson street
                    Lambeth

177. JAMES CLARK ROSS TO FRANCIS CROZIER, 6 JANUARY 1848

                                        Aston House
                                        Aylsebury
                                        6 January 1848

My Dear Frank,

Altho I can entertain only a very feeble hope of this reaching you I cannot let the Plover leave England without conveying a few lines from your old friend and messmate in the assurance of that continued regard and friendship which has been the source of so much happiness to us both. The Plover will convey letters also from your family and Moore will afford you any information relative to public affairs so that I can have little to say beyond that which relates to myself. We are settled very quietly in the country and it will be a great happiness to see you again at our fireside. If we don't hear of you having passed the Behring Strait & being on your way home before the end of the month the Admiralty have determined to send two ships after you by Lancaster Sound and the command of the Expedition is to be in my hands & with Old Bird as my second I feel satisfied we shall not be found wanting altho' I most sincerely trust there will be no occasion for our services. By the time this reaches you (if at all) we shall be at the East end of the Passage pushing our researches in all directions under the apprehension that some calamity may have befallen one of the ships or that they may both be enclosed in some harbour from which they cannot be extricated.

The Admiralty have behaved throughout with admirable liberality and judgements & I am sure will leave nothing undone that ought to be done. If we do not meet on our former ground of exertion how happy will be our meeting when we return to Old England, which I confidently hope may be the case before the end of the present year.

Anne is writing a note to accompany this and with the assurance of our united warm regards believe me to remain your attached friend & old messmate.

Jas. C. Ross

178. ANN ROSS TO FRANCIS CROZIER, JANUARY 1848 (ENCLOSED WITH PREVIOUS LETTER)

My dear Captain Crozier

Although I hear from my husband that he considers that there is but small probability of your falling in with the Plover yet I will not lose the bare possibility of sending you all the kind wishes of this New Year and the assurance that 'Frank and Franklin' are always specially mentioned along with 'all our friends.' We are still looking for your happy and triumphant return this month, arguing your success from your prolonged absence, and amidst all the congratulations of the country and of friends you will receive ours most warmly & sincerely, and how delighted shall we be to see you.

Should such results not crown your arduous efforts then it will be a satisfaction to think that the government has not been dilatory on this occasion in arranging a very complete system of communications with you, for in addition to the Plover & Sir John Richardson's expeditions, in the event of your further delayed return, your faithful friend, whom I may truly rejoice to call my dearest James, is prepared to take command of a third by way of Baffin's Bay, and both our hearts are ardent in the cause. I will not however lengthen this note as we may perhaps shake hands in the place of your receiving it, and with a prayer of God's blessing upon you & your enterprise & my kind love, I am,

My dear Frank,
yours most truly,
Ann Ross

179. JOHN AND PHOEBE DIGGLE TO JOHN DIGGLE [SON], 4 JANUARY 1848

January 4th, 1848

Dear Son

I Wright these few lines to [you] in hopes to find you and all your Shipmates in both Ships well as it leaves us all at Present thank God for that but our fears his wee shall Never see you again seeing the Account in the Newspaper how you have been Situated what with been frozen inn and having that Dreadful Disorder the Schervey wich [leaves] us in little hopes of seeing you again but we trust in God. When HMS Plover Reaches you our thoughts will be Flusterated and Joyful news it will be for us to hear in her return to England that you and all the Crew are well. Please God it may be so.

Dear Son your brother in law William Windchip and I have had some conversation together has he knows the Nature of the Voiage he told mee more about it then i Could see in the Newspaper and he Hartley wishes to see you and your shipmates Safe in England again. William & T. Budington his sill in their situation and very comfortable.

Your Dear Mother prays to Almighty God for your safe Return likewise your fellow Sufferers. Joseph Wallace R. Chipps & there Wife's Charlotte Phoebe Edith Sarah & Harriet all join in Love to you and hopes to Congratulate you on your safe Return.

Dear Son I Conclude with our Unbounded Gratitude to you

Your loving Father & Mother

John & Phoebe Diggle and God bless you

No. 13 Daeve St. West

180. ELEANOR FRANKLIN TO JOHN FRANKLIN [FATHER], 29 APRIL–9 MAY 1848

Remember me very kindly to Captain Crozier & the other officers
I wrote to Captain Crozier by Sir John Richardson

21 Bedford Place
29th April 1848

My dearest Father

Again we begin letters to you in the hope that one, at least of the
Expeditions which take them will fall in with you – it is impossible to
picture to ourselves your present position, and it seems our duty, so far
as we can, not to endeavour to do so – we must leave you entirely in
His keeping "who doeth all things well" – praying for you that you may
find Him your refuge & strength, & a very present help in trouble." &
for ourselves that whatever He ordains respecting you, we may have
strength to say from our hearts "Thy will be done." – It is often a great
source of comfort to recall to mind & to turn into prayer the closing
words of your last letter to me "Thy will be done" we should earnestly
pray "– I pray that the events of this Expedition may bring me closer to
Christ" may your prayer have been indeed abundantly answered. & may
many of your companions, nay all, have been stimulated by your example & precepts, to run with patience the race set before them.

2nd you will be interested to hear that by the last Gazette, Admiral
Beaufort is made a Knight Commander of the Bath – he was not told of
it beforehand – so that it came quite like a shock upon him – the order
is now given away for civil services, as well as military – Sir E. Parry is
now Governor of Haslar Hospital, & likes his post much – but he is
now so far up in the List in consequence of the numbers who were put
on the retiring list last year: & the many deaths at the beginning of this
winter, that he almost fears he will be an Admiral before his five years at
the Hospital are at an end.

Mary Ann Kendall is now about to live in Sir John Richardson's house to
take care of it during his absence. We heard of his arrival at New York the
other day – You will be glad to hear of Dr. Richardson's being knighted, no
doubt your letter to Lord Minto on leaving had a great deal to do with it,
but the ostensible reason given was that Sir John Barrow in writing his summary of the polar voyages was struck by the fact that Dr. Richardson was
the only one of the Explorers who had not received this acknowledgement

of his services. His marriage to Miss Fletcher (sister in law of Dr. Davy) &
dear Mary Richardson's great friend has I think been a great relief to his
mind whilst engaging in the Expedition in search of you. Lady Richardson
is a very sensible & intellectual person, & truly excellent; she seems most
devoted to the children & anxious to carry out what she feels to be their
mother's wishes. She & Sir John spent two or three weeks with us, as did
Sir James and Lady Ross. Mama took a lodging near here, for the purpose.
What a pleasure it will be to you if you meet your old friends again in
those regions – how much they will have to tell you, & you to tell them.
I dare hardly dwell on this prospect, however. Sir James is very sanguine
about finding you – he thinks you are blocked up about 75°N. & 105° W.
How interested you will all feel in hearing of the public events which have
lately passed, & are passing now. France a Republic, and Louis Philippe a
fugitive & Refugee in England – but what is more important to us English
people – the quiet way in which the Chartist demonstration of the 10th
April has passed off – it was indeed most truly gratifying to observe the
loyal spirit pervading London – almost very respectable man from the
peers of the realm down to the labouring classes – enlisted himself as a
special Constable for the occasion, & as many as were wanted, patroled
the streets in the absence of the police, who were sent to defend the House
of Commons & other public buildings. Lord Glenelg was on duty I heard
for more than two hours – we often meet him at Sir Robert Inglis's, & he is
always very kind. Sir R & Lady Inglis too are full of kindness & sympathy
towards us, as are also Sir Francis Beaufort & Dr. Fitton. We have seen
Mr. Elliot occasionally he has lately married a daughter of Sir Edmund
Antrobus, a lady whom he has known for very many years. He hopes not
to have to return to St Petersburg.

You will long to know something about V.D. Land & the success of your
pamphlet – an almost forgotten subject now – I think the general feeling
respecting it is satisfaction, both here & in V.D.Land – & the circumstance
of Mr. Montagu's never having attempted to answer it, is considered conclusive as to his guilt – poor Mr. Forster died very soon after the book
reached VD Land – he died suddenly, & was much in debt. Sir Eardley
Wilmott too is dead – he was removed from the Government in consequence of his behavior to six members of the Legislative Council who
resigned their seats in consequence & petitioned for his removal – their
desire was granted, he was removed instantly & Mr Latrobe ordered at
24 hours notice to assume the Government pro tempore – Unfortunately,
Mr Gladstone who was then Secretary for the Colonies accompanied
his despatch to Sir E. Wilmot announcing his recall, with a private one

to the effect that in consequence of the reports which had reached him concerning his moral character, he must not expect to receive office under his Government again – Sir E.W. laid this letter before the Council, & a board of enquiry was appointed him – the matter has since been brought before parliament & he has been exculpated to an extent which he certainly did not deserve, tho' doubtless many of the reports which were circulated about him were false – the Archbishop & the Bishop have unfortunately been brought forward in the matter thro' what I must call the betrayal of Mr Gladstone. The Bishop of Tasmania was in England the whole of last year; he came to get the Colonial Chaplain question settled more to his mind, but without success. he collected however a considerable sum of money for his Diocese which in some degree made amends for the failure of his mission – he seemed sadly disheartened at the state of the Colony. You will I am sure be sorry to hear that Mr. Gell has not returned to England yet, tho' I fully expect he will be leaving v.d. Land about the end of this month, as the Bishop must be very near arriving by this time, & he was to leave immediately after the Bishop arrived – indeed judging from his last letters, which implied a hope of being here this month, I think he will be vexed at this long detention & especially as it is to little purpose, after all, for the Bishop did not take out a Warden for the College, & will only appoint a temporary successor, till Mr. Gell can select a suitable person in England. The College has been in existence about a year & a half, & thrives well – the Hutchin's School & a Grammar school at Launceston have been founded in conjunction with it – the first scholarship endowed at the College is called "The Franklin Scholarship" in grateful memory of you, their founder.

9th May. Sir James Ross has this morning paid us a parting visit – he seems to hope he will return with you this year – what a happiness it will be if this is the case. But if it is God's will that we should still be kept in anxiety about you – I trust God will give us patience & resignation to His will, & fulfil His promise to us "As thy day, so shall thy strength be" I leave all the members of our family in England to speak for themselves, at least such as are writing. The Prices are now at Norfolk Island, Mr. Price being Commandant. Transportation of men has at least nominally, if not altogether practically ceased for two years, in consequence of the urgent petition of the V.D.Land Colonists – the home government do not seem to have determined what they shall do with the Convicts – Sir William Denison is the present Governor of V.D.Land a brother of the Bishop of Salisbury he has indifferent health, being subject to epileptic fits, & as he has had several since he has been in V.D.Land, one dreads that he may have to resign – he seems on the whole to be a good Governor, tho' people complain that he takes the minutiae of Government too much upon himself – he does not seem very popular – just now he is in an awkward predicament thro' Sir E.W.'s misgovernment – for when the six members of Council resigned their seats, Sir E.W. after the seats had gone begging for some time, prevailed on six other persons to take them – then when Sir E.W. was recalled on the petition of the six members who resigned came the question, which of the two sets of members were to be in the Council, whereupon the matter was referred to the V.D.Land law officers who have found some legal flaw, which prevents either party from taking their seats, & consequently the Governor cannot assemble his Council until the decision of the law officers in England is known – the Governor has made great reductions in the salaries of the Government officers – which of course does not please them at all.

Both William & Henry Kay are married William to Miss Elwall (Mrs Jawcub's sister) & Henry to Miss Meredith – they both seem very happy. W. is Colonial Architect & Director of Roads, & Henry is still at the Observatory, longing to come home & vexed that he has not yet got his promotion. You will be interested to see the changes in the navy list. You are already on the 14/6 list – Lieutenants Gore & Little were made Commanders, soon after you left – Mr. Couch a Lieutenant – and Captain Fitz James a Post Captain – Admiral Beaufort went on the retired list – he could not hold the post of hydrographer as a full Admiral. I believe Captain Owen Stanley is gone to survey Torres Straits, Mr Dayman is with him – Captain Stokes is gone on a surveying voyage to New Zealand – We sometimes see the Bishop of Norwich – he still takes a warm interest in Arctic matters – his son Captain Ed. Stanley is Private Secretary to Sir W. Denison – Sir George Gipps did not long survive after his return to England, he died from disease of the heart, brought on by his exciting work in Sydney – we have lately had melancholy news from Sydney, in the death of Lady Mary Fitzroy the wife of the present Governor Sir Charles Fitzroy – from the overturn of their carriage. Sir E Charles was on the box driving – & seems to have been injured by the fall but was recovering, when we last heard from Sydney.

We sent letters to you to St. Peter & St. Paul, in April /47 & again by the "Plover" which sailed in January in search of you, by way of Behring's Straits & again by Sir John Richardson, who left England at the end of March – one scarcely knows how sufficiently to admire & feel grateful to Sir John Richardson for this noble act of self devotion in going in search of you – at his age & with his young family & with the consciousness that he cannot add to his fame in as much as there is no new country for him to explore where he is going – nothing but the purest sense of duty, & strong attachment to you – dear Papa has prompted him to the undertaking. He said once, "As Franklin has set such an example, I should never forgive myself if I did not follow it, & go in search of him" Mr. Rae, a Hudson's Bay Officer, & the late explorer of Boothia accompanies him he is a young, active, cheerful, young man, one who does not make difficulties & who is enured to fatigue & hardships. There has been much to interest the thoughtful with regard to the Church of England – since you left – there were many secessions to Romanism in the Autumn of /45 – amongst others, Mr Newman "went over" as it is called, & is now a Romish Priest – The Archbishops of York & Canterbury died within a few months of each other. The Bishop of Hereford, Dr. Musgrave, a tailor's son was translated to York, & the Bishop of Chester, Dr. Sumner, whose lectures on the Creation pleased you so much, has just been translated to Canterbury. By this last appointment, Lord John Russell, the present prime minister, has made himself popular, & has disposed people to forgive him, for his, to say the least, very injudicious appointment of Dr. Hampden to the vacant see of Hereford, he being a man whose writings had been condemned as heterodox by the University of Oxford, some years back thirteen of the Bishops & the Dean of Hereford, & many clergy & laymen, petitioned Lord John not appoint him, & there was a great disturbance in Bow Church at the confirmation, but all to no purpose, except to open the eyes of Church people to the inequity of the obsolete law of "Praemunire" – this event tends much towards that which we cannot but dread may someday take place – the disunion of Church & State – It is interesting to see how as a nation, we have lately been acknowledging God in our ways. The Fast day of last year – in consequence of the Irish Famine, the Thanks giving, when an abundant harvest was given us, & the prayer which is now being offered up for the maintenance of peace & tranquility, testify that in the midst of all the dreadful wickedness, which late years have disclosed as existing in London, particularly, there is still a leaven of much good amongst us.

I have forgotten to mention that one of the good service pensions has been awarded to you £150 per anum. Lord Auckland, the present First Lord of the Admiralty takes a most kind personal interest in our anxieties respecting you & has written several kind notes to Mama – & asked us to dine with him the other day, at a farewell dinner to Sir James Ross – but we did not go. Lord Grey is now at the Colonial Office – Mr Stephen has retired on account of his health, & has just been made a K.C.B.

Aunt Simpkinson begs me to say that she had fully meant to write to you today, but has been prevented. Mr Simpkinson was knighted on the occasion of the Queen's visit to Lincoln's Inn at the opening of the new Hall – he was Treasurer & is consequently now Sir Francis Simpkinson. John S. is one of the masters at Harrow, his friend, Dr. Vaughan being the much esteemed Head Master. Some people wish Mr. Gell to take a mastership when he comes home but I rather hope he will prefer a curacy & pupils. I have said little about ourselves – we have wandered about a good deal having been to Madeira, the West Indies, the United States & Canada, & subsequently to Sicily & Italy. The latter excursion was made partly for my health's sake – as I had the meazles at the end of /46. & my chest was not very strong afterwards. But I am well again now, I am thankful to say, tho' beginning to look old, people tell me – dear Mama you will find much the same as when you left, often suffering from her head, but when travelling, as capable of enduring fatigue as ever –

Now my dearest Father I will bid you good bye – may God be with you to bless & protect you – may you feel Him your Refuge & Strength, a very present help in trouble – & may He bring you safely & speedily back again – is the prayer of your very affectionate daughter

      Eleanor Isabella Franklin

181. JANE FRANKLIN TO JOHN FRANKLIN, 8–9 MAY 1848

           8th & 9th May 1848
           Bedford Place

My dearest love,

May it be the will of God if you are not restored to us earlier that you should open this letter & that it may give you comfort in all your trials. I feel sure that you must all have suffered much & perhaps when you are met with it may be in a state of great exhaustion, & your numbers even may be diminished, & many a bitter trial you may have had to bear. May you have found your refuge & strength in Him whose mercies you have so often experienced when every human aid was gone. If the prayers of all who love you can have availed with that Merciful God whose ear is ever open to the cry of all who trust to Him, you will yet be spared to us – but we know that His ways are not always such as we can adore without the subjection of many human feelings & the exercise of the humblest & deepest faith. I try to prepare myself for every trial which may be in store for me, but dearest, if you ever open this, it will be I trust because I have been spared the greatest of all. Next to you I think of dear Captain Crozier – I trust you have never been forced to separate & that you have been a mutual comfort to each other – And your own officers, may they also have been preserved to you. Yet amidst all the perils to which you have all been exposed, I scarcely dare to trust that some casualty has not happened to either of the ships during so long an absence. We have not had any serious uneasiness about you till lately. I felt sure you <u>meant</u> to have returned last autumn tho' your letter to me from Disco contemplates the possibility, at least the words were capable of this interpretation, of staying out a third winter, & every body thinks you would not return till forced by the want of provisions. Sir James Ross thinks you have been sent by poor instructions to a part where you could hardly fail of being inextricably entangled in the ice somewhere about 73N & 105W indeed I believe he thinks you can never unassisted get out of such a position. Richardsons' expedition (for he too is in search of you) goes on the supposition that you may have made your way in boats to your former haunt of the Mackenzie or Coppermine while Lieutenant now Commander Moore (formerly of the Erebus I believe) has been sent to Behring's straits with provisions, tho' we have very little hope of your being met with in that direction.

He sailed in January in the Plover & was to be accompanied by the Herald, Captain Kellett, now on S. American station, also loaded with stores. About the month of April 1847 (last year) all the Arctic officers were applied to by Government to know what they thought of the then probable position & prospects of the expedition, or whether any & what stores were necessary to take for your assistance. This was probably owing to some published letters of Dr. King (formerly Captain Back's surgeon) which were intended to alarm the public mind as to your safety. The reply of Parry, Ross, Richardson &c was to the effect that there was no reason whatever at that time for alarm or uneasiness, that it might be desirable to offer rewards to whalers to bring information, and that if the following autumn arrived without your return it would then be necessary to send in search of you, & Richardson on his part devised a scheme for exploring the coast between the Mackenzie & Coppermine & the opposite shores of Victoria & Wollaston Land which he said he was ready to conduct himself. This noble & generous offer was at once accepted since for its proper accomplishment it was necessary that the canoes & provisions should be prepared & dispatched beforehand. This was accordingly done & 20 picked men. 4 canoes & loads of pemmican were conveyed to America by the Hudson's Bay ships of last spring. Ross also volunteered to command an expedition in search of you if it should be become necessary. I had previously expressed to him my ardent desires on this head, but I have an entire conviction that he would have offered all the same, if I had said nothing.

It is a beautiful thing to see these 2 friends thus eager to devote themselves to this noble service & the public sense of this, or rather perhaps the sense of their friends was lately shown by a dinner given by 12 of them at the Athenaeum to Ross & Richardson just on the eve of the embarkation of the latter in March last for America. This dinner was first conceived by Mr. Brown, who invited Sir Geo. Back to take the chair (Admiral Beaufort having declined) an arrangement not pleasing to Ross & perhaps not to Richardson, but which however they made the best of. Indeed Sir George Back has done his best to make himself agreeable both to Richardson & ourselves & has invited us to his house to dinner which we accepted – have I not yet told you that he is married, it must have been in autumn of /46 that he took to wife the widow of Mr. Hammond, a well known rich stock broker who left her with a fortune of about 2000 a year & a house in Gloucester Place where they live. She, Lady Back is a good-natured amiable little person, tolerably good-looking, but said to be a few years older than himself.

·I must tell you a similar piece of news respecting Sir John Richardson – (he was knighted very soon after your departure, Sir John Barrow takes upon himself the credit of it, but I think your letter had also something to do with it) & was married last August to Miss Fletcher, the daughter of Mrs. F (a lady of great celebrity [?] for her beauty & talents) & sister of your old acquaintance Mrs. Davy. Lady Richardson was also a friend of poor Mary's & she has entered on her new duties of mother to her children in the highest & noblest spirit – dear Dr. Richardson seems to have enjoyed much increased happiness since this event & the children take to their new mother very affectionately particularly the younger ones. Lady Richardson is about 48, so the family is not very likely to be increased – she is extremely tall & thin – her face, except that she has a bad mouth is rather pretty but she has the misfortune of a very ugly, croaking, monotonous voice, not very intelligible either – she is not only a woman of very superior mind, as I believe all the Fletcher family are, but is an authoress – a good many years ago when keeping her bed from sickness she wrote a novel called "Concealment" which was lent to me by Mrs. Maconochie at Hobarton. She has a villa built by herself at

Grasmere in that fine lake country, where her mother lived with her & now lives, Mrs. Davy being in the same neighbourhood.

I think you will be pleased to hear that in order to shew my regard & gratitude to both Richardson & Ross, I hired a house in this neighbourhood Charlotte St. Bedford Square in February last, in order to receive them both in it – first we had the Richardsons who were with us between 2 & 3 weeks, & when they left the Ross' who also spent a fortnight with us. This plan also enabled me to ask occasionally a few other friends to dinner, as your dear old friend Robert Brown, the Beauforts, Barrows, Dr. Fitton &c. My scheme seemed to answer very well, particularly in bringing me intimately acquainted with Lady Richardson & Lady Ross. The latter remains in Buckinghamshire during her husband's absence with her 2 children, a boy & a girl. Lady Richardson joins her mother at Grasmere with the children, & the empty house at Haslar is kindly lent by them to Mary Ann Kendall & her family to occupy– she will have close & kind neighbours in the Parrys, Sir Edward being now Captain Superintendant of Haslar Hospital – Clarence Yard, a place which suits him much better & gives him more leisure than that he has quitted. The old Admirals have been dying off with such extraordinary rapidity this last sickly winter, that Sir Edward begins to be afraid he may not have ran out his arm at Haslar himself before he gets his flag. About a year ago Captain Beaufort was induced to become a retired rear-admiral, rather than wait a short time longer for his flag, in order to retain his hydrographer's place. It was thought shabby of the admiralty not to let him keep it & make him an effective admiral too – however a very distinguished honor has been within a few days conferred on him, that of making him a Lord Knight of the Bath. This proceeded from Lord Auckland, the present 1st Lord of the Admiralty, who gave him no intimation of it beforehand, so that he knew of it for the first time by the gazette. There has been lately an alteration in the rules of the order, & now in each class of C.B., KCB., & G.C.B. there are 3 divisions, Civil, Military & Foreign – the 1st list after this recent alteration, includes Admiral Beaufort's name. A little while ago, he was knocked down by a cab & injured his head, but he says the sight of this gazette was a much harder blow to him.

Lord Haddington did not remain long in office after you went – he retired from ill health & was succeeded by Lord Ellenborough who went out with the Peel administration in 1846, & Lord Auckland has held it ever since under the premiership of Lord John Russell – I have certainly every reason to speak well of him – last year while in Italy, I received an extremely kind note from him saying that he had conferred on you the Good Service Pension, lapsed by the promotion of Sir H Willoughby & hoped I should see in this act, in which the whole board had unanimously concurred, a proof of the estimation in which your character & services were held by them. In my reply, I told him that I felt sure the value of this act would be enhanced by the circumstance of its being conferred during your absence & quite independent of any success which might (or might not) attend your expedition – in November last, he wrote to me again to tell me what he had just decided on respecting the sending out of expeditions & told me that any suggestions I would make "would be earnestly attended to". I did not scruple to avail myself of this privilege, nay, whether I had been so invited or no, I should not have failed to say to him all I thought necessary for your welfare – many letters have passed between us and I do not think I have ever written in vain. Besides this, he was kind enough to pay us a visit of an hour long while we were in Charlotte St, & he lately asked us to his house to a farewell dinner to Sir [James] Ross, but this we declined, for I do not like farewells. Besides the Good Service Pension, you have now been for some little time on the 14/6 a day list.

The promotion of your officers you will hear fully about – pray congratulate them from me. I will try to write a line to Captain Crozier & Fitzjames, but my time for writing is sadly reduced from what I expected it to be this morning, Sir James Ross having called to take his leave of us & having told us we must send our letters to him by 8 this evening – We were in hope to have had several days longer.

I send you the vols of the Illustrated London News which have come out since your departure. The last 2 months have been wonderful times Louis Philippe dethroned & in exile in England, a fierce democracy ruling France, almost all the kingdoms of Europe in commotion, England alone steady & erect amidst the crash of thrones & dynasties.

You will be pleased to see your own pamphlet in its complete & finished form & still more so to learn that its success has been most triumphant & conclusive – what can be a better proof of this than the profound silence of Mr. Montagu – not one word in reply from him or from any one, tho a copy was sent to him from the Colonial Office. It is thought at the Colonial Office that this silence says more in your favour than any thing you could say for yourself, but besides this there are innumerable positive testimonies,

to the convincing truthfulness, manliness, clearness & candour of the narrative. Lord Glenelg said one day to Eleanor either in allusion to your
pamphlet or to the sins of Sir E. Wilmot, or to both that "you were well
revenged" & Mr. Hawes, the present Under Secretary of State in the room
of Mr. Hope told your friend Robert Brown that he had read it through
& was quite convinced by it. It seems too that not long ago Mr. Gordon
Gardner who is again in the VDL. department was present at a discussion
at the Colonial Office on the services or merits of Montagu when some
one brought up against him his conduct towards you. "Ah! that was a
bad business", said Mr. Gardner & walked away to the other end of the
room – I suppose his own conscience smote him too. I have innumerable
testimonies both at home & from VDL of the satisfaction it has given – in
VDL. they said it was like yourself, noble, manly, like a lion, like a 'prince of
a man', candid, forbearing – Forster wrote to Montagu to entreat him not
to get himself deeper in the mire by attempting to answer it, & Turnbull,
upon Montagu writing him a letter intending to involve him again in the
prosecution of the affair, wrote him such a letter as would have ruined him
more than any thing he had written before had it ever seen the light.

Had Montagu answered your pamphlet I should have had nothing to
do but to publish that new letter of Dr. Turnbulls – Poor Forster was
no doubt frightened for himself & well he might be – his tricks were
found out. It became too clear that he was grossly deceiving the home
Government as to the state of things in his department, & his removal
was decided upon at home when news arrived of his rather sudden death,
leaving his wife & children with nothing but his debts – it was then
made known that he was most deeply involved with Rowlands, (also
since dead) hence the disgraceful intimacy between them. Mr. Young to
whom we sent one of the pamphlets was highly delighted at receiving
it. We had the satisfaction of hearing also that Sir George Arthur highly
disapproved of Montagu's conduct & this was indirectly confirmed to us
not long ago, by the marked attentions we have received from Sir George
who returned about 2 years ago from India in very ill health, but is now
recovered. We met him at Sir Robert Inglis' & he afterwards called twice
on us, stopping a couple of hours (at his last visit) talking over VDL.
persons & things constantly mentioning your name & coming so close
repeatedly to that of Montagu that I felt assured he desired nothing so
much as an opportunity of saying something about him. This however
I did not give him – he spoke very highly of Dr. Turnbull which was of
itself quite sufficient to shew he disapproved of Montagu, & told me he
had never interfered in any way whatever in the affairs of VDL. since he

left, except in the affair of Mr. Gregory who had shewed him his correspondence with you, of which he (Sir George) entirely disapproved – he
regretted the affair had not been made up since you came home, but said
it was for Mr. Gregory to come forward to you & not you to him.

On going away Sir George said he knew I was surrounded by many &
kind friends & therefore he could not presume to offer his services – if
however at any time he could be of the least use to me, he hoped I would
commend him.

I must leave VDL. Affairs, to be discussed between you & Sir James Ross,
who will tell you of the ignominious recall of Sir Eardley Wilmot by Mr.
Gladstone (then Secretary of State) & his subsequent death in the colony,
of the interregnum of Mr. Latrobe & the appointment of Sir William
Denison (Captain of Engineers) the present Governor. Also of the death
of Sir George Gipps, soon after his return home, a complete victim to
his unparalleled exertions in his Government. He was succeeded by Sir
Charles Fitzroy, Governor of Antigua, elder brother of Captain Fitzroy
of New Zealand, who has recently met with the most sad misfortune
by the violent death of his wife Lady Mary F. whom he was driving at
Paramatta with 4 skittish horses which ran away with them – poor Lady
Mary & the Aid de Camp were killed on the spot & the Governor himself was severely injured. Captain Fitzroy of New Zealand was recalled
I think sooner after your departure, much blamed for some of his public
but much commiserated by his many friends of whom Admiral Beaufort
you know is one of the warmest. He has been succeeded by Captain
Grey of South Australia, recently made a Knight of the Bath.

Captain Maconochie after having been promised (last autumn) by Sir
George Grey the superinten[den]ce on his own plan of a gang of convicts
at Portland Island, Dorsetshire, has not yet received his appointment
owing it is supposed to the difficulties made to his system by one or two
of the Inspectors of Prisons. In the mean time they have given a clerkship
in the Home Office to his eldest son Alexander a very elegant & pleasing
young man. I believe he is in great embarrassment what to do with the
other sons. –

We never see Mrs. Maconochie, but he is as kind & attentive as it is possible to me, never so happy as when he can be doing us some kindness
or service. I have got in writing his warm & hearty approbation of your
pamphlet.

Another person, still nearer to us who has been a most kind & useful friend is Mr. Majendie – in the bringing out of the pamphlet he spared no pains & in every thing else, I have only to ask him to do a thing & he does it. As an advisor & manager in the Clavering property I don't know what Sir Francis would do without him – The farm buildings there (not the farmhouse) have lately been burnt down. They were insured for £1000 which is sufficient to reconstruct them, some of the materials of the Old Bury(?) or Manor House have been used for the purpose, & the Manor House itself, thus reduced, has been patched up & is to furnish us with 2 or 3 rooms to which to retire to when we wish to ruralize. If there is to be any more book writing, it will be good for a retreat & at all events I think you will be glad of a little place to which to run occasionally. I think it is since your departure, tho' it seems a long while ago, since Mr. Majendie returned in triumph to Hedingham Castle, bells ringing, color flying – All his debts paid & a grand dinner given to him at the Bell by the gentry & tenants. He has ever since continued to be in high repute, is put forward at all the public meetings, looked up to as a high authority in all agricultural matters, & in every respect is highly esteemed & respected. My father seems now to be again proud of him, & Fanny bears a very high character as being the main agent by which all this has been brought about – one of his great hobbies now is the improvement & adornment of his parish church. Mr. Morgan is at last retired & a respectable clergyman who can be heard, has taken his place. Mr Morgan's Cottage at the gate is now occupied by a school for children supported at Fanny's whole expence.

I hope you will tell Captains Crozier & Fitzjames any thing that you think will interest them, but I suppose they & all the officers have a mass of letters – pray excuse me to Captain Gore for not writing to him & thanking him for his most beautiful drawing of the packing of the ships which has been greatly admired by every body

Sir James Ross is of opinion you have been sent by your instructions just where you ought not to have been. It appears it was Parry who drew up your instructions or at least who wished you to avoid Melville island, & here is the great point of difference. Ross thinks that W of Melville island is the passage. Dr. Scoresby has some doubt whether there is any passage at all – This gentleman Dr. S. has been extremely kind to me.

I do not know what Sir James Ross means to do if he finds you coming out of Davies Straits as he is going in – he is fully equipped with ships like rocks for 3 years – and it seems a pity he should not go on – but he does not admit that such is in his contemplation or instructions – when he has sailed, I shall ask Lord Auckland to let me see his instructions, I asked him for yours, & obtained a copy directly. You will be glad to hear how well Eleanor has got thro' this winter in London – it has been a remarkably mild one, I leave it her to talk of Gell, except that I will tell you I propose bringing about their union as soon as he returns which on every account I think desirable – I have no doubt of his getting at once an eligible curacy, & of getting a few pupils at high salaries, which will soon lead to something better. Willingham continues to behave very kindly to all his relatives & particularly to those who want it most as Aunt or Sister Betsey. The Cracrofts have already written to you, but whether now or not I do not know – your sister seems more contented at Winchester than I have ever known her before. I hope you have had every reason to be satisfied with your officers & particularly that Mr. Stanley has proved to be skilful & attentive my kind remembrances to him & all the others particularly Captain Gore – I have written a few lines to Captains Crozier & Fitzjames.

We meet with the greatest kindness from the Inglis's. My father is wonderfully well – my poor aunt losing her memory fast. I will leave any forgotten or unmentioned things for Sir James to tell you – I have written in a great hurry, not knowing till this morning that we had not got 2 or 3 days before us, & now being hurried off today. God bless you my own dearest love – how ardently we pray for you you will not doubt. It was settled between us & the Bishop of Tasmania who has lately left us that on 16 July next, prayers should be put up in VDL in every church & chapel for you & all the expeditions. It would have been a less trial to me to come after you, as I was at one time tempted to do, but I thought it my duty & my interest to remain, for might I not have missed you, & would it have been right to leave Eleanor – yet if I had thought you to be ill, nothing should have stopped me. God bless you again. You will be welcomed back with joy & honor by your friends & family & country – <u>most</u> of all by your

affectionate & devoted wife

Jane Franklin

[note on envelope of this letter]

to the care of <u>Sir James Ross</u>

182. CHARLES THOMPSON TO JAMES THOMPSON [BROTHER], 25 APRIL 1849

Leeds April 25th 49

Dear Brother

I send you a few lines. But what to talk to you about I am at a loss. It will be four Years come the seventeenth of May since I left you on Board the "Terror" It would give me very great pleasure, should I have to write to you saying I acknowledge the Receipt of your Letter But at present we must overlook that. Well I write to you a few lines and I hope that you have received them by Lieutenant Moore of the Plover, and again by Sir James Ross in his Expedition in search of Sir John Franklin and now again by the North Star. – – – – – – – -

Your Father & Mother likewise Sisters & Brothers are all very well at Present, and we shall be very glad to see you at Home in Leeds when you return to England – It is now four years since, since Susannah brought word that you had some thoughts of going with Sir John Franklin in search of a Northwest passage. She is in London again at the present Time. I do expect that your Brother John will write to you for he is still living at 28 Thomas St Gibson St Lambeth <u>London</u> I do not know whether you will take any interest in the following lines which I send you or not. But we do, they have appeared in some of the English Newspapers – likewise Prayers have been read in some of the Churches for your safe return. – – – – – –

"The Artic Expedition A series of Papers relating to the Artic Expedition has been printed and presented to Parliament They form a continuation of the Parliamentary papers in 1848 but the greater portion of their contents have been from time to time laid before our readers. Indeed the only document which is new is that entitled, Purport of Instructions intended to be sent to Sir James Ross, by the North Star This ship it will be remembered is to carry out supplies to Sir James Ross but as some difficulty may be found in communicating with the latter officer the Admiralty have ordered twelve cylinders to be constructed each containing a copy of the dispatch to that officer one of these cylinders is to be carefully deposited at each of the following Places Whaler-Point, Cape York, Cape Crawford, Cape Hay, Possession's Bay, Ponds Bay, Agnes' Monument, or if this should not be practicable in any conspicuous place on the same line of coast – observing however that these named have been specially selected by Sir James Ross himself and are therefore by far the most important –

The following mode of depositing the cylinders is recommended as most likely to ensure the intended purpose. A spot is to be selected conspicuous to a boat rowing near the shore and not very far from the sea. The cylinder is then to be buried from a foot to eighteen inches beneath the surface the ground being made quite smooth again and covered with a large heap of stones with a staff in the centre. Beside this caches four watertight casks are to be fitted with a short pole carrying a small flag or tin vane and one of the above cylinders is to be inclosed in each cask – which latter are to be dropped in different places four of five leagues apart as far to the westward as possible in Lancaster Sound but in those parts where the sea is most generally free from ice should the Investigator or her boats not be fallen in with the commander of the North Star will be directed to land the supplies in sufficient time to secure his return across Baffins Bay to the eastward The instructions to Captain Sir James Ross are to the iffect that as the Expedition under his orders will only really commence its search this year the Investigator is to remain out in company with the Enterprise, a fact which we announced several weeks ago –

The papers before us contain further instructions to Captain Kellett of the Herald ordering him to fill the Herald with all the provisions which she will stow and to lose no time in sailing from the coast of Mexico so as if possible to reach Woahoo by the 1st of May – In the event of finding the Plover at the latter place to which port she may have fallen back from a late arrival last autumn at Behring's Straits the Herald and Plover are to sail in company on the 10th of May or as soon after as may be practicable – and proceed together direct to Behring's Straits Captain Kellett is enjoined to use every exertion to communicate with the Plover and supply her with provisions – so that she may be enabled to pass the winter of 1849–50 in Behrings Straits and make such search for the Erebus and Terror as was intended should have been made during the winter of 1848–49. – – –

We may take the opportunity of stating that the Admiralty have expressed their willingness to place a ship at the disposal of the Liverpool Shipowners Association for the purpose of being fitted for searching the Artic Seas. The cost of preparing the vessel would have to be defrayed by public subscription as well as that of navigating her. The subject is under consideration. Letters from the relatives and friends of the officers and seamen serving in the Artic seas in Her Majesty's ships Erebus & Terror Enterprise and Investigator will be forwarded by Her Majesty's ship North Star if sent to the Secretary of the Admiralty on or before first of May." – – – – –

Sir John Franklins Expedition To Mariners

The following [h]as been Received at Lloyd's from the Admiralty Twenty thousand pounds sterling reward (Lady Franklin [h]as offered Three Thousand) to be given by her Majesty's Government to such private ship or distributed among such private ships or any exploring party or parties of any country as may in the judgment of the Board of Admiralty have rendered efficient assistance To Sir John Franklin his ships or their crews and may have contributed directly to extricate them from the ice – signed H. G. Ward Secretary to the Board of Admiralty 23rd March 1849 – – – – – The attention of Whalers or of any other ships or parties disposed to aid in this service is particularly directed to Smith's Sound and Jones's Sound in Baffins Bay to Regents Inlet and the Guelf of Boothia as well as to any of the inlets or channels leading out of Barrow's Straits particularly Wellington Strait or the sea beyond either northward or southward vessels entering through Behring's Strait would necessarily direct their search North and South of Melville Island – – –

Sergeant Major Williamson died in his 100 year on the 15th of May, 1848. – – – – –

Your Father continues to receive your half-pay excuse all Blunders from your affectionate
Brother C. Thompson 8 Fleece Yard Meadows Lane Leeds

183. JANE ROSS GOODSIR TO HARRY GOODSIR [BROTHER],
26 APRIL 1849

My dear Henry

We saw in the Newspaper the other day that if we had letters ready before the first of May, they might reach you, by some Means, but as we have had little time, we must just write a few lines;

We need not speak of our terrible anxiety about you, and indeed all in your Ships, the length of time you have been away has put the whole country in a state of the greatest distress, although many people, able to judge, say, there is yet no need to be over-alarmed God grant it may be so, and that we shall have the great joy and thankfulness of welcoming you home during this Summer some time.

You will be astonished to hear, that Robert set out from Dundee in a Whaleship with the strong hope of aiding in the search after Your Expedition. He sailed on the 8th of March, in a very good Ship the Captain's name is Penny, and they have dispatches on board from Government; and I think Robert had a letter from Lady Franklin; they were to push up Lancaster Sound, as far as they possibly could. Captain Penny is a very respectable active young man, a native of Aberdeen.

My dear Henry, we have to tell you of two sad events, which have taken place during the past year; and I fear if our letters reach you, it will give you a very great shock to learn the painful tidings. Poor Papa died on the 7th. of June last, and our dear Archie died on the 20th. of last March. Archie had an attack of cold in his chest nearly two years and six months ago, but he got better, and just two years ago, on the 1st. of April, John sent him to study in Germany, there he had a bad return of his cold and cough, and when he returned home last Spring he was found to be far gone in Consumption. He was a great sufferer all along, and so much so at the last, that we were thankful to see him laid at rest. He died in perfect peace and quietness. Papas fearful anxiety about you – and agony to see Archie's state, brought his heart complaint to a climax, and at the last he died suddenly.

I can venture to say no more upon this melancholy breaking up, in our family. You and Robert being both away, there are but three of us now at home – and a sad change it is – but your coming back will be an unspeakable comfort to us all, Poor Archie spoke often of you; and Robert had to bid him farewell, knowing he never could see him again, though Archie hoped, for long, that he would get better. If God grants our meeting, you shall hear all particulars as to both these departed members of our family.

On the other hand, many worldly changes, have taken place amongst us, John has been Professor of Anatomy in Edinburgh for three Winters now, and has had an immense Class every year, he lives in George Square, and

Papa had a little cottage at Morningside where he died! Poor man after making it as neat, as neat could be. I have been living in Edinburgh for the last three years, and had scarcely left Archie during the last year for a day. Joseph is well, and still at Largo. Uncle and Aunt well, and sorely afflicted about Archies death. I have been here at Carnbee for a month serenity[?] after my attendance on Archie.

I must conclude with the earnest prayer, that you will soon return in health and safety as well as the many companions you have with you.

Believe me
Your affectionate Sister
Jane Ross Goodsir

Carnbee Manse
April 26th, 1849

184. ELEANOR FRANKLIN TO JOHN FRANKLIN [FATHER],
6 MAY 1849

21 Bedford Place London
Sunday 6th May 1849

My very dear Father

We hear the "North Star" is about to sail, so I think I cannot do better than begin a letter to you today – you know I am not an advocate for Sunday letter writing, but the painful suspense in which we are concerning you & your companions, seems so to hallow every thing connected with you, that it seems like a sacred duty to write to you – 7th I was interrupted yesterday you must picture me to yourself seated in my own little room off the drawing room, with Phillips large portrait of you hanging over the mantlepiece, & a smaller bronze one of you below – often, often are my eyes & thoughts directed to them with the prayer that you may be brought back to us in safety, or if not, that we may have strength given us to say "Father thy will be done."

It is indeed an unexpressable comfort to me to feel that you have committed yourself as we have committed you, into our heavenly Father's hands, & that you have sought his guidance in every perplexity, his succour in every danger – we know he is watching over you, keeping you as the apple of his eye, from all that can really hurt you because even death itself is no injury, but only gain to the Christian –& I feel sure that tho' God's dealings with you & us, seem mysterious now, we shall hereafter know why He has thus dealt with us; and feel that all has been done in love, with a view of bringing us into closer union with himself.

Since we wrote to you at this time last year, I do not think anything very important has occurred in our family, except that which concerns me more deeply than any one else – the return of Mr. Gell to England – I am sure it will give you joy to think that he is with us, cheering & helping & counselling us. I have had much anxiety respecting his leaving V.D. Land, owing to the Bishop's urgent entreaties for his staying – so that I seemed sometime as if I should be overwhelmed with the two anxieties together – but God in mercy removed the trial of his absence, just at the time when the suspense about you became more painful.

However when you read this there will speedily be an end to this suspense; may God bless the efforts which have been & will be made, to search for & succour you. Mama has been very active in stirring up people to consider the necessity of searching every where at once – it was mainly thro' her exertions & Sir Thomas Acland's that a Reward was offered about the end of March of £20,000 to any ship or land party who should find you – unfortunately this Reward was offered too late for the English Whalers – but we hope the Americans will do something, by Bhering's Straits –

We have been very anxious that the "North Star" should be allowed to remain out to search thoroughly Wellington Channel – & many have been the means tried to get the Admiralty to consent to this; I went myself to Sir Francis Baring (the 1st Lord) – a few days ago – but tho he listened very kindly & patiently, I fear the Board will not consent – they say it is not the money they grudge but the risk of life. You may be sure that universal sympathy is felt for you & for us – not long ago public prayers were offered for you in many Churches throughout England – This gave me great hope, & I am sure it was the best thing we could do for you. The day chosen was March 18th but in some Churches it is done once a month – at Alverstoke every Sunday – & in some places the prayer used at sea was with proper alterations used.

I think all our family are much as when we wrote by Sir James Ross. Aunt Cracroft continues comfortably settled at Winchester – Catherine (Kitty) is now in much better health, I am thankful to say. Sophy is with us in Town just now. Louisa Turner has within the last few weeks been sent for by her husband, & is now living with him in his parish – Anne Weld within the last few months has become a mother. Willingham was married last August – to a Miss Murdoch whose mother was a niece of Lord Gambier's & is living now at Lutterworth – the Simpkinsons & Grandpapa are much as usual. Aunt Betsey has been ill this winter, but is better now again.

We have not been out of England since we last wrote – but in the summer we took a tour first in Somersetshire, & then in Kent, & then remained until December, quiet at Tunbridge Wells – a place which reminded me much of you. In December we came to Town, & have remained here ever since, with the exceptions of a few days now & then – Our future plans are yet hardly thought about – when every measure connected with search for you has been taken we shall then have more leisure to think upon what course we ought to pursue in your absence – it will be most painful to me to marry in your absence, & yet I feel that if you could send us word you would say that you wished us no longer to delay – if proper arrangements can be made – our homeless, unsettled life, makes such a step perhaps more desirable, & the want of all other relative ties has made me feel that in you & John all my strongest affections are con- centred, & now that you have been so long removed from us, I feel as if almost every earthly tie were concentred in him.

In all our thoughts of home – the hope that our home will be yours is mixed up – and if I ever form dreamy plans for the future – the one I cling to most is that after all your wanderings, you will settle down quietly to be well cared for, in the peaceful home of your loving son & daughter. It has always been a very great source of joy, dear Papa, to know how much you love my dear John, & how much he loves & respects you – I wished much you could have been with us yesterday, to hear him read prayers & preach & help in the Communion. I know how much you care for the prayers being well read & I think his way of performing this service would be just what you like – simple & varied & yet with true earnestness & devotion – the sermon was the one we heard him preach at Port Phillip from Col iii 12 & 13th v, but his manner of delivery is much improved since then, & people think it very striking –

I was very much pleased yesterday to see the effect a speech he made at a Propagation Society meeting made upon his Vicar's mind, by the very pointed attention he drew to it in his sermon – not at all by way of com- pliment, but merely as the natural expression of his feelings about it. I have not yet heard him speak at a public meeting – but I have often heard of his speeches – & I hear the Propagation Society want him to become

one of their travelling secretaries in order that he may go about to meetings about once a week. Indeed he seems I think a very great favorite so
far as he is known. As to myself, I feel more & more how very thankful
I ought to feel for being so loved by him & having so happy & peaceful
a home in store for me – not that I expect freedom from sorrow at any
time – but every sorrow will be lightened by being shared by him, whilst
every duty will be made pleasant by being done with him. I am learning
something of the duties of a clergyman's wife by visiting amongst the
poor as a District Visitor in this parish – a work which interests me much
– I am not very strong & cannot therefore do all I could wish – but I am
certainly in much better health than when you left, & much thinner.

By the way you will find Mr. Gell looking older & stouter – but this gives
him a more commanding appearance. Mama is much the same as when
you left – in the summer, she was lame, from a weakness in one knee,
but she seems to have got over it now. A week or two ago a report was
circulated that you had arrived or been heard of – fortunately it did not
reach our ears until it was proved to be false. At the risk of your being
shocked about Mesmerism I think I must just tell you that a few weeks
ago a clairvoyante said she could see you – that you were very well, but
very sorry – Captain Crozier was not seen but Sir James Ross & Sir John
Richardson were. This report has cheered us up but she is afraid of trusting too much to it – no one has been informed of it but ourselves. Now,
may God bless & keep you, my dearest Father, & comfort & direct you
is the heartfelt prayer of your ever affectionate daughter,

Eleanor Isabella Franklin

Every kind expression of regard to Captain Crozier. I have told you no
public news, expecting Mama would do that.

185. JANE FRANKLIN TO JOHN FRANKLIN,
15 MAY 1849

21. Bedford place
15 May 1849

My own dearest love
    May a merciful God have preserved you to open this letter! – May He
have been your comfort & support, a tower of strength to you! – And
even should your great sufferings & privations have ever made your
faith to waver or your courage to fail, He will have pity on you, because

it is not the heart, but the sinking body & the enervated brain which is the cause and He knoweth the secrets of the soul. How often do I pray for you that He will remember your faith & love & pity & pardon if it ever have failed you in the hour of need! Remember dearest that it is even His best beloved whom He often tries the most fearfully, that the most awful calamities sometimes fall on his best-beloved children!

I am sure one of your severest trials has been knowing what we have been suffering on your account, and indeed could I have shared your sufferings with you, it would have been better than to think of you bearing their burden without you – I told Captain Fitzjames that if you did not return at the end of 3 years, I should come out to look for you – and at the end of 4 years nearly, I have strived to come out in this store ship which carries my letter, but they would not let me. I could hardly perhaps expect it to be otherwise & I strive to console myself by feeling & knowing I am of use to you, to all of you, at home – I do not let the Admiralty rest about you, & though they do not do all I desire, & all perhaps that the public in their great sympathy would approve of, yet have they done a good deal & have undoubtedly an anxious interest in your preservation. I do not intend to abuse them to you tho' they are whigs! £20000 reward have been offered for finding & succouring you, & tho' this announcement was not made till all the Whalers had sailed, yet it seems to have had its effect upon the Yankees & they say an expedition is organizing to look after you – May you rather be saved by Ross & his gallant crews, yet Heaven bless the Yankies if they are the means of rescuing you.

Our own private impression is that you will be found in the Northern Channel where no one has been before, but I wish every place to be searched, because you may have been driven into parts the least expected. If there were half a dozen searching ships, it would not be too many.

Eleanor has written to you & I believe told you whatever news may most interesting to you. We have been wonderfully preserved in our great trials on your account & I trust are prepared to submit ourselves to Gods' will in all things. You need not make yourself uneasy about E's marriage being delayed on your account, since it cannot take place till Gell has some ecclesiastical promotion which he is sure of in time – In the mean time they are much together & happy in each other. Sophy is now with me & a great comfort all your sisters as well as usual Willingham married, very steady & a very affectionate nephew – his wife thro' her mother who was a Gambier must be connected with Fitzjames.

You have had the good service pension of £150 a year for the last 2 years – the good Lord Aukland wrote me a most kind letter about – The Simpkinsons are titled (or did this take place before you left?) Mr. Majendie restored with great honor to his castle & estates & acting the country gentleman & Fannys' is the squires wife[s] part with great credit to themselves – your pamphlet to Lord Stanley has been greatly admired & could not be answered – not a word from Montagu in reply

[written on small piece of paper with letter]

While you thought yourselves deserted & unlooked for (but could you ever think so!) every heart has been turned towards you & unheard of efforts have been made for your rescue – it has been the business of my life to instigate & set in motion as far as my feeble means admitted of it much that has been done & it has pleased God to crown my efforts with success

[notes on envelope of this letter]

left behind by mistake –now sent by American ship of war Captain Wilks

Dear Eleanor was married yesterday 7th June

[rest of letter missing]

186. JANE FRANKLIN TO JOHN FRANKLIN, 9 JUNE 1849

21. Bedford Place
9th June 1849

My dearest Love
    We have written many letters to you but omit no opportunity of writing again –

Since I last wrote dear Eleanor's union with Gell has taken place, last Thursday 7th June was the day. They were married at St George's Bloomsbury, by Mr. Villiers Mr. Sellwood gave her away – There were many relations & friends – I left them after the ceremony, because in your absence I could not bear any festivities & employed the afternoon in going to Stanmore & visiting the old church in which we were married & which I am sorry to say is going to be pulled down – poor old Mr. Chaunce died 2 years ago – The bride & bridegroom went to Eastbourn to the house of Mr. Davies Gilbert which is lent to them.

Mr. Gell is one of the Curates of St Martin's, & this curacy with £100 a year from his father & about £50 from the Propagation of Gospel Society or one of their agents, brings him in a small fixed income, to which I add an allowance sufficient to make it up to £500 a year until the time of your return, there being every reason to hope that he will very soon get a living & be independent.

They are going to take ready furnished lodgings in St Martin's parish – I hope if you ever open this note that this news may be a comfort to you – God grant you may have opened others of our notes before this – you are in my thoughts day & night & my fervent prayers are offered up incessantly for you. May a merciful God have enabled you to bear your great trials & yet restore you to us. I feel sure of your faith & love, and even if in weakness & suffering your trust should ever for a moment have failed, God will have had pity on man's weakness, he will revive & strengthen you again – the greater part of my letter to you by the North Star was left behind & is forwarded by the American ship of war which is gone in search of you.

God bless you, my own, my dearest – kindest regards to your officers & particularly to Captain Fitzjames & Gore – also to dear Captain Crozier – I wrote 2 hurried lines to each of them last time.

> Ever your most devoted & affectionate wife
> Jane Franklin

I add a line now at a much later date (this letter which went out by a whaler having been brought back to me) to say we are all well as far as our great anxiety for you will allow us to be, yet we are not yet without hope. May you have been sustained & comforted in your severe & protracted trials is the fervent prayer night & day of your devoted wife – this letter now goes out again in the Prince Albert private expedition under command of Mr. Kennedy – dear old Hepburn on board – Stromness May 26, 1851

187. JANE FRANKLIN TO JOHN FRANKLIN,
C. 1849–1850 [FRAGMENT]

part of letter sent by Captain Forsyth

<u>2</u>

this should be the happy ship to bring you succour, it will be strange and wonderful indeed! This last vessel is one that has been got up by private funds for the search of Regent Inlet & the Western Coast of Boothia & the passages whether of land or water connecting them together or dividing them from one another. It is commanded by your old friend of VD Land Forsyth, now a Commander who offered his services gratuitously – He will tell you of all the other expeditions afloat, including the American one, for in consequence of a letter I wrote to the President of the United States, even another nation is in the field, gloriously engaged in the common cause.

Your dear friend Richardson set off in 1848 in company with the Hudson's Bay Company's officer Mr. Rae to search for you along the coast between the Mackenzie & the Coppermine & Sir James Ross the same year sailed in command of 2 ships for Lancaster Sound. Richardson returned in safety, tho unsuccessful, last autumn, & so also did Sir J. Ross, much sooner than was expected, owing to fortuitous circumstances – but the search is going on again actively in various quarters – amongst others old Sir John Ross, at past 70, has with assistance of H. Bay Company & other subscriptions got up a vessel, to perform the promise he says he made you at parting to search for you in places which he pointed out to you in the way to Melville Island. It has been the sole business of my life to instigate & set in motion as far as my feeble means could admit of

[start and end of letter missing]

188. JANE FRANKLIN TO JOHN FRANKLIN, 11 APRIL 1850

33. Spring Gardens. London.
11th April 1850.

My own dearest love

May it be the will of God if you are not restored to us earlier that you should open this letter & that it may give you comfort in your great trial. I feel sure that you must all have suffered much, & perhaps when you are met with, it may be in a state of great exhaustion, & your numbers may be diminished & many a bitter trial you may have had to bear. May you have found your refuge & strength in Him whose mercies you have so often experienced when every human aid was gone. May He in his infinite mercy have forgiven you if thro' human infirmity and weakness, even your faith should ever have been shaken thro' extremity of suffering! The spirit indeed is willing, but the flesh is weak. If the prayers of all who love you can have availed with that merciful God whose ear is ever open to the cry of all who trust in Him, you will yet be spared to us.

But we know that His ways are not our ways, are not always such as we can adore without the subjection of many human feelings & the exercise of the humblest & deepest faith. I try to prepare myself for every trial which may be in store for me, but dearest, if you ever open this, it will be because I have been spared the greatest trial of all.

Next to you I think of dear Captain Crozier & then of our other dear friends, Fitzjames & Gore & the others. I trust you have all been a mutual comfort to each other. Yet amidst the perils to which <u>you have all</u> been exposed, I scarcely dare to trust that some casualty has not occurred to some if not to many of you during so long an absence. If you are restored to us in any way, enfeebled as you may be, I shall still bless God for the mercy. If you live to receive this, & to receive my fondest blessing, I will thank Him still! I desire nothing but to cherish the remainder of your days, however impaired & broken your health may be, but in every case, I will strive to bow to the Almighty's Will, and trust thro' His mercy for a blessed reunion in a better world!

I wish you could have known the intense sympathy that has been felt for you, not by us alone, nor by this nation alone, but by the whole civilized world!

You will hear from those who find you all the measures that have been taken for your rescue by the Government & how one expedition after another has been sent in search of you. Everyone vying with one another in such a cause. Your devoted friend Richardson has again been exploring the Arctic Shore from the Mackenzie to the Coppermine & returned at the close of last year. Sir James Ross also has been sent out & returned in safety, without having been able to penetrate far. Other expeditions are now afloat, one from Behring Strait commanded by Captain Collinson and one from Davis Strait under Captain Austin but that which has now the happiness of meeting with you is the only one I need dwell upon, because you will hear of the others from books & the personal communications of the present party. It was by my earnest desire & by our special efforts supported by our few dear friends at the Admiralty that Captain Penny of the Whaling trade was put in possession of his 2 fine vessels manned & officered with people of his own selection & of all the expeditions afloat there is none which possesses heartier public sympathy than this. Captain Penny is a man of great experience & enterprise, with a fine generous heart & a noble zeal in the cause, which is enhanced I am sure by his personal friendship for myself. I hope he will take on board with him as Surgeon Mr. Robert Goodsir, a younger brother of your Assistant Surgeon. £20,000 reward is offered by Government for your rescue, open to ships of all nations.

But the hope of pecuniary reward has I am sure much less to do with the general eagerness & zeal than the impulse of humanity & the love of glory. A rich American gentleman has sent 2 vessels after you, one of which like Captain Pennys ship is called the "Lady Franklin". Captain P's was so named by Sir F Beaufort who also named the companion the "Sophia" in compliment to Sophy Cracroft my attached friend & companion who has long been to me as a daughter. Eleanor has been married nearly a year to Mr. Gell I allow them enough to make their income £500 a year till you return, by which time I hope they will have an independence. I shall leave to Eleanor to tell you of her married life. We have been singularly free from domestic losses during your absence, but you will not be surprised to hear of the death of poor Betsey – all your other sisters are much as usual – my dear old father is still going & in full possession of his faculties.

Mr. Simpkinson is now Sir F. Simpkinson. John S. has lately married the sister of Dr. Vaughan of Harrow. Sir F. Beaufort is a Civil Knight of the Bath having first accepted the Retired Rear Admiral ship – Richardson was knighted soon after you left, & is married again to a sister of Mrs. Davey, (Miss Fletcher) a lady of 48 with whom he seems very happy. Sir Edward Parry is Supt of Haslar Hospital & Clarence Yard. Dr. Robert Brown is well & loves you as much as ever.

Lord Haddington did not remain long in office. He was succeeded by Lord Ellenborough & then by Lord Auckland who died last autumn, & now it is Sir F. Baring. In 1847 Lord Auckland gave you the Good Service Pension in a most handsome manner. Old Sir John Ross has got one since & he too is commanding a ship of search. The Majendies are living in comfort and honor at Hedingham Castle, all debts paid, & he returned with bells ringing & a grand dinner given to him by the gentry. As for the pamphlet which you did not see quite the end of when you sailed, it has been most triumphant. Montagu has not had a word to say in answer. Mr. Gregory has got the Government. rather a poor one at the Bahamas. Captain Maconachie is pulling out his convict plans at Birmingham in a new prison.

Since I began this letter I have had such incessant interruption relating to the instant departure of Captain Pennys ships that the post time is at hand, or I would fain write more, things crowd upon me to tell you, but I have mentioned some of the chief. I have written to you by every ship – Dearest love be comforted by this pleasant news, God has blessed & comforted us – I live in you my own dearest – I pray for you at all hours – give my affectionate remembrance to Captain Crozier, Fitzjames, Gore, Little, all Captains now. The Arctic Service is the high road to promotion.

God bless you – ever your most devoted & affectionate wife
                                          Jane Franklin

[Note on envelope of this letter] Sent afresh 22nd April 1852 by Sir E. Belcher with additions

189. SOPHIA CRACROFT TO JOHN FRANKLIN, 11 APRIL 1850

London. 11th April.

My dearest Uncle

We send our letters by Captain Penny with great hope that he will reach you & be the happy means of relieving and restoring you to us, which may God in mercy grant. Deeply indeed you must have suffered during these long years of detention & latterly of privation, but I am persuaded that He whose power to help you have so fully tested has been ever present with you, as He has been with us – especially with my dearest Aunt who could never unsupported have gone through the trial of suspence & anxiety which has been her portion since the third year of your departure. You may wonder at my saying that even you do not know your own wife, but in as much as her devotedness, courage, fortitude, and extraordinary mental endowments have never been tested as of late, so you have never known the full extent of her rare qualities. I cannot express to you how entirely I honor as well as love her & what a privilege I feel it to be with her, I share as far as may be her sorrow at your protracted absence. What a compensation will be your return, under any circumstances, prepared as we are to see the effects of anxiety and even of want of proper food. Still we have <u>hope</u>, & this, together with the great exertions made by the country to rescue you, keeps her up. Without the last, she would utterly sink. But an active spirit of sympathy is aroused throughout the whole nation & this is no small consolation under the circumstances. I must tell you however that it is to my dear Aunts personal influence and most wonderful efforts that the existence of this feeling is mainly due.

Throughout the length & breadth of the land is she honored and respected, and sympathy to her has been expressed & conveyed to herself by all ranks from the Queen down to the lowest of her subjects – and this, notwithstanding the most shrinking anxiety to avoid notice or comment or observation. You could not find in all England a woman more universally honored and admired & respected, than your own wife. I could write pages on this theme my dearest Uncle & no one has a better right to do so than myself since no one can know so well as myself what she really is, from the circumstance of my having been with her constantly since Eleanors marriage & witnessed her efforts not merely as most others in their results, but in the manner of their accomplishment. It will be a futile subject if it please God to restore you to us. Eleanor will write to you herself of her married happiness & I shall therefore leave it to her to do so. My own dear family are well thank God & have been residing for some years at Winchester which suits us extremely well. Dear Mama is in excellent health and looks.

You will not be surprised to hear that it has pleased [God] to remove dear Aunt Betsey, her sufferings were repeatedly intense, but her last illness was but short. She was taken away in January last. The Wrights are much as usual as are Uncle & Aunt Booth, the former getting older, not so my Aunt. Willinghams marriage will please you, you will a little grand niece both there & at the Welds, who remain at the Royal Society. Emily & her father reside at Eastbourne and of late we have had the happiness of seeing the reunion under very promising circumstances of Louisa and her husband – both have greatly changed for the better, and seem excessively attached to each other & very happy. Foster remains with my Aunt, a most attached & faithful servant. I am sure you will be glad to think she has continued in her service. My Aunt will tell you of her own family, of Mr. Griffin especially how wonderfully his life is prolonged. You will indeed not find many changes among your friends. The Navy list which Captain Penny has with him will show you a total change in the rules of promotion. The Admirals list is kept up to its present number by placing upon it the Senior Captain upon the death of an Admiral. This regulation places you very high up, and we may hope to see you one day an Admiral. You will see the Good Service Pension before your name, certainly a well earned reward. Pray remember me very kindly to Captain Crozier. I need hardly say that next to you, we think most frequently of him. You indeed are ever present, in sleeping as well as waking hours. May God in His great mercy bring us face to face once more. Ever my dearest Uncle
      Your attached niece
      Sophia Cracroft

190. SOPHIA CRACROFT TO JOHN FRANKLIN, 12 APRIL 1850

London.
12th April.
1850.

My dearest Uncle

If this reaches you, it will be given by our American friends, for <u>friends</u> we must call any who aid in restoring you to us in safety. It is believed to be without a precedent that a nation should send forth an expedition to rescue from danger & from death, the people of another, and that noble instance of liberality, this glorious example is afforded, is due solely to my dearest Aunt. You will find that she is spoken of with enthusiasm by the Americans & well may it be so for she has moved them to do great things. Last year she wrote a letter to the President & received a reply calculated to excite, not only admiration, but the strongest hopes that the Government would immediately send out an Expedition to seek for yours.

This letter & the reply was republished from the American Papers into our own, & it (my Aunt's) was spoken of in the House of Commons by Sir Robert Inglis, as the most admirable letter ever addressed <u>by</u> man or woman, <u>to</u> man or woman. It has everywhere excited the deepest sympathy & admiration. Unhappily last year the American Government were unable to fulfil their benevolent intentions. Congress was not then sitting & it was besides (in April) too late to begin preparations, no vessels fitted for the service being attainable.

Meanwhile my Aunt kept up frequent communication with the United States & particularly with a Mr. Silas Burrows who formed her acquaintance in England last summer. Her letters to himself were seen by Mr. Henry Grinnell of New York, one of the Merchant Princes of that City, & so strongly influenced his mind that he proposed heading a subscription for fitting out a private Expedition with 5000 dollars, soon after he raised it to 10,000 dollars, & upon seeing my Aunts next following letter, written a fortnight after the first I have alluded to, he made his contribution $15,000. Upon hearing of his 1st donation my Aunt wrote to thank him for it, and when he read this letter, he immediately augmented his subscription to the splendid gift of $<u>30,000</u> – selected his vessels, & his officers, who belong to the U. States Navy, and, with probably some assistance, will send them off early in May in search of you.

You must not suppose that my Aunt has attained this wonderful result, by using entreaties, or by beseeching help. It has been accomplished by the force of dignity, simplicity & earnestness, united to a most extraordinary extent in herself.

And to these qualities may in very great degree be attributed the universal sympathy now experienced in England, for there is not a woman in the kingdom so universally honored & esteemed as your wife. I cannot express to you how entirely I honor and love her, & to be permitted to endeavor to comfort her & share her sorrow, is a privilege which I value above every other. Her devotedness, her perseverance, and entire acquaintance with every part of the question of search for you, combined with her extraordinary mental endowments have given her an influence which is really wonderful, & of which people in general see only the results. It is only for one who like myself has witnessed her efforts fully to recognize & appreciate them, tho' there are some who do so nearly to the utmost, and these are your nearest & dearest friends. Full & complete indeed, will be her reward if you are restored to her in safety, compensation even for all she has suffered.

I could long dwell upon this subject my dearest Uncle – God grant we may soon enter upon it face to face, for it will be a welcome theme to you, and there will be many to place it before you.

My Aunt is entering into family & other details & it will be a great comfort to you to learn what she writes, for there have been on the whole few changes. We have very suddenly and at short notice learned this opportunity for writing to America, not in time to send to Eleanor, as my Aunt will explain. Our letters too are shorter than they might otherwise have been.

Will you remember me very kindly to Captain Crozier, I am sure, I need not tell you that next to yourself, we think oftenest of him. May God in his great mercy bring you safely to us my dearest Uncle

> Your attached niece
> Sophia Cracroft

191. JANE FRANKLIN TO JOHN FRANKLIN, 21 MAY 1850

> 33. Spring Gardens
> 21st May. 1850.

My dearest love

May it be the will of God if you are not restored to us earlier that you should open this letter & that it may give you comfort in all your trials! This is the 6th or 7th letter I have written to you by different ships, & I say nearly the same in all knowing that in all probability it will be one only that you will receive. I feel sure that you must all have suffered much & perhaps when you are met with it may be in a state of great exhaustion, and your numbers even may be diminished & many a sore trial you may have had to bear. May you have found your refuge & strength in Him whose mercies you have so often experienced when every human aid was gone. If the prayers of all who love you can have availed with that Merciful God whose ear is open to the cry of all who trust in Him, you will yet be spared to us! But we know that His ways are not always such as we can adore without the subjection of many human feelings & the exercise of the humblest & deepest faith. I try to prepare myself for every trial which may be in store for me but, dearest, if you ever open this, it will be cause I have been spared the greatest of all. Next to you I think of dear Captain Crozier – I trust his health improved after his departure & that you may not have been forced to separate & that you have been a mutual comfort to each other – and your own officers. May they also have been preserved to you – yet amidst all the perils to which you have all been exposed, I scarcely dare to trust that some casualty has not happened to either of the ships during so long an absence – indeed we are all prepared to hear that you have been forced to abandon them, or that one of them at least is lost.

If you are only restored to us in any way, enfeebled as you may be, I shall bless God for the mercy. If you live to read this & receive my fondest blessing, I will thank Him still. I desire nothing but to cherish the remainder of your days, however injured & broken your health may be, but in all cases, I will strive to bow to the Almighty Will & trust in his mercy for reunion in a better world. Your greatest trial I am sure has been the thought of what we have been suffering, yet we have been greatly supported. I wish you could all of you have known the intense sympathy that has been felt for you not by me alone, not by this nation alone, but by the whole world! You will hear from those who find you all the measures that have been taken for your rescue by the government & how one expedition after another has been sent in search of you. The present one, which brings you this letter is a private expedition under the command of Sir John Ross who on the ground of having given you his word, as he has publicly stated that he would come to look for you after 3 years, did, in the year 1847, apply to the Admiralty to be employed on such an expedition, but at that time it was thought premature & his declarations were not attended to & when in 1848, the first expedition of search set forth, the command was given to his nephew, who returned prematurely owing to various causes, having accomplished very little.

This year there are 3 in search of you and on Government orders & no less than 3 private ones, viz this of Sir John Ross defrayed partly by Hudsons Bay Co. & partly by public funds another on eve of starting, defrayed by public & private funds under command of Captain Forsyth, once of the Beagle who knew you in VDLand & lastly, an American expedition defrayed at the expense of a private individual named Grinnell, aided by the U.S. government. Besides this your old friend Richardson set off in 1848, accompanied by a H. Bay officer named Rae to search for you between Mackenzie & Copper Mine – he returned safe last autumn.

And now for some domestic information – Thank God very little has happened of a painful nature – all my family is living & well, even my old father, still in full possession of his faculties, tho' feebler in body. Mr. Gell returned last Xmas twelve month & was married to Eleanor last June, upon a curacy in London & upon funds drawn from the income you left me, till they could secure an independence, or till you return, for I allow them much more now than we could afford to do if we were keeping house together. She is very well & has lately given birth to a little girl. The Majendies well, living in honor & credit at Hedingham.

Mr. Simpkinson knighted – his son one of the masters of Harrow & lately married to sister of Dr. Vaughan. Your sisters well except one poor Betsey who will not be surprised to hear has at last paid the debt of nature. Sophy is the kindest of daughters to me I would say more but am forced in great hurry to conclude. My kindest affectionate remembrances to Captain Crozier, Captain Fitzjames now Post Captain) Captain Gore &c &c none forgotten God bless you dearest love – we pray day & night that you may be supported & comforted as we are –

Your devoted & affectionate wife
Jane Franklin

This is shorter letter than others, as less likely to reach you in my opinion.

[note on envelope of this letter]
by Sir John Ross & returned
again by Lt Pim & returned

192. SOPHIA CRACROFT TO JOHN FRANKLIN, 26 MAY 1851

<u>Stromness</u>
May 26/51

My dearest Uncle

Although we feel that little can be added to our former letters, yet that little must be written – and having said briefly that all dearest to you are well. I would rather tell you of my dear Aunt how wonderfully God has supported in the deep trial she is called upon to endure. Her trust and humble dependence upon Him has been met by great blessings, for she has had not only strength, but wisdom given her, by which she has accomplished more for your deliverance, if indeed such a blessing be in store for us, than ever our imagination could have anticipated. Her extraordinary powers both of character & mind seem to have been developed, used there, combined with the results most justly attributed to her, have procured for her such an amount of sympathy, respect, & affection as has been without any parallel, there is not a woman in any part of the civilized world who is more universally & truly honored than your wife. She has had homage enough to turn any other woman's head, used she is but all the more unpretending & anxious to escape obser-vation. I feel that all this is grateful to your heart, and I will only add that no one in the world but yourself can love and reverence her more than myself – it would be strange indeed if I did not. I am sure it will cheer you after all your suffering to see the zeal & devotedness of those who have gone in search of you – they are but the representatives of a whole nation – nay of many nations, and will prepare you in some sort for the enthusiasm with which your return will be hailed – the thankful joy of some is more than we dare yet anticipate, but God will with the unspeakable blessing, give us also strength to bear it.

My Aunt will tell you that Eleanor is extremely well, and has lately had a son in addition to her little girl. My dearest mother is very well as are my sisters. Will you remember me very kindly to Captain Crozier and let him be assured that we often think and talk of him.

That God in mercy to us, may restore you in safety is the constant prayer of your attached niece

Sophia Cracroft

[written on reverse of this letter]

<u>1851</u>
S.C. to Sir John Franklin
(copied by desire of Lady F)

193. JANE FRANKLIN TO JOHN FRANKLIN,
10 DECEMBER 1851

Bedford Place
<u>10th Dec 1851</u>

My own dearest love

The enclosed letter was brought back to me this autumn by Sir John Ross on his return from Lancaster Sound. To our extreme disappointment all the ships sent out in search of you [by] the government returned also. These included 4 under Captain Austin, & 2, called the "Lady Franklin" & the "Sophia" under Captain Penny, the Whaling Captain. Captain Austin during last spring sent off travelling parties to Melville Island (where I felt sure you would not be found at least on the S side) & also S.W. of Cape Walker where they judged no ships could ever have passed. Captain Penny took another direction & went up Wellington with sledge & convinced himself you had gone that way in open water. They all had previously found your winter quarters in 1845.6 at Beechey Island. Penny had not materials to pursue his search another year so returned home this autumn as well as the rest & now another expedition will start in the spring to pursue the course thro' Wellington Channel.

The little "Prince Albert" private expedition is attempting to get to James Ross' Strait & Simpson's Strait to search for you in that direction – dear old Hepburn is on board – he would not be left behind. This is the 2^d voyage of the Prince Albert – she is now under the command of Mr. Kennedy late of the Hudsons Bay Co. whose father was governor of Fort Cumberland – Besides this, Mr. Rae is seeking for you in a boat about Wolstenholme & Victoria Land & Banks Land.

On the other or Behring Strait sides, Captain Collinson & Captain McClure have passed thro' Behring Strait Eastward towards Melville Island but I fear in too low a latitude to fall in with you & too near the coast of America to be able to get along. Lastly, the bearer of this letter Lieutenant Pim RN. has gone out alone supported by the Russian authorities to seek for you on the N & E coasts of Siberia & the islands lying to the North where if God in his great mercy should bless his endeavours, you may open this letter full of consolation & joy I trust to your broken down & suffering heart.

I hope you have never for a moment thought that your country had forgotten you or left you to your fate – you have felt sure that I could never never rest till we had some tidings of you. It is my mission upon earth – my heart's sole thought, the one only object & occupation of all my faculties & energies – dearest love, I live only for you.

Eleanor & her husband are going on well in the same position in London she has a 2^d child, a boy. Sophy lives almost constantly with me & is to me as a daughter – without her aid I should never have been to get thro' the work which God has assigned me & which my heart has accepted as its own, that of striving for your rescue. Willingham has been married 2 years has 1 little girl & a nice wife who is about to be confined of her 2^d, he has lately bought a beautiful estate in Northamptonshire & has become a most respectable & active country squire.

Mr. Pim who is now generously devoting himself to your service can give you news of many of your other old friends, as Richardson, John Barrow (his father Sir John is no more) Beaufort, Brown, & many others perhaps – Sir Roderick Murchison again President this year of the Geographical has taken the most active interest in promoting the expedition of Lieutenant Pim by writing to the Emperor of Russia on his behalf & it is this thro' the Emperor that we hope he will be enabled to execute his mission. Remember me again & again most kindly & affectionately to your friends & companions. Mr. Barrow has given to Mr Pim a Halkett boat, having christened it in remembrance of the friend he loves so well, the "James Fitzjames". Sophys' heart is devoted to you – May we be united again in time & for eternity – your most devoted &
affectionate wife

Jane Franklin.

[note on envelope of this letter]
by Lt Pim

194. JANE FRANKLIN TO JOHN FRANKLIN, 6 JULY 1852

Bedford Place
6th July 1852

My dearest love

I have written many letters which I think have a better chance of falling into your hands than this, but I cannot let any opportunity escape which offers any hope whatever of communicating with you. I live only for your sake and have no other object in life than to seek to save you.

The vessel which carries this letter was originally destined to go to Behring Strait to look for you – we failed in our endeavours to dispatch it on that search & then I offered it to Captain Inglefield to do what he best could with it, but if he is ever enabled to give you this letter he will tell you all this and much more, how we have been preserved and strengthened for our work and how not only those who personally love you, but the whole world is interested in your safety and rescue – Oh! if my efforts should be so blessed as to save you or any of you, I shall be rewarded indeed for all my sufferings!

Dear Sophy, my adopted daughter and faithful helpmate joins me in fondest love and in affectionate regards to all our dear friends, your companions, who may by God's mercy have survived your hard trials and are yet by your side.

May that God of Mercy support me and you still, my own dearest husband and restore us to one another even in this world, but above all in the world to come, redeemed and sanctified by Him for ever. This is the constant prayer of your most affectionate and devoted wife

Jane Franklin

I have not said any thing about Eleanor, because she has an opportunity of writing for herself, and will probably do so if she thinks there is any probability of this ever reaching you –

195. JANE FRANKLIN TO JOHN FRANKLIN,
30 MARCH 1853

London

30th March 1853

My dearest love

Should this letter ever be opened by you after the many I have written to you in vain it will be a happiness indeed! Would that I could make sure of such a consolation to your broken down and suffering heart! I do trust that never for a moment have you thought that your country & your friends had forgotten you or left you to your fate. You must always have felt sure that I could never rest till we had some tidings of you. It is my mission upon earth. It keeps me alive – it is my hearts's sole thought, the one only object & occupation of all my faculties & energies – My own dear husband, it is for you I live –

My present expedition of the "Isabel" was to have sailed last year under a different commander a merchant captain who misled & deceived me – the vessel then was his, it has now become mine. Mr. Kennedy, the Commander is an excellent man he will tell all he has done already in the cause & all that is now doing by Government. I do not wish to over-whelm you with news – it would not be good for you – you will learn every thing in time – those nearest & dearest to you are well.

I have had great trials independent of the greatest one of my ignorance of your fate – but I will not enter upon them. Sophy I find has been writing you a long letter & I dare say has entered upon all the events which have occurred to us –

For many years, things remained much in the same state as when you left – latterly changes have taken place, but few however in your own immediate family. Sophy lives almost constantly with me & has been to me as a daughter since Eleanor's marriage – without her aid, I should not have been able to get through the work which God has assigned me & which my heart has accepted as its own, that of striving for your rescue.

The faithful Foster too is still with me & I believe nothing now would make her leave me – she remembers your injunction on this subject – but we are all growing old & shattered, grey-haired & half toothless (I do not include Sophy in this) and yet still you would know us again as the same persons – I know <u>you</u> must all be changed also, what must you not have suffered!

Remember me most kindly & affectionately to your friends & companions. I scarcely dare to name them since those whose names I might first utter may not be amongst the number of the living.

I do not know whether Sophy has told you that owing to new regulations of the Admiralty which place many old officers on the retired lists, you were raised a few months ago to the rank of Rear Admiral, on the active list, by this promotion you have ceased to enjoy the Captain's Good Service Pension which in the year 1847 was conferred upon you by Lord Auckland, then 1st Lord of the Admiralty. God grant you may read this pleasant news – It is I who hold your commission.

And now dearest love once more may Heaven bless & preserve you – May we be united again in time & for eternity – a blessed eternity! Ever your most devoted & affectionate wife

Jane Franklin

[note on envelope written by Sophy Cracroft]

Sent by the "Isabel" to the Pacific,
returned to, & kept by my aunt
dated 30th March   1853

APPENDICES

APPENDIX A

Harry Goodsir's "Zoology from the Arctic Expedition," with a fragment of a letter to Edward Forbes

This article was commissioned by William Jerdan (1782–1869), the editor of the *Literary Gazette and Journal of Belles Lettres*. Goodsir chose to write his report in the form of a letter and while it duly appeared in the *Literary Gazette*, its final paragraph – being more personal in nature – was omitted. When it was republished some twenty-four years later in *The Leisure Hour*, Jerdan added a brief note; the version below restores Goodsir's last few lines.

I hope this last record of my lamented friend, Harry Goodsir will be found of some public interest. He sailed with Franklin and Crozier on their fatal Arctic expedition, and perished with them. Not of rank enough to have his name blazoned and his fate lamented, like those of his leaders, he yet stood so high in the estimation of all who knew him, and stood on so high a ground as an illustrator of natural science, that even now, after the lapse of a quarter of a century, there are many still left to recall his memory to their hearts, as I do, with the deepest sorrow and regret. The letter speaks for itself, and needs no introductory comment.

– William Jerdan.

"ZOOLOGY FROM THE ARCTIC EXPEDITION"

Before presenting our readers with the following communication, the first from the Arctic Expedition, and of high interest to natural history, we may notice that Professor . Forbes has been pursuing his submarine researches on the coasts of Zetland [Shetland Isles] and the Hebrides, and with great success, adding much to the stores of knowledge his indefatigable exertions (with those of his dredging friends) have contributed to this branch of zoological inquiry.

Whale Fish Islands, Baffin's Bay

July 7, 1845.

Dear Sir, – After a passage of nearly two months we have at length arrived at this place, which in all probability will be the last opportunity at present afforded me of acquainting you with the success of our proceedings so far as we have yet gone. I was very sanguine, before leaving England, of success as regarded the zoological productions of these latitudes, and certainly have not been disappointed.

Our passage out was rather tedious, in consequence of the adverse nature of the winds; and during that part of it from Stromness to Cape Farewell, we were forced to proceed so far to the north and east of our course as to be in hourly expectation, during the 11ᵗʰ, of seeing Hecla in the distance. In this, however, all were disappointed; for the wind becoming favourable during the night, we made for Cape Farewell, which we were off by Sunday the 22ᵈ.

The whole of this time I was prevented making any observations in consequence of the boisterous state of the weather, with the exception of two days; the animals, however, which were then obtained, from their beauty and unknown characters, made up for the previous and succeeding loss of time. It was during the 10ᵗʰ ult., while in lat. 61° 47', and long. 14° 14', that I first obtained specimens of a new species of Briareus, which proved a most important addition to our knowledge of these animals, inasmuch as cilia were observed fringing the bifurcated portions of the lateral extremities of the body. This fact decides the position of these very remarkable creatures in the animal scale; so that Quoy and Gaimard's supposition regarding its mollusciform character is incorrect.

At the same time a very beautiful crustacean was obtained – the type of a new genus of Pontia, allied to Irenæus. It is characterised most prominently by the great size and by the enormous length of the four central tail -filaments, the inner of which are not armed with filaments, all the others being so; each of the antennæ are armed with a joint at the distal part of the first third, by which means the animal is able to bend them up so as to conceal them beneath its body; altogether it is one of the most beautiful and characteristic forms of the family I ever saw. All the Medusæ obtained at that time were ciliogrades; one of these, the most interesting, is peculiar, in so far that, instead of the ribs bearing the cilia being in a longitudinal direction, they are transverse – the cilia rising from either edge of the rib. The minute structure is very complicated, and, so far as I am at present aware, proves its affinity to the Diphydæ, as well as the Salpæ.

A small specimen of Clio was obtained along with the above-mentioned species; but it was only after entering Davis's Straits on the 23^{d} that these beautiful Pteropoda were seen in abundance along with Spiratella. Both of these creatures, while swimming in the water, are very active, and exceedingly beautiful, being adorned with the brightest colours. They only make their appearance on the surface of the water in the still of the evening, and in calm weather. From observations made on them, I am enabled to corroborate those of Eschricht, with the exception of one or two points, which want of time prevents me taking notice of in this place.

On Tuesday we saw land to the eastward, and the following morning, passed several large icebergs. The wind, which had been falling away since Monday night, now fell off altogether, and my harvest began. Ever since I have been completely engaged without intermission in drawing those animals which cannot be preserved, and in describing all that are procured. I can assure you, although a labour of love, it is not without its fatigues; for my fellow-officers are so anxious to procure specimens for me, that I never want fresh matter to work on. Owing to the constant light, also, I am enabled to work without intermission until all the specimens are secured. My work, therefore, does not cease until a change of weather puts a stop to it. On the 27th soundings were got in forty-one fathoms; so that a dredge was put over, which came up containing numerous valuable and interesting animals a nondescript species of Caprella, Amphipoda to great numbers, several Asteriadæ, a Terebratula, along with several Mollusca, and the type of a new genus of Isopod allied to Murina, a very beautiful ascidian, and three species of fish – Cyclopterus, Liparis, Ammodytes, and a very beautiful species new to me. Towards the evening of this day a large shoal of the Caaing whale (*Phocæna melas*) passed the ship, apparently on their way towards the south. The next day (28th) the dredge was again put down in 300 fathoms, and produced many valuable specimens, which are extremely interesting, both from their peculiar characters and the great depth at which they were got. Amongst the many that were obtained, I observed Fusus, Turitellæ, Venus, Dentalium, some very large forms of Isopoda, along with Annelides, Zoophytes, Corallines, and many other forms of interest. The species obtained on this last attempt, which were of most interest to me, on account of the bearings regarding the distribution of the species, were the *Brissus lyrifer* of Forbes, and the *Alauna rostrata*, first got by myself at the Firth of Forth.

On the 1ˢᵗ inst. I procured several specimens of Sagitta, and two of a small Medusa (*Beroe*), which presented some very interesting peculiarities regarding the process of development. In this animal a thick germinal membrane of a red colour was observed lining the central cavity of the body, in which both male and female cells appeared to be developed. The ova, after a certain time, having arrived at some size, project so far out as to become pedunculated, and so hang from the membrane into the cavity. The male cells are also developed in the same membrane.

Within the last few days I have been examining the minute or microscopic structure of the ice forming the bergs. The first and most striking peculiarity regarding it is its perfect freshness and freedom from salt, producing most excellent water. So far south as this, and during this moist warm weather, it is disappearing very rapidly, and it is curious to observe how the action of melting goes on. When the surface of a mass is examined when melting, numerous flat concavities are seen upon it, all of the same size and form, without any interruption, excepting the ridges forming the walls of separation. A portion being taken up in the hand, a loud crackling noise is heard issuing from it, small particles occasionally flying off. Both of these phenomena appear to arise from the peculiar nature of the minute structure of the ice, which consists of three series of cells. Two of these series traverse the mass in the same direction; the third at right angles to the course of the two former. One of the former series has the cells of some size, and quite globular – the size being very regular throughout; they have also exactly the appearance of nucleated cells, owing to the existence of a small globule of a peculiar fluid contained within it. The other series are of an oblong sausage-shape, and also contain small globules, but generally several instead of one. These may be formed in consequence of several of the smaller globular-shaped cells conjoining; but this is a mere conjecture, and not very likely to be correct, because if it were so, these oblong cells would not assume the same direct linear course which they always have. It appears to me that the two series of cells just spoken of are the causes of the phenomena mentioned above as taking place when the mass is liquefying – several globules falling into one, and thereby forming a receptacle for water. The chuckling noise is easily accounted for. The mode of formation, however, and the nature of the fluid contained in the cells, is a much more difficult subject. Is it likely to be similar in any way, or similarly formed, to the fluid described by Sir David Brewster as existing in the small cells of topaz and some other precious stones?

The third series of cells are very minute, and thickly studded in very well-defined wavy bands, which run across the lines formed by the other series at right angles. These bands are of an opaque white colour, owing to the cells being so closely placed together, and in all probability the berg derives its opaque white snow- like colour from this circumstance. Regarding this, however, as well as many other points relative to these interesting bodies – such as the formation, &c. – I expect to have further and better opportunities of making observations.

The shores of these islands offer many very beautiful illustrations of the action of floating ice upon rocks. (Their mineralogical structure is entirely granitic, of a greyish colour, with occasional long narrow undulating bands of white and red quartz.) All within the tidemark, and in some places considerably above it, being rounded off, long irregular ridges and intervening sulci, marking the action of the half- floating masses. Of the particular action, however, I shall be enabled to speak more in detail after witnessing the breaking up of the ice next spring. The shores afford many species of seaweed; the islands themselves also produce some very beautiful mosses and lichens, with several of the higher forms of plants, all of which I have already gathered.

The Esquimaux are in a state of half-civilisation, there being a Danish settlement for the purpose of collecting seal-oil, narwal-teeth, &c. The sea produces numerous very beautiful forms of Medusæ, Mollusca, &c.; and as we are to remain here until Thursday the 10th, I expect to complete the Fauna, Flora, and Mineralogy of the whole group.

You are already, ere you reach this part of this tiresome letter, heartily tired of it. You must excuse its many imperfections, for I am too anxious to get on with my work to be able to correct them. When you see any of my friends in London, pray be so good as to remember me to them, and

Believe me yours very faithfully,

Harry D.S. Goodsir

FRAGMENT OF A LETTER TO EDWARD FORBES, UNDATED

In one of Harry Goodsir's last letters to Professor Edward Forbes – date unknown – he wrote about the sea creatures he was studying. Forbes embeds quotations from Harry's descriptions of his work in his book *The Natural History of the European Seas* (London: John Van Voorst, 1859, 51–2).

"Ever since I have begun work, the officers have been exceedingly zealous in procuring animals for me, so that my time is completely

occupied, almost day and night, for, from the constant light, and
having generally lots of animals on hand, I am anxious that none
should be lost. All are anxious to assist, down to the men, who have
got several very good things for me. The boatswain is sometimes seen
running after a specimen with the large net in hand." On the 25th of
June (1845), when in Davis Straits, soundings were taken in forty
fathoms, when a small dredge was put over. It brought up starfishes,
echini, Mollusca, crustacea, and annellida. Among the shells was a
small *Terebratula*. On the 28th, they sounded in three hundred fathoms, and sank the dredge at that great depth. The bottom proved to
be of greenish mud, and they had "a capital haul, – Mollusca, crustacea, asteridae, spatangi, corallines, a nondescript *Fusus*, Isopoda,
and what is interesting to me, my genus *Alauna*, and your *Brissus
lyrifer* (a curious sea-urchin), and some fine corals." The floor of the
sea was composed of very fine green mud, which when placed under
the microscope, appeared to be composed "of granitic particles." The
next day they sounded in two hundred and forty fathoms, and met
with the same green mud, but when, this time, it was placed under the
microscope, it appeared to be composed of sandstone particles, with
small fragments of shells, and of spines of *Echinus*, and *Spatangus*,
mingled with great quantities of mucus.

Unattributed Letters in the Press

There are three unattributed letters, two of which appeared in the public press in August of 1845, shortly after the return of the *Barretto Junior*. One was printed in the *Greenock Advertiser*, Friday, 15 August 1845, along with a notice mentioning the return to England of the *Baretto Junior*, and credited simply to "one of the principals." The details of both letters are certainly authentic, and while it may be impossible to firmly assign authorship, the leading candidate for the first would surely be James Fitzjames – twice in his letters (134 and 141) he noted James Reid's observation that there would be "no ice but the bergs," which seemed to him incredibly droll; the letter's phrase "no ice except bergs, which are considered as such by the whalers" suggests the letter was his, as does its lighthearted tone and gentle humour. The second, quite a brief excerpt, appeared in the "Naval Intelligence" section of *The Times* of London of 11 August 1845. Its one notable additional detail is the writer's high opinion of the Inuit, and a clear indication of barter between them and the crews of the ships.

A third letter has recently been located; it first appeared in the *Morning Chronicle* on 25 September 1851 and was reprinted in the *St. James's Chronicle* (27 September), the *Westmeath Guardian* (2 October), the *Newry Telegraph* (2 October), and the *Kilkenny Moderator* (8 October). The reprinted versions omitted parts of the original text from the *Chronicle*, possibly because of space considerations, and the *Newry Telegraph* version also removed the writer's stronger criticisms of Crozier (see notes for details). Given the proximity of Newry to Crozier's hometown of Banbridge, this may well have been a deliberate attempt to soften the letter writer's criticisms of a native son.

There are a number of reasons to support the conjecture that the writer of this letter was George Henry Hodgson (b. 1817), the second lieutenant aboard *Terror*. For one, the letter writer mentions doing magnetic observations with Fitzjames; Hodgson is several times mentioned by him as having done so (Letters 130, 141, and 164). For another, the writer speaks of experiencing improved health after reaching calmer waters off the coast of Greenland; Hodgson is mentioned as looking ill by Fitzjames (Letter 134, entry for 26 July) and then as appearing "better" after the weather had grown calm (Letter 135, entry for 29 July). Lastly, there is the curious attribution of the text to a newspaper in India; Hodgson's family had connections to the East India Company, his sister Henrietta having married Oswald Smith, the son of one of its directors, in 1824. Several relations, including George's brother Robert Francis Hodgson (1810–1871), took up posts with the company in India. It may well have been he who provided the original letter to an Indian paper, as this would match with the reference to his "beloved brother."

A LETTER FROM ONE OF THE PRINCIPALS

Whale Fish Islands, July 11

Here we are, laden and moored in a snug little cove among the Whale Fish Islands, east coast of Greenland, lat. 69.9., long. 53.10. W. One would have hardly thought it possible for two such ships as the Erebus and Terror to have taken board all the provisions. &c., that were on board the transport, but with very little exception such is the case. I certainly never saw any ship so deep before, and I felt anxious, like the boy with walnut shell in a basin of water, to see if the vessels could bear It. One thing is certain, our fellows, who are high spirits, and in robust health, will make a large hole in the comestibles every day, and therefore we shall 'improve our sailing qualities as we lighten,' as they say of the surveyor's ships.

The weather here is delightful. We have the sun all the hours, and the middle of the day is really very warm, notwithstanding from the top of the island you can count, speaking within bounds, at least thousand icebergs.

The transport leaves to-morrow, and we pursue our voyage on Monday. We have received accounts from the Danes that the state of the ice northward is very favourable to our enterprise. This is very gratifying, and will be additional incentive to our gallant chief to push on, though with all the stability, prudence and caution of the sexagenarian: and while considering the glorious advantages which he would reap from complete success, he, nevertheless, calculates the sacrifice which he must inevitably risk. But who knows? We may get through this year. Then how delighted I should be to pitch an upper deck-load overboard, consisting of 40 tons, and nearly 100 casks.

Our passage out was very fair one; but small allowance of bad weather, and that not very bad for us to feel it much.

Large collections have already been made in natural history, especially in marine animals, such crustaciæ, medusæ, &c., several hundred in number, and great many of a new kind.

We are working away here from four the morning until six. We have then some shooting until noon. There are quantities of eider duck here; they resort to this latitude in the breeding season.

As yet we have seen no ice except bergs, which are considered as such by the whalers. For two days previous to our reaching here we were threading our way through them. It is a grand sight witnessing one of the icebergs capsize; they come over with the reverberating noise of thunder, and, generally speaking, gradually fall to pieces.

P.S. I have written this hasty letter by the midnight sun.

THE ARCTIC EXPEDITION

"Letters have been received at Woolwich, dated her Majesty's ship Erebus, Whalefish Islands, Davis's Straits, July 8, 1845, from one of which the following is an extract:

"We are discharging the transport as quickly as possible, for the season is far advanced and we are in a great hurry to get up the country; but we have plenty of time yet if the weather keeps fine. We calculate on being absent two years and a-half at most, unless we get through to the Southern Ocean, when it may be three or four years before we return. We are all well, and I am very happy. We have the best treatment, and one of the best of captains, and a good set of officers throughout. The Barretto Junior, the transport ship, sails the day after tomorrow (July 10) on her return. The natives here are civilized, and as shrewd at making a bargain as you or I would be in any transactions at home."

SIR JOHN FRANKLIN'S EXPEDITION

[from the *Morning Herald*. 25 September 1851]

"At the present moment, when public attention is more than ordinarily excited by the reports of traces of Sir John Franklin, the following letter addressed to an Indian paper, will be deemed interesting: –

"Dear Sir, – So deep and melancholy an interest is attached to the expedition under Sir John Franklin to the North Pole, that a letter from a young and able officer written from the last starting point in Baffin's Bay can hardly fail of proving acceptable to many of your readers; for though none in this country, like myself, may be so unhappily situated so to have a beloved brother in the expedition, yet its unknown fate is so universally deplored and sympathised in, that few, it is presumed, can peruse these unpremeditated passages, penned in light-heartedness and in the youthful confidence of success, without contrasting the sanguine feelings of hope that glowed in the bosom of the writer with the dismal uncertainty that now surrounds his fate, and that of his brother officers –

"Seven years and more have passed since the expedition, full of life and joy, left the shores of England, and all the late energetic efforts of England, and of that noble-minded woman Lady Franklin, have, alas! up to this hour, proved ineffectual in discovering any satisfactory traces of its existence; but hope though desponding does not yet despair. Many persons fully competent to offer an opinion are still confident that the expedition will yet be heard of. It is well known that it was amply supplied with provisions for five years, which, with care and prudence, might easily be doled out to last seven. Fresh search is still being made, and ere hope dies within us we may well permit another season to pass away. The prospect indeed is gloomy, but their advent some day, like a ray of sunshine in a wintry sky, may yet burst upon us, and diffuse in our hearts a joy the more grateful from its being so long deferred.

"The extract here appended is from a letter dated from the island of Disko, in lat. 69 50 N, and long. 53 30W, the place from which the transport was discharged. The expedition lay at anchor there for eight days, and left on the 12th of July, 1844, on its almost hopeless enterprise amidst the thick-ribbed ice. Six long years have, indeed, passed without hearing from them, but God's hand is not shortened; He may yet preserve and restore to their homes and country the

grey-headed chief and the noble spirits that accompanied him in this
daring expedition.

"Her Majesty's ship Terror, Davis Straits, June 28, 1845.

"Our passage across has been a most tedious one, for since we
left we have had nothing but a succession of westerly winds. We
parted from the steamer on the 4th, and only made the land of
Greenland on the 25th, which, considering the distance is only
1400 miles, is a very long time. Owing to the west winds we were
obliged to go to the northward, and at one time were only 60
miles from Zealand, and should have made the island had the
same wind continued. A fair start, however, came, and we bore
away for Cape Farewell.

"On the 22d, when about 90 miles from the cape, a most furi-
ous gale of wind came on, luckily in the right direction, and we
were obliged to take in nearly all sail; the sea ran very high, and
owing to our being so deeply laden, several heavy waves struck
us, but did no harm except wetting through all who happened to
be on deck. If we had been amongst ice it would have been very
dangerous, but luckily we found none.

"This breeze carried us round the Cape (which we did not see)
into Davis's Straits, when the water became much smoother, and
on the 25th it moderated and became fine. On that day we saw
icebergs and the land, and all were running on deck to see so fine,
and what was to many a new sight. The bergs, however, were not
large, at least in comparison with those we shall see when we get
further north. The land, from which were distant some 50 miles,
was very high, and had a most bleak and desolate appearance, not
a vestige of vegetation was visible, and the tops of the mountains
were covered with perpetual snow. As our fancies, however, had
not led us to expect noble forests and flowery fields, this first sight
of Greenland did not disappoint us.

"Our occupation during our passage out consisted in keeping our respective watches, taking numerous observations, and
making remarks on the different temperatures of the water
and the air, and, as Captain Crozier unfortunately keeps us on
three watches, you may imagine that we have not much time
for reading. I have, however, managed to get through nearly
all the Polar voyages, which I thought necessary to read, with
a view of acquainting myself with ice navigation, and to know

what hardships and difficulties were in store for us. From all I
have read, I feel convinced that our success and getting through
depends not so much on our energy and perseverance as upon
our having the good fortune to have one open season during the
three or four years we may be up here, for if the ice does not give
way, in time, the obstacles it presents are so tremendous, that,
notwithstanding all our means and resources, I do not think it
possible they can be overcome.

"Some on board the Erebus fancy they will slip through this
season, but they are too sanguine, and have not well calculated
all the difficulties we shall have to encounter. If we get through,
and it is just within the bounds of possibility, we should probably touch at an island called St. Peter and St. Paul, a Russian
settlement, on the coast of Kamschatka, and from thence go on
to Panama; so pray write to me to both these places, sending to
the first place through the Russian ambassador, and to the second,
care of the consul.

"Since we have been in the Straits we have had most lovely
weather – the water beautifully smooth, and the sky without a
cloud. We all enjoyed it the more after the rough weather we
experienced outside, and though the thermometer has been at 34
to 35 degrees, still we have not found it at all cold. In England, at
that temperature, we should all have been huddling round the fire.
During the last few days we have had most capital fun in fishing;
finding ourselves sailing over a bank, the lines were got out, and
in the course of an hour upwards of 50 fine cod were caught; and
yesterday and to-day as many more. Tell this to –––––––––, and
ask him if he does not call that fair sport. Several times I caught
two at once, each fish weighing about 10 lb. When we get to
Disko's Island, we expect some good reindeer shooting.

"During our passage we have had several visits to the Erebus,
and they to us, for the sake of a little change of society. They are
very comfortable, and say Sir John is the kindest and most delightful person they ever sailed with. He joins in all their amusements
and occupations, and every day two or three dine with him –
Fitzjames always. Sir John is full of activity and vigour and looks a
great deal better than when we started. In the Terror, I am sorry to
say, it is very different; for Captain Crozier is most unsociable; he
hardly ever speaks to us, none of us ever go into his cabin, and he
likes solitude so much that he even thinks going on board to dine
with Sir John Franklin a great bore. It is very unfortunate that he is

so unsociable; for if otherwise it would be far more agreeable, and we should all feel so much more interest in our duties if he entered into them with us, or even seemed pleased with what we did.

"He has, however, many good qualities, and has great experience in the navigation of these seas; and though it would be more agreeable if he mixed with us more, we all respect him, and make every allowance for his peculiarities. Luckily we are very happy amongst ourselves: Little is a capital fellow; Hornby is most light-hearted, and singing all the day. As yet we have lived like fighting-cocks, which always keeps people in good humour.

"Having now crossed the Arctic circle, we have daylight during the 24 hours, which to us, who have never been in these high latitudes before, appears strange. It is with difficulty that we can remember when bedtime comes; for while the sun is shining brightly in the heavens, bed is the last thing thought of. And last night I found myself walking the deck at half-past eleven, with the sun staring me hard in the face. In a short time we shall, I suppose, get used to this new state of things, and then we shall go to our cabins at the regular time, and make it night by closing our shutters and lighting the lamps. We ought to be and are very thankful for this continuous day, for without it these seas would be unnavigable, and we ought to make the most of it while we can; for in a few short months the reverse will be the case, and we shall have no day, but one dreary night. You cannot think how much our appetites have increased since we have been up here; what was ample for us some time ago, is now not sufficient, and when the cold weather sets in we shall be still more ravenous. I hope there will be grub sufficient, for I do not think this great increase of appetite was duly taken into consideration.

"July 5 – We anchored at the Whale Fish Islands (a small cluster of rocks near the large island of Disko) yesterday, and most heartily glad we were to find ourselves snugly moored here, after all the knocking about at sea. The great business of clearing the transports has now commenced, and this quiet nook is become a scene of bustle and excitement. In one of the islands there are about ten families of Esquimaux, and the whole population turned out on our account. They are, without exception, the ugliest, dirtiest set of beings I ever beheld, and smelling so strong of seal oil that it is disagreeable to come within five yards of them. We allowed several to come on board, and each brought up a bag with him, containing the things he had to barter. These people are very poor and wretched, and had nothing worth having. Each man comes off in a separate canoe, it being only made to contain one. It is the only neat thing they seem to possess. It is very light, made of sealskin stretched over a frame, and in the middle is a hole into which the man's legs go, and where he stores all his provisions and utensils for fishing, &c. If we were on our way home I would certainly get one for the water at B ————, though I do not think O ———— would keep it very long, as it capsizes with the least motion. Several of us have had a ducking; but these fellows fish, throw their spears, and do everything, without causing a roll.

"Their huts are more dirty and disgusting than their inhabitants. In one that we went into, there was a man very ill with rheumatism, and affection of the lungs, yet the grass was growing close under his bed, and the floor of this pigsty was several inches deep in mud. It really made me feel very small when I remembered I was of the same species as these creatures, and I thanked God that I was not born an Esquimaux.

"These are, however, a very bad example of the race, for they have Danish blood in them, which has not improved the breed. At present they are in very great distress for want of fuel and provisions. When we arrived they had been two days without anything to eat, the seals, upon which they nearly depend for subsistence, being very scarce.

"I have given you a long account of these people, but as they are the only human beings that we shall see, I thought you would like to know something about them.

"From the information we have been able to collect it seems that we are likely to make a good passage across the Bay, as the ice this year is very clear, and the summer very early. Upon our getting across Baffin's Bay our progress this year chiefly depends.

"July 11. – From the day I last wrote up to this, I have been constantly employed with Fitzjames and Captain Crozier in making observations. Some here are impressed with the idea that I am a very scientific sort of fellow, but nothing is more purely mechanical than the use of these instruments, and it does not at all follow that because a man observes well he must be clever. I, for one, certainly am not; and though I understand the practice, I know very little of the theory. This is, however, a most capital opportunity of studying, of which I hope I shall take advantage.

"The transport is now clear, much to our satisfaction, for the men have had a very hard week's work in discharging her cargo, and now we are all anxious to be off. Tomorrow we shall swing the ship for the magnetic attraction, and the same evening, or Sunday morning, we shall sail.

"I have told you almost all that has happened since we sailed; but as yet our voyage has been so much like any other one that no incident of any interest has occurred. We are all longing to reach some unknown ground, and are determined, if we do not get through this year, to winter to the westward of Parry's Land.

"The lovely weather we have had has put me to rights, and I feel better now than I have done since leaving England. There is something very invigorating and delightful in the feeling of the air here, and though the thermometer has been as high as 65 degrees, still we all wear warm clothing, for there is a sharpness in the air which we should feel much were we not to do so. I have been drawing a good deal, and send to L.——— a sketch of the anchorage, but the effect of the icebergs and snow is lost on the white paper. I also enclose a track chart of the course we have made already, and our probable line after leaving this, but everything depends on the movements of the ice.

"The next letter you receive will, I hope, be dated from some spot in the Pacific, when we shall be recruiting our strength after our Polar winter. If we do not touch at the places I have mentioned, we shall go to the Sandwich Islands, but an officer will be sent home via Panama, and he will forward all letters for the expedition, so fail not to write. February will be the best time to write to St. Peter and St. Paul, and June to Panama."

Franklin's Two Official Despatches to the Admiralty

Franklin sent two official despatches to the Admiralty, the first – in May of 1845 – in reply to directions he had received, and the second – on 12 July, the day the Transport headed home – as a sort of interim report on the progress of the expedition to date. They are letters of a sort – but they are mainly formal reports to his superiors. The hand is not that of Franklin, but of someone capable of a reasonably good "copperplate" script. Due to last-minute crew changes, the *Erebus* had ended up without a clerk; in Letter 159 Franklin mentions giving the latter of these "for Mr Osmer to copy," so it was most likely his in both cases (Osmer's personal letters here are only known from copies by others, so it is not possible to compare the hands).

FRANKLIN'S OFFICIAL DESPATCH OF 29 MAY 1845

Her Majesty's Ship Erebus off Aberdeen – 29 May 1845

Sir,

I have the honor to acknowledge the receipt of your letter of the 23rd instant, just delivered to me by Captain Stanley of Her Majesty's Steam Vessel Blazer, signifying to me the directions of the Lords Commissioners of the Admiralty that if the wind continues in the present quarter (N.E.) with the appearance of lasting, I should immediately proceed with the Ships under my command down Channel – And I beg to acquaint you, for their Lordships information that, except on one occasion since our leaving the anchorage off Aldborough, we have found the winds to be favorable for the continuing of the course by the Orkneys.

The "Rattler" not being in company at the time the "Blazer" joined us, and the Monkey having been sent back to Woolwich, I considered it best in order to take all the advantage we could of the present moderate weather to retain the Blazer for the purpose of towing us, which she did, taking each ship alternately up to windward. I therefore ventured on giving Captain Stanley an order to remain with me, which I trust will meet their Lordships' approbation.

It having been found on Monday the 26th instant when off the Farn Islands, that the wind and sea were too high for the Erebus and Terror being kept in tow by the Rattler without repeatedly carrying away the Hawsers, and exposing the Ships to come in contact with each other, I caused them to be cast off. The weather at the time being very thick, I sent the Rattler to communicate the Rendezvous to the Transport which was far to windward; the Rattler parted company as well as the Transport on this occasion. Commander Smith however very judiciously availed himself of this circumstance to proceed into a Port that he might replenish her coal, and, what was of equal importance, get her screw freed from the turns of the hawser, which had wound round the screw when it last parted and greatly impeded her speed.

Captain Stanley informed me that he had this morning been on board the "Rattler" at Cromarty, and brought me a message from Commander Smith, to say that he hoped to rejoin us in the course of the day.

I have the honor to be, Sir, Your most obedient humble Servant
John Franklin, Captain.

FRANKLIN'S OFFICIAL DESPATCH OF 12 JULY 1845

Her Majesty's Ship Erebus
Whale Fish Islands, 12 July 1845

Sir,

I have the honor to acquaint you for the information of the Lords Commissioners of the Admiralty that Her Majesty's Ships Erebus and Terror, with the Transport, arrived at this anchorage on the 4th instant, having had a passage of one month from Stromness – The Transport was immediately taken alongside this ship that she might be the more readily cleared, and we have been constantly employed at that operation 'till last evening, the delay having been caused not so much in getting the stores transferred to either of the ships as in making the best stowage of them below as well as on the upper deck – the Ships are now complete with supplies of every kind for three years. They are therefore very deep – but happily we have no reason to expect much sea as we proceed further.

The Magnetic Instruments were landed the same morning, so also were the other instruments requisite for ascertaining the position of the Observatory, and it is satisfactory to find that the results of the observations for Latitude and Longitude accord very nearly with those assigned to the same place by Sir Edward Parry. Those for the Dip and Variation are equally satisfactory, which were made by Captain Crozier with the Instruments belonging to the "Terror" and by Commander Fitzjames with those of the "Erebus."

The Ships are now being swung for the purpose of ascertaining the Dip and Deviation of the Needle on board, as was done at Greenhithe, which I trust will be completed this afternoon, and I hope to be able to sail in the night.

The Governor and principal persons are at this time absent from Disco, so that I have not been able to receive a communication from Head Quarters as to the State of the Ice to the North. I have however learnt from a Danish carpenter, in charge of the Esquimaux at these Islands, that though the winter was severe, the Spring was not later than usual, nor was the ice later in breaking away hereabout; he supposes also that it is now loose as far as 74° latitude and that our prospect is favorable of getting through the barrier and as far as Lancaster Sound without much obstruction.

The Transport will sail for England this day. I shall instruct the Agent, Lieutenant Griffiths, to proceed to Deptford and report his arrival to the Secretary of the Admiralty. I have much satisfaction in bearing my testimony to the careful and zealous manner in which Lieutenant Griffiths has performed the service entrusted to him, and would beg to recommend him, as an Officer who appears to have seen much Service, to the favorable consideration of their Lordships.

It is unnecessary for me to assure their Lordships of the energy and zeal of Captain Crozier, Commander Fitzjames, and of the Officers and men with whom I have the happiness of being employed on this Service.

> I have the honor to be,
> Sir,
> Your most obedient
> humble Servant
> <u>John Franklin</u>, <u>Captain</u>

APPENDIX D

A Brief Account of the Role of Steam Power in the Launch of the Expedition

SKETCH OF SCREW PROPELLERS, WITH CAPTION,
ON THE INSIDE OF AN ENVELOPE DATED 3 MARCH 1845,
SENT BY HENRY T.D. LE VESCONTE TO HIS FATHER
(LETTER MISSING)

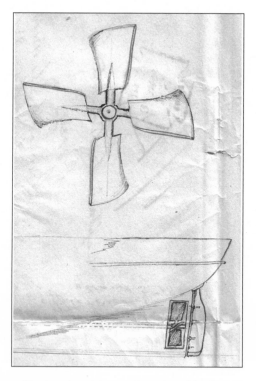

Smith's screw propeller | various sizes and angles of inclination to the water have been tried also different numbers of blades from two to six but it does not appear to be decided which is the best – it is plain that a ship's stern from the large space left for the screws must be very liable to serious injury from getting on shore.

While Le Vesconte's drawing shows a four-bladed propeller with distinctive squarish blades, those outfitting *Erebus* and *Terror* were actually quite different, being two-bladed Smith's pattern propellers. The drawings show that Le Vesconte was generally well informed about the principles of screw propulsion and ways in which ships in service could be modified to use it, and aware of some of the potential drawbacks. One month later he would report that the conversion of the ships was in progress.

The Navy's transition from sail to steam had begun in 1822 with their first paddle steamer, Comet, employed as a tug. The vulnerability of the paddle wheels to enemy shot limited their use on warships. Arctic explorer Sir Edward Parry headed the department managing this new technology, overseeing the steam factory at Woolwich Dockyard, the engineering establishment that supported the new steam navy. Parry had previously insisted that ships sent on distant expeditions have identical machinery to allow a common stock of spare parts and he was an early proponent of standardized screw threads.

Three steam vessels assisted the sailing ships on their way to the North Atlantic:

- *Monkey*: 212 tons, 80 HP. Paddle steamer built 1821. Served as a packet vessel for the Post Office as *Lightning*, later *Royal Sovereign*. Transferred to the Navy as Monkey in 1837, used as a tug.
- *Blazer*: 527 tons, 136 HP. Paddle steamer built 1834. Rated as a sloop. Used as a survey ship from 1843. The figurehead is on display at the National Museum of the Royal Navy, Portsmouth.
- *Rattler*: 888 tons, 200 hp. Screw Sloop built 1843. Used in an extensive series of trials to compare the merits of screw against paddle wheel, the most celebrated being the "tug of war" with HMS *Alecto* on 3 April 1845.

(Note that the given tonnages are builder's measure and horsepower nominal)

For comparison, *Erebus* and *Terror* were both rated at 30 horse power with tonnages of 378 and 326 respectively.

A practical system of screw propulsion was first demonstrated by Francis Petit Smith (1808–1874) in 1836, leading to the first screw-propelled steamship, *Archimedes*, built in 1839. Smith's work convinced Isambard Kingdom Brunel to change his design of the SS *Great Britain*, then being built, and spurred the Admiralty to build the Rattler, leading to its general adoption. Smith became popularly known as "Propeller Smith" (see Letter 112) and he himself was aboard the *Rattler* when she assisted *Erebus* and *Terror* on their way up the east coast of Britain in 1845. Her propeller has survived and is on exhibit in the SS *Great Britain* Museum in Bristol.

The respected firm of Maudslay, Sons & Field, of Lambeth, London, was contracted to supply engines for Erebus and Terror. In consideration of the tight deadline, they were permitted to modify second-hand railway locomotives on condition that the results were "perfectly efficient." Maudslay's would have had their pick of around hundred engines from the nearby depot at New Cross, where the three local railway companies had combined their locomotive operations. With so many to choose from, there would have been no difficulty in selecting a suitable pair to modify in line with Parry's requirements. The most likely candidates are locomotives named Archimedes and Croydon, built by the firm of G. & J. Rennie. Maudslay's were also tasked with finding suitably skilled engineers to operate and maintain the engines during the voyage. The men selected were John Gregory and James Thompson, both of whom had experience working with the firm.

The engines supplied to Franklin were anticipated to be used solely in times of calm, and the ships were provided with only enough coal for this purpose. According to Lieutenant John Irving (Letter 78), it amounted to sufficient fuel for twelve days of use. Although the ships took on some additional coal from the Transport in Greenland ("some hundred bags," according to Edward Couch in Letter 148), the sum total probably did not greatly extend this period. Inuit testimony, whereby a ship with a "burning mast" was reported, suggests that at least one of the engines was used; photographs taken of the wreck of the *Terror* by Parks Canada indicate that the smokestack – which was removable – was not in place.

APPENDIX E

A Note on the Proposed Route of the Expedition

INSTRUCTIONS ADDRESSED TO FRANKLIN
BY THE ADMIRALTY

Lancaster Sound, and its continuation through Barrow's Strait, having been four times navigated without any impediment by Sir Edward Parry, and since frequently by whaling ships, will probably be found without any obstacles from ice or islands ; and Sir Edward Parry having also proceeded from the latter in a straight course to Melville Island, and returned without experiencing any, or very little, difficulty, it is hoped that the remaining portion of the passage, about 900 miles, to the Bhering's Strait may also be found equally free from obstruction ; and in proceeding to the westward, therefore, you will not stop to examine any openings either to the northward or southward in that Strait, but continue to push to the westward without loss of time, in the latitude of about 74 ¼ degrees, till you have reached the longitude of that portion of the land on which Cape Walker is situated, or about 98 degrees west. From that point we desire that every effort be used to endeavour to penetrate to the southward and the westward in a course as direct towards Bhering's Strait as the position and extent of the ice, or the existence of land, at present unknown, may admit.

One of the more striking things that is not often remarked upon about the mission of the Franklin expedition is that, in comparison with the areas that had been charted either from the east or from the west, relatively little remained to be explored. The route directly west via Lancaster Sound was the given starting point, and the instruction to head southwest from Cape Walker simply indicated the most direct route into the heart of this blank on the map. This direction was preferred over the due west route, as the heavy ice encountered by Parry in 1819 was assumed to be a likely obstacle; that route also had the advantage of offering the greatest

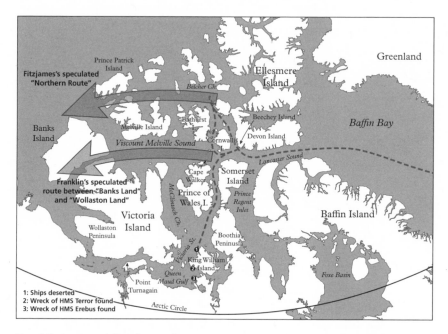

Franklin's potential and actual routes

possibility of connecting with earlier surveys of the northern coasts by Franklin himself, as extended by the land expedition of Peter Warren Dease and Thomas Simpson. Had, however, this route proven impassable, due either to ice or land being in the way, the Admiralty was open to alternatives, mentioning the ascent of Wellington Channel northward from its opening between North Devon and Cornwallis lands.

Franklin himself, in his discussions with his officers reported here, had clearly considered a more northerly route. He wondered whether or not Wollaston Land (now known to be a peninsula of Victoria Island) and Banks Land might be connected (in fact, Banks and Victoria Islands are separated by the Prince of Wales Strait, which, as Franklin imagined, could have provided a route through, were it not for the near-constant presence of heavy sea ice). James Fitzjames, for his part, seems to have been a keen advocate for a still more northerly route even before the expedition sailed; in his letter to John Barrow Jr of 2 January 1845, he declared:

> It does not appear clear to me what led Parry down Prince Regents Inlet after having got as far as Melville Island before – the N. W. passage is certainly to be gone through by Barrows Straits but whether

South or North of Parrys group remains to be proved. I am for
North edging N.W till in Longitude 140° if possible. (Letter 14)

A route such as this, going north of Melville Island, would have been quite
risky, but Fitzjames's advocacy for it seems to have had at least some influence on Franklin, and on those searching for him as well. In Jane Franklin's
later letters regarding the search for her lost husband, there is even a sense
that she gave credence to the great chimera of the age, the "Open Polar Sea."
For advocates of this idea, open water around the pole offered a quick shortcut – if only one could get through the "ice barrier"; the awareness that the
entire pole was covered with a cap of heavy ice did not arrive until much
later in the century. Some – including Dr Elisha Kent Kane, who commanded
the second Grinnell search for Franklin – even claimed to have discovered it,
though what they had seen must have been no more than a large polynya.

It appears, from the lone official record we so far have – the "Victory
Point" note – that the ships did indeed try the northern route at some
point between 1845 and 1847, and though apparently unable to proceed
to the westward, returned by the further coast of Cornwallis, showing it to
be an island. They next proceeded southwest as directed, presumably via
Peel Sound, only to find their ships icebound off the northwestern coast
of King William Island. This was known territory – James Clark Ross had
reached the western coast of King William in 1830 – but in crossing over
the ice he mistook the eastern passage around King William for a bay,
naming it Poets Bay (which mapmaker John Arrowsmith inexplicably gar-
bled as "Poctes Bay"). This is now the James Ross Strait, and would have
offered at least one possible alternative, although the shallow water and
shoals there might well have proven as treacherous for Franklin's ships
as the ice to the west. But this choice was yet far in the future at the time
these letters were written.

In the end, as we now know, both of Franklin's ships somehow made it
through the passage to the west of King William Island; the Erebus was
found in 2014 off the Adelaide Peninsula to the south, and the *Terror* in
(of all places) Terror Bay on the southern coast of King William. Whether
the ships arrived at these locations under human command, or simply
drifted to them in the ice, is not yet known for certain, though it is to
be hoped that the ongoing underwater archaeological work by Parks
Canada will someday recover evidence one way or the other. If they do,
there is every likelihood that it will come in the form of written documents, and that we may again hear these voices, whose sudden cessation
as the mailbag was stitched shut on 12 July 1845 marks the beginning of
a period of which – as yet – there is only silence.

Capsule Biographies of the Writers of These Letters

HMS *EREBUS*

Captain Sir John Franklin (1786–1847)   Franklin, the overall commander of the expedition, was an Arctic veteran, having participated in three previous expeditions, and commanded the latter two of them. He was born in 1786 in Spilsby, Lincolnshire, the ninth of twelve children born to Willingham and Hannah (née Weekes) Franklin. His father was a merchant, and his mother's family were farmers. He entered the Royal Navy in 1800 at the age of fourteen, serving first aboard HMS *Polyphemus*. In 1801 he accompanied his uncle Matthew Flinders on an expedition to survey the coasts of Australia. After his return, Franklin continued his naval service; he was at the Battle of Trafalgar aboard HMS *Bellerophon*.

His career as an explorer began in 1818, in command of the *Trent* under Captain David Buchan aboard the Dorothea; their attempt to set a new record for furthest north fell short, as both ships were damaged by ice and forced to retreat. He returned to the Arctic the next year in command of a small naval land expedition to the mouth of the Coppermine River, in 1819–22; a disastrous shortcut on his return trek led to the deaths of eleven of the twenty men in his command, along with a murder and likely cannibalism. Reduced to eating boiled leather and *tripe de roche*, he only barely survived, but returned home to considerable fame as "the man who ate his boots."

On a second, more successful land expedition he charted considerable additional northern coastline, such that the Northwest Passage – had he attained it – would have brought him to familiar shores. He accepted the command of the present expedition after it was declined by James Clark Ross, and brought his personal reputation and expertise as offsets to his age – fifty-nine – which was said to be concerning to some. He had most recently served as the lieutenant governor of Van Diemen's Land, a post from which he was abruptly recalled; some portion of his energy early in the voyage was taken up with a "Pamphlet" he had written and printed, outlining what he felt was the unfairness of his dismissal. By the account of nearly everyone who served under him, he was a beloved "chief," and his was the only date of death noted in what is so far the lone official record of the crew's later doings, the "Victory Point Record." Andrew Lambert's *Franklin: Tragic Hero of Polar Exploration* (2009) is the most recent biography.

Commander James Fitzjames (b. 1813) Fitzjames entered the Royal Navy at the age of twelve in 1825, distinguishing himself on the Euphrates Expedition (1836) and in the Egyptian-Ottoman War (1839–41) and the First Opium War (1841–42), serving aboard HMS *Cornwallis*, whose surgeon, Stephen Samuel Stanley, was later to serve under him aboard *Erebus*. Thanks to his friendship with John Barrow Jr, Fitzjames benefitted from the powerful patronage of Sir John Barrow senior; he had initially even hoped to command the new expedition himself. In the end he was given a slightly subsidiary role – becoming, as Franklin put it in Letter 92, "a Commander unsolicited on my part." He and Franklin nevertheless appear to have enjoyed a happy working relationship. His "Journal," a series of letters written to his sister-in-law Elizabeth Coningham, was published early in the period when the expedition's fate was uncertain, and provided – until the present volume – the most complete portrait of his fellow officers. The Coninghams were his adoptive family; from the letters it seems that he and others were aware that his natural father was Sir James Gambier (1772–1844). William Battersby's *James Fitzjames: The Mystery Man of the Franklin Expedition* (2010) is the authoritative biography.

Lieutenant Henry Thomas Dundas Le Vesconte (b. 1813) Le Vesconte came from a large family, originally from the Channel Island of Jersey. He entered the Royal Navy in 1829, serving aboard HMS *Calliope* in the war with China; his later service included serving as second-in-command to James Fitzjames aboard HMS *Clio*. His father and sisters had already emigrated to Canada at the time of his sailing with Franklin, and his letters are preserved in the Archives of Newfoundland and Labrador (ANL).

Lieutenant James Walter Fairholme (b. 1821) Fairholme entered the Royal Navy in 1834, serving at the West India station and later in Africa. In 1839 he served with Fitzjames aboard HMS *Ganges*, after which he became part of the Niger Expedition under Captain Henry D. Trotter. He was promoted to lieutenant in 1842 and served on other vessels, most lately HMS *Excellent*, before joining the Franklin expedition on Fitzjames's recommendation.

Edward Couch, Mate (b. 1823)   Couch was born in Camberwell in 1823; he served aboard HMS *Excellent* with James Fitzjames and also saw action in the First Opium War. His father, Captain James Couch RN, was a veteran of Trafalgar and the inventor of the solid channels (chain-wales) which were a distinctive feature of ships strengthened for polar service.

James Reid, Ice Master (b. 1801)   Reid was born in Montrose, some forty miles south of Aberdeen; he was a veteran of numerous whaling and other voyages aboard Aberdeen-based ships. Along with Thomas Blanky aboard HMS *Terror*, Reid was engaged because the Admiralty had come to believe that an experienced ice pilot would be an asset to the expedition.

Stephen Samuel Stanley, Surgeon (year of birth unknown)   Stanley entered the Royal Navy as an assistant surgeon in 1838, and served aboard HMS *Cornwallis* with James Fitzjames; it was likely he who removed the bullet from a wound Fitzjames suffered during this period. His background and training are unclear, though it seems that he studied with Robert Knox (1791–1862) in Edinburgh, and for a time he worked as an assistant to Knox's associate Sir William Fergusson (1801–1877). Unbeknownst to his shipmates, he had married a woman named Mary Ann Windus scarcely ten days before the expedition sailed; her son from a previous marriage, Samuel Speight, later went by the name Stanley. Harry Goodsir's opinion of Stanley, originally high, went rapidly down as he became aware that Stanley's knowledge of natural history was in fact extremely limited (see, for example, Letter 65).

Harry Goodsir, Assistant Surgeon (b. 1819)   Harry (full name Henry Duncan Spens Goodsir) was one of a distinguished group of brothers whose father was John Goodsir, an Edinburgh-trained doctor in Anstruther, Fife. His brother John became a distinguished anatomist and pioneer in cell theory; his brother Joseph became an influential minister and theologian; his brother Robert was a surgeon and later participated in two search expeditions for Franklin; his youngest brother, Archibald ("Archie" in his letters), also qualified as a surgeon, though he died at a young age from tuberculosis. Harry was enormously active in the burgeoning field of natural history, most recently serving as the conservator of the museum at Surgeons' Hall in Edinburgh; the figures with whom he met in London while the expedition was being prepared are practically a Who's Who of natural science at the time. A skeleton was brought back from King William Island in the Arctic by Charles Francis Hall in 1870 and shipped to England; it was originally thought to be that of Le Vesconte; modern analysis has shown features, and isotopes in the teeth, that make it much more likely that this skeleton is Harry's.

Charles Hamilton Osmer, Purser (b. 1799)   Osmer entered the Royal Navy in 1819 as a clerk. He had previous Arctic service aboard HMS *Blossom* under Frederick Beechey to the coast of Alaska; according to Richard Cyriax (*The Last Arctic Expedition of Sir John Franklin*), he had subsequently served on the Canadian lakes.

Daniel Bryant, Sergeant of the Marines (b. 1814)   Bryant was born in the village of Shepton Montague in Somerset, and joined the Royal Marines as a private in 1828, making him the longest-serving of all the marines in the expedition. See Ralph Lloyd-Jones, "The Royal Marines on Franklin's last expedition," *Polar Record* 40 (215): 319–26 (2004).

John Gregory, Engineer (b. 1806)   Gregory was not a naval man but was appointed to the crew to be in charge of the engine installed in HMS *Erebus*. He had been employed by the firm of Maudslay, Sons & Field, a marine engineering company based in Lambeth that had been selected to handle the engines (see Appendix D). According to Admiralty records, "This Engineer was recommended by Messrs Maudslay to serve in the Vessels employed on the Arctic Expedition having been accustomed to locomotive engines his pay to be double of that allowed to 1st class Engineers"; an identical statement was recorded for his fellow engineer James Thompson (ADM 29/105). He was born in Salford, now part of Manchester, on 22 September 1806; his father, William, was a grocer on Chapel Street. Many of his descendants were also engineers, with the notable exception of his grandson Edward John Gregory (1850–1909), an acclaimed painter and member of the Royal Academy. In March of 2021, Gregory had the distinction of being the first crewmember identified by means of DNA evidence; see Douglas R. Stenton, Stephen Fratpietro, Anne Keenleyside, and Robert W. Park, "DNA identification of a sailor from the 1845 Franklin northwest passage expedition," *Polar Record* 57 (e14), 1–5. His remains were found at NgLj-3, a site on Erebus Bay where the Schwatka expedition had reburied bones they found nearby.

HMS *TERROR*

Captain Francis Rawdon Moira Crozier (b. 1796)   Crozier came from a protestant Anglo-Irish family in Banbridge, County Down, now Northern Ireland; his father, George, was a solicitor who worked with other established families in that area. His fifth son and eleventh child was named after Francis Rawdon, Earl of Moira, a well-known army officer and governor-general of India, who was born not far from Banbridge. Francis joined his first ship, HMS *Hamadryad*, in 1810, a few months shy of his fourteenth birthday, under the auspices of Sir Thomas Staines.

Crozier, who was known as "Frank" to friends and family, got his first taste of Arctic exploration when he joined HMS *Fury* as a midshipman (although having passed his exam as mate in 1817) in William Edward Parry's second Northwest Passage expedition from 1821 to 1823. During this expedition he met fellow midshipman James Clark Ross and the two men formed a lifelong friendship. Crozier also participated in Parry's third attempt for the Northwest Passage of 1824 in HMS *Hecla*. The expedition had to be abandoned in 1825 when HMS *Fury* was damaged beyond repair at Fury Beach on Somerset Island, prompting both crews to abandon the *Fury* and return home in *Hecla*.

In 1827 Crozier, now a lieutenant, again joined HMS *Hecla* under Parry, this time in the unsuccessful attempt to reach the geographic North Pole via Spitzbergen. During the absence of the higher-ranking officers, Crozier, who did not participate in Parry's and Ross's attempt to reach the pole by sledges and boats, temporarily held command of the *Hecla*. The expedition returned home in October 1827 for Crozier to learn that he had been elected a fellow of the Royal Astronomical Society thanks to his work on Parry's previous expeditions.

In 1839, now holding the rank of commander, Crozier again joined James Clark Ross for an expedition to Antarctica as second-in-command and captain of HMS *Terror*, a ship that had previously been in the Arctic under George Back. Ross captained HMS *Erebus*. As it was not possible to winter on the Antarctic mainland, they spent two winters in Hobart (then Hobart Town), establishing Rossbank Observatory and becoming friends with Sir John Franklin, who was at that time governor of Tasmania (then Van Diemen's Land). While there, Crozier fell unhappily in love with Sir John Franklin's niece Sophia Cracroft, who rejected his proposal. After the expedition's return in 1843, Crozier's scientific work during the Antarctic expedition and his expertise in terrestrial magnetism earned him another fellowship, this time of the Royal Society. In 1841 he had also been promoted to post-captain.

In 1844 Crozier and Edward Bird, another old shipmate from Parry's expeditions, served as best men at James Clark Ross's wedding with Ann Coulman. Later that year, without employment and still depressed by Sophy's rejection, Crozier decided to join family members and friends for a prolonged stay in Italy. It was there in Florence that the news reached him of the Franklin Expedition, which he officially joined in March 1845, again serving as second-in-command and captain of HMS *Terror*. When Sir John Franklin died on King William Island on 11 June 1847, Francis Crozier became senior officer and assumed the position of expedition leader. Along with most other members of the expedition, his trace vanished on 25 April 1848, after signing the only written record that has yet been found, the "Victory Point Note."

Michael Smith's *Captain Francis Crozier: Last Man Standing?* (2014; second edition as *Icebound in the Arctic: The Mystery of Captain Francis Crozier and the Franklin Expedition*, 2021) is the definitive biography.

Lieutenant John Irving (b. 1815) Irving was born in Edinburgh; his father was a childhood friend of Sir Walter Scott. He joined the Royal Navy in 1828 but left in 1837 to settle in New South Wales in Australia with his younger brother David. Their sheep farm proved unprofitable and Irving returned in 1843 and rejoined the navy. Frederick Schwatka, in his search for traces of Franklin in 1879, discovered a grave marked by a maths medal awarded to Irving; he brought the skeleton back with him, and it was subsequently interred at Edinburgh's Dean Cemetery. Irving's religious background made him an unusual figure; see Ralph Lloyd-Jones, "An evangelical Christian on Franklin's last expedition," *Polar Record* 33 (187): 327–32 (1997).

Thomas Blanky, Ice Master (b. 1800) Blanky (whose name was sometimes spelled Blenky) was born in Whitby. He first went to sea at the age of eleven, joining the Royal Navy in 1824 as a seaman aboard HMS *Griper* under George Francis Lyon as part of Edward Parry's Northwest Passage Expedition. He returned to serve under Parry on HMS *Hecla* on his North Pole attempt in 1827. In 1829 he signed up with Sir John and James Clark Ross for their private expedition aboard the *Victory* (1829–33), during which the ship had to be abandoned and the men made a difficult year-long trek overland to Barrow Strait, where they were rescued by a passing whaler. He was the most experienced Arctic veteran aboard either of Franklin's ships, with the exception only of Franklin himself.

Alexander McDonald, Assistant Surgeon (b. 1817)   McDonald was
born in Laurencekirk, Scotland, some thirty miles south of Aberdeen.
He studied medicine in Edinburgh, and became a licentiate of the Royal
College of Surgeons in 1838, later serving as surgeon on a number of
whaling vessels. His friendship with whaling captain William Penny
led to his involvement with Eenoolooapik, an Inuk from Baffin Island
whom Penny had brought back to Aberdeen; McDonald published a
book about him in 1841. Franklin apparently knew of this work, and
it may have played a role in McDonald's appointment as assistant surgeon aboard the Terror. See Ian Barrie, "Alexander M'Donald L.R.C.S.E.
(1817–c. 1848)," *Arctic* 62, 2 (June 2009): 239–40.

Alexander Wilson, Carpenter's Mate (b. 1818)   Wilson was born on
Lindisfarne, the "Holy Island," in Northumberland. He was apparently
previously acquainted with two other crew members, Able Seamen John
Handford and James Walker.

James Thompson, Engineer (b. 1810)   Thompson was born in Leeds,
and like his fellow engineer John Gregory (*see above*), had been recommended by his employers, Maudslay, Sons & Field, for service thanks to
his familiarity with railway engines.

Acknowledgments

Above all, the editors would like to thank the executors of the Roderic Fenwick-Owen Literary Estate for their generous support for the maps and for the volume as a whole; we feel honoured to be associated with his name and work, particularly his pioneering *The Fate of Franklin* (1978). We are also grateful to both Kenn Harper and Doug Wamsley for their wise counsel as well as their financial support, and for Doug's contribution of letters.

Numerous archives and archivists have been essential to our undertaking from the start; in particular we would like to thank: Neil Bettridge of the Derbyshire Record Office for his many kindnesses and for making key material readily available; Naomi Boneham of the Scott Polar Research Institute; Andy Carr of the State Library of New South Wales; Val Nelson of Jersey Heritage; Heather McNabb of the Musée McCord; Beatrice Okoro of the National Maritime Museum; and Melanie Tucker at the Archives of Newfoundland and Labrador.

We have also benefitted from the generous assistance of many other scholars and Franklin aficionados: Alexa Price, who located the James Reid letters at the State Library of New South Wales; Rick Burrows, Reid's descendant, who was enormously helpful in providing relevant family history; and Alison Alexander, Jane Franklin's biographer, who helped with the tricky bits in Jane's letters and with details of the couple's time in Tasmania. We are also grateful for: Matthew Betts's incomparable knowledge of Franklin's ships; Logan Zachary's innovative and persistent research on all things Franklin; Frank Michael Schuster's gifted research and insights; D.J. Holzhueter's research on the Hartnell family; Olga Kimmins's discovery of the third unattributed letter; and Alison Freebairn's incisive familiarity with the Goodsir papers. Kevin Paul McKenzie was also of great assistance with genealogical research on the family of Le Vesconte. Special thanks are due to Jonathan Moore of Parks Canada's Underwater Archaeology Team, which discovered, and has been working to excavate, the wrecks of the *Erebus* and *Terror*; his meticulous review of our manuscript was invaluable. We are also very much indebted to our editor, Jonathan Crago, who has offered his wise counsel and support throughout the many years of this long undertaking. Lastly, we are deeply grateful to Mike Tracy, one of Harry Goodsir's closest living relations; his insight into Harry's life, family, and career has been absolutely vital to this undertaking.

Notes and Sources

ABBREVIATIONS

ARCHIVAL SOURCES

AMS   Aberdeenshire Museums Service

ANL   Archives of Newfoundland and Labrador

BNA   British Newspaper Archive online

DRO   Derbyshire Record Office

DNB   Oxford Dictionary of National Biography

LA   Langney Archive, East Sussex (Private Collection, Mary Williamson)

MMC   McCord Museum, Montreal

NA   National Archives (UK) at Kew

NMM   National Maritime Museum, Greenwich

RGS   Royal Geographical Society

RSGS   Royal Scottish Geographical Society

SLNSW   State Library of New South Wales, Sydney

SPRI   Scott Polar Research Institute, Cambridge University

UT   Royal Society of Tasmania & University of Tasmania Library Special and Rare Materials Collection, Australia

PC   Other private collections (identified, if permission has been granted to do so)

PRINT SOURCES

BB   Benjamin Bell. *Lieutenant John Irving, R.N. of H.M.S. "Terror" in Sir John Franklin's Last Expedition to the Arctic Regions: A Memorial Sketch with Letters* (Edinburgh: David Douglas, 1881).

GM   George Mackaness, ed. *Some Private Correspondence of Sir John and Lady Jane Franklin, with an introduction, notes and commentary by*

George Mackaness (Tasmania 1837–45) (Sydney: George Mackaness, 1947).

MJR   M.J. Ross. *Polar Pioneers: John Ross and James Clark Ross* (Montreal · and Kingston: McGill-Queen's University Press, 1994).

FLM   Francis Leopold McClintock. *The Voyage of the 'Fox' in Arctic Seas*, 5th edition (London: John Murray, 1881).

CHAPTER ONE: ANTICIPATION

Letter 1   John Goodsir [father] to Harry Goodsir, 11 June 1844. RSGS ARC.4.3/2   These and all other Goodsir letters were originally kept in a bound album by Harry's sister, Jane Ross Goodsir; they have since been separated and moved into acid-free folders. "Mr. O" has not been identified. "Captain Ross" was Sir James Clark Ross (1800–1862), a successful naval officer and explorer of both the Arctic and Antarctic regions; he had just returned from Antarctica in September of 1843, and it was widely expected that he would command any upcoming polar expedition. "I know of no one save Admiral Durham to whom I can write": "Admiral Durham" was Sir Philip Charles Henderson Calderwood Durham (1763–1845), a noted naval commander also from Fife; as fate would have it, he died less than a year after this letter was written. "Drumrack, Kingsmuir, &c." were all homes in Goodsir's general area of practice in Fifeshire. "Mrs. Farmer" has not been identified. "Lady William Douglas" was Elizabeth Irvine (1798–1864), the wife of Lord William Douglas (1783–1859) of Grangemuir, Fifeshire; Lord Douglas served a number of terms as one of the Lords Commissioners of the Admiralty. Jane was Jane Ross Goodsir, Harry's sister (see above). "Trotter" was evidently a physician of whose practices the Goodsirs disapproved; there are references to both a "T. Trotter" and "C. Trotter" in the Goodsir letters; "C. Trotter" might possibly be Charles Y. Trotter, who received his diploma from the College of Surgeons in 1829. "John & Archie" were Harry's brothers John Goodsir (1814–1867), who became a distinguished anatomist and pioneer in cell theory, and Archibald Goodsir (1826–1848), who died of tuberculosis at the age of twenty-two (see Letter 183).

Letter 2   Robert Goodsir to Harry Goodsir [brother], 11 June 1844. RSGS ARC.4.3/2   "Forbes" was Edward Forbes (1815–1854), a botanist and marine biologist and mentor of Harry's; he was at the time professor of botany at King's College, London; see also Letters 20 & 38. "Mr. Cleghorn" was Hugh Francis Clarke Cleghorn (1820–1895), a classmate of Harry's at the University of Edinburgh who later became a botanist and a significant figure in forestry in India. "Professor Bell" was the eminent zoologist Thomas Bell (1792–1880); he and Harry were good friends, sharing an interest in crustacea; Harry sent him a large number of specimens.

Letter 3 Harry Goodsir, to John Goodsir [father], 11 June 1844 RSGS ARC.4.3/2 "Mr. Nasmyth" was Robert Nasmyth (1791–1870), a Scottish dental surgeon, considered by some the "father of Scottish dentistry"; he was a friend of Harry's father, and Harry's brother John worked as his apprentice. Among his innovations was the use of gold in dental fillings, a possibly significant fact because the skeleton brought back from the Arctic by Charles Francis Hall and now believed to be Harry's, has a gold filling in one tooth. Sir George Ballingal (1780–1855) was a prominent Edinburgh physician and professor of military surgery at the University of Edinburgh. "Dr. Gairdner" was John Gairdner (1790–1876), a prominent member and past president (1830–32) of the Royal College of Surgeons. For "Admiral Durham" see note to Letter 1. "Captain Nairne" was Captain Alexander Nairne (1785–1866). Nairne's naval career began in 1801; he retired sometime after 1824; by Harry's account he had at one point been a shipmate of Franklin's (see Letter 63). He spent the rest of his life as a director of various marine and shipping companies, and was said to "aid many young men in their pursuits of life, and not a few of those for whom he has obtained employment have been connected with Fife, his native county" (*Fifeshire Biography*). "Dr. Henderson" was William Henderson (1810–1872), physician and later chair of pathology at the Edinburgh Medical School. For "John Reekie" see note to Letter 50. "Bob" was Harry's brother Robert Goodsir (1824–1895), who later joined two search expeditions for his missing brother.

Letter 4 John Goodsir [father] to Harry Goodsir, 12 June 1844. RSGS ARC.4.3/2 "Sir Philip" was Admiral Durham (see note to Letter 1). For "Dr. Gairdner" see note to Letter 3. "Joseph" was Harry's brother Joseph Goodsir (1815–1893), a Scottish minister and theological writer; although the longest-lived of the brothers, he suffered later in life from periodic bouts of severe mental illness which necessitated his hospitalization; the last, from which he never recovered, came in 1881.

Letter 5 Joseph Goodsir to Harry Goodsir [brother], 12 June 1844. RSGS ARC.4.3/2 "Professor Jamieson" was Robert Jameson (1774–1854), an eminent naturalist, for fifty years Regius Professor of Natural History at the University of Edinburgh; he was one of Charles Darwin's more influential teachers. "Dr. Abercrombie" was John Abercrombie (1780–1844), a renowned doctor who held the post of Physician to the King for Scotland; he died very suddenly a little more than five months after this letter was written, on 14 November 1844.

Letter 6   John Goodsir [father] to Harry Goodsir, 14 June 1844. RSGS ARC.4.3/2 "Mr. Roughead" was William Roughead, who operated a shirt-making and hosiery shop then located at 24 Prince's Street in Edinburgh. "Mr. Scott" was William Scott (1788–1862), an old friend from Anstruther, who was a member of the London Stock Exchange; John hoped he could help Robert find a position. "Mr. Forman" has not been identified. "Mr. Lumsdaine" was probably James Lumsdaine (1783–1853), from Kilconquhar, Fife. "Mr. Urquhart [in] Newburn" was the Rev. Dr Alexander Urquhart, the minister of Newburn Church in Largo. For "Dr. H.," see note to Letter 3.

Letter 7   William Douglas to Harry Goodsir, 15 June 1844, enclosing copy letter Douglas to Thomas Hamilton 11 June 1844 (8a), and letter Hamilton to Douglas, 13 June 1844 (8b). RSGS ARC.4.3/2

Letter 8a   William Douglas to Thomas Hamilton, 11 June 1844 [enclosed with 7] RSGS ARC.4.3/2 "two letters which I have received this morning from the Messrs Goodsir"; these presumably included the "application" alluded to by Harry's father, John, at the start of Letter 6, along with a letter from Harry's brother John.

Letter 8b   Thomas Hamilton, to William Douglas, 13 June 1844 [enclosed with 7], RSGS ARC.4.3/2   This note was enclosed within Letter 7. Thomas Hamilton, 9th Earl of Haddington (1780–1858) was the First Lord of the Admiralty from 1841 to 1846. "Sir James Ross has married a wife": this was Ann Coulman (1817–1857); Ross's marriage was a possible factor in his declining the command of the Northwest Passage expedition; some sources say that he promised his new wife that he would stay close to home. She wrote a letter to Crozier in 1848 (Letter 178).

Letter 9   James Fitzjames to John Barrow Jr, 3 November 1844. RGS REG/LMS F 6   John Barrow Jr (1808–1898) was the second son of Sir John Barrow (see note to Letter 10); Fitzjames and he had met in the course of the China Wars and remained fast friends; the connection is often credited as a reason for Fitzjames's rapid rise in the ranks and his selection for the Franklin expedition. Barrow was at the time the head of the Admiralty Record Office. Fitzjames's brusque tone here, and reckless "plan" to simply "walk to the Pole" are clear evidence that he did not as yet appreciate the true hazards of the Arctic. "Captain Beaufort" was Sir Francis Beaufort (1774–1857), the hydrographer of the Navy. The Beaufort Sea is named for him, and the "Beaufort Scale" describing wind conditions at sea is still used today.

Letter 10 John Franklin to James Clark Ross, 24 December 1844. SPRI
248/316/16 "your confidential communication": apparently Ross had written
directly to Franklin to let him know that he intended to decline the command of
the new expedition for the Northwest Passage. Sir John Barrow (1764–1848)
held the influential position of Second Secretary to the Admiralty for many
years, and was the main force behind all the many Arctic and Antarctic expeditions of the period from 1818 to 1845. "Beaufort & Parry": for "Beaufort" see
note to Letter 9; Parry was Sir William Edward Parry (1790–1855), the most
experienced Arctic commander of his day; he participated in five expeditions,
and commanded four of them, between 1818 and 1826. "I shall certainly offer
myself for the Command of it": this, along with Franklin's earlier allusion to a
private communication with Ross, strongly suggests that it was Franklin himself, rather than anyone lobbying on his behalf, who sought the command; Ross
likely understood that Franklin would only have advanced his own claim if he
knew for certain that Ross planned to decline the post. "best wishes for the
Baby": this was the Rosses' newborn son, James Coulman Ross (1844–1916);
see also Letters 12 and 31.

Letter 11 Francis Crozier to James Clark Ross, 30 December 1844. SPRI
248/364/21 For "Captain Parry" see note to Letter 10. "I hesitate not a
moment to go second to Sir John Franklin": when read alongside Letter 10, this
strongly suggests that Ross, having already deferred to Franklin for the post,
was eager to arrange for his old second to serve under him. "Thot" was Crozier's
nickname for Ann Ross, *née* Coulman (1817–1857); she and James Clark Ross
had just married in 1843 (see Letter 8b).

Letter 12 Francis Crozier to James Clark Ross, 31 December 1844. SPRI
248/364/22 For "Captain Parry" see note to Letter 10. "Master James" was
the Rosses' infant son; see note to Letter 10. "Wilkes" was the American lieutenant Charles Wilkes (1798–1877), commander of the United States Exploring
Expedition to the south seas (1838–42) and in some ways a rival to James Clark
Ross; Crozier was wondering whether Wilkes's account of his voyage has
appeared in print (it had in fact been published earlier that year). "Colonel
Sabine" was Sir Edward Sabine (1788–1883); Crozier refers to him as "Colonel,"
a rank to which he had been promoted in 1841. Both Crozier and Sabine were
from established Anglo-Irish families. Early in his career, Sabine had also been
on two Arctic expeditions (under John Ross in 1818 and Edward Parry in 1819–
20), and he was a central figure in the quest for mapping, and understanding, the
earth's magnetism ("The Magnetic Crusade"). "Mr. Thomas" may have been
Henry Thomas, a magistrate in Glamorganshire (Lord Adare's home district as

an MP). "Lord Adare" was Edwin Richard Windham-Quin, 3rd Earl of Dunraven and Mount Earl, and Viscount Adare (1812–1871). He was a passionate amateur scientist with interests in astronomy, archaeology, and geology; in 1837 he was elected a Fellow of the Royal Geographical Society.

Letter 13   John Franklin to Jane Franklin, 31 December 1844. SPRI 248/303/83   For "Beaufort" see note to Letter 9; for "Barrow" see note to Letter 10. "Mr Copeland" was William Taylor Copeland (1797–1868), a British politician; he was the son of William Copeland, Josiah Spode's late partner in his eponymous pottery business. "Nairne" was William Edward Nairn (1812–1869), a public servant and politician, who emigrated to VDL in the same ship as the Franklins, arriving in 1837. He served in a number of government posts. "Spode" was Josiah Spode (1790–1858), a member of the Spode pottery family and naval veteran, who emigrated to Van Diemen's Land in 1821, and later became the supervisor of the convict system. "Montagu" was John Montagu (1797–1853), the colonial secretary in Van Diemen's Land from 1834 to 1842; having earned the enmity of the Franklins over a variety of issues, he was dismissed by Sir John in 1842, but on returning to London persuaded Lord Stanley (Edward Smith-Stanley, the 14th Earl of Derby (1799–1869) and then secretary of state for war and the colonies, to recall Franklin as governor. Stanley was three times prime minister of the United Kingdom. "Seymour," according to an earlier letter by Jane Franklin, was "a stupid, incapable young man" who was befriended by Montagu on the latter's return voyage to England (GM II 44). "The Reverend Mr Bawdler" has not been identified. "my dear Eleanor": this was Franklin's daughter, Eleanor Isabella Franklin (1824–1860); in 1849 she married John Philip Gell (see note to Letter 100). The "Archdeacon" was Fitzherbert Adams Marriott (1811–1890); see note to Letter 100.

Letter 14   James Fitzjames to John Barrow Jr, 2 January 1845 RGS REG/LMS F 6 Abraham Rose Bradford (1807–1884) was a naval surgeon who had seen service aboard convict ships headed to Van Diemen's Land; he later served aboard HMS *Resolute* when it was the flagship for Horatio Thomas Austin's 1850–51 Franklin search. "youngster": this was D'Arcy Edward Norcliffe Wynyard, a younger man for whom Fitzjames hoped to secure an appointment to the expedition. His bid was rejected, whereupon Fitzjames apparently helped find Wynyard a berth on HMS *Pandora*, aboard which he unfortunately died in March of 1849 at the age of eighteen. "Conway" was HMS *Conway*, aboard which Wynyard had served. "Mrs. Basil Hall" was a well-travelled woman of strong opinions; her letters were collected in 1931 under the title *The aristocratic journey: being the outspoken letters of Mrs. Basil Hall written during a fourteen months' in America 1827–1828.* "Charlewood" was Edward Philip Charlewood (1814–1894), whom

Fitzjames met early in his naval career, serving aboard HMS *Euphrates*. According to Fitzjames's biographer William Battersby, they became lifelong friends. "Zeno": this is a reference to the fourteenth-century Venetian navigators Nicolò and Antonio Zeno; letters published in 1558 by a descendant, Nicolò Zeno the Younger, claimed they had made a variety of new discoveries in the North Atlantic and the Arctic. Their "discoveries" match very imperfectly with existing land masses, and the letters are generally now believed to be forgeries. "Ross & Back": this would be James Clark Ross (see note to Letter 1) or possibly his uncle Sir John Ross, who explored the central Arctic together in 1829–33 aboard the *Victory*, and Sir George Back (1796–1878), a veteran of several Arctic expeditions, including Franklin's Coppermine Expedition (1819–22) and his own expedition aboard HMS *Terror* (1836–37). "the Fury is broken up": this was HMS *Fury*, which was heavily damaged and forced ashore by ice in 1825 at a place now known as Fury Beach; that Fitzjames would have even briefly entertained the notion that she was salvageable shows how little he understood the Arctic and ice at this time. "I am for North": this is the earliest instance of Fitzjames's oft-expressed view that a navigable passage lay to the north of Melville Island. "Bakalim": this word, which means "let's see" in Turkish, may have been picked up by Fitzjames during one of his visits to Constantinople (Istanbul) in 1832 and 1839. "a Master named Forster": a person of this name, aboard the same ship at an earlier date, was credited for his observations of the comet of 1821 (*Edinburgh Philosophical Journal* 7 (1822), 382). "Captain Bethune" was Charles Ramsay Drinkwater-Bethune (1802–1884), who commanded HMS *Conway* from 1836 to 1842, including service in the First China War; in 1846 he was among the founders of the Hakluyt Society. "Cornwallis" was HMS *Cornwallis*, aboard which Fitzjames himself had served. The "Campbells" were Henry Dundas Campbell (1798–1872) and his family. Campbell was a decorated soldier and later a colonial governor who had befriended Fitzjames early in his career, helping him secure an appointment as Midshipman in 1831.

Letter 15   James Fitzjames to John Barrow Jr, 4 January 1845 RGS REG/LMS F 6
Robert Jenner was a naval lieutenant who had most recently served aboard HMS *St Vincent* under Richard Freeman Rowley. For Captain Beaufort see note to Letter 9. For D'Arcy Wynyard, see note to Letter 14. "Mrs Hall's boy": this was evidently a son of the Mrs Basil Hall mentioned in Letter 14. "the Firebrand": HMS *Firebrand* was a wooden paddle-steamer commissioned in 1842.

Letter 16   John Franklin to James Clark Ross, 9 January 1845. SPRI 248/316/17 "your suggestion"; this implies that Ross had recommended Crozier as Franklin's second; see Letter 10 and notes. "having a Commander only in the 2nd ship": the Board of the Admiralty had apparently decided against such a plan, but it did appoint Fitzjames as commander under Franklin aboard *Erebus*; Franklin refers to this again in Letter 26, as well as in Letter 92, where – apparently forgetting his earlier view – he says, "the Admiralty have appointed a Commander unsolicited on my part to my ship." "two persons of that rank whom they have in their eye": one of these was surely Fitzjames; it is unclear who the other one was. "perhaps to put my age and Croziers together and fancy that it makes a somewhat heavy amount": there is a widely circulated story that, when Lord Haddington expressed concern about Franklin's age (which he thought was sixty) he was met with the reply, "No, my lord, I am only fifty-nine." The anecdote first appears in Sherard Osborn's 1860 biography and is repeated by Clements Markham in his, but its source is unclear; this appears to be the only reference by Franklin himself to any concerns about his age (Crozier was forty-eight). "a sister in Lincolnshire": this was probably Elizabeth "Betsey" Franklin (1777–1850); she had long been in ill health, and her death was noted by Jane in Letter 188 and Sophy in Letter 189 to John, both remarking that he would "not be surprised" to learn of it.

Letter 17   John Franklin to James Clark Ross, 17 January 1845. SPRI 248/316/17   This somewhat cryptic letter seems to allude to some "notes" about plans for the expedition prepared by Barrow senior that he wanted Franklin and Ross to read before their meeting with Lord Haddington. The involvement of John Barrow Jr in conveying them is a sign of his growing role here, less than a fortnight before his father's official retirement. Some time later, in a scrapbook now held by the UK National Archives in Kew, John Barrow Jr noted that he *himself* had written out the final draft of his father's letter of 27 December 1844 to be sent to Lord Haddington, and then had his father sign it. On the page preceding the letter, Barrow Jr wrote: "from the first commencement I have been deeply interested & much occupied in all that relates to this now painful subject."

Letter 18   James Fitzjames to John Barrow Jr, 19 January 1845. RGS REG/LMS F 6   Fitzjames here demonstrates both a passion for the historical weight of the search for the Passage, along with a strong appreciation of Sir John Barrow, who was on the brink of retirement on 27 January. He also shows his frustration with the pace of the process of appointments – particularly his own – and the lack of news.

Letter 19   Francis Crozier to James Clark Ross, 23 January 1845 SPRI MS 248/364/23   For "Thot" see note to Letter 11. For "Barrow" see note to Letter 10. "Smith of China" was Henry Smith (1804–1887), who had distinguished himself in the China War; he and "Mrs. Smith" (Anna, *née* Costigin) were married at the British Embassy in Switzerland the previous September, and were likely on their honeymoon. "The Grand Duke" was Leopold II, Grand Duke of Tuscany (1797–1870). "Richards": this was Charles Richards (d. 1844), who had served alongside Ross and Crozier under Parry; Richards Bay near Hecla and Fury Strait is named after him. "buisiness" is so spelled in the original. "old Bird" was Edward Joseph Bird (1798–1881), who had served under Ross in Antarctica; he commanded HMS *Investigator* under James Clark Ross on Ross's search for Franklin in 1848–49. "Sir William Parker" (1781–1866) was a distinguished naval commander; it was aboard his flagship HMS *Cornwallis* that the Treaty of Nanking was signed; a period print of the event shows both Le Vesconte and James Fitzjames to be present (see Battersby, *James Fitzjames: The Mystery Man of the Franklin Expedition*, 133–4). "Lord George Paulet": Admiral George Paulet (1803–1879) was a naval officer chiefly remembered for his five-month occupation of Hawaii in 1843. "librarian to the Grand Duke of Tuskany": in 1845, this would have been Giuseppe Canestrini (1807–1870), though he was not born in Sweden. For "Wilkes" see note to Letter 12. "Belfast Bazaar": bazaars were common in major Irish cities, often serving as fundraisers for good causes; they were most common around Christmas. "alabaster head": an image of this bust, which still exists, is in on page 170 of Michael Smith's *Icebound in the Arctic*. "Blackheath" was Ross's neighbourhood in South East London.

Letter 20 Edward Forbes to Harry Goodsir, 24 January 1845. RSGS ARC.4.3/2 The triangles – one opposite the header and the other above Forbes's signature – are drawn on the original letter; it was an important symbol to Forbes. He used it as the central sign of a fraternity, the "Universal Brotherhood of the Friends of the Truth," which he helped found in the late 1830s at the University of Edinburgh. The motto of the society was (in Greek) "wine, love, learning," symbolized by "an equilateral triangle, meaning: the wine was not excessive; the love was brotherly love; the learning was of a high order" (see Michael T. Tracy, "John Goodsir (1814–1867): A Scottish Anatomist and Pioneer of the Study of the Cell," Royal Society of Edinburgh biography at https://www.royalsoced.org.uk). The triangle also carried special symbolism for the endeavour of natural science, as the side of the naturalist's dredge formed a triangle as well; Forbes alluded to this in his "Song of the Dredge," penned for the 1839 meeting of the British Association. Its first stanza goes:

> Hurrah for the dredge, with its iron edge,
> And its mystical triangle.
> And its hided net with meshes set
> Odd fishes to entangle!

"Barrow is retiring from the Admiralty": Barrow did indeed retire on the twenty-seventh of that month, but his departure did not have the effect Forbes feared of altering plans for the expedition. "Stokes" and "Broderip": Charles Stokes FRS (1784–1853) was a London stockbroker who took a very active interest in natural history; he was good friends with Forbes. At the time this letter was written, he was working closely with James Clark Ross on the scientific appendices to Ross's narrative of his Antarctic expedition (published in 1847). William Broderip FRS (1789–1859) was a lawyer and an eminent naturalist. "Deshayes Conchology": the multi-volume compendium by Gérard Paul Deshayes (1795–1875) published in Paris between 1839 and 1857.

Letter 21   John Franklin to Thomas Hamilton, 24 January 1845. NA ADM 7/187 (4)   "the questions your Lordship did me the honor of putting to me this morning": this must have been the meeting anticipated in Letter 17. "that space between Cape Walker & Banks's land of Parry": this blank on the map was to be the one to which the Admiralty directed Franklin to proceed; see Appendix E on the proposed routes of the expedition. "the advantage of steam": while this shows that the plan to add steam engines to *Erebus* and *Terror* was well along, the actual advantage granted by them was modest; see Appendix D.

Letter 22   John Franklin to James Clark Ross, 31 January 1845. SPRI 248/316/20   Between Letter 17 and this letter, it would seem that, in the wake of his father's retirement, John Barrow Jr was becoming increasingly involved in some of the details relating to the expedition. "an engraving on the pedestal of the ships wintering … if this device of the ships be adopted, it must be instead of Sir John Barrows Coat of Arms": these details concern a silver candelabrum which was being commissioned as a retirement gift for Sir John Barrow; it was presented to him in late March of that year. See "TESTIMONIAL TO SIR JOHN BARROW, BART." in the *London Evening Standard*, 28 March 1845, 3. Parry, Franklin, James Clark Ross, and Sir George Back were listed at the head of the committee presenting it. The present whereabouts of the candelabrum is unknown.

Letter 23   James Fitzjames to John Barrow Jr, on or before 7 February 1845. RGS REG/LMS F 6   This letter can confidently be dated thanks to the fact that Franklin's new appointment on 7 February would presumably have reached Fitzjames fairly quickly. "Sir James Ross who has refused it": Fitzjames is correct on this point. "Captain Stokes" was John Lort Stokes (1811–1885); Lieutenant Graham Gore had served under Stokes aboard HMS *Beagle*; Stokes recommended him for a promotion on their return in 1843, but Gore was not given it; in Stokes's words, he was "compelled to seek it by a second voyage to the North Pole." (See Stokes's *Discoveries in Australia: With an Account of the*

Coasts and Rivers Explored … during the voyage of H.M.S. *Beagle*, London: T. and W. Boone, 1846 Vol. II, 527). "Parry's 1ˢᵗ expedition sailed on the 1ˢᵗ May": in these and other notations of date, Fitzjames seems not fully aware of the high variability of ice conditions regardless of date; as fate would have it, the Franklin expedition would not in fact reach this point until after 12 July. For "Charlewood" see note to Letter 14.

Letter 24 John Franklin to James Clark Ross, 8 February 1845. SPRI 248/316/21 This letter gives Franklin's own account of receiving the news that he was to command the expedition. "determined on writing to Crozier at once": Ross was now able to tell Crozier that he would be able to serve as Franklin's second.

Letter 25 Sir John Franklin to Isabella Cracroft [sister], 8 February 1845, SPRI 248/298/18-20 "Lord H" was Lord Haddington; see note to Letter 8b. "Jarman" was John James Jarman (1804–1874), a cabinetmaker in St Ives, Huntingdonshire, who among other specialties made cabinets for entomologists.

Letter 26 John Franklin to James Clark Ross, 10 February 1845. SPRI 248/316/22 "your father in law in a less dangerous state than you expected": this was Thomas Coulman (1781–1852), who evidently survived his bout of ill health. "promote Kendall": this was Franklin's old friend and fellow Arctic explorer Edward Nicholas Kendall (1800–1845), who was married to his niece Mary. Kendall had extensive Arctic service, beginning with Sir Edward Parry's expedition in 1824; after that he joined Franklin's second overland expedition of 1825–27, during which he discovered Wollaston Land. Franklin's mention of him may have been an effort to secure a better pension for his widow, as Kendall was quite ill and would in fact die two days after the date of this letter; see Franklin's Letter 169 to Mary Kendall and note. "being so near Hull": Hull was at the time one of the busiest ports of the whaling trade, which was rapidly expanding into the Arctic. "Ice Masters and leading men for both ships": it seems that it had already been decided that a pilot with Arctic experience would be appointed to each vessel. "Mr Innes of the Admiralty speaks well of the Purser": this was Charles Hamilton Osmer (see Letters 98, 103, 109, 111, 125, 136, 139, 145, and 173), who was indeed appointed purser. "Mr Griffin … is daily gaining strength": this was Henry John Griffin (1757–1852), Jane Franklin's father; see Letter 87 for Franklin's last letter to him. "the experience of the Masters of the Whalers for some years past": here Franklin is hoping that Ross might gather some intelligence on whaling vessels that have lately followed parts of his anticipated route; he is particularly interested in the area to the southwest of Cape Walker, toward which his instructions explicitly directed him.

Letter 27   James Fitzjames to John Barrow Jr, 11 February 1845. RGS REG/
LMS F 6 "Captain Curry" was Commander Douglas Curry; he had served
under Franklin aboard the *Rainbow* in the Mediterranean. Sir Thomas Herbert
(1793–1861) commanded HMS *Calliope* and other vessels during the China
War. "Mrs. Gee" was the wife of Richard Gee, the vicar of St Lawrence, Abbots
Langley, from 1844 to 1878; Mary Ann Jackson was her maiden name; Abbots
Langley is a village in Hertfordshire where Fitzjames spent many years with his
adopted family. HMS *Daphne* was the ship aboard which John Milbourne
Jackson (1819–1883) was then serving under John James Onslow; his service,
however uncomfortable, earned him a promotion to lieutenant while on board.
"Captain Kellett" was Sir Henry Kellett (1806–1875), who commanded HMS
Herald and later HMS *Resolute* in Belcher's Squadron as part of the Franklin
search. At the time of this letter, he was about to depart in command of HMS
Herald on a surveying expedition along the western coasts of South America.

Letter 28   James Fitzjames to John Barrow Jr, 12 February 1845. RGS REG/
LMS F 6 Hodgson was indeed selected for the expedition; Forster was not (for
him see note to Letter 14). "Bradford" was Abraham Rose Bradford (1807–
1884); he later served aboard HMS *Resolute* while she was in Austin's squadron
in 1850–51. "Actaeon": HMS *Actaeon* was a 26-gun sixth-rate frigate of the
Royal Navy which had returned to Plymouth from service in South America in
1842. "Euphrates Expedition": this was an expedition (1835–37) to test the
navigability of the Euphrates River; Fitzjames distinguished himself on it.
"Columbine": HMS *Columbine* was a sloop which accompanied the expedition
in the Mediterranean. "Francis Marten" had been promoted to lieutenant on
20 November 1844 hence described as "just made." The check marks next to
the names are in blue pencil. "Friday": since the 27th was a Wednesday, this
indication suggests that this portion or the portion just above was added on
Friday the 29th.

Letter 29   James Fitzjames to John Barrow Jr, probably 13 February 1845. RGS
REG/LMS F 6 The notation "Brighton Thursday Evening" is written at the bottom of this letter; the 13th of February was a Thursday and best matches the general
timeline of events; it may have been enclosed with Letter 28, which has the indication "Brighton Friday" near the bottom. "young Jackson" was Charles Keats
Jackson, with whom Fitzjames had served aboard HMS *Cornwallis* in the China
War. For Kellett see note to Letter 27. HMS *Dido* was a Royal Navy corvette.

Letter 30   Francis Crozier to James Clark Ross, 15 February 1845. SPRI
248/364/24 "Levinge" was Reginald Thomas John Levinge (1813–1848),
who like Crozier was from an Anglo-Irish background and who had apparently

lobbied for the post (see also Letter 31). In the end, although Franklin wrote of Levinge, "he can of course have him" (Letter 37), Crozier chose Little. Levinge, sadly, did not long outlive his would-be shipmates; he died aboard HMS *Penelope* on 24 April 1848, just one day before the amended Victory Point record was deposited on King William Island by Crozier and his officers.

Letter 31   Francis Crozier to James Clark Ross, 18 February 1845. SPRI 248/364/25   "Lord Haddington" was the First Lord of the Admiralty; see note to Letter 8b. "Sir George C." was Sir George Cockburn (1772–1853), at that time First Sea Lord; Cockburn Island at the tip of the Antarctic Peninsula was named for him by Ross. "I am of opinion Sir George C. will not approve of two captains being employed on that service Expense etc.": apparently, despite his being summoned to serve as Franklin's second, Crozier was still unsure whether or not the second vessel might yet be commanded by a commander on account of the cost. For Levinge, see note to Letter 30.

Letter 32   Harry Goodsir to John Goodsir [father], 18 February 1845, RSGS ARC.4.3/2   Harry here is concerned both with securing his title as "Naturalist" and with getting support for his appointment. "Professor Simpson" was James Young Simpson (1811–1870), an Edinburgh-trained physician best known as an obstetrician and later as an advocate for anæsthesia during labour and delivery. For "Admiral Durham" see note to Letter 1. The Earl of Haddington was the First Lord of the Admiralty; see note to Letter 8b.

Letter 33   Francis Crozier to Charlotte Crozier [sister], 19 February 1845. SPRI 1372/2   "Mr. Hill" was George Hill, the proprietor of Hill's Hotel in Charing Cross. "Henry" may have been John Henry Loftie (1808–1860), who had married Crozier's niece Jane in 1838. "the Parson" was Crozier's brother Graham Philip Crozier (1801–1872), whose parish was in Rathconnell, County Westmeath. For Levinge, see note to Letter 30.

Letter 34   James Fitzjames to John Barrow Jr, 20 February 1845. RGS REG/ LMS F 6   "Mr Dawson" was George Robert Dawson (1790–1856); he served as MP for Londonderry from 1815 to 1830. "John Boyd" was John McNeill Boyd (1812–1861), a childhood friend of Fitzjames's; they served together aboard the *St Vincent*. In 1861 Boyd was drowned while trying to rescue the survivors of wrecked ships off the pier at Dun Laoghaire; his impressive memorial at St. Patrick's Cathedral in Dublin is said to be haunted by the ghost of his faithful Newfoundland dog. Henry Thomas Dundas Le Vesconte's father, Henry Le Vesconte, served on HMS *Ville de Paris* for about six months in 1811 while Francis Beaufort was acting captain and commanding officer. Hodgson and Dès

Veaux were indeed appointed to the expedition, although Fitzjames's young friend Wynyard was disappointed (see note to Letter 14).

Letter 35   John Franklin to James Clark Ross, 21 [February] 1845. SPRI 248/316/19   The month is inferred from the context and the fact that 21 February was a Friday that year. "Beverley" was Charles James Beverly FRS (1788–1868), a naval surgeon and naturalist who had served under Parry on most of his Arctic expeditions; at the time of this letter he was the medical super-intendent of the Bethnal Green Lunatic Asylum. "Sir William Gage" was Sir William Hall Gage (1777–1864); he was at this time the Second Naval Lord. James Clark Ross named "Cape Gage" on Ross Island in the Antarctic after him.

Letter 36   John Franklin to John Richardson, 22 February 1845. DRO D8760/F/ FJR/1/1/90   Sir John Richardson (1787–1865) was a naturalist and explorer; he and Franklin were both members of the Coppermine Expedition of 1819–22, which ended in the deaths of eleven men out of the party of twenty and sugges-tions of cannibalism by one of the guides; Richardson also accompanied Franklin on his second Arctic land expedition (1825–27). They remained firm friends, and Richardson joined Dr John Rae in the very first search for Franklin's party in 1849. "accouchement": French term for childbirth, used here as a sort of euphemism. "I do not think we shall have room for any Naturalist": it makes sense for Richardson, himself a naturalist, to advocate for one; apparently Goodsir's lobbying had not yet borne fruit. In Letter 32 of 18 February, Goodsir tells his father he is: "very busy getting some certificates regarding my qualifica-tions as a Naturalist." "all you are doing for poor Mary Anne": this was Mary Anne Kendall, Franklin's niece and just now the ten days' widow of his old friend Edward Kendall (see note to Letter 26). Sir John Richardson would later arrange for her to stay in his home (see Letter 180 and note); the baby on whose birth Franklin was writing to congratulate the Richardsons was christened Edward Kendall Richardson. "Paine" has not been identified, but was appar-ently a family friend who was assisting Mary Anne; in Letter 169 of 12 July to her, Franklin writes: "you have a most judicious friend to advice you in Mr. Paine – I do not remember having met any person who seizes upon and acts with more promptness on the best points of a case."

Letter 37   John Franklin to James Clark Ross, 24 February 1845. SPRI 248/316/23   "a letter just received from him dated 15th February": in fact, this intelligence was already out of date; Crozier received Ross's letter of 6 February on 15 February and replied that he was "all ready" (Letter 30). For "Sir George Cockburn" see note to Letter 31. "1st Lieutenant of the Terror" ... "If he reaches Mr Levinge he can of course have him – Lieutenant Little is however quite ready to go if Crozier wishes to have him": for "Mr Levinge" see note to Letter 30; Crozier chose Little. For "Beverly" see note to Letter 35. "Lord Northampton" was Spencer Joshua Alwyne Compton, 2nd Marquess of Northampton (1790–1851); he was president of the Royal Society from 1838 to 1848. "Treakle Posset" was a hot beverage made with milk and molasses, thought to be efficacious for colds. "How did the young Hero bear the inoculation?": this was the Rosses' infant son James (see note to Letter 10); the "inoculation" was that for smallpox, which was widely given at the time; with the 1853 Vaccination Act, it became compulsory.

Letter 38   Edward Forbes to Harry Goodsir, 24 February 1845. RSGS ARC.4.3/2   Sir William Burnett (1779–1861) was the physician-general of the Navy and thus the final authority on any appointments.

Letter 39   John Irving to Catherine Irving [sister-in-law], 28 February 1845. BB   This and all of Irving's letters are reproduced from Benjamin Bell's book *Lieutenant John Irving, R.N. of H.M.S. "Terror" in Sir John Franklin's Last Expedition to the Arctic Regions: A Memorial Sketch with Letters* (Edinburgh: David Douglas, 1881); the whereabouts of the originals are unknown. Catherine Irving, *née* Cadell (1817–1890) came from a genteel family; she married John's brother "Lewie," the Rev. Lewis Irving (1806–1877) in 1840. It is apparent from the letters that she and John had become fast friends. The Irvings had six children; the fourth was named John after his uncle, and became the minister of the Free Church at Innellan.

Letter 40   John Franklin to John Richardson, 1 March 1845. PC Collection of Douglas W. Wamsley   For John Richardson, see note to Letter 36. "Mr Grant" was Thomas Tassell Grant FRS (1795–1859), who held the office of Storekeeper at the Royal Navy's Clarence Victualling Yard (rising to Comptroller of Victualling and Transport Services). A noted inventor, he developed the steam-powered machinery for making ship's biscuits and "Grant's patent fuel for steam boats," which was supplied to the Franklin expedition. He would have been in a position to attend to various prepared items supplied to the expedition. For "Sir William Burnet" see note to Letter 38. "Mary" was Richardson's wife (*née* Booth, she was Franklin's niece); the "Baby" was Edward Kendall Richardson (1845–1855), named after Edward Kendall (see note to Letter 26). Lieutenant Halkett" was Peter Halkett (1820–1885), the inventor of several types of inflatable boats made of rubberized cloth. One version was a cloak which could be inflated to become a boat. Several Halkett boats were sent with Franklin, as well as with subsequent search expeditions; James Fairholme describes a test of one in Letter 140, and Jane Franklin mentions another being sent with searchers in Letter 193.

Letter 41   Harry Goodsir, recipient unspecified, 13 March 1845. RSGS ARC.4.3/2   This was presumably written in response to an official communication from the Admiralty that he was to be appointed to the expedition.

Letter 42   James Reid to Ann Reid [wife], 22 March 1845. SLNSW MLDOC 446   Reid's wife was Ann Reid (*née* Walker) (1797–1871). "William" was William W. Reid (1826–1860), James and Ann's fourth son, who eventually died in transit at Calcutta, India. He says of William, who would have been about nineteen, that he wants to go to sea. By 1845 they had already lost Alexander (1821–1837) and David (1824–1839), who was lost at sea. "Mr. Enderby" was either Charles or George Enderby, grandsons of whaling merchant Samuel Enderby Jr (1719–1797), who at that time jointly operated the whaling firm of Enderby & Sons. "James" was Reid's son (1819–1857), who in 1850–51 served as second mate of the *Sophia* as part of the search for Franklin. "Mr. Ronald's sister" has not been identified. "my three Darulins": Reid's spelling here for "Darlings" – these were the Reids' youngest children, Ann (1833–1899), Mary (1835–1909), and Alexandrina (1838–1901).

Letter 43   Alexander McDonald to William Penny, 24 March 1845. SPRI 116/45/5   William Penny (1809–1892) was an experienced Arctic whaling captain under whom McDonald had sailed before; it was with Penny that he met the Inuk hunter Eenoolooapik, about whom he wrote a book, *A Narrative of some passages in the history of Eenoolooapik, a young Esquimaux ... An account of the discovery of Hogarth's Sound: Remarks on the northern whale fishery, etc.* (Edinburgh: Fraser & Co., 1841). "I have twice written to Mr Hogarth": this was William Hogarth (1804–1867), a merchant and shipowner in Aberdeen, whom McDonald believed owed him some back wages; he was later involved in providing and outfitting the Franklin search vessel *Prince Albert*; see Gillies Ross, *Hunters on the Track*, 19–20. "Mr George Davidson" was another Aberdeen ship owner, who in 1850 was a subscribing owner of the search vessel *Lady Franklin*. "Miss Kennedy" has not been identified.

Letter 44   James Reid to Ann Reid [wife], 26 March 1845. SLNSW MLDOC 446   "Anns most welcome Letter" must have been from his daughter Ann (see note to Letter 42), who would have been about twelve years old at the time. "St. Catreenes Dock" was St Katharine Docks on the Thames, then in active use as a port for ships. "Langester" is Reid's spelling of "Lancaster." "It is no use lying at home being allwise in measurie the thoughts of your leg and leaving the family is worse than the Voyage": "allwise in measurie" may be Reid's spelling of "always in misery." He seems to suggest that neither his sadness at leaving nor his worries about his wife's leg are reasons for him not to go on the voyage. "just

such ships as the Hecla but not Quite so Large": HMS *Hecla* (1815) was used by
Parry on four of his expeditions; like *Erebus* and *Terror*, she was a bomb ship,
of 375 tons burthen; *Erebus* was 372 tons and *Terror* was 325 tons, so Reid was
correct as to their relative size. "Mr. Enderby hase bean a good friend": see note
to Letter 42 for Reid's relationship to the Enderbys. "and Bring them <u>bagen</u>" –
this may be Reid's spelling of "begging" – i.e., if one were to stay at home and
not take employment at sea, one would bring one's family to begging. "Clark
might write me" – there were several ship's masters with this name.

Letter 45   James Fitzjames to John Barrow Jr, 27 March 1845 RGS REG/LMS F
6   For "Colonel Sabine," see note to Letter 12. Fitzjames's audacious plan for
returning overland via Siberia would seem to verge on the reckless; his proposed
route would have been roughly 9,350 km in length (5,850 miles). "Okhotsk,"
"Yakoutsk," "Irkoutsk," "Tomsk," and Tobolsk would have been Russian cities
on his route (Fitzjames's spelling accords with period maps). It would also have
been quite unprecedented for a senior officer to leave his ship before its return
to home port.

CHAPTER TWO: PREPARATION

letter 46   Francis Crozier to John Franklin, March or April 1845. PC Collection
of Douglas W. Wamsley   Sir John Hill (1774–1855) was the captain-super-
intendent of the dockyard at Deptford.

Letter 47   John Franklin to Jane Franklin, 1 April 1845. SPRI MS
248/303/85   The modern address for "40 Lower Brook Street" is now simply
"40 Brook Street"; see Map 1. The palatial Somerset House was at the time
home to the Navy Victualling Office. "Mr Phillot" was apparently Franklin's
physician; there was a practitioner, John Stephen Phillot, in Mortlake in 1844–
46. "the Drawing Room": this may be a reference to the Drawing Room at
Admiralty House, or possibly the Queen's drawing room at Buckingham Palace,
both places where the "squeeze" of society might well have been uncomfortable.
"the substitution in the news papers of my return from foreign service, for the
Government of VDL" – this apparently refers to the omission of some recognition
the Franklins had anticipated in the press. The last two paragraphs contain two
areas – roughly six in the first and fifteen in the second – of inked-over words that
cannot be recovered. "Mr Phillot has given me Quinine": Quinine was made
from the bark of the Cinchona tree and was used against malaria, as well as to
treat fevers generally; it remains an ingredient in modern "tonic" water. "Love to
Sophy": this was Franklin's niece Sophia Cracroft (1816–1892). A free spirit, she
twice rejected proposals of marriage from Francis Crozier, but found her calling

as the "constant companion" of Jane Franklin. Throughout the Franklin search era, Cracroft served as coordinator and gatekeeper for Lady Franklin's efforts; the two also travelled together extensively for many years, visiting such places as the eastern Mediterranean, Yosemite in California, Alaska, and Hawaii. After Jane's death, Sophy kept the flame, helping to ensure that her uncle's reputation was never dimmed in the public eye. Sir John wrote to her on 3 June 1845 (Letter 124), and she wrote several letters to him (Letters 189, 190, and 192).

Letter 48 John Franklin to Jane Franklin, 2 April 1845. SPRI 248/303/86 "Crozier & the Purser": presumably this was Osmer. "daily reminders from Parry": this was William Edward Parry (see note to Letter 10), who was in charge of obtaining and installing the engines (see Appendix D). For "Mr Phillot" see note to Letter 47. "Lady Ross" was Ann Ross; see note to Letter 8b. For "Mr Grant" see note to Letter 40. For Mary Richardson, see note to Letter 40; news of her death reached Franklin on 10 April (see Letter 58); "Lady Haddington" was Maria Parker (1781–1861), wife of Lord Haddington (see note to Letter 8b); "Mr Hope" was George William Hope (1808–1863), then undersecretary of state for the colonies, thus Lord Stanley's deputy. "William" has not been identified.

Letter 49 Henry T.D. Le Vesconte to Henry Le Vesconte [father], 2 April 1845. ANL "Captain Beaufort" was Sir Francis Beaufort; see note to Letter 9. For "Sir John Barrow" see note to Letter 10. William LeFeuvre 1799–1867 was a prosperous merchant and shipping agent from an old Jersey family. A prominent citizen of Southampton, Hampshire, he served there as a magistrate, sheriff in 1828, and three terms as mayor in 1824, 1835, and 1846. Prior to his departure in 1845, Henry Le Vesconte was engaged to William's nineteen-year-old daughter Henrietta Mansell LeFeuvre. Henrietta died in 1868 aged forty-one and is buried in the family vault in Southampton Old Cemetery with her father and other family members. "we take a transport to the edge of the ice": this is the first reference in the letters to the *Baretto Junior*, although almost no one referred to her by name.

Letter 50 Harry Goodsir to John Goodsir [father], 3 April 1845. RSGS ARC.4.3/2 "none of the Officers live in the hulk but in Lodgings on shore": there seem to have been exceptions to this, as with Le Vesconte, who as early as 2 April dates his letters from on board ship. "Dr. Kerr" may have been Dr James Kerr, (c. 1769–1848). "Bob Robertson" was a grocer in Anstruther; his son Robert (1867–1930) became a doctor and attended both Jane and Robert Goodsir in their final days.

Letter 51   Harry Goodsir to John Goodsir [brother], 3 April 1845. RSGS
ARC.4.3/2   "Bell, Yarrell, Falconer, Spence, Dr. Good, Forster": for Bell, see note
to Letter 2; William Yarrell (1784–1856) was an English zoologist and naturalist,
known for his History of British Fishes (1836); Hugh Falconer (1808–1865) was a
Scottish geologist, botanist, and palaeontologist; "Spence" was William Spence (c.
1783–1860), a British economist and entomologist; "Dr Good" has not been identified; "Forster" was Edward Forster the younger (1765–1849), an English banker
and botanist. "Cumming the Conchologist" was Hugh Cuming (1791–1865), a
noted collector who specialized in conchology. "Milne Edwards" was Henri Milne-
Edwards (1800–1885), an eminent French zoologist. "Kolliker" was Albert von
Kölliker (1817–1905), a Swiss anatomist. It can be inferred from this who's who of
natural history, zoology, and other related fields that Goodsir was seeking advice
from all of them in terms of what specimens to gather, and what areas of inquiry
they thought would be most valuable to undertake during the expedition.

Letter 52   James Fitzjames to John Barrow Jr, before 4 April 1845. RGS
ARC.4.3/2   The meeting of the Royal Society alluded to took place on 5 April,
thus the presumed date; in Letter 49 (2 April), Le Vesconte mentioned that the
engines were to be put in "next week." "Kelly of Conway" has not been identified, but was likely a man of that name aboard HMS Conway. For "Wynyard"
see note to Letter 14. For "Charlewood" see note to Letter 14. "Peter Barlow"
was Peter W. Barlow (1809–1885), an English civil engineer known for his work
on railways and bridges. He was indeed elected a member of the Royal Society
in November of 1845. "Becher" was Rear-Admiral Alexander Bridgeport Becher
(1796–1876); he served in the Hydrography Department under Sir Francis
Beaufort and was founding editor of The Nautical Magazine (where, years later,
Fitzjames's shipboard letters were to appear). Becher also instituted a system of
mapping ocean currents using bottles thrown from ships at sea; the Victory
Point Record is written on a form printed for this purpose.

Letter 53   Harry Goodsir to Jane Ross Goodsir [sister], 5 April 1845. RSGS
ARC.4.3/2   "The Queen it is said is going to pay us a visit on Tuesday, but
unfortunately I have not got my uniform yet!!": this visit appears not to have
occurred; there is no note of it either in the daily Court Circular or in Queen
Victoria's diaries. "Duprez as Arnold in William Tell": Gilbert Duprez (1806–
1896) was then appearing at Drury Lane in the role of Arnold in Rossini's
masterpiece, Guillaume Tell. Duprez was famed in his time for being the first to
sing a "high C" from his chest. Interest in his appearance was high and, although
Her Majesty did not visit the ships, she did go to Drury Lane to hear Duprez for
herself on 29 April.

Letter 54   John Franklin to James Fitzjames, 5 April 1845 NMM MRF/89   For
"Sir George Cockburn" see note to Letter 31. "Mr Miles" was Alfred Miles
(1796–1851), a long-serving naval assistant in the Hydrographic Department of
the Admiralty. "Hoar" was Edmund Hoar (b. 1821), whom Franklin wanted to
serve as his steward aboard *Erebus*; he is mentioned again in Letter 159. For
"Lord Haddington" see note to Letter 8b.

Letter 55   Henry T.D. Le Vesconte, to Sarah Le Vesconte [mother], 8 April
1845. ANL   "Miss Sarah Le Feuvre" (b. 1802) was a sister of William Le Feuvre;
"her niece" was Le Vesconte's intended, Henrietta (see note to Letter 49). Philip
was Le Vesconte's younger brother Dr Philip John Le Vesconte (1816–1894).
"Mrs John" was probably Mary, wife of Le Vesconte's maternal uncle John
Wills (1794–1878); at this time they were living at Waddon in Newton Abbot,
but both emigrated to Ontario in 1847. "Mary Kendell" has not been identified.
"aunt Betsy" was Le Vesconte's mother's sister Elizabeth Wills (1789–1847).
"William writes from Ipplepen a hurried scrawl": "William" was Le Vesconte's
uncle on his mother's side, William Wills (1804–1889); he emigrated to Australia
in 1853, where his son William John Wills (1834–1861) completed the first
north-south traverse of the continent; it ended tragically in a manner reminis-
cent of the Franklin expedition. "house and practice at Totnes": Totnes, where
Dr Wills's practice was apparently located, and Ipplepen are neighbouring towns
in Devonshire. "Mrs W": presumably this refers to William's wife, Sarah Wills,
née Calley (1800–1880). "Mr Nantes" was Lieutenant Richard Nantes (1792–
1871), who was married to Le Vesconte's mother's sister Anna Wills; in October
of 1844 he had received an appointment as one of the Military Knights of
Windsor, a sinecure for retired military officers which came with a pension and
an apartment – hence Le Vesconte's asking if Nantes has yet gone to Windsor.

Letter 56   Harry Goodsir to John Goodsir [father], 9 April 1845. RSGS
ARC.4.3/2   "Rickards" appears to have been a London merchant; there were
several firms of that name. "The Queen visits us on Tuesday next": no such visit
occurred; see note to Letter 53. For "Forbes" see note to Letter 2, and Letters 20
and 38. F: a pointing hand is drawn at this point in the letter. "Aunt Ann" was
Anna (Anne) Monro Taylor (1789–1864), Harry's maternal aunt, who resided
with her brother, the Reverend Anstruther Taylor, at Carnbee Manse, Fife (see
Letter 60). "Walkers" may be a reference" to Harry's cousins; Walker was his
grandmother's maiden name. "Traill" was probably Thomas Steward Traill
(1781–1862), a Scottish physician and zoologist; he was professor of medical
jurisprudence at the University of Edinburgh and later president of the Royal
College of Physicians.

Letter 57   Harry Goodsir to John Goodsir [brother], 11 April 1845. RSGS ARC.4.3/2 "John Christie" may have been the person of that name who owned a farm, Pitgorno, in Fifeshire; both he and John Goodsir were members of the Royal Highland and Agricultural Society, for which John provided veterinary examinations. "Dandy Dinmont" is a breed of terrier. "Taylor" was Richard Taylor (1781–1858), the editor of the *Annals and Magazine of Natural History*, to which Harry contributed several articles, including one that was still in preparation for the press; see note to Letter 129. For "Forbes," see note to Letter 2, and Letters 20 and 38.

Letter 58   John Franklin to John Richardson, 12 April 1845. SPRI 1503/30/8; DRO D8760/F/FJR/1/1 "the awful announcement" was of the death of Richardson's wife, Mary, who was also Franklin's niece; see note to Letter 40.

Letter 59   Harry Goodsir to John Goodsir [brother], 13 April 1845. RSGS ARC.4.3/2 "Gray" was John Edward Gray (1800–1875) an eminent British zoologist, and longtime Keeper of Zoology at the British Museum. He shared an interest in *mollusca* with Goodsir, and collaborated with John Richardson on the zoological supplement to James Clark Ross's account of his Antarctic voyage with *Erebus* and *Terror*, published in two volumes in 1844 and 1875. "Hookers Surgeon was mad": this seems to refer to Robert McCormick (1800–1890), the surgeon aboard HMS *Erebus* on Ross's Antarctic expedition on which Joseph Dalton Hooker served; McCormick fancied himself a naturalist and (by this report) may have regarded Hooker as a rival and sought to impede his work. For "Nasmyth" see note to Letter 3. "Wardrop" was Dr James Wardrop (1782–1869), author of the magisterial *On the nature and treatment of the diseases of the heart: With some new views of the physiology of the circulation* (1837). For "Forbes" see note to Letter 2. "Waterhouse" was probably the astronomer John Waterhouse (1806–1879). "Dalrymple" was probably Sir Adolphus John Dalrymple (1784–1866), a cousin of Sir John Ross who took a keen interest in Arctic exploration. "King (the letter man)" was likely Richard King, known for his polemical missives; see note to Letter 181. For "Kolliker" see note to Letter 51. For "Richard Taylor" see note to Letter 57. "Young" was Robert Young (1813–1858), a writer (clerk) and the owner of Milton Muir, a well-known farm in Anstruther Wester. The missing words near the end of this letter are due to a fragment of paper having been cut away. For "Falconer" see note to Letter 51.

Letter 60   Harry Goodsir to Anne Monro Taylor [aunt], 17 April 1845. RSGS ARC.4.3/2 "Each officer is required to have at least 2 pairs of each": the silver plate that was so troublesome for Harry to acquire illustrates an old tradition among naval officers, who were expected to equip their own mess. Harry, having never been in the position, had to scramble, while veteran officers already had what was needed. Franklin himself splurged on a large new set from a prestigious London silversmith. These utensils, curiously, have been among the most frequently recovered relics of the men; often they bear an officer's crest or initials on one side, and an ordinary seaman's scratched initials on the other – a sign that, at some point, they were distributed in hopes that they would carry a message in trade or acquisition. Of Harry's silverware, just two pieces – a silver table fork and a table spoon – have been the only items recovered.

Letter 61   James Fitzjames to John Barrow Jr, 17 April 1845. RGS REG/LMS F 6 "April 17, Thursday": the date added top right, is in a different hand. "Hungerford Market" was a public market near the banks of the Thames; it was demolished in 1860 to make way for Charing Cross Station. Fitzjames's directions would have taken Barrow to the old Charing Cross pier. "Steam Boats": paddle-wheel steamboats had been in service from around 1830 for Thames crossings. For "Captain Beaufort" see note to Letter 9. "I hope the Queen will come & see us" – such a visit was mentioned by Harry Goodsir as well (see Letters 53 and 56), but in the end did not take place. "his broad pendant": this is the regulation spelling, describing a personal pennant allotted to those with the rank of commodore, which would have been a promotion for Franklin.

Letter 62   John Irving to Catherine Irving [sister-in-law], 18 April 1845. BB "Captain Back" was Sir George Back (1796–1878), a veteran of several Arctic expeditions including Franklin's Coppermine Expedition (1819–22) and his own expedition aboard HMS *Terror* (1836–37).

Letter 63   Harry Goodsir to John Goodsir [brother], 21 April 1845. RSGS ARC.4.3/2   "David Forbes" (1828–1876) was the brother of Edward Forbes, and known as a mineralogist. For "Nasmyth" see note to Letter 3. For "Dalrymple" see note to Letter 59. "Gulliver" was George Gulliver (1804–1882), an English anatomist and physiologist. For "King" see notes to Letters 59 and 181. "Carpenter" was William Benjamin Carpenter (1813–1885), a noted zoologist. "Dr. Grant" was likely Robert Edmond Grant (1793–1874), a British zoologist and one of Darwin's mentors. For "Waterhouse" see note to Letter 59. The book in question was *Anatomical and Pathological Observations*, published in Edinburgh in 1845; John and Harry were credited as co-authors. "Dr. Wilson" was likely George Fergusson Wilson (1822–1902), a wealthy industrialist and amateur botanist. "Dr. Maclagan" was Sir Andrew Douglas Maclagan (1812–1900), a prominent Scottish surgeon and toxicologist. For "Kolliker" see note to

Letter 51. "Oken" was Lorenz Oken (1779–1851), an eminent German naturalist. "Siebold" was Philipp Franz Balthasar von Siebold (1796–1866), a well-
known German botanist. For "Richard Taylor" see note to Letter 57. "Owen &
Robert Brown": "Owen" was Sir Richard Owen (1804–1892), a noted naturalist, critic of Darwin, and coiner of the word "dinosaur." For "Robert Brown" see
note to Letter 127. For "Grey" see note to Letter 59. "Highland plaid, Mackenzie
tartan, directed to Frederick Hornbey": this was Frederick John Hornby, a Mate
aboard HMS *Terror*, with whom Harry had apparently formed a friendship; a
"plaid" would have been a rectangular length of tartan fabric, customarily worn
over the shoulder. For "Captain Nairne" see note to Letter 3. The presence of all
these eminent men of science in London at the time was due in part to a meeting
of the Royal Society on 5 April.

Letter 64   Henry T.D. Le Vesconte to Henry Le Vesconte [father], 2 May 1845.
ANL   For "William Le Feuvre" and "Henrietta" see note to Letter 49. "Madame
Adelaide" was Louise Marie Adélaïde Eugénie d'Orléans (1777–1846), the sister of the then King of France, Louis-Philippe I. "the Red Rover and water
witch": The *Red Rover* was a clipper ship built in 1829; the *Water Witch* was a
clipper built in 1831; both saw use in the opium trade and were likely familiar
to Le Vesconte from his service in China. "Aunt Judith" was Judith Ann Le
Feuvre (1790–1845), the older sister of Henrietta's father, William. "Maria
Kilroy" (1807/8–1892) was a close family friend and Judith Le Feuvre's goddaughter; her husband, Alexander Kilroy (1806–1872), was a surgeon in the
Royal Navy. In February of 1845 he was appointed to the convict ship *China*.
"Fairholme was on the Niger expedition," "The surgeon was in the Cornwallis":
Le Vesconte neatly states both men's acquaintance with Fitzjames, who lobbied
for their appointments. "Lord Forbes" was Walter Gammell Forbes, 18th Lord
Forbes (1798–1868), whose sister, Caroline Elizabeth Forbes (1793–1865),
married George Fairholme (1789–1846); Lieutenant Fairholme was their son."
"We have a queer fellow for an acting master": Le Vesconte, at least as far as the
letters testify, seems to have been in a distinct minority in not welcoming Reid's
presence. "Fitzjames wants to go through Siberia": this oft-expressed preference
of Fitzjames's is difficult to account for – a more impractical route of return is
hard to imagine; see note to Letter 45. "Captain Austin" was Sir Horatio Thomas
Austin (1800–1865): hitherto known for his circumnavigation of the Southern
Hemisphere in 1828–30, he would later play a key role in the search for Franklin,
commanding HMS *Resolute* in 1850–51. "the 79th sent to make discoveries in
the Polar seas": the exact source of Le Vesconte's figure is hard to determine,
though if one goes back to John Cabot in 1497, the number may approach this
figure. "Edmund," "Frederick," and "Mary" were the siblings of Le Vesconte's
intended fiancée (see note to Letter 49).

Letter 65   Harry Goodsir to John Goodsir [brother], 2 May 1845. RSGS
ARC.4.3/2   "Plaid & Silver spoons": the "Plaid" was apparently the one Harry
had requested for his friend Frederick Hornby (see note to Letter 63); the silver
spoons were to help him fill out the required set (see Letters 60 and 63). "Bob"
was Harry's brother Robert Goodsir (later in this same letter referred to as
"Robert"). For "Falconer" see note to Letter 51. For "Forbes" see note to Letter
2. For "Robert Brown" see note to Letter 127. For "George Wilson" see note to
Letter 63. "Peddie of the Terror is a Montrose man": it is not quite clear what
Harry meant by this; Peddie was, like himself, a graduate of the Royal College
of Surgeons. It may be worth noting that Montrose was the name of Scotland's
first lunatic asylum (so called at the time).

Letter 66   Harry Goodsir to John Goodsir [father], 6 May 1845. RSGS
ARC.4.3/2   For "Captain Nairne" see note to Letter 3. For "Young" see note to
Letter 59. For "William Scott" see note to Letter 6; Scott was Nairne's brother-
in-law. "Harris & Co" may have been the Scottish wine merchant Quarles,
Harris & Co.; it seems that Robert was seeking clerical employment there
(Harry later notes that "as a banker or a wine merchant he can never can expect
to rise above a Clerkship"). "The 1st. Lieutenant of the Erebus has got a dog":
this would have been Graham Gore; in his table in Letter 134. Fitzjames lists
"Lieutenant Gore and his black Labrador dog." "I have received the Plaid for
Hornby": see note to Letter 63. For "the Annals of Natural History" and
"Taylor" see note to Letter 57.

Letter 67   James Fitzjames to Elizabeth Coningham [sister-in-law], 10 May
1845. NMM MRF/89   "Shell who is with me": Shell appears to have been a
devoted and likely long-serving domestic attached to the Coninghams. "Parry"
was likely William Edward Parry; see note to Letter 10. For "Lord Haddington"
see note to Letter 8b; "Ross" would have been James Clark Ross (see note to
Letter 1); "Back" would have been Sir George Back (see note to Letter 14); John
Pelly (1777–1852) was the governor of the Hudson's Bay Company. "Barrow"
was Sir John Barrow (see note to Letter 10); Beaufort was Sir Francis Beaufort
(see note to Letter 9); Sabine was Edward Sabine (see note to Letter 12); "Sir
William Gage" was William Hall Gage (1777–1864), the second sea lord at the
time. "Icheboe" was Ichaboe, an island heavily covered with guano – to a depth
of seven meters! – off the coast of Namibia, which Fitzjames had visited in 1844,
in an effort to impose some order on the many groups trying to take advantage
of what was then a valuable commodity. He later referred to it as "the Father of
all Dung-Hills." Haddington's joke about "Caesar passing the Rubicon" was a
scatological *double entendre*. For "Lord Northampton" see note to Letter 37.
"Captain Hoskins" is Fitzjames's misspelling of the surname of James Hosken

(1798–1885), the captain of the *Great Britain*. "the children": Fitzjames was looking forward to a trip to see the ships the following day with a party that included the Coninghams' children. "The Colonel" would have been Edward Sabine; see note to Letter 12.

Letter 68   James Fitzjames to Elizabeth Coningham [sister-in-law], [11] May 1845, enclosing letters from Fanny and Maria Jane Campbell to James Fitzjames, both undated. NMM NRF/89 "little Fanny" was Eliza Frances Campbell (1833–1869), daughter of Fitzjames's friend Henry Dundas Campbell)see note to Letter 14). The letters appear to have been enclosed within a letter from the children's' mother (see Letter 67, where Fitzjames says "I have had a long letter from Mrs Campbell begging me to try & persuade you to go to Portsmouth, in which Missie joins"). "a letter written in a very extraordinary hand": this hints at the possibility that Elizabeth's older child, Elizabeth Meyrick Coningham (1841–1858), may have been its writer; the letter is missing.

Letter 68a   Fanny Campbell to James Fitzjames [enclosed with 68]   "when your poor toes are freezing with cold": Fanny seems here almost to conceive of the cold as a sharp reminder to Fitzjames to pay her a longer visit next time.

Letter 68b   Maria Jane Campbell to James Fitzjames [enclosed with 68]   This letter is by Fanny's sister Maria Jane Campbell (1832–1924). "Northend House" was the Campbells' residence in Portsmouth, which seems to have been associated with Henry's position as deputy-lieutenant for Hampshire. "Captain Fisher" has not been identified. "Missie's dog": Missie was apparently another sister of the two young girls, either Eliza (who would have been ten) or Harriet (who would have been sixteen); see note to Letter 68. "Mrs Gambier" was Hester Gambier, *née* Butler (1800–1885), the wife of Fitzjames's half-brother Robert Fitzgerald Gambier (1803–1885).

Letter 69   James Fitzjames to William Coningham [brother], [11] May 1845. NMM NRF/89 This letter is dated "Sunday 10th" but Sunday was the 11th; as the letter describes events planned for Sunday, it must have been written later that day. For "Shell" see note to Letter 67. Their visit to the "Great Britain" has additional possible significance, as a small medal commemorating that ship was found years later along with other relics of the expedition. "the children" refers to William and Elizabeth's children Elizabeth Meyrick Coningham (1841–1858), whom Fitzjames calls "Minney," and William John Capper Coningham (1843–1899), whom he often refers to as "my Godson." Their parents were in Antwerp, and the children were being cared for by the family's nurse, Sarah Pritchard. "Captain Hoskins": this again is Fitzjames's misspelling for "Hosken" (see note to Letter 67). "John B" was John Barrow, Jr (see note to Letter 9). "the commission": Fitzjames had been angling for a promotion to captain before sailing; in the end he received the promotion by gazette, dated 31 December 1845.

Letter 70   James Fitzjames to Elizabeth Coningham [sister-in-law], 12 May 1845 NMM NRF/89   "Minney" was Elizabeth's daughter Elizabeth Meyrick; see note to Letter 69. "Sarah" was Sarah Pritchard, the Coninghams' nurse (see note to Letter 69). "Hodgsons mother": this would have been Mary Hodgson, née Tucker (1778–1863), the mother of Lieutenant George Henry Hodgson, who served with Fitzjames on HMS *Cornwallis* and had been appointed to *Terror* at his recommendation. "your letter from Bruges": the Coninghams had apparently travelled there from Antwerp during the previous two days. "Sarah sends her love": this was family nurse Sarah Pritchard. "Old Shell has a new lease of his life": this phrase again suggests that "Shell" was a fellow servant of Sarah's, and one of long standing. "Excuse small paper": Fitzjames has had to use very small sheets, which necessitated cross-writing at the end.

Letter 71   James Reid to Ann Reid [wife], 13 May 1845. SLNSW MLDOC 446   The "King of Denmark" was a pub located at 24 Wapping High Street; its proprietor was listed as Robert Laws in *Pigot's Directory* for 1839. "British Linnin Company": this was an Edinburgh-based industrial corporation that by this time had become an active banking concern; it was later acquired by Barclays and ultimately sold to the Bank of Scotland in 1970. "£63 „ „ sore against my will": The Navy's practice of having the officers pay for their own mess was onerous to Reid, as it was to Goodsir (see Letter 60 and note). "Brinkly" was of course Thomas Blanky. "Mr. Finlason the Tailor": there was an Eric Finlason, "tailor and clothier," listed in the 1844 Aberdeen directory at 26 Marischal-street; he was apparently a bit too generous in giving credit, as by 1851 he had filed for bankruptcy. "Mr. Valentin[e] wase casten for the Scurvey in his Leges and the others for several things an the Black Ladi wase casten for his Leg having once Broken": Reid is using "casten" in the Scots sense, meaning "cast off or away"; these were late volunteers for the expedition who were rejected. Mr. Valentine was George Valentine of Dundee, who according to the muster book was discharged on 25 April 1845. The "Black Ladi": given the Scots use of "laddie" to mean a young man, he may have been a young Black sailor who was also rejected for service at this time. On Black sailors during this period, see Philip K. Allan's "Black Tars: The Role of Black Sailors in the Navy in the Age of Fighting Sail," on the Dawlish Chronicles site: https://dawlishchronicles.com

Letter 72   Harry Goodsir to John Goodsir [father], 13 May 1845 RSGS ARC.4.3/2   "the old House at Anstruther": this had indeed been listed for sale, as a "large and commodious DWELLINGHOUSE, and OFFICES attached, with the beautiful GARDEN in front, situated on the eminence to the North of the Town of Anstruther, belonging to, and long possessed by, Mr Goodsir, Surgeon" (*Fife Herald*, 21 March 1844), but was apparently taken off the market subsequently, of which decision Harry seems to have approved. "swinging the vessels": in order to account for minute variations of the compass due to metallic objects and fixtures aboard ship, the vessel was rotated through all eight major compass bearings, with observations of fixed objects calculated to determine the precise variation at each point. "Joseph would not part with Cæsar": Harry had previously suggested Cæsar as a ship's dog, but had written to withdraw the request after he found the *Erebus* already had a dog (see Letters 57, 66, and 134). "Granton Steamer": Granton was the main port area of Edinburgh on the Firth of Forth; steamers left from there twice a week. For "Mr. Scott" see note to Letter 6. For "Captain Nairne" see note to Letter 3. Sir William Burnett was the Physician-General of the Navy (see note to Letter 38). "the actual title of Naturalist": Harry had been very keen to have this title, but here seems willing to wait until his return, when a future appointment carrying it would likely have been made; see Letters 1, 2, 5, 6, 32, and 65.

Letter 73   James Fitzjames to John Barrow Jr, 14 May 1845. RGS REG/LMS F 6   "Chronology of North Polar Voyages": this was Sir John Barrow's *A chronological history of voyages into the Arctic regions; undertaken chiefly for the purpose of discovering a north-east, north-west, or polar passage between the Atlantic and Pacific* (London: John Murray, 1818). "Beechy's last book": this would have been Frederick William Beechey's *A Voyage of Discovery Towards the North Pole: Performed in His Majesty's Ships Dorothea and Trent, Under the Command of Captain David Buchan, R.N.; 1818* (London: R. Bentley, 1843).

Letter 74   James Fitzjames to William Coningham [brother], 14 May 1845 NMM MRF/89   "swinging the ship": this process, as Fitzjames explains, involved testing the compass at different parts of the ship to calculate any local deviation. "The Pictorial Times" was a short-lived (1843–48) rival to the *Illustrated London News*, whose own feature appeared on 26 May; its woodcut of Fitzjames's cabin is reproduced as Figure 1. "Captain Robert Gambier" (1791–1872) was Fitzjames's cousin on his father's side; "on purpose" suggests Fitzjames wished to emphasize this visit as a sign of his birth family's support for his new command. "Fitzgerald & a party": this was Robert Fitzgerald Gambier, Fitzjames's half-brother; see note to Letter 68. "the children's visit to the Dockyard": this was the visit described in Letter 70 to which Fitzjames refers. "Old Shell stood on the wharf": it seems from this description that he felt considerable sadness at what he (correctly) imagined would be his last parting from Fitzjames.

Letter 75   Henry T.D. Le Vesconte to Sarah Le Vesconte [mother], 15 May 1845. ANL   "a certain young very dear friend of mine": for this and "Henrietta" see note to Letter 49. "Mrs. Kendell" has not been identified. "by the Vesuvius": this was HMS *Vesuvius*, which had seen preliminary service from 1839–45 in the Mediterranean and Syria; her commander was Erasmus Ommaney (1814– 1904), who later commanded HMS *Assistance* as part of Captain Horatio Austin's search for Franklin in 1850–51. In March of 1845, Vesuvius was recommissioned and sailed for North America. "Messrs. Shewells" have not been identified, although there was a share-brokering firm of that name in London. "There is a man onboard sent down by Lady Franklin to take <u>all</u> our portraits": this was the camera operator for the firm of Richard Beard (see note to Letter 90). "Aunt Lily" has not been identified. "Cousin Nymphe" was Nymphe Prudente Le Vesconte (1819–1902), the daughter of Henry's uncle Phillip. "Mr. John Wills" was an unidentified relation on Henry's mother's side. "Mr. Rainier" has not been identified.

Letter 76   Henry T.D. Le Vesconte to Rose Le Vesconte [sister], 15 May 1845. ANL   A large number of Le Vesconte's family had already emigrated to Canada as of this time, his father and his sister Rose among them.

Letter 77   James Reid to Ann Reid [wife], 16 May 1845 SLNSW MLDOC 446   The loss of text in this letter is due to a thin strip having been torn off along one side of both leaves. The "Brig Flora" was a brigantine built by Alexander Hall in 1841 of 148 tons; she was reported by the *Dundee Courier* as having been wrecked in 1846 "on the coast of Patagonia." The mentioned "Parcel" evidently consisted of fabric for Ann to make a frock for their daughter Alexandrina, with the remaining cloth to be used if possible for the other daughters. "Mr. Bannerman & Mr. Adam of the [news]Paper": "Bannerman" was Sir Alexander Bannerman (1788–1864), a successful wine merchant in Aberdeen who also had investments in the whaling business; his visit to Reid is mentioned in a news clipping preserved with Reid's letters. "Mr. Adam" has not been identified. "Vouge": this may be a variant of the Scots word "Vaige" meaning "voyage," also extended to mean any sort of journey. "Murray th[e] Watch Maker" may have been James Murray (1780–1847), chronometer- and watch-maker, 1 Royal Exchange, London; one of his chronometers (no. 819) was taken by William Edward Parry on his Arctic expedition of 1824.

CHAPTER THREE: SAILING

Letter 78   John Irving to Catherine Irving [sister-in-law], 16 May 1845. BB "two days ago": Irving is incorrect; the ships left Woolwich and arrived at Greenhithe on the twelfth. "Our engine once ran somewhat faster on the Birmingham line": this is one of two references to a railway on which the engines previously ran; the other is Crozier's in Letter 172, where he places it on the "Dover line." Research by William Battersby and Peter Carney has shown that the more likely candidates were two engines from the London and Croydon line. See their "Equipping HM Ships Erebus and Terror, 1845," *International Journal for the History of Engineering and Technology* 81: 2 (July 2011), 192–211, as well as Appendix D. "Lewie" was Irving's brother Lewis (see note to Letter 39).

Letter 79   James Fitzjames to Horatio Austin, 16 May 1845. RGS REG/LMS F 6   Austin was Captain Horatio Thomas Austin (1800–1865); he had served on a scientific expedition to the South Pacific, and in 1850 would command a squadron of four vessels (*Resolute, Assistance, Pioneer,* and *Intrepid*) in search of Franklin.

Letter 80   James Fitzjames to William Coningham [brother], 16 May 1845 NMM MRF /89   "6000 cases of soup": this was the final delivery of Stephen Goldner's tinned food, which apparently was one factor among many that delayed the ships' departure. "Sir John w'ont sail on Sunday": Franklin's deep-felt religious view against working on Sundays is remarked at several points in these letters. "who takes us all with the Daguerreotype": this was the operator from Richard Beard's establishment (see note to Letter 90). "I have got a second for Elizabeth": Beard's operator took two portraits of each officer; in Fitzjames's case both survive. "He comes on board tomorrow": this suggests that there was a second day of photography. "2 more one for Fitzgerald & one for Mrs Campbell": these would have been Mary Campbell, wife of Fitzjames's friend Henry, and Robert Fitzgerald Gambier (see note to Letter 68). "All the Gambiers ... Gloucester also came from Dover" – this group included two half-brothers in addition to Fitzgerald: William Gambier (1802–1860) and Gloucester Gambier (1813–1872). "on purpose": the same phrase occurs in Letter 74, and here further underlines Fitzjames's sense of their support, which he mentions himself a few lines later: "I can have no doubt of their real feeling of regard for me." "Mrs. Norris" was William Gambier's twin sister, who married Richard Norris (b. 1795) in 1820. "the Board w'ont promote me" (see note to Letter 69).

Letter 81   James Fairholme to George Fairholme [father], 17 May 1845. DRO D3311 58   Fairholme mentions the monkey, which was named "Jacko," again in Letter 140: "The Doctor declares that Jacko is in a rapid consumption, & he certainly has a very bad cough, but the only other symptom I see of it, is the rapid consumption of everything eatable he can lay his paws on" (it may be noted here that monkeys, like humans, are susceptible to tuberculosis).

Letter 82   Francis Crozier to Charles Magee [brother-in-law], 17 May 1845. AMS   Charles Robert Magee was married to Crozier's youngest sister, Margaret, and had apparently been put in charge of Francis's finances while he was away. "Mrs. Crozier" has not been identified. "Mary Little" has not been identified. "Mae & Mrs" have not been identified. "Within an hours walk to Ross's during my Stay at Woolwich": James Clark Ross's home at Blackheath was within walking distance of the ships; it appears that Crozier was a frequent visitor. The Rosses removed to their country home prior to or just when the ships sailed; in Letter 172 Crozier writes: "I hope the little son is going on well, the mild weather of the interior must be to him beneficial. That Bleakheath was a scorching place."

Letter 83   James Fitzjames to Sir John Barrow, 17 May 1845. RGS REG/LMS F 6 This is one of several letters from Fitzjames excerpts of which were copied by Lady Franklin (SPRI 248/380); this first is to Sir John Barrow, while the rest – here as Letters 97, 104, 115, and 120 – were to his son John Barrow, Jr. "the rating of midshipman in the St Vincent": though he had joined the Navy in 1825, Fitzjames had been unable to secure a post as midshipman until he was appointed to the St Vincent in 1830. "appointed to Sir William Parker's Flag ship": This was HMS Cornwallis, aboard which Fitzjames served with distinction in the First Opium War; see note to Letter 19. "put in command of the Clio": it was then that Fitzjames achieved the rank of commander, a meteoric rise ensured by Barrow's support. "your glorious son John": this was John Barrow Jr; see note to Letter 9.

Letter 84   John Franklin to Isabella Cracroft [sister], 18 May 1845 SPRI 248/298/19 "soon be going to Hedingham": this was Hedingham Castle in Essex, the estate of Ashurst Majendie (1784–1867), husband of Jane Franklin's sister Frances (Fanny); he was a barrister, antiquary, and geologist.

Letter 85   James Fitzjames to John Barrow Jr, 18 May 1845 RGS REG/LMS F 6 "river pay": this was the customary pay for the period when ships were stationed on the Thames before sailing; the phrase "never expressed any dissatisfaction but much dis-appointment" suggests that the men may at first have believed that they might not receive their pay, but that they were never less than "satisfied" all the same. "a cast iron fever": this phrase only appears elsewhere in a few sea-narratives published at the same time; it seems to have been the naval equivalent of getting one's knickers in a twist. "If you were to send me my Captains commission": this is a roundabout way of saying that he would rather have his present post than any speedier prospect of promotion without it. "Lord Haddington or Captain Hamilton": Lord Haddington was at this time the First Lord of the Admiralty; Captain William Alexander Baillie-Hamilton was the Second Lord; the two had visited *Erebus* and *Terror* together on 9 May 1845 ("Naval Intelligence," *London Evening Standard*, 10 May 1845, 1). Hamilton's name – as "W.A.B. Hamilton" – was prominently affixed to the later notices advertising a reward for any intelligence about Franklin's ships. "qui que ce soit": French for "anybody." "Petro Paulovski": this is Petropavlovsk, in Russia, one of the expedition's potential ports of call after completing the passage – also mentioned by Fairholme and McDonald (see note to Letter 162).

Letter 86   Harry Goodsir to John Goodsir [brother], 18 May 1845. RSGS ARC.4.3/2   "thro the Bulls eye": i.e., water was leaking around the circular glass "Preston Patent Illuminator" in his cabin ceiling. "Newport" was George Newport (1803–1854), a noted entomologist and Fellow of the Royal Society. "Thompson of Belfast" was William Thomson (1805–1852), an eminent Irish naturalist. "those of the Sydenham": this is a reference to the Sydenham Society, which from 1844–57 issued annual volumes of current medical and scientific work. "Edmonston has got the one for the Californian Coast": "Edmonston" was the gifted young botanist Thomas Edmonston (1825–1846), who served as naturalist aboard HMS *Herald*, which was sent to the Galapagos and then to survey the western coasts of North America under the command of Henry Kellett; Edmonston died early on the Galapos expedition, killed by the accidental discharge of a firearm near the coast of Ecuador. Kellett later undertook three voyages as part of the search for Franklin. For "Forbes" see note to Letter 2. "Van Hoorst" was probably John Van Voorst (1804–1898), an English publisher who specialized in books of natural history; he brought out Robert Goodsir's memoir of his search for his brother in the Arctic in 1850. "Davy" was probably Edmund Davy (1785–1857), a chemist and member of the Royal Society; "a desperately outspoken obstreperous fellow, but goodhearted": many of Davy's contemporaries remarked on his admixture of restless energy and kindheartedness (DNB). "I hope Robert did not send Cæsar": this was one of the dogs Goodsir had intended for the *Erebus* before he realized there was already a ship's dog. "I gave it t[o] Stanley t[o] be put into the Post": this is the first reference in the letters to Owen Stanley (1811–1850); he had served aboard HMS *Terror* in 1836 under George Back, and was in command of the steamer HMS *Blazer*, which was, with the *Rattler*, one of the steamers sent to tow *Erebus* and *Terror* as far as Stromness; one of Stanley's regular tasks was to bring any mail ashore at the next port.

Letter 87   John Franklin to John Griffin [father-in-law], 18 May 1845. SPRI MS
248/307; LA /19/10   For Griffin see note to Letter 26. The copy letter in LA has
a separate note attached to it in Jane Franklin's hand: "The last letter written by
Sir John before he sailed. Copied out by Lady F."

Letter 88   James Fitzjames to William Coningham [brother], 18 May 1845
NMM MRF/89   "The men were paid their money yesterday": this was the men's
"river pay," to cover work prior to sailing; Fitzjames also mentions it in Letter
85; the exact nature of the mix-up is unclear. "The Rattler": this was HMS
Rattler, one of the first Royal Navy ships to be equipped with a screw propeller.
"a small steamer for the Transport": this was the *Monkey*, a paddle-wheel
steamer. "'Baretto Junior'": this vessel, often referred to in these letters simply as
"the Transport," was engaged to carry extra stores and supplies as far as
Greenland, where they were to be stowed aboard *Erebus* and *Terror*.

Letter 89   James Fitzjames to John Barrow Jr, n.d. (before 19 May) RGS REG/
LMS F 6   "Admiralty Bibles": according to R.J. Cyriax, it was at Sir John
Franklin's request that the Admiralty supplied one hundred Bibles (along with
Prayer Books and Testaments) to the expedition; he also notes that, due to
"friends and various societies," more than enough of these were donated, and so
the Admiralty ones were not needed (Cyriax, *Sir John Franklin's Last Arctic
Expedition*, 44).

Letter 90   Harry Goodsir to Jane Ross Goodsir [sister], 19 May 1845. RSGS
ARC.4.3/2   The Bishop of Norwich would have been Edward Stanley (1779–
1849), who was also at that time the president of the Linnean Society, the leading organization of natural historians, and thus someone Harry would have
been eager to meet with. Harry's disclosure that "our Surgeon who is a humbug
had been stuffing the Right Reverend with all sorts of nonsense" further highlights Harry's rapidly diminishing opinion of him, which went from positive –
"a very excellent fellow" (Letter 50) to "a would be great man" (Letter 65), and
finally to "a little better than Trotter" (Letter 138). "Lady Franklin has sent
down a Talbotypist to take the portraits of all the Officers of the Erebus": this
is a reference to the photographer from the firm of Richard Beard (1801–1885),
but the process used was that of the daguerreotype. The mistake may seem
unusual, but Harry would not necessarily have been able to tell the process by
looking at the camera; the Talbotype process, developed by William Henry Fox
Talbot (1800–1877), was far more common in Scotland, and Harry himself had
previously sat for one. In addition to the officers of the *Erebus*, Crozier alone of
the *Terror* was photographed. "You may get all or any of the likenesses to purchase": although the daguerreotype process produced a one-off metal plate, it

could be copied by the same process, or (more commonly) using Talbot's, which produced a copy on paper (this must have been the practice, as, according to Reid, Beard's offered to send a copy to his wife "by Post free of expence," see Letter 121). A set of these paper copies, which preserve an image of the since-lost daguerreotype of Crozier, is in the Derbyshire Record Office, and may have been the property of Sophia Cracroft. "a sketch of the Gun room": on most ships of the Royal Navy, the "gun room" was a space set aside for the junior officers' mess; the senior officers (lieutenant and above) had a separate mess room known as the "ward room," while warrant officers had a third, smaller mess. Aboard both *Erebus* and *Terror*, presumably for reasons of space – and to allow for hatches to be added above the engine room – the gun room and the ward room had been combined into a single space. In Letter 143, Goodsir remarks: "The Officers mess consists of 12," which confirms that the two messes had likewise been merged. At times, their duties may have separated them; in Letter 119 Goodsir mentions that the "Gun Room Officers" specifically had been invited to dine aboard the *Rattler*.

Letter 91   Harry Goodsir to Joseph Goodsir [brother], 19 May 1845 RSGS ARC.4.3/2   "General Assembly": this was the General Assembly of the Church of Scotland, which met at the time at Victoria Hall at the top of the Royal Mile in Edinburgh; the meetings took – and take – place in May. As a minister, Joseph would have been expected to attend. "your catechism": this was Joseph's *Sacramental Catechism*, which was published in 1845 in Edinburgh by Myles Machphaill.

Letter 92   John Franklin to Dr Adam Turnbull, 19 May 1845. UT RS 18/7   This letter was first published in GM; at that time (1947) the original was in the possession of one Dr Clifford Craig of Launceston, but its present whereabouts is unknown. There is a typewritten copy in the Royal Society of Tasmania & University of Tasmania Library Special and Rare Materials Collection, Australia (UT); words underlined in this copy are italicized in GM; we have generally followed the UT text, which likely better reflects the original. Adam Turnbull (1803–1891) was an Edinburgh-trained physician as well as a minister; he emigrated to Tasmania in 1825. During Franklin's term as lieutenant governor (1837–43), he filled several different government positions, ultimately finding himself in the unenviable position of middleman between Franklin and Montagu. Apparently, from the warm tone of this and other letters, Franklin felt Turnbull had discharged his duties well. "most opportunely": this is the UT text; GM has "opportunitely." For "Montagu" and "Stanley" see note to Letter 13. "the Pamphlet" was *Narrative of Some Passages in the History of Van Diemen's Land During the Last Three Years of Sir John Franklin's Administration of its*

Government, which had been prepared by Sir John in order to rebut the implied slight of his having been recalled from the lieutenant-governorship of Van Diemen's Land by Lord Stanley. It's actually a fairly substantial booklet of 157 pages; it was, as indicated on the title page, "not published" but intended only for private circulation. A partial copy of the page proofs, with the rest in manuscript, was brought on board by Sir John, and this he circulated among his officers, noting with satisfaction their generally positive reviews (see Letters 152 and 159). It was republished by Platypus Publications in Hobart, Tasmania, in 1967 and can now be had via Google Books. For "Mr. Hope" see note to Letter 48. "Mr. Aislabie" was William John Aislabie (1805–1876), a minister involved in "the Coverdale case": this was a situation arising when the district medical officer, Dr Coverdale, was reported to have refused to attend a man who had been run over by a cart. Montagu claimed the doctor had not justified his actions and dismissed him; this led to a petition by local residents for his reinstatement. Lady Franklin, who was friends with Coverdale, persuaded Sir John to reinstate him; this led to a final rift between Franklin and Montagu. "Sir James Graham" (1792–1861) held several posts in government including first lord of the Admiralty (1830–34 and again in 1852–55); "Graham Land" in Antarctica is named after him. "a Commander unsolicited on my part": this was Fitzjames; see note to Letter 16. "my dearest wife my child and niece assembled with the crew": these were of course Jane, Eleanor, and Sophy; their visit is also mentioned by Franklin in Letter 84, Fairholme in Letter 81, and Goodsir in Letter 90. "my personal desire": this follows the UT text; GM reads "my fervent desire."

Letter 93   James Reid to Ann Reid [wife], 19 May 1845. SLNSW MLDOC 446   "Lady Franklin hase ordered all the officers Likeness to bee taken": this is a reference to Beard's daguerreotypes; see note to Letter 90. For "Finlason the Tailor" see note to Letter 71. "David Leys is not Quartermaster": David Leys (b. 1808) joined HMS *Terror* as an able seaman. He was apparently known to Reid and his wife, Ann; Leys was from Montrose, near Ann's home town of Dun, and James and Ann were married in Montrose. Reid mentions him again in Letter 161.

Letter 94   Harry Goodsir to Anne Monro Taylor [aunt], 19 May 1845 RSGS ARC.4.3/2   For "Captain Nairne" see note to Letter 3; for Mr. Scott see note to Letter 6. For "Grangemuir Family" and "Lord William" see note to Letter 1. "Robert Macadam" was apparently a close friend of the Goodsirs; Robert inscribed to him a copy of his book, *An Arctic Voyage to Baffin's Bay and Lancaster Sound in Search of Friends with Sir John Franklin*, which came up for auction in 2017. "Wakifeild" has not been identified.

Letter 95 Harry Goodsir to John Goodsir [father], 19 May 1845 RSGS ARC.4.3/2 "the Surgeon of a Greenland Ship" has not been identified. "Shoemaker Dowie" was Archibald Dowie of Fife (d. 1883). "Dr. Lankester Golden Square" was Edward Lankester, who was elected a fellow of the Royal Society in December of that year. For "Mr. Scott" see note to Letter 6; for "Captain Nairne" see note to Letter 3.

Letter 96 James Fitzjames to Elizabeth Coningham [sister-in-law], 19 May 1845 NMM MRF/89 "Mrs. Norris" was Wilhelmina Gambier (see note to Letter 80); her daughter, the "agreeable girl of about eighteen," was Jemima Norris (c. 1826-1883). "Mrs. F. Gambier" was Hester Gambier; see note to Letter 68b.

CHAPTER FOUR: LONDON TO STROMNESS (MAY–JUNE 1845)

Letter 97 James Fitzjames to John Barrow Jr, 20 May 1845. RGS REG/LMS F 6 "the Nore": this is a prominent sandbank at just the point where the Thames reaches the North Sea; ships might have to wait here if the tide or winds were unfavourable. "off Harwich": Harwich, in Essex, would have been a logical next stop. "Stanley has come off in a cutter": Owen Stanley was the captain of the *Blazer*; see note to Letter 86. "wishes [for] a sight of Cape Farew[ell]": the southernmost point of Greenland, and thus the first to come into view – see Map 4.

Letter 98 Charles Osmer to Eliza Osmer [wife], probably 23 May 1845. (copy) SPRI 248/449/1–2 These and all others of Osmer's letters are from a copy in another hand; they were not copied out in chronological order, and how many of them may have been separate – or serial – letters is unknown. They are treated here largely as separate. Eliza Osmer, *née* Eliza Butt Scott (1819–1894) was recorded as attending the dedication of the Franklin memorial at Westminster Abbey in 1874. "Aldborough": this was the period spelling for Aldeburgh on the Suffolk coast.

Letter 99 John Franklin to the Reverend Philip Gell, 23 May 1845. DRO D3311 32 1 Philip Gell (1783–1870) was the father of John Philip Gell (see note to Letter 100). "indisposition from Influenza, and by the death of my much esteemed niece Mrs Richardson": see Letters 48 and 58. "the College": see note to Letter 100. "1st Warden": see note to Letter 100. "should the Expedition prove successful this Season we may hope to reach England again in 18 months, but if we have to winter we must be about three years": this is one of the very few occasions on which Franklin himself ventured an estimate; he seems to have given the shortest – and the longest – possibilities.

Letter 100   John Franklin to John Philip Gell, 23 May 1845. DRO D3311 32 3
"Gell" was the Reverend John Philip Gell (1816–1898), to whom Franklin's
daughter Eleanor was engaged. He was still out in VDL at that time. Franklin
had requested a well-qualified person to be headmaster of the planned college in
VDL, and Thomas Arnold (1795–1842), headmaster of Rugby (whom Franklin
already knew), sent out Reverend Gell in 1840. There he met Eleanor Franklin.
Both John and Jane Franklin approved of the match. For "Lord Stanley" see
note to Letter 13. "College": the Franklins continued to lobby for such an institution, but little further progress was made in its establishment for some time.
"Dayman" was Lieutenant Joseph Dayman RN, a skilled nautical surveyor; as
part of James Clark Ross's Antarctic expedition, he was stationed at the
Rossbank Observatory in VDL; later in his career he made soundings for the
laying of the North Atlantic cable. The "Bishop" was Francis Russell Nixon
(1803–1879), the first Anglican bishop of Tasmania, who arrived in 1843,
shortly before the Franklins left. Letters written by Nixon's wife show the couple
were sympathetic to the Franklins; he later attended Jane Franklin's funeral. "to
be placed entirely under the Bishop" and "independent of the Government":
rivalries between Nixon and the government of VDL, as well as between him
and certain branches of the church there, led him and Franklin to urge this
course. The college, known as "Christ's College," opened its doors in 1846, but
its remote location and financial problems led to its closure just ten years later.
In 1879 it re-opened as a secondary school, but closed again in 1892. It finally
re-opened on a limited scale in 1911, but it was not until it received substantial
government support in 1926 that it really took form; in 1933 it became part of
the University of Tasmania. Its first functioning "Warden" – the position Franklin
had hoped Gell would fill – was appointed in 1929. Two of its current buildings
bear familiar names: Gell and Nixon. "providing you saw any immediate prospect of the College succeeding": Gell foresaw the financial problems the college
would face, and returned to England. He and Franklin's daughter Eleanor were
married on 7 June 1849 (see Jane's note to Letter 185 and Letter 186). "Marriott"
(referred to in other letters as "the Archdeacon") was Fitzherbert Adams
Marriott (1811–1890), a friend and ally of Nixon; he arrived in VDL in 1843.
He was back in England at this time to try to shore up Nixon's claim for authority over the chaplains in the Convict Department at VDL. For "Parry" see note
to Letter 10. "the Bishop of Norwich" was Edward Stanley, also a noted naturalist; see note to Letter 90. The "Arch Bishop of Dublin" would have been Daniel
Murray (1768–1852). "Mr Arnold" could not have been Thomas Arnold, since
he had died three years earlier, but may be a reference to his son Matthew
Arnold (1822–1888), who had recently graduated from Oxford and was teach-
ing at Rugby in 1845. "Sir Robert Peel" (1788–1852) was at the time prime
minister. "Sir Eardley" was Sir John Eardley-Wilmot, who succeeded Franklin as

lieutenant–governor; see note to Letter 116. For "Mr Hope" see note to Letter 48. "Lathrope Murray" was Robert Lathrop Murray (1777–1850), a convict and later journalist in VDL who loudly supported Franklin's critics. "Grace Darling's memorable Exploit" was her rescue of survivors from the wreck of the *Forfarshire* in 1838, for which she was awarded the Silver Medal for Bravery by the Royal National Institution for the Preservation of Life from Shipwreck. "I have written to your Father": this is in very small letters, and refers to Letter 99.

Letter 101 Harry Goodsir to John Goodsir [father], 23 May 1845 RSGS ARC.4.3/2 "Let me know what you have done about Cæsar": see note to Letter 72.

Letter 102 Daniel Bryant to Mary Ann Bryant [wife], 25 May 1845. PC This letter was preserved by Daniel's family, and a photostat – the only known copy – was shared with us by his descendant Julie Shaw. "Anne" was Ann Bryant, *née* Mary Ann Oxford (1810–1881). "Herridge" is Bryant's spelling of Harwich. "the 17th Chapter of the first Book of Kings": this is the story of how Elijah kept a widow in the city of Zaraphath alive; following God's instructions, the widow used the flour ("meal" in the King James version) from her barrel and the oil from her jug, and they never ran out. "please to excuse": this phrase, repeated twice in the postscript (which ends by going up the right side of the final leaf of the letter), seems to be an apology for a hastily written letter. The bottom line of the letter, marked by [...] is illegible in the photostat.

Letter 103 Charles Osmer to Eliza Osmer [wife], 29 May 1845. (copy) SPRI 248/449/1–2 "Stromness": Osmer must mean he is *en route* to Stromness, as in his letter the next day (Letter 109) the ships were still only off Peterhead. "hope to be in England in August 1846": this wish, expressed again later in the letter, puts Osmer among the officers' most optimistic voices.

Letter 104 James Fitzjames to John Barrow Jr, 29 May 1845 RGS REG/LMS F 6 "Stanley just found in Blazer": the ships periodically lost sight of their companion vessels; see details in Franklin's despatches in Appendix C. "Cromarty" is a small port in the Highlands area of Scotland. "Peterhead" is a port in Aberdeenshire, then home to a whaling fleet that included many that sailed to the Arctic. "Buchan Ness" is a point with a lighthouse near Peterhead.

Letter 105 James Fairholme to George Fairholme [father], 29 May–1 June 1845. DRO D3311 58 "William" was probably James's older brother William Fairholme (1819–1868), who apparently had expressed a desire to join the expedition. "We were very fortunate in getting a good steward only 2 days before we sailed": on 22 March, James Reid had remarked that they had "no servant, we must find one." For whatever reason, the position of steward was often one of the last filled; Crozier replaced his previous steward with Thomas Jopson only a few days before sailing as well (see Letter 128: "I am happy to say I am most comfortably fixed with my old Servant – the one I had found was too smart for me and I am delighted I got rid of him as I am induced to think he would have been a troublesome fellow if not a great rogue – The one I have knows me and that is a great matter on a voyage of this kind.")

Letter 106   Francis Crozier to Charlotte Crozier [sister], 29 May 1845. SPRI 1372/3   Fortfield refers to Fortfield Lodge in Dublin, the residence of Crozier's brother William Crozier.

Letter 107   James Fitzjames to William Coningham, [brother], 29 May 1845 NMM MRF/89   "This goes in to Aberdeen … by the Blazer": the steamers, which often had to return to port to stock up on coal, served as informal mail packets for the expedition. "a few fathoms of hawser": this was even mentioned by other writers; though a (perhaps unavoidable) hazard of screw propulsion, such accidents seem not to have caused substantial damage. "determined to go this way": upon leaving the Thames, the ships had two possible routes – one up the east coast, one back around Cornwall – and greatly preferred the former. "my new Goddaughter which the Charlewood's have got": this was Annie Sophie Charlewood (1844–1900), the daughter of Fitzjames's great friend. "I think I cleared Shell": this again implies that Shell was a servant, and perhaps also that Fitzjames had specifically engaged him for additional services.

Letter 108   James Fitzjames to William Coningham, [brother], 29 May–2 June 1845 NMM MRF/89   "like the little ships one sees in a very blue sea in musical clocks"; Fitzjames makes the same comparison in Letter 112, where he illustrated the ships, here reproduced as Figure 3. "The Blazer brought orders to go round by the Lizard": this was Lizard Point in Cornwall (see note to Letter 112). For "Propeller Smith" see note to Letter 112. "Beechey's voyage towards the North Pole": this was *A voyage of discovery towards the North Pole: performed in His Majesty's ships Dorothea and Trent, under the command of Captain David Buchan, R.N.; 1818* (London: Richard Bentley, 1843). "Captain Flinders" was Matthew Flinders (1774–1814), Franklin's uncle, who was the first to circumnavigate Australia. "another forest springs up consisting of a different species of tree": Fitzjames overstates the case, but the phenomenon was remarked upon in nineteenth-century sources; see "Forest Fires," *House of Representatives Miscellaneous Documents 1881–1882*, pp. 226–7. "Stanley" was Owen Stanley (see note to Letter 86). "O'Callaghan's friend" has not been identified; George

William Douglas O'Callaghan (1811–1900) was the new commander of HMS *Vesuvius*, which had just returned from the Mediterranean under Erasmus Ommaney (1814–1904), who later commanded HMS *Assistance* as part of the search for Franklin. "young East" has not been identified. "the Hague" appears to have been the Coninghams' last stop before Bruges. "w'ont move or shew themselves seeing that it is the Sabbath": Scots Presbyterians were strict in their observance of the Sabbath. For "his daughter just born" see note to Letter 107.

Letter 109   Charles Osmer to Eliza Osmer [wife], 30 May 1845. (copy) SPRI 248/449/1–2

Letter 110   Harry Goodsir to John Goodsir [father], 31 May 1845 RSGS ARC.4.3/2   "Buchan Ness" is a point with a lighthouse near Peterhead. "a paper about the General Assembly": this was the annual May meeting of the Church of Scotland which Joseph was to have attended. "not be in my power ... to write as I intended to Uncle Anstruther": but he did, on 2 July; see Letter 143.

Letter 111   Charles Osmer to Eliza Osmer [wife], 31 May 1845. (copy) SPRI 248/449/1–2   "fully occupied in purchasing Oxen": the *Barretto Junior* had originally carried eighteen; Fitzjames in Letter 115 noted that "4 bullocks having died we want to fill up their stalls": this were presumably the number Osmer was sent to obtain. In the end, only three survived the crossing to Greenland (see Letter 158). "Sir John being too strict in his observance of the Sabbath": his observance was noted by many of his contemporaries, but it was personal only – unlike the "Sabbatarians" of this period, he did not necessarily forbid *others* to do their work on that day.

Letter 112   James Fitzjames to John Barrow Jr, 31 May 1845. RGS REG/LMS F 6   "divers notes from me written in a hurry": these are likely the short letters – numbers 97, 104, and 120 in this collection. "round by the Lizard": Lizard Point in Cornwall, known for bad weather and adverse currents, would have been on the expedition's route had the ships sailed up the western coasts of Britain. "Inshallah!" literally "if Allah wills it": the phrase was a more common one in English in the 1840s than today, and was used interchangeably with "God willing." "we were like little ships in musical clocks that bob up & down in a very solid green sea": Fitzjames illustrated the ships' pitching on the page; it is here reproduced as Figure 3. "Captain Smith" was Commander George Woodberry Smith (1799–1854), the captain of HMS *Rattler*; there has in the past been some confusion as to his identity, as he relieved the *Rattler*'s regular captain, Commander Henry Smith (1797–1854), for the duration of this voyage only. "Bryant" was William Bryant (1792–1851), the captain of the *Monkey*.

"Propeller Smith" was Sir Francis Petit Smith (1808–1874), the inventor of an early screw propeller, and an advocate for it to supplant the paddle-wheel in driving steam ships.

Letter 113   James Fitzjames to Elizabeth Coningham [sister-in-law], 31 May 1845 NMM MRF/89   "Bruges": this appears to have been the last stop on the Coninghams' tour before they headed back toward home, presumably by way of Calais. "the old Terror pitches so much we call her our friend & pitcher" (see note to Letter 115). For "Beechys North Polar Voyage" see note to Letter 108.

Letter 114   James Thompson to Charles Thompson [brother], 1 June 1845. NMM AGC/T/7(2)   "Nore Light": this was a lightship on the Nore, a sandbank near the mouth of the Thames; the same location is referenced by Fitzjames in Letter 97. "Harwick" is Harwich; "Alborough" is Aldbrough; like his fellow engineer John Gregory, Thompson's spelling is indifferent and often phonetic. "Stoarm Ness" is Stromness. This and other correspondence at the National Maritime Museum indicate the family's roots in Leeds, where Thompson's parents and his brother Charles still lived. "Mother January," "Bob & Beard likewise Bienham": these names have not been identified.

Letter 115   James Fitzjames to John Barrow Jr, 1 June 1845. RGS REG/LMS F 6 "Prince Albert's kiss": this is accompanied by a small sketch – the substantial side-whiskers of Prince Albert were well known at the time. Jane made her own version of the sketch in her copy; both are here reproduced in Figure 5. "Massey's log" was a patented device which, towed behind a ship, gave an indication of its speed by means of a brass rotator and recorder. "Sabbath strictly": thus no opportunity to acquire new livestock. Osmer, who was the one sent to obtain the bullocks, added that Franklin himself was "too strict in his observance of the Sabbath for any duty to be done on that day." "4 bullocks having died": fourteen of these animals were originally brought, but only three were to survive the full journey to Greenland. "a dissolute island" – thus written: Fitzjames probably meant "desolate"; the confusion of the two words is common enough to be noted in the OED (dissolute def. 6). "a rotten old Fox": Fitzjames is referring to his magnetic dipping-circle; he refers to it as "rotten" again in Letter 130. "Kellett": apparently the better "Fox" had been sent off with Captain Henry Kellett, who left England at nearly the same time for a survey of the Galapagos Islands and the western coasts of the Americas; see note to Letter 27. "Panama on Speck": Panama was another of the ports at which the expedition, if successful, might have received letters; "on Speck" is Fitzjames's spelling of "on spec." "Stanley calls the Terror his friend and pitcher": his friend, because the ships travelled in company, and "pitcher" because she pitched about so much. He gave that same title to a sketch of the "Terror" under tow, dated 30 May 1845; the phrase likely came to mind thanks to a comic song "My Friend and Pitcher," part of William Shield's and John O'Keefe's comic opera *The Poor Soldier* (1785), which was often featured in other productions in the years following, including one in London in 1838:

> My friend so rare, my girl so fair!
> With such, what mortal can be richer?
> Give me but these, a fig for care!
> With my sweet girl, my friend and pitcher.

Letter 116   John Franklin to Jane Franklin, 1–3 June 1845. LA/19/12   "proceed down Channel": this would have been the alternative course (referred to as "round by the Lizard" by Fitzjames in Letter 112). "Captain Stanley" was Owen Stanley, the captain of the *Blazer* (see note to Letter 86). "Farr Islands": Franklin means the Farne Islands off the coast of Northumberland. "Mr Smith" was Sir Francis Petit Smith (see note to Letter 112). For "the Pamphlet" see note to Letter 92. For "Dayman" see note to Letter 100. "Sir E. Wilmot" was Sir John Eardley-Wilmot (1783–1847), who succeeded Franklin as lieutenant-governor. Although Franklin was not to know it, Wilmot fared even worse than his predecessor, being ignominiously recalled for no specified reason in April of 1846; the event affected him so much that it contributed to his decline and death early in 1847 (see Letter 180 for Eleanor's account of this). For "Mr Nixon" see note to Letter 100. "old Bedford" was William Bedford (1781–1852), an Anglican clergyman who arrived in Hobart in 1823, to serve in St David's Church and proved to be a thorn in nearly everyone's side; his refusal to recognize Bishop Nixon's authority led to a protracted quarrel. "Edward Bedford" (1809–1876) was William's son; he did his medical training in London and eventually became one of Hobart's most successful doctors. "Fry" was Henry Phibbs Fry (1807?–1874), an Anglican clergyman who arrived in VDL in 1839. He mainly served in the Hobart churches of All Saints and St George's; he and Nixon did not get along. "Gregson" was Thomas Gregson (1796–1874), who arrived in VDL as a free settler in 1821. He enjoyed politics and was a bit of a loose cannon, but he was hospitable and cheerful, and the Franklins liked him, often visiting his home. "Gunn" was Ronald Campbell Gunn (1808–1881), a botanist and public servant. He arrived in VDL in 1830 and held various positions in the public service, including as Franklin's private secretary. When the Franklins left, Gunn was in charge of Jane Franklin's land in VDL, which was probably why he was writing about buying more land there. "Captain Smith" was George W. Smith, captain of the *Rattler* (see note to Letter 112). For "Mr Hope" see note to Letter 48. "Captain Washington" was John Washington (1800–1863), a naval officer; he was one of the original members of the Royal Geographical Society, and later succeeded his friend

Beaufort as hydrographer of the Navy. "Simpkinson" was Sir John Augustus Francis Simpkinson (1780–1851), who was married to Jane Franklin's sister Mary (1793–1854). "Sabine Brown Parry Richardson Ross": see Letters 126, 127, and 154; Franklin's surviving letters to Parry and Richardson are later than this one (Letter 150 of 7 July to Richardson, and Letter 157 of 10 July to Parry). "Elliot" may have been Sir Henry George Elliot (1817–1907); he had accompanied the Franklins to VDL as an aide-de-camp to Sir John, returning to England in 1840 to take up a post in the Foreign Office. As Alfons Korn notes in *The Victorian Visitors*, Elliot and Sophy Cracroft had "conducted a pleasant but perfectly casual flirtation" via a series of letters. "Lord Bloomfield" would have been Benjamin Bloomfield, 1st Baron Bloomfield (1768–1846); his son John Arthur Douglas Bloomfield (1802–1879) was at the time British minister to Russia.

Letter 117   Alexander Wilson to Sarah Wilson [wife], 1–2 June 1845. PC Wilson Family   This was Sarah Wilson, *née* Rear; no details known, but she may have been the individual of that name listed in the 1851 census, who was born in 1819 in Tynemouth. "Heaton" has not been identified. "Handford" was John Handford, an able seaman also aboard *Terror*; Handford was listed as from Sunderland; Wilson was from Holy Island; "Walker" was James Walker, another able seaman, from South Shields. It seems that these men had known one another prior to sailing; one possible explanation is that Wilson's marriage to his wife, Sarah, took place in 1839 in Bishopwearmouth, which is in Sunderland, a fact that suggests they may have made their home there. "Mrs Meirifield and Mr Tolpin and Edward and also ... Elisabeth and Ann ... Spraggon ... elisabeth and Isabella": these have not been identified.

Letter 118   John Irving to Catherine Irving [sister-in-law], 2 June 1845. BB   "The third steamer" was HMS *Monkey*; after losing her anchor and forty feet of cable in a gale on 22 May she went into Harwich for repairs; it was apparently decided that she was not in fit shape to continue. See the *London Evening Standard* for 24 May 1845.

Letter 119   Harry Goodsir to John Goodsir [brother], 2 June 1845. RSGS ARC.4.3/2   "Gun Room Officers": the junior officers, whose mess was usually in the "gun room" forward of the senior officers' wardroom; aboard *Erebus* and *Terror* these rooms were combined (see note to Letter 90). "Chambers" was Robert J.B. Chambers (1810–1875), the surgeon aboard HMS *Rattler*. "Crowner" has not been identified. "Baillie Robertson": in Scotland, "Baillie" was an honorific for a town magistrate; this may have been John Robertson, the proprietor of a livestock insurance firm in Stromness, who served as a town magistrate there. "a nephew of Lord Forbes": see note to Letter 64.

CHAPTER FIVE: STROMNESS TO GREENLAND

LETTER 120   James Fitzjames to John Barrow Jr, 3 June 1845. RGS REG/LMS F 6   "More postage to pay for I have no <u>heads</u>": "heads" was at the time a colloquial term for postage stamps, particularly penny stamps (OED "head," 4c); Fitzjames had also mentioned his lack of stamps in Letter 115. This addendum was apparently given to one of the steamers to return via the post; it is written on three narrow leaves of a different dimension than the main part of the letter. Letters delivered without stamps required that the recipient pay the postage due. "on speck," i.e., on speculation, more commonly spelled "on spec"; Fitzjames uses the same phrase in Letters 115 and 131.

Letter 121   James Reid to Ann Reid [wife], 3 June 1845. SLNSW MLDOC 446 Reid's persistent checking on whether his "Likeness" has been received seems to bely his earlier sense of sitting for it reluctantly (see Letter 93). "Aunty Edger" has not been identified.

Letter 122   John Franklin to James Clark Ross, 3 June 1845. SPRI 248/316/24

Letter 123   John Franklin to Eleanor Franklin [daughter], 3 June 1845. DRO   The "him who is so dear" was John Philip Gell (see note to Letter 100). For "Captain Smith" note to Letter 112; for "Captain Stanley" see note to Letter 86; they were in command of the two steamers.

Letter 124   John Franklin to Sophia Cracroft [sister], 3 June 1845. MMC P242/A.08   "Mr Lacys safe arrival": this was Thomas S. Lacy, Sophia's brother-in-law; see note to Letter 165. For "Lieutenant Dayman" see note to Letter 100. For "Gregson" see note to Letter 116. "Tom" was Thomas Cracroft (1820–1845), Sophy's brother, who died in VDL later that year. "I have written to Richardson, Brown Sabine Parry & Ross – I will write to Sellwood if possible": see Letters 127 (Brown), 153 (Sabine), and 154 (Ross); his surviving letters to Richardson and Parry are later than this one (Letter 150 of 7 July to Richardson, and Letter 157 of 10 July to Parry).

Letter 125   Charles Osmer to Eliza Osmer [wife], 3 June 1845. (copy) SPRI 248/449/1–2   Osmer describes the parting from the *Rattler* and *Blazer* in considerably more detail in Letter 136 (10 July 1845).

Letter 126   John Franklin to Edward Sabine, 3 June 1845. NA BJ 3/18   For "Captain G W Smith" see note to Letter 112.

Letter 127   John Franklin to Robert Brown, 3 June 1845. LA/19/11 [copy in another hand]   Brown (1773–1858) was a botanist, Franklin's shipmate in the *Investigator* under Matthew Flinders in 1801–03, and a lifelong friend. At the time of the expedition's sailing, he was keeper of the Banksian Botanical Collection at the British Museum; in this capacity, he had consulted with Harry Goodsir on 20 April, on which occasion, by Harry's account, they "spent the whole forenoon ... looking over the collections of Arctic plants" (see Letter 63). "Fitton" was Dr William Henry Fitton (1780–1861), a doctor and geologist who had worked closely with Franklin, Richardson, and other Arctic explorers from the 1820s onward; he wrote the geological appendix for George Back's narrative of his Arctic expedition of 1833–35. For "the Pamphlet" see note to Letter 92. "Bicheno" was James Ebenezer Bicheno (1785–1851), a gifted amateur naturalist and member of the Linnean Society; from 1843 to his death in 1851 he served as colonial secretary in VDL.

Letter 128   Francis Crozier to Charlotte Crozier [sister], 3 June 1845. SPRI 1372/4   "most comfortably fixed with my old Servant" – this was Thomas Jopson (b. 1816), who had previously served Crozier aboard *Terror* on Ross's Antarctic voyage. The "first Lieutenant" was Edward Little. "the Doctor our only married man": this was Dr John S. Peddie (b. 1816). "Robertson" was John Robertson, the surgeon aboard HMS *Terror* on that same voyage. "Fortfield" was Fortfield Lodge in Dublin, the residence of Crozier's brother William Crozier (see also Letter 106); "dear Jane" was William's daughter Jane, who in 1838 married John Henry Loftie (1808–1860); see also Letters 33 and 147. "Sally & Sarah" were Crozier's other sisters.

Letter 129   Harry Goodsir to John Goodsir [brother], 3 June 1845. RSGS ARC.4.3/2   For "Mr. Chambers" see note to Letter 119. For "Baillie Robertson" see note to Letter 119. "Description of the Plates": these plates were likely those associated with his article "*On several new species of Crustaceans allied to Saphirina*," which appeared in Taylor's *Annals* in Volume 16, No. 106 (November 1845), 325–7 (see note to Letter 57); the plate is reproduced here as Figure 6. "Jerden" (Harry's habitual misspelling) was William Jerdan (1782–1869), the editor of *The Literary Gazette, and Journal of Belles Lettres, Arts, Sciences*, for publication in which Goodsir wrote a report in the form of a letter (see Appendix B). "a brother of Sir J. Macgregor": this may be a reference to Sir James McGrigor (1771–1858), a Scottish physician and botanist; he and John Goodsir (Harry's brother) were both members of the Wernerian Natural History Society, an offshoot of the Royal Society of Edinburgh. However, both his brothers had died some years previously. For "Mr. Nasmyth" see note to Letter 3.

Letter 130 James Fitzjames to Edward Sabine, 3 June 1845. NA BJ 3–17 "Terror's Unifilar": this was one of several types of magnetometers and other instruments taken to make measurements for the "Magnetic Crusade." "Fox which is <u>rotten</u>": this was a type of "dipping circle" invented by Robert Were Fox (1789–1877) and thought especially fitted for polar observations – apparently there was some fundamental problem with Fitzjames's; see note to Letter 115. "Crozier has been trying vibrations with Hansteen": this was another type of magnetometer, designed by the Norwegian mathematician Christopher Hansteen (1784–1873); James Clark Ross was a promoter of this instrument.

Letter 131 James Fitzjames to William Coningham [brother], 3 June 1845 NMM MRF/89 "Cape Farewell" is the southernmost point of Greenland; see Map 4.

Letter 132 James Reid to Ann Reid [wife], 4 June 1845. SLNSW MLDOC 446 "Barra and Rona" was then a common way to refer to the remote islands now known as Sula Sgeir and North Rona. "Brazier" is Reid's spelling of "Blazer," and perhaps a sort of pun. For "Mr. Beards Process of Photography" see note to Letter 90. "the 2^d one is from Fife Shire": this of course is Harry Goodsir. "him & I is Quite chief": "chief," in Scots, means "intimate or friendly." "Fairom" was James Fairholme, born in Kinnoul, Scotland; Reid's acquaintance with people from Aberdeen is not surprising.

Letter 133 James Fitzjames to Elizabeth Coningham [sister-in-law], 4 June 1845 NMM MRF/89 "Minney" was the Coninghams' daughter Elizabeth Meyrick; for descriptions of the visit see Letters 69 and 70.

Letter 134 James Fitzjames to Elizabeth Coningham [sister-in-law], 6–25 June 1845. NMM MRF/89 Fitzjames's letters to Elizabeth were privately published by the Coninghams, and also appeared (lightly censored) in the *Nautical Magazine* and in Charles Dickens's *All the Year Round;* see also note to Letter 135. In these letters, Fitzjames regularly uses planetary signs to represent the days of the week, a not uncommon nautical practice. We have replaced them with the names of the days, but for the curious, they are:

☉	Sunday
☽	Monday
♂	Tuesday
☿	Wednesday
♃	Thursday
♀	Friday
♄	Saturday

"No ice at <u>arl</u> about it Sir, unless it be the <u>bergs</u>": Fitzjames's droll imitation of Reid's statement is similar to that in the "letter from one of the Principals": "we have seen no ice except bergs, which are considered as such by the whalers," suggesting Fitzjames may be its author; he makes a similar quote in Letter 141; see Appendix B. "the Purser, Osmar, who is delightful": Fitzjames's summary of Osmer's career is an accurate one. "The second master Collins ... is <u>mad</u>": the passage from here to "make something of him" was censored in the printed version; all deletions were presumably made by William Coningham. "Captain Buchan" was David Buchan (1780–1838), under whom Franklin had served on his first Arctic voyage in 1818. "mollimauk" – this was a mollymawk, a species of albatross. "his upper lip projects beyond his lower" ... through to "more of it," along with the phrase "like a yard of pumpwater" was censored. "I have been reading Sir John Franklin's vindication of his Government of Van Diemen's Land": this of course was the Pamphlet; see note to Letter 92. "Couch is a little bullet-headed – blackhaired – smooth-faced lump of inanity": "bullet-headed" and "lump of inanity" were censored. The unkind statements about Stanley being "flabby as if from drinking beer" and "what is called a 'good fellow' ... vulgar to a certain extent" were also removed. "assisted by Baillie somebody or other": this means assisted by a town Bailiff or other such person whose name Fitzjames can't recall. "Valparaiso" in Chile might conceivably have been a stop on the way home, were the ships to return via Cape Horn. "the Sandwich Islands": Franklin's sailing orders (which Fitzjames, earlier in the journal, notes he has shared with him) suggested a call there after achieving the passage. "Sweethearts and Wives" was a well-known toast; it expressed the wish that the two would never meet. The salutation to Elizabeth of 18 June, and the words from "I left off journalizing" to "down paper and grin" were omitted from the printed text. "the India rubber boat": this was the Halkett boat (see note to Letter 40). "when you came to Woolwich": the words from "to bully me" to "getting near the ice" were omitted in the printed text. "To day we arranged all our books in the mess and find that we have a very capital library"; later in the Journal, on 18 June, he notes that a catalogue was made; according to James Fairholme in Letter 140, this catalogue included books in both ships; Goodsir, as "librarian," could use it to locate any volume wanted. The words from "I think I have now written enough nonsense" to Fitzjames's signature were omitted from the printed version. "Waterloo day" was June 18, commemorating the victory of the Duke of Wellington in that battle on 18 June 1815; it is to his health that they drink. A "Brevet" would have been an honorary promotion given out on such a holiday. "I now seldom think about": in fact, he seems to have thought about at least once before, as it is mentioned in Letter 88. "in petto" means "in secret" or discreetly. "named, I think, Akatcho": this was Akaitcho, a Dene chief who had lent valuable assistance to Franklin's first land expedition. "Lichtenfels" was the name of the Moravian mission station; the site is now known as Akunnat. "Couch turns out a very nice little obstinate chap": this sentence was omitted in the printed version. "boots like John Coninghams": this appears to be a private reference of some kind. "'Huski-mays', which ... are 'vulgarly' called Yaks by the whalers, – & 'Huski's' for shortness": these were terms then in use for the Kalaallit people of western Greenland, and other Inuit with whom the whalers came into contact; all would be considered derogatory today. "Hodgson came looking very ill": the nature of his illness is not specified; by 29 June, he had apparently recovered (see Letter 135).

CHAPTER SIX: LAST PARTINGS

Letter 135   James Fitzjames to Elizabeth Coningham [sister-in-law], 27 June–6 July 1845. NMM MRF/89   A large section of the opening of this letter, from the initial salutation through to "prosecution of our journey," was omitted in the printed version. "Lancaster Sound" was the presumed entry point for nearly all possible passages; "Parry was fortunate enough, in his first voyage to sail right across in 9 or 10 days a thing unheard of before or since": no nineteenth-century expedition was ever to improve on his furthest west; see Appendix E for details. "Wednesday 2nd" – the first sentence of this entry, from "Soon after" to "nearly brushed," was omitted from the printed version of the letters, as was a second passage, from "Ice bergs –Grand and fantastic" to "till it clears." "Pour quitter ce triste Sol / Je m'embarque à Liverpol": "to leave this unhappy land, I embarked at Liverpool": the source of this couplet has not been identified. "This will show you that we are": the text following, up through "few hours sleep," was omitted in the printed version. "Waigaut Channel" was the "Waygat Passage," the passage between Disko Island and the Nursoak Peninsula to its north, today known as Sullorsuaq Strait; see also note to Letter 140. "Friday 4th": the first sentence of this entry was omitted from the printed version, as was much of the second paragraph and several other shorter passages. "plan of the place": Fitzjames drew a very similar sketch-map in Letter 141, which is reproduced here as Figure 10. "Fox" was Fitzjames's magnetic dipping circle; see letter 115. "a façon de parler" means "a manner of speaking." "This will go by the Transport": this entire passage, ending with Fitzjames's signature, was omitted from the printed version.

Letter 136   Charles Osmer to Eliza Osmer [wife], 27 June–10 July 1845. (copy) SPRI 248/449/1–2   "the Late Wars": Osmer likely refers to recent British engagements in Afghanistan, Syria, and China. "the farthest limit West reached by Captain Sir Edward Parry": this was Winter Harbour on Melville Island; the ice to its west is heavy Arctic Ocean ice, impassable to ships of this time; Parry's achievement was to have gotten further west than any vessel from the east in that century. "Bank's Land," now more properly Banks Island, lies to the southwest of Melville Island. "Wellington Channel" was a still more northerly route; see Appendix E. "some snug and secure anchorage": this would be a fair anticipation of the expedition's actual first wintering, in Erebus and Terror Bay on Beechey Island near the south entrance to Wellington Channel.

Letter 137   Harry Goodsir to John Goodsir [brother], 28–30 June 1845. RSGS ARC.4.3/2 "allied to my Irenæus": Goodsir is describing crustaceans and comparing one to *Irenæus Goodsir*, which he first identified in 1843. For "Jerden," see note to Letter 129. "Eschricht" was the Danish zoologist Daniel Frederik Eschricht (1798–1863). "the Gun Room was floating & all drenched": aboard *Erebus* and *Terror* the gun room and the ward room had been combined into a single space, which Goodsir must be referring to here; see note to Letter 90. "sitting in the main chains": this refers to the chain plate, which on *Erebus* and *Terror* took the form of an ice chock, anchored the shrouds (lines that hold the mast). Matthew Betts, an authority on the construction of the ships, notes that it would be "a logical place to sit as the shrouds provide something to hold on to, and the ice chock or bumper would provide a platform overhanging the water." "the only idle hand is the Surgeon who appears to spend the greater part of his time reading novels in bed": this jesting deprecation shows Goodsir's declining view of Stanley, but also his good humour. "Stanley tried to perswade them, they were not": another example of the surgeon being a "humbug." "deep sea Cod at Cellardyke": Cellardyke was a village to the immediate east of Goodsir's home at Anstruther. "300 fathoms": this would be a depth of 1,800 feet. "Forbes Brissus Lyrifer and my own Alauna in great abundance": these were *Brissus Lyrifer Forbes*, first identified by him in 1841, and *Alauna Goodsir*, identified by Harry in 1843. "Sir H. De la Beche" was Sir Henry Thomas De la Beche (1796–1855), an English geologist who was the first director of the Geological Survey of Great Britain. "Sea Horse": a common name at the time for walrus. "I have also got a good friend in the Ice Master": this shows that Reid's regard for Goodsir was returned. For "David Forbes" see note to Letter 63; for Edward Forbes see note to Letter 2. "Syme" was Dr James Syme (1799–1870), a noted surgical pioneer and professor of clinical surgery at the University of Edinburgh. "Duncan" was probably James Duncan (1810–1856), a Scottish surgeon who later made a fortune as the leading manufacturer of chloroform in Britain. "the enclosed packet of Disco Flowers": Harry's parcel, which included these and other flowers, along with "a little eider down and a few bottles" and Goodsir's article for Jerden, was safely received on 19 August by his brother John (RSGS Goodsir papers, page 32). "Mrs. Duncan" was Margaret Balfour (1819–1895), James Duncan's wife. "There are several Danes on board of us as seamen so having no difficulty with language": one of the Danes is mentioned by Osmer in Letter 145 in a similar context.

Letter 138   Harry Goodsir to John Goodsir [father], 30 June–2 July 1845. RSGS ARC.4.3/2 "Our Surgeon is a little better than Trotter": this is a reference to the surgeon Stephen Stanley's being only a slight step above "Dr Trotter," a country practitioner of whom the Goodsirs apparently thought very little; see note to Letter 1. "What is poor Dog doing now?": this may be a reference to one of the dogs Goodsir had earlier hoped to bring on board (see Letter 57). "New Hernhuth": this was New Herrnhut, a mission station established in 1733 and abandoned in 1900; the site is now within the modern city of Nuuk, the capital of Greenland. "a good hearted rough old sailor ... through him ... I expect to get all the Seals, Sea, Horses & Whales, Sea Unicorns &c.": again a sign of warm regard, but also Harry's having cultivated the friendship to be sure he didn't miss seeing any of these creatures. "Mr. Goodall, Samuel St. Woolwich" may have been William Goodall, a joiner at the Woolwich dockyards.

Letter 139   Charles Osmer to Eliza Osmer [wife], 1 July 1845. (copy) SPRI 248/449/1–2 "sixty five Ice Bergs": the ships were not far from the well-known "Icefjord" near Illulisat (then known as Jakobshavn). The large glacier there sends numerous icebergs down a long "chute" formed by the fjord. The berg that sank RMS *Titanic* likely came from here. "one or more opportunities of sending letters home to England by the Greenland Whale Ships": several officers spoke of this possibility, but no letters beyond those returned via the *Baretto Junior* on 12 July are known.

Letter 140   James Fairholme to George Fairholme [father], 1–5 July 1845. DRO D3311 58 "Cape Wrath" is the furthest northwest point in Scotland. "Cape Farewell" is the southernmost tip of Greenland. "we met an Aberdeen brig out on a speculation": this was almost certainly the *Banchory* later mentioned by James Reid (see Letter 161); Harry Goodsir also mentions it in Letter 137: "A brig from Aberdeen was out on a Speculation fishing for Cod." "Fortnum & Mason have done their part well": many of the officers obtained provisions from this storied London victualler, which continues in business today in its 315th year. "Sir John is a new man since we left": many writers commented on their commander's improved health. On "Peter Halketts boat": see note to Letter 40. "its rate with the chronometers varying a few seconds only each day": a key task of the lieutenants was to keep the chronometers wound and compare their rates; each ship had ten of them. Their key use was in calculating longitude. "Whewell's Indications": this was William Whewell's *Indications of the Creator: Extracts, Bearing Upon Theology, from the History and the Philosophy of the Inductive*

Science (1845); "Vestiges" was Robert Chambers's *Vestiges of the Natural History of Creation* (1844). Fairholme took a great interest in the books brought on board; he seems to have worked closely with Harry Goodsir, who (as he mentions later in this same letter) became the *de facto* librarian of the expedition: "when a book is wanted, the Librarian (Goodsir) will at once know which ship & what cabin it is in." "now reading a book which I strongly advise you to look at": this was Pawel Edmund de Strzelecki's book about Australia and Tasmania; see note to Letter 152. "I have no doubt George met him out there": Fairholme's brother George was a settler in New South Wales, not VDL; see end of notes for this letter. "the <u>dirtiest</u> race I ever came across": this prejudice, unfortunately, seems to have been widely shared by Franklin's officers, though not by Franklin himself. "Ross' <u>red snow</u>": when Sir John Ross returned from his controversial survey of Baffin Bay in 1818, he was pilloried for making much of what were considered (at the time) trivial discoveries. The "red snow" he observed was made much fun of. "They are very different in appearance to any Indians that I have seen": it was a common mistake at this time to regard the "Esquimaux" as a variety of "Indians," whereas their lineage is completely different. "I assisted Goodsir yesterday in collecting words for a vocabulary, & we were very much struck with the resemblance between their language & what we know of the Tartar & Kamschatadate": this is remarkable, as the Inuktitut language and its dialects are indeed distantly related to those of Mongolia; this work, had it survived, would have been among the earliest to recognize this connection (see Louis-Jacques Dorais, *The Language of the Inuit: Syntax, Semantics, and Society in the Arctic* [Montreal & Kingston: McGill-Queen's University Press, 2010: 91–3]). "Mr. Warre & Dr. Richardson": "Mr. Warre" may have been John Ashley Warre (1787–1860), a fellow of the Royal Society, who apparently made a gift of a sextant. For "Dr. Richardson" see note to Letter 36. "Uncle Walter" was Walter Forbes (1798–1868), later the 18th Lord Forbes. "Charley is now in the Superb": this may have been Charles Blatchford; he was the only sailor with that given name aboard HMS *Superb* in 1845. "Petropaulowsky": this is Petropavlovsk; see note to Letter 162. "Libbity" was Fairholme's sister Elizabeth Marjery Fairholme (1826–1888); "William" was Fairholme's brother William Fairholme (see note to Letter 105). "George" was Fairholme's brother George Knight Erskine Fairholme (1822–1889); he emigrated to Queensland in 1838 and remained there until 1852; a capable amateur artist, his portfolio of lithographs, "Fifteen Views of Australia in 1845," includes some of the earliest depictions of Brisbane. "Waygat passage": an obsolete name for the passage between Disko Island and the Nursoak Peninsula to its north, today known as Sullorsuaq Strait.

Letter 141   James Fitzjames to John Barrow Jr, 1–11 July 1845. RGS   "Lichtenfels" was a Moravian mission settlement in southwestern Greenland; the site is now known as Akuunat. "Lievely," now known as Qeqertarsuaq, is a settlement is on the south coast of Disko Island. "Waigaut" is "Waygat Passage"; see note to Letter 140. "This is the harbour": what follows is a key to the sketch Fitzjames drew within this letter; it is reproduced here as Figure 10.

Letter 142   Henry T.D. Le Vesconte to Sarah Le Vesconte [mother], 2 July 1845. ANL

Letter 143   Harry Goodsir to Anstruther Taylor [uncle], 2 July 1845. RSGS ARC.4.3/2   In Scottish usage, "Burgoo" is a kind of oatmeal porridge; it appears that Goodsir's suggestion was to take all the ingredients mentioned and stir them together with porridge, the better to prevent the men "tumbling over their dishes." "10,000 cases of preserved ready cooked meats on board the Erebus alone so you see there is no chance of Starving" – this is a reference to Stephen Goldner's tinned preserved meats and soups, which – though blamed by later sources for spoilage or excessive lead content – appear to have been a reasonably good and valued source of nutrition, at least for the first few years of the expedition (see page 7 and note). "Sir Howard Douglas" was General Sir Howard Douglas, 3rd Baronet (1776–1861); he was one of the founders of the Royal Geographical Society and had an interest in steam-powered vessels. "Lord Williams" was probably meant to be "Lord William's" and thus a reference to Lord William Paget (1803–1873), a British naval commander and at that time Member of Parliament for Andover.

Letter 144   Henry T.D. Le Vesconte to Henry Le Vesconte [father], 2 July 1845. ANL   "the case with the officers of the Isabella and Alexander and Dorothea and Trent in 18" – Le Vesconte alludes to the two polar expeditions, commanded by John Ross and David Buchan respectively, which were launched in 1818. Ross was widely faulted for failing to probe Lancaster Sound, and Buchan's voyage, as Le Veconte describes, turned back after the Dorothea was damaged in the polar ice; neither commander was promoted. For "Henrietta" see note to Letter 49. For "Louis Phillipe and Madame Adelaide" see note to Letter 64.

Letter 145   Charles Osmer to Eliza Osmer [wife], 4–9 July 1845. (copy) SPRI 248/449/1–2   "one of our Sailors (a Dane)": this most likely refers to a sailor who had come aboard from the Danish port (see Harry Goodsir's mention of them in his postscript to Letter 137), though it has been suggested that it might have been Henry Lloyd, a seaman aboard Erebus who was born in Kristiansand, Norway, which until a few years prior had been in a political union with Denmark. "I dined on board the Terror to day and was much entertained by the surmises of the different Officers as to our intended route – nobody but Sir John and myself being acquainted with it": certainly it seems that Franklin took

Osmer into his confidence, but at the same time, it is very unlikely that Crozier would have known less of it than Osmer. For an account of the possible routes and alternatives, see Appendix E.

Letter 146 Francis Crozier to John Henderson, 4 July 1845. NMM AGC/C/5/1 "Jack" was John Henderson, a fellow midshipman of Crozier's aboard HMS *Fury* during Parry's 1821–22 expedition. The nature of the accident to which Crozier refers is not known. Point Henderson on Southampton Island is named after him.

Letter 147 Francis Crozier to unknown correspondent, c. 4 July 1845 [excerpt] FLM 1881 One possible candidate for the "Henry" of this letter is John Henry Loftie (1808–1860), who married Crozier's niece Jane in 1838; in later years he was a respected magistrate in Banbridge. Crozier's nephew Henry Crozier has been thought by some to be the "Henry" mentioned here, but as he was only nine or ten years old at this time, this is almost certainly mistaken; the tone of the excerpt is not that of a letter to a child. Loftie may also have been the "Henry" referred to in Letter 33. This brief excerpt is known only from its appearance in the fifth edition of Francis Leopold McClintock's *The Voyage of the 'Fox' in Arctic Seas* (London: John Murray, 1881). For this edition, McClintock prepared a new introduction which included a selection of letters from various officers, all but Crozier unnamed. This particular excerpt was the last (numbered 15); McClintock states that "the last of these extracts is from a letter of Captain Crozier's, written from the Whalefish Islands, and was one of the last letters ever received from the expedition." The date is inferred from the fact that a nearly identical phrase – "All going on as well as I could wish" – also appears in Letter 146.

Letter 148 Edward Couch to James Couch and Mary Couch [parents], excerpts only [copy], 4–11 July 1845. SPRI 248/363 This is a copy in another hand; the transcriber has apparently used sequences of "x x x x" to indicate illegible words; no other copy is known. "(Terror ?)": this is transcribed exactly as written by the copyist. "making Sir John a signal book": this must be the new book of signals mentioned by Franklin in Letter 159. "an English barque": this is likely the *Banchory* again. "lent me one of his sextants to use instead of my old quadrant": a sextant would generally be a preferred instrument to the bulkier and less precise quadrant.

Letter 149 John Franklin to Eleanor Franklin [daughter], 6 July 1845. DRO D3311 28 14 "Bartimaeus," according to the Gospel of Mark, was the name of a blind man healed by Jesus as he was leaving the city of Jericho; the version in

Luke does not name the man. "David wishing to purchase Araunah's threshing Floor": a reference to a passage in 2 Samuel: 24, 18–25, where David purchased a threshing floor from Araunah the Jebusite in order to erect an altar to the Lord; David insisted on paying for the threshing floor, as otherwise it would not be a proper sacrifice of his material wealth. The "Fairlie" was a ship of the East India Company aboard which Franklin and his family first sailed to VDL; the "Rajah" was a vessel aboard which they sailed from Melbourne to London in January of 1844. "Arnolds sermons": "Arnold" was Thomas Arnold (1795–1842); the missed volume was his *Sermons, preached mostly in the Chapel of Rugby School* (1841); the volumes that Franklin did have were Arnold's *History of Rome* (1840) and the *Life of Arnold* by Arthur Penrhyn Stanley (1844). "Their faces as well as those of their children were clean": Franklin's assessment contrasts with that of the men who accompanied him – that they were, in Osmer's words, "one mass of dirt." "the Carpenter": this man's identity is not known, but see note to Letter 153. For "Mr Gell" see note to Letter 100; "I do not imagine that he will remain very long in VDLand – nor at all after the Archdeacon returns": this suggests that Franklin was not sanguine as to the likelihood of Gell's remaining to work on the college; "the Archdeacon" was Fitzherbert Marriott (see note to Letter 100).

Letter 150   John Franklin to John Richardson, 7 July 1845. DRO D3311 58 39; copy at SPRI MS 248/314   "with which branch of Natural History he is perhaps the most acquainted": the use of "perhaps" suggests that Franklin had gained some idea of the limits of Stanley's acquaintance with natural history. "Wollaston Land with that of Banks": Wollaston Land was in fact a peninsula of neighbouring Victoria Island. "how the Musk Oxen got to Melville Island": Musk oxen are, in fact, excellent swimmers. "Regents Inlet" is Prince Regent Inlet; there is indeed a route to the west that way via Bellot Strait, which was not discovered until 1852. "Wellington channels": this more northerly route would not have been an easy passage, but the expedition *did* ascend the channel, returning via the other side of Cornwallis Island (according to the Victory Point record). For more on these and other possible routes, see Appendix E. The gaps at the end of this letter are due to the signature having been cut away.

Letter 151   Harry Goodsir to John Goodsir [father], 7 July 1845. RSGS ARC.4.3/2   "that in the Gallery of the College of Surgeons": this was a kayak donated to the Museum of the College of Surgeons circa 1800, which has since been transferred to the National Museum of Scotland, where it is currently catalogued as 1995.886. It is of West Greenlandic design, and may indeed have originally been brought to Edinburgh by a whaler from someplace not far from where Harry was at this moment.

Letter 152   Sir John Franklin to Robert Brown 9 July 1845; see note to Letter 127. SPRI 248/296/20; LA/19/11 contains a copy in another hand, but the original is our copytext. "Streleski" was Sir Pawel Edmund Strzelecki (1797–1873), an early explorer of Tasmania, where he penetrated the Snowy Mountains; he also explored the Australian mainland, where he named – and was the first to climb – Mount Kosciuszko, its highest peak. He and the Franklins became fast friends, and Sir John and Lady Jane supported his endeavours during their time there. Strzelecki dedicated his 1845 book, *Physical description of New South Wales and Van Diemen's land*, to Franklin, and this letter makes it clear that a copy was on board HMS *Erebus* (Fairholme mentions in Letter 140 that he is reading it). Franklin's response to this dedication is also attested to in a letter to Strzelecki by William Edward Parry: "On my final visit to our dear friend Franklin at Greenhithe on Saturday, his eyes overflowed when he told me of your having dedicated your Work to him, I can only say, that he is worthy of all the regard you can pay him; – for "take him for all in all, we nee'er shall look upon his like again" (19 May 1845; collection of Douglas W. Wamsley). "Your neighbour, Arrowsmith": this was John Arrowsmith (1790–1873) the principal maker of maps and charts for the Admiralty, as well as for private publication.

Letter 153   Sir John Franklin to Edward Sabine, 9 July 1845. NA BJ 3/18 "an intelligent Dane (who has been here 13 years ... the Carpenter in charge of the Esquimaux station on these Islands": It is tempting to think this may have been Johan Carl Christian Petersen (1813–1880), who became a prominent figure as a guide and interpreter for many later Franklin searchers, including William Penny and Francis McClintock. However, it is said that he left Lievely on Disko for Upernavik in 1841, so this is probably a different intelligent Danish carpenter. "au fait" means having an up-to-date knowledge of something. "on the gun line": the naval phrase refers to the gunwales (pronounced "gunnels"): this complements Goodsir's own "sitting in the main chains" (see note to Letter 137), and suggests that specimens were being laid out on the gunwales for the officers and men to see (thanks to Matthew Betts for this note). "The Surgeons part is that of ornithology": given Goodsir's firm conclusion that Stanley was a "humbug," the study of birds may have been a convenient ruse for his having a serious purpose. "not as yet been favoured with the sight of a Bear leaping from a floating Iceberg": this is an allusion to a famous lithographic plate "A bear plunging into the sea," which appeared in Sir John Ross's *A Voyage of Discovery, made under the Orders of the Admiralty, in His Majesty's Ships Isabella and Alexander, for the Purpose of Exploring Baffin's Bay, and Enquiring Into the Probability of a North-west Passage* (1819).

Letter 154   John Franklin to James Clark Ross, 9 July 1845. SPRI 248/316/25 "the Yachts": a lightly jesting reference to *Erebus* and *Terror*. "a Carpenter by trade": see note to Letter 153. "the space between Bank's Land and Wollastons": see notes to Letters 150 and 154, and Appendix E. "The Musk Oxen on Melville Island" ... "never ... swam far": see note to Letter 150. "If the western shore of Boothia should stretch from your Southern point to Cape Walker as I believe you supposed it to do": the shore is almost continuous, broken only by the Bellot Strait, which was not discovered until 1852. "Wellington Channel" ... "if baffled to the South of Bank's Land it is the next place I shall try": it appears likely that Franklin did exactly that, either in 1845 or 1846, but apparently found no passage west there either, returning south and thereby circumnavigating Cornwallis Island (see Appendix E). "Baron Wrangle": this was Ferdinand von Wrangel (1796–1870); Wrangel Island was named after him by Thomas Long, as Wrangel had deduced its existence from the observation of seabirds, though he never found it.

Letter 155   John Gregory to Hannah Gregory [wife], 9 July 1845. SPRI 824/1   John Gregory was born in 1806, and one of the older of the men who served with Franklin; his wife was Hannah, *née* Wilson (1801–1873). Their grandson Edward John Gregory (1850–1909) was an acclaimed painter and member of the Royal Academy. "1 welsh wig": this knitted headgear, made famous recently by its use in the costumes for the AMC series "The Terror," was meant to keep the men's heads and ears warm while dressed otherwise in regulation gear. "as presents": this was a mark of distinction, as usually sailors were charged for much of what was provided them. "There are a few inhabitants of the Esquimaux Tribe most of whom have been on board the ships bartering with the crew": this is one of two clear accounts of barter having taken place; for the other see the second letter in Appendix B. "see Mr Fitzpatrick with respect of the Money you may place in Mr Maudslays hands": this is likely a reference to John's half-pay, which sailors counted on to sustain their families while they were away. "Mr Fitzpatrick" has not been identified; "Mr Maudslay" refers to one of the sons of Henry Maudslay (1771–1831), founder of Maudslay, Sons, and Field, who had been Gregory's employers prior to his transfer into *Erebus* to serve as its engineer; it was they who had prepared and installed the engines (see Appendix D). "Mr & Mrs Haviland, also Mr Harts": these individuals have not been identified. "Mr Rose" and "Mr Pile" have not been identified, but may have been associated with Maudslay's. "Mr and Mrs Empey" have not been identified. "Fanny is improving in her business" ... "James is giving every satisfaction": apparently these children were already employed in some line of work. "Edward, Fanny, James, William, and Kiss baby for me": this is a full list of John and Hannah's living children; the "baby" was Frederick, born on 6 December 1844.

Letter 156   James Thompson to Charles Thompson [brother], 10 July 1845.
NMM AGD/T/7 (3)   "A quantity of Provisions for private use": any member of
the crew who had the means and the opportunity could purchase their own
stores. "the Ships allowance": this is remarkable testimony as to what the men
ate while on board; contrary to what has sometimes been claimed, they were
apparently issued "Preserved Meat" three times a week. "Lime juice": lemon
juice rather than lime was issued to the expedition. "An Aberdeen Fishing Boat":
this was the *Banchory*; see note to Letter 161. "A harmless set of People and very
honest I had two of the Men to supper on Munday Night": Thompson's positive
view of the local Inuit stands in contrast to that of the officers. "1 Welch Wig":
see note to letter 155. "1 A Marien the Armerer and the sale maker": these fortunate men were sent home; Crozier mentions them in Letter 172: "I have been
obliged to send home our armourer & Sailmaker being perfectly useless either
at their trade or anything else." "be like the Hibernian bring it myself": this
seems to be a reference to a story in which an Irishman accidentally delivers his
own letter; such a tale was part of the plot of James Planché's farce *The Irish
Post*, but since that play wasn't staged until 1846, Thompson's reference must
be to some earlier version.

Letter 157   John Franklin to Edward Parry, 10 July 1845. SPRI 438/18/7   "there
exists much land between the Wollaston and Banks Lands which I hope may be
found to be separated into Islands; and also I trust we may be able to penetrate
through a channel between them": see note to Letter 135 and Appendix E.
"Signal Books": see notes to Letters 148 and 159. For "Beaufort" see note to
Letter 9.

Letter 158   John Irving to Catherine Irving [sister-in-law], 10 July 1845.
GM   "10th July": the printed version of the letter – our only source – gives
"Probably 10th July" as its date. "three of the cattle" – out of an original eighteen
– seems a sad remainder. They were to be slaughtered to provide fresh meat for the
first post-Greenland leg of the expedition." "Inchkeith" is an island in the Firth of
Forth in Scotland. "a library of the best books of all kinds, consisting of 1200
volumes": the exact number of books brought by the expedition has been difficult
to determine; Osmer gives the figure of 1700 books in Letter 139. "God has been
with us in all our wanderings": Irving was second perhaps only to Franklin himself in his religious zeal; see Ralph Lloyd-Jones, "An evangelical Christian on
Franklin's last expedition: Lieutenant John Irving of HMS *Terror*," *Polar Record*
33 (187) 327–32 (1997). "Tripe de Roche" was rock tripe, a lichen that famously
had helped sustain Franklin on his first land expedition. "I send you a sketch of
our ships at this place": a woodcut of this sketch is here reproduced as Figure 12.

Letter 159   John Franklin to Jane Franklin, 1–12 July 1845 LA/19/13, parts transcribed by Eleanor Franklin DRO D8760/F/FLJ/1/4   The original is our copytext, but Eleanor's partial transcript was of help in deciphering several of the difficult bits. "a letter for Mrs Foster from Hoar … expressed his hope that she would remain with you till our return": this must have been Edmund Hoar, who was Franklin's steward aboard *Erebus*; the reference, with the forwarded letter (since lost) suggests that there was a previous acquaintance between Hoar and Jane's maid, the "faithful Foster" of Letter 195. Mary Foster (1805–1858) entered into service as Jane's "Lady's Maid" sometime after they returned from VDL and is listed in her household in the 1851 census; she died in 1858 in Pera, Turkey (modern Beyoğlu), while accompanying Jane and Sophy on a Mediterranean tour. The newspaper notices of her death described her as "the faithful servant and beloved friend" of Lady Franklin (*Evening Mail*, 4 August 1858, 8). "communicated with an English Brig": this was the brig *Banchory* of Aberdeen described by Reid in Letter 161; see also Letters 140 and 156. "his immediate Senior": this would have been Stanley; while we don't have a record of Richardson's concerns, we do know that Stanley was described as a "humbug" by Harry Goodsir; see Letter 90. "Sir George Staunton" was George Thomas Staunton, 2nd Baronet (1781–1859), MP for Portsmouth. Barrow had been Staunton's teacher and both had travelled with with Lord Macartney's diplomatic mission (1792–94) to the Chinese Imperial court. "unfortunate son Peter": this was Peter Barrow (b. 1813), who settled in Western Australia in 1840 and briefly held the posts of magistrate and "Protector of Aborigines." He was apparently quite headstrong, disappointed in his salary, and infuriated when Bishop Nixon refused to ordain him; he abruptly resigned his positions and returned to England less than two years after arriving. Details on his later life are scant and the date of his death is unknown. For "Lord Stanley" and "Montagu" see note to Letter 13. For "the Pamphlet" see note to Letter 92. "Code of Signals": in his daguerreotype portrait, Le Vesconte is shown holding a copy of Frederick Marryat's widely used "Code of Signals," but it was not unusual for individual expeditions to devise their own when the need arose; the need here was apparently related to the ships' steam engines. "nor Ross's (Sir John I mean)": Sir John Ross (1777–1856), James Clark Ross's uncle, had sailed twice to the Arctic, the second time with his nephew. Despite his age, the elder Ross returned to search for Franklin in 1850; he left his yacht *Mary* behind at Beechey Island in case Franklin might make use of it. The remains may be seen to this day. "reading again the voyages of the earlier Navigators": Franklin here seems to be referring to articles and summaries; the "Edinburgh Cabinet Library" published a volume surveying past expeditions in 1830 (because of its date, it would not have included Sir John Ross, Dease and Simpson, or other later expeditions mentioned here). It appears likely that the complete volumes of these and other expedition journals were also aboard. "the Commentaries of Henry upon it": this was Matthew Henry's extensive *An Exposition on the Old and New Testament*, originally published in 1708–10; there were a number of editions contemporary with Franklin, most of which had been extended and edited by later figures. For "Captain Smith of the Rattler" see note to Letter 112. "off Lievely"; now known as Qeqertarsuaq, this settlement is on the south coast of Disko Island. "Way-gat passage": see note to Letter 135. "Mosquitoes however are most abundant": an issue mentioned by many crewmembers, summed up by James Thompson's remark in Letter 156 that they are "more venemous than the English Bugg." "Moravians": the Moravian Church had founded a number of missionary stations on the coast of Greenland, and also in Labrador. "La Trobe" is probably a reference to Peter La Trobe (1795–1863), an English-born Moravian bishop then in London; the Franklins had visited his brother Charles, a colonial official in Australia, in Melbourne in 1843. "Woman's Islands": a reference to the former name of Upernavik. "Lady Cust" was Mary Anne Cust (1799–1882), a naturalist and scientific illustrator who gained renown for her book *History and Diseases of the Cat*. "Lieutenant Griffiths the agent of Transport": this was Edward Griffiths (1792–1883) of the Royal Navy's Transport Service. As the last naval officer to see Franklin alive, his recollections and opinions were eagerly sought once Franklin was missed; when the scandal over the quality of the tinned foods supplied to the Navy erupted in 1852, he wrote a letter to *The Times* averring that he had dined on the tinned foods with Franklin and that they had found them "of excellent quality." "Mr Stilwell" was the head of the firm of Stilwell & Sons in London, a naval agent with whom Franklin apparently had an understanding. "Huggins" was Iden Huggins, master of the *Baretto Junior*. "Mr Gunn to sell the land at Port Phillip": see note to Letter 116. "the land at the Huon": the Huon River lies to the south of Hobart; Jane Franklin bought a large parcel of land there and rented it cheaply to deserving free settlers, whom she thought the government did not help enough. This was probably her most successful venture in the island. The settlement was later called Franklin in her honour; Gunn ran it for her after she left. "Dunn's Bank": this was the bank established in 1829 in VDL by John Dunn (1790–1861). "McLachlan": McLachlan's was the Bank of Van Diemen's Land, whose director was Charles McLachlan (1795–1855). "Mr. Gell to commence now with the formation of the College Library at Ancanthe": For Mr. Gell, see note to Letter 100. Ancanthe was a Greek-revival building in Hobart which Jane had caused to be built to house a natural history collection she hoped would be the centrepiece of an intended school/college (see note to Letter 100). The building was neglected for years, but eventually restored by the City of Hobart; at present it houses the Art Society of Tasmania. The "Tasmanian Journal" was the *Tasmanian Journal of natural science, agriculture, and statistics*;

it was established by Sir John Franklin and published its first issue in 1841. For "The Bishop" see note to Letter 100. For "Mr Hope" see note to Letter 48. "Sir Robert Inglis" was Sir Robert Harry Inglis (1786–1855), a conservative member of Parliament who was later a vocal supporter of Lady Franklin's campaign to mobilize searches for her lost husband; see also Letters 180 and 190. "Tom Cracroft" was Thomas Cracroft (1820–1845), Sophy's brother, who died in VDL later that year. "when Ross & I went there": this was Sir James Clark Ross, who visited Hobart while on his Antarctic expedition. "He dined with me and was more cheerful": Franklin here is wondering when – or whether – to broach the subject of Sophia Cracroft's rejection of Crozier's offer of marriage. "Ross had not stuck closer at his publication": J.C. Ross had taken longer than usual to publish the traditional book-length account of his expedition; it did not appear until 1847, four years after his return.

Letter 160   John Franklin to Henrietta Wright [sister], 11 July 1845. DRO D8760/F/FSJ/1/15/47   This letter is known only from a typed copy at the Derbyshire Record Office. Henrietta Franklin (1794–1878) was married to a clergyman, Rev. Thomas Bailey Wright (1790–1858), referred to as Mr. Wright in the letter. "Mr. Montague and Lord Stanley": see note to letter 13. "write to _____": since this letter is extant only in a typed copy, it is impossible to know the reason for this blank.

Letter 161   James Reid to Ann Reid [wife], 11 July 1845. SLNSW MLDOC 446   "Whalers having got fish": among whalers, a whale was referred to as a fish. "My Brother 2 if not 3": this was James's brother Charles (b. 1798), named later in the letter, who was the master of the *Alexander* that season. In 1850 Charles wrote to Lady Franklin in hopes of gaining an appointment "to go in search of my absent brother" (*Arctic Blue Books* 1850a, 135). "St. Andrew 1 if not 2": a ship of this name was in a Davis Strait whaling fleet. "Parker from Hull": another Davis Strait whaler. "Mannager of the Alexander": apparently in order to let them know sooner of the success of their ship that season. For "David Leys" see note to Letter 93. "Dr. Kid[d] on the whaler": this was the illustrious Dr James Kidd of Aberdeen (1761–1834), described in a contemporary biography as "one of the very greatest religious forces with which this part of the country was ever favoured." The reference to a whaler here is unclear. "Lost my Spy Glass": this would have been the one he's pictured holding in the daguerreotype portrait by Richard Beard. "Mr. Enderby": see note to Letter 42. "William Gaudy" has not been identified, though there was a miller of this name in the town of Lunan, some fifty miles south of Aberdeen. "Miscatties": Reid's spelling of mosquitoes. "Robert Forbes" has not been identified. "the Brig Banchory of Aberdeen" may have been among the last vessels to meet with

Franklin's ships. "Mowat master," according to the Aberdeen Built Ships database, the master's name was "M. Mouet." Although Reid's report of her success sounds positive, she was put up for sale by her owners in December of 1845, being described as of 129 tons, with "new Top-sides, Decks, Fastenings, and Spars" (*Aberdeen Journal*, 31 December 1845, 1).

Letter 162   Alexander McDonald to James Clark Ross, 11 July 1845. SPRI 312/3   "Petropolski": McDonald means Petropavlovsk; the idea that Franklin's ships – or ships that encountered them – could have called at Petropavlovsk was not out of the question; when Lady Franklin visited Sitka, Alaska, with Sophy in 1870, she sought to inquire about any letters or documents that might have arrived via that route. "the Sandwich Islands," now known as Hawaii, were indeed included in the sailing orders, apparently for some R&R for the crew after the hoped-for passage. Lady Franklin and Sophy visited there in 1861; see Alfons L. Korn, *The Victorian Visitors* (Honolulu: University of Hawaii Press, 1969). "Panama": this was also mentioned in the sailing orders.

Letter 163   James Fitzjames to William Coningham [brother], 11 July 1845. PC   This letter was edited for the printed version, and the salutation changed to 'Dear Coningham." "Elizabeths bundle of yarns" – this refers to the running "Journal" that Fitzjames sent to Elizabeth Coningham; in this volume it is broken up into Letters 134 and 135. These letters were the first to be published, appearing in the *Nautical Magazine* as well as in Charles Dickens's *All The Year Round*, where an abridged version appeared with an introduction by Wilkie Collins under the title, "Last Leaves of a Sorrowful Book" in the number for 30 July, 1859. The last sentence of the first paragraph was omitted in the printed version, as was the entire paragraph beginning with "I was on shore" and ending with "a great many people." "If you go to John Barrow": this sentence was also omitted, as was "a letter via Petersburg to Petro Paulowski" as well as "and Elizabeth and the children."

Letter 164   James Fitzjames to Edward Sabine, 1 July 1845. NA BJ 3/17   "Captain Crozier has I know written to you fully": the whereabouts of this correspondence is unknown. "Fox" was Fitzjames's dipping circle; see note to Letter 115. "I can only suppose that it was supposed my observations would not be of use as compared to Captain Crozier's"; here Fitzjames betrays a touch of insecurity; he was a relative newcomer to magnetic observations, whereas Crozier's outstanding work in this field had already earned him election to the Royal Society in 1843. "Robinson": this was another manufacturer of magnetic instruments; McClintock found a dipping circle of theirs on King William Island. "Lloyd": this was yet another type of dip circle, recently introduced by

Humphrey Lloyd (1800–1881), a professor at Trinity College, Dublin. "Riddell" was Charles James Buchanan Riddell (1817–1903), a close associate of Sabine's and the author of the authoritative "Magnetical Instructions for the Use of Portable Instruments adapted for Magnetical Surveys and Portable Observatories, and for the Use of a Set of Small Instruments for a Fixed Magnetic Observatory," which had just been published by the Admiralty in 1844.

Letter 165   John Franklin to Isabella Cracroft [sister], 11 July 1845 SPRI 248/298/18–20   "Mr Lacy" was Thomas S. Lacy; he married Isabella's daughter Isabella (1816–1883) in 1840.

Letter 166   Harry Goodsir to John Goodsir [father], 12 July 1845. RSGS ARC.4.3/2 "the other Surgeons are great bores regarding all these things": another snipe at Stanley.

Letter 167   Harry Goodsir to John Goodsir [brother], 12 July 1845 RSGS ARC.4.3/2   "I send a small box": see note to Letter 137; it was received by John on 19 August. "casts of the head and face": this sort of skull-oriented anthropology was common in its day. "Professor Forbes" was Edward Forbes; see note to Letter 2. "Jardines Gazette": this was William Jerdan's magazine; see note to Letter 129 and Appendix A.

Letter 168   Henry T.D. Le Vesconte to Henry Le Vesconte [father], 12 July 1845. ANL   For "Henrietta," see note to Letter 49.

Letter 169   John Franklin to Mary Anne Kendall [niece], 12 July 1845. NMM FRN/1/26   Mary Anne Kendall (1808–1869) was Franklin's niece (the daughter of his first wife's sister Sarah Porden) and the widow of Franklin's fellow explorer (see note to Letter 26). Kendall & George Back produced the drawings that appear in Franklin's published account. Mention is made in the letter to the one of Fort Franklin. See *Narrative of a second expedition to the shores of the Polar Sea, in the years 1825, 1826, and 1827* (London: John Murray, 1828). "Admiral MacKinley & his family": this was Vice-Admiral George McKinley (1760–1852). "Miss Garrett" has not been identified.

Letter 170   Stephen Stanley to John Richardson, 12 July 1845. SPRI 248/476   This is Stanley's only known letter, and it is a relatively formal one, along the lines of a medical report on Franklin's health.

Letter 171   Thomas Blanky to Esther Blanky [wife], 12 July 1845. BNA   Aside from its appearance in the *Evening Standard* (25 February 1852) and other newspapers, no source for this letter is known. Blanky's wife, Esther (*née*

Walker), was born in 1797. In the 1851 census, she listed her occupation as "wife of Ice Master RN"; in 1854 she was declared bankrupt, but in 1856 she was the recipient of a benefit fund raised by John Barrow Jr (the contributors included Sir John Richardson, Dr John Rae, and Sir James Clark Ross). In 1858 she again became bankrupt and lost the tobacconist's shop she had established. She attended the dedication of the Franklin memorial at Westminster Abbey in 1874; in a diary entry describing the occasion, Franklin's niece Catherine Rawnsley noted that "the poor Ice Master's widow was quite overcome." Esther Blanky died in Islington in 1879.

Letter 172   Francis Crozier to James Clark Ross, 12 July 1845. SPRI 245/364/26 "I cannot bear going on board Erebus": in context, this indicates how much he misses Ross, and how being aboard Ross's old ship exacerbates that feeling – not to any ill-will between him and Franklin. "He has Fitzjames and 2 officers every day": this line is followed by three lines that have been completely obliterated with ink. "What I fear is that from our being so late we shall have no time to look round and judge for our selves, but blunder into the Ice and make a second 1824 of it": Crozier here refers to his second Arctic expedition with Parry; the ice in 1824 was very unfavourable and they did not reach Lancaster Sound until 10 September. They were forced to winter over in Prince Regent Inlet, and the following summer HMS *Fury* was driven against the shore and wrecked; the site is now known as "Fury Beach." "Thot" was Crozier's nickname for Ross's wife, Ann (see note to Letter 11). "Blackheath" – later in the letter "Bleakheath": the latter is Crozier's wry comment on Blackheath, the location of Ross's city home, just south of Greenwich Park. "I would like to have seen your place": this would be Ann's family's country home in Whitgift, Yorkshire, where they went from London, or the home at Aston Abbots in Buckinghamshire that Ross rented (it's not clear whether Crozier would have known of the latter). "No congenial Spirit": Crozier clearly meant this, but he puts the phrase in quotes – one possible source is the anonymous novel *Oldcourt* (1829). "again on the Dover line": see note for Letter 78. "has not the leading stoker": this was leading stoker John Torrington, who died in January of 1846 and was the first buried at Beechey Island. "to assist him in doing nothing": the engineer aboard *Terror* was James Thompson; the implication is that he was, having no duties when the engine was not in use, idle. "a poor thing by Pastorelli": this was a family firm of barometer makers in London, active from the 1790s to the 1850s. "Fitzjames is appointed to superintend the Magnetic observations": Crozier was clearly disappointed that an inexperienced officer like Fitzjames was given this role rather than he himself, who had been made a fellow of the Royal Society in recognition of his work with terrestrial magnetism.

Letter 173   Charles Osmer to Eliza Osmer [wife], 12 July 1845. (copy) SPRI 248/449/1–2   As the ship's purser, Osmer would have been in charge of the mailbag, and thus the last person able to add a letter to it.

CHAPTER SEVEN: LETTERS TO THE LOST

Letter 174   Charles Hartnell to John and Thomas Hartnell [brothers], 23 December 1848. PC   Charles, despite his recently having enlisted in a volunteer military unit (see note to Letter 175), turned out to be the longest-lived of the Hartnell brothers; he died in 1900 at the age of 72, and most of the known current descendants are his. "borden" is the village of Borden, about eight miles from Gillingham. "Uncle Ford," "Uncle and Aunt Hoar," and "Mrs Goldie" have not been identified. "three years less to serve": Charles apparently refers to the term of his enlistment (see note to Letter 175). "Mother is going to Finish": Charles's letter is written on the lower right quarter of the same large sheet of paper as Sarah's; this suggests that his was written first.

Letter 175   Sarah Hartnell to John and Thomas Hartnell [sons], c. 23 December 1847 PC   The Hartnells – Thomas (1789–1832) and Sarah (*née* Friar, 1792–1854) – were a family of sailors and shipwrights; their sons John (1820–1846) and Thomas (b. 1822) both joined the Franklin expedition. Thomas, interestingly, had previously sailed to VDL aboard HMS *Tortoise*, on an 1841 voyage carrying convicts, the present editor's great-great-grandfather among them. "rhumatiss[m]s" – this is written as a superscript in tiny letters, but seems to be a version of either "rheumatism" or "rheumatiss" (a further variant also attested at this time). "at her place" suggests Mary was a domestic servant; Mary Ann (b. 1826), Betsy (b. 1832), and Charles (b. 1828) were among the remaining siblings. "we have a Soldier in our family" ... "they have six pence an hour for exercise" – apparently Charles had joined one of the volunteer corps established at HM Dockyards by the Admiralty in 1846; in exchange for being willing "to serve her Majesty in any department to which they may be called," the men were given uniforms and paid "sixpence per hour while at exercise" (*Dublin Weekly Nation*, 19 December 1846, 4). "C. Barlow" may have been Caroline Emily Barlow (born 1820 in Gillingham); "Goose" may refer to the family's neighbour Sarah Gosling; she attended St Mary Magdalene Church and was a year older than John. "Old Dray" may have been George Dray, ropemaker, of the nearby Park Place neighbourhood. John and Margaret Gardener are mentioned in the District 12 Gillingham Census in 1840, including a son John born in 1820. Mary Ann Hammond lived in the Park Place neighbourhood with her family, including her father, who was a shipwright at Chatham Dockyard. Mary Ann was also born in 1820. "Hary Bane" may be Henry Banes, a hatter who was thirty at the time of the 1841 census and lived nearby at High Street. With the exception of Dray and Banes, the names mentioned are nearly all those of men and women close in age who were probably childhood playmates of John and Thomas; most of them likely attended church at St Mary Magadelene.

Letter 176   John Thompson to James Thompson [brother] 3 January 1848. NMM AGC/T/7 (4)   "plover": HMS *Plover* had sailed on 11 January for the Bering Strait; the families of Franklin and his men had been informed that she would carry letters with the hope of delivering them if the ships were found. "Dr Rae returned without either hearing off or seeing you": this is a reference to John Rae's expedition of 1846–47, which, though not specifically designed to search for Franklin, brought back news in November of 1847 that they had found no evidence of his whereabouts (*Staffordshire Advertiser*, 6 November 1847, 6). "famine in Ireland": this was the Great Starvation, which lasted from 1845 to 1852. "a money panic": this was the "Panic of 1847," associated with the end of the 1840s railway boom. "A kind of Influenza": this was the 1847–48 flu, which affected one in four Londoners, but was generally mild; see K. David Patterson, "Pandemic and Epidemic Influenza, 1830–1848," *Soc. Sci. Med.* 21:5 (1985), 571–80. "you must practice artificial memory": this unusual phrase evokes James's study, with its books, papers, and magazines; John assures him that they have been left just as they were, so he might see them in his mind's eye. "Marsh gate" was a turnpike at the junction of Lower Marsh with Westminster Bridge Road; tolls were collected for its upkeep until 1844. In 1847 the property was sold; according to the *Illustrated London News*: "the materials of upwards of twenty houses, on the west side of Westminster Bridge Road, near the old Marsh-gate, were sold for the extension of the South Western Railway to the proposed new terminus in the York Road." "Watchorns" was a nearby retail establishment and wine merchant, said by *Punch* in 1843 to be "a favourite resort of holiday makers." "A little alteration in all the worlds … a great increase of publication": Thompson is referring in a broad way to developments in all aspects of society, and particularly to the rise of periodical publications – of which his brother was evidently fond – in the years since 1845. "28 Thomas Street gibson street Lambeth": This was Thomas Street, a short crossroad to Gibson Street, just south of the intersection of Waterloo Road with Lower Marsh and New Cut; the terminus of the South Western Railway was nearby.

Letter 177   James Clark Ross to Francis Crozier, 6 January 1848. MJR   "the Plover": this was HMS *Plover*; see note to Letter 176. For "Old Bird" see note to Letter 19.

Letter 178   Ann Ross to Francis Crozier, January 1848. MJR   For the "Plover" see note to Letter 176. "Frank and Franklin": to his intimate friends, Crozier was universally known as "Frank"; Ann's formality in addressing him as "My dear Captain Crozier" earlier is probably a sort of a humorous overly formal "wink." "Sir John Richardson's expeditions": this refers to his upcoming search with Dr John Rae.

Letter 179   John and Phoebe Diggle [parents] to John Diggle, 4 January 1848. NMM AGC/D/12/1   John Diggle had the unusual experience of having served aboard HMS *Erebus* on the Ross Expedition to the Antarctic, then as cook on HMS *Terror* on the Franklin expedition. "Schervey" is scurvy. For "HMS Plover" see note to Letter 176. "William Windchip," "William & T. Budington," and "Joseph Wallace R. Chipps & there Wife's Charlotte Phoebe Edith Sarah & Harriet" have not been identified.

Letter 180   Eleanor Franklin to John Franklin [father], 29 April–9 May 1848 DRO D3311 28 15   For "Admiral Beaufort" see note to Letter 9. "Sir E. Parry" was Sir William Edward Parry; see note to Letter 10. For "Mary Ann Kendall" see Letter 36 and note. "Lord Minto" was Gilbert Elliot-Murray-Kynynmound, 2nd Earl of Minto (1782–1859), who was First Lord of the Admiralty from 1835 to 1841. For "Sir John Barrow" see note to Letter 10; his "summary" was published as *Voyages of discovery and research within the Arctic regions, from the year 1818 to the present time* (1846). "Miss Fletcher" was Mary Fletcher (1802–1880), whom Richardson married in 1847 (curiously, all three of his wives were named Mary). "Dr. Davy" was John Davy (1790–1868), an eminent chemist. "Lady Richardson" – here Eleanor gets formal – is Mary Fletcher again. "France a Republic": this was the short-lived Second Republic (1848–51). "Louis Philippe" was the freshly deposed Louis Philippe I (1773–1850). "The Chartist demonstration of the 10th April": this was the great mass meeting of the Chartists – a loosely organized but vocal coalition of campaigners for universal suffrage and other reforms – on Kennington Common. There was considerable anxiety about the event – the Duke of Wellington was put in charge of arranging troops if needed to quell any riots, and more than 170,000 special constables were sworn in (including the unnamed person in Eleanor's letter). In the event, it passed peacefully but ended up marking the decline of the movement's effectiveness. "Lord Glenelg" was Charles Grant, 1st Baron Glenelg (1778–1866). For "Sir Robert Inglis" see note to Letter 159. For "Fitton" see note to Letter 127. For "Mr. Elliot" see note to Letter 116. "Sir Edmund Antrobus" (1818–1899) was a British politician. "hopes not to have to return to St Petersburg": Elliot had been an attaché there early in his diplomatic career. For "Montagu" see note to Letter

13. "Forster" was Matthew Forster (1796–1846), a loyal supporter of Montagu's in VDL. For "Sir Eardley Wilmot" see note to Letter 100. "Latrobe" was Charles Joseph La Trobe, who briefly stepped in as administrator of VDL from 1846–47; for his brother Peter, see note to Letter 159. "Gladstone" was William Ewart Gladstone (1809–1898), a British politician who succeeded Lord Stanley as secretary of state for war and the colonies. "The Bishop of Tasmania" was Francis Russell Nixon (see note to Letter 100); he was in England to lobby for authority over the convict chaplains in VDL. "Mr. Gell has not returned to England yet, tho' I fully expect he will be leaving V.D. Land": this was John Philip Gell, Eleanor's intended and later husband; see note to Letter 100. "The College": this was the never-quite-fully-launched College that Gell was intended to supervise; see note to Letter 100. "thrives well": it did not, in fact. "Hutchin's School": this was a grammar school in Hobart dedicated to the memory of William Hutchins (1792–1841), a Church of England archdeacon who had arrived in VDL with the Franklins in 1837 and was a friend and counsellor to them; not long before his death, he gave the blessing at Franklin's dedication of the cornerstone of the college. "Sir James Ross has this morning paid us a parting visit": Ross was about to embark on his unsuccessful search for Franklin in command of the ships *Enterprise* and *Investigator*. "Mr. Price being Commandant": this was John Giles Price (1808–1857), an advocate of strict treatment who did not believe convicts could be reformed; he governed the convict settlement at Norfolk Island from 1846 to 18 January 1853, when he was stoned to death by angry convicts. Price was married to Franklin's niece Mary (1814–1894), the illegitimate daughter of Franklin's brother Major James Franklin. "Sir William Denison" (1804–1871) was then lieutenant governor of Van Diemen's Land; unlike those of his immediate predecessors, his seems to have been a good and (relatively) uneventful administration, despite the initial difficulties described here. "William" was probably William Kay, the brother of Henry Kay; "Henry Kay" was Joseph Henry Kay (1815–1875), a nephew of Franklin's who served aboard HMS *Terror* under Francis Crozier during the Ross Antarctic expedition; he remained in Hobart as the director of the magnetic observatory. "Miss Elwall" was Clara Ann Elwall (1816–1903); "Mrs Jawcub" has not been identified. "Miss Meredith" was Maria Meredith, the daughter of George Meredith (1777–1856), a key early settler of VDL. For "Captain Stokes" see note to Letter 23. The "Bishop of Norwich" was Edward Stanley; see note to Letter 90. For "Captain Owen Stanley" see note to Letter 86. "Captain Ed. Stanley" was Captain Charles Edward Stanley (1819–1849); he died quite suddenly in August of 1849 in the midst of his duties. For "Dayman" see note to Letter 100. "Sir George Gipps" (1790–1847) was governor of New South Wales. Charles Augustus FitzRoy (1796–1858) succeeded Gipps; his wife Mary (*née* Lennox, daughter of the Duke of Richmond) was killed, as Eleanor notes, in a coach accident in December of 1847. "Sir E Charles"

must refer to FitzRoy, as he was driving the carriage. "St. Peter & St. Paul": that is, Petropavlovsk. For "Plover" see note to Letter 176. For "Mr. Rae" see note to Letter 191. "many secessions to Romanism": Eleanor means many conversions to Catholicism; John Henry Newman (1801–1890) was the most prominent. "Dr. Musgrave": Thomas Musgrave, (1788–1860) was Archbishop of York from 1847–60. "Dr. Sumner" was John Bird Sumner (1780–1862); he was made Archbishop of Canterbury in 1848. "Dr. Hampden" was Renn Dickson Hampden (1793–1868), who, although he did not convert to Catholicism, supported the admission to Oxford and Cambridge of Catholics and others who did not conform to the Church of England; his election as Bishop of Hereford was highly controversial, as Eleanor notes. "good service pensions": these were awarded, though not automatically, to flag officers and captains of the Royal Navy. For "Lord Auckland," see note to Letter 181. "Mr Stephen" was Sir James Stephen, (1789–1859), undersecretary of state for the colonies, 1836–47. "Aunt Simpkinson" was Jane Franklin's sister Mary, who was married to Sir Francis Simpkinson (see note to Letter 116); "John S." was his son John Nassau Simpkinson (see note to Letter 191); ditto for Sir Francis. "Dr. Vaughan" was Charles John Vaughan (1816–1897); he resigned from the headship in 1859 after what some historians believe was a suppressed homosexual affair. "a mastership": this would have been a role as a school master, but Eleanor (like her father) preferred a curacy, which, though often modest in pay, offered more room for advancement. On the back of the last leaf are these words: "Written to Sir John Franklin by my mother to accompany Sir Jas Ross' expedition & brought back to her"; the note is signed "JFG," which must represent Eleanor's son, John Franklin Gell (1851–1884).

Letter 181   Jane Franklin to John Franklin, 8–9 May 1848. LA/3/21   "Mrs. Maconochie" was Mary, née Hutton-Browne, the wife of Captain Alexander Maconochie (1787–1860), a Scottish naval officer, geographer, and penal reformer. Captain Maconochie had been one of the founders of the Royal Geographical Society (1830) and its first secretary before he sailed to VDL in the capacity of Sir John Franklin's secretary; he later became known as a penal reformer. In 1844 he too was recalled to England. "Commander Moore" was Thomas Edward Laws Moore (1819–1872), who in fact served as the mate of HMS *Terror* (not *Erebus*) during J.C. Ross's expedition; during the Franklin search, he commanded HMS *Plover* into the Behring Straits (see note to Letter 182). Later in his career he served as governor of the Falkland Islands. "Captain Kellett" was Sir Henry Kellett (1806–1875), who commanded HMS *Herald* and later HMS *Resolute* in Belcher's squadron, part of the Franklin search. "Dr. King" was Richard King (1811?–1876), who served as surgeon with George Back on his Arctic expedition (1833–35) as well as aboard HMS *Resolute* in the

Franklin search. King was known for his adversarial relationship with the naval men of the "Arctic Council," and published broadsides arguing for where to look for Franklin that turned out to be more accurate than theirs. For "Mr. Brown" see note to Letter 127. "widow of Mr. Hammond": this was Theodosia Elizabeth Hammond, *née* Gostling (1789–1861), the widow of Anthony Hammond, a wealthy stockbroker; as Jane mentions, she and George Back married in October of 1846. For "Miss Fletcher" see note to Letter 180; the novel mentioned, *Concealment: A Novel*, was published anonymously in 1821 by John Warren in London. "Sir Edward" is William Edward Parry (see note to Letter 10), who was in 1846 appointed captain superintendent of Halsar Hospital; he got his "flag" in 1852 when he was promoted to rear-admiral. "Lord Auckland" was George Eden, 1st Earl of Auckland (1784–1849); he became first lord of the Admiralty in 1846 in Lord John Russell's first government, holding the office until his death three years later. "Lord Ellenborough" was Edward Law, 1st Earl of Ellenborough (1790–1871); he succeeded the Earl of Haddington as first lord of the Admiralty but lost the office at the end of Sir Robert Peel's second government in July of 1846. "Sir H Willoughby" was Sir Henry Willoughby (1796–1865), a Conservative member of Parliament. "Mr. Hawes" was Benjamin Hawes (1797–1862), who (as Jane notes) served as under-secretary of state for war and the colonies. "Gordon Gardner" was an official in the Colonial Office, said to be a close friend of Sir George Arthur (1784–1854), Franklin's predecessor as lieutenant-governor of Van Diemen's Land (1824–36); see the *Bristol Mirror* for 8 January 1842, 5. "Rowlands" was Thomas Wood Rowlands (1800–1847), a disreputable attorney and newspaper editor who frequently attacked the Franklins in the press. "Mr. Young" was Thomas Young (1793–1866), another attorney in VDL who sparred with – and brought an action of battery against – Thomas Rowlands. "Mr. Gregory" was John Gregory (1795–1853), colonial treasurer in VDL. "Captain Fitzroy of New Zealand" was Robert FitzRoy FRS (1805–1865), the captain of HMS *Beagle* during Darwin's famous voyage, inventor of the weather "forecast" including the word, and the younger brother of Sir Charles FitzRoy; see note to Letter 180. "Captain Grey of South Australia, recently made a Knight of the Bath": this was George Grey (1812–1898), an explorer, colonial administrator, and writer who became governor of New Zealand from 1845–54 (following Robert Fitzroy). For "Mr. Majendie" see note to Letter 84. "Dr. Scoresby" was William Scoresby (1789–1857), a former whaling captain and author of the authoritative *An Account of the Arctic Regions and Northern Whale Fishery* (1820). "Willingham" was Willingham Franklin (1823–1860), John Franklin's nephew (see notes to Letters 184 and 185).

Letter 182   Charles Thompson to James Thompson [brother], 26 April 1849. NMM AGC/T/7(6)   "Lieutenant Moore of the Plover": this was Thomas Edward

Laws Moore (1816–1872), who had served aboard HMS *Terror* on Ross's Antarctic expedition; he is also mentioned in Letters 180 and 181. For details on the *Plover*, see note to Letter 176. "Sir James Ross in his Expedition": this was Ross's search of 1848–49. "Brother John will write to you": this was John Thompson; see Letter 176 and notes. "A series of Papers": the following section of this letter consists of two long quotations copied from newspaper articles of the day; the first, beginning with "The Artic [*sic*] Expedition" to "before first of May," appeared on 24 April 1849 in the *Manchester Times* and numerous other papers; the second, beginning with "Sir John Franklins Expedition To Mariners" and ending with "Melville Island," was from 28 April 1845, and appeared in the *Northampton Mercury* (BNA). The first article concludes by stating that "Letters from the relatives and friends of the officers and seamen searching in the Artic seas in Her Majesty's ships *Erebus* & *Terror Enterprise* and *Investigator* will be forwarded by Her Majesty's ship *North Star* if sent to the Secretary of the Admiralty on or before first of May." This notice was the reason for the writing of this letter; see Letter 183 for another example. For "Captain Kellett of the Herald" see note to Letter 27. "Woahoo": this is an older spelling of Oahu, the third-largest of the Hawaiian islands. "The Liverpool Shipowners Association": there seems to be little documentation of this effort, but the association was thanked for having offered similar assistance in a public letter by Sir Francis Leopold McClintock some years later (*Dublin Evening Mail*, 5 June 1857). The notice for "Sergeant Major Williamson" may be that of a relative. "8 Fleece Yard Meadows Lane <u>Leeds</u>"; a William Thompson, victualler, is listed at 87 Meadow Lane in an 1842 City Directory for Leeds.

Letter 183 Jane Ross Goodsir to Harry Goodsir [brother], 26 April 1849. RSGS ARC.4.3/2 As Jane notes, their brother Robert was away searching for Harry in the Arctic at this time. "the Captain's name is Penny": this was William Penny (1809–1892), a whaler and one of the most intrepid searchers for Franklin. He commanded three search expeditions – his aboard the whaler *St Andrew* in 1847 was the first; in 1849 he returned aboard the *Advice* – in both cases he was turned back by adverse ice conditions. In 1850–51 he commanded the brigs *Lady Franklin* and *Sophia*, and a detachment from his ships – which included Robert – was the first to find the graves on Beechey Island. "Papa" was John Goodsir, senior; "Archie" was Harry's youngest brother, Archibald, who had died of tuberculosis at the age of twenty-two the year before. "If God grants our meeting": this echoes Sarah Hartnell's lines which form the title of the present volume. "John has been Professor of Anatomy in Edinburgh for three Winters now"; John's success as a professor and anatomist was stellar, though there is a sense – as here with "immense Class" – of his being a bit of what we today might call a "workaholic."

Letter 184   Eleanor Franklin to John Franklin [father], 6 May 1849. DRO D3311
118 1   "North Star" was HMS *North Star*, which sailed to the Arctic in 1849
under the command of James Saunders; like HMS *Plover* the previous year, she
carried a number of letters for Franklin's men (see note to Letter 176). She returned
to the Arctic in 1852 as part of Belcher's squadron, and when seaman Thomas
Morgan died on board, he was buried next to Franklin's men on Beechey Island.
"Phillips large portrait" was the oil portrait of Franklin by Thomas Phillips RA
(1770–1845); the "smaller bronze one of you" is a bronze medallion (dated 1829)
by Pierre-Jean David d'Angers (1788–1856), sculptor and medallist. For "Mr.
Gell" see note to Letter 100. "Sir Thomas Acland" was Sir Thomas Dyke Ackland,
10th Baronet (1787–1871), a member of Parliament for North Devon, who had
lobbied for the £20,000 reward. "Sir Francis Baring" was Sir Francis Thornhill
Baring, 3rd Baronet (1796–1866); he held office as chancellor of the exchequer
and was first lord of the Admiralty from 1849–52. "Aunt Cracroft" was John
Franklin's sister Isabella Cracroft, *née* Franklin (1791–1883). "Kitty" was
Catherine Cracroft (1824–1885), sister of Sophy Cracroft. "Louisa Turner," *née*
Sellwood (1816–1879), was a niece of John Franklin through his sister Sarah
Franklin (1788–1816), who married Henry Sellwood (1781–1867), a solicitor
and attorney in Horncastle, Lincolnshire. Louisa married Charles Tennyson
Turner (1808–1879), older brother of Alfred Tennyson (who married Louisa's
sister Emily). "Anne Weld" (1814–1894) was the third Sellwood sister; in 1842
she married Charles Richard Weld (1813–1869). Willingham Franklin married
Fanny Lydia Murdoch in 1848. He trained as a barrister but in the 1850s he
bought the Haselbech estate in Northamptonshire and became a country squire.
"Aunt Betsey" was John Franklin's sister Elizabeth Franklin (1777–1850); see
note to Letter 16. "Col iii 12 & 13th": this would be chapter three, verses 12 and
13 of St Paul's epistle to the Colossians: "Put on therefore, as the elect of God,
holy and beloved, bowels of mercies, kindness, humbleness of mind, meekness,
long suffering; Forbearing one another, and forgiving one another, if any man
have a quarrel against any: even as Christ forgave you, so also do ye." (KJV). The
"Propagation Society" was the Society for the Propagation of the Gospel in
Foreign Parts, founded in 1701; it dispatched Anglican clergymen and religious
materials to British colonies such as VDL. "a clairvoyante": Lady Franklin and
Sophy called upon a number of these; for an account of them see W. Gillies Ross,
"Clairvoyants and Mediums search for Franklin," *Polar Record* 39 (208): 1–18
(2003).

Letter 185   Jane Franklin to John Franklin, 15 May 1849. LA/3/21   "Ross &
his gallant crews": this was James Clark Ross, whose search expedition with the
ships *Enterprise* and *Investigator* was just departing. "the Yankees": Jane was to
be disappointed that the American search was not launched until the following

year. "the Northern Channel": this may be a reference to Wellington Channel; see Appendix E for more details. "Willingham married, very steady & a very affectionate nephew – his wife thro' her mother who was a Gambier must be connected with Fitzjames": this was Franklin's nephew Willingham Franklin (1823–1860), who had married Fanny Lydia Murdoch (1827–1900), the daughter of Caroline Penelope Gambier (1799–1866), who was herself the daughter of Admiral Samuel Gambier (1752–1813), the brother of Fitzjames's natural father James Gambier. Jane seems to have known of Fitzjames's true parentage; this wedding made him into a relation. For "Mr. Majendie" see note to Letter 84.

Letter 186 Jane Franklin to John Franklin, 9 June 1849. LA /3/22 "Mr. Villiers" was Henry Montagu Villiers (1813–1861), then the rector of St George's; he later became the Bishop of Durham. "Mr. Sellwood"; John was the last surviving Franklin brother, so it was fitting that his brother-in-law Henry Sellwood was asked to give Eleanor away. "Eastbourn"; Eleanor and her new husband stayed at the home of the Gilbert family in Eastbourne; "Mr. Davies Gilbert" (1767–1839) had been a long-standing family friend of the Griffins; his daughter Annie Gilbert (1817–1892) corresponded with Eleanor. "Prince Albert" was the ketch *Prince Albert*, launched in 1851 under the command of William Kennedy (1814–1890), a Canadian fur trader and explorer. "dear old Hepburn" was John Hepburn (1794–1861), who had been the sole ordinary seaman on Franklin's Coppermine Expedition (see note to Letter 36). He accompanied John Franklin & party to VDL, working as superintendent of Government House and then at the Point Puer convict establishment. He remained in VDL until 1850, then returning to England and joining the *Prince Albert*.

Letter 187 Jane Franklin to John Franklin, c. 1849–50 [fragment]. LA/3/21 "your old friend of VD Land Forsyth" was Charles Condrington Forsyth (c. 1810–1873), who had known the Franklins in VDL while he was engaged as a surveyor. In 1850 he was appointed by Jane to command the *Prince Albert* on the first of several searches she sponsored; this fragment is part of a letter sent out with him. His service was not particularly distinguished; he returned without having pursued any fresh areas of search, the first of Lady Franklin's many disappointments.

Letter 188 Jane Franklin to John Franklin, 11 April 1850 (copy) LA/3/22 "Captain Penny of the Whaling trade": this was William Penny; see note to Letter 43. "poor Betsey": this was Franklin's sister Elizabeth; see note to Letter 16. "Lord Haddington did not remain long in office": this was Thomas Hamilton (see note to Letter 8b); he served as first lord of the Admiralty for six years, so Jane must mean he did not remain long after Franklin's departure; the

number of successors in that office were the result of the reshuffling of the
second Peel administration, followed by the first Russell government. For "Mr.
Simpkinson" see note to Letter 116; he was indeed knighted in 1850, and died
in 1851. "John S." was his son John Nassau Simpkinson.

Letter 189   Sophia Cracroft to John Franklin, 11 April 1850. LA/3/24   For
"Captain Penny" see note to Letter 43. For "Aunt Betsey" see note to Letter 16.
"The Wrights are much as usual": this was Franklin's sister Henrietta, who was
married to Thomas Wright; see note to Letter 160. "Uncle & Aunt Booth": this
was Hannah Booth, *née* Franklin (1776–1867), Sir John's sister, who married
John Booth (1779–1854). For "Willinghams marriage" see notes to Letters 184,
185, and 193. "Foster remains with my Aunt, a most attached & faithful servant": this was Jane's lady's maid Mary Foster (see note to Letter 159). "Mr.
Griffin especially how wonderfully his life is prolonged": this was Jane's father;
in fact he had scarcely two years to live.

Letter 190   Sophia Cracroft to John Franklin, 12 April 1850. LA/3/24   "the
most admirable letter ever addressed <u>by</u> man or woman, <u>to</u> man or woman": this
was Jane's letter to President Zachary Taylor; while widely admired, the letter
failed to have immediate effect; President Taylor could not by himself allocate the
requisite funds, and it was not until Congress acted and Henry Grinnell (1799–
1874) added his support (as detailed in this letter) that the expedition, the "First
Grinnell," was launched, a few weeks after this letter, under the command of
Lieutenant Edward De Haven; its surgeon, Dr Elisha Kent Kane (1820–1857)
returned in command of the "Second Grinnell" expedition in search of Franklin
in 1853–55. "a Mr. Silas Burrows": this was Silas Enoch Burrows (1794–1870),
a merchant from Stonington, Connecticut, a key backer of the Franklin search in
America; as Wamsley notes, "the part played by Burrows in response to Lady
Franklin's heartfelt plea produced perhaps the most meaningful privately funded
source of support for her benefit." See Douglas Wamsley, "Silas Enoch Burrows
and the Search for Franklin," *Coriolus*, Vol. 8, No. 2, 25–41.

Letter 191   Jane Franklin to John Franklin, 21 May 1850. LA/3/22   Note:
there are various marks down the side of this letter, explained by Jane sideways
down the page: "I have taken a sheet which was written on for some other purpose." "May it be the will of God": the first paragraph of this letter is remarkable; Jane Franklin, in her earlier correspondence with her husband and others,
rarely so much as spoke of religion. A "private expedition under the command
of Sir John Ross": this entailed Ross's yacht the *Felix*, which towed a second
smaller vessel, the *Mary*. For "Captain Forsyth" see note to Letter 187. "an
American expedition": this was that commanded by Edward De Haven. "your

old friend Richardson ... accompanied by a H. Bay officer named Rae": for Richardson see note to Letter 36; "Rae" was of course Dr John Rae (1813–1893), whose later searches led to the first major find of Franklin relics, along with Inuit tales of starvation and cannibalism that turned Lady Franklin against him. "Mr. Gell returned last Xmas": see note to Letter 100. For "Simpkinson" see note to Letter 116; his son John Nassau Simpkinson (1817–1894) was assistant master at Harrow from 1845–55. "Sophy" was of course Sophia Cracroft. "Captain Fitzjames ... Captain Gore": these officers had all since received promotions announced in the *London Gazette* (this was called being "gazetted"), though of course they were unaware of them.

Letter 192   Sophia Cracroft to John Franklin, 26 May 1851. LA/3/24   This is a copy. "Eleanor is extremely well, and has lately had a son": this would have been the aptly named John Franklin Gell (1851–1884); "her little girl" was Eleanor Elizabeth Franklin Gell (1850–1909).

Letter 193   Jane Franklin to John Franklin, 10 December 1851. LA/3/23   "all the ships sent out in search of you": the 1850–51 season was a high point for searchers, although other than the expedition's first winter camp at Beechey Island, their findings were slight. "S.W. of Cape Walker where they judged no ships could ever have passed": this is a slightly muddled reference to Peel Sound, which appeared entirely icebound to the searchers; its changeable nature was not understood. "The little 'Prince Albert' private expedition is attempting to get to James Ross' Strait & Simpson's Strait": this would have been the right area to search, but although the expedition, commanded by William Kennedy (1814–1890), discovered the Bellot Strait, it was unable to press further to the west due to extreme weather. "Captain Collinson & Captain McClure have passed thro' Behring Strait Eastward towards Melville Island but I fear in too low a latitude to fall in with you": The ships of Collinson (HMS *Enterprise*) and McClure (HMS *Investigator*) became separated; Collinson made it as far as Cambridge Bay, but McClure's ship found itself trapped in "Mercy Bay" on Banks Island. After being rescued in 1853 by Belcher's squadron, McClure and his men eventually made it through the passage from west to east; although part of that travel had been on foot or by other ships, his transit was recognized by Parliament as an achievement of the Northwest Passage. "Willingham has been married 2 years has 1 little girl & a nice wife who is about to be confined of her 2$^{\rm d}$": For Willingham, see notes to Letters 184 and 185; the children would be Edith Jane Franklin (1849–1931) and Catherine Elizabeth Franklin (1852–1920). "Pim" was Lieutenant Bedford Clapperton Trevelyan Pim (1826–1886), who in 1852 found and helped rescue Robert McClure's *Investigator*. For "Richardson" see note to Letter 36; "John Barrow" was John Barrow Jr; see note to Letter 9. "his father Sir John is no more": Sir John Barrow had died in 1848. "Sir Roderick Murchison" was Sir Roderick Impey Murchison, 1st Baronet (1792–1871), an eminent geologist. The "Emperor of Russia" at this time would have been Nicholas I (1796–1855).

Letter 194   Jane Franklin to John Franklin, 6 July 1852. LA/3/23   "Sophy, my adopted daughter": this is perhaps Jane's strongest statement about the woman more often described as her "constant companion." "Captain Inglefield": this was Edward Augustus Inglefield (1820–1894); in addition to his largely unsuccessful voyage with the *Isabel*, he later commanded HMS *Phoenix* in support of Belcher's squadron; among his returning passengers was Samuel Gurney Creswell, originally of HMS *Investigator*, who became – by arriving in England before his commander, Robert McClure – the first man to traverse the Northwest Passage (albeit in part on foot over sea ice) from west to east.

Letter 195   Jane Franklin to John Franklin, 30 March 1853. NMM AGC/F/9/1, copy at LA/3/23 with original envelope   "My present expedition of the 'Isabel' was to have sailed last year": the *Isabel* proved to be a vexed ship; she was originally intended for the Franklin search in 1851, but funds proved insufficient. In 1852 she sailed again under Inglefield (see note to Letter 194), but no further traces were found. In 1853, with the aid of considerable public subscriptions from "VDL," she sailed again with William Kennedy in command, only to have the crew mutiny at Valparaiso. The *Isabel* was eventually sold and the proceeds used to help acquire the "Fox," which ultimately, in 1857–59 under the command of Leopold McClintock, succeeded in bringing back the best evidence of Franklin's fate. "The faithful Foster too is still with me": see note to letter 159.

APPENDIX A:
HARRY GOODSIR'S "ZOOLOGY FROM THE ARCTIC EXPEDITION"

Caaing whale (*Phocæna melas*) – contempory names for the long-finned pilot whale (*Globicephalus melas*). Mistranscribed in both printed sources: the *Literary Gazette* has "Caring whale (D. locæna melas)"; the *Leisure Hour* has "Lowing whale, Phocæna melas."

APPENDIX B:
UNATTRIBUTED LETTERS IN THE PRESS

Letter 3   [from the *Morning Herald*]   The *Herald*'s version is the most complete. "Dear sir ... so long deferred": this opening paragraph, by the brother of the letter's writer, was omitted in some republications. "The expedition lay at anchor there for eight days, and left on the 12th of July, 1844" [1845]: this mistaken date occurs in all printed versions. "at one time were only 60 miles from Zealand": this is an error for "Iceland"; the figure of 60 miles is also mentioned in Letter 134 and elsewhere. "This breeze carried us ... did not disappoint us": this paragraph was omitted in some republications. "In the Terror, I am sorry to say ... pleased with what we did": this paragraph was omitted in the *Newry Telegraph* of 2 October 1851, possibly to avoid offending local sensibilities, as Newry is only fifteen miles from Crozier's hometown of Banbridge. "clearing the transports": "transport" should have been singular; this error appears in all printings. "July 11 I have been constantly employed ... I shall take advantage": this passage was omitted in some republications.

Index

Items in **bold** refer to letters sent or received by the indexed person; items with an "*n*" are found in the Notes.